T0377401

THE EUROPEAN UNION

*

VOLUME I
European Integration Outside-In

Volume I examines the history of the European Union from an outside-in perspective, asking the following questions: how does the European Union look from the outside, and which outside forces shaped and guided the process of European integration? Split into three parts, the first addresses the main external events that have steered the European integration process, with emphasis placed on critical junctures following the Second World War, such as the division and reunification of Germany and the Eastern enlargement. Part II considers the various international trends that have shaped European integration, with particular focus on globalisation and geopolitics. While the first two parts pay special attention to institutions, countries, international organisations and the main actors, Part III focuses on the role of ideas, networks, public opinion and memory that influenced the development of the European Union.

MATHIEU SEGERS is Professor of Contemporary European History at Maastricht University. His book on the Netherlands and European Integration was awarded the Dutch prize for best political book in 2013. He is a member of The Netherlands Scientific Council for Government Policy (WRR) and the SSH Board of the Dutch Research Council (NWO).

STEVEN VAN HECKE is Professor in Comparative and EU Politics at the Public Governance Institute of the University of Leuven. His research focuses on EU institutions, political parties and the history of European integration.

THE CAMBRIDGE HISTORY OF
THE EUROPEAN UNION

Split into two volumes, *The Cambridge History of the European Union* focuses on European integration from a diachronic, multidisciplinary and multi-institutional angle to provide the most comprehensive and contemporary history of the European Union to date. The volumes do not present a strict timeline of historical events; instead they look at the various themes and changes over time in order to shed light both on the more well-known and on the lesser-known moments in European history. Ranging from the first steps of European integration to the latest developments, the fifty essays from experts across the field provide a wholly unique perspective that changes the way we look at European integration history. This is a much-needed addition to the history of the European Union.

VOLUME I

European Integration Outside-In

EDITED BY MATHIEU SEGERS AND STEVEN VAN HECKE

VOLUME II

European Integration Inside-Out

EDITED BY MATHIEU SEGERS AND STEVEN VAN HECKE

THE CAMBRIDGE
HISTORY OF
THE EUROPEAN UNION

*

VOLUME I
European Integration Outside-In

*

Edited by
MATHIEU SEGERS
Maastricht University
and
STEVEN VAN HECKE
University of Leuven

 CAMBRIDGE
UNIVERSITY PRESS

Shaftesbury Road, Cambridge CB2 8EA, United Kingdom

One Liberty Plaza, 20th Floor, New York, NY 10006, USA

477 Williamstown Road, Port Melbourne, VIC 3207, Australia

314–321, 3rd Floor, Plot 3, Splendor Forum, Jasola District Centre,
New Delhi – 110025, India

103 Penang Road, #05–06/07, Visioncrest Commercial, Singapore 238467

Cambridge University Press is part of Cambridge University Press & Assessment,
a department of the University of Cambridge.

We share the University's mission to contribute to society through the pursuit of
education, learning and research at the highest international levels of excellence.

www.cambridge.org
Information on this title: www.cambridge.org/9781108490405

DOI: 10.1017/9781108780865

© Cambridge University Press & Assessment 2024

First published 2024

Printed in the United Kingdom by TJ Books Limited, Padstow, Cornwall

A catalogue record for this publication is available from the British Library

A Cataloging-in-Publication data record for this book is available from the Library of Congress

Two-Volume Set ISBN 978-1-009-28437-0 Hardback
Volume I ISBN 978-1-108-49040-5 Hardback
Volume II ISBN 978-1-108-47893-9 Hardback

Contents

PART I
CRITICAL JUNCTURES

Contents

PART II

MULTILATERALISM AND GEOPOLITICS

Contents

Figures

Contributors to Volume I

STEFANIA BERNINI is Adjunct Professor in the Department of Asian and North African Studies at Ca' Foscari University of Venice

KATJA BIEDENKOPF is Associate Professor, Leuven International and European Studies (LINES) at the University of Leuven

ANNA BROSIUS was Postdoctoral Researcher, Amsterdam School of Communication Research at the University of Amsterdam

MARTIN DAUNTON is Emeritus Professor of Economic History, Faculty of History at the University of Cambridge

MATTHEW D'AURIA is Associate Professor of Modern European History, School of History at the University of East Anglia

TOM DELREUX is Professor of Political Science, Institute of Political Sciences Louvain–Europe at the University of Louvain

EDITH DRIESKENS is Associate Professor of International Relations, Leuven International and European Studies (LINES) at the University of Leuven

ANDREAS C. GOLDBERG is Associate Professor, Department of Sociology and Political Science at the Norwegian University of Science and Technology (NTNU), Trondheim

GILLES GRIN is Director of the Jean Monnet Foundation for Europe and Lecturer at the University of Lausanne

FERENC LACZÓ is Assistant Professor, History Department, at Maastricht University

JOEP LEERSSEN is Emeritus Professor of European Studies at the University of Amsterdam

LORENZO MECHI is Professor in History of International Relations, Department of Political Science, Law and International Studies at the University of Padua

MADALENA MEYER RESENDE is Assistant Professor, Portuguese Institute of International Relations at NOVA University Lisbon

GUIA MIGANI is Associate Professor in Contemporary History at the Department of History and Archaeology, University of Tours

ANA MILOŠEVIĆ is Postdoctoral Researcher, Leuven Institute of Criminology (LINC) at the University of Leuven

EMMANUEL MOURLON-DRUOL is Professor of History of European Cooperation and Integration in the Twentieth Century at the European University Institute

SERGEI A. MUDROV is Associate Professor, Department of Social Communications at Polotsk State University

LEOPOLDO NUTI is Professor of International History, Department of Political Science at the University of Rome Three

LUCA RATTI is Associate Professor of History of International Relations at the University of Rome Three

KOLJA RAUBE is Assistant Professor for European Studies, LINES International and European Studies, Faculty of Social Sciences and Leuven Centre for Global Governance Studies at the University of Leuven

ANGELA ROMANO is Senior Researcher, Department of Political and Social Sciences at the University of Bologna

GILES SCOTT-SMITH is Professor of Transnational Relations and New Diplomatic History at Leiden University

MATHIEU SEGERS is Professor of Contemporary European History and European Integration at Maastricht University

CRIS SHORE is Professor of Social Anthropology, Department of Anthropology at Goldsmiths University of London and Research Director, Helsinki Collegium for Advanced Studies

EMMANUEL SIGALAS is Policy Analyst at the European Education and Culture Executive Agency of the European Commission and Research Fellow at the Public Governance Institute of the University of Leuven

RENITA THEDVALL is Associate Professor, Department of Social Anthropology at Stockholm University

MARKUS THIEL is Associate Professor, Politics and International Relations, Steven J. Green School of International and Public Affairs at Florida International University

HENNING TÜRK is a researcher at the Leibniz Centre for Contemporary History Potsdam (ZZF)

MATHILDE UNGER is Associate Professor of Public Law at the University of Strasbourg

STEVEN VAN HECKE is Professor in Comparative and EU Politics at the University of Leuven Public Governance Institute

Antonio Varsori is Professor emeritus of History of International Relations, Department of Political Science, Law and International Studies at the University of Padua

Claes H. de Vreese is University Professor of AI and Society and Professor of Political Communication at the University of Amsterdam

Kenneth Weisbrode is Assistant Professor at the Department of History, Bilkent University

Jan Zielonka is Professor of Politics and International Relations at the University of Oxford and at Ca' Foscari University of Venice

Acknowledgements

Editing a study like this is a team effort. *The Cambridge History of the European Union* (CHEU) aims to be a comprehensive, multidisciplinary, diachronic and transnational history of the process of European integration based on original archival and primary source research. The outline of the two books was first conceived in 2017. Since then, the project has developed into a major international, multidisciplinary *and* inter-generational project that resulted in two volumes that reflect the richness of the state-of-the-art research in the broad field of 'European Studies' with a focus on the topical and often even feverish urge to better understand what the Europe of European integration was, is and represents. Therefore, we hope that this scholarly project will serve not only as a source of reference, insights, analysis, inspiration and stimulation for our fellow scholars, students, policy-makers and other experts, but also as an accessible introduction to the history, present and future of the European Union for a wider public.

We thank all of the contributors for the spirit of cooperation, the concentration on content and the willingness to revise their contributions and work together on overlapping and inter-linked topics. And this all took place despite the pandemic, which made our work on the project even more challenging in unforeseen ways. Nonetheless, we managed to keep up with the original planning, although, regretfully, we had to cancel all our plans for working conferences.

We, the editors, are grateful for the uniquely cross-disciplinary and inspiring cooperation with all the contributors in this project. We remain indebted to all of them for their commitment to the CHEU. Next to that, a limited but crucial number of others deserve a huge thank you for all their efforts to pull off the CHEU. Our editorial assistants in different stages of the project, Annelies van Rijen, Toine Paulissen, Kate Rudd and Lucas Robbroeckx, have been indispensable in realising our ambitions – within this reliable team of young colleagues Angus Foster deserves our special gratitude for his year-long, consistent and professional role as the anchor in coordinating the editorial process. Michael Watson, Liz Hanlon, Emily Sharp, Lisa Carter, Steven Holt and Victoria Inci Philips, our editorial team at Cambridge University Press, formed a rock-solid basis throughout the whole process right from the inception of the project. We feel both lucky and grateful for the unique opportunity the CHEU has offered us to intensely collaborate on the subject that keeps us working, thinking and reflecting and stirs our passions in so many ways. It has brought, and still brings, us so much more than what we hoped for.

Abbreviations

ACP	African, Caribbean and Pacific
ACUE	American Committee on United Europe
ACUSE	Action Committee for a United States of Europe
AEC	Atomic Energy Commission
AI	Atlantic Institute
ASEAN	Association of Southeast Asian Nations
AU	African Union
BTO	Brussels Treaty Organization
CAI	China Investment Agreement
CAP	Common Agricultural Policy
CCP	Common Commercial Policy
CDE	Conference on Disarmament in Europe
CDU	Christlich Demokratische Union
CEC	Conference of European Churches
CEN	Comité Européen de Normalisation
CENELEC	Comité Européen de Normalisation Électrotechnique
CERN	Centre for European Nuclear Research
CERV	Citizens, Equality, Rights and Values programme
CET	Common External Tariff
CETA	Comprehensive Economic and Trade Agreement
CFSP	Common Foreign and Security Policy
CGIL	Confederazione Generale Italiana del Lavoro
CGT	Confédération Générale du Travail
CHAN	Centre historique des archives nationales
CIDCC	Comité International de Défense de la Civilisation Chrétienne
CMEA	Council for Mutual Economic Assistance
CoE	Council of Europe

COMECE	Commission of the Bishops' Conferences of the European Union
Comecon	Council for Mutual Economic Assistance
Cominform	Communist Information Bureau
Comintern	Communist International
COREPER	Council of Representatives to the European Union
CPSU	Communist Party of the Soviet Union
CROCEU	Committee of the Representatives of the Orthodox Churches in the European Union
CSC	Church and Society Commission
CSCE	Conference on Security and Cooperation in Europe
CSDP	Common Security and Defence Policy
CSR	Corporate social responsibility
CVCE	Centre Virtuel de la Connaissance sur l'Europe
DG	Directorate General
DG DEVCO	Directorate General for International Cooperation and Development
DG ECFIN	Directorate General of Economy and Finance
DG EMPL	Directorate General of Employment and Social Affairs
DM	Deutsche Mark
DNE	Detached national expert
EBRD	European Bank for Reconstruction and Development
EC	European Community
EC	European Council
ECA	Economic Commission for Africa
ECA	European Cooperation Administration
ECB	European Central Bank
ECE	Economic Commission for Europe
ECF	European Cultural Foundation
ECHR	European Convention on Human Rights
ECITO	European Central Inland Transport Organisation
ECJ	European Court of Justice
ECO	European Coal Organisation
ECOSOC	Economic and Social Council
ECSC	European Coal and Steel Community
ECU	European Currency Unit
EDC	European Defence Community
EDF	European Development Fund
EEA	European Economic Area

EEAS	European External Action Service
EEC	European Economic Community
EECE	Emergency Economic Committee for Europe
EFTA	European Free Trade Association
EGD	European Green Deal
EGNOS	European Geostationary Navigation Overlay Service
EKD	Evangelische Kirche in Deutschland
ELDO	European Launcher Development Organisation
ELEC	European League for Economic Cooperation
EM	European Movement
EMS	European Monetary System
EMU	Economic and Monetary Union
ENEA	European Nuclear Energy Agency
EP	European Parliament
EPA	European Political Authority
EPA	Economic Partnership Agreement
EPC	European Political Community
EPC	European Political Cooperation
EPP	European People's Party
EPU	European Payments Union
ERP	European Recovery Programme
ERT	European Round Table of Industrialists
ESA	European Space Agency
ESDP	European Security and Defence Policy
ESM	European Stability Mechanism
ESP	European Space Policy
ESRO	European Space Research Organisation
ETS	Emission Trading System
ETSI	European Telecommunications Standards Institute
EU	European Union
EU-27	European Union, remaining twenty-seven members after Brexit
Euratom	European Atomic Energy Community
Eurochemic	European Company for the Chemical Processing of Irradiated Fuels
Eurodif	European Gaseous Diffusion Uranium Enrichment Consortium
EUROGROUP	Independent European Programme Group
EUSP	European Union's space policy

FBR	Fast breeder reactor
FRG	Federal Republic of Germany
FSU	Financial Services Union
FYROM	Former Yugoslav Republic of Macedonia
GATT	General Agreement on Tariffs and Trade
GDP	Gross domestic product
GDR	German Democratic Republic
GFC	Global Financial Crisis
GHG	Greenhouse gas
GLONASS	Global'naya Navigatsionnaya Sputnikovaya Sistema
GMES	Global Monitoring for Environment and Security
GNSS	Global Navigation Satellite System
GOVSATCOM	Governmental Satellite Communication
GPS	Global Positioning System
GSP	Generalised Scheme of Preferences
G7	Group of Seven
G10	Group of Ten
G77	Group of Seventy-Seven
HAEU	Historical Archives of the European Union
HEH	House of European History
HR	High Representative
IAEA	International Atomic Energy Agency
IGC	Intergovernmental conference
IMF	International Monetary Fund
INFCE	International Nuclear Fuel Cycle Evaluation
IR	International Relations
ITO	International Trade Organization
LAS	League of Arab States
LDC	Least developed country
MEP	Member of the European Parliament
Mercosur	Mercado Común del Sur
MLF	Multilateral nuclear force
MRP	Mouvement Républicain Populaire
NAC	North Atlantic Council
NATO	North Atlantic Treaty Organization
NEI	Nouvelles Équipes Internationales
NIEO	New International Economic Order

NPT	Treaty on the Non-proliferation of Nuclear Weapons
NSC	National Security Council
NSC	New Strategic Concept
OAU	Organisation of African Unity
OAS	Organization of American States
OECD	Organisation for Economic Co-operation and Development
OEEC	Organisation for European Economic Co-operation
ONEm	National Employment Office
OPEC	Organization of the Petroleum Exporting Countries
PPP	Public–private partnership
PRC	People's Republic of China
REH	Reconciliation of European Histories
RTD	Research and technological development
SACEUR	Supreme Allied Commander in Europe
SAEF	Service des archives économiques et financières
SDRs	Special drawing rights
SEA	Single European Act
SED	Sozialistische Einheitspartei Deutschlands
SGP	Stability and Growth Pact
SMEs	Small and medium-sized enterprises
SMP	Single Market Programme
SSA	Space Situational Awareness
STABEX	System for the Stabilisation of Export Earnings
SWU	Separative work unit
TENs	Trans-European networks
TEU	Treaty on the European Union
TFEU	Treaty on the Functioning of the European Union
TTIP	Transatlantic Trade and Investment Partnership
UC	Units of account
UEF	Union Européenne des Fédéralistes
UK	United Kingdom
UN	United Nations
UNCTAD	United Nations Conference on Trade and Development
UNECE	United Nations Economic Commission for Europe
UNESCO	United Nations Educational, Scientific and Cultural Organization
UNGA	United Nations General Assembly
UNSC	United Nations Security Council
USSR	Union of Soviet Socialist Republics

VP	Vice President
WEU	Western European Union
WMD	Weapons of mass destruction
WTO	World Trade Organization

Reflections on the History and Historiography of European Integration

MATHIEU SEGERS AND STEVEN VAN HECKE

Introduction

European integration is not the result of a preconceived plan. It rather consists of messy procedures and heated discussions. Ad hoc decision-making, crises and even utter chaos have been constants in the history of the European Union (EU). This complex reality has induced scholars to zoom in on its infamous 'muddling through' to better understand what is going on in European integration. Consequently, the primary focus of research has been on ways, means and outcomes: inter-state bargaining, and the resulting treaties and European institutions. However, this focus on institutional ways and means, and on the outcomes of inter-state bargaining, has implied that ideas about Europe's future mostly have been treated as proxies of specific, rather one-dimensional, state, or institutional, interests. This leads to distorted images of history. If the recent crisis years made one thing very clear, it is this: that it proves quite complex to adequately analyse the multilevel, multipolicy and *demoi-cracy* muddling through that characterises the EU's laborious management of crises and day-to-day politics and policies, let alone that a mere focus on institutional interests would be sufficient. Putting it even more strongly, existing theories to understand European integration, which were developed mostly during the heyday of integration, turn out to be insufficient to fathom the evolution of European integration, especially since the Treaty of Maastricht (1992).

Indeed, the Treaty of Maastricht redefined European integration afresh in terms of 'deepening' and 'widening' in the totally new, and largely unforeseen, situation of a post-Cold-War world order. Stylised images of conflicting national interests, archetypical antitheses between federalist Europhiles and patriotic Eurosceptics, or one-dimensional alternatives in terms of supra-national versus intergovernmental integration proved insufficient to grasp the essence either of this plot of history or of its narrative, let alone to understand why and how European integration engaged itself in the highly risky undertakings of a single currency and an unprecedented enlargement process on 'shaky foundations', as the former German minister of Foreign Affairs, Joschka Fischer, characterised the state of play in the EU in terms of institutional groundwork in 2011.

To get an answer to (revived traditional) grand questions like whether the Treaty of Maastricht was a crucial moment of metamorphoses of European integration or an episode of continuation, or what the 'nature' of the historical process of European integration in essence entails, research ought to delve into the history underneath the surface of European integration's day-to-day institutional development. On that deeper level, we find that European integration is drawn from an ongoing 'battle of ideas' concerning what Europe may or should become in the future. Indeed, European integration is the product of never-ending battles among such plans, which have sprung from ideas (both causal and principled) as well as from ideals. In addition, these ideas and ideals often have been working across national frontiers, crosscutting member states, as well as political parties and conventional political camps within them.[1] Rival designs and grand designs for Europe continuously usher in rivalling concrete proposals in various policy fields, which then become the subject of European negotiations on different levels. However, the continuous competition of concepts and plans this induces has often been hidden from public and scholarly view, also because 'loser grand designs' disappear in the *ex post facto* depictions that dominate the historiography.

European Integration: What It Is and What It Is about

After they had actively engaged themselves in integration through the establishment of the European Coal and Steel Community (ECSC) in 1951, the governments of the six founding members (Belgium, France, the Federal Republic of Germany, Italy, Luxembourg and the Netherlands) were able neither to escape the ongoing battles of ideas over the future of European

---

1 C. Parsons, *A Certain Idea of Europe* (Ithaca, NY, Cornell University Press, 2003); J. Vanke, *Europeanism and European Union* (Palo Alto, CA, Academica Press, 2010).

integration, nor to control what sprang from the widely popular idea of European unification. Instead, the new phenomenon of European integration penetrated domestic politics and caused deep splits within cabinets and parliaments, crosscutting conventional political camps, and stirring up national versions of heated debate between federalists, confederalists, Eurosceptics and others. At the same time, however, behind the scenes, the lack of national control of this process encouraged unorthodox coalition formation across national frontiers, bureaucracies and transnational lobbies and networks – as recent archival research and fresh investigations within the neo-functionalist approach underscore. Moreover, European negotiations encapsulated both state and non-state actors right from the start – including transnational lobbies such as Jean Monnet's Action Committee and the Roundtable of Industrialists, but certainly also less well-known lobbies such as those organised in the world of churches and international banking, allowing for coalition formation across national frontiers and state and European institutions, such as the European Commission and the European Parliament (then still in the making). Influencing the integration process thus presupposed a certain 'transnationalisation' of European policies right from its earliest days.

This all has been underrated in the historiography. And there is an empirical reason: the governments' convincing but false claim to control the integration process. However, the idea of a striking match between the emerging integration and clear-cut national economic and/or geopolitical rationales essentially was an *ex post facto* depiction of largely unforeseen developments, in which ad hoc issue linkages and path dependences have been shaping forces. The situation was continually characterised by contested actor positions and unclear coalitions. This is the 'normal condition' in the unprecedented process of European integration. In such instances, ideas can facilitate institutional reform and/or radical policy change, for instance, through redefinition of actors' interests as a result of 'inter-elite persuasion'.[2]

So far, research has had serious difficulties in the attempt to master these national *ex post facto* rationalisations. Moreover, state-centric and issue-specific subdivisions still hinder the design of projects concerned with 'European' path dependences and issue linkages from a more diachronic

2 M. M. Blyth, '"Any More Bright Ideas?" The Ideational Turn of Comparative Political Economy', *Comparative Politics* 29, no. 2 (1997): 229–50; M. Blyth, *Great Transformations: The Rise and Decline of Embedded Liberalism* (Cambridge, Cambridge University Press, 2002).

perspective. In the exceptional cases in which these phenomena have been studied over a longer period, the scope has been limited to either path dependence or issue linkage. This is a serious shortcoming in the historiography, for instance because long-term institutional consequences may well have been 'by-products' of actions taken for short-term reasons inherent in specific issue linkages in earlier episodes.

During the 1940s the western quest for more international stability and coordination resulted in an institutional 'system' that the American political scientist John Ruggie famously described as the 'regime of embedded liberalism'.[3] Although the scholars of embedded liberalism never really engaged with it,[4] European integration may have formed an integral and inspirational – yet subdued – part of this primary financial-economic dimension of the *pax Americana*. After all, if they were to stand a chance, plans of European integration had to be nested within the transatlantic institutional structures that were already in the making. Pre-1950 western multilateralism built a 'laboratory' in which different initiatives for European integration were developed and tested, long before the process of European integration took root. The evolution of ideas for a new order in Europe within this transatlantic world was shaped by ongoing – and still highly topical – debates about the 'dialectics' of free world capitalism, such as those between domestic and international stability and social cohesion and competitiveness. To a certain extent institutions like Land-Lease, Bretton Woods, the International Monetary Fund (IMF), the International Trade Organization (ITO, later General Agreement on Tariffs and Trade, GATT), the Marshall Plan, the Organisation for European Economic Co-operation (OEEC, later Organisation for Economic Co-operation and Development, OECD), the European Payments Union (EPU), the ECSC and the European Common Market were all part of the same quest for welfare and stability via resilient capitalism and democracy, with a special focus on Europe and/or western Europe. Regarding the latter, the fact that early common market grand designs were often inspired by Cold War and/or colonial geography has long been omitted in the existing literature. It is telling in this regard that the inter-linkage of the process of European integration with the history of

3 J. G. Ruggie, 'International Regimes, Transactions, and Change: Embedded Liberalism in the Postwar Economic Order', *International Organization* 36 (1982): 379–415.
4 G. J. Ikenberry, 'The Liberal International Order and Its Discontents', *Millennium: Journal of International Studies* 38, no. 3 (2010): 509–21.

decolonisation has scarcely been researched as an integral part of European integration.[5]

In more general historical terms, the evolution of the Common Market can be considered illustrative for the dynamics sketched out above. Europe's market project has been offered detailed counter plans and nuanced alternatives ever since its inception. Starting from the treaty negotiations over the European Economic Community (EEC) during the mid 1950s, premature EEC concepts clashed with other plans, among others, plans for a European free trade area (which later became the European Free Trade Association, EFTA), a plan for an institutionalised Atlantic market and schemes for a (non-American) continental market. This can be considered a striking example of an ongoing battle of ideas, in the form of clashing grand designs for a future Europe of cooperation. Moreover, the above-mentioned EFTA and Atlantic market plan implied the membership of the United Kingdom (UK), whereas the EEC concepts were very sceptical about this, and continental schemes argued in favour of widening towards eastern Europe, instead of in Atlantic directions. Moreover, traditional historiography paid little attention to the neo-colonial undertones that were very present in the first plans and practices concerning the European common market, and connected this project to a history that stretched back far beyond the Second World War and the twentieth century – it is only very recently that historians of European integration have begun to take this dimension and its imperial and racial features more seriously as an integral part of the history of European integration (see below).

The crucial point here is that the existing historiography merely deals with the EEC extensively. The EFTA appears only at the margins. There is a simple reason for this. Plans and projects like the EEC and EFTA can be attributed to the conflicting 'national interests' of France and the UK, respectively. History has been bent accordingly, and a biased image of the history of the making of Europe's common market may have been the result. The consequences thereof still resonate in (mis)understandings of what is going on in the Europe of integration until today, while European integration, in essence, is a history of many plans and ideas, not just one, as is so

---

5 Important exceptions are M.-T. Bitsch and G. Bossuat (eds.), *L'Europe unie et l'Afrique: De l'idée d'Eurafrique à la Convention de Lomé I* (Brussels, Bruylant, 2005); P. Hansen and S. Jonsson, *Eurafrica: The Untold History of European Integration and Colonialism* (London, Bloomsbury, 2014); N. P. Ludlow, 'European Integration and the Cold War', in M. P. Leffler and O. A. Westad (eds.), *The Cambridge History of the Cold War* (Cambridge, Cambridge University Press, 2010), vol. II, pp. 179–97.

often claimed and believed. Indeed, no idea, ideal, plan, design or grand design has ever been strong enough to continuously subordinate the alternatives to its institutional logic, despite the fact that post-war European integration did channel Europe's (classic) drift towards unification within an unprecedented institutional framework of 'community method integration' and its self-reinforcing boundaries of integration–expansion (see, for example, Articles 38, 39 and 237 of the EEC Treaty).

If we want to better understand why things went how they did in European integration, we must do more work on the reconstruction of this unique episode in contemporary history that continues until today, by both broadening the conceptual scope (in multidisciplinary and interdisciplinary ways) and deepening the historical perspective (by stretching European integration history, harking back to histories before 1950 and the Second World War). This is exactly what this *Cambridge History of the European Union* (CHEU) aims to do.

The Genealogy of Post-war (Western) Europe[6]

The unprecedented stability and prosperity realized in (western) Europe in the second half of the twentieth century was neither 'evident in 1945' nor 'an automatic consequence' of the horrors of the Second World War. While the western Europe that was to emerge in the first post-war decades started to take shape in the mid 1940s, this 'new Europe' was not created during or after the Second World War. Instead, crucial pieces amongst the wreckage of the first decades of the twentieth century formed its central building blocks. The post-war developments in western Europe were strongly linked to the inter-war years, when, on the one hand, the juxtaposed processes of 'de-globalisation' and 'nationalisation', accompanied by a transnational 'turn to private corporatism', shook up the societal and political order, while, on the other hand, possibilities for 'one-worldism' and lofty pacifism were being explored in international politics.[7]

---

6 This section is based on M. Segers, *The Origins of European Integration: The Pre-history of Today's European Union, 1937–1951* (Cambridge, Cambridge University Press, 2023), Chapter 1.

7 A. Preston and D. Rossinow (eds.), *Outside In: The Transnational Circuitry of US History* (New York, NY, Oxford University Press, 2017), pp. 1–2; M. Hewitson and M. D'Auria (eds.), *Europe in Crisis: Intellectuals and the European Idea, 1917–1957* (New York, NY and Oxford, Berghahn, 2012), p. 13; P. F. Kjær, 'The Transnational Constitution of Europe's Social Market Economies: A Question of Constitutional Imbalances?', *Journal of Common Market Studies* 57, no. 1 (2019): 143–58; D. W. Ellwood, *The Shock of America: Europe and the Challenge of the Century* (Oxford, Oxford University Press, 2016), p. 182.

After the unmatched horrors of the First World War, American President Woodrow Wilson's call for a 'worldwide settlement' gained traction at the Paris Peace Conference. Hopes were high that, as the British commentator and writer H. G. Wells had put it during the first year of the Great War, this war would be 'the war that will end war'.[8] At Versailles in 1919, the 'Big Four' powers – the United States, the UK, France and Italy – knew all too well 'that there had never been an attempt at a worldwide settlement'; indeed, as the historian Margaret McMillan wrote in 2013, 'there has never been one since'. While the post-Great War period was unique in that the populations of the warring states were ready and keen to embrace universalism and world peace, McMillan noted that, if anything, the Treaty of Versailles made the Great War into 'the war that ended peace'.[9] In other words, the peace settlement of 1919 failed to 'make the world safe for democracy' (this is the phrase Wilson used on 2 April 1917 in a speech before Congress to obtain permission to declare war against Germany, which he obtained 4 days later) – quite the contrary. Moreover, this was the moment the United States became definitively involved in European and world politics. By the time Wilson was bypassed as presidential candidate for the 1920 elections, his 'Fourteen Points' outlining his principles of peace had already been dead in the water for quite some time. Wilson's proactive and idealistic vision for world cooperation became buried under the essentially reactive and opportunistic cost–benefit reasoning enshrined in the agreements of the Versailles Peace Treaty. This was also 'an illustration of how ill-defined Wilson's ideas were as practical politics'.[10]

The brute reality on the ground in Europe tore down the American-inspired aspirations for a better world and relegated them to naïve utopianism, ultimately symbolised by the fate of the League of Nations, which proved to be tragically dysfunctional in the inter-war years. Europeans turned a deaf ear to the politics of reconciliation touted by politicians such as Gustav Stresemann and Aristide Briand.[11] What re-emerged was a Europe of conflict, violence, uncertainty and poverty. It was a Europe that was plunging into even greater darkness than before, transfixed by a feverish search for an escape. This was the Europe of the Spanish Civil War and of Pablo Picasso's *Guernica* (1937), the mural-sized painting portraying the suffering of people

---

8 H. G. Wells, *The War That Will End War* (London, Frank & Cecil Palmer, 1914).

9 M. McMillan, *The War That Ended Peace: The Road to 1914* (London: Profile Books, 2014).

10 A. Williams, *Failed Imagination? The Anglo-American New World Order from Wilson to Bush*, 2nd ed. (Manchester, Manchester University Press, 2007), pp. 19–21, 38–44.

11 H. Kissinger, *Diplomacy* (New York, NY, Simon & Schuster, 1994), pp. 266–88.

and animals during the bombing of the eponymous city by German and Italian aircraft. This was the Europe of rampant poverty and gloom, which the young American journalist Walter Lippmann had implicitly warned about in his coverage of the Paris Peace Conference. This was the Europe that was captured by the German-Swiss painter Paul Klee in his painting *Europa* (1933): a goddess still, but one of wild despair and expressionism.

A new generation of American descendants of well-to-do East Coast families came to know Europe while living there during the inter-war years as part of the twentieth-century American variant of the Grand Tour, often travelling together with the intellectual American *avant-garde* in Paris. It was this generation of Americans that fell in love with the struggling old continent, and it was this emotional attachment that partly explains why key figures among these Americans – who were to take up influential positions in government and business during the 1940s – pushed passionately for a brighter European future after the Second World War. Indeed, the outlook of their generation would carry the 'American century' along with an emerging, 'altogether new, emblematic, Atlantic world, bound together in mind and deed'.[12] Politically, their activism often had its origins in the direct involvement of the United States in the post-First World War peace negotiations, then also labelled 'America's geopolitical coming-out party',[13] where many of them had been present as diplomatic youngsters or journalists.

Indeed, the American point of view on the Second World War was that it was the Great Depression and the devastating inequality, nationalism and racism it had unleashed that were at the root of the extraordinary violence that ravaged Europe during Hitler's war. This meant that the work of the many American diplomats, policy-makers, journalists, businessmen and politicians involved in the American mission of 'building Europe' entailed a dual battle against both poverty and the collapse in international coordination. This mission eventually culminated in the Marshall Plan in 1947 – the programme Wilson didn't have.

It was crucial, however, that the Europeans themselves promote and defend the new transnational policies of international organisation, mobilising the commitment of their fellow Europeans to embrace a radically different post-war experience from the one 25 years earlier. To American analysts, it was immediately obvious that making this work would be no walk in the

---

12 K. Weisbrode, *The Atlantic Century: Four Generations of Extraordinary Diplomats Who Forged America's Vital Alliance with Europe* (Cambridge, Da Capo, 2009), p. 10.

13 N. D. Lankford, *The Last American Aristocrat: The Biography of Ambassador David K. E. Bruce* (New York, NY, Little, Brown, 1996), pp. 42–3.

park, to say the least.[14] Or, to put it in more cynical terms: to be acceptable, and paradoxically enough, real unity was not allowed to exist.[15] This was the harsh dictum on a continent of warring nation-states. It also was one of the key lessons of the failure of Wilsonian idealism in 1919. Any new Europe must also remain an old Europe. In practice, this meant that post-war Europe was still to be based on its nation-states (no matter how worn out and discredited they may have been) and their traditions (no matter how dark these may have been). Moreover, the 'new Old World' of post-war Europe would remain an ongoing experiment in new and more just forms of capitalism and democracy, oscillating between the past and the future, the national and the supranational.[16]

Planning a New Europe

But whatever the ideas of politicians and intellectuals, one constant remained dominant in Europe's realities: the ordinary people of Europe were not really interested in the grandiose plans of the elites. Matters of individual security, food, housing and clothing simply took precedence. Indeed, this was the most evident continuity in the lives of many Europeans.[17] It made European societies fundamentally insecure, uncertain and desperate for stability and security. That was the case after the Second World War, just as it had been before that war had started.

The uncertainty that accompanied these parallel developments – the increasingly nationalist focus of governments in parallel with talk of a world government – did not arise in a historical vacuum. According to the Romanian-British policy expert and scholar David Mitrany – the father of functionalism and champion of post-war functionalist planning – it was during the nineteenth century that two political trends emerged that 'moved on two and opposite lines'. The first line enhanced 'the enfranchisement of the individual, the person becoming a citizen' (anchored in the Renaissance, humanism and anti-totalitarianism). The second line led to 'the enfranchisement of national groups through states of their own' –

---

14 Nationaal Archief, Dutch National Archives (DNA), The Hague, 2.21.408 (Nalatenschap Beyen), B.2.2.2.1, 71; 'Anglo-American Relations in the Post-war World', Yale Institute of International Studies, May 1943, pp. 5f. See also Weisbrode, *The Atlantic Century*, p. 104.

15 P. Mélandri, *Les États-Unis face à l'unification de l'Europe, 1945–1954* (Paris, Éditions A. Pedone, 1980), p. 26.

16 P. Anderson, *The New Old World* (London, Verso, 2011).

17 Preston and Rossinow (eds.), *Outside In*, pp. 1–2; Hewitson and D'Auria (eds.), *Europe in Crisis*, p. 13; P. F. Kjær, 'The Transnational Constitution of Europe's Social Market Economies', 146; A. Shennan, *Rethinking France: Plans for Renewal 1940–1946* (Oxford, Clarendon Press, 1989), p. 13.

a process that would radically intensify during the first five decades of the twentieth century, when Europe's nation-states became more ethnically homogeneous, often as a result of very violent politics.[18] Mitrany stressed that it was the task of post-war Europe 'to reconcile these two trends'.[19] Indeed, this may have been the key challenge of the post-war era in western Europe, given that the uncertainty mentioned above persisted into the first post-war years.

This confronted the planners of the post-war West, and European integration in particular, with the dilemma endemic to the multilateral management of interdependence. The 'two trends' identified by Mitrany continued unabated in a geopolitical and geo-cultural context marked by unremitting ambiguity. On the one hand, this context was characterised by nation-states that were increasingly becoming culturally homogeneous. On the other hand, it was coloured by the phenomenon of economic, political and cultural 'Americanisation', especially in western Europe,[20] where societies increasingly became spellbound by the United States and its films, its music, its automobiles, its stimulation of the senses, its money.[21]

This cultural–commercial trend was mirrored in new political visions. The backdrop of Americanisation allowed the idea of an 'Atlantic Community' to win relevance in western Europe. But it had been the outbreak of the war against Hitler's Germany that allowed this idea to truly catch the mood of the time, as the concept of the Atlantic Community could be easily linked to Allied cooperation, in particular to the politics and policies that sprang from the strongly intensified Anglo-American partnership but also to the drafting of plans for post-war Europe by the European exile governments in wartime London.[22] Nonetheless, the translation of this 'easy link' into a concrete and coherent grand design ultimately failed. As a result, the visionary concept of an Atlantic Community was put on the back burner and turned into

18 T. Judt, *Postwar: A History of Europe since 1945* (London, Pimlico, 2007), pp. 27–8; I. de Haan, 'The Western European Welfare State beyond Christian and Social Democratic Ideology', in D. Stone (ed.), *The Oxford Handbook of Postwar European History* (Oxford, Oxford University Press, 2012), pp. 299–318, 305, 312.

19 D. Mitrany, *A Working Peace System: An Argument for the Functional Development of International Organization* (London, Royal Institute of International Affairs, 1943), pp. 26–7.

20 B. L. Blower, *Becoming Americans in Paris: Transatlantic Politics and Culture between the World Wars* (Oxford, Oxford University Press, 2011).

21 P. Gassert, 'The Spectre of Americanization: Western Europe in the American Century', in D. Stone (ed.), *The Oxford Handbook of Postwar European History* (Oxford, Oxford University Press, 2012), pp. 180–200, 184.

22 M. Conway, 'Legacies of Exile: The Exile Governments in London during the Second World War and the Politics of Post-war Europe', in M. Conway and J. Gotovitch (eds.), *Europe in Exile: European Exile Communities in Britain 1940–45* (New York, NY, Berghahn, 2001), pp. 255–74.

a transatlantic politico-economic incubator space facilitating the international cooperation of open societies and promoting 'liberalism as a pan-Western exercise' but remaining 'unguided by overall strategy'.[23]

Be that as it may, the 'better world' envisaged during the inter-war decades and the war years did build the foundation for stability, prosperity and well-being in post-war western Europe. Moreover, despite the global aspirations often simmering below the surface in post-war planning, this new reality of free societies, progress and international cooperation remained a strictly Western affair for more than four decades, crafted from ideas of an 'Atlantic civilisation' and a distinct and coherent Western unity – or even union – and identity. In the 1966 republication of his influential pamphlet *A Working Peace System* (first published in 1943), David Mitrany starts the reworked introduction as follows: 'When this short study was first published in the summer of 1943, there was great confidence in the unity which had grown up during the war, and [we] were thinking mainly of how to consolidate that unity and expand it.'[24] However, when the time was ripe to put such ideas into practice in post-war western Europe, this 'Atlantic imagination' of a 'better world'[25] had already lost much of its power. In its place, a messier western European variant emerged, morally indebted to its American precursors, yet focused in practical terms on devising a European method of American-inspired socio-economic and financial-economic planning, a European style of state intervention, inter-state coordination and supranational organisation.

If there was a clean historical break with the post-First World War past after 1945, it was reflected in the modern phenomenon of economically legitimised state intervention elaborated in projects of planning and the policies of the welfare state. The credibility of planning and policy offered a fresh solution to the political problems that had torn Europe apart in the first decades of the twentieth century. During the 1940s, planning and policy even evolved into something much bigger than a set of instruments to organise society. It became a belief, a movement, a kind of pseudo-religion. It became the binding mission that drove the Western quest for a resilient,

---

23 V. R. Berghahn, *Europe in the Era of Two World Wars: From Militarism and Genocide to Civil Society, 1900–1945* (Princeton, NJ, Princeton University Press, 2009), p. 6; Gassert, 'The Spectre of Americanization', p. 196; J. Gillingham, 'From Morgenthau to Schuman Plan: The Allies and the Ruhr, 1944–1950', in J. Gillingham, *Coal, Steel, and the Rebirth of Europe, 1945–1955: The Germans and French from Ruhr Conflict to Economic Community* (Cambridge, Cambridge University Press, 1991), pp. 97–117, 111.

24 D. Mitrany, 'Author's Foreword, 1966', in D. Mitrany, *A Working Peace System* (Chicago, IL, Quadrangle Books, 1966 [1943]), p. 25.

25 A. S. Milward, *The Reconstruction of Western Europe 1945–51* (London, Methuen, 1984), p. 55.

free world: 'if a democracy was to work, if it was to recover its appeal, it would have to be *planned*';[26] and primarily economically planned, focused on the battle against unemployment and on providing 'welfare for all'.[27]

In taking on this mission, the leading planners designed a society that was more organised than the inter-war societies had been when Europeans had experimented with a mix of wild capitalism and even wilder politics. These experiments had only led the continent into economic depression and societal unrest. Given this dark historical backdrop, it was felt that the adventures of the inter-war years had to be avoided at all costs. Planners now took the lead, presenting themselves as unsullied by political ideology. And there was a reason. They were not only able to learn from their own sobering experiences of the 1920s and 1930s, but also had recourse to the preparatory work carried out by the bureaus of the League of Nations and its academic and non-governmental partners. The moribund committees and bureaus of the League – which had found themselves increasingly orphaned in a Europe under the spell of fascism, nationalism and Nazism – had formed a breeding ground for what would turn out to be an 'epistemic community in the making'.[28] With the benefit of hindsight, the broad, loose and diverse community of internationally oriented and universalistic inspired people, scattered over and around the League's committees and secretariats, can be seen to have been a kind of 'training centre' for the post-war years of reconstruction. It was here that thinking was focused on practical and implementable plans.

These planners and designers helped politicians build their promised 'better world' of prosperity and multilateralism by drawing up a programme of practical politics that the Western world had lacked. This earned them political trust, and it made their claim that rational policies of international cooperation could prevent disaster even more convincing and thus appealing. The most prominent of the planners even presented themselves as 'statesmen of interdependence' – as apolitical experts operating within an emerging international order based on the cooperation of free and open societies, social justice and the practical and material benefits of functionalism

26 Judt, *Postwar*.
27 D. de Bellefroid, 'La Commission belge pour l'Étude des Problèmes d'Après-Guerre (CEPAG), 1941–1944' (degree thesis, University College London, 1987), pp. 124–9.
28 K. K. Patel, *The New Deal: A Global History* (Princeton, NJ, Princeton University Press, 2016), p. 292; P. Clavin, *Securing the World Economy: The Reinvention of the League of Nations, 1920–1947* (Oxford, Oxford University Press, 2013).

and market expansion, cheap production and mass consumption.[29] Initially, this conversion of American ideas into Atlantic and western European practices of international cooperation and organisation was achieved mainly by promoting and managing economic interdependence in the fields of monetary policy, trade and financial-economic affairs.

Renewing the Historiography of European Integration

The work undertaken by the planners of a new (western) Europe was soon given a powerful boost by the success story – unparalleled in history – of economic growth, prosperity and general progress. As Alan Milward has noted, 'nothing in the history of western Europe resembles its experience between 1945 and 1968 ... the material standard of living for most people improved uninterruptedly and often very rapidly'.[30] In combination with the geopolitical and ideological black-and-white logic of the Cold War, this makes it seem – *ex post facto* – as though the early post-war rationalist planners had triumphed. This influential perception, however, is fundamentally incomplete because it obfuscates the non-economic origins of European integration and falsely portrays European integration as a purely rational affair.

This notion forms the starting point for the historical research that underpins the CHEU and mirrors a relatively recent development in the historiography of European integration.[31] The CHEU aims to make an important contribution to the existing historiography by integrating three relatively new insights from the emerging revisionist literature into a new comprehensive approach.

The first new insight derived from the revisionist literature is that the governments involved in initiating European integration were unable to control what emerged out of the widely popular idea of European unification. Once the genie was let out of the bottle, European integration took on a life of its own, penetrating domestic politics and causing deep splits within

---

29 F. Duchêne, *Jean Monnet: The First Statesman of Interdependence* (New York, NY, W. W. Norton, 1994); compare John Foster Dulles quoted in Berghahn, *Europe in the Era of Two World Wars*, p. 136.

30 Milward, *The European Rescue of the Nation-State*, p. 21.

31 For a useful and complete overview of the historiography concerning European integration, see K. K. Patel, 'Widening and Deepening? Recent Advances in European Integration History', *Neue Politische Literatur* 64 (2019): 327–57.

cabinets and parliaments, cutting across conventional political camps and stirring up heated debates between federalists, confederalists, isolationists, nationalists and so on. The lack of national control over this process of integration also led to the formation of unorthodox transnational coalitions, lobbies and networks. Moreover, the transatlantic and European negotiations that prepared the ground for the revolutionary first steps of European integration involved both state and non-state actors from the very beginning, which meant that the drafting of plans and the formation of coalitions occurred across national frontiers and that state and non-state institutions worked together. This was, in essence, its own 'polity' in the making.[32] Influencing the integration process presupposed access to this polity. In addition, there was a certain degree of 'transnationalisation' of European politics and policies from its earliest days. This has not been given sufficient attention in the historiography, and the CHEU strives to correct this.

The second new insight is the need to delve deeper into the past to understand the origins of European integration. The state-centric and issue-specific historiography mentioned above impedes efforts to understand transatlantic path dependences and issue linkages from a more diachronic perspective. In the rare cases in which these phenomena have been studied over a longer period, the scope has been limited either to intellectual history or to institutional path dependence or issue linkage within and between certain policy domains – of which the latter two typically remain limited to the traditional timeframe of European integration, meaning post-1950 or even post-1990.[33] Obviously, this is a major shortcoming in the literature, for instance because long-term institutional consequences may well have been

---

32 W. Kaiser, B. Leucht and M. Rasmussen (eds.), *The History of the European Union: Origins of a Trans- and Supranational Polity 1950–72* (London, Routledge, 2008). The importance of factoring in the transnational and polity dimensions has been underscored by relatively recent studies of diplomatic history, as well as research within the neo-functionalist tradition in political science research, for instance, Weisbrode, *The Atlantic Century*; M. Segers, 'Preparing Europe for the Unforeseen, 1958–63: De Gaulle, Monnet and European Integration beyond the Cold War: From Cooperation to Discord in the Matter of the Future of the EEC', *International History Review* 34 (2012): 347–70; A. Niemann, *Explaining Decisions in the European Union* (Cambridge, Cambridge University Press, 2006).

33 See, for example, Hewitson and D'Auria (eds.), *Europe in Crisis*; P. Pierson, 'The Path to European Integration: A Historical Institutionalist Analysis', *Comparative Political Studies* 29, no. 2 (1996): 123–63; W. Sandholtz and A. Stone Sweet (eds.), *European Integration and Supranational Governance* (Oxford, Oxford University Press, 1998); L. Friis, '"The End of the Beginning" of Eastern Enlargement – Luxemburg Summit and Agenda-Setting', *European Integration Online Papers* 2, no. 7 (1998), 16 pp.

'by-products' of decisions taken for short-term reasons inherent in specific issue linkages (of earlier episodes). It is essential for historians to go back beyond 1950, beyond 1945, and even beyond the Second World War to the inter-war period and the First World War in order to widen their diachronic scope of research.[34] The 'new Europe' of cooperation and integration was not created from scratch after the Second World War; instead, post-war developments were deeply rooted in the inter-war years, if only because it was ultimately the Great War that plunged Europe into a period of 75 years of war, unrest and division – 'the longest of its civil wars'[35] – that ended only in 1990 with the Treaty on the Final Settlement with Respect to Germany allowing the two German states to reunite. It was this treaty that laid the foundations for the end of the Cold War and the reunification of Europe, facilitated by the process of European integration and re-enshrined in the Treaty on European Union in 2007. Together, these treaties explicitly built on the multilateral order of the post-war West and its ideals of international cooperation and human rights. The CHEU also entails an effort to reconstruct this fragmented history of the Western world in the twentieth century in which post-war (western) Europe was – and still is – so firmly embedded.

The third new insight that has emerged from recent historiography is the conviction that to understand how European integration developed the way it did, historians must delve beneath the surface of day-to-day politics, diplomacy and the development of institutions. On that deeper level, it becomes apparent that European integration was drawn from a relentless 'battle of ideas' over Europe's future. It was not the result of a preconceived plan but the product of never-ending battles over such plans – battles that were fuelled by ideas and ideals that crossed national frontiers as well as political parties. Grand designs for a new European, regional and world order inevitably ushered in a competition of proposals from very general and political ones to ones that were extremely technical and focused on very specific policy fields. This ceaseless competition between different concepts and plans is key to understanding what happened and why. And yet the unsuccessful grand designs are largely neglected in the *ex post facto* depictions that dominate the historiography. The CHEU hopes to paint a more com-

34 Hewitson and D'Auria (eds.), *Europe in Crisis*.
35 N. Davies, *Europe: A History* (London, Bodley Head, 2014), p. 14.

plete picture of these ideational dynamics and struggles than is usually presented in scholarly works on European integration.

Other ways in which the CHEU aims to enrich the existing literature on European integration are the addition of innovative conceptual elements (from disciplines other than contemporary history) and the highlighting of key dimensions in the history of European integration that often have been overlooked, such as the above-mentioned neocolonial dimension, which was very present in the initial phases of European market integration. Another example of such an overlooked dimension is the (very) active role of the churches and leading ecclesiastics, often made possible through the trans-European and transatlantic networks of Christian Democracy, especially in the first phases of European integration. This represented a vital political force in all free societies of post-war Europe, where political, technocratic and clerical networks often overlapped in an emerging world of transatlantic cooperation that fostered partnerships that were pivotal in the post-war West. The interconnectedness of the world of the churches and the process of (re)building Europe has been largely ignored in the historiography.[36]

Theorising European Integration: A Brief History

Generally speaking, European integration theories, fuelled by various strands of political science, have taken these insights – like the role of ideas or non-state actors and the power of path dependence or transnational networks – into account. Historically, these theories – borrowed from international relations, comparative politics and public management and applied to a unique case often labelled as sui generis – followed clear trends in trying to explain the range, degree and speed of European integration, or the lack thereof. The big questions of how and why followed certain waves, clearly corresponding to the ups and downs of the process of (political) integration itself.

---

36 Recent attempts to fill this gap in the historiography include W. Kaiser, *Christian Democracy and the Origins of the European Union* (Cambridge, Cambridge University Press, 2007); S. Shortall, *Soldiers of God in a Secular World: Catholic Theology and Twentieth-Century French Politics* (Cambridge, MA, Harvard University Press, 2021); G. Chamedes, *A Twentieth-Century Crusade: The Vatican's Battle to Remake Christian Europe* (Cambridge, MA, Harvard University Press, 2019).

Neo-functionalism was the first theory trying to explain this unique phenomenon in international politics.[37] Neo-functionalism explained the coming about of the ECSC and the Rome Treaties (EEC and Euratom) by noting the internal logic and dynamics of the integration process, with special emphasis on processes of socialisation. Its failure to provide explanations for certain shortcomings or even stagnation in the process of European integration – such as the failure of the European Defence Community (EDC) or the Empty Chair Crisis – triggered a renewed attention towards actors' self-interests and preferences, first and foremost driven by national interests of the member states. This theory of inter-governmentalism became dominant when neo-functionalist (and rather linear) explanations and predictions had been disavowed by events like the failure of the EDC.[38] Intergovernmentalism assumes that integration proceeds only when states envisage more benefits than costs in cooperating with each other. Consequently, intergovernmentalists consider European integration to be the reflection of the national interests of the most powerful states and corresponding policy choices, be they 'geopolitical', 'socio-economic' or 'commercial', under the banner of 'liberal intergovernmentalism'.[39]

These long-dominant 'varieties of intergovernmentalism', however, share comparable problems in their efforts to capture the institutional dynamics of the Community system, as this system clearly contains normative features, transnational dynamics, fragmented national governments, caprices of public support for European integration, and non-state actors – and also in the accurate and/or balanced use of sources.[40]

---

37 E. B. Haas, *The Uniting of Europe: Political, Social and Economical Forces, 1950–1957* (Notre Dame, IN, University of Notre Dame Press, 1958).

38 S. Hoffmann, 'Obstinate or Obsolete? The Fate of the Nation-State and the Case of Western Europe', *Dædalus* 95, no. 3 (1966): 862–915.

39 H.-J. Küsters, 'West Germany's Foreign Policy in Western Europe 1949–1958', in C. Wurm (ed.), *Western Europe and Germany* (Oxford and Washington, DC, Berg, 1995), pp. 55–85; Milward, *The European Rescue of the Nation-State*; A. Moravcsik, 'Liberal Intergovernmentalism and Integration: A Rejoinder', *Journal of Common Market Studies* 33, no. 4 (1995): 611–28; A. Moravcsik, *The Choice for Europe: Social Purpose and State Power from Messina to Maastricht* (London, UCL Press, 1998); A. Moravcsik, 'De Gaulle between Grain and Grandeur' (Parts 1 and 2), *Journal of Cold War Studies* 2, no. 2 (2000): 3–43 and 2, no. 3 (2000): 4–68; A. Moravcsik, 'Preference, Power and Institutions in 21st-Century Europe', *Journal of Common Market Studies* 56, no. 7 (2018): 1648–74.

40 M. Kleine and M. Pollack (eds.), 'Special Issue: Liberal Intergovernmentalism and Its Critics', *Journal of Common Market Studies* 56, no. 7 (2018); L. Hooghe and G. Marks, 'Is Liberal Intergovernmentalism Regressive? A Comment on Moravcsik (2018)', *Journal of European Public Policy* 27, no. 4 (2019): 501–8; Niemann, *Explaining Decisions in the European*

From this perspective it may not be a surprise that the quest for a grand theory – shaping much of the infant historiography in the early decades of integration – that can explain the overall European integration process has been increasingly abandoned by scholars in the past two decades.[41] Instead, so-called meso-theories (such as social constructivism, multilevel governance and 'Europe as an empire') tried to analyse specific elements or phenomena within European integration, which seem located at the heart of the process – for instance the variation inherent in it.[42] Most of the time, however, this has been done by borrowing frameworks and concepts from existing academic disciplines and subdisciplines, mainly in the social sciences, which were not focused on European integration per se.[43] Even the efforts to theoretically explain 'the age of crisis' (the euro and Schengen/migration, 'the two flagship integration projects of the 1990s'),[44] as well as forms of 'differentiated integration' and disintegration,[45] particularly Brexit, did not preclude the appearance of a new grand theory. What did happen was the adaption and nuancing of the 'old grand theories' so as to include new insights and relate them to a decade of crises. This led to theories such as postfunctionalism (which assesses the causes and effects of the increasing 'politicisation' of European integration) and new varieties of 'liberal intergovernmentalism'.[46] The communis opinio more and more seems to be that the relevance of European integration theories lies in 'elucidating the EU's polycrisis or its distinctive features', also given that 'one theory might not be apt for explaining all the crises the EU has faced since 2009, different theories explain distinct empirical realities'.[47]

Union; Kaiser et al. (eds.), *The History of the European Union*; R. H. Lieshout, M. L. L. Segers and A. M. van der Vleuten, 'De Gaulle, Moravcsik, and the Choice for Europe: Soft Sources, Weak Evidence', *Journal of Cold War Studies* 6, no. 4 (2004): 89–139.

41 S. Hix and B. Høyland, *The Political System of the European Union* (New York, NY, Red Globe Press, 2011).

42 F. Schimmelfennig and B. Rittberger, 'The EU as a System of Differentiated Integration. A Challenge for Theories of European Integration?', in J. Richardson and S. Mazey (eds.), *European Union: Power and Policy-Making*, 4th ed. (London, Routledge, 2015), Chapter 2; E. Hirsch Ballin, E. Ćerimović, H. Dijstelbloem and M. Segers, *European Variations as a Key to Cooperation in the European Union* (Cham, Springer, 2020).

43 S. Hix, 'The Study of the European Community: The Challenge to Comparative Politics', *West European Politics* 17, no. 1 (1994): 1–30.

44 F. Schimmelfennig, 'European Integration (Theory) in Times of Crisis. A Comparison of the Euro and Schengen Crises', *Journal of European Public Policy* 25, no. 7 (2018): 969–89.

45 H. Vollaard, *European Disintegration: A Search for Explanations* (London, Palgrave Macmillan, 2018).

46 Hooghe and Marks, 'Is Liberal Intergovernmentalism Regressive?'

47 S. Gürkan and N. Brack, 'Understanding and Explaining the European Union in a Crisis Context: Concluding Reflections', in N. Brack and S. Gürkan (eds.), *Theorising the Crises of the European Union* (London, Routledge, 2020), p. 247.

Interestingly, by giving up the ambition to understand what is going on in Europe in a more general sense, the 'new theories' do generally indicate that the Treaty of Maastricht has been a turning point in the history of European integration. In other words, 'Maastricht' may have changed the nature of the integration process as such. For some 'Maastricht', for instance, finally proved that the ultimate nature of European integration is in building a common political future and for the EU to become a more political player, both internally and externally, in one way or another.[48] And there is an obvious, albeit still not much mentioned, direct reason for this turn to *Realpolitik*: the post-Maastricht era was also characterised by geographical 'widening' of integration, next to nation-state penetrating 'deepening'; the latter especially via the Economic and Monetary Union (EMU).

Indeed, what the last 30 years of European integration do force us to confront is the far-reaching significance of a Europe of the euro, namely the money and the banks. That Europe has actually been achieved. The deep grooves that the euro crisis has gouged across the EU and its member states have pushed the history of the EU towards other, new perspectives. It is difficult as yet to see what they are, but we can already conclude that the origins of the monetary dimension of European integration will perhaps prove even more important for the history of integration than was long asserted, believed or estimated. That is one reason why the CHEU devotes considerable attention to the origins and developments of the EMU, and the 'order of Maastricht' (replacing the 'order of Rome'), within which the EMU became a reality. Moreover, the pre-history of the EMU explains much of the how and why of the Europe of European integration and its endemic internal and external struggles. All in all, the state of the art of the historical research on the EMU, as presented in the CHEU, provides new insights into the tangled state of crisis in which the *enlarged* Europe of European integration of today finds itself.

It is, however, only since the EU launched its overwhelming enlargement policy towards the central and eastern European countries that enlargement has become a serious topic of scholarly debate.[49] Until now,

---

48 L. van Middelaar, *De nieuwe politiek van Europa* (Groningen, Historische Uitgeverij, 2019).

49 N. Nugent (ed.), *European Union Enlargement* (New York, NY, Red Globe Press, 2004).

studies have either presented insightful, yet single, case studies focusing on specific key dimensions and/or actors,[50] or remain preoccupied by post-Cold War eastern enlargement as the ultimate falsification of rational choice theories.[51] These shifts in scholarly efforts to elucidate what European integration is have implications for the study of the general phenomenon itself.

Moreover, these shifts suggest that new ways of thinking and other disciplines (next to the usual suspects and their 'European studies' sub-branches: history, political science, law and economics) ought to be encapsulated in the study concerning the 'why and how' of European integration, to rejuvenate the research and anticipate new perspectives the transformation of 'Maastricht' may require. At the same time, however, the traditional 'big questions' of European integration history, about the role of ideas, interests and institutions, have neither been answered sufficiently nor lost their relevance. One of the most prominent of these concerns the position of reunified Germany, 'the German Question' in the reality of post-Cold War history. Since 'Maastricht', and even more so since the euro crisis, the migration crisis, the Covid-19 crisis and the Russian war in Ukraine, this old European question has again become very topical and is hotly debated. The same holds true for that other traditional European question: the British relationship with the continent. The latter is more topical than ever in the present context of Brexit – a feverish search to understand why and how the British struggle with post-Maastricht Europe culminated in the Brexit vote. Or, more generally, the geopolitical questions: what role is left for the EU, next to its Anglo-Saxon allies, in the immediate neighbourhood of the western Balkans, along its unstable borders in the east and the south, vis-à-vis openly revisionist powers like Russia and China.

50 F. Kaiser and J. Elvert (eds.), *European Union Enlargement: A Comparative History* (London, Routledge, 2004); H. Sjursen (ed.), *Questioning EU Enlargement: Europe in Search of Identity* (London, Routledge, 2006).
51 F. Schimmelfennig, 'The Community Trap: Liberal Norms, Rhetorical Action, and the Eastern Enlargement of the European Union', *International Organization* 55, no. 1 (2001): 47–80; F. Schimmelfennig and U. Sedelmeier, 'Theorizing EU Enlargement: Research Focus, Hypotheses, and the State of Research', *Journal of European Public Policy* 9, no. 4 (2002): 500–28; U. Sedelmeier, *Constructing the Path to Eastern Enlargement: The Uneven Impact of EU Identity* (Manchester, Manchester University Press, 2005).

Aim and Organisation of the CHEU

The CHEU offers a unique opportunity to open up a truly diachronic research scope on the history of European integration. Next to that, it also offers a rare opportunity – on the basis of this research scope – to re-conceptualise the history of European integration, taking on board the latest insights from sub-branches of the study of European integration and interdisciplinary research on the theme. In other words, the CHEU entails a re-visiting of the big questions of the why and how of this European integration process. Indeed, the CHEU offers the opportunity to take on this challenge from an interdisciplinary and empirically, historically, informed angle, which fits the essentially sui generis aspects of the process. The key questions are as follows: why did we do it, and how does it work? How does the interplay between contingency, clashing ideas and the inherent urge for endurance and expansion of the integration process function? What are the outcomes of this interplay?

In order to find answers to these questions, the present book studies European integration history from a (1) diachronic, (2) multidisciplinary and (3) multi-actor angle in order to present an innovative, comprehensive and up-to-date CHEU. Therefore, unlike many textbooks as well as edited volumes on this topic, we do not organise the two volumes along a strict and classical timeline, starting with the first steps of European integration and finishing with the latest developments. Instead, time and change over time are integrated within the various chapters. Moreover, we invited historians as well as political scientists (and other social scientists and colleagues from other disciplines) to shed light both on traditional topics (such as foreign policy or economic and monetary cooperation and integration) and on non-traditional topics of European integration (like the role of narratives). Such a multidisciplinary approach is guaranteed between but also often within the different chapters. Finally, we neither analyse the European integration process from a state-centric perspective (with chapters on Germany, France, the UK, etc.), nor with a primary focus on European institutions (the European Commission, European Parliament, etc.). Instead, we introduce a thematic approach in which countries and institutions will be discussed from a variety of angles.

In the first volume of the CHEU the outside-in approach is dominant: what does the EU look like from the outside, and which outside forces shaped and co-designed the process of European integration? External events have played a major role in the tempo and direction of European integration. Moreover, research on European integration was nourished by a fairly long tradition of deep interest from US scholars – the influence of their 'eye of the beholder' perspective on European integration has been profound, both in the reality of the making of European integration and in the historiography concerning the why and how of the take-off of European integration and its development. This volume builds on these insights, yet also on recent developments in history and political science that have laid more emphasis on the limits of a Western or western European perspective. In addition, this volume of the CHEU also benefits from how European integration is understood outside the typical European Studies disciplines.

- Part I (Critical Junctures) pays attention to the main external events that have steered the European integration process. Instead of treaties, the emphasis is on 'critical junctures', defining moments in post-Second World War world history, as well as in international geopolitical arenas, in which (western) Europe evolved, found its form and transformed into the EU; this includes the division and reunification of Germany, the history of the Cold War and its legacy, decolonisation and the EU's eastern enlargement.
- Part II (Multilateralism and Geopolitics) considers various international trends that are not unique to the European integration process, but have been strong shaping forces in European integration, such as globalisation and (the return of) geopolitics (to post-war Europe). The analyses in this second part of the first volume specifically focus on causes and effects of these trends on the market, in society and with regard to global challenges adopted by the Europe of European integration. This 'outside-focus' mirrors the 'inside-focus' on instruments of the Europe of integration discussed in the second part of the second volume (see below).
- While the first two parts have institutions, countries and international organisations as the main actors, Part III (Perspectives and Ideas) focuses on the role of ideas, people, networks, public opinion, culture, religion and memory in the development of what is today the EU. Non-exclusive to the EU but increasingly salient within contemporary academic research, the analyses of these phenomena by scholars from various disciplines certainly contribute to an innovative take on the history of European integration.

The second volume takes an opposite perspective by looking at European integration from an inside-out perspective, an 'inside the black box' approach with a keen eye for the outside effects of internal dynamics in the process of European integration. This means that the authors first of all focus on the internal developments that have shaped the European integration process.

The aim of the volume is to shed light on the most important aspects of this process by looking at this process from an inside-out perspective. With the benefit of hindsight and with the typical academic distance, we cover the main events, instruments of European integration and narratives that have shaped the internal development of European integration.

- The scope of Part I (Milestones) concerns the basic rules that have defined European integration. In other words, in this part of the CHEU the treaties and their many changes are (chronologically) analysed by referring to the partly event-driven internal dynamics that have led to the establishment of a legal and political architecture of European integration. Brexit is considered here as a milestone in the history of European integration.
- Part II (Instruments of Integration) zooms in on the different instruments within the architecture of European integration and elucidates how policies are developed, with a special focus on the (pre-)history of the EMU and the euro, so central to today's European integration. To a certain extent similar to political entities at lower levels, the Europe of European integration has rules, money and coordinated management of economic and monetary policies at its disposal to steer the behaviour of public and private organisations, as well as that of its citizens. To make the system work, it also produces specific internal and external policies. In other words, by studying these instruments this part will make clear how European integration developed (in terms of politics and policy-making) within an expanding range of competences (policies). Special attention is paid to enlargement and the wider challenges of expansion of European integration, because, amongst other reasons, the (unforeseen) swift accession of new countries to the EU has had a profound impact on the internal development of European integration.
- In Part III (Narratives and Outcomes) the focus is on the many narratives the Europe of European integration is historically linked to and/or produced itself for internal use. More *'longue durée'* concepts, goals and ideas such as peace, (the promise of) prosperity, (the lack of) solidarity and democracy over time have all played a crucial mobilising role in the making of European integration (both in material terms and in mental and (collective) psychological terms). These concepts and ideas, as well as their evolutions and impact, deserve a critical and innovative analysis, since they constitute an essential force in the history of European integration, and determine how the process both spoke and failed to speak to the hearts and minds of Europeans.

The choice of this particular organisation of the two volumes, especially the outside-in and inside-out perspectives (in that order) is a deliberate choice by us, the editors. We believe it offers the best chances for an adequate, up-to-date and innovative approach to the history of the Europe of European integration and enables us to present the wide variety of relevant insights and perspectives in the making of the history *and* historiography in a comprehensive way.

Outlook

History is never finished, and neither is historiography. This also applies for the EU, and its still fairly recent history and pre-histories. Nonetheless, its past determines to a great extent its present and prefigures its future in ways we do not know yet.

Knowing and understanding integration history helps us to distinguish between what is acquired – like peace (or the absence of war) in (the western part of) the European continent – and what is not, and what is at stake. This is an urgent matter, not only of the research agenda of European integration history. The achievements of more than seven decades of European integration – economic prosperity, solidarity and democracy – are increasingly under pressure. On the one hand this is happening from within: think about the rise of illiberalism in a number of member states and the difficulties in coping with that for the EU institutions. But certainly the pressure is coming also from outside, with the volatility of the United States, the aggression of Russia and the so-called new Cold War with China. It puts the very idea of European integration under stress. This *project* is criticised because of its ambitions and goals ('why European integration?') that are never really reached, or tend to satisfy too few. Also its compe-tences, institutions, modes of decision-making and geographical scope trigger multiple unanswered questions. Evidently, the complexity of the EU is more of a certainty than its results. Given the fact that there is no consensus on what the project is and where it should lead, it is easier (but also elucidatory) to focus on the *process*. This means that European integra-tion might be defined not by its destiny (like the United States of America) but rather as a permanent series of actions, in reaction to but also anticipat-ing events. From this perspective, EU history often seems a flux of conflicts, crises and compromises.

The latter view is certainly true for the way in which the EU handled the Covid-19 pandemic and the war Russia started in Ukraine on 24 February 2022. After a decade in which European integration was almost identified with crisis management, these extraordinary new challenges shook the foundations of the EU anew. The jury is still out as the long-term consequences of the Covid-19 crisis are still unclear at the time of writing, and the horrific war in Ukraine is radically changing Europe's post-war history and the history of the EU while the two volumes of the present Cambridge History are being copy-edited and produced. The complete manuscript of the CHEU was handed in on 1 February 2022. This means that these two volumes cover the history of European integration until the Russian war in Ukraine.

In relation to the Covid-19 pandemic, three things are already clear. First of all, like many previous crises, it did not in the end lead to a quantum leap in European integration. Secondly, it did trigger some change within the EU, but without entirely changing the EU itself.[52] Here too, resilience is a characteristic of (the empirical) reality in the first place, although many would like to attribute it more to the EU itself. Thirdly, the crisis management of the pandemic reaffirmed that European integration is about messy procedures and heated discussions. Ad hoc decision-making, crises and even utter chaos have been constants in the recent history of the EU, as the EU's reaction to the war in Ukraine reconfirms once more. And yet, at the same time, the history of European integration also remains a history of persistent ideas about some sort of European unity and purpose in world history – these ideas represent a deeper and older Europe, an undercurrent to the history of treaties of European integration, a history regarding which we feel that it must not be neglected in analysing the latest trends and modes, if only because it represents a certain resilience of European civilisation and its promises, an urge – despite everything – to look forward, to define a purpose, to imagine a better world.

Note on Archival and Primary Sources

Given the 30-year rule of archival release (that mostly applies for key archives), most relevant archival sources are accessible to researchers of the history of European integration only after that period of 30 years. Consequently, broad international archival research into the history of European integration did not really start until the beginning of the 1980s (and now extends up to the end of the 1980s). Since then, time and time again, one conclusion has proved inescapable: none of the parties involved – the

---

52 S. Van Hecke, H. Fuhr and W. Wolfs, 'The Politics of Crisis Management by Regional and International Organizations in Fighting against a Global Pandemic: The Member States at a Crossroads', *International Review of Administrative Sciences* 87, no. 3 (2021): 672–90.

governments of the member states, European institutions and their predecessors, the business community, lobbies, political parties, individuals and so
on – have ever been able to control the integration process, let alone
dominate it, not even for a short time. The process has been uncontrollable
from the very beginning, even for the United States.

This general insight into the history of European integration has consequences for the research agenda. From an operational and methodological
perspective any research approach that sets itself the task of attempting to
fathom what has been going on in the history of European integration must
build also on multinational and/or transnational archival research. Every
chapter in the CHEU is based on original multinational archival research, or
(regarding the chapters dealing with the more recent history) on new
primary sources (for instance those made available through the EU institutions), new combinations of primary sources, or new original empirical
research. All of the chapters encapsulate the ambition to stretch the research
across the boundaries of 'silo studies' (on, for example, the Marshall Plan,
Bretton Woods, the European Payments Union, the ECSC) and try to
approach their subject matter from a richer and more comprehensive perspective, including a keen eye for the inter-linkages between the silos.

Vast collections of governmental and European documents are accessible
for the period from 1950 up to the early 1990s, including the key episodes
around the coming about and first crystallisations of the Treaty of Maastricht.
Moreover, for the more recent history, a significant number of published
sources, EU sources and private paper collections/ego-documents are
available and accessible already, also in the form of interviews with key
figures and numerous ego-documents, and – most notably – in other, and
in a way enriching, forms, such as films and interactive datasets. Indeed, the
list of relevant archives is extensive, and includes, next to the national
archives, among many others 'European archives' such as the Historical
Archives of the EU (HAEU) in Florence, the Jean Monnet Foundation in
Lausanne, the Archives of European Integration (AEI) at the University of
Pittsburgh, the Centre Virtuel de la Connaissance sur l'Europe (CVCE) in
Luxembourg, and national, European and trans-European political party
archival collections.

Thanks to its initial focus on archival and primary source research, the
CHEU unearthed a true wealth of archival and empirical sources. This
obviously includes the archives from numerous EU member states and
key countries outside the EU, including the United States, the UK and
Switzerland, but, in addition, many of the CHEU's chapters also build

upon in-depth research in private paper collections and non-governmental archival collections all over the world, many of them less well known. References to the archival and primary sources used are available in detail in the footnotes to each chapter. We, the editors, believe that this makes these sources checkable and accessible for follow-up research in the most adequate way.

PART I

★

CRITICAL JUNCTURES

The Emergence of a Divided World and a Divisible West

KENNETH WEISBRODE

Introduction

Before the Great War of 1914–18 ended, the successor states of four Eurasian empires split into conservative, liberal and revolutionary camps; ideological battles that had been waged for nearly a century were resumed like trench warfare in the streets of cities, in diplomatic salons, in the pages of broadsheets and in parliamentary halls. By the middle of the 1930s these ideological battles had again brought forth a civil war, this time in Spain, which came as an augury, tragic and bloody, conjoining the past, present and future in a grim garden of forking paths. This was the setting after the Second World War in which some western European nations sought to lay the basis for what would come to be called 'an ever closer union', whilst a rather different 'union' settled upon their eastern neighbours under Soviet rule. The processes of unification in eastern and western Europe were reactions and stimuli to the diminution of European power during the post-war period.

The world of the second half of the twentieth century therefore was a divided world. It was divided by politics, society, economics, culture, history and, above all else, ideology. It was a world whose actors had yet to recover from the great sundering of beliefs, kinships, institutions, manners and traditions that had begun with or soon after the Great War. The Second World War perpetuated the sundering as it was fought to resolve a dispute over geopolitical mastery. 'Men are ever ready to accuse statesmen of backing into the future', Raymond Aron has written; 'determined to prevent yesterday's disaster, they bring on tomorrow's'.[1] To state the point more

---

1 R. Aron, *The Century of Total War* (Garden City, NY, Doubleday, 1954), p. 149.

precisely, that war was fought by Germany and Japan to defeat two empires – Soviet and British – and by the United States to defeat one concept of empire and to replace it with another that did not regard itself as imperial. And after that war came a new 'cold' war between East and West. It emerged from the disease and desolation that followed the slaughter of millions of Europeans and their society.

This chronology begins after the middle of the Second World War, in 1943. By spring, the tide of the war had turned in favour of the Allies in North Africa and along the eastern front. The Nazi New Order stalled; the British began assisting communist partisans in Yugoslavia. In March, Winston Churchill spoke up against tyranny and for a post-war Council of Europe; in the spring, Wendell Willkie's bestseller *One World* appeared, followed in the summer by David Mitrany's *A Working Peace System* and in the fall by Richard Coudenhove-Kalergi's autobiography, *Crusade for Pan-Europe*. In November, the 'Big Three' – Churchill, Franklin Roosevelt and Joseph Stalin – held their first wartime conference together at Tehran. They debated but barely settled their many disagreements over what to do after the war was over, and over, presumably, in their favour. Meanwhile, the Soviet ambassadors to Britain and the United States were recalled and replaced by less pliant envoys.

This chronology ends 20 years later, in 1963. Europe was stable. It had grown more prosperous. But it remained divided between east and west, with a barbaric concrete wall that sealed off Europe from itself, and a shrill ideological frontier in Asia; and between north and south, with splenetic gradations of race, status, wealth and power. Stability in Europe notwithstanding, it was part of a world that stood in fear of weapons which, for the first time in history, had the capacity to destroy most life on earth. That prospect forever changed the calculus of power, not least for the United States, which possessed a short-lived monopoly on such weaponry. Yet, there were still terrible wars fought by 'conventional' means in other parts of the world which were interrelated in one way or another with the post-war divisions that emanated from Europe.

The events of these years mark the study of contemporary history as the moment when 'the problems which are actual in the world today first take visible shape', as the scholar Geoffrey Barraclough defined it.[2] Most historical literature on the contemporary period in European history employs this

---

2 G. Barraclough, *An Introduction to Contemporary History* (Harmondsworth, Penguin, 1967 [1964]), p. 20.

definition, and adheres to the standard twentieth-century chronology with a beginning, a middle and an end. The historical literature of the Cold War also tends to follow a narrative arc, which starts in about 1946, culminates between 1956 and 1962, and ends in or about 1989 – at least from the perspective of most European capitals.[3]

For participants in this history to claim that Europe needed the Cold War in order to unite and prosper was not incorrect. It was also correct to claim that, in a more limited sense, the Cold War needed Europe to divide if one imagines Europe as a geopolitical buffer zone and magnet for two superpowers trapped in mutual antagonism. Europe was divided and united in parts by the Cold War and a type of regional unification that goes by the name of Europeanisation, whilst the world outside Europe was divided from Europe by Europeanisation and joined to it by the ideological, military, political and social divisions enacted by the Cold War. As European external power waned, the internal, cultural sense of being 'European' waxed.

A more procedural term to describe this four-part phenomenon is 'integration', which may recall Max Weber's denunciation of German unification as a youthful prank inflicted upon the world by an old nation, or, in this instance, by an old continent. Integration is rarely uniform, but it was the twentieth century's principal response to instability and interdependence. Those conditions and the response to them extend to the historiographies of Europeanisation and the Cold War.[4] Contending interpretations – supranational, intergovernmental, functionalist and so on – have produced a large, variable social science literature. Ernst Haas, for example, would go on to renounce his own celebrated 'neo-functionalist' approach following the Gaullist interventions of the 1960s.

In truth, the divided world of the twentieth century was a world that featured not only a rhetoric of liberation but also a movement of cultural, industrial, moral, political and territorial consolidation that went by many

---

3 Cf. M. Connelly, *A Diplomatic Revolution* (Oxford, Oxford University Press, 2002); P. Grosser, *L'histoire du monde se fait en Asie* (Paris, Odile Jacob, 2017); T. Judt, *Postwar* (New York, NY, Penguin, 2005); D. Reynolds, *One World Divisible* (New York, NY, Norton, 2000). Other interpretive surveys from various ideological positions include J. L. Harper, *The Cold War* (Oxford, Oxford University Press, 2011); W. I. Hitchcock, *The Struggle for Europe* (New York, NY, Doubleday, 2003); E. Hobsbawm, *The Age of Extremes* (London, Michael Joseph, 1994); M. P. Leffler, *For the Soul of Mankind* (New York, NY, Hill and Wang, 2007); M. Mazower, *Dark Continent* (New York, NY, Knopf, 1998); R. Vinen, *A History in Fragments* (London, Little, Brown, 2000); I. Woloch, *The Postwar Moment* (New Haven, CT, Yale University Press, 2019).

4 Standard rationales are given in E. B. Haas, *The Uniting of Europe* (Stanford, CA, Stanford University Press, 1958); R. Mayne, *The Community of Europe* (New York, NY, Norton, 1963).

names: *unification, integration, amalgamation, annexation, solidarity, convergence, confluence, fusion, domination, swallowing* and so on. There were discrete differences between these concepts, but all derived from persistent efforts to mitigate, obstruct or undo the process of bifurcation into opposing camps. And yet, nearly every effort created additional divisions – camps within camps – or perpetuated and made clearer the divisions that already existed, beginning with the division between the past and the present. The binary trope of unity and division appears often in the historical literature.[5]

It is tempting for the historian to view the twentieth century thus, dialectically, as interdependent cycles of unity and division – between continents, empires, ideas, institutions, ideologies, nations, narratives and technologies – each rising or falling in relation to the others over time. Where peace, liberty and prosperity thrived in one place whose people imagined themselves superior, the opposite was bound to happen somewhere else.[6] Had this not been the record of European history for several centuries? If a set of inverse relationships did exist, and moreover if the Soviet Union and the United States each lay along the 'periphery' of Europe, were peace and sovereignty in both places – core and periphery – not also inversely co-dependent? Perhaps smaller powers in the 'centre' were now forced to choose, or be chosen by, one extra-European master or the other. But was there no middle ground for them to choose between truth and compromise?

Those abstract questions date back to the formulation of the European state system in the middle of the seventeenth century and to its national reformulation in the middle of the eighteenth and nineteenth centuries. But like many abstractions, the terminology of geopolitics is imperfect. That was the case during the years 1943–63 when a remarkable attempt was made in western Europe to bury national rivalries with a grand project for solving or managing problems collectively. The nation-state appeared once again as an artefact in a new age of continental, super- or 'global powers'.[7] That the project succeeded had as much to do with the persistence of its makers as it did with a divisible geopolitical system. The nation-state was, on balance, a durable beneficiary of that system,

---

5 See, for example, P. M. H. Bell, *Twentieth Century Europe* (London, Hodder, 2006).
6 C. Burney, *The Dungeon Democracy* (London, Heinemann, 1945), p. 40; F. Ninkovich, *Modernity and Power* (Chicago, IL, University of Chicago Press, 1994), pp. 172, 182; J. B. Priestley, *Russian Journey* (London, Writers Group of the Society for Cultural Relations with the USSR, 1946), p. 36.
7 Kurt Riezler quoted in K. H. Jarausch, *Out of Ashes* (Princeton, NJ, Princeton University Press, 2015), p. 48.

however much the proponents of European integration proclaimed Europe to be progressive, post-national and post-participatory.

Partisans of the nation-state and integration came to know the limits of their contradictions. Whereas the Cold War may ultimately have done more to bring Europe together than to drive it apart, beyond Europe the opposite occurred. Arthur M. Schlesinger, Jr. wrote in 1967 that 'the difference between America and Russia in 1945 was that some Americans fundamentally believed that, over a long run, a modus vivendi with Russia was possible; while the Russians, so far as one can tell, believed in no more than a short-run modus vivendi with the United States'.[8] If that was true, then the European project, by its simultaneous attempt to narrow the scope and strengthen the will for unification, probably exacerbated existing divisions more than it created new ones.

The Emergence of the 'Yalta Order'

The 'Yalta Order', named after the conference in that place during February 1945, is a familiar but deceptive shorthand formula to describe the period after the war.[9] It was not actually an order as the term is usually understood; neither did it emerge in the usual sense, but was rather dictated, purportedly, by the logic of *tertius gaudens*; and that happened at least 2 years before the Yalta conference itself and continued to be reworked, refined and challenged in the years after the conference, albeit by a generation of mainly pre-war politicians.

In January 1943, Churchill and Roosevelt met at Casablanca and improvised the policy of 'unconditional surrender' for the end of the war. The rhetoric accompanying the policy was an acknowledgement of the reality of 'total war'. It sent a signal to the Axis enemies and to a resolute and more confident Soviet ally: in theory, there would be no partial victory. In practice the implementation of the policy would be mixed, for even a prostrate Japan was allowed to keep its emperor in 1945 (on the condition that he acknowledge for his country's armed forces the policy of 'unconditional surrender'). Thus commenced in Europe the effort to capitalise upon Axis losses in North Africa and in the Soviet Union, and then, ultimately, to destroy the Axis and, along with it, Nazi Germany.

---

8 A. M. Schlesinger, Jr., 'Origins of the Cold War', *Foreign Affairs* 46, no. 1 (1967): 22–52, 50.
9 See F. J. Harbutt, *Yalta 1945* (Cambridge, Cambridge University Press, 2010).

Allied successes accumulated during the first half of 1943. The Soviets managed to hold on in Leningrad (the siege was broken in January 1944) and relieved Stalingrad with a decisive offensive in February 1943. Stalin directed Igor Kurchatov to develop an atomic bomb. The British meanwhile obtained evidence of the German V1 and V2 weapons programmes. The Warsaw ghetto uprising began in April. During the same month the Soviet Union severed diplomatic relations with Poland following the Polish appeal to the International Committee of the Red Cross to investigate the graves of massacred Polish officers at Katyń. 'Poland', the exiled diarist Andrzej Bobkowski wrote at the end of April, 'sticks in everyone's throats'.[10] In Italy in July came the dramatic fall of Benito Mussolini and his fascist party.

Yet the war had come to resemble a war of attrition, which gave advantage to the side with more resources, and more human blood to shed, not including, of course, the blood of the victims of Nazi mass murder, which had also begun in earnest. The USSR, which was doing much of the fighting, received significant assistance as part of the American lend-lease programme, something a generation of Soviet citizens and their descendants did not forget. (A museum of the Allies and lend-lease opened in Moscow in 2004.) In the summer of 1943 came the Allied invasion of Sicily and subsequently of Italy itself, whose army surrendered in September, only to have the war continue there between German and Allied forces. These military events occasioned the meeting of Allied foreign ministers at Moscow in October and then of the Big Three the following month at Tehran. Their discussions centred on plans to coordinate strategy for the remainder of the war – the timing of a second front in the west being the most urgent topic – and for the post-war period. Churchill and Stalin discussed the map of Europe, using matches to represent Poland's borders, but Roosevelt demurred when Stalin drew lines showing where he thought the borders should be.[11] There was an election coming up in the United States and Roosevelt admitted that he could not afford to lose votes – namely Polish votes – if word got out about plans for the Polish borders.

Stalin's attitude towards Poland was as predictable as his concentration on territorial matters; Roosevelt's suggestion that Germany be divided into seven parts was not; but a fuller discussion on borders and related topics would await the next meeting at Yalta. For then the Soviet Union was in a strong position to dictate policies, starting with the creation of a buffer

10 A. Bobkowski, *Wartime Notebooks*, trans. G. Drabik and L. Engelstein (New Haven, CT, Yale University Press, 2018), p. 441.
11 C. E. Bohlen, *Witness to History* (New York, NY, Norton, 1973), pp. 144, 151–2.

along its western border. The extent and dimensions of that buffer – one plan for a 'neutral zone' had included Austria, Denmark, Germany, Italy and Switzerland – were unresolved; but post-war lines would run between the east and the west, not between the north and the south or between regional blocs, such as a Scandinavian or a Danubian federation. The Soviet Union would keep control over many of the central European territories it had already incorporated by separation from traditional neighbours and hinterlands. Borders would move and so would populations. Poland, for example, shifted to the west as millions of Belarusians, Germans, Poles, Ukrainians and others went with it. This created much work for the United Nations Relief and Rehabilitation Administration, which was established in 1943.

Over the course of 1944 the Red Army defeated Germany throughout much of the Balkans and restored control over the Black Sea. For their part, the Americans and the British had finally made good on their promise to open a second front in the west, with the Normandy invasion of June 1944. It succeeded. The second front was in the northwest rather than the southeast, which again meant that post-war Europe would be divided along a north–south axis. Now, the final race was on to defeat German power, which the Allies did, notwithstanding terrible fighting in the Ardennes in the winter of 1944–5. Rome was liberated in June 1944; Paris in August; Berlin finally in May of the following year as the Red Army begun its race to the Elbe. There Americans saw Russians digging trenches on the other side.[12]

These liberations were not all combined operations. The first two were carried out by American, British and other Allied troops, the final one by the Red Army. The Soviet Union did not take part in the invasion or occupation of Italy. The wish by some British and American commanders to march on to Berlin was not granted by the Supreme Allied Commander, General Dwight Eisenhower, adhering to plans of the US Joint Chiefs of Staff which did not seek a large post-war occupation of Germany.[13]

The outlines of post-war Europe were set by the time of the final wartime conference at Potsdam in the summer of 1945. The Allies were united, ostensibly, but also divided, as later, 'in a fog of cross-purposes'.[14] The liberators and now occupiers set about clearing, collectivising and integrating disparate territories as had begun to occur in other regions around the world. In March 1945 the collective defence of the western hemisphere was

12 T. H. White, *Fire in the Ashes* (New York, NY, Sloane, 1953), p. 25.
13 C. Eisenberg, *Drawing the Line* (Cambridge, Cambridge University Press, 1997 [1996]), pp. 51, 74.
14 Priestley, *Russian Journey*, p. 11.

formalised in the Act of Chapultepec. That month the Arab League was created. Starting in April at San Francisco, the United Nations (UN) worked to establish the UN organisation. The first session of its general assembly would take place at London in January of the following year.

Neither the San Francisco nor the Potsdam conference made a formal peace like the ones at Westphalia in 1643–8, Utrecht in 1713–15, Vienna in 1814–15 or Paris in 1919–20. Here a general settlement would come only in 1975 with the Helsinki meeting of the Conference on Security and Cooperation in Europe, but even then there was no treaty, only an agreement. Following Potsdam came several contentious meetings of foreign ministers. The most contentious subject was Germany.

Germany joined much of Europe in being occupied. In Germany's case, the occupiers were Americans, British, French and Soviets. Each had a designated sector which was governed according to multiple longstanding preferences of each occupier. Their aims, in contested order of priority, were to reconstruct the German economy, notably its industry, and to reconstruct the political culture so as to ensure that Germany would no longer threaten its neighbours or the general peace.[15] Deep within the Soviet sector lay Berlin, which itself was divided into sectors. At first the four powers coordinated their occupation. By the middle of 1946, however, their collaboration had dissolved in suspicion and acrimony. Berlin would be divided during the next 2 years into western ('bizonia', then 'trizonia') and eastern sectors.

Berlin's division was coterminous with the eventual hardening of the country's division into East and West Germany. Hardening resulted from diverging interests and policies, such as those regarding industrial reparations and the status of the Ruhr, but also from the incompatibility of the above-mentioned aims with the perpetuation of a single German state and, at the same time, with the reintegration of Germany into the European and international economy. Such reintegration would happen, but mainly in the western sectors; the eastern one remained, like most of central Europe, a 'stony world ... merciless and bare'.[16]

The rhetorical association of economic recovery with German and European unity lasted longer than a recognition of any real contradiction between the aims and realities of post-war policy. A united Germany was potentially too dangerous – to Europe or as allied to either superpower, which meant that Germany could be rehabilitated, reconstructed, reformed

---

15 W. Laqueur, *Europe since Hitler* (Harmondsworth, Penguin, 1972 [1970]), p. 101.
16 C. Miłosz, *The Captive Mind*, trans. J. Zielonko (London, Penguin, 2001 [1953]), p. 127.

and ransomed, but not by all four occupiers in unison. Instead, just as there were to be two Chinas and two Koreas, there would be two Germanies and two Berlins.

'The struggle over Germany ended', W. R. Smyser has written, 'only when all participants received what they had needed from the beginning, although none received it in the form in which they had first thought they wanted it.'[17] This division of aspirations and accomplishments – and of declaratory and actual policy – culminated in a series of Berlin 'crises' lasting from 1948 to 1962. The first saw the provision of an 'airlift' to supply the western sectors of the city that were threatened with Soviet-imposed isolation following the introduction of a new western currency. The airlift was a galvanising force and a propaganda coup for the western powers. They declared West Berlin, a theoretically indefensible western exclave, to be defended at all costs. A divided Berlin had become Europe's main prize and the *sine qua non* of prestige, resolve and unity for each side in the Cold War.

Western unity was bolstered by the signing of the Brussels Pact in 1948 and the North Atlantic Treaty Organization (NATO) in 1949 (see below). The Soviet Union went on to construct its own alliance, the Warsaw Pact, in 1955, which, like NATO, would later be armed with intercontinental ballistic missiles. Finally, in 1961, the Soviets, at the behest of the East German authorities, allowed the Berlin Wall to be constructed through the middle of the city after stopping the movement of Berliners from east to west. That policy was received with relief in the west, not least by US President John F. Kennedy, who remarked glibly that it was 'a hell of a lot better than a war'.[18]

Kennedy nearly did get his war. The following year, in October, the Soviet premier, Nikita Khrushchev, oversaw the placement of nuclear missiles on the island of Cuba, 90 miles off the coast of the United States, in a manner that reminded many people, not least the US president, of Berlin, where large pipelines to the West German border had recently been lain. Thirteen days later, the Soviets agreed to remove their missiles from Cuba. That the Berlin crises were suspended by a missile crisis halfway across the world was remarkable but not unbelievable. It demonstrated that the Cold War, which had begun over Germany, had acquired a global dimension and that Europe remained dependent upon the whims, passions and lapses of the two superpowers.

---

17 W. R. Smyser, *From Yalta to Berlin* (New York, NY, St. Martin's Press, 1999), pp. xvii, 138.
18 Ibid., p. 161.

The Globalisation of the 'Yalta Order'

Cold War interdependence had already existed for more than a decade by the time of the Cuban missile crisis. In the summer of 1950, South Korea was invaded from the north after the communist leader Kim Il-sung had obtained Stalin's assent to unify Korea under communist rule. After having been repelled by UN troops led by the United States, Kim was assisted by the People's Republic of China, which had joined the communist bloc the previous year after Mao's victory in China's civil war. Now Stalin, having just endured the challenge of wilful Yugoslavia (described below), faced the likelihood of dealing with a much bigger 'junior partner' in China. For his part, the US president, Harry Truman, depicted the Korean problem less as a matter of geopolitics and more as a simple test of his backbone. Each man's response brought to mind the remark of Stalin upon seeing Ivan Pavlov, the great scientist and convert to atheism, cross himself: 'There he goes again – a slave to his reflexes.'[19]

The Korean War led to the extension of the Cold War to Asia and ultimately to the major split within the communist camp Stalin had tried to avoid. It also brought about the militarisation of the Cold War in Europe. The Warsaw Pact, as noted, was established in response to the creation of NATO. The western alliance, at the time of the signing of the North Atlantic Treaty 6 years earlier, had no army; George Gershwin's 'I got plenty o' nuttin' and 'It ain't necessarily so' were played at the signing ceremony in Washington, DC. Following the Korean invasion, it became necessary to create such an allied army, which would include West Germany.

German rearmament would happen when West Germany (known since 1949 as the Federal Republic) joined NATO, also in 1955. It capped a consolidating and energising global trend that had underwritten the Truman Doctrine, announced in March 1947, according to which the United States vowed to assist any nation menaced by communism. In September the Rio Pact, building on the Act of Chapultepec, was signed, followed in April 1948 by the Pact of Bogotá creating the Organisation of American States. In November 1950, the United States got the UN General Assembly to pass a 'Uniting for Peace' resolution for collective security.

Truman's vow gained material backing with the Bretton Woods institutions (the International Monetary Fund and World Bank), invented back in 1944, which moved to underwrite economic stability and growth. Then came

---

19 Quoted in R. H. B. Lockhart, *My Europe* (London, Putnam, 1952), p. 45.

the Marshall Plan, a recovery, reconstruction and, in effect, insurance programme for the European economies of approximately $13 billion,
announced in June 1947 and followed by a conference at Paris in July to
which the members of the nascent Soviet bloc, the Cominform (succeeding
the Comintern, which had been dissolved back in 1943), were invited. In
marking the birth of the Cominform that autumn, the Soviet ideologue
Andrei Zhdanov announced the division of the world into two 'camps' –
democratic and imperialist. Czechoslovakia, which accepted the invitation to
the Paris conference, reversed itself; its long-suffering president, Edvard
Beneš, had a stroke. (Czechoslovakia had also been one of the original
signatories of the General Agreement on Tariffs and Trade (GATT).) Stalin
presently saw to the toppling of the government there in a coup in
February 1948. This produced fear and outrage to varying degrees in the
west, which eased the passage of appropriations for the Marshall Plan
through the US Congress. Partition had become popular. Even trade unionists organised rival world federations.

Few measures had been taken to guarantee western European unity
until the Prague coup. After it, they came in short order. In March 1948
Britain, France and the Benelux states (Belgium, Luxembourg and the
Netherlands) signed the Brussels Treaty (the 'Brussels Pact') of collective
defence. (The Benelux states had already signed monetary and customs
conventions during the war.) In April the Organisation for European
Economic Co-operation (OEEC) was established to give institutional
coherence to the Marshall Plan. In May the Congress of Europe was
held, which led the following year to the creation of the Council of
Europe, one month after the North Atlantic Treaty was, as noted, signed
by twelve nations.

Retrenchment in the East and West

The Schuman Plan for the European Coal and Steel Community followed in
May 1950. Its name came from the French foreign minister, Robert Schuman,
whose family was from Lorraine and Luxembourg. West Germany was led by
a man from the Rhineland, Konrad Adenauer. Adenauer was about as far as one
could be from ambivalent Prussian *Schaukelpolitik* (oscillation). His Germany
looked towards its west: in 1955 West Germany proclaimed the policy later
known as the 'Hallstein Doctrine', which conditioned diplomatic relations with
other states upon their refusal to recognise East Germany. French governments,
which had looked towards France's east, that is, towards Germany, now bought

into the Marshall Plan for European, including German, rehabilitation, reconstruction and reintegration.

Schuman's announcement was dramatic, but the plan itself was modest; or, as Richard Mayne has written with regard to the later mantra, 'ever closer union', it was a gesture that had 'the double advantage of being at once spirited and imprecise'.[20] It called merely for the combination of the French and German coal and steel industries, but was regarded with suspicion by some. The US Secretary of State, Dean Acheson, remembered thinking it was the 'damndest cartel I had ever heard of in my life'.[21] But he and other Americans came round to supporting the plan. The widening of European economic and political integration continued with the deepening of a belief in the indivisibility of security – or, in Acheson's words, the refusal to see its various ingredients 'be separated in the intellectual equivalent of a cream separator'.[22]

On both sides of the Atlantic, through the methodical integration of their economies, nations had created a certain stability that went by the name of the welfare state. It coexisted with a capitalist economy and a brand of politics called 'hegemonic democracy'.[23] Christian and Social Democratic parties went from being ideological foes to pragmatic collaborators. Their use of socio-economic planning buttressed wartime practices as they aimed to overcome pre-war political and social divisions and prevent a return to 'the frowzy and fidgety little hole called Europe'.[24] To say that western stability was co-dependent by collective association with peace, prosperity, integration and the Cold War is simplistic and possibly overstated, but not ironic insofar as it liberated rulers whilst constraining the ruled. The beneficiaries of the welfare state would become at once more hierarchical, incremental, aspirational, predictable, conservative, technocratic, nationalistic and entrenched, not to mention preponderantly male, middle class and middle-aged.

Eastern integration was at once both more and less uniform than its western counterpart. The Soviet domination of what were called in the

20 Mayne, *Community of Europe*, p. 13.
21 Quoted in L. S. Kaplan, 'Dean Acheson and the Atlantic Community', in D. Brinkley (ed.), *Dean Acheson and the Making of U.S. Foreign Policy* (New York, NY, St. Martin's Press, 1993), p. 38.
22 Quoted in W. LaFeber, *America, Russia, and the Cold War* (New York, NY, Wiley, 1967), p. 102.
23 M. Conway, *Western Europe's Democratic Age* (Princeton, NJ, Princeton University Press, 2020), pp. 2, 79–81.
24 Harold Acton quoting Norman Douglas, in D. Pryce-Jones, *Signatures* (New York, NY, Encounter, 2020), p. 7.

west 'captive nations' was apparent before the end of the Second World War, but it had already begun to weaken. Under the leadership of Josip Broz Tito – a communist who freed his country from Nazi rule with the help of the USSR – Yugoslavia left the Cominform in June 1948 following the Prague coup and a dispute with Stalin over Albania. A few months later, in January 1949, the Council for Mutual Economic Assistance (Comecon) was set up and later, as noted, the Warsaw Pact. Following the Prague coup, the Soviets and their allies would find themselves policing and putting down more such uprisings: in East Germany in 1953, in Hungary in 1956, and in Czechoslovakia and Poland during the same year. For his part, Tito would co-found his own organisation of like-minded states, the Non-Aligned Movement, in 1961.

Western communist parties, despite their democratic vigour, were mostly loyal to Moscow and exercised restraint for fear of triggering too forceful a reaction as the foil of 'democratic' parties. By the 1950s the possibility of any of them coming to power on their own appeared slight. Eastern communist parties, in contrast, were less numerous and less popular, but also less supine. By now they presided over single-party states. Political rivalries in the east and west, with the partial exception of Berlin, usually came from within the same ideological camp and the assertiveness of 'local' actors seeking advantages vis-à-vis outside powers and interests.

German rearmament again offers an example of such rivalries. The prospect of German rearmament during the Korean War drove a wedge between western powers unable to find the political wherewithal to support or to oppose rearmament. The French premier, René Pleven, and Jean Monnet, the president of the High Authority of the European Coal and Steel Community, devised a solution to that quandary in the form of a European army, called the European Defence Community (EDC). Once assured of its compatibility with NATO, the Americans backed the EDC proposal with the passion of the converted. The French people then felt otherwise. The National Assembly voted down the EDC Treaty in August 1954. The vote took place just after a meeting at Geneva, called to settle the Korean War, but diverted by the French defeat at Dien Bien Phu in French Indochina to discuss the colony's future. It was alleged but never proven that the Soviet Union conspired with the French government to assist with France's extrication from Indochina in exchange for quashing the EDC. France presently began the effort to build a nuclear weapon; occupied Austria regained its independence as a neutral power; and a rearmed West Germany, as noted, joined NATO in May of the following year. East Germany remained a Soviet satellite.

After the EDC defeat, the founders of the European movement met at Messina in June 1955. Monnet had announced his resignation from the High Authority following a stroke brought on, it was said, by the EDC saga. At Messina the other founders laid the foundations of the Treaties of Rome (1957), which established the next two European communities: the Common Market and the European Atomic Energy Community. Both treaties, like their predecessor at Paris in 1951 establishing the Coal and Steel Community, were modest. 'Community' fell short of 'union'. But even 'community' was a difficult sell for some countries, such as France, whose efforts at integration had boosted the appeal there of opponents like the Poujadist movement, which gained a short-lived but intense popularity.

Those early efforts nonetheless gained benefits from certain divisions. Integration meant different things to different people. To some opponents, integration was the kernel of a German-dominated European renaissance, or a thin substitute for it. To others, it was a French-dominated attempt to counterbalance German power, or to connive in it for the benefit of French industry and, later, agriculture. To others it was an American import meant to subordinate European economies and to subvert national sovereignty and institutions.[25] To some proponents, it was meant to reinforce both economies and institutions, as was critical for western well-being; or to redirect attention, resources and devotion away from former colonies; or to establish the 'conditions . . . for transforming so-called peaceful coexistence into genuine peace'.[26] To others, it was simply a way to advance efficiency in order to attain or otherwise accompany higher levels of industrialisation, growth, productivity and investment.

The first decade after the end of the Second World War therefore was characterised by centripetal tendencies within western Europe and centrifugal tendencies beyond it. The subsequent decade was characterised by the opposite. This pattern coincided with a shift in focus of the major powers of western Europe towards European integration, and away from the decolonising, or 'third', world at the moment when Africa, Asia and Latin America began to attract more attention from the Soviet Union and the United States.

25 As summarised by E. Benoit, *Europe at Sixes and Sevens* (Westport, CT, Greenwood Press, 1982 [1961]), p. 68.
26 Jean Monnet quoted in F. Duchêne, *Jean Monnet* (New York, NY, Norton, 1994), p. 380.

Retrenchment in the North and South

Another international conference besides Messina took place in 1955. This was again at Geneva, in July. It was the first time the leaders of the major powers of the world – the old 'Big Three' in addition to France – had met since the war. Stalin had died in March 1953. It was not certain who would replace him, until Geneva, that is, when US president Dwight Eisenhower and a few others present noticed the members of the Soviet delegation, led ostensibly by Nikolai Bulganin, deferring to Nikita Khrushchev.

Little of substance was agreed at Geneva. The rhetoric of 'peaceful coexistence' notwithstanding, the Cold War would remain in place. This coincided with another, warmer development around the world, which fell under the broad term 'decolonisation'. By 1960 there were some forty new independent states, many of which nonetheless retained their colonial borders. The concurrent waging of independence struggles, however violent or peaceful, alongside the waging of the Cold War suggests that, in their interrelationship, they were not disconnected from global trends, and the Cold War was not entirely cold. This was in fact a global Cold War. It was not a single conflict but rather multiple intersecting conflicts that involved as many local and regional rivalries as transnational ones.

Alignments between decolonisation, the Cold War and European integra-tion were complicated. The Treaties of Rome were signed in 1957 with the divisions of the previous year's Suez crisis, in which British, French and Israeli forces intervened against Egypt, still fresh in the public mind. European imperialism – in Egypt, at least – was becoming passé, yet one of its legacies persisted. After 1919, the founders of the nation-states that emerged from the collapse of four European empires exhibited greater allegiance to, and received more support from, the rulers of two overseas empires – the British and French – as well as from two nascent empires or 'multinational states' – American and Soviet – than did fellow nationalists seeking self-determination in Africa or Asia. Likewise, during the Second World War, the Allies and their colonial possessions were ostensibly united against fascism, but behind such unity were divisions challenging the moral integrity of each side. After all, the borders of the United States and the USSR – two nominally anti-colonial powers – had each been defined in part by force of arms.

One of the most telling divisions was therefore racial. 'Toward the end of the last century', John Lukacs wrote in 1961, 'Bismarck said that the most important factor in the next century would be that Americans, after all, spoke

English. The most important factor in the second half of this century may be that, after all, the Russians are white.'[27] Opposition to racial hierarchies challenged the wider Eurocentric world system that upheld what is today called globalisation but that also unleashed cultural, ideological and political forces globalisation was able to enlist and mobilise against itself. 'Liberation' from colonial rule often led to disappointment, however, starting with the institutions that inherited (or seized) power, namely militaries and the closed, dysfunctional states they protected, and accompanied in Europe by a 'pall of negation' that bemused, panicked or discomfited elites long accustomed to European rule.[28]

The normative attempt to export a west European-style democratic peace to Africa and Asia did not succeed as some had hoped. Liberal ideology had grown stale and, in 'decolonised' context, hypocritical. More notable were the efforts of the decolonised themselves: the Conference of African and Asian Peoples, which first met at Bandung, Indonesia, in 1955, made a mark. The Non-Aligned Movement, as noted, joined several of these countries with fellow travellers such as Cuba and Yugoslavia. Few were genuinely non-aligned. But both movements, despite having different aims and justifications, acquired cachet and made *tiers-mondisme* a force in domestic and international politics. Its importance is reflected in the recent historiography of the Cold War, European integration and what is known today as the Global South.[29]

In 1957 Mao Zedong declared the coming of an 'east wind'; nearly 3 years later the British prime minister, Harold Macmillan, pronounced a 'wind of change' blowing across Africa. Charles de Gaulle returned to power in France in 1958, established the Fifth Republic, and acceded to Algerian independence after a bloody war. The leader of independent Ghana, Kwame Nkrumah, declared, also in 1958, that 'force alone is no longer a decisive factor in world affairs'.[30] In the United Kingdom the Campaign for Nuclear Disarmament was born. What came to be called the 'third world' had become, by way of a 'pre-emptive cringe', an important ground

27 J. Lukacs, *A New History of the Cold War* (Garden City, NY, Anchor Books, 1966 [1961]), p. 396.
28 G. K. Young, *Masters of Indecision* (London, Methuen, 1962), p. 15.
29 For example, P. T. Chamberlin, *The Cold War's Killing Fields* (New York, NY, HarperCollins, 2018); G. Garavini, *After Empires*, trans. R. R. Nybakken (Oxford, Oxford University Press, 2012).
30 Quoted in W. S. Thompson, *Ghana's Foreign Policy* (Princeton, NJ, Princeton University Press, 1969), p. xi.

of geopolitical and moral contestation, dependent upon, but divided from, a retreating Europe.[31]

Some Africans and Asians continued to assert themselves collectively in ways familiar to Europeans. In February 1958 Egypt and Syria formed the United Arab Republic. In April representatives of eight northern and western African states met at Ghana in a Conference of Independent African States. By December, several non-governmental groups had joined them in an All-African People's Conference. In June 1959 seven west African states formed a customs union. In January 1961 several went further in the Charter of Casablanca, which anticipated a common market in addition to a collective security organisation, a payments union and a development bank. One could add here the founding in 1960 of the Organization of the Petroleum Exporting Countries. And in January 1962, twenty other African governments agreed to create an Organisation of African States. Thirty-two established the Organisation of African Unity the following year.

The Re-emergence of the West

Western Europe's own relations with former colonies were now dominated by trade and other economic matters. When the Common Market was established after 1957, overseas colonies and other territories were, directly or by 'association', part of it. But as the latter gained independence and the former grew protectionist – for instance, under the Common Agricultural Policy (CAP) – economic relationships required redefinition. That happened with the Yaoundé (1963) convention and in the Dillon (1960–2) round of the GATT. Together the negotiations aimed to facilitate a single trade policy for the Common Market, which by 1963 had also affirmed a legal personality with the decision by the European Court of Justice in the case of *Van Gend & Loos*. Later, with the Kennedy Round (1964–7), the Common Market asserted itself as a single economic – and an embryonic political – actor.

Yet, Europe not only remained divided but appeared to be closing in upon itself. That was the paradox of '*ridimensionamento* . . . to which André Malraux once referred when he pointed out that continents had replaced countries as the effective units of world power'.[32] The Common Market was not a country, and not quite continental. In economic relations it is customary to speak of a single 'centre', which the Common Market was, potentially,

---

31 J. B. Kelly quoted in Pryce-Jones, *Signatures*, p. 152; Conway, *Western Europe's Democratic Age*, p. 281.
32 Mayne, *Community of Europe*, p. 28.

but by now there were multiple peripheries: not only the seven members of the European Free Trade Association (EFTA, formed in 1960) that remained outside the Common Market, but also the European members of neither organisation as well as erstwhile colonies beyond Europe.

The Common Market emerged alongside a number of other institutions with overlapping and mutually serviceable memberships, including EFTA and the OEEC (after 1960, the Organisation for Economic Co-operation and Development, OECD). Relationships amongst these institutions varied. Some European integrationists, and some of their opponents, sought a total break between the Common Market and everyone else; others, a doubling down on one or more sets of relationships; still others, an even more intimate or extensive association amongst them – for example, the British Commonwealth and 'Eurafrique'. It was not unusual for proponents to claim that one or other preferred arrangement was in the best interests of Europeans and non-Europeans alike.[33] European aid and development pro-grammes towards former colonies were characterised accordingly, where, again, memories of colonial attitudes and practices remained strong and dynamic in, for example, the movement towards the establishment of the G77, the group of developing nations, starting in 1962 and formally estab-lished 2 years later. Such variations hindered the concurrent development of transatlantic relations outside NATO and, at the same time, distracted from campaigns for socio-economic reform, notably those coming from the political left.[34] For its part, the United States continued to play the role of midwife, arbiter and occasional enforcer of consensus, recovery and growth within and amongst the various organisations and their members up to the point when, after 1959, a gold and balance of payments problem demanded greater policy consolidation. That in turn meant a stronger US effort to harmonise transatlantic positions on fiscal policy – known as 'bur-den-sharing' – with its commitments to European integration and trade liberalisation.

This was one side of the coin of prosperity. The other side was the daily experience of Europeans, especially in the most prosperous nations, of participating in a more informal, individualistic, confident, mobile, diverse society – not least because of changing demographics. The *trente glorieuses* – as the period of west European prosperity that followed the twentieth

33 Benoit, *Europe at Sixes and Sevens*, pp. 9, 27 n. 17, 112 n. 28, 202; Thompson, *Ghana's Foreign Policy*, p. 217; K. K. Patel, *Project Europe*, trans. M. Dale (Cambridge, Cambridge University Press, 2020), p. 10.
34 See D. Johnstone, *Circle in the Darkness* (Atlanta, GA, Clarity Press, 2020), pp. 57–69.

century's own 30 years' war was called – required many more workers and consumers. Many of them came from the decolonised states of Africa and Asia, and from southern and eastern Europe. Many also prospered and came to see themselves, and their children, as Europeans. Some of them and some in their host societies would not, giving the underbelly of 'integration' an ambivalent, darker meaning as a record of failure. But Europe had grown peaceful. Mass murder at the hands of the state would continue to occur outside Europe but no longer inside it, at least until the 1990s. Still, in the east, the gulag endured, abetted now by the use of psychiatry whereby dissidents were sent to re-education camps in the guise of mental hospitals.

Conclusion

After the Cuban missile crisis in 1962, the Soviet Union and the United States entered a period of détente in Europe. The following year they and the United Kingdom signed the first nuclear arms control treaty: the Limited Test Ban. The signing of the Limited Test Ban irked Charles de Gaulle, who was not party to the negotiations, as well as Mao Zedong, whose nuclear weapons ambitions, along with those presumed to possess the leaders of West Germany, the treaty was meant to proscribe. The following year, France granted diplomatic recognition to communist China, which would go on to conduct its first successful nuclear test, as France had done after the Suez crisis. Nuclear diplomacy, therefore, served at once to draw together the interests of the superpowers and to drive a wedge between them and their nominal allies.

The two superpowers *manqués*, China and France, took separate advantage, not only of a nuclear test ban but also of tensions in the third world. The Sino-Soviet split, which began more than a decade earlier between Stalin and the people he called 'margarine Communists', worsened after 1962. That year Kwame Nkrumah was awarded the Lenin Peace Prize, and China fought a war with India. Seven years later China and the Soviet Union would also engage in open conflict along their border. On reflection it is remarkable that it took western governments, notably in the United States, so long to believe the split was real.

NATO fared better overall, but France would go on to withdraw from its unified military command and to expel the headquarters of the alliance from Paris (in 1966), a few months after de Gaulle suspended the French role in decision-making in the Common Market, prompting the 'empty chair crisis'. (In 1961–2, French foreign minister Maurice Couve de Murville 'stopped the clock' of changes to EEC decision-making for 2 weeks, but in 1965 he refused to do so, opting instead for a boycott lasting nearly 6 months.) These disruptions, de Gaulle claimed, were not meant to advance a neutralist alternative, but rather to strengthen France by raising it to the level of a 'third force', or perhaps a 'second force in the west'. Most attempts to establish a second force in the east met with a harsh reaction from the Soviet Union.

Some of de Gaulle's related gestures, such as the 'Fouchet Plan' for a European political directorate, did not succeed, but galvanised those who sought a more intergovernmental path of European integration. As he had done throughout his career, de Gaulle split opinion as he acted to consolidate it. He was not uniformly against integration or even unity, and may have endorsed an economic combination back in 1943, the year in which Altiero Spinelli founded the European Federalist Movement.[35] Several wartime leaders signed the *Déclaration des résistances européennes*, a call for European unity, at Geneva the following July. But liberating his country from colonial interdependence would, as de Gaulle's defenders have claimed, allow France greater freedom of manoeuvre; so, unlike Spinelli's federalists, there should be no federal citizenship and also less interdependence vis-à-vis Europe and the United States.[36]

During the 1960s, Gaullism would appear to decline and fall, but its reassertion of the national prerogative, of particular national interests within international organisations and of the value of the modern nation-state would endure and advance, in Europe and elsewhere. In East Asia the material rise of Japan, South Korea and Taiwan had begun under the rule of single-party or authoritarian governments. It was from these states, and from the successful city-state of Singapore, that China's leaders a generation later would draw inspiration for transforming their own country from humiliating poverty to boastful prosperity. So, too, began, by way of an alternative economic model, the dawn of a more pluralistic, or perhaps another Asian, age.

The year 1963 is a convenient point at which to pause in this story of the second half of the twentieth century. If, in Winston Churchill's phrase, 1943 was the year after the end of the beginning of the Second World War, 1963 marked another end of a beginning – of the end of the European era that Geoffrey Barraclough described. 'Russia grows and grows', Kurt Riezler had

35 Mayne, *Community of Europe*, pp. 68–9, 167 n. 1.
36 Connelly, *Diplomatic Revolution*, p. 277.

written in 1914. 'She has become a nightmare.'[37] The nightmare seemed at last to recede. Philip Larkin called 1963 an *annus mirabilis*, the year in which sexual intercourse began. California's population became the largest in the United States. An environmental movement, boosted by the publication of Rachel Carson's *Silent Spring* the previous year, gained international support. The use of computers became widespread. The ecumenical council known as 'Vatican II' had been convened, and centre-left parties were once again ascendant as the 'sixties' saw the 'Baby Boom' generation reach political and other forms of consciousness. Sylvia Plath published *The Bell Jar*, while John F. Kennedy delivered two of his most notable speeches, one at the American University in Washington, DC, and the other in Berlin. The Berlin speech, where the American president declared himself to be a citizen of that divided city, was also meant as a rebuke to de Gaulle, who had concluded the Élysée Treaty with West Germany. That was perceived, in turn, as a rebuke to NATO and, specifically, to the 'Anglo-Saxons' whom de Gaulle had denounced when rejecting the British application for membership in the Common Market also back in January. Adenauer, also wary of Harold Macmillan and his presumed influence over Kennedy, went along with de Gaulle even though the Bundestag added a preamble to the treaty affirming transatlantic solidarity. For their part, the British had yet to decide firmly whether the benefits of European integration were better accrued from inside or outside supranational institutions. De Gaulle thus did not destroy the European movement, but did hinder the wider movement towards an Atlantic community. Along with Martin Luther King's 'I Have a Dream' speech in August, the interlude marked a climax of Cold War-era idealism. In the Soviet Union, Khrushchev and his charismatic style would give way to new leadership under Leonid Brezhnev. In the United States, President Kennedy was assassinated.

Thus came an accelerated period of moral contestation in both Cold War blocs and, alongside, the attenuation of the civilisational discourse of Atlanticism by Europeanisation amidst the Americanisation of European culture. 'Europe' had already ceased being a cultural or geopolitical term and instead had become a political ideology and a measure of patriotism.[38] In West Germany the long chancellorship of Adenauer neared an end as Jürgen Habermas, denouncing elective monarchy, published *The Structural Transformation of the Public Sphere*; and the German people finally began an

---

37 Quoted in N. Stone, *World War One* (London, Penguin, 2008 [2007]), p. 24.
38 L. van Middelaar, *The Passage to Europe*, trans. L. Waters (New Haven, CT, Yale University Press, 2020 [2013]), p. 222.

open discussion of the war's horrors and crimes. (Adolf Eichmann was tried, found guilty of crimes against humanity and hanged in 1962.) Europe may not yet have become, in the words of one American observer, 'a kaleidoscopic sideshow', but it was no longer in the foreground of world politics.[39] Nor did its ideologues still wield the power of great religions or revolutions. The Cold War had reached a point of stabilisation at its European centre and had begun to tilt in favour of the west beyond Europe. Europe was still divided along the same lines that had been set in 1943 as it espoused the cause of freedom and unity, but détente suggested another path ahead. It happened with the small beginning of an *Endkampf*, the *Wandel durch Annäherung*, 'change through coming together', which the West German statesman Egon Bahr announced in July 1963. Today that shift appears less the culmination of a clash within modernity than a mature interregnum, Europe's swan song.

'He who is to perform a horrendous act should imagine to himself that it is already done, should impose upon himself a future as irrevocable as the past.'[40] Jorge Luis Borges published that sentence back in 1941. Four years later humanity witnessed an enormous destructive capacity, with tens of millions murdered and the sudden prospect of many millions more. It was in the shadow of that realisation and the rupture of total war that a chastened people inherited, imagined and, over the next two decades, began to invent another Europe.

Recommended Reading

Grossman, V. *Stalingrad*, trans. R. and E. Chandler (New York, NY, New York Review of Books, 2019 [1952]).
Romero, F. *Storia della guerra fredda* (Turin, Einaudi, 2009).
Sheehan, J. J. *Where Have All the Soldiers Gone?* (Boston, MA, Houghton Mifflin, 2008).
Wylie, P. *Generation of Vipers* (New York, NY, Rinehart, 1942).

39 R. Steel, *Pax Americana* (New York, NY, Viking, 1967), p. 73.
40 J. L. Borges, 'The Garden of Forking Paths', in *Fictions*, trans. A. Hurley (New York, NY, Penguin, 2000), p. 78.

2

European Integration and the Temporary Division of Germany

HENNING TÜRK

Introduction

On 3 October 1990, something very strange happened. The European Community (EC) expanded without formally acquiring a new member. The reason for this was the reunification of Germany – on this day, the German Democratic Republic (GDR) acceded to the constitution of the Federal Republic of Germany (FRG). As a result, the FRG gained five new federal states, which then also became part of the EC.

This expansion 'by the back door' was somewhat inadvertent. The EC had just completed its 'southern enlargement' with the accessions of Greece (1981), Spain and Portugal (both in 1986), with which it hoped above all to stabilise these fledgling democracies. Because the process of economically integrating these three southern countries put a strain on the Community, the EC had decided to halt further expansion. These plans were scuppered by the surprising developments in central and eastern Europe.

The expansion to include the five East German states spelt the end of one of the basic constellations of the European integration process. The founding of the two German states in 1949 was a key factor in the establishment of the western European organisations, as these also served to firmly anchor the FRG in the Western camp. In the following, we shall take a closer look at this basic constellation. What role did the partition of Germany play in the European integration process? What repercussions did the European integration process have for the partition of Germany?

To answer these questions, four key aspects of the relationship between European integration and German partition will be considered more closely.

I would like to thank Joy Titheridge for the translation of this chapter.

The first is the founding phase of European organisations following the Second World War. In what way were they connected with the incipient Cold War and the division of Germany? We will then turn our attention to trade between the two German states. To what extent was the GDR involved in the EC through trade with the FRG? Thirdly, we will analyse the process of rapprochement between the two German states from the 1960s onwards and its implications for the external relations of the EC. Finally, I would like to take a closer look at the reunification process of 1989–90. What role did it play for the EC, and how was the EC involved in the reunification process? Were there any alternatives to the back-door accession of the five new states to the EC?

Research Literature

There has not been any systematic investigation to date of the relationship between the division of Germany and European integration. Instead, the research literature thus far has concentrated on individual aspects. There has been a particular focus on trade between the two German states, which was granted special status when the European Economic Community (EEC) was created.[1] This special status in the European integration process has been studied extensively in the contemporary political science and legal literature.[2] Overall, the research deems untenable the allegation that the GDR was a 'secret member' of the EC due to the exceptions for trade between the two Germanies.[3] There was too little trade between East and West Germany

1 D. Nakath, 'Die DDR – "heimliches Mitglied" der Europäischen Gemeinschaft? Zur Entwicklung des innerdeutschen Handels vor dem Hintergrund der westeuropäischen Integration', in F. Knipping and M. Schönwald (eds.), *Aufbruch zum Europa der zweiten Generation: Die europäische Einigung 1969–1984* (Trier, Wissenschaftlicher Verlag Trier, 2004), pp. 451–73; M. Graf, 'Die DDR und die EWG 1957–1990', *Revue d'Allemagne et des pays de langue allemande* 51 (2019): 21–35.
2 P. Scharpf, 'Die Bedeutung des innerdeutschen Handels für die Beziehungen der EWG zur DDR', *Deutschland-Archiv* 7 (1974): 260–6; P. Scharpf, 'Europäische Wirtschaftsgemeinschaft und Deutsche Demokratische Republik: Die Entwicklung ihrer Rechtsbeziehungen seit 1958 unter besonderer Berücksichtigung des innerdeutschen Handels' (PhD Thesis, Universität Tübingen, 1973); R. Biskup, *Deutschlands offene Handelsgrenze: Die DDR als Nutznießer des EWG-Protokolls über den innerdeutschen Handel* (Berlin, Ullstein, 1976); B. Jansen, *EWG und DDR nach Abschluß des Grundlagenvertrages* (Baden-Baden, Nomos, 1976); K. A. Hobson, 'The European Community and East–West German Relations', *Virginia Journal of International Law* 19 (1978): 45–68.
3 Graf, 'Die DDR und die EWG', 22.

for this to be the case, and besides, the GDR's inclusion on the basis of trade between the two German states pertained only to certain domains of integration.

Another key area of research is the 1989–90 reunification process. The role of the EC in this regard was analysed by political scientists immediately following reunification, drawing on publications and newspaper reports.[4] These studies emphasised the strong influence of the Commission,[5] a finding confirmed by the recently published study on the history of the EC Commission between 1986 and 2000.[6] The research also shed light on how the process of European integration was accelerated by German unification.[7]

The greatest gaps are in the analysis of the interactions between the phases of the Cold War in Europe, the transformation of intra-German relations and the changes in the EC.[8] In particular, the phase of easing tensions from the 1960s onwards is central here.[9] It was not only the views of the two German

4 B. Lippert, 'Die EG als Mitgestalter der Erfolgsgeschichte. Der deutsche Einigungsprozeß 1989/90', in B. Lippert (ed.), *Die EG und die neuen Bundesländer: Eine Erfolgsgeschichte von kurzer Dauer?* (Bonn, Europa-Union Verlag, 1993), pp. 35–102; P. von Ham, *The EC, Eastern Europe, and European Unity: Discord, Collaboration, and Integration since 1947* (London, Pinter, 1993); C. Meyer, *Die Eingliederung der DDR in die EG* (Cologne, Verlag Wissenschaft und Politik, 1993); B. Kohler-Koch (ed.), *Die Osterweiterung der EG: Die Einbeziehung der ehemaligen DDR in die Gemeinschaft* (Baden-Baden, Nomos, 1991).
5 Lippert, 'Die EG als Mitgestalter', pp. 97–8; Meyer, *Die Eingliederung der DDR*, pp. 64–5.
6 M. Gehler and A. Jacob, 'Die Eingliederung Ostdeutschlands und die Erweiterungen', in É. Bussière, P. Ludlow, F. Romero, D. Schlenker, V. Dujardin and A. Varsori (eds.), *Die Europäische Kommission 1986–2000: Geschichte und Erinnerung einer Institution* (Luxembourg, Amt für Veröffentlichungen der EU, 2019), pp. 548–59. See also N. P. Ludlow, 'A Naturally Supportive Environment? The European Institutions and German Unification', in F. Bozo, M.-P. Rey, N. P. Ludlow and L. Nuti (eds.), *Europe and the End of the Cold War: A Reappraisal* (London, Routledge, 2008), pp. 161–73.
7 See, for example, W. Loth, *Building Europe: A History of European Unification* (Berlin and Boston, MA, De Gruyter, 2015), pp. 310–22; G. Clemens, 'Die deutsche Frage und Europa', in H. Reinitzer (ed.), *Deutschland und Europa: Wächst zusammen, was zusammen gehört?* (Berlin, De Gruyter, 2013), pp. 15–26, 25; H. J. Küsters, *Der Integrationsfriede: Viermächte-Verhandlungen über die Friedensregelung mit Deutschland 1945–1990* (Munich, Oldenbourg, 2000), pp. 865–6, 877.
8 On the long-neglected relationship between the Cold War and European integration, see, for example, U. Krotz, K. K. Patel and F. Romero (eds.), *Europe's Cold War Relations: The EC towards a Global Role* (London, Bloomsbury, 2019); N. P. Ludlow, 'European Integration and the Cold War', in M. P. Leffler and O. A. Westad (eds.), *The Cambridge History of the Cold War* (Cambridge, Cambridge University Press, 2010), vol. II, pp. 179–97 and Chapter 1 by Kenneth Weisbrode in this volume.
9 N. P. Ludlow (ed.), *European Integration and the Cold War: Ostpolitik–Westpolitik, 1965–1973* (London and New York, Routledge, 2007); K. K. Patel, 'Who Was Saving Whom? The European Community and the Cold War, 1960s–1970s', *The British Journal of Politics and International Relations* 19 (2017): 29–47.

states towards the EC that changed during this period[10] – the perceptions and expectations of the other countries vis-à-vis the EC did as well. We have yet to fully gauge the impact of this change in the way the European integration process was viewed.[11] How, for instance, did the conclusion of the Basic Treaty between the GDR and the Federal Republic influence the role of the EC in international relations in the 1970s? What did the associated relinquishing by the Federal Republic of its claim to sole representation of the whole German nation (the exclusive mandate) mean for the external relations of the EC? The present chapter seeks to shed some light on these questions.

Two Camps: The Division of Germany and the Beginnings of European Cooperation

The European integration process was closely linked to the basic international constellations following the Second World War. One lesson from the years between the wars, and especially from the Great Depression of 1929, was that the international organisations had been too weak to stabilise Europe's fledgling democracies and protect the established order against authoritarian regimes. As a result, the Allies began planning strong international organisations and a coordinated approach for the post-war period, even as the Second World War was still unfolding. Early examples of this policy include the three organisations emerging in 1945 from British– American cooperation, the Emergency Economic Committee for Europe (EECE), European Coal Organisation (ECO) and European Central Inland Transport Organisation (ECITO), which were intended to facilitate a coordinated reconstruction of Europe. The United States and Great Britain were therefore keen for membership to be as broad as possible, and this was to some extent achieved. The USSR, Poland and Czechoslovakia

---

10 On the GDR's view of the EC, see K.-P. Schmidt, *Die europäische Gemeinschaft aus der Sicht der DDR 1957–1989* (Hamburg, Dr Kovacs, 1991); S. Schwarz, 'Der lange Weg der DDR nach Brüssel. Von der Verurteilung zur Kooperation mit der Europäischen Gemeinschaft', *Deutschland-Archiv* 36 (2003): 574–87; J. Wüstenhagen, '*Blick durch den Vorhang*': *Die SBZ/DDR und die Integration Westeuropas (1946–1972)* (Baden-Baden, Nomos, 2001); J. Scholtyseck, 'Die DDR und Europa', in H. Timmermann (ed.), *Die DDR in Europa – zwischen Isolation und Öffnung* (Münster, LIT, 2005), pp. 88–99. On the Federal Republic's position on European policy from the end of the 1960s onwards, see C. Hiepel, *Willy Brandt und Georges Pompidou: Deutsch-französische Europapolitik zwischen Aufbruch und Krise* (Munich, Oldenbourg, 2012); H. Türk, *Die Europapolitik der Großen Koalition, 1966–1969* (Munich, Oldenbourg, 2006).

11 Some initial considerations are offered by, among others, A. Romano, 'Untying Cold War Knots: The EEC and Eastern Europe in the Long 1970s', *Cold War History* 14, no. 2 (2014): 153–73.

were members of ECITO. Poland and Czechoslovakia joined the ECO, where the German occupied zones were represented by delegates from the occupying powers.[12] This approach encompassing eastern and western Europe, which was also manifest in the creation of the Economic Commission for Europe (ECE) in 1947 as the European regional organisation of the United Nations (UN), ended with the Marshall Plan.[13] The associated creation of the Organisation for European Economic Co-operation (OEEC) as a Western organisation and the Council for Mutual Economic Assistance (Comecon) as its Eastern counterpart then symbolised the start of the Cold War on the level of the European organisations as well. The Federal Republic of Germany, founded in May 1949, then joined the OEEC on 31 October 1949, and the GDR, founded in October 1949, became a member of Comecon in September 1950.

The building of the supranational communities in a small circle of six European states then also served from 1951 onwards to monitor the Federal Republic's economic recovery and make its benefits available to the western European countries. The newly created European Coal and Steel Community (ECSC), the European Economic Community (EEC) and the European Atomic Energy Community (EURATOM) offered a number of advantages for the Federal Republic. Within this framework it could now, for the first time, act as an equal member of the international community. Moreover, Federal Chancellor Konrad Adenauer hoped that close integration in the Western community would guard West Germany against a disastrous seesaw policy between East and West. European integration was also intended to strengthen the western European countries economically, thus immunising them against the communist temptations from eastern Europe and the Soviet Union. The European Communities also accepted the Federal Republic's claim to be, until such time as Germany was reunified, 'the sole legitimate state organisation of the German people'[14] (the exclusive mandate). The Federal Government had reinforced this in 1955 with the

12 Y. Berthelot and P. Rayment, *Looking Back and Peering Forward: A Short History of the United Nations Economic Commission on Europe, 1947–2007* (New York, NY, United Nations, 2007), p. 6.

13 D. Stinsky, 'Western European vs. All-European Cooperation? The OEEC, the European Recovery Program, and the United Nations Economic Commission for Europe (ECE), 1947–1952', in M. Leimgruber and M. Schmelzer (eds.), *The OECD and the International Political Economy since 1948* (Basingstoke, Palgrave Macmillan, 2017), pp. 65–88.

14 'Bundeskanzler Adenauer an den Geschäftsführenden Vorsitzenden der Alliierten Hohen Kommission, McCloy', in Institut für Zeitgeschichte (ed.), *Akten zur Auswärtigen Politik der Bundesrepublik Deutschland 1949/50* (Munich, Oldenbourg, 1997), p. 10.

Hallstein Doctrine, whereby any country recognising the GDR diplomatically was threatened with retaliatory action by the Federal Republic.

This anchoring of the three European communities in the Western camp of the Cold War also coloured the GDR's perception of European integration.[15] It saw European integration primarily as an attempt by the United States to secure its hegemony in the Western capitalist world and as a means to stepping up its battle against the socialist states. The European communities, it believed, were also propping up the dominant position of monopoly capital in the Western world. In the medium term, however, the GDR leadership expected European integration to fail as a result of the internal contradictions inherent in the capitalist system. The government of the GDR rejected western European integration from an intra-German perspective as well. It maintained that the Federal Republic was reinforcing the division of Germany through its membership in the European communities, impeding reunification. As the West German opposition likewise used this reasoning to attack the policies of the Federal Government, the Federal Government was anxious to counter this impression in its negotiations of the treaties establishing the European communities. This was particularly apparent when it came to the subject of trade between the two German states, which will be examined more closely in the following.

The GDR as a Secret Member of the EC? Trade between the Two Germanies and EC Trade Policy

Trade between East and West Germany had been subject to specific regulations since the creation of the two German states. These were first established in October 1949 with the Frankfurt Agreement, which was superseded in September 1951 by the Berlin Agreement. This 'interzonal agreement' was repeatedly adjusted, but essentially remained in effect until reunification in October 1990. On the basis of this agreement, trade between the two German states was conducted bilaterally via clearing accounts. For clearing, one East German mark was equivalent to one West German mark – a principle that was very advantageous for the GDR. In addition, it was possible to overdraw the clearing accounts up to a certain amount. This 'swing' was granted to the

---

15 On this and the following, see Schmidt, *Europäische Gemeinschaft*, pp. 101–47; Wüstenhagen, *'Blick durch den Vorhang'*, pp. 118–41; M. Lemke, 'Die Position der SED zur EWG 1949–1957. Ideologische Grundlagen, Motive und Argumente', in H. Wagner (ed.), *Europa und Deutschland – Deutschland und Europa: Liber amicorum für Heiner Timmermann zum 65. Geburtstag* (Münster, LIT, 2005), pp. 356–72.

GDR at no interest. The import of GDR goods to the Federal Republic was not considered international trade, so no duties or levies were collected.[16]

The system of trade between the two German states, which benefited the GDR economically and enabled the Federal Republic to exert political influence, was, in the Federal Government's view, not to be affected by the integration of the Federal Republic in the emerging European communities. In this way it hoped to avoid the accusation that its policy of alignment with the West was increasingly distancing the German states from one another, rendering reunification impossible.[17] In the negotiations on the creation of the ECSC, then, the Federal Republic was committed to ensuring that trade with the GDR in coal and steel should not be restricted by the provisions of the ECSC Treaty. The governments included trade between the Federal Republic and the GDR relating to coal and steel in the 'Convention on the Transitional Provisions' which was annexed to the ECSC Treaty. Section 22 of the Convention stipulated that trade between the Federal Republic and the GDR was to be 'regulated in agreement with the High Authority'.[18] In other words, the Federal Republic subsequently informed the High Authority of its trade with the GDR in coal and steel, but essentially remained free to act as it pleased.

The six countries of the EEC addressed trade between the two German states in much greater detail in the EEC founding treaties. In the 'Protocol on German Internal Trade',[19] the founding members accepted that trade between the Federal Republic and the GDR was to be considered trade within Germany and hence would remain untouched by the provisions of the EEC Treaty. This meant that trade between the two German states was not affected by the development of a unified economic area in the EEC mainly consisting of a customs union with a common external tariff and the removal of internal customs borders. In accordance with the protocol, all countries were also obliged to inform the Commission of any trade agreements with the GDR.

This arrangement meant that goods from the GDR reached the territory of the EEC via the Federal Republic duty-free. Despite the fact that uniform customs tariffs had applied since 1 July 1968 and the Common Market entered

16 Nakath, 'Die DDR – "heimliches Mitglied"', pp. 453–5.
17 See, for example, the Bundestag debate on the EEC Treaty on 21 March 1957: Bundestag minutes, second legislative period, 200th session of 21 March 1957, pp. 11327–72.
18 Section 22 of the Convention on the Transitional Provisions (ECSC), in Jansen, *Die EWG und die DDR*, pp. 125–6.
19 Protocol on German internal trade and connected problems (EEC), in Jansen, *Die EWG und die DDR*, p. 125.

its final phase by contractual agreement on 1 January 1970, the customs union was de facto incomplete. It had a hole in the Federal Republic.

This affected not only industrial and consumer goods but also the common agricultural market, which came to spearhead integration in the 1960s.[20] The EEC promoted internal trade in this sector by developing an agricultural policy based on import levies and export refunds. But how was the GDR to be dealt with in this regard? There was fierce debate about this, particularly as the other EEC countries began to apply for export refunds for their exports to the GDR under the common agricultural policy. These were initially approved by the EEC after 1962–3, but the Federal Republic then tried to block this provision, arguing that it meant the EEC was treating the GDR like a normal third country and thus implicitly recognising it. In 1966, the EEC countries agreed that the interzonal agreement would remain applicable for German–German trade in agricultural goods and that, for the other five countries, the GDR did not constitute a normal third country. This meant that they could not receive any export refunds from the EEC. Instead, the EEC allowed them to cover these through national payments.[21] This compromise satisfied the Federal Government, as through this workaround it retained its exclusive mandate.

When it came to industrial goods, the application of the specific provisions for interzonal trade remained unproblematic as long as trade between the two Germanies was relatively small. This changed over the course of the 1960s. Towards the end of Federal Chancellor Ludwig Erhard's administration, and much more so with the formation of the Grand Coalition in December 1966, the Federal Government was already seeking to expand trade with the GDR and the countries of eastern Europe with a view to strengthening political ties as well. This resulted in increasing complaints from the other EEC countries that the GDR was exporting its goods to their countries duty-free via the Federal Republic, culminating in the allegation that the provisions concerning trade between the two Germanies made the GDR a 'secret member' of the EEC.[22]

The Socialist Dutch Member of the European Parliament and later EC Commissioner for Social Affairs Henk Vredeling was particularly persistent at

---

20 On this and the following, see K. K. Patel, *Europäisierung wider Willen: Die Bundesrepublik Deutschland in der Agrarintegration der EWG 1955–1973* (Munich, Oldenbourg, 2009), pp. 334–42.

21 The full text of the resolution can be found in Biskup, *Deutschlands offene Handelsgrenze*, p. 77.

22 Nakath, 'Die DDR – "heimliches Mitglied"', p. 470.

this stage, repeatedly addressing parliamentary questions to the Commission and the Council of Ministers to investigate what exactly German–German trade meant for the countries of the EEC.[23] There were also individual complaints from the governments of the Netherlands and others, such as France. The Commission and the Council would not openly get involved in any discussion and generally noted that, while there were isolated cases in which the interzonal trade regulations were abused, trade between the two Germanies did not represent a serious gateway for GDR products to enter the Common Market.

Internally, however, the matter was the subject of intense debate in the EC institutions at this time. The Federal Government vehemently defended its approach in order to prevent the EEC from interfering in its intra-German policy. This had much to do with the Federal Government's concern that the contractually agreed broadening of the EEC's trade policy on 1 January 1970 could affect trade with the GDR. The Federal Government therefore submitted a memorandum explaining its position in May 1969,[24] in which it insisted that trade with the GDR was domestic trade for the Federal Republic and external trade for the other five countries. Trade with the GDR was therefore 'sui generis trade'[25] and did not fall within the competence of the EEC. The latter could not impose regulations governing trade with the GDR. Instead, the Federal Government maintained, the individual countries must continue to conduct trade with the GDR in accordance with national regulations. The countries should, however, ensure that their national regulations did not conflict with the EEC guidelines for trade with third countries. But the resolution to this effect that the Federal Republic hoped to mediate among the five other EEC members could not be achieved. Resolving the problem legally in all its details would have raised all too complex questions. For instance, the Commission's Legal Service expressed serious doubts about the

23 See, for example, 'Schriftliche Anfrage Nr. 98 von Herrn Vredeling an die Kommission der EWG, 19. Januar 1966', *Amtsblatt der Europäischen Gemeinschaften* 9, no. 72, (1966): 7–8; 'Schriftliche Anfrage Nr. 119 von Herrn Vredeling an die Kommission der EWG, 18. Februar 1966', *Amtsblatt der Europäischen Gemeinschaften* 9, no. 108 (1966): 4–6; 'Schriftliche Anfrage Nr. 428/69 von Herrn Vredeling an den Rat der Europäischen Gemeinschaften, 16. Januar 1970', *Amtsblatt der Europäischen Gemeinschaften* 13, no. C/62 (1970): 1–3.

24 On this and the following, see Ambassador Hans-Georg Sachs to the Vice-President of the EEC Commission Sicco Mansholt, Brussels, 7 May 1969, Historical Archives of the European Union (HAEU), Klaus Meyer papers (KM), vol. 0097.

25 Memorandum from the General Secretariat of the Commission of the European Communities for the members of the Commission re: 516th session of the Committee of Permanent Representatives on 12 June 1969, Brussels, 13 June 1969, HAEU, Klaus Meyer papers (KM), vol. 0097.

German interpretation in an internal report.[26] So the subject more or less tacitly went by the board, and the practice simply continued as it had previously.[27]

Change came about only with the Basic Treaty between the Federal Republic and the GDR, which the two governments concluded in December 1972 and which came into force on 21 June 1973. Under the treaty, the two German states each accepted the existence of the other, without recognition under international law. The Federal Republic thus relinquished its exclusive mandate, with the result that numerous countries subsequently established diplomatic relations with the GDR, including the Federal Republic's partners in the EEC. The two German states then joined the UN on 18 September 1973.

During the negotiations between the Federal Republic and the GDR, the West German Foreign Office had already been considering the implications of a German–German treaty for intra-German trade within the context of the EC.[28] The Foreign Office drew particular attention to the fact that under the Basic Treaty, steering clear of recognition of the GDR under international law by the Federal Republic, the legal situation would not change. The protocol on interzonal trade was thus to remain in force. The Foreign Office concluded by recommending that the German government should not raise the subject in Brussels.

But the other EC countries and the Commission were quick to seize on German–German trade. It became apparent that the Federal Republic would have to make concessions with regard to trade between the other EEC countries and the GDR. In April 1973, the Commission suggested that the other EEC countries conduct trade with the GDR on the basis of the Community regulations, while trade between the two Germanies would continue to be conducted on the basis of the 1957 protocol.[29] This proposal was initially resisted by the French government, which did not want to lose its right to conclude independent trade agreements with the GDR. But the pressure from the Commission and the other countries did not let up, and France finally relented. In the spring of 1975, a redefinition of the EC's relationship to the GDR was achieved. The GDR was now classified as

26 Memorandum of the Legal Service of the Commission re: regulations concerning trade with the German territories outside the scope of the Basic Law of the Federal Republic of Germany, Brussels, 12 June 1969, HAEU, Klaus Meyer papers (KM), vol. 0097.

27 Biskup, *Deutschlands offene Handelsgrenze*, p. 79.

28 Memorandum by the Head of Department Herbst: Trade between the two Germanies in connection with the conclusion of a Basic Treaty between the Federal Republic of Germany and the GDR, Bonn, 13 September 1972, in Institut für Zeitgeschichte (ed.), *Akten zur Auswärtigen Politik der Bundesrepublik Deutschland 1972* (Munich, Oldenbourg, 2003), pp. 1263–70.

29 On this and the following, see Biskup, *Deutschlands offene Handelsgrenze*, pp. 96–9.

a state-trading country, and the existing EC framework for trade with these countries was applied to the GDR as well. This meant, for example, that the EC was now responsible for the trade agreements of the eight non-German member states with the GDR. The EC framework for industrial and agricultural trade now also applied to the GDR. The special provisions for the agricultural market created in 1966 were repealed. This did not, however, affect trade between the two Germanies, which continued to be governed by the 1957 protocol.

The Basic Treaty of 1972 thus rendered untenable the Federal Government's previous assertion that trade with the GDR was sui generis trade. General international recognition of the GDR meant that the EC treated it as it did the other socialist countries. But it was crucial for the West German government, however, that the exceptions for trade between the two Germanies could still stand. With the help of close economic connections it hoped to strengthen personal contacts and political ties with the GDR. The EEC had essentially not touched the rules for the two Germanies since 1957, nor was there any legal reason to do so, because the Federal Republic had only accepted the existence of the GDR with the Basic Treaty and still did not recognise it under international law. The EC's divided approach to the GDR therefore continued until German reunification in October 1990. As a consequence, the GDR was relatively immune to the expansion of the EC's trade policy in the 1970s and 1980s that posed major challenges to the export policies of the other socialist countries. This enabled the GDR to agitate vehemently in the Eastern bloc against the establishment of close contacts with the EC.[30]

The Development of the EC's External Relations: The Rapprochement between the Two Germanies in the Context of Détente and Its Consequences

The easing of tensions in the East–West conflict from the 1960s onwards made the Federal Republic's tough position on the GDR increasingly untenable. The exclusive mandate associated with the Hallstein Doctrine appeared more and more anachronistic and restricted the Federal Republic's foreign policy options. The Federal Republic's Ostpolitik and its stance on the GDR was already beginning to shift during the administration of the Grand

---

30 On this issue, see in particular M. Graf, 'Nichtanerkennung zu eigenen Lasten? Die DDR und die EWG in den "langen 1970er-Jahren"', *Jahrbuch für Historische Kommunismusforschung* 28 (2020): 225–38.

Coalition from 1966 to 1969, with the government increasingly positioning its intra-German policy within the framework of European unification. In a keynote address on the Federal Government's European policy on 30 November 1967, the Social Democrat Foreign Minister Willy Brandt pointed out that the solution to the German question was dependent on 'what becomes of the relationship between the two halves of Europe'.[31] Over and above the unification of western Europe, he said, the aim was to bring the countries of western and eastern Europe back together 'under changed circumstances, on a new basis'.[32] The Common Market, whose economic potential could not be ignored by the East, would play an important role here. Brandt went on to explain that the economic appeal of the Common Market raised the question of cooperation based on 'real interests', irrespective of the different political systems.[33]

Paul Frank, head of the subdivision for European affairs of the Foreign Office, explored how such a conception of intra-German policy and Ostpolitik would affect the Federal Government's European policy in a memorandum on the 'Guidelines for Germany's European Policy' on 4 October 1967. Frank saw the long-term goal of West Germany's European policy as 'the reorganisation of pan-European affairs, including the problem of Germany, in the form of economic and political cooperation between eastern and western Europe (European peace order)'.[34] Before this cooperation was expanded to include eastern Europe, it was first necessary for all of the western European countries to be involved in it. An expansion of the EEC to include Great Britain and other interested countries thus represented 'a necessary transitional phase towards pan-European cooperation encompassing both East and West'.[35] To make an active intra-German policy possible within this framework, it was necessary to avoid 'the European Economic Community becoming a part of the East–West conflict'.[36] The strengthening of western Europe must therefore no longer serve as a bulwark against communism, as it had in the early days of the European project, but instead should serve to 'establish

31 W. Brandt, 'Die Verantwortung der Deutschen gegenüber Europa. Vortrag auf der Jahrestagung des Kuratoriums der Friedrich-Ebert-Stiftung in Düsseldorf am 30. November 1967', in W. Brandt, Außenpolitik, Deutschlandpolitik, Europapolitik: Grundsätzliche Erklärungen während des ersten Jahres im Auswärtigen Amt (Berlin, Berlin-Verlag, 1968), pp. 149–64, 152.
32 Ibid.   33 Ibid.
34 Memorandum by Paul Frank, Head of the subdivision for European affairs: Guidelines on Germany's European Policy, 4 October 1967, p. 11, Politisches Archiv des Auswärtigen Amts (Federal Foreign Office Political Archive, PAAA), B1, vol. 324.
35 Ibid.   36 Ibid., p. 7.

a dialogue between western and eastern Europe'.[37] Frank concluded that the main task of the West German government was to align its European policy with the long-term goal of a European peace order. The development of Ostpolitik therefore changed not only the perception of European integration and its benefits for the Federal Republic but also the expectations about the future tasks of the Communities.

These considerations fuelled the policy towards the EC that Brandt developed as Foreign Minister and, from October 1969, as Federal Chancellor. He sought to push the development and enlargement of the EC to make it more attractive for cooperation with the countries of eastern Europe. Thus, on 13 November 1973, in the first speech by a West German Chancellor to the European Parliament, he stressed the importance of the EC 'for cooperation and communication with the eastern European countries and the Soviet Union'.[38] At the same time, with his strong commitment to Europe he was able to undergird his policy of opening up to the countries of eastern Europe while demonstrating to his western European partners that he was not solely focused on eastern Europe, but also dedicated to policy as regards the western European countries and the EC. In this way, he was able to allay the concerns of the other countries that the focus of West German policies was shifting towards eastern Europe and that the Federal Republic would come to occupy a politically neutral position between East and West.[39]

Among the first fruits of the new Ostpolitik were the Federal Republic's treaties with the Soviet Union and Poland and the Four Power Agreement on Berlin, which came into force on 3 June 1972. These were followed a year later by the Basic Treaty with the GDR and, in 1974, the treaty with Czechoslovakia. The Federal Republic's rapprochement with the GDR, the eastern European states and the USSR had a clear impact on the external relations of the EC, which had been constrained by the Federal Republic's exclusive mandate and the EC positioning itself squarely in the Western camp in the Cold War. This was reflected in the EC's relationship to the Soviet Union and to Comecon, which in the 1950s and 1960s was dominated by Soviet accusations that the EC was an extension of monopoly capital and a vassal of the United States. This attitude began to shift with the negotiations

---

37 Ibid., p. 17.
38 Speech by Federal Chancellor Willy Brandt to the European Parliament in Strasbourg, 13 November 1973, www.willy-brandt-biografie.de/wp-content/uploads/2017/08/Bra ndt_Rede_Europa-Parlament_1973.pdf.
39 On Willy Brandt's European policy, see C. Hiepel, 'Europakonzeptionen und Europapolitik', in B. Rother (ed.), *Willy Brandts Außenpolitik* (Wiesbaden, Springer, 2014), pp. 21–91.

on the Treaty of Moscow between the Federal Republic and the USSR. During the ratification debate for the treaty in the Federal Republic, Leonid Brezhnev, General Secretary of the Communist Party of the Soviet Union (CPSU), surprised the EC countries with a conciliatory statement. In a speech to Soviet trade union officials on 20 March 1972, he said:

> The Soviet Union does not ignore the reality that has emerged in Western Europe, particularly the existence of an economic group of capitalist countries such as the 'Common Market'. [. . .] Our posture toward its members will depend on the extent to which they, for their part, recognize the reality in the socialist part of Europe, particularly the interests of the member-states of the [Comecon].[40]

This appeared to be a sign that the Soviet Union's previously hostile attitude towards the EC was beginning to crumble. Drawing on Soviet documentation, Wolfgang Mueller has shown that the Soviet leadership's change in position was related to Soviet concerns that the Treaty of Moscow might be rejected by the German Bundestag. The Christlich Demokratische Union/Christlich-Soziale Union opposition had repeatedly accused Brandt of promoting Ostpolitik at the expense of European integration. The Soviet leadership wanted to support Brandt by invalidating this argument.[41]

But there were other considerations underlying the Soviet Union's new policy direction as well. For one thing, the EC took over key trade policy functions from the member states and began to standardise the criteria for its trade policy towards the state-trading countries. This made it necessary for the Soviet Union to establish closer contacts with the EC. In addition, the Soviet Union wanted to achieve a unified position towards the EC among the member states of Comecon, and in so doing to pin the other countries down to the Soviet position.

While the realignment of the Soviet Union and Comecon did result in closer ties between the Eastern economic organisation and the EC Commission in the years that followed, these contacts remained informal. One reason why they could not be formalised was that the Comecon member states had no desire to be pinned down to a common line by the Soviet Union. Another was that the EC countries and the Commission were not interested in cementing the Soviet Union's hegemonic position over the

40 Cited in W. Mueller, 'Recognition in Return for Détente? Brezhnev, the EEC, and the Moscow Treaty with West Germany, 1970–1973', *Journal of Cold War Studies* 13 (2011): 79–100, 85.
41 Ibid., 87–96.

other Eastern bloc countries by establishing diplomatic relations with Comecon.[42]

A further illustration of the changing role of the EC in the context of détente and the West German easing of tensions with the East is the Conference on Security and Cooperation in Europe (CSCE), which met from 1973 to 1975. It had been instigated primarily at the insistence of the Soviet Union, which hoped to achieve a consolidation of the status quo in Europe. The Federal Republic, on the other hand, saw the CSCE primarily as a step on the path towards a pan-European peace order. The Federal Government was anxious that the possibility of a peaceful change to the borders be mentioned in the final document to leave the door open for the unification of the two German states. It therefore put a lot of energy into working out a western European position for the CSCE, as this placed the Federal Republic's interests on a broader foundation.[43] For the EC countries, the CSCE conference also provided an opportunity to utilise and strengthen the newly created European Political Cooperation (EPC). A number of working groups were set up within the EPC to elaborate the western European positions, in order to ensure that the EC countries entered into negotiations with a common approach. The working groups also consulted the Commission to help work out their negotiating positions for the matter at hand. The EPC proved to be a highly effective instrument of coordination in the context of the CSCE negotiations, and the western European countries were largely able to achieve their objectives. Moreover, Italian Prime Minister Aldo Moro signed the Final Act of the CSCE Summit explicitly also in his capacity as President of the Council of the European Communities.[44] The countries and institutions of the EC were thus able to demonstrate their ability to act in the pan-European and international context – something which was also acknowledged by the East.[45]

A third aspect that points to the change in the EC's external relations brought about by détente in Europe is the role played by the EC in the UN General Assembly.[46] Since the early 1970s, the EC Commission had

---

42 L. Ferrari, *Sometimes Speaking with a Single Voice: The European Community as an International Actor, 1969–1979* (Brussels, Peter Lang, 2016), pp. 86–7; Romano, 'Untying Cold War Knots', 159.

43 P. Hakkarainen, *A State of Peace in Europe: West Germany and the CSCE, 1966–1975* (New York, NY, Berghahn, 2011).

44 A. Romano, *From Détente in Europe to European Détente: How the West Shaped the Helsinki CSCE* (Brussels, Peter Lang, 2009), pp. 210–12.

45 Schwarz, 'Der lange Weg der DDR', 578–80.

46 On this and the following, see Ferrari, *Sometimes Speaking with a Single Voice*, pp. 97–102; L. Ferrari, 'How the European Community Entered the United Nations, 1969–1976,

considered applying for admission to the UN General Assembly on multiple occasions. But the EC member states were reluctant, not wanting to cause friction with the Soviet Union and its allies in the General Assembly, who rejected the EC's proposal. Moreover, certain countries wanted to resist the admission of Comecon, which such a step was likely to entail. The situation now changed after the entry into force of the Basic Treaty between the Federal Republic and the GDR, with the two German states being admitted to the UN on 18 September 1973. This seemed also to pave the way for the EC to be admitted to the General Assembly. In November of the same year, the Commission convinced the EC members to take this step and subsequently submitted its request to the UN. On 11 October 1974, the UN finally accepted the EC Commission as a Permanent Observer of the General Assembly and also granted this status to Comecon. The diplomatic standing of the EC representation at the UN improved over the following years, and in 1976 it officially received diplomatic status.

All in all, the rapprochement between the two German states and the easing of relations between the Federal Republic and the eastern European states in the context of the overall détente in the East–West conflict laid the foundations for the EC's growing role as an international player in the early 1970s. The EC was able to develop its external relations to individual states or international organisations that had previously been inhibited by the tensions of the East–West conflict. But its relationship to the eastern European states and to Comecon remained problematic and tended to be limited to 'technical' contacts. This situation did not change until the 1980s.

A European Framework: The EC and German Unification

In the late 1980s, the Eastern bloc under the leadership of the Soviet Union began to erode. This development took many politicians by surprise. It was closely tied to the policies of Mikhail Gorbachev, who was elected General Secretary of the Central Committee of the CPSU in March 1985. Gorbachev was no longer willing to provide emergency military support to the governments of central and eastern Europe, so the centrifugal forces in east central Europe gained the upper hand.

and What It Meant for European Political Integration', *Diplomacy & Statecraft* 29, no. 2 (2018): 237–54.

The changes in the communist sphere of influence did not leave the GDR untouched, where the opposition movement was increasingly gaining support. The GDR administration and the leadership of the Socialist Unity Party of Germany (Sozialistische Einheitspartei Deutschlands, SED) lost control of the opposition groups over the course of 1989, and with the surprising and uncontrolled opening of the wall on 9 November 1989, there was euphoria throughout the country. It was in this situation that West German Chancellor Helmut Kohl pressed ahead with a ten-point programme that he presented to the Bundestag on 28 November 1989. The programme developed a long-term path towards unification on a federal basis, beginning with a 'contractual community' between the two German states and a subsequent confederation. This process was to be embedded in the European structures.[47]

With his ten-point plan, Kohl deftly seized the initiative in the question of reunification. But he also snubbed his European partners, having failed to discuss the plan with them in advance.[48] Some countries began to fear that the Federal Republic might act unilaterally with regard to reunification. Moreover, some European politicians were wary of a reunified Germany adopting a politically neutral position between East and West and abandoning the structures that had been carefully developed to contain Germany. British Prime Minister Margaret Thatcher in particular warned of dire consequences and opposed reunification due to fears of German dominance in Europe. French President François Mitterrand also initially expressed reserve, but adjusted to developments and was subsequently much more constructive than Thatcher in supporting the reunification process.[49]

For Kohl and his Foreign Minister Hans-Dietrich Genscher,[50] then, it was crucial at this time to maintain the international confidence the Federal Republic had built up in the decades since the Second World War in order to allay the other countries' concerns about German unilateralism. The plans

47 On the unification process in general, see A. Rödder, *Deutschland einig Vaterland: Die Geschichte der Wiedervereinigung* (Munich, C. H. Beck, 2009).

48 Loth, *Building Europe*, p. 306.

49 On the European countries' various views on German unification, see, for example, M. Gehler and M. Graf (eds.), *Europa und die deutsche Einheit: Beobachtungen, Entscheidungen und Folgen* (Göttingen, Vandenhoeck & Ruprecht, 2017); H. Kohl, *Berichte zur Lage 1989–1998: Der Kanzler und Parteivorsitzende im Bundesvorstand der CDU Deutschlands* (Düsseldorf, Droste, 2012), pp. 27–8, 57–8, 70, 130, 170.

50 On Genscher's commitment to European unification, see, for example, G. A. Ritter, 'Deutschland und Europa. Grundzüge der Außenpolitik Genschers 1989 bis 1992', in K. Brauckhoff and I. Schwaetzer (eds.), *Hans-Dietrich Genschers Außenpolitik* (Wiesbaden, Springer, 2015), pp. 209–41.

already developed in the EC for the Economic and Monetary Union (EMU) worked to Kohl's advantage here. They envisaged a three-step approach to the EMU.[51] In the first stage, the margins of fluctuation of the currencies' exchange rates in the European Monetary System (EMS) would be narrowed. In addition, the role of the central bank presidents would be strengthened and the national economic policies brought closer together. The second stage envisaged the creation of an independent European Central Bank. In the third stage, the single currency would be introduced and the national economic and monetary policy competencies transferred to the European level. The European Council had accepted this roadmap at its meeting in Madrid in June 1989 and set 1 July 1990 as the date for the three-stage plan to begin. The timeframe for the start of the second and third phases, however, remained open.

So the monetary union was not the price Germany had to pay for acceptance of reunification, because the EMU was already under way. It was rather a question of when and under what conditions it would be achieved. The reunification process accelerated the plans and led to Kohl taking bolder decisions than he had originally intended.[52] Thus, chiefly to allay French concerns, he agreed at the meeting of the European Council in Strasbourg on 8 December 1989 to an intergovernmental conference to develop the second and third stages of the EMU, which would meet in late 1990. Concerning reunification, the twelve Heads of State and Government stated in the Council conclusions:

> We seek the strengthening of the state of peace in Europe in which the German people will regain its unity through free self-determination. This process should take place peacefully and democratically, in full respect of the relevant agreements and treaties and of all the principles defined by the Helsinki Final Act, in a context of dialogue and East–West cooperation. It also has to be placed in the perspective of European integration.[53]

In the context of an accelerated European integration policy, Kohl was able to take the developments in the GDR on board and tie them in with his reunification policy. Following the first democratic elections for the People's

---

51 On this and the following, see Loth, *Building Europe*, pp. 294–7; G. Brunn, *Die Europäische Einigung von 1945 bis heute* (Bonn, Bundeszentrale für politische Bildung, 2005), pp. 263–4.
52 Loth, *Building Europe*, p. 308; W. Loth, 'Helmut Kohl und die Währungsunion', *Vierteljahrshefte für Zeitgeschichte* 61 (2013): 455–80.
53 Conclusions of the Presidency, European Council, Strasbourg, 8–9 December 1989, p. 16, www.consilium.europa.eu/media/20580/1989_december_-_strasbourg__eng_.pdf.

Chamber in the GDR in March 1990, the monetary, economic and social union between the Federal Republic of Germany and the GDR that came into force on 1 July 1990, and the negotiation of the Unification Treaty, German unity then became a reality on 3 October 1990. International safeguards on the process took the form of negotiations between the four Allied powers of the Second World War and the Federal Republic and the GDR, known as the 'two-plus-four' negotiations. The six nations signed the Two-Plus-Four Agreement on 12 September 1990. This defined the borders of the reunified Germany. In addition, the four Allied powers gave up their remaining rights over Germany as a whole, and the united Federal Republic attained full sovereignty over its internal and external affairs. The Federal Republic reaffirmed its renunciation of the manufacture or possession of nuclear, biological or chemical weapons and limited its armed forces to a total of 370,000 men.[54]

The unification of the Federal Republic and the GDR also meant that the five new federal states joined the EC. Surprisingly, most of the standard literature on the history of European integration devotes only a few sentences to this remarkable process. It had an enormous impact on the situation in the new federal states, which were integrated into the comprehensive EC law and jurisdictional framework, and it also had a bearing on the situation of the EC with what was a sort of 'back-door' accession.

And there was scarcely any groundwork to build on, as the EC's relations to the GDR were still virtually non-existent. Even Gorbachev's policy of reform had done little to change this. It is true that this policy had resulted in the establishment of diplomatic relations between the EC and Comecon on 9 July 1988, whereupon the GDR and the EC also established official diplomatic relations.[55] But these were largely just formalities. At the time the GDR was still resisting the entire reform process in central and eastern Europe, so it had no interest in closer ties with the EC.

The EC institutions initially took a somewhat distanced and sceptical view of the developments in the GDR in the autumn of 1989 and the first steps taken by the Federal Government towards a subsequent unification of the

---

54 Treaty on the Final Settlement with Respect to Germany with agreed protocol note, in Auswärtiges Amt (ed.), *Außenpolitik der Bundesrepublik Deutschland: Dokumente 1949 bis 1994* (Cologne, Verlag Wissenschaft und Politik, 1995), pp. 699–703. On the negotiation of the Two-Plus-Four Agreement, see in particular Institut für Zeitgeschichte (ed.), *Die Einheit: Das Auswärtige Amt, das DDR-Außenministerium und der Zwei-plus-Vier-Prozess* (Göttingen, Vandenhoeck & Ruprecht, 2015); Küsters, *Der Integrationsfriede*.

55 'Signing of the EC/Comecon Joint Declaration: Luxembourg, 25 June 1988', https://ec.europa.eu/commission/presscorner/detail/en/MEMO_88_97.

two German states. This changed only after February 1990, as it became apparent that an expeditious process towards German unity was getting under way. At this stage, both the European Parliament and the Commission took the developments on board and sought to understand the significance of the changes in the GDR for the EC. To do this, the European Parliament set up a 'temporary committee' on 15 February 1990 to investigate the impact of the German unification process on the EC.[56] Commission President Jacques Delors signalled publicly that the EC was willing to integrate the GDR, whatever form this might take. Delors also recognised that the unification process could be an opportunity to deepen integration.[57] The Commission, in cooperation with the Council and the European Parliament, subsequently became the main institution for the handling of the unification process within the EC.

The Commission saw three options for the integration of the GDR.[58] The first option involved the conclusion of an Association Agreement to be negotiated with the GDR. An association along these lines was also the preferred option of the GDR administration under Hans Modrow. But the Federal Government disapproved, arguing that this would again foreground and bolster the GDR's now teetering legitimacy as an independent state.

The second option was the GDR joining the EC straight away. But the other member states rejected this in the Council at the beginning of 1990, believing it would shift the institutional balance in favour of the Germans. Such a step would also have been politically highly sensitive, as the GDR was still a member of the Warsaw Pact defence alliance. The Commission likewise rejected proceeding in this way, and the Federal Government expressed concerns that, as with association, formal membership could stabilise the GDR government and the GDR as an independent state.

Everything thus pointed to the third solution. This involved the GDR acceding via unification with the Federal Republic. Like the Federal Government, the EC institutions favoured the accession of the GDR to the Federal Republic under Article 23 of the Basic Law. This provided that the Basic Law would apply to other parts of Germany if they acceded to the Federal Republic. The EC Commission held that reunification along these lines did not require any amendments to the European treaties. It argued that the EC Treaties merely listed the states' names, so the scope of the EC Treaties followed from the territory of the state in question. A change

---

56 European Parliament (ed.), *The European Parliament and German Unification* (Luxembourg, European Communities, 2009), pp. 9–11.
57 Meyer, *Die Eingliederung der DDR*, p. 28.
58 On this and the following, see Meyer, *Die Eingliederung der DDR*, p. 30.

to the territory's boundaries therefore did not raise any legal problems, particularly as the Federal Republic remained a subject of international law. So from this perspective, too, there was much to be said for the path that was ultimately chosen, namely reunification under Article 23 of the Basic Law.

The Commission's approach coincided precisely with the plans of the Federal Government, which accepted the Commission playing a significant role in the unification process and provided it with detailed reports on developments in the relationship between the two German states.[59] The last GDR government under Prime Minister Lothar de Maizière did try to gain more influence on the EC. One demand was for representatives from East Germany to be included in the committees tasked with developing the EC single market project, the monetary union and the political union.[60] These demands did not get very far, however, as the Commission largely aligned itself with the Federal Government and events continued to unfold at a rapid pace, quickly making the proposals of the GDR government appear anachronistic.

The EC Commission then set up a number of high-calibre working groups to establish the legal processes for the integration of the territory of the GDR. In particular, the Commission officials were to ensure that the integration of the GDR did not jeopardise the single-market process and the Commission could demonstrate its effectiveness in the unification process. This, Delors reasoned, would boost the Commission's standing in the following negotiations on the institutional changes.[61]

The Commission subsequently sought to retain control over the process of integrating the GDR. It framed it as an 'administrative Community measure',[62] to be carried out as quietly as possible below the political decision-making level. The process proceeded smoothly, but in the final phase the Commission came under pressure with the accelerated pace of developments. Originally the Commission had assumed reunification would take place on 1 January 1991, but the two Germanies unexpectedly brought it forward to 3 October 1990. In response, the Council and the European Parliament adopted an extraordinary resolution authorising the Commission to provisionally enact the transitional provisions for the integration of the five

59 Gehler and Jacob, 'Die Eingliederung Ostdeutschlands', p. 554.
60 Lothar de Maizière to Jacques Delors, Berlin, 21 May 1990, HAEU, Georges Rencki papers, vol. GR-0162.
61 Meyer, *Die Eingliederung der DDR*, pp. 35–6.   62 Ibid., p. 64.

new federal states into the EC. These were then to be formally approved by the EC institutions by 31 December 1990.[63]

The Commission thus managed, with a major effort, to hammer out the provisions for the accession of the East German states in parallel with the reunification process. The provisions set out a transitional period running until 31 December 1992 for many domains, particularly trade, the common agricultural market, and environmental protection. The aim was, on the one hand, to allow the economy of the former GDR access to the Common Market, while, on the other, avoiding competitive disadvantages for the existing EC countries due to lower economic norms and standards in the five new federal states. The territories of the former GDR were then to be fully integrated into the EC on 1 January 1993. An offer by Commission President Delors to support the new region of the EC financially was declined by Kohl, because he knew about the concerns on the part of the other countries, particularly those of southern Europe, that they would bear some of the cost of unification through the EC.[64]

Alongside these developments towards German unification, over the course of 1990 politicians stepped up discussions about deepening integration with a view to the reunited Germany becoming still more closely involved in European integration. The road to the Maastricht Treaty was therefore crucially influenced by the developments of German unification. It acted as a catalyst for the treaty reforms and the introduction of new policy areas such as the EMU. The reforms now seemed imperative in order to integrate the enlarged Germany and make the benefits of its strength available to all countries. There are therefore analogies between the situation in 1989–90 and the founding phase of the European communities, as one central theme of the development of supranational European structures consisted in integrating the newly founded Federal Republic and monitoring its economic recovery. For the Federal Government, European integration, both in the 1950s and in 1989–90, had the advantage of allaying the concerns and fears of its European neighbours.

Concluding Remarks

The division of Germany from 1949 to 1990 was interwoven with the European integration process in many ways. It influenced the reasons for the European integration process and the member states' expectations of the

---

63 Submission by von Kyaw, Head of Directorate 41, for Foreign Minister Genscher, 24 August 1990, in Institut für Zeitgeschichte (ed.), *Die Einheit*, doc. 141, pp. 662–6.
64 Gehler and Jacob, 'Die Eingliederung Ostdeutschlands', p. 555.

European organisations. During the founding phase, integration enabled the Federal Republic to return to the international stage as an equal member and to establish itself in the Western system of alliances. West Germany's neighbours expected the European organisations to control the German recovery and to integrate its economic potential. Meanwhile, the GDR joined Comecon and watched western European integration with suspicion, viewing it primarily as an instrument of US domination.

The inclusion of the Federal Republic in the Western and the GDR in the Eastern organisations threatened to deepen the division between the two German states. The Federal Government was therefore anxious to maintain and strengthen the opportunities for contact between the two Germanies. One key way of ensuring this was intra-German trade. In its negotiations for the Treaties of Rome, the Federal Government was able to ensure that trade between the two Germanies was treated as domestic trade and thus that the EEC's trade policy provisions did not apply. The Federal Republic was able to achieve this in 1966 for the common agricultural market as well.

The rapprochement between the two German states with the entry into force of the Basic Treaty in 1973 rendered this system no longer entirely tenable. The improved international diplomatic standing of the GDR resulted in the EC introducing a split system. The EC regulations governing trade policy and the agricultural market applied to the EC member states' relations with the GDR, with the exception of the Federal Republic. The latter was able to continue conducting its trade between the two Germanies on the basis of the 1957 protocol. This remained the situation until 1990.

The relationship between the two German states, and hence also their influence on European integration, was closely tied to the overall development of the Cold War. This is evident in the phase of détente in Europe, which is also the context in which the Basic Treaty between the Federal Republic and the GDR must be viewed. The rapprochement between the two German states and the easing of tensions in Europe changed the perceptions and expectations of the EC. Détente was thus pivotal in the European integration process. Seen prior to this largely as an instrument for the defence of the Western capitalist economic system, the integration process now increasingly looked like an opportunity to develop relations with the eastern European countries and hence facilitate pan-European contacts. This liberation from the straitjacket of the East–West confrontation was reflected in the external relations of the EC. The antagonism between the EC and Comecon eased. In addition, the EC countries were able to take a coordinated stance in the CSCE, thereby achieving recognition for their work from the countries of eastern Europe. The coordination of positions in the context of the EPC had proven effective here. Furthermore, after the two German states joined the UN, the EC Commission succeeded in securing participation at the UN General Assembly.

The division of Germany had been a constant of European integration for more than 30 years; with the process of German unification in 1989–90, the system began to totter. At this stage the Federal Government was able, as in the founding phase of the 1950s, to relieve its neighbours' concerns and fears of a dominant Germany by stepping up its commitment to European integration. In this way, German unification acted as a catalyst for the process of EC reform that was initiated in the mid 1980s. Especially the projects of a political union and an EMU with a common currency at its core gained impetus from the German developments. The interconnectedness of German unification and European integration therefore accelerated the negotiations on the way to the Maastricht Treaty that entered into force in November 1993.

For the EC, German unification also meant expansion 'by the back door'. By acceding to the territory of the Federal Republic on 3 October 1990, the five new federal states also joined the EC. Ironically, this meant that the first former socialist state to become a member of the EC was the one that had most vehemently resisted establishing closer ties with the Communities.[65] The Commission in particular constructively supported the accession process and drafted the legal framework for the accession. By treating the process as a technical issue, it was able to keep it away from the higher political levels. It hoped that its role in the unification process would also increase its future importance in the institutional architecture of the EC.

This brought the period of German partition to an end for the EC. The division of Germany and the relationship between the two German states had influenced the European integration process on multiple occasions, sometimes impeding and sometimes accelerating it. In the initial phase it proved advantageous that only one part of Germany, the Federal Republic, became a founding member of the European communities. The distribution of power in the communities was balanced, due mainly to the relative equilibrium between the three large countries, France, Italy and the Federal Republic.[66] With unification in 1990, this balancing act became more complicated. The integration of the largest member state still poses major challenges for the EU to this day.

---

65 Graf, 'Die DDR und die EWG', 33.
66 Ludlow, 'European Integration and the Cold War', p. 191.

Recommended Reading

Gehler, M. and M. Graf (eds.). *Europa und die deutsche Einheit: Beobachtungen, Entscheidungen und Folgen* (Göttingen, Vandenhoeck & Ruprecht, 2017).

Graf, M. 'Die DDR und die EWG 1957–1990', *Revue d'Allemagne et des pays de langue allemande* 51 (2019): 21–35.

König, M. and M. Schulz (eds.). *Die Bundesrepublik Deutschland und die europäische Einigung 1949–2000: Politische Akteure, gesellschaftliche Kräfte und internationale Erfahrungen* (Stuttgart, Steiner, 2004).

Krotz, U., K. K. Patel and F. Romero (eds.). *Europe's Cold War Relations: The EC towards a Global Role* (London, Bloomsbury, 2019).

Küsters, H. J. (ed.). *Deutsche Europapolitik christlicher Demokraten: Von Konrad Adenauer bis Angela Merkel (1945–2013)* (Düsseldorf, Droste, 2014).

Ludlow, N. P. (ed.). *European Integration and the Cold War: Ostpolitik–Westpolitik, 1965–1973* (London and New York, Routledge, 2007).

Patel, K. K. 'Germany and European Integration since 1945', in H. Walser Smith (ed.), *The Oxford Handbook of Modern German History* (Oxford, Oxford University Press, 2011), pp. 775–94.

3

Europe, Decolonisation and the Challenge of Developing Countries

GUIA MIGANI

Development policy is currently one of the pillars of external action of the European Union (EU). The volume of official development assistance disbursed by the EU and its member states makes the EU one of the world's largest donors.[1] Despite its significance today, development assistance was not discussed in the meetings of the Spaak Committee in 1955–6 and was only later placed on the table during negotiations for the EEC Treaty.

One reason for the emergence of European development policy was that some countries – notably France – were still colonial empires during negotiations for the Rome Treaty. As a result, many studies have focused on the continuities between the colonial regime and the Euro-African association.[2] The regional orientation of the policy of the European Economic Community (EEC) reinforced these colonial continuities, as it focused for a long time on sub-Saharan Africa, a region which had been part of the colonial empires. In this regard, the old dream of Eurafrica persisted until at least the mid 1960s.[3] However, the EEC development policy's emergence did not stem solely from this colonial past. The Cold War provided EEC member states with a significant incentive to finance development plans outside

---

1 Organisation for Economic Cooperation and Development, 'European Union Institutions' (2022), in *Development Co-operation Profiles*, www.oecd-ilibrary.org/development/development-co-operation-profiles_coadrfod-en.
2 C. Unger, 'Postwar European Development Aid: Defined by Decolonization, the Cold War, and European Integration?', in S. J. Macekura and E. Manela (eds.), *The Development Century: A Global History* (Cambridge, Cambridge University Press, 2018), pp. 240–60; V. Dimier, *The Invention of a European Development Aid Bureaucracy: Recycling Empire* (New York, NY, Palgrave Macmillan, 2014); T. Chafer and N. Cooper, 'Introduction', *Journal of Contemporary European Studies* 11, no. 2 (2003): 159–66; M. Lister, *The European Union and the South: Relations with Developing Countries* (London, Routledge, 1997).
3 P. Hansen and S. Jonsson, *Eurafrica: The Untold History of European Integration and Colonialism* (London, Bloomsbury, 2014).

Europe. From this point of view the EEC, which was (mainly) an economic organisation, could intervene and maintain Western influence in countries where the stakes were high but the political risks were lower.[4]

Nonetheless, neither the continuation nor the features of the Euro-African association were dependent on the Cold War. From a political and economic point of view, the significance of French–African relations in the 1960s explains the terms of the Yaoundé Conventions (signed in 1963 and 1969 by the EEC and eighteen French-speaking African countries).[5] Furthermore, the idea of promoting the development of newly independent states was gaining traction,[6] which placed the Six under pressure collectively and separately. By the 1960s the debate inside the European Community (EC) was no longer about whether a development policy should exist but rather about the approach to be taken: should European development policy be regionalist (aimed at African and Mediterranean countries) or universalist?

The Lomé Convention, which was signed between the EEC and forty-six African, Caribbean and Pacific (ACP) states for the first time in 1975 and renewed every 5 years until 1989, has been studied extensively. Part of the historiography stresses the new elements of the Lomé Convention: how it resonated with the New International Economic Order (NIEO) sought by the Third World and how it was an example of North–South dialogue.[7] Some studies have highlighted the role of the 1973 oil-price shock empowering the Organization of the Petroleum Exporting Countries (OPEC) countries and raw materials suppliers in general, as well as the new political climate in Europe, which made European leaders more responsive to the requests of left-wing social groups,[8] whereas others have emphasised the continuity of Euro-African relations. The structural weakness of the African countries persisted throughout this period, as did the dominance of European economic interests in

---

4 S. Lorenzini, *Global Development: A Cold War History* (Princeton, NJ, Princeton University Press, 2019).

5 C. Balleix, 'La politique française de coopération au développement. Cinquante ans d'histoire au miroir de l'Europe', *Afrique contemporaine* 236, no. 4 (2010): 95–107; J.-P. Bat, O. Forcade and S. Mary (eds.), *Jacques Foccart: Archives ouvertes (1958–1974): La politique, l'Afrique et le monde* (Paris, PUPS, 2017); F. Turpin, *De Gaulle, Pompidou et l'Afrique, 1958–1974: Décoloniser et coopérer* (Paris, Les Indes savantes, 2010).

6 L. Emmerij, R. Jolly and T. G. Weiss, *Ahead of the Curve? UN Ideas and Global Challenges* (Bloomington, IN, Indiana University Press, 2001); O. Stokke, *The UN and Development: From Aid to Cooperation* (Bloomington, IN, Indiana University Press, 2009).

7 F. A. M. Alting von Geusau (ed.), *The Lomé Convention and a New International Economic Order* (Leyden, A. W. Sijthoff, 1977); C. Cosgrove-Twitchett, *A Framework for Development: The EEC and the ACP* (London, Allen and Unwin, 1981); I. Gruhn, 'The Lomé Convention: Inching towards Interdependence', *International Organisation* 30, no. 2 (1976): 241–62.

8 G. Garavini, *After Empires: European Integration, Decolonization, and the Challenge from the Global South, 1957–1985* (Oxford, Oxford University Press, 2012).

defining EEC development policy.[9] Yet the idea of continuities has been challenged, at least partially, by some specialists, who note the significance of structural economic changes in the 1980s and the impact of the neoliberal revolution. Faced with globalisation and new challenges posed by the post-Cold War international order, EEC development policy and Euro-African relations had to adapt to new priorities and constraints.[10]

The aim of this chapter is to analyse the evolution of EEC development policy from the EEC Treaty (1957) to Lomé 4 (1989) and the relationship between the EEC and the African countries. I will point out the continuities and reasons behind important changes, providing a periodisation of the evolution of EEC development policy. First, I will focus on the implications for France of taking part in the EEC with or without its colonial empire and the negotiations for the Association regime in 1956–7. In the second part, I will discuss the impact of the independence of the African states on the Association regime. In the third part, I will focus on the Yaoundé Conventions negotiated by the newly independent French-speaking African countries. Then I will focus on the reasons behind the changes in the 1970s and how the new context permitted the conclusion of a new 'revolutionary' convention, signed in Lomé in February 1975. The last part will discuss the evolution of the Lomé Convention from 1979 (Lomé 2) to 1989 (Lomé 4), analysing how the neoliberal revolution, new international economic priorities and the first manifestations of globalisation changed ACP–EEC relations.

France and the Negotiations of the Rome Treaties: The Association Policy as a Colonial Accident

European development policy, initially referred to as the Association Policy, was imposed by France as a condition for its accession to the EEC. France, which along with its colonies was already part of a common

9 J. Ravenhill, *Collective Clientelism: The Lomé Conventions and North–South Relations* (New York, NY, Columbia University Press, 1985); O. Mailafia, *Europe and Economic Reform in Africa: Structural Adjustment and Economic Diplomacy* (London, Routledge, 1997); L. Drieghe and J. Orbie, 'Revolution in Times of Eurosclerosis: The Case of the First Lomé Convention', *L'Europe en formation* 353–4 (2009): 167–81; S. K. B. Asante, 'Africa and Europe: Collective Dependence or Interdependence?', in A. Sesay (ed.), *Africa and Europe: From Partition to Interdependence or Dependence?* (London, Crom Helm, 1986), pp. 183–221; E. Grilli, *The European Community and the Developing Countries* (Cambridge, Cambridge University Press, 1993).
10 W. Brown, *The European Union and Africa: The Restructuring of North–South Relations* (London, I. B. Tauris, 2002); K. Arts and A. K. Dickson (eds.), *EU Development Cooperation: From Model to Symbol* (Manchester, Manchester University Press, 2004).

market, could not enter the European Common Market without making arrangements for its colonies.

In 1956, during the negotiations leading to the Treaties of Rome, France retained an empire, known as the *Union française*, which included part of west and central Africa and Madagascar. Economically, the sub-Saharan African territories formed part of the franc zone, with the CFA franc as their currency, pegged to the French franc and guaranteed by the French treasury. The franc zone was a protected market with guaranteed prices (that were higher than world prices) for colonial products. However, this price guarantee system, known as the *surprix* system, had led to such a degree of overproduction that the French market could no longer absorb it. The economic burden of the colonies was growing and becoming increasingly difficult to sustain.[11]

In 1956 Paris faced a complex set of challenges. France was engaged in the Algerian War. The French government and political class were still far from accepting Algeria's independence, but the war was extremely expensive and placing pressure on France's public finances. The situation in the sub-Saharan African territories was less dramatic but there was an urgent need for political evolution as Ghana, a British west African colony, was due to gain independence the following year. This meant that French-oriented African leaderships were facing growing pressure from their own populations to reclaim more power. In this context the Loi-Cadre Defferre (named after Gaston Defferre, the socialist Minister for Overseas France) was adopted, which marked an important step towards the self-administration of the African colonies.[12]

Negotiations for the relaunch of European integration took place at a delicate time for the Union française: most of the French political class still backed the continuation of the war to keep Algeria under French rule, while part of the Ministry for Overseas France was working on a crucial reform to grant a new status to the sub-Saharan African territories. The French colonial administration, which was aware of the work of the Spaak Committee in Brussels, stressed the need to include the sub-Saharan African territories in any European project. A report from the Ministry for Overseas

---

11 Ravenhill, *Collective Clientelism*, pp. 48–9. For more general details, see J. Marseille, *Empire colonial et capitalisme français: Histoire d'un divorce* (Paris, Albin Michel, 1984).
12 T. Chafer, *The End of Empire in French West Africa: France's Successful Decolonization?* (Oxford and New York, NY, Berg, 2002), pp. 165–72.

France defending this perspective insisted on the potential for making Eurafrican cooperation a reality:

> Faced with the American technical assistance and the new but symptomatic interest which the USSR is showing towards the underdeveloped countries, Europe must appear to the African countries as a power endowed with equally great means and as sure of itself and its civilising mission. [. . .] The main interest of Euratom, which is one of the particular but essential aspects of a collective aid plan for the underdeveloped countries of Africa, is the creation of industrial and technical relations between Europe and Africa.[13]

The idea of Eurafrica occupied a prominent place in France, especially among the socialists, as it represented a third international force, which was autonomous both from the United States and from the Soviet Union. But Eurafrica appealed to those outside the socialist party for other reasons. For supporters of European integration, it permitted the reconciliation of the (French) empire with the dream of a federal Europe. In fact, many Europeanists did not think it possible for a European organisation to exist without the resources of the African colonies.[14]

Writing to the then Prime Minister, Gaston Defferre noted the contradiction implied by France entering a European Common Market while continuing to be part of a French–African Common Market. France's withdrawal from the French–African Common Market had the potential to result in the independence of the African territories: a possibility that the French government rejected. However, it would be extremely difficult for France to simultaneously form part of two separate economic areas, particularly given the economic situation of the African territories and the efforts made by the French economy to support their development.[15] In the subsequent weeks, Paris decided to make the French African territories' inclusion in the EEC a condition *sine qua non* of French accession to the Common Market. Consequently, during the Conference of Foreign Ministers in Venice,

---

13 Centre des archives d'outremer (henceforth CAOM), FM 60, 2316/5, Note au sujet du projet Euratom, 2 February 1956.

14 Y. Montarsolo, *L'Eurafrique contrepoint de l'idée d'Europe: Le cas français de la fin de la deuxième guerre mondiale aux négociations des traités de Rome* (Aix en Provence, Presses universitaires de Provence, 2010); A.-I. Richard, 'The Limits of Solidarity: Europeanism, Anti-colonialism and Socialism at the Congress of the Peoples of Europe, Asia and Africa in Puteaux, 1948', *European Review of History* 21, no. 4 (2014): 519–37; Hansen and Jonsson, *Eurafrica*, pp. 71–146.

15 CAOM, FM 60, 2317/1, Le Ministre de la France d'outremer au Président du Conseil, 22 May 1956.

Christian Pineau approved the Spaak Committee's report on behalf of his government, but stated that France could not form part of a European Common Market without its colonies. The Five agreed to discuss the issue during the negotiations.

Some weeks later, the French delegation, with Belgian support, asked for the association of the African territories with the Common Market. Although Belgium did not have the same economic relations with its colonial empire as France, it stood to gain from a political and economic relationship between the Common Market and the colonial territories. Moreover, Paul-Henri Spaak, the Belgian Foreign Minister presiding over the negotiations, believed that France would be more open to reaching a compromise were it not completely isolated and at odds with the Five.[16]

Paris did not ask for the integration of its colonies into the Common Market, since that would have been extremely difficult given the huge differences in economic status (and development) between the European states and the African territories. The association was based on the opening of the African territories to European exports in exchange for their exports being granted preferential treatment. The creation of a Eurafrican free trade area was proposed, which would include a fund of at least $1 million for the 'communitarisation' of development efforts in these territories.[17]

The European partners' critiques of the French–Belgian proposal for an association between the EEC and the African colonies focused on its terms rather than the principle of the association itself. Bonn and The Hague were the most reluctant, as they were wary of becoming involved in the French colonial world – in particular the French–Algerian war. Discussions about how the association should be organised proved to be protracted and difficult. Criticisms of the proposal were levelled at the economic advantages which would be granted to the African territories, the size of the fund and how it was intended to work, as well as the long-term engagement in African territories that it would imply, among other things. The strategy adopted by France was to stress the advantages of a Eurafrican association, such as how Europe would benefit from access to African raw materials and how the

---

16 Archives diplomatiques françaises (henceforth AD), DE-CE (Papiers Bruneau), 867. Exposé de M. Moussa à la réunion du Comité monétaire de la zone franc, 7 November 1956. Cf. V. Dujardin, 'Le monde politique belge face au traité d'associa- tion des PTOM au Marché commun', in M.-T. Bitsch and G. Bossuat (eds.), *L'Europe unie et l'Afrique: De l'idée d'Eurafrique à la Convention de Lomé I* (Brussels, Bruylant, 2005), pp. 291–318.

17 AD, DE-CE 1945–1966, 719. Note d'information sur les territoires d'outremer et le Marché Commun, undated.

association would prevent the expansion of Soviet influence in Africa.[18] Despite Paris' efforts to show how Eurafrica could be reinvented in a post-Second World War world, the Five remained sceptical. They refused to apply the same regime negotiated for European agricultural products to African ones or to finance a fund of the size requested by Paris. They were not prepared for the long-term commitment sought by France and did not consider the concessions it was willing to grant – the gradual opening of markets in the French overseas territories – sufficient. The situation was summarised in a note for Pierre Moussa, Director of Political Affairs at the Ministry for French Overseas Territories:

> Under these conditions, we are not in a strong position. If we obtain a satisfactory result, it will be:
> – either because if they want to take us, they will also take the Overseas Territories
> – or because the idea of making an effort to develop the underdeveloped countries is also beginning to gain some support in certain German circles.[19]

Only after a meeting of the Heads of State and Government in February 1957 were the Six able to reach a last-minute compromise. The principles of the association (the economic and social development of the associated territories and the establishment of a close economic relationship between them and the EEC) would be included in the Treaty, while a protocol valid for only 5 years specified the terms of the association. The territories included in the association were the French and Belgian colonies, Somalia (under Italian authority) and some overseas Dutch territories. A fund of 581 million units of account (uc) was set up for the development of the associated territories. The European Development Fund (EDF) was to be managed by the Commission, which was tasked with evaluating the projects submitted by the competent authorities in the associated territories. All EEC companies would be allowed to compete for the projects financed by the EDF. The Five refused to provide any guarantees regarding the associates' exports, but the associates were exempt from paying the Common External Tariff (CET). The preferential treatment granted to the colonial power was to be extended to the other five member states. The preferences granted by the associated countries to the EEC member states (reverse preferences) and those granted by the EEC member states to the associated territories (direct

18 R. Schreurs, 'L'Eurafrique dans les négociations du traité de Rome, 1956–1957', *Politique Africaine* no. 49 (1993): 82–92.
19 CAOM, FM 60, 2317/1, Note pour le Directeur des Affaires Politiques, undated.

preferences) were intended to lead to a Eurafrican free trade area. The free trade area argument was used at the General Agreement on Tariffs and Trade (GATT) negotiations to defend against criticism from Latin American states which were worried about the new preferential treatment being granted to the associates' exports by the Six.[20]

The association regime was imposed by France.[21] In exchange for the association, France made important concessions which had an impact on the evolution of its colonies and contributed – in the medium term – to their decolonisation, due to the new constraints they imposed on the French government. Having obtained only half of the funds requested from the Five, Paris was forced to choose where to focus its resources. It could either modernise the French economy before entering the Common Market or finance the development of the African territories. Moreover, it was forced to abandon the surprix system in force in the franc zone because it was incompatible with the Common Market and Paris had accepted that the franc zone would open to the economic influence of the Five. The association regime was not established with a view to the independence of the African territories, a possibility which would not yet have been tolerated by the French political class. However, it was a first step towards the Europeanisation of French–African relations, from which the other European countries had thus far been excluded.[22]

The Independent African Countries and the Association Regime

The EEC and Euratom treaties, signed on 25 March 1957, entered into force in January 1958. The Commission Directorate General (DG) VIII was presided over by the French Commissioner, Robert Lemaignen,[23] who was in charge of managing the association regime and setting up the EDF. Defining how the EDF would work was no easy task. It was necessary to establish the association regime, to specify the roles and responsibilities of the Council of Ministers and the Commission and to identify the associate's local authorities

20 Grilli, *The European Community and the Developing Countries*, pp. 11–13.
21 A.-S. Claeys, '"Sense and Sensibility": The Role of France and French Interests in European Development Policy since 1957', in Arts and Dickson (eds.), *EU Development Cooperation*, pp. 113–32; Dimier, *The Invention of a European Development Aid Bureaucracy*, pp. 10–21.
22 AD, DE-CE 1945–1966, 613, Note, 20 April 1956.
23 On the Commission and DG VIII's beginnings, see R. Lemaignen, *L'Europe au berceau: Souvenirs d'un technocrate* (Paris, Plon, 1964).

with which to discuss the implementation of the association regime. It was also necessary to reassure the French government, which considered the Commission was acting too independently.[24]

In 1960 the independence of the African territories cast doubt on the legitimacy of the association regime. Given that it had been negotiated when the African territories were still under the authority of a colonial power, was it still in force? The debate inside the EC revealed different positions. In the Commission's opinion the association regime could remain in force, with the consent of the associates. Paris supported the Commission, as it felt it too soon to negotiate a new Convention of Association (and that the result would be too unpredictable). For the Netherlands the independence of the associated territories signalled the end of the association regime: it wanted to end preferential treatment of the associates, while allowing them to continue to benefit from the EDF. In the end, the Six agreed to compromise: the convention would remain in force provided that the associated states explicitly agreed to it. In reality, ending the association regime could have had political repercussions as it could be interpreted as sanctioning the independence of the African states. It was also decided that the African governments could choose whether to appoint an ambassador to the EEC or to delegate a representative of an EEC member state. The associates themselves would present the projects to be financed by the EDF, and collective meetings would be organised to discuss issues concerning the association regime.

All the newly independent states confirmed their association with the EEC, which lasted until its expiration date, in 1962. The association regime itself, which was conceived in 1956, when the African countries were still under colonial rule, rapidly became outdated. Yet the aims of the association – the economic and social development of the associated territories and the establishment of close economic relations between them and the EEC – remained far from being accomplished. The associates' development was a distant goal, and trade between the two regions had barely increased in the preceding 5 years, with France remaining the associates' main economic partner. In contrast, economic

---

24 Sciences Po Archives, Fonds Debré, 2 DE 21, Lettre au ministre des Affaires étrangères, 3 March 1960; V. Dimier, 'The Birth of a European Diplomatic Service: From *contrôleurs-techniques* to the Delegates of the Commission in ACP Countries', in A. Deighton and G. Bossuat (eds.), *Les Communautés européennes, acteurs de la sécurité mondiale: Bilan de cinquante ans de relations extérieures* (Paris, Soleb, 2007), pp. 114–29.

relations between the Five and the English-speaking African countries were growing.[25]

In addition to these unremarkable outcomes, the association regime received heavy political and economic criticism. The Latin American countries protested inside the GATT against the trade preferences granted to the associates. But insofar as independent African countries were concerned, the Economic Commission for Africa (ECA) played a more important role than the GATT. The ECA was created in 1958 under the authority of the United Nations (UN) Economic and Social Council. It was composed of European and African states and offered the independent African states the perfect platform on which to confront the Europeans about the creation of the Common Market and the association regime. From an economic perspective, the African states insisted that the association would lead to an unfair increase in the associates' exports to the EEC. Others noted that the association regime was hindering the industrialisation of the African states by preventing them from imposing tariff protections against the EEC's exports. Furthermore, the association regime was criticised for serving as a barrier to the creation of an African Common Market. Guinean leader Sékou Touré and Ghanaian Prime Minister Kwame Nkrumah claimed the EEC was a neo-colonialist organisation exploiting the African countries and contributing to the division of the African continent.[26] The association's renewal in 1963 did nothing to assuage their views on Euro-African relations.

Negotiating a New Convention

Yaoundé 1 (1963)

With the association regime due to expire at the end of 1962, negotiations for its renewal started in 1961. They ended in July 1963 with the signature of a convention in Yaoundé (Cameroon). Yaoundé 1 and its renewal, Yaoundé 2 (signed in July 1969), amounted to the prosecution of the association policy defined in 1957.

During the negotiations, the French delegation relinquished its use of the Eurafrican argument to defend the association. Instead, Paris insisted on the need to keep the associated countries safe from Soviet influence, stressing

---

25 Service des archives économiques et financières (henceforth SAEF), Fonds Trésor, B 17.726, Note sur le commerce des États de la zone franc associés à la CEE, August–September 1961.
26 Historical Archives of the European Union (henceforth HAEU), BAC 26/1969, (524), Note d'Information, 27 February 1961.

Europe's responsibility towards part of the developing world.[27] For their part, West Germany and the Netherlands sought to overhaul the association regime, withdrawing the preferences granted to the associated states in exchange for increased financial aid, arguing that the preferences failed to help these countries compete internationally.[28]

Negotiations with London, following the first British request to join the EEC, interfered with those involving the associated states. After the French veto on British membership in 1963, the signing of the new convention was delayed by the Netherlands and Italy. The end of the Algerian War in 1962 also had an indirect impact on the negotiations. France was now free to re-examine its relations with the Third World and to develop new forms of cooperation with Asian and Latin American countries. Consequently, it was important for it not to favour the interests of French-speaking African states over those of other developing states. As a result, France was prepared to compromise on the CET for tropical products in exchange for the convention's renewal.[29]

The final agreement confirmed the creation of a Eurafrican free trade area. The lowering of the Six's national custom duties would be speeded up for the benefit of the associates but – at the request of the Netherlands and West Germany – the CET on some key tropical products (such as coffee and cocoa) was reduced, as was the preferential treatment granted to the associates' exports. Furthermore, the Five refused to replace the surprix system, which had until then been in force in the franc zone, or to provide compensation for its abolition as they felt that Paris was attempting to pass the cost of its colonial policy on to the EEC. Despite pressure from the French, the Five argued that the price support of tropical agricultural products or raw materials exported by the associates should be addressed at the international level, rather than inside the EEC. Their only concession was to provide the associates with 230 million uc as aid to finance production and diversification. A compromise to increase the second EDF from 581 to 730 million uc (including production and diversification aid) was eventually reached only when the Italian government agreed to significantly increase its contribution.[30] During the negotiations questions were raised about other

27 AD, Papiers Wormser, 35, Note, 15 May 1961.
28 HAEU, BAC 118/1986, (1663), Réunion du Conseil de la CEE, 25 July 1961.
29 Centre historique des archives nationales (henceforth CHAN), Fonds public Foccart, 2612, Télégramme pour l'Ambassade française à Bruxelles, 28 May 1962.
30 G. Migani, 'La CEE et l'Afrique, quel projet de développement pour la coopération eurafricaine?', in Bat, Forcade and Mary (eds.), *Jacques Foccart*, pp. 309–22; Mailafia, *Europe and Economic Reform in Africa*, pp. 45–8.

aspects of the French African policy: the franc zone was highly criticised by the Five, who pointed out that a devaluation of the CFA franc would make the associates' exports more internationally competitive. However, France dismissed this, arguing that a devaluation would only worsen the associates' economic position because it would increase the cost of imports.[31] In the end, joint institutions, comprising an Association Council, a Euro-African Parliamentary Conference and a Court of Arbitration, were created to oversee the convention.

The African states were disappointed with the outcome of the negotiations and asked for the continuation of the surprix system, guarantees for the sale of tropical products, the elimination of national taxes on tropical products and to benefit from the Common Agricultural Policy (CAP) for their agricultural exports. However, they obtained nothing.[32] The only undertaking of the Six to the African states was to consider the associates' interests when setting up the CAP. The EEC states also refused to allow the associates any involvement in the EDF. The end of the surprix system and the EEC's refusal to take any initiative to stabilise raw material or agricultural product prices were major losses for the associates. Nonetheless, they agreed to sign the convention because the positive aspects outweighed the negative ones: their preferential tariff treatment was extended and they received a new EDF for the following 5 years. Given their limited diplomatic resources, another positive element for associated African and Malagasy states was the opportunity to develop their relations with the Six in Brussels, in a privileged context. The convention's preamble, which declares 'a mutual willingness for cooperation based on complete equality' (volonté mutuelle de coopération sur le plan d'une complète égalité), was symbolic and arrived at a crucial moment in the consolidation of their then recent independence.

Yaoundé 2 (1969)

Although Yaoundé 2 did not differ in its essence from Yaoundé 1, the negotiations proved to be more difficult than ever. In Europe, the debate focused on the special treatment granted to the associated states. During the second UN Conference on Trade and Development (UNCTAD), in New Delhi (1 February to 29 March 1968), the Six accepted the principle of a Generalised Scheme of Preferences (GSP) for developing states. But how could a GSP be created that was compatible with the Convention of

---

31 SAEF, Fonds Trésor, B 62.169, Réunion des Ministres des Finances, 30 November 1961.
32 HAEU, BAC 118/1986, (1664), Tableau synoptique des positions prises par les États associés et de la Communauté, April 1962.

Association, which already granted special treatment to the associated states? In the opinion of the Dutch and German governments, which advocated a universalist approach, the new convention should prepare the transition towards a European development policy addressing all of the Third World. The Hague asked for the end of the reverse preferences which had been granted by the associated states to the Six, the lowering of the CET on tropical products and a declaration that the new agreement would not hinder the adoption of the GSP. However, France, which advocated the regionalist approach, wanted a renewal of the association regime without any significant changes. Paris was experiencing difficult times (May 1968 and the end of de Gaulle's presidency), and was not prepared to compromise on reverse preferences. The French representative argued that these were an essential element of the Eurafrican free trade area, were economically significant (at least for France) and represented the African states' contribution to the association. Paris was prepared to accept a reduction in the CET, but only for products that did not compete with the associates' exports and if the principle of a Eurafrican free trade area was preserved.[33]

The associated states highlighted the shortcomings of Yaoundé 1, requesting the maintenance of tariff preferences, along with stronger measures to support the commercialisation of their products and export price guarantees (based on the CAP model). However, all these requests were refused. At the end of the negotiations the free trade area was preserved, while the CET on coffee, cocoa and palm oil (three key exports from Latin America and Asian countries) was lowered. Aid for diversification, which was introduced during Yaoundé 1 to compensate for the end of the French surprix system, was eliminated. An Emergency Fund, financed by the EDF, would be made available in exceptional circumstances, such as sharp drops in world prices. The new EDF would be 900 million uc, including European Investment Bank loans of 90 million uc.

The association regime, which was renewed in 1969 for a further 5 years, was based – as in 1957 – on tariff preferences, financial aid and technical cooperation. However, the global effect of tariff preferences on trade remained slight: the EEC's trade with the associates grew at a slower rate than with other developing countries. The associates preserved their position only on the French market. Rules of origin were another difficult issue: the associates argued that the EC demanded too large a percentage of local value added to industrial products for them to be considered as having

---

33 AD, De-Ce 1967–1975, 804, Télégramme 413–20, Bruxelles, 27 March 1969.

originated in their territories (and therefore eligible for CET exemption).[34] In terms of financial aid and technical cooperation, the funds provided by the EDF consisted mainly of grants, with a small portion of subsidised loans. Aid was not tied, but it was disbursed slowly – especially at first – and no clear apportionment criteria were established. Most of the funds were allocated to infrastructure and rural production, while the industrial sector was under-represented throughout the period 1958–69.[35] By the end of the 1960s disillusionment was palpable among the associates and the European states. The associates were disappointed with the outcomes of the Yaoundé Convention, in particular France's incapability or unwillingness to defend a European alternative to the surprix system, and they were concerned about the increasing importance of the EEC's relations with other developing states. In the Five's view, the failings were also clear: the Yaoundé Convention had not made the associates more competitive and was too closely connected to Europe's colonial past. The reverse preferences and accusations of dividing the African continent or exploiting the associated states were a growing embarrassment to the EEC.

The 1970s: Entering a New Arena

At the dawn of the 1970s, internal and external factors led to changes in the EEC's association policy. First, the negotiations for British accession placed relations with the Commonwealth on the table. During the 1960s, the EEC had already established some relations with English-speaking African countries, signing agreements with Nigeria in 1965 and with the East African Community (Kenya, Tanzania and Uganda) in 1968. The Lagos agreement with Nigeria, with clauses on commercial relations and tariffs, failed to enter into force due to the Nigerian Civil War and France's support of Biafra. The Arusha Agreement (signed in 1968 and renewed in 1969) granted the east African countries a trade regime like that of the Yaoundé Convention but with restrictions on coffee and other products competing with the associates' exports. It did not include financial or technical assistance and lasted for 5 years.[36] Neither of these agreements could be compared to the Yaoundé

---

34 Ravenhill, *Collective Clientelism*, pp. 57–65.
35 Ibid., pp. 66–72; M. Rempe, 'Entangled Industrialization. The EEC and Industrial Development in Francophone West Africa', in C. Grabash and A. Nützenadel (eds.), *Industrial Policy in Europe after 1945: Wealth, Power and Economic Development in the Cold War* (New York, NY, Palgrave Macmillan, 2014), pp. 236–55.
36 Mailafia, *Europe and Economic Reform in Africa*, pp. 51–4.

Convention, which the English-speaking African countries did not seek to join. When the Lagos agreement was negotiated, neither the French government nor the Nigerian government – for opposite reasons – wanted it to resemble the Yaoundé Convention. In the case of the Arusha agreement, the east African states had no sponsor among the European states: the opening of an East German consulate in Dar es Salam and the pro-communist attitude of the Tanzanian government made West Germany and the Netherlands, which usually favoured English-speaking African countries, less keen to defend their requests.[37]

The negotiations for British accession were the occasion to discuss both the renewal of Yaoundé 2 and relations with the developing countries of the Commonwealth. Paris was in a difficult position because it could not refuse the accession of the English-speaking African countries to the Yaoundé Convention without putting the convention itself at risk; West Germany and the Netherlands wanted to enlarge the EEC's relations with the whole of the developing world. The problem was that enlarging the association to so many states would dilute its meaning and decrease the magnitude of its commercial and financial advantages.[38] The British position was influenced by the economic and political interests of the Commonwealth. The Commonwealth Sugar Agreement – according to which the United Kingdom (UK) imported a fixed quantity of sugar produced by the Caribbean countries every year at an agreed price – was a particular concern, since it would expire in 1974 and could not be renewed after British accession to the EEC. At the end of the negotiations with London, given the complexity of the situation for the Commonwealth countries, it was decided to offer them a range of options. The English-speaking African and Caribbean countries (the so-called associables) could choose:

- to participate in the negotiations for the renewal of the Yaoundé Convention.
- to negotiate a new agreement like the Arusha agreement.
- to negotiate a simple commercial agreement.

Other developing countries (notably the Asian countries, whose population size and level of development differed from those of the African states) would be offered ad hoc agreements with the EEC.

---

37 G. Migani, 'Avant Lomé: La France, l'Afrique anglophone et la CEE (1961–1972)', *Modern & Contemporary France* 26, no. 1 (2018): 43–58.

38 CHAN, 5AGF/2576, Note du SGCI sur l'Afrique noire francophone, 15 June 1970.

Other international factors compelled the EEC to re-evaluate its relations with the African countries and more generally with the Third World. At the beginning of the 1970s, the Third World was a challenging actor in the international arena. Inside UNCTAD the Group of Seventy-Seven (G77) contested more and more fiercely the international economic order dominated by the Western states. During the 1970s North–South dialogue, focusing on issues such as trade and tariffs, the just price of raw materials, international finance, foreign aid and the governance of international institutions, was the instrument through which the developing countries sought to impose crucial reforms on industrialised states to create a more just and equitable international economic order.

The end of the Bretton Woods monetary system in 1971 and the oil-price shock in 1973 made the western European countries more sensitive to the need to secure supplies of raw materials. The oil-price shock triggered a similar rise in the prices of other commodities, causing 'widespread insecurity about raw material supplies to the industrialized countries'.[39] In this context the EEC member states had to re-engage in dialogue with the Third World, or at least a part of it.[40] At the same time, the international détente combined with the perceived weakness of the United States encouraged the EEC to develop new international ambitions. In October 1972 at the Paris Summit, the Nine agreed on a declaration establishing the EEC's guiding principles and aims for the decade ahead. Insofar as the Third World was concerned, the declaration mentioned old and new priorities, stressing the need for a world-wide development policy, at the request of the Netherlands and West Germany, and the special status of the associated (African) states and Mediterranean countries, which was a priority for the French government.[41]

As agreed with London, the English-speaking African countries were offered the opportunity to take part in the negotiations for the renewal of Yaoundé 2.[42] However, initially they refused. Nigeria played an important role in this refusal, although its attitude was largely shared by the other countries. The term 'association' was categorically refused as being symbolic of a neo-colonialist policy. London and the ECA's secretary, Robert Gardiner,

39 Brown, *The European Union and Africa*, p. 50.   40 Garavini, *After Empires*, pp. 184–200.
41 *Bulletin of the European Communities*, 'Statement from the Paris Summit', 10, 1 October 1972.
42 O. Akinrinade, 'Associates and Associables: The Failure of Commonwealth Bridge-Building, 1971–3', *The Journal of Modern African Studies* 27, no. 2 (1989): 177–99.

put great effort into explaining the advantages of negotiating with the EEC.[43] The two Commissioners for development during the negotiations, Jean Deniau and Claude Cheysson, played an important role in showing that the EEC was open to discussion without imposing any preconditions. The associates, for their part, were being pulled in opposing directions: while an agreement to be open to the largest possible number of members would be less advantageous for them, it was difficult to refuse the associables participation because of the appeal to African unity and because a larger coalition meant greater leverage during negotiations. In the end, the combined efforts of the Commission and the British government with the ECA's assistance succeeded: the associables agreed to take part in the negotiations, although they refused – much to Paris' chagrin – to discuss the renewal of the Yaoundé regime.

In fact, the French government was forced to recognise that its aims – to preserve the essential elements of the Yaoundé regime or to exclude the associables (by making acceptance of the terms of the Yaoundé Convention a precondition for the opening of negotiations) – were destined to fail. None of the other member states, or the Commission, wanted the associables to reject the EEC's offer and all were amenable to reviewing the terms of the Yaoundé Convention. The creation of an African bloc, composed of the associables and the associates, was the next step. However, this took a long time to become a reality. One of the main disagreements concerned reverse preferences: the associables sought their abolition, whereas the associates wished to preserve them to defend their privileged position on the EEC market at the GATT (using the Eurafrican free trade area argument). In the end, the English-speaking countries prevailed and, during an Organisation of African Unity conference held in Lagos in July 1973, the African countries adopted a common position. During the negotiations, the associates and the associables formed a common group, the ACP countries, which was formalised by the Georgetown Agreement in June 1975.

Negotiating Lomé: A New Development Cooperation Policy

Inside the EEC the debate on the future convention was opened by the Commission. The Deniau Memorandum, in March 1973, presented the possible terms of the new convention and proposed a new set of instruments.

---

43 British National Archives (BNA), FCO 30/1266, Protocol 22 of the treaty of accession, undated.

It played a key role in defining the main topics for the renewal of Yaoundé 2 and showed that the EEC was ready to include delicate new issues that had been discussed at the UNCTAD gatherings. The memorandum succeeded in convincing the associables that the best way to protect their interests was by negotiating with the EEC and reassured the associates that they would not receive benefits that would be of lesser magnitude than in the previous agreements.[44] Concerning the reverse preferences, the memorandum specified that the association would be based on the principle of a free trade area, but the associates would be entitled not to grant preferences to the EEC. This was a contradictory promise, as noted by Paris, which sought to oppose this concession. The memorandum's most interesting proposal was the creation of a new price support system for agricultural exports. The issue of a just price for raw materials and agricultural exports was discussed extensively during the North–South dialogue. Falling export prices was one of the main problems faced by developing countries. Inside UNCTAD they proposed various solutions, without success. In fact, following the abolition of the surprix system in the franc zone, there was no longer any kind of support system for developing states' agricultural exports. From this point of view, the CAP was both a model in terms of guarantees and a focus of criticism because it penalised exports that competed with European products. The Commission's proposal to create a compensatory financing scheme – although limited to ACP countries' exports to the EEC – was a huge commitment that was met with little enthusiasm by Western countries inside UNCTAD. The memorandum did not mention any specific amount of financial aid, but did specify that the enlargement of the association regime would not lessen the associates' benefits.

The negotiations, which officially started in July 1973 and ended in February 1975, proved extremely difficult on almost all fronts. The ACP countries requested free entry into the Common Market, without reciprocity, for all their exports, including agricultural products covered by the CAP – a concession the Europeans refused to make. Concerning the rules of origin clause, the ACP countries wanted as broad a definition as possible. After prolonged discussions, the EEC agreed to consider ACP countries as a single producing area to favour their regional cooperation. The price stabilisation scheme for export earnings was criticised by the ACP countries for not being ambitious enough. They also refused to make any undertakings regarding the volume of exports to be delivered to the Common Market.

44 Ravenhill, *Collective Clientelism*, p. 82.

The oil-price shock and the prospect of establishing more producers' cartels in the Third World had strengthened their bargaining position.[45]

For its part, France refused to abandon the reverse preferences and criticised what it considered the English-speaking African countries' overly prominent role in the negotiations. France, and to some extent the Commission, wanted to maintain the reverse preferences for two reasons: first, they protected the convention inside the GATT from the protests against the preferential treatment of the associated states; and secondly, they helped to distinguish the convention from the GSP that the EEC had granted to all developing states in 1971.

The first months of 1974 were particularly difficult, and the negotiations were even suspended after the election of a new Labour government in the UK. London demanded a world-wide development policy and wanted to divide the EEC's aid equally between the associates and non-associates. Negotiations were resumed, in part because of pressure being placed on London by the ACP countries, and in July 1974 at the Kingston Conference the Heads of State and governments achieved a breakthrough. The Nine finally conceded that the new convention would not be based on reverse preferences. A US declaration promising not to dispute the preferential access granted to ACP countries contributed to the adoption of this solution. The end of the reverse preferences marked an important change from the previous conventions. It represented the end of the idea of a Eurafrican free trade area, which had been one of the pillars of the association policy since 1957. The Nine also agreed to propose a better offer for agricultural products and agreed on a scheme to stabilise ACP countries' export earnings, the future Système de Stabilisation des Recettes d'Exportation (System for the Stabilisation of Export Earnings, STABEX).

The ACP countries insisted on managing STABEX with the Community, enlarging the list of products covered by the system (obtaining only the inclusion of iron) and exonerating the least developed countries (LDCs) from reimbursing the loans. They also rejected any limitation on how to use STABEX funds. At the end of the negotiations, STABEX was fully controlled by the EEC. Money was paid as interest-free loans to cover shortfalls in export earnings to the EEC for each of the commodities. The ACP countries, except for the LDCs, were supposed to reimburse the loans. Payments for the export earnings losses were made to governments without

---

45 Brown, *The European Union and Africa*, pp. 54–6.

any requirement that they be spent on the product in question. Governments were asked merely to send a report on how they had used STABEX funds.

STABEX became one of the most important commitments of the new convention, which symbolised the old and the new facets of the Euro-African relationship. On the one hand, it was possible only because the oil-price shock and the new assertiveness of the G77 had given the ACP countries greater leverage. The ACP countries were able to use STABEX funds with only nominal oversight by the EEC. In fact, the ACP states were largely free to define their development priorities – a possibility which would be drastically curbed in the next decade. On the other hand, the fact that the EEC made such a commitment exclusively towards ACP countries was symbolic of the significance of old colonial links. The fact that the guarantees operated only in respect of agricultural exports was also seen as a manifestation of a persisting neo-colonial relationship.

Two questions remained to be decided on the last days of negotiations: the amount of financial aid and the quantity of sugar the EEC would absorb. Discussions about the final amount of the EDF remained under the strict control of the Nine, who refused to let the ACP countries participate in any way. The EDF was more than tripled, taking it to 3 billion European Currency Units (ECU), while the number of developing countries that were parties to the agreement had only doubled, from nineteen to forty-six. However, in the opinion of the ACP countries, this increase was not sufficient. Decision-making about the contributions of the Nine to the EDF took quite some time because London did not wish to contribute the same amount as France and Germany. In the end, it was decided that France and Germany would contribute 25.95 per cent of the total, whereas the UK would contribute 18.7 per cent – less than Bonn and Paris but more than London had proposed initially.

Finally, a sugar protocol was annexed to the convention. The British Sugar Agreement, under which London imported sugar from Caribbean countries, expired in 1974 and was not renewable after the British accession to the EEC. In the protocol annex, the EEC agreed to import 1,275,000 tons of sugar from ACP countries, which would benefit from guarantees relating to its price and sale. In practice, this meant that the CAP would be extended to ACP sugar. This protocol had a special status, since its term was indefinite.

Lomé 1 was the best convention negotiated by the ACP states. It represented a significant improvement on the Yaoundé regime, with the ACP states obtaining the end of reverse preferences, a new system for the stabil-isation of export earnings, special guarantees for sugar and even a protocol on industrial cooperation. The international crisis and the oil-price shock reinforced the leverage of countries exporting raw materials such as the ACP states. The experience of the G77 inside UNCTAD was very useful. After years of debates, the developing states now had theories, arguments and a list of requests at their disposal. The Global South was united in its request of an NIEO, which was approved by the UN General Assembly in May 1974. From this point of view, Lomé can be considered the European answer to the Global South's request to reform the international economic system. Even the convention's language alluded to the NIEO, with the need to establish 'a new model for relations between developed and developing States, compatible with the aspirations of the international community towards a more just and more balanced economic order' being mentioned in the preamble.

Many factors contributed to the signing of the new convention: France and the UK were committed to maintaining a special relationship with ACP countries, whereas West Germany and the Netherlands were in favour of expanding the EEC's relations with the English-speaking developing world. Moreover, since commodity prices were rising unpredictably and the security of supplies was not guaranteed, securing relations with the sub-Saharan African countries, which were important producers of raw materials, was a wise move. The EEC's development policy had distinct aims from those of the old association policy: it did away with the most criticised aspects of the Yaoundé regime and was capable of serving as a positive example in the North–South dialogue at the UNCTAD conferences. This helped it to gain the support of social-democratic governments in the EEC and of left-wing parties, which had long been suspicious of the Yaoundé policy.

More generally, Lomé was also a manifestation of the European desire to play a more assertive role in the international arena. In a context where Washington appeared relatively weak following the Vietnam War, the EEC could play a useful role in Africa, and especially in the former colonies, by financing their economic development and opposing the expansion of Soviet influence. The EEC's decision in 1976 to allocate funds to Asian and Latin American countries for the first time and to establish a new emergency fund for all the LDCs also signalled its growing inclination not to limit its activities (and possible influence) to the African region. Furthermore, during the same period the EEC established more formalised relations with some key Third World countries and organisations, such as India in 1973, China in 1978 and the Association of Southeast Asian Nations in 1980.

Lomé in Question: Re-discussing Its Terms

Lomé 2: Preserving the Essential

As soon as Lomé was signed, an intensive propaganda campaign was launched to promote its progressiveness. This marked the beginning of a new relationship with the ACP countries. However, within a few years the shortcomings of the convention became evident: the new partnership, though an improvement on what had come before, was never really equal. The EEC kept the EDF's management strictly under its own control. The CAP protected European agricultural products, and the Nine had recourse to safeguard clauses to protect their most exposed industrial sectors. Industrial cooperation failed to blossom and the ACP countries remained confined to the role of supplying raw materials and agricultural products, reproducing old colonial patterns of trade. Although Lomé was more than a neo-colonial policy, EEC–ACP trade betrayed the 'persisting influence of colonially-inherited relations'.[46]

At the end of the 1970s, EEC–ACP relations changed as a result of neoliberalism, new international economic priorities (due to the debt crisis and the economic growth of the east Asian states) and the first signs of globalisation. Lomé 2, signed in October 1979, was affected by this climate. Disappointed with the outcomes of Lomé, the ACP countries requested full access to the EEC market for all their agricultural products, changes to the rules of origin to facilitate their exports to the Common Market and an end to the EEC's safeguard clauses. They asked for true joint administration powers for the new agreement, criticising the Commission's excessive control in administering aid and the slow aid disbursal rate. Lastly, they demanded that the amount of the new EDF cover the inflation rate as well as the entry of new members.[47] The EEC, which was facing its own problems, including recession, institutional changes and internal conflict, wanted to maintain the main features of the Lomé system, with financial adjustments and minor improvements.[48] For the first time the question of human rights hindered the negotiations: London and The Hague wanted to make EEC aid subject to respect for human rights. The British government was forced to take this initiative following major human rights violations in Uganda, which had

---

46 Brown, *The European Union and Africa*, p. 53; Mailafia, *Europe and Economic Reform in Africa*, pp. 78–81.

47 HAEU, BAC 48/1984 (877), Extrait du compte rendu de la Conférence ministérielle ACP–CEE, 4 May 1979, p. 2.

48 HAEU, BAC 48/1984 (869), Note à l'attention des membres de la Commission, Bruxelles, 25 July 1978.

a strong impact on public opinion in the UK. But the proposal divided the European governments.[49] Lomé 2 did not include a clause on human rights because of the ACP countries' steadfast refusal to allow this, but from that point on the matter would be openly discussed during negotiations for future treaties.[50]

In the end, Lomé 2 did not contain any important amendments with respect to aid, trade or industrial cooperation. The EDF was confirmed but its amount (4,542 million ECU) barely covered the inflation rate. The convention reinforced the programming phase: from then on ACP countries were required to prepare National Indicative Programmes approved by the Commission before requesting EDF funds. The most important innovation was a system to promote ACP countries' mineral production and to assist them in stabilising export earnings derived from minerals. In fact, the EEC, and especially West Germany, was increasingly worried about the African mining sector. The European states feared that declining mining investment in ACP countries would threaten their raw materials supplies. So, the Commission proposed a system called SYSMIN, which operated like STABEX but with some important differences. Since its aim was to create a viable mining industry in ACP countries, SYSMIN funds were linked to the mining sector and governments could not change their allocation.[51] In contrast, STABEX funds went directly to ACP countries' national budgets and could be used freely with minimum control by the EEC.

Lomé in the 1980s: The EEC Takes Back Full Control

During the 1980s the European development policy evolved to adapt to the new international context. Some continuities persisted, but by the end of the decade the European development policy had integrated features that fundamentally changed the EEC–ACP relationship. One of the first new elements was a renewed interest in the agricultural sector, driven by the famine in the Sahel and Ethiopia. This interest in agriculture – which contrasted with the industrial focus of the 1970s – was connected to the environmental priority which emerged in the 1970s. The environmental evolution of the EEC development policy was favoured by the new Development

49 HAEU, BAC 48/1984 (868), Note à l'attention des membres de la Commission, Bruxelles, 3 June 1978.
50 CHAN, Fonds 5AG3, 1420, télégramme circulaire n. 458, Paris, 19 July 1978; HAEU Archives, BAC 48/1984 (877), Extrait du compte rendu de la Conférence ministérielle ACP–CEE, 30 April 1979, p. 2.
51 HAEU Archives, BAC 48/1984 (877), Note à l'attention des membres de la Commission, 23 May 1979.

Commissioner, Edgar Pisani, appointed in 1981. He remained at the Commission for a short but intense period (1981–4) which included the adoption of the memorandum on development cooperation policy (October 1982) and the negotiations of Lomé 3 (1983–4). After arriving in Brussels, Pisani mobilised his DG in a collective effort to rethink the EEC's cooperation policy. Pisani saw various reasons for revising European aid; the difficulties faced by developing countries and especially Africa, which was the focus of European aid, cast doubt on the strategies that had thus far been adopted. Pisani's main proposals included the adoption of sectoral strategies, particularly in agriculture, and the introduction of a policy dialogue. Adopting sectoral strategies meant placing the emphasis on programmes rather than projects, as had been the practice in the past. The Pisani memorandum also acknowledged that the EEC's policy should promote the self-reliant, sustainable development of developing countries, particularly the poorest.[52]

In 1984 Lomé 3 provided a good indicator of the EEC's changing priorities. Environmental protection was addressed in Article 1, before agriculture, nutrition and rural development. By introducing the policy dialogue, Lomé 3 represented another step towards greater control by the Commission of European funds. In fact, Pisani wanted to establish a policy dialogue between the Commission and the ACP countries that was something different from the International Monetary Fund (IMF) and World Bank conditionality. The policy dialogue was intended to help ACP countries to identify the sectors in which to concentrate European aid to maximise its effects.[53] However, the ACP countries opposed the proposal because they feared that the policy dialogue would limit their freedom to define their development priorities.[54] Indeed, for some EEC member states the policy dialogue was a welcome step towards imposing greater conditionality on aid.[55] Apart from the policy dialogue, Lomé 3 imposed greater control by the Commission on STABEX funds and assigned greater importance to the elaboration of National Indicative Programmes, which were conceived with the help of the Commission. The Commission also took on greater involvement in EEC–ACP political relations. Despite the

---

52 'The Community's Development Policy', *Bulletin of the European Communities*, Supplement 5/82, p. 14.
53 HAEU, BAC 16/2006, Communication de la Commission 'Orientations des prochaines négociations CEE/ACP', 25 March 1983.
54 HAEU, BAC 19/2001 (1), Négociations CEE–ACP. État d'avancement des travaux, Bruxelles, 17 February 1984.
55 AD, De-Ce 1981–83, 2029, Note d'information, 16 August 1983; HAEU, BAC 19/2001 (1), Résumé du mémorandum ACP pour les négociations, 5 September 1983.

ACP countries' opposition, a reference to the UN Charter and respect for human rights was included in Lomé 3's preamble. This reference was intended to demonstrate the ACP countries' concern about the EEC's relations with South Africa, as well as the Nine's concern about human rights violations in ACP countries.[56]

Lomé 3 provided the first framework for the promotion and protection of private investments in the ACP states. The proposal had been discussed in the past but the ACP countries had always refused to accept it. However, they now agreed that creating a good climate for private (foreign) investments would be important for their own development. The shift from development based mainly on public funds to private investments was another fundamental change in this decade. Although the leading role of the private sector in the economy was a neoliberal idea, it was brought about by the major reduction in official development assistance. Given the economic context, even maintaining the value of the EDF in real terms was extremely difficult. Its amount (7,400 million ECU) was one of the last questions to be negotiated. It was not until contributions from Spain and Portugal – neither of which was yet an official EEC member – were taken into account that a compromise was reached.

These trends continued for the rest of the decade. Lomé 4 was signed in December 1989 for a term of 10 years. It reflected a new political relationship between the ACP countries and the EEC. Regarding the environment, in 1987 the Brundtland report formalised the idea of sustainable development, placing it within the economic and political context of international development.[57] The EEC enshrined the principles of the Brundtland report in Lomé 4, with Article 1 of the convention setting out the objectives and terms of environmental cooperation, and sustainable development featuring throughout the text. For example, the article on mining and energy placed emphasis on energy conservation and the promotion of new and renewable sources of energy. The convention banned the export of toxic waste from the EEC to ACP countries and prohibited ACP countries from accepting this kind of waste from the EEC or other countries. Lomé 4 was the first convention to officially include a financing facility (1,150 million ECU) to enable the ACP states to adopt the reforms recommended by the Bretton

56 Speech of Rabbie L. Namaliu, President of the ACP Council of Ministers, *The Courier* 89 (January–February 1985): 4.
57 World Commission on Environment and Development, *Our Common Future* (Oxford, Oxford University Press, 1987); W. M. Adams, *Green Development: Environment and Sustainability in the Third World* (London, Routledge, 1990), p. 70.

Woods institutions, thus sanctioning the EEC's alignment with the Washington Consensus. Cooperation with the Bretton Woods institutions increased in the second half of the 1980s: in 1987 the EEC took part in the special programme launched by the IMF and the World Bank for the African states; and in 1988 the EC Council of Ministers adopted structural adjustment as an element of the EEC's development policy towards African countries.[58] The EC declaration stated the need to implement a more pragmatic version of the structural adjustment policy to minimise the social costs of the reforms, but in practice the differences were insignificant.[59] Economic conditionality came with greater political conditionality. Respect for human rights had already been mentioned in the preamble of Lomé 3 in 1984 and 2 years later the EC Council of Ministers adopted a declaration making respect for human rights one of the principles of the EEC's external action. Lomé 4 made respect for human rights an 'essential element' clause of EEC development policy.[60] Lastly, the EDF was established at 12 billion ECU – a 40 per cent increase in nominal terms but only 20 per cent in real terms. In per capita terms the increase was even less, given the rate of population growth in ACP countries since 1984 and Namibia's accession to the convention in 1990.[61]

Conclusions

In analysing more than 30 years of EEC development policy, we have identified some turning points and fundamental changes. From its inception in 1957, the association policy was connected to the Six's colonial past. This connection was apparent not only in terms of the countries that benefited from European aid but also in the way the association policy functioned. This policy, which predated the African states' independence, comprised financial aid and technical assistance, as well as extending to the Five the trade regimes previously in force between the French colonial power and its territories. The Eurafrican free trade area played an important role as a project allowing western Europe to keep up with the United States and the Soviet Union and

---

58 Council Resolution on the Economic Situation and Adjustment Process in Sub-Saharan Africa, 31 May 1988; 'The Adjustment Process in Africa: A European Council Resolution', *The Courier* 111 (September–October 1988): 73.
59 B. Petit, 'L'ajustement structurel et la position de la Communauté européenne', *Revue Tiers Monde* 34, no. 136 (1993): 827–50.
60 L. Ferrari, 'The European Community as a Promoter of Human Rights in Africa and Latin America, 1970–80', *Journal of European Integration History* 21, no. 2 (2015): 217–30.
61 *The Courier* 120 (March–April 1990): 3; Brown, *The European Union and Africa*, p. 90.

as a tool to oppose communist influence. During the 1960s the idea of Eurafrica gradually lost its appeal and was replaced by North–South dialogue.

A first turning point can be identified at the Paris Summit, in 1972, where the EEC agreed on new goals for the decade ahead. In terms of development policy, the Nine agreed to take measures in respect of the whole Third World and new issues, such as stabilising the prices of raw materials, were included. Lomé, in 1975, represented an important shift away from the Yaoundé regime and was marked by the abandonment of the term 'association', which the English-speaking African countries refused. Lomé integrated new tools and new aims. Lomé even acknowledged the need for ACP states to protect their market from European competition by eliminating reverse preferences. This signified the end of the Eurafrican free trade area, which had been a pillar of the association policy since 1957. Moreover, for the first time the EEC made new (albeit limited) commitments towards the rest of the Third World, with the GSP entering into force in 1971, increased food aid and the EEC offering financing for Latin American and Asian countries from 1976.

That is not to say that its colonial past was forgotten – the most visible sign of this situation being the fact that EEC development policy was still based on a regional approach that focused on the former colonies. Some of the new measures were reminiscent of the colonial period. For example, the Sugar Protocol was requested by London to replace the Commonwealth Sugar Agreement. STABEX, too, was reminiscent of the surprix system that had been in force in the Union française, although the issue of a just price for raw materials and agricultural products had been discussed extensively during the UNCTAD gatherings. However, the fact that this effort was made only for the ACP countries was another sign of old colonial links.

A second turning point came at the end of the 1970s, the consequences of which were visible in Lomé 3 and especially Lomé 4. The EEC development policy changed again in the 1980s in terms of its aims and tools. Slowly but surely the EEC development policy's regionalist approach was challenged, with the ACP states becoming less of a priority. During this decade the political and economic significance of other developing regions grew, as the EEC signed agreements with the most politically and economically powerful Asian and Latin American countries. The ACP states' poor economic performance contributed to the EEC's growing disinterest, but other factors must also be considered. First, globalisation deeply impacted North–South relations, weakening the Third World and ACP countries. In this context, the debt crisis and the growing influence of the Bretton Woods institutions in managing the debt crisis made it impossible for the

Commission not to seek greater cooperation with the World Bank and the IMF.[62] Although EEC development policy retained a greater degree of social orientation than the World Bank and the IMF, it adopted their priorities in the long term. Furthermore, the EEC's choice of globalisation[63] – managed by the creation of the World Trade Organization – implied the end of the ACP countries' special status. From this point of view, Lomé 4 was the last convention of its kind.

Recommended Reading

Bitsch, M. T. and G. Bossuat (eds.). *L'Europe unie et l'Afrique: De l'idée d'Eurafrique à la Convention de Lomé I* (Brussels, Bruylant, 2005).

Dimier, V. *The Invention of a European Development Aid Bureaucracy: Recycling Empire* (New York, NY, Palgrave Macmillan, 2014).

Garavini, G. *After Empires: European Integration, Decolonization, and the Challenge from the Global South, 1957–1985* (Oxford, Oxford University Press, 2012).

Hansen, P. and S. Jonsson. *Eurafrica: The Untold History of European Integration and Colonialism* (London, Bloomsbury, 2014).

Ravenhill, J. *Collective Clientelism: The Lomé Conventions and North–South Relations* (New York, NY, Columbia University Press, 1985).

Unger, C. 'Postwar European Development Aid: Defined by Decolonization, the Cold War, and European Integration?', in S. J. Macekura and E. Manela (eds.), *The Development Century: A Global History* (Cambridge, Cambridge University Press, 2018), pp. 240–60.

62 HAEU, Interview with Bernard Petit, https://archives.eui.eu/en/oral_history/INT1104.

63 S. Meunier, 'Managing Globalization? The EU in International Trade Negotiations', *Journal of Common Market Studies* 45, no. 4 (2007): 905–26.

4

European Integration and Globalisation since the 1970s

EMMANUEL MOURLON-DRUOL

Introduction

In 2020, 'strategic autonomy' became a buzzword in Brussels. The phrase catches different meanings, ranging from the self-sufficiency of the European Union (EU) to the management of interconnectedness in a globalised world. In EU parlance, 'strategic autonomy' is used in a sense that aims to be different from the traditional concepts of sovereignty and power, but should, however, not be read in contradiction with free trade. 'Strategic autonomy' seems to have been articulated first by President of the European Council Charles Michel in two speeches in September 2020.[1] But in reacting to the clichés that US President Donald Trump voiced against the EU in January 2017, German Chancellor Angela Merkel had already expressed her desire for European autonomy in declaring that 'we Europeans have our fate in our own hands'.[2] French President Emmanuel Macron has regularly used

I wish to thank Alexis Drach, Laurent Warlouzet and the editors for comments on an earlier draft of this chapter, and Catherine Lefèvre for research assistance. This chapter builds on a project that has received funding from the European Research Council under the EU's Horizon 2020 research and innovation programme (grant agreement No. 716849). The project is entitled 'The Making of a Lopsided Union: Economic Integration in the European Economic Community, 1957–1992 (EURECON)'.

1 C. Michel, 'Recovery Plan: Powering Europe's Strategic Autonomy – Speech by President Charles Michel at the Brussels Economic Forum', 8 September 2020, www.consilium.europa.eu/en/press/press-releases/2020/09/08/recovery-plan-powering-europe-s-strategic-autonomy-speech-by-president-charles-michel-at-the-brussels-economic-forum; C. Michel, '"Strategic Autonomy for Europe – the Aim of Our Generation" – Speech by President Charles Michel to the Bruegel Think Tank', 28 September 2020, www.consilium.europa.eu/en/press/press-releases/2020/09/28/l-autonomie-strategique-europeenne-est-l-objectif-de-notre-generation-discours-du-president-charles-michel-au-groupe-de-reflexion-bruegel.

2 '"Europe's Fate Is in Our Hands": Angela Merkel's Defiant Reply to Trump', The Guardian, 16 January 2017, www.theguardian.com/us-news/2017/jan/16/europes-fate-is-in-our-hands-angela-merkels-defiant-reply-to-trump.

the related concept of 'European sovereignty' since his speech on Europe at the Sorbonne in 2017.[3] Regardless of the origin and meaning of the phrase, 'strategic autonomy' touches therefore on a perennial motif of European integration that largely predates the 2010s, namely the place and role of the EU in a globalising (or globalised) world.

European integration and globalisation form a tumultuous duo. To some, the latter dictates the former. The EU is helpless – or worse, complicit – in letting the neoliberal forces of global markets impose their rule on European lives. But to others, the former regulates the latter. The EU is a heavyweight in many policy areas. The EU allows otherwise too small individual European nation-states to make their voice collectively heard, and matter, in international arenas. Whatever the interpretation, the interaction between European cooperation and globalisation is therefore a given. And this has remained true over the past half a century, in spite of the dramatic changes that have taken place, between what the European Economic Community (EEC) looked like when globalisation restarted, around 1970, and what it is today. Between 1970 and 2023, the integration of European nation-states moved from a Community of six members to a Union of twenty-seven, with a peak at twenty-eight members between 2013 and 2020, and from a single currency area of eleven members in 1999 to twenty members in 2023 – all this in spite of repeated predictions by authoritative pundits about the imminent disintegration of the EU or the eurozone, or indeed both, especially from 2008 onwards. Between 1970 and 2023, globalisation moved from being a fledgling (and restarting) phenomenon to a seemingly inescapable trend, reinforced by the end of the Cold War and by the emergence of China and its inclusion in the international multilateral capitalist system, but again put at risk by the coronavirus pandemic. Globalisation remains severely criticised, regularly challenged and liable to setbacks, but it continues to be a driving force. The EEC/EU's share of world gross domestic product (GDP) has steadily declined since the 1990s – in spite of its enlargements – going from its peak at 28 per cent (1995–2002) to 23 per cent in 2019 (Figure 4.1). However, in more than half a century, the EEC/EU's share of world population has remained relatively stable over time, at about 7 per cent, due to its successive enlargements (Figure 4.2).

3 E. Macron, 'Initiative pour l'Europe – Discours d'Emmanuel Macron pour une Europe souveraine, unie, démocratique', 26 September 2017, www.elysee.fr/emman uel-macron/2017/09/26/initiative-pour-l-europe-discours-d-emmanuel-macron-pour-une -europe-souveraine-unie-democratique.

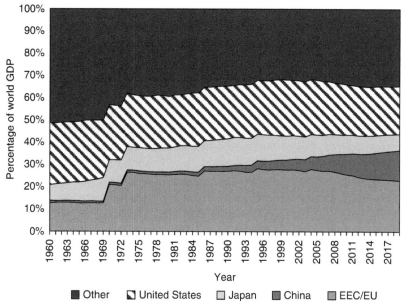

Figure 4.1 EEC/EU GDP as a share of world GDP since 1957. Source: World Bank, constant 2010 US$.

Beyond these basic indicators, the role of the EEC/EU has also markedly changed. In 2023, the EU is the largest trading block in the world, most of its member states share a single currency that is the second-most-traded internationally after the dollar, and its regulatory influence, that Anu Bradford recently dubbed the *Brussels Effect*, spreads well beyond the borders of the EU.[4] All these elements, and indeed many others that are not included in this shortlist, were far from being a given in 1970. In examining the interplay between European integration and (economic) globalisation, this chapter thus attempts to capture the main trends of a relationship that is in constant flux, with each element having also its own endogenous dynamics. How does European integration contribute to, and how is it influenced by, the course of globalisation? What tools has the EEC/EU built, failed to build or considered building, to enhance its status in a globalised world?

This chapter is divided into two sections, revolving around two major turning points: 1989–1991 and the mid 2010s. As with any chronological

4 A. Bradford, *The Brussels Effect: How the European Union Rules the World* (Oxford, Oxford University Press, 2020).

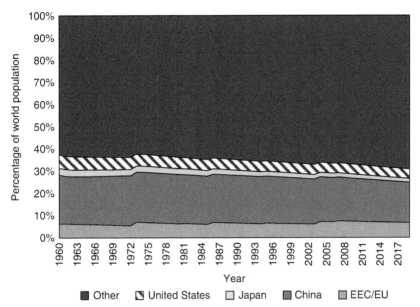

Figure 4.2 EEC/EU population as a share of world population since 1957. Source: World Bank.

division in writing history, this reflects a deliberate choice to highlight the coherence and continuity of some periods over others. The first section covers the restart of globalisation around 1970 until the end of the Cold War and the signature of the Maastricht Treaty creating the EU. This was a time when the main challenges to the post-war order emerged, and when the first EEC responses to globalisation were being devised. The second section analyses how the Maastricht Treaty, and the end of the Cold War, changed the stakes of the globalisation–European integration relationship. It looks at the early hopes for genuinely global governance and the first seemingly successful decade of the euro, and then it turns to the global financial crisis and the crisis then reforms of the euro area, before scrutinising the challenges posed by the rise of China. Finally, a long concluding section starts from the middle of the 2010s, when the crisis of the euro area was over, at least in its most acute form, and the consequences of the failures of globalisation started to manifest themselves in their most acute form. This includes the UK's referendum decision to leave the EU in June 2016, the internationalisation of the euro, climate change, the challenges brought by the digital and the Covid-19 crisis. (Since this chapter was written before Russia's attack on Ukraine, it does not include discussion of this topic.) Given its scope and contemporary nature, this concluding section is much more forward looking than the previous ones.

The End of the Transatlantic Cocoon (1970–1990)

How did the EEC fit in the global conversation about some key issues of globalisation before Maastricht? This first section looks into the governance of four key policy areas for Europe in a globalised world: trade, finance, macroeconomic relations and capital liberalisation. It then analyses separately the making of the Single European Act and the Maastricht Treaty as responses to international challenges.[5]

The Governance of International Trade Relations

Trade was one of the policy areas where the EEC's power and influence over international negotiations could, and still can, be felt most clearly.[6] The General Agreement on Tariffs and Trade (GATT), signed in 1947, aimed at promoting the liberalisation of international trade by reducing tariff barriers after the end of the Second World War. A series of 'rounds', lasting several months or years, covering specific subjects (textiles, dumping, agriculture ...) and involving a number of countries, were organised in order to reach a negotiated outcome. One of the first major rounds, the so-called Kennedy Round, lasted from 1964 until 1967. Overall, the EEC, as such, championed a liberal attitude in the industrial sector but a protectionist one in agriculture. But, crucially, the Kennedy Round of talks showed the interest of the then six EEC member states in attempting to reconcile their internal quarrels in order to present a united regional front in the negotiations in Geneva. Overcoming these quarrels was surely no easy task, but the prospect

---

5 A. Andry, E. Mourlon-Druol, H. A. Ikonomou and Q. Jouan, 'Rethinking European Integration History in Light of Capitalism: The Case of the Long 1970s', *European Review of History: Revue Européenne d'histoire* 26, no. 4 (2019): 553–72.

6 P. Ludlow, 'The Emergence of a Commercial Heavy-Weight: The Kennedy Round Negotiations and the European Community of the 1960s', *Diplomacy & Statecraft* 18, no. 2 (2007): 351–68; L. Coppolaro, 'In Search of Power: The European Commission in the Kennedy Round Negotiations (1963–1967)', *Contemporary European History* 23, no. 1 (2014): 23–41; L. Coppolaro, *The Making of a World Trading Power: The European Economic Community (EEC) in the GATT Kennedy Round Negotiations (1963–67)* (Farnham and Burlington, VT, Ashgate, 2013); F. McKenzie, *GATT and Global Order in the Postwar Era* (Cambridge, Cambridge University Press, 2020); A. Sapir, 'EU Trade Policy', in H. Badinger and V. Nitsch (eds.), *Routledge Handbook of the Economics of European Integration* (Abingdon, Routledge, 2019), pp. 205–19.

of being able to have considerable weight in the global negotiations and ultimately attain a dominant position in world trade helped sideline these difficulties, even if eventually the EEC did not move the talks ahead, leaving that task to the United States. EEC member states carefully defined the European Commission's room for manoeuvre so as to preserve what they perceived as their own national interests and to enhance at the same time their common position. Whereas in the preceding Dillon round the six EEC member states kept attending negotiation sessions with speaking rights, for the Kennedy Round they let the EEC Commission become the sole negotiator.

The Kennedy Round thus marked, as Lucia Coppolaro argued, the EEC's 'first act of foreign policy'.[7] Later rounds confirmed the importance of the EEC as a world trading power, further reinforced by the EEC's enlargement. But the 1960s remained the defining time period when these choices granting significant power and autonomy to the European Commission were made. In subsequent rounds, especially the so-called Tokyo Round, which lasted from 1973 until 1979, and the so-called Uruguay Round, which lasted from 1986 until 1994, the EEC (and later the EU) continued to put forward preferences that confronted those of the United States in particular, while promoting the development and strengthening of the rules of the multilateral trade regime aimed at regulating globalisation, up until the creation of the World Trade Organization (WTO) in 1995.

Europe and the Vicissitudes of International Finance and Energy

At first, the evolution of the international monetary system and of European currency relations seemed unconnected. When the EEC was being negotiated in 1955–7, the European Payments Union (EPU), an organisation created to facilitate the convertibility of European currencies, was still in operation (it was wound up in December 1958), and the international monetary system was considered stable. So stable, in fact, that the negotiators of the Treaty of Rome largely omitted the topic in drafting the treaty. In short, western Europe started its economic integration in what was widely perceived to be an international monetary cocoon.

---

7 L. Coppolaro, 'In the Shadow of Globalization: The European Community and the United States in the GATT Negotiations of the Tokyo Round (1973–1979)', *The International History Review* 40, no. 4 (2018): 752–73; L. Coppolaro, 'Globalizing GATT: The EC/EU and the Trade Regime in the 1980s–1990s', *Journal of European Integration History* 24, no. 2 (2018): 335–52.

The vicissitudes of international monetary relations, however, offered an early opportunity to highlight the necessity and the difficulty of finding a common European solution. They equally spurred hopes that the EEC, as such, could become a regional unit of stability and thus protect itself in an unstable world. In spite of the European Commission's activism to find an EEC-wide solution, in particular with the creation of the Committee of Governors of the Central Banks of the EEC in 1964, the crises of the 1960s were not auspicious. Instead of coordinated EEC solutions, EEC member states most often considered bilateral options (with the United States) or global multilateral options (with the International Monetary Fund (IMF) or the World Bank).[8] In April 1969, the Commissioner in charge of economic and financial affairs, Raymond Barre, lamented: 'What we want is that the currency problems of the Community can be examined at the Community level and can be treated at the Community level. If ever it happens that these problems must be examined in a wider framework, then the Community as such can participate in the debates that take place at the IMF, or in the Group of Ten (G10). But we are at present in a situation where there exists a Community in trade, there exists a Community in the economic realm, but when there are monetary consequences of the existence of the Community in the economic realm, and in the trade realm, then the Community does not exist.'[9]

In the 1970s, the problem of international and European monetary coordination remained, and European policy-makers kept on discussing the possibility of devising a coordinated response. The end of the Bretton Woods system pressed European policy-makers to envisage creating a new European framework able to provide some currency stability to EEC member states, without having to rely on the evolution of the discussions about the future of the international monetary system. President of the European Commission François-Xavier Ortoli declared in January 1974: 'It is essential that the problems linked to international monetary relations [...] be treated as Community problems [*problèmes communautaires*] and that Europe speaks

---

8 H. James, *Making the European Monetary Union: The Role of the Committee of Central Bank Governors and the Origins of the European Central Bank* (Cambridge, Belknap Press, 2012), pp. 36–88; E. Mourlon-Druol, 'History of an Incomplete EMU', in F. Amtenbrink and C. Herrmann (eds.), *The EU Law of Economic and Monetary Union* (Oxford, Oxford University Press, 2020), pp. 13–36.

9 Historical Archives of the European Union, PE0 19402, Intervention prononcée par M. Barre devant la Commission économique du Parlement européen, 14 April 1969 (my translation).

with one voice in these negotiations.'[10] In September of the same year, Ortoli further added that 'the common dependence of outward-looking economies which rely on the growth of trade for maintaining full employment implies that Europe must effectively participate, that is to say as a unit, in international discussions and must contribute towards defining a new, stable and lasting international monetary and commercial order'.[11]

In 1977, still in the same vein, President of the European Commission Roy Jenkins argued that a single European currency could contribute, alongside the dollar, to a more stable international monetary system. In a famous speech calling for the monetary integration of Europe at the European University Institute in Florence, he said: 'The benefits of a European currency, as a joint and alternative pillar of the world monetary system, would be great, and made still more necessary by the current problems of the dollar, with its possible destabilising effects. By such a development the Community would be relieved of many short-run balance-of-payments preoccupations. It could live through patches of unfavourable trading results with a few-points drop in the exchange rate and in relative equanimity. International capital would be more stable because there were fewer exchange risks to play on, and Europe would stand to gain through being the issuer of a world currency.'[12] Even if the creation of the European Monetary System (EMS) was quite a long way from being the same as introducing a European single currency, the dynamic was comparable, and it represented an attempt to provide a coordinated European response in a world of fluctuating currencies.[13]

International financial relations offered another early opportunity to show the weaknesses of European coordination. From the 1960s, the development of the so-called euromarkets exemplified the inability of Europeans to act in unison. The development of the euromarkets provided another global challenge to international financial relations and European integration.

---

10 Archives historiques de la Commission européenne, Collection des discours, François-Xavier Ortoli, Declaration on the State of the Community, 31 January 1974 (my translation).

11 Archives historiques de la Commission européenne, Collection des discours, François-Xavier Ortoli, 'The Personality of Europe and Economic and Monetary Union', 25 September 1974 (my translation).

12 R. Jenkins, *Europe's Present Challenge and Future Opportunity* (Florence, European University Institute, 1977).

13 E. Mourlon-Druol, *A Europe Made of Money: The Emergence of the European Monetary System* (Ithaca, NY, Cornell University Press, 2012).

The origins of the Euromarkets are still being debated.[14] The prefix 'euro' in euromarkets does not relate to the European single currency or even to the European continent. It means 'offshore', that is, something that is done outside the normal area of jurisdiction. Euromarkets are, broadly speaking, markets that operate outside their home country. Eurodollars, the most common form of euromarket, refer to dollars traded outside the United States. London was the leading international financial centre for this trade. Several factors contributed to the development of euromarkets, including the desire to evade regulations (in particular US Regulation Q), the benevolence of British regulators and the fact that, during the Cold War, the Soviet Union held many dollars but did not want to store them in a location where they could be seized by the US authorities. The Soviet Union thus preferred trading them in London. The banks that started trading in this market were British-based, in particular the Midlands Bank.

The main challenge posed by this market was that, because it was based offshore, that is, outside the conventional apparatus of a state authority, it was unregulated. Euromarkets called into question monetary sovereignties. But, just as much as the United States, the UK or the G10, the EEC was unable to regulate them, in spite of the creation of a new institution, the Euro Currency Standing Committee, by the governors of the G10.[15] Furthermore, the EEC was also unable to develop a genuine capital market of its own. This represented a potential twinned failure of European integration: the inability both to develop a capital market in the EEC and to regulate the one that had developed in Europe, but outside EEC jurisdiction. The question of the liberalisation of capital movements will be addressed later in this chapter.

Finally, the oil-price shock of 1973 also laid bare European disagreements on the global stage. European positions were not always well coordinated in

14 S. Battilossi, 'International Money Markets: Eurocurrencies', in S. Battilossi, Y. Cassis and K. Yago (eds.), *Handbook of the History of Money and Currency* (Singapore, Springer Singapore, 2019), pp. 1–46; B. Braun, A. Krampf and S. Murau, 'Financial Globalization as Positive Integration: Monetary Technocrats and the Eurodollar Market in the 1970s', *Review of International Political Economy* 28, no. 4 (2020): 1–26; C. R. Schenk, 'The Origins of the Eurodollar Market in London: 1955–1963', *Explorations in Economic History* 35, no. 2 (1998): 221–38; G. Toniolo and P. Clement, *Central Bank Cooperation at the Bank for International Settlements, 1930–1973* (New York, NY, Cambridge University Press, 2005); K. Yago, *The Financial History of the Bank for International Settlements* (London and New York, NY, Routledge, 2012).
15 See A. Drach, *Liberté surveillée: Supervision bancaire et globalisation financière au Comité de Bâle (1974–1988)* (Rennes, Presses universitaires de Rennes, 2021); C. Goodhart, *The Basel Committee on Banking Supervision: A History of the Early Years, 1974–1997* (Cambridge, Cambridge University Press, 2012).

the Group of Seven (G7).[16] This partly stemmed from the fact that EEC member states fared very differently in response to the oil-price shock, and their energy and geopolitical situations varied from one to another. The oil-price shock also contributed to the further development of the euromarkets, in that they were used for recycling the surpluses of the producing countries. Finally, as I will explain in greater detail in the section on Covid-19, the oil-price shock spurred the creation of a new EEC financial mechanism to support the balance of payments difficulties of EEC member states. With the benefit of hindsight, this move has gained in significance, as this was historically the first time that the EEC, as such, borrowed on international capital markets.

A New European and Global Institutional Framework

The beginning of the 1970s witnessed a major reconfiguration of European and global institutions to deal with a new wave of challenges spurred by the restart of globalisation, which had to be addressed respectively at European and global level.[17] The international and European monetary and financial issues that have been set out above featured prominently, but they were not alone in motivating institutional change.

Two new institutional frameworks emerged. The first was designed to cope more specifically with economic challenges, and increasingly political challenges. In 1974, EEC heads of state and government met at a summit in Paris, to discuss the current state of European integration. They decided, among other things, that such meetings would from then on become regular, three times a year and whenever necessary, in what was to be called the 'European Council'. In November 1975, the leaders of the six most industrialised countries met in Rambouillet to discuss the state of the West's economic problems, and in particular the future of the international monetary system. They did not decide straight away to make their meetings regular – this decision was not taken until 1977 – but they quickly decided to meet up again.

---

16 N. Bonhomme, 'Les Européens au G7: Entre intérêts communautaires et gouvernance mondiale (1975–1985)', *Les cahiers Irice* 9, no. 1 (2012): 73–89.

17 E. Mourlon-Druol and F. Romero, *International Summitry and Global Governance: The Rise of the G7 and the European Council, 1974–1991* (London, Routledge, 2014); N. P. Ludlow, 'The Real Years of Europe? U.S.–West European Relations during the Ford Administration', *Journal of Cold War Studies* 15, no. 3 (2013): 136–61; E. Mourlon-Druol, 'Adjusting an Institutional Framework to a Globalising World: The Creation of New Institutions in the EEC, 1957–1992', *Journal of Economic Policy Reform* 23, no. 3 (2020): 273–89.

Both types of meeting had roots in previous ad hoc and informal meetings. From the early 1970s, the so-called Library Group, named after the location of the meetings in the Library of the White House, gathered the finance ministers (not heads of governments) of France, the UK, West Germany and the United States. From the creation of the EEC onwards, heads of state and government met occasionally, in ad hoc summit meetings, to discuss the state of European integration. Both experiences inspired the creation of the European Council and the G7, although both of these new institutions were specifically aimed at filling an international and European institutional void: the regular meeting of heads of state and government. Until then, the only occasions at which European heads of state and government normally met were state funerals.

The second stream of institutional reform focused on financial challenges. It involved again both a global trend and a distinctively European regionalism. Faced with an increase of coordination challenges, European banking regulators and supervisors decided to convene on a regular basis in a so-called Contact Group from 1971–2. A few years later, in 1974–5, after the outbreak of several major banking crises, including the Lugano scandal and the failure of Bankhaus Herstatt, Western financial regulators and supervisors decided to create the Basel Committee on Banking Supervision, housed at the Bank for International Settlements in Basel.[18] Just as with economic and political coordination, the coordination of financial regulation therefore originated from a regional endeavour, which was soon accompanied and partly superseded by a global effort.

European-Inspired or US-Inspired: The Liberalisation élan of the 1980s

The 1980s witnessed the rise to power of neoliberal ideas and their implementation in policy terms. European and global dynamics converged, with the two most famous neoliberal leaders – US President Ronald Reagan and UK Prime Minister Margaret Thatcher – being elected on the two sides of the Atlantic. The reforms of the 1980s provide another example of mutual

18 C. Schenk, 'Summer in the City: Banking Scandals of 1974 and the Development of International Banking Supervision', *English Historical Review* 129, no. 540 (2014): 1129–56; E. Mourlon-Druol, '"Trust Is Good, Control Is Better": The 1974 Herstatt Bank Crisis and Its Implications for International Regulatory Reform', *Business History* 57, no. 2 (2015): 311–34; Goodhart, *The Basel Committee on Banking Supervision*; A. Drach, 'A Globalization Laboratory: European Banking Regulation and Global Capitalism in the 1970s and Early 1980s', *European Review of History: Revue Européenne d'histoire* 26, no. 4 (2019): 658–78; Drach, *Liberté surveillée*.

influences between European integration and globalisation.[19] Rawi Abdelal famously argued that, while the shift towards the liberalisation of capital movements had long been perceived as US-centred and US-driven, it had been European-inspired and French-engineered.[20] Jacques Delors (president of the European Commission), Michel Camdessus (director general of the IMF) and Henri Chavranski (president of the Committee on Capital Movements and Invisible Transactions of the Organisation for Economic Co-operation and Development (OECD)) were at the helm of those financial reforms. Abdelal highlights how these French politicians and civil servants, often linked to the French Socialist Party, first implemented the opening of the French economy to international financial markets and then worked to liberalise capital movements through the OECD, the IMF and the EEC.[21] While French policy-makers fully embraced the liberalisation of the 1980s, they aimed at creating new rules at the international and European levels to govern this liberalisation.

Key to these developments, so Abdelal argues, was the work done within the EEC. Liberalisation was not only accepted as a critical component of the European project, but was being devised in the most liberal sense. No distinction was made according to the origins and destination of capital movements: whether from outside or within the EEC, capital could move freely. The EEC thus established a model of 'open regionalism' – an expression that Peter Katzenstein coined, and that Abdelal uses with reference to the European setting – that critically influenced the course of global finance.

A final feature highlighted by Abdelal is the common ideological background of the French policy-makers involved in the effort to liber-alise international and European capital movements. This elite was often left-wing, which is surprising given the policy options implemented in favour of capital. Several reasons contribute to explaining these choices. French policy-makers argued that, before liberalisation, capital controls were a failure: rules were constantly evaded by the rich at the expense of the working class and the poor. Unable to regulate this, they decided to liberalise everything. Another factor was that national public debt

19 A. Drach and Y. Cassis (eds.), *Financial Deregulation: A Historical Perspective* (Oxford, Oxford University Press, 2021).

20 R. Abdelal, *Capital Rules: The Construction of Global Finance* (Cambridge, MA, Harvard University Press, 2007).

21 R. Abdelal, 'Le consensus de Paris: La France et les règles de la finance mondiale', *Critique internationale* 28, no. 3 (2005): 87–115.

was high, and liberalising capital markets would decrease the cost of servicing it.[22]

The story of the liberalisation of capital movements within the EEC is one of stop and go: early moves (1960–2) were followed by standstill until the mid 1980s, with occasional introduction of greater constraints in the 1970s and full liberalisation in the second half of the 1980s.[23] The Treaty of Rome originally set out four freedoms of movement: for goods, people, capital and services. But Article 67 on the free movement of capital was devised with some restrictions, in that it should happen only 'to the extent necessary for the proper functioning of the Common Market'. This restrictive phrasing was largely influenced by the view that capital movements could have destabilising effects. In the early 1960s, the European Commission pushed for greater liberalisation, which materialised in two directives (dated 11 May 1960 and 18 December 1962). Given the disagreements among EEC members, in particular with France being against and Germany in favour, no consensus was reached on a third directive as the European Commission envisaged. The efforts for liberalisation stalled afterwards, and indeed some greater restrictions were put in place in the 1970s. The French U-turn on the subject in the early 1980s allowed the formation of a new consensus in favour of removing restrictions. The free movement of capital was now seen as a useful constraint imposed on the national individual economic policies of EEC member states in the framework of the EMS. Further to this, and regardless of the time period, the free movement of capital was a prerequisite to the European monetary union: whether in 1970 or in 1989, restrictions on capital movements had to be lifted in order for the monetary union to become a reality. The EEC Commission's White Paper of June 1985 gave a central position to the liberalisation of capital movements. The full liberalisation of capital flows was eventually adopted in June 1988.

The French and EEC role, while indeed central as Abdelal contends, should, however, be qualified. Alexis Drach argues that two elements must be borne in mind.[24] First, French policy-makers were not alone in pushing for the liberalisation of capital movements: so did British and German

---

22 O. Feiertag, 'Financial Deregulation in France: A French "Big Bang"? (1984–1990)', in Drach and Cassis (eds.), *Financial Deregulation*, pp. 121–54; L. Quennouëlle-Corre, 'Les réformes financières de 1982 à 1985: Un grand saut néolibéral?', *Vingtième Siècle. Revue d'histoire* 138, no. 2 (2018): 65–78.

23 A. F. P. Bakker, *The Liberalization of Capital Movements in Europe* (Dordrecht, Springer Netherlands, 1996); A. Drach, 'Removing Obstacles to Integration: The European Way to Deregulation', in Drach and Cassis (eds.), *Financial Deregulation*, pp. 76–100.

24 Drach, 'Removing Obstacles to Integration'.

policy-makers, who, in addition to liberalisation, pushed for financial deregulation. The UK view was that liberalisation should not be accompanied with re-regulation at the European level; quite the contrary, London fought against any attempt at reinforcing the role and competences of the EEC. Secondly, the EEC's programme for liberalisation covered many policy areas other than capital movements, including, for instance, stock markets. In these other areas, French policy-makers were far from being enthusiastic supporters of a systematic liberalisation. One further argument, at the heart of the investigation of this chapter, should be added to these two. The liberalisation of capital movements in the EEC was also part of an ambition to re-assert EEC sovereignty over European capital markets. As mentioned earlier, the development of euromarkets took place in Europe but offshore, outside any EEC jurisdiction. As Padoa-Schioppa noted in 1982, 'Instead of the development of an integrated European capital market, we have witnessed the remarkable growth of a parallel and unregulated world-wide financial market, the so-called Euromarket.'[25] The liberalisation of capital movements within the EEC aimed at contributing to the creation of a genuine EEC market under EEC jurisdiction.

The Single Market and the Single Currency as European Responses to Globalisation

At its heart the single market was a re-enactment of the goals of the Treaty of Rome and its four freedoms.[26] The reason why this re-enactment was needed was that the authors of the Treaty of Rome had not anticipated the development of non-tariff barriers, such as consciously imposed administrative delays, that could limit these free movements. In so doing, the development of the European single market set out a new institutional and legal framework that considerably reinforced the regulatory power of the EEC. Far from being ideologically monolithic, as Laurent Warlouzet argues, the EEC pursued many different options in trying to regulate globalisation: at times socially oriented, at times neomercantilist, and at times market-oriented. The

---

25 Archives historiques de la Banque de France, 1489200205/222, T. Padoa-Schioppa, 'European Capital Markets between Liberalisation and Restrictions', Speech to the Second Symposium of European Banks, Milan, June 1982. See also Commission of the European Communities, Communication to the Council, Financial integration, COM (83) 207, 20 April 1983.
26 M. Egan, *Constructing a European Market: Standards, Regulation, and Governance* (Oxford, Oxford University Press, 2001).

first option aimed to diminish social inequalities, the second focused on maximising industrial output and the third promoted free-market reforms [27]

With the movement of capital fully liberalised in the EEC, exchange rates had to be locked to ensure the survival of the single market. It was not just that currency fluctuations constituted a non-tariff barrier. It was more that incessant currency fluctuations, and in proportions that would render intra-marginal interventions within the EMS framework impossible, put the single market at risk. To the famous inconsistent trinity originally set out by Robert Mundell in the early 1960s, according to whom it was impossible to have at the same time fixed exchange rates, free capital movements and independent national monetary policies (one had to give), the vice-director of the Banca d'Italia and former head of Directorate General II Tommaso Padoa-Schioppa added free trade (the single market) and dubbed this the 'inconsistent quartet'.[28] This reasoning was at the heart of the renewed *élan* in discussing the possible creation of a European Economic and Monetary Union (EMU) in the second half of the 1980s.[29] As the next section will show, the creation of EMU – and the deepening of European integration in general – further complexified the relationship between the EU and globalisation.

One Mirage and Two Crises (1991–2015)

The end of the Cold War and the creation of the EU changed the dynamics of the relationship between European integration and globalisation. The end of the Cold War gave birth to a wave of hope for a better world, the governance of which would become truly multilateral, including former communist countries. For European integration, it opened the way for an eastern enlargement. The creation of the EU presented European policy-makers with some new tools, most importantly the European single currency. But the twenty-first century quickly made these hopes fade away and contrasted them with a range of new (or seemingly new) challenges. This section analyses the impact of these changes across five themes: the hopes of

27 For more details, see L. Warlouzet, *Governing Europe in a Globalizing World: Neoliberalism and Its Alternatives Following the 1973 Oil Crisis* (Abingdon, Routledge, 2018).

28 R. Mundell, 'Capital Mobility and Stabilization Policy under Fixed and Flexible Exchange Rates', *Canadian Journal of Economic and Political Science* 29, no. 4 (1963): 475–85; T. Padoa-Schioppa, 'Capital Mobility: Why Is the Treaty Not Implemented? [1982]', in T. Padoa-Schioppa, *The Road to Monetary Union in Europe: The Emperor, the King, and the Genies* (Oxford, Clarendon Press, 1994), pp. 26–43.

29 K. H. F. Dyson and K. Featherstone, *The Road to Maastricht: Negotiating Economic and Monetary Union* (Oxford, Oxford University Press, 1999); James, *Making the European Monetary Union*, especially Chapters 6 and 7.

global governance, the first decade of the euro, the outbreak of the Global Financial Crisis (GFC) and the crisis of the euro area, the reform of the euro area and finally the challenges posed by the rise of China.

The End of the Cold War and the Dream of Global Governance

The end of the Cold War engendered hopes about a new world order based on multilateralism. While the international system that emerged after the Second World War was in principle universal, it was only with the enlargement of the Bretton Woods institutions to the countries of the former Soviet bloc, and then to the WTO incorporating China, that it became truly so. Trade continued to expand, in particular in services, but without corresponding international rules. Emerging economies had increasing importance globally, and thus also for the EU, but this role was not reflected in international governance. The remit of the Uruguay Round (1986–94) thus became larger and included services, intellectual property and investment. The creation of the WTO in 1995 materialised the American–European efforts to strengthen the international system. Unlike the GATT, the WTO was a full-fledged international institution, with a binding dispute settlement mechanism. China first requested access to the GATT in 1986, and eventually joined the WTO in 2001. While China aimed at gaining export markets, the United States and EU aimed at inserting China into a rules-based international trade system.[30] The 1990s therefore progressively marked the end of a system that had hitherto been dominated by the United States and (west) European countries. This system had become challenged, both because geopolitics had changed and because the reality of world trade had considerably evolved. But once this new international architecture was set in place, coordination stalled, and the hopes for successful international collective action faded in the late 1990s.

The First Decade of the Euro

With the benefit of hindsight, the first decade of the euro emerges as a stereotypical moment of quietness before the storm. Against the scepticism that surrounded its creation, in particular among US economists, the first decade of the euro proved better than expected. This was so on at least two counts. First, the transition to the single currency was smooth. This was no small feat, since it was a monumental logistical task. Secondly, in terms of

---

30 For an examination of China's WTO membership, see P. C. Mavroidis and A. Sapir, *China and the WTO: Why Multilateralism Still Matters* (Princeton, NJ, Princeton University Press, 2021).

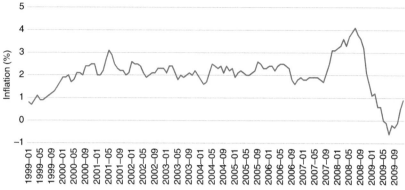

Figure 4.3 Euro area inflation, 1999–2009. Source: ECB.

various basic economic metrics, the first decade of the euro was far from the disaster predicted: the European Central Bank (ECB) mandate of price stability was broadly respected, with inflation remaining around 2 per cent except in 1999–2000 and 2008–9 (Figure 4.3); yearly growth rose to about 4 per cent in 2001, then fell to about 1 per cent in 2002–3 and rose again slightly until the GFC (Figure 4.4); unemployment decreased until 2001, then rose slightly until 2004 and decreased again until the GFC (Figure 4.5). Reflecting on the first 10 years of the euro, the European Commission concluded in 2008 that it was 'a resounding success. Ten years into its existence, it has ensured macroeconomic stability, spurred the economic integration of Europe – not least through its successive enlargements –, increased its resilience to adverse shocks, and become a regional and global pole of stability. Now more than ever, the single currency and the policy framework that underpins it are proving to be a major asset.'[31] The European Commission's positive assessment was not without substance, but the EMU's structural weaknesses identified at Maastricht were still there, and they were only partly and poorly addressed in the rest of the 1990s with the creation of the Stability and Growth Pact (SGP).[32] But 10 years after the introduction of the single

31 European Commission, Directorate General for Economic and Financial Affairs, *EMU@10: Successes and Challenges after Ten Years of Economic and Monetary Union* (Luxembourg, Publications Office of the European Union, 2008).
32 The nature of the SGP is highly political, see M. Segers and F. Van Esch, 'Behind the Veil of Budgetary Discipline: The Political Logic of the Budgetary Rules in EMU and the SGP', *Journal of Common Market Studies* 45, no. 5 (2007): 1089–109; M. Heipertz and A. Verdun, *Ruling Europe: The Politics of the Stability and Growth Pact* (Cambridge and New York, NY, Cambridge University Press, 2010).

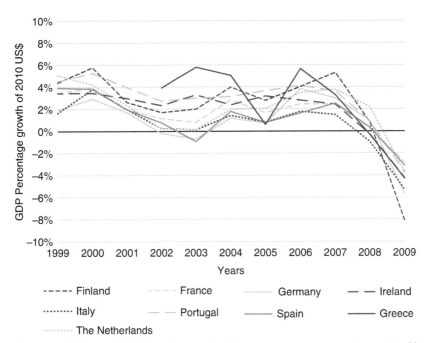

Figure 4.4 GDP growth of selected countries in the euro area, 1999–2009. Source: World Bank, World Development Indicators – GDP (constant 2010 US$).

currency, many of the disadvantages put forward by economists and political scientists warning against the introduction of the euro had simply failed to materialise.[33] In assessing the first 10 years of the euro, Henrik Enderlein and Amy Verdun concluded that 'almost all of the highly pessimistic views on the creation of EMU have proven to be wrong'.[34] They do, however, strike a note of caution, observing that the 'EMU's success is rather puzzling, since it is based on a peculiar mixture of outcomes that no one predicted, and which was not thought to lead

33 A comprehensive review can be found in A. Verdun, 'Ten Years EMU: An Assessment of Ten Critical Claims', *International Journal of Economics and Business Research* 2, no. 1–2 (2010): 144–63, 144.
34 H. Enderlein and A. Verdun, 'EMU's Teenage Challenge: What Have We Learned and Can We Predict from Political Science?', *Journal of European Public Policy* 16, no. 4 (2009): 490–507, 491.

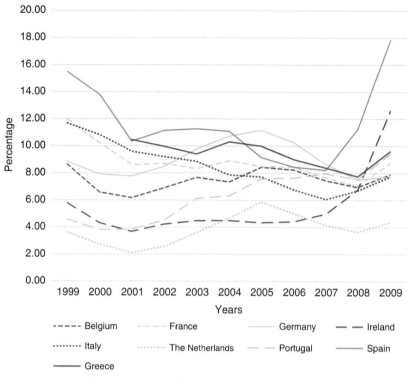

Figure 4.5 Unemployment in some selected countries in the euro area, 1999–2009 (as percentage of total labour force, national estimate). Source: World Bank.

to success.'[35] Writing in 2009, they duly highlight that the main challenge will be how the euro area will fare through the GFC.

A Transatlantic Financial Crisis?

Since 2007, the GFC and the crisis of the euro area have challenged the foundations of both globalisation and European integration. Both crises had well-known immediate triggers. The bankruptcy of Lehman Brothers on 15 September 2008 signalled the former. Greek prime minister George Papandreou's disclosure in October 2009 that Greece's budget deficit would be nearly twice the original estimate heralds the latter. Their

35 Ibid., 491.

interconnection is also traditionally well known. Borrowing costs rose as a consequence of the GFC, and Greece then became unable to service its debt, which in turn triggered a wider crisis of public debt in the EU. There would appear to be some sort of domino effect in this narrative, which is comforting but not wholly accurate.[36]

The 2008 crisis is often depicted as being of US origin. It originated from the 2007 subprime mortgage crisis and the practice of securitisation. A subprime mortgage is a loan offered to a borrower with a low credit rating and hence at a higher cost. Securitisation is the pooling of different types of debts, including subprime mortgages, then called mortgage-backed securities. Rating agencies kept rating these securities highly in spite of the poor quality of these financial assets, which in turn blinded investors about the risks incurred. A decline in home prices led to a devaluation of mortgage-backed securities, which spurred a classic domino effect on the entire economy: mortgage delinquency and foreclosure, bank losses, bank failures, a liquidity crunch and increasing unemployment. The crisis erupted in the United States, and only after some time had elapsed was the crisis 'imported' to the European side of the Atlantic. Once it had reached Europe, the crisis took the form of the European debt crisis, which in turn gave birth to the so-called eurozone crisis.

Or did it? Adam Tooze calls for a geographical change of focus and argues that the 2008–9 crisis, instead of being purely American-led in origin, was transatlantic in the making.[37] Tooze documents how European banks were part and parcel of the US financial landscape. While European policy-makers were quick to criticise American mistakes in the run-up to the crisis, in reality European banks actively participated in the construction of that system and were implicated in the securitisation system.

The Crisis and Reform of the Euro Area under International Pressure

Whether the trigger was extra-European or not, the crisis of the euro area had distinctively European features and exposed a number of issues that European policy-makers had failed to solve ever since the very first debates

---

36 There is insufficient space here to recount in detail the chronology of these crises. For more details, see A. Tooze, *Crashed: How a Decade of Financial Crises Changed the World* (London, Allen Lane, 2018), 42–71. The Federal Reserve Bank of St Louis provides a useful timeline of events: Federal Reserve Bank of St. Louis, 'Federal Reserve Bank of St. Louis' Financial Crisis Timeline', 1 April 2021, https://fraser.stlouisfed.org/timeline/financial-crisis#11. Charles H. Ferguson's documentary *Inside Job*, which won an Oscar in 2011, also remarkably documents the crisis, including the pre-2001 period of regulation/deregulation and the formation of the bubble between 2001 and 2007.

37 Tooze, *Crashed*, pp. 72–90.

about the making of an EMU.[38] Even before the crisis broke out in the euro area, it was well known that the Eurozone did not have a common framework to deal with the case of a member state being unable to service its sovereign debt; that the redistributive dimension of its common budget was not large enough and would not allow a member state hit by an external economic shock to recover financially; that there was no common supervisory and regulatory framework in the euro area to deal with the actions, difficulties and/or outright failure of a bank; and, finally, that the political setting in which decisions about the single currency were taken was unsatisfactory.

While it is surely difficult to disentangle euro area reforms that have an endogenous origin from those that have an exogenous origin, the GFC had a clear impact on European integration. The creation of the banking union was spurred by the need to break the vicious circle between debt and sovereigns that the GFC laid bare. The so-called Troika, composed of the European Commission, the ECB and the IMF was a stereotypical example of the intertwining of globalisation and European integration. The Troika was the group of institutions that negotiated the bailouts of several euro area countries (Cyprus, Greece, Ireland, Portugal and Spain) from 2010 onwards. In exchange for bailouts, the Troika required the implementation of several economic reforms, or adjustment programmes, composed of austerity measures aimed at cutting these countries' government expenditures. The IMF's involvement was not a given. Originally, European institutions wished to keep the resolution of these crises to EU institutions as this was an EU matter. But they progressively came to realise that the intervention of the IMF as an outsider which had much experience in dealing with such crises, and was considered to be neutral, would be useful.

Further to the IMF's involvement, the euro crisis posed another challenge to European integration in that it led to the creation of institutions to deal with the crisis that were outside the regular EU treaty framework, in a separate treaty: the European Financial Stability Facility, the European Financial Stability Mechanism and later the European Stability Mechanism (ESM).[39] In contrast, the European Banking Union was created within the

---

38 A timeline of the crisis is available at Bruegel, 'Euro Crisis Timeline', *Bruegel Blog* (blog), 16 September 2015, www.bruegel.org/blog-post/euro-crisis; M. Sandbu, *Europe's Orphan: The Future of the Euro and the Politics of Debt* (Princeton, NJ, Princeton University Press, 2015); E. Mourlon-Druol, 'Don't Blame the Euro: Historical Reflections on the Roots of the Eurozone Crisis', *West European Politics* 37, no. 6 (2014): 1282–96.

39 R. Christie (ed.), *Safeguarding the Euro in Times of Crisis: The Inside Story of the ESM* (Luxembourg, Publications Office of the European Union, 2019).

regular EU treaty framework.[40] The reform of the euro area remains a work in progress, the outcome of which could tend to reinforce or weaken the EU's 'strategic autonomy'.

The Rise of China

As Tooze reminds us, what was expected to be the real international economic issue of the 2010s was not US subprime mortgages and the travails of the euro area, but rather US–Chinese economic imbalances.[41] As the world's large deficit economy, the United States was vulnerable to a loss of confidence from investors, which could lead to a depreciation of the dollar and a hike in interest rates. But as an ever-larger surplus economy that accumulated currency reserves and invested them in US government debt, China was less vulnerable but could also be hit by the imbalances of the world economy. Niall Ferguson and Moritz Schularick called this symbiotic relationship between the United States and China 'Chimerica'.[42] A crisis resulting from these imbalances was not what really happened, but the concern about this issue revealed the further politicisation of international economic and financial relations that is also at play in EU–China relations.

China has long been on the radar of the EEC and its member states.[43] Just as Nixon visited Beijing in 1972 – which is widely seen as the start of the normalisation of US–China relations – EEC member states had already recognised and developed relations with the People's Republic of China (PRC). And only 2 years later, in 1974, the EEC, as such, signed its first trade agreement with the PRC, whereas the United States did so only in 1979.

After this early development of economic and political relations, the rise of China to world-leading status since the 1990s has posed at least three different types of challenges to the EU.[44] First, the different bilateral relationships that

---

40 P. G. Teixeira, *The Legal History of the European Banking Union* (London, Hart Publishing, 2020). For the most recent analyses, see F. Amtenbrink and C. Herrmann, (eds.), *The EU Law of Economic and Monetary Union* (Oxford, Oxford University Press, 2020).
41 Tooze, *Crashed*, pp. 25–41.
42 N. Ferguson and M. Schularick, '"Chimerica" and the Global Asset Market Boom', *International Finance* 10, no. 3 (2007): 215–39; O. A. Westad, *Restless Empire: China and the World since 1750* (London, Bodley Head, 2012), pp. 365–404.
43 A. Romano and V. Zanier, 'Circumventing the Cold War: The Parallel Diplomacy of Economic and Cultural Exchanges between Western Europe and Socialist China in the 1950s and 1960s: An Introduction', *Modern Asian Studies* 51, no. 1 (2017): 1–16; M.-J. Chenard, 'The European Community's Opening to the People's Republic of China, 1969–1979: Internal Decision-Making on External Relations' (PhD thesis, London School of Economics and Political Science, 2012).
44 J. Pisani-Ferry, G. B. Wolff, J. Shapiro, E. Ribakova and M. Leonard, 'Redefining Europe's Economic Sovereignty', Bruegel Policy Contribution (2019), www.bruegel.org/policy-brief/redefining-europes-economic-sovereignty.

China develops with individual EU member states risks compromising the EU's ability to reach a single cohesive position. This was apparent with the Belt and Road Initiative, whereby China seeks to improve transportation infrastructures leading from China to Europe in order to support trade. Some European countries are liable to benefit from this policy, and its associated investments, more than others. This was also the case of Chinese foreign direct investment in Europe.[45] Secondly, China's interests in economic, military and security affairs are blurred. This poses a challenge for the EU in that economic matters become closely intertwined with political issues. For instance, competition in the field of new technologies takes on a strategic dimension which it would not necessarily have with other countries in the world. The third challenge is common to other countries – such as the United States under the Trump administration between 2016 and 2020 – and concerns deviation from multilateral standards. This challenge comes from the fact that, with its growing financial and economic importance, China does not necessarily want to follow the rules that the United States and European nations established after the end of the Second World War. For all three of these reasons, the rise of China since the 1990s has added a layer of complexity to the EU's place and role in globalisation.

The Challenges of 'Strategic Autonomy' since 2016

Just as the crisis of the euro area seemed to depart from its most acute phase, other longstanding or new challenges at the heart of the global–European nexus came into the open. This concluding section briefly looks at five of these challenges: the possible global consequences of the EU's internal challenges of Brexit and the rise of illiberal democracies, the question of the internationalisation of the euro, climate change, the regulation of the digital and the recent Covid-19 crisis.

The EU's Internal Challenges and Globalisation

The UK's decision to leave the EU following the result of the referendum held on 23 June 2016 was made in reaction not just to European integration problems, but also to more broadly globalisation-related challenges. In that sense, Brexit illustrates the constant interplay between domestic politics, European integration and globalisation. The relationship between the UK

---

45 S. Meunier, 'Divide and Conquer? China and the Cacophony of Foreign Investment Rules in the EU', *Journal of European Public Policy* 21, no. 7 (2014): 996–1016.

and the EEC/EU is the subject of a large historiography that cannot be reviewed here. One issue of the UK–EEC/EU relationship has always been the claim that the UK viewed its role in the world differently. The UK political elite used the EU as a convenient scapegoat to blame for the economic distress of its population during elections – as indeed did many other political elites in the rest of the EU. The UK's departure from the EU has, however, overall not yet resulted in a weakening of the EU, but this will have to be judged over the longer term. In political terms, the EU member states displayed considerable unity during all stages of the Brexit negotiations, in spite of the repeated attempts by the UK to divide their united front.

The development and consolidation of what has been called 'illiberal democracies' has persisted throughout the 2010s. Kelemen has powerfully argued that, while many commentators and scholars criticise the EU's 'democratic deficit', they probably do not think about the one it really has.[46] It is true that democratisation of EU institutions, not least in the framework of the EMU, is needed. But, more worryingly, the EU as such, and the EU member states, have allowed dangerous backsliding away from democracy by several of the EU member states, especially Hungary since the election of Viktor Orbán in 2010 and Poland since the victory in the 2015 parliamentary elections of the ultra-conservative party PiS. These developments make it more difficult for the EU to claim to be promoting democracy and good governance abroad when domestically some of its members do not respect such rules.

The Internationalisation of the Euro

The possible greater internationalisation of the European single currency, which has been a longstanding issue in international economics, raises important questions for the euro area and the EU.[47] While the euro is already the second-most-traded currency internationally, the international monetary system remains largely dollar-based. Dollar dominance can be used by US administrations as a tool against the interests of any other country or group of

---

46 R. D. Kelemen, 'Europe's Other Democratic Deficit: National Authoritarianism in Europe's Democratic Union', *Government and Opposition* 52, no. 2 (2017): 211–38.

47 E. Mourlon-Druol, 'The International Use of the Euro: What Can We Learn from Past Examples of Currency Internationalisation?', *Bruegel Blog* (blog), 15 October 2018, www .bruegel.org/blog-post/international-use-euro-what-can-we-learn-past-examples-currency -internationalisation; F. Papadia and K. Efstathiou, 'The Euro as an International Currency', Bruegel Policy Contribution (2018), www.bruegel.org/policy-brief/euro-international-currency; B. Eichengreen, 'International Currencies in the Lens of History', in Battilossi et al. (eds.), *Handbook of the History of Money and Currency*, pp. 1–25.

countries in the world, including the EU. This possible challenge became most apparent under Donald Trump's presidency, when US sanctions threatened European companies doing business in Iran.[48] Only a few weeks later in September 2018, the president of the European Commission, Jean-Claude Juncker, called for a strengthening of the international role of the euro, without, however, making any explicit connection between this call and the US sanctions. Juncker declared in particular that 'The euro must become the face and the instrument of a new, more sovereign Europe.'[49] The main benefit of a greater international use of the euro would be to increase the euro area's financial autonomy.[50] The extraterritorial reach of US rule is effective because the dollar is widely used in international transactions, hence the idea of reducing use of the dollar by replacing it with a greater use of the euro. Such a rebalancing exercise would also be welcomed by other countries in the world, such as China, as it would mean reducing US dominance of international currency relations.

Climate Change

Fighting against climate change poses the most immediate and pressing challenge to globalisation. As it is a collective challenge, it also raises specific issues for European integration in a globalised world. Early attempts to create an internationally binding framework largely failed, first at Kyoto in 1997 and then in Copenhagen in 2009. With the worsening of the analysis of the scale of climate change, and a new popular *élan* to promote change after the early attempts to create an internationally binding framework (Kyoto 1997 and Copenhagen 2009), the agreement reached in Paris in 2015 was surrounded by much greater hopes. However, the election of Trump and the withdrawal of the United States from the agreement during his mandate severely limited the effectiveness of the deal.

Climate actions have foreign policy implications: dropping fossil-fuel consumption leads to major changes in relationships with suppliers, which in turn can destabilise their economies. As in other policy areas, climate change leads the EU to consider what unified policy it follows, and in what international framework relevant issues can be discussed and agreed upon.

48 M. Peel, 'US Warns European Companies Not to Defy Iran Sanctions', *Financial Times*, 7 September 2018, www.ft.com/content/f6edbfc8-b1ec-11e8-8d14-6f049d06439c.
49 J.-C. Juncker, 'State of the Union 2018. The Hour of European Sovereignty', 12 September 2018, https://ec.europa.eu/info/priorities/state-union-speeches/state-union-2018_en.
50 Papadia and Efstathiou, 'The Euro as an International Currency'.

In 2019, the European Commission presented the European Green Deal, which aims to make the EU climate neutral by 2050.[51] Many international economic and geopolitical challenges are implied by this Green Deal, further compounded by Russia's war against Ukraine.[52] The EU's decision to move to carbon neutrality by 2050 implies first a drop of its oil and natural gas imports and secondly a reflection on the logic of European decisions: many European products are manufactured in China, and European policy-makers will need to take this into account. Climate change, a global challenge par excellence, therefore calls for decisive actions by the EU.

Regulating the Digital

Another area where globalisation and European integration have interacted most recently is in the governance of the digital.[53] The digital includes a variety of issues, ranging from social network regulation to 5G and cloud computing. All these issues provide several challenges to polities: they are subject to rapid change, their use and mastery in the population is unequal, they may not recognise the state's borders and they can at the same time be used – by other states or by non-state organisations – to attack a state. Such attacks can be multifaceted and range from the spread of disinformation to outright attacks on digital infrastructure. In short, the digital is not only about economics, but concerns a broader set of issues that affect European integration and globalisation in their broadest senses.

Global and without borders by definition, the Internet challenges traditional models of regulation. For the EU, the Internet has created a new dimension to the single market: the digital single market. Just as non-tariff barriers had not been envisaged by the authors of the Treaty of Rome, so too the possible digital obstacles to the free movements of goods, people and services that the EU now has to work on removing had not been foreseen.

---

51 European Commission, 'A European Green Deal' (2021), https://ec.europa.eu/info/strategy/priorities-2019-2024/european-green-deal_en.
52 M. Leonard, J. Pisani-Ferry, J. Shapiro, S. Tagliapietra and G. Wolff, 'The Geopolitics of the European Green Deal', Bruegel Policy Contribution (2021), www.bruegel.org/sites/default/files/wp_attachments/PC-04-GrenDeal-2021-1.pdf.
53 C. Hobbs (ed.), *Europe's Digital Sovereignty: From Rulemaker to Superpower in the Age of US–China Rivalry*, European Council on Foreign Relations (2020), https://ecfr.eu/publication/europe_digital_sovereignty_rulemaker_superpower_age_us_china_rivalry; Bradford, *The Brussels Effect*, pp. 131–69. Given how fast moving this field is, it is best to refer to the ongoing reflections of think tanks' webpages dedicated to the topic, for instance Bruegel's Digital Economy and Innovation, www.bruegel.org/topic/digital-economy-and-innovation, or the Centre for European Policy Studies Digital Forum, www.ceps.eu/ceps-digital-forum, in addition to the EU website for up-to-date information on legislative initiatives.

The global landscape is now well known: the United States has a dominant position on all things digital, and China is seen as both an economic and a political competitor on the world's stage. For the EU, this global situation poses two challenges: one of innovation (how to develop homegrown future technologies, in particular in the field of artificial intelligence) and one of regulation (how to make the EU's voice heard in a discussion dominated by the two heavyweights). Digital innovation is associated with Silicon Valley, but digital regulation is increasingly associated with the EU. The General Data Protection Regulation implemented in the EU since 2018 increasingly sets an international standard in the field. In digital affairs, the EU has thus, again, an important role to play.

Covid-19

Finally, the Covid-19 pandemic offers a further illustration of the mutual interaction between European integration and globalisation. Just like climate change and digital issues, the Covid-19 pandemic is global par excellence. But here the Covid-19 pandemic spurred a radical internal change in the attitude of EU member states. For the first time, they agreed on the fact that the EU, as such, could borrow large sums of money on the international markets in its own name in order to redistribute them among its members so as to support the European economy. Borrowing by the EU was not something new per se. As mentioned earlier, the EEC borrowed on international capital markets in the 1970s to fund momentary balance of payments deficits due to the oil-price shock.[54] But this scheme – the Community Loan Mechanism – was meant only for balance-of-payments difficulties, not for large investments. Under NextGenerationEU, the European Council agreed in July 2020 that the EU would borrow €750 billion to set up the EU Recovery Fund. While the eventual impact of this investment remains to be seen, the move is unprecedented, and highlights once more the continued interaction between global events and European integration.

Conclusions

While the phrase 'strategic autonomy' has gained wide currency in the EU since the late 2010s, this chapter showed that the EEC/EU's quest for its independence from other powers in some key policy areas directly affected

54 S. Horn, J. Meyer and C. Trebesch, 'European Community Bonds since the Oil Crisis: Lessons for Today?', Kiel Policy Briefs (2020), www.ifw-kiel.de/publications/kiel-policy-brief/2020/european-community-bonds-since-the-oil-crisis-lessons-for-today-14037.

by globalisation – including trade, international banking regulation, international capital markets and climate change – has a long history. True, it is difficult to compare the magnitude of the stakes in the 2020s and what they were the 1970s. But the key question remains the same: how can European nation-states organise themselves to preserve more efficiently through a collective regional effort what they perceive as their common interests against potentially disruptive global events?

The EEC/EU's answers to this question have varied across time. Sometimes the EEC/EU was simply unable to provide a coordinated and coherent answer to well-identified challenges, such as the troubles of the international monetary system in the 1960s and the rise of the euromarkets. On other occasions, the EEC/EU managed to put forward a response – whether one judges this response adequate or not retrospectively is another matter – such as in the 1980s with the liberalisation of capital movements, the creation of the European single market and the introduction of the euro. And more often than not the EEC/EU responses were incomplete, such as indeed in these three cases, and in most of the cases outlined in the last section of this chapter. This is certainly frustrating. But this is also to a large extent unavoidable, since the EU remains, except in its domains of exclusive competence, bound to implement what EU members states agree to do. The economic response to the Covid-19 pandemic offers one such example. While the EU Recovery Fund is certainly a historical step due to the size of the fund, it can still be criticised for being too modest and too slow in its implementation, and in any case falls short of instituting any genuine fiscal union that the euro area would need. But this is due to the EU member states' opposition to such an outcome, rather than to an intrinsic inability of the EU to devise one.

The efficiency of the EEC/EU responses to those challenges is a more difficult question to tackle. While there is little doubt that a coordinated action of European nation states will have more weight on the international stage than individual actions, the definition of the collective EEC/EU position is subject to debate and scrutiny. Further democratising the EU remains therefore one of the key challenges to overcome in order to make the EU's responses – whether 'domestic' or global – more effective.[55]

---

55 A. Vauchez, *Democratizing Europe* (Basingstoke: Palgrave Macmillan, 2015).

Recommended Reading

Drach, A. and Y. Cassis (eds.). *Financial Deregulation: A Historical Perspective* (Oxford, Oxford University Press, 2021).

James, H. *Making the European Monetary Union: The Role of the Committee of Central Bank Governors and the Origins of the European Central Bank* (Cambridge, MA, Belknap Press, 2012).

Mourlon-Druol, E. and F. Romero. *International Summitry and Global Governance: The Rise of the G7 and the European Council, 1974–1991* (London, Routledge, 2014).

Schenk, C. R. *International Economic Relations since 1945* (Abingdon, Routledge, 2021).

Tooze, A. *Crashed: How a Decade of Financial Crises Changed the World* (London, Allen Lane, 2018).

Warlouzet, L. *Governing Europe in a Globalizing World: Neoliberalism and Its Alternatives Following the 1973 Oil Crisis* (Abingdon, Routledge, 2018).

5

A Europe of Reunification?

STEFANIA BERNINI AND JAN ZIELONKA

The beginning of European integration was portrayed as a process of reconciliation among former enemies, Germany and France most prominent among them. Extending cooperation in various functional fields was seen as a step towards eventual unification. Throughout the Cold War, this project was confined to the western part of the continent; the events of 1989, however, changed both the scope and the meaning of integration. After the fall of the Berlin Wall, a broad agreement arose that Europe should be made 'whole and free'.[1] The eastward enlargement of the European Union (EU) became the main instrument of the continent's reunification. There was always a clear discrepancy, however, between the political rhetoric of Europe's reunification and the nitty-gritty of integration. In daily politics, regulatory realignment, expressed in an ever-growing body of laws dealing with disparate issues, dwarfed initiatives in the fields of Europe's memory, culture and inheritance. While the requirements of institutional integration were clearly spelled out (and imposed on the new candidate states), the question of what a reunified Europe should amount to faded rapidly away.

This tension was not unique to the post-Cold War enlargement. In fact, at no stage of the integration 'project' was the European Community (EC)/EU able to spell out either where Europe ended or who exactly should be reunited. The tension between the functional and spatial dimensions of integration accompanied the European project from the beginning, giving rise to a paradox which is still to be fully confronted. On the one hand, the spatial dimension of integration has usually been seen as undermining

---

1 G. Bush, *Remarks to the Citizens in Mainz Rheingoldhalle*, speech delivered in Mainz, 31 May 1989, https://usa.usembassy.de/etexts/ga6-890531.htm.

convergence and complicating the European decision-making process. On the other, the EC/EU extended its territory several times and each of the successive enlargements has had a considerable impact on the nature of the integration project. The British accession in 1973 provided probably the greatest shock to the system; Brexit shows that the European institutions never recovered.

The post-1989 enlargement process brought into the Union a large number of states whose historical legacies, socio-economic characteristics and political concerns differed from those of western and southern Europe. While the rhetoric of reunification celebrated the newly found wholeness of Europe, the subsequent three decades showed how elusive that goal was. From the perspective of today, it is easy to see not only that the east–west divide has not been fully bridged, but also that new cleavages have opened up: between creditors and debtor countries; between those within and those outside the Eurozone; between migrant-receiving and non-receiving countries. These divisions have joined the east–west divide in threatening the continent's unity and in suggesting that the spatial and functional dimensions of European integration have not been effectively harmonised.

This chapter will tackle this dilemma by focusing on the following questions. Why has the EC/EU enlarged several times in its history? How were successive waves of enlargement conceived and organised? How has the geographical widening of the integration project affected its functional deepening? What form of Europe has emerged as a result of successive enlargements?

The chapter will argue that the technocratic mode of enlargement neglected the political and economic challenges generated by merging diverse economies and cultures. Moreover, the EU's institutional structure proved ill-suited to governing diversity and inequality within the enlarged European space. EU technocrats managed to dominate policy-making; parochial populists, however, have increasingly dominated politics, with detrimental effects for the process of European unification.

These problems and challenges created pressure on the EU to confine further enlargement to the history books. However, the full-scale Russian invasion of Ukraine in 2022 has reopened the enlargement debate, with voices demanding that Ukraine should be granted 'fast-track' entry to the EU. This in turn revived prospects of the EU enlarging further in the western Balkans and possibly also to Moldova.

Competing Narratives

As John H. Elliott put it: 'Europe is a mental construct, born of the conjunction of memory with aspiration ... the tension between the aspiration after unity and the intractable reality of diversity has been a permanent characteristic of the European past and present.'[2] Throughout history, the notion of European unity has been conceived either as an imperial project or as a remedy to the ongoing wars.[3] European unity acquired a new dimension with the birth of the post-Second World War integration project. Striving for unity, however, was not synonymous with aiming at Europe's reunification. In the integration discourse, unity was chiefly about issues such as sharing sovereignty, abolishing barriers to trade or forging a common stance on foreign policy issues. The term reconciliation, rather than reunification, was used to characterise the Franco-German joint ventures in the early 1950s.[4] When the fascist regimes of southern Europe finally collapsed, the accession of Spain, Portugal and Greece to the European Economic Community (EEC) was presented chiefly as a project aimed at consolidating nascent and fragile democracies. Little was said about the ambition of bringing under one roof all European nations.[5] After all, a large part of Europe was still under Soviet rule at the time of the Mediterranean accession, with little hope for a breakthrough.

The narrative was very different in the 1990s. The fall of the Berlin Wall on 9 November 1989 symbolised the end of the division of Germany, and of the whole European continent. The geopolitical order put in place by the Cold War unravelled rapidly and with momentous consequences for European integration. Germany's reunification and the emergence of Austria, Finland

---

2 J. Elliott, 'The Difficulties of Unity 1500–1750', in *The Pursuit of Europe* (2012), https://axsonjohnsonfoundation.org/seminars/2012-the-pursuit-of-europe.

3 P. Pasture, *Imagining European Unity since 1000 AD* (Basingstoke, Palgrave Macmillan, 2015).

4 See U. Krotz and J. Schild, *Shaping Europe: France, Germany, and Embedded Bilateralism from the Elysée Treaty to Twenty-First Century Politics* (Oxford, Oxford University Press, 2013). See also K. K. Patel, 'Germany and European Integration since 1945', in H. W. Smith (ed.), *The Oxford Handbook of Modern German History* (Oxford, Oxford University Press, 2011), pp. 775–94. For the Dutch and Belgian perspective, see S. Nasra and M. Segers, 'Between Charlemagne and Atlantis: Belgium and the Netherlands during the First Stages of European Integration (1950–1966)', *Journal of European Integration History* 18 (2012): 183–206.

5 L. Tsoukalis, *The European Community and Its Mediterranean Enlargement* (London, Allen & Unwin, 1981); G. Pridham, 'European Integration and Democratic Consolidation in Southern Europe', in A. Costa Pinto and N. S. Teixeira (eds.), *Southern Europe and the Making of the European Union, 1945–1980s* (New York, NY, Columbia University Press, 2002), pp. 183–208.

and Sweden from the geopolitical limbo in which they had existed since the end of the Second World War represented the first steps of what would soon become the most ambitious enlargement process ever pursued by the EC/EU.

Initially only Germany was reunited, to the amazement, if not irritation, of some European leaders unable to steer a largely spontaneous unification process. A unified Germany would certainly transform the existing balance of power in Europe, which made numerous European politicians feel uneasy. They feared that fostering the enlargement to the east, where Germany was a key player, would upset this balance further.[6] These geopolitical speculations were undermined by the eruption of violence in the Balkans. The catastrophic break-up of Yugoslavia showed the explosive potential of the ongoing changes, especially when dangerous situations were left unattended. Developments in Russia and in the former Soviet states were not reassuring either. It was in this context that the narrative of Europe's reunification picked up, not just in newly 'liberated' states, but also in the western part of the continent. Bringing central and eastern Europe back into the European fold was increasingly seen as the most effective means of securing peace and prosperity for the continent. East central Europe was not to become an unstable German periphery, but would be integrated as part of the European family. These noble policy objectives legitimised the painful adjustment process demanded by this unprecedented wave of enlargement. Never before had the EU admitted so many states, and states that were so different. Both for the EU and for candidate states the task was enormous and required a narrative powerful enough to justify the compromises and sacrifices ahead.

Throughout the first four decades following the Second World War, western Europe alone had been integrating, and the notion of unity was subject to conflicting interpretations. For some activists and intellectuals such as Altiero Spinelli, unity was about constructing a European federation able to overcome once and for all 'the division of Europe into national sovereign states'.[7] For others, such as Massimo Cacciari, integration was about multiple

6 P. Anderson, *The New Old World* (London and New York, Verso, 2009), pp. 38–9, and more specifically on 'the role of Germany in the new Europe', pp. 51–6; T. Judt, *Postwar: A History of Europe since 1945* (London, William Heinemann, 2005), pp. 638–42.

7 A. Spinelli and E. Rossi, *Per un'Europa libera e unita: Progetto d'un Manifesto* (Milan, Feltrinelli, 2017 [1941]); for a later appraisal of the relationship between European integration and nationalism, see A. Spinelli, 'Démocratie et nationalisme II', *Le Contrat Social: Revue historique et critique des faits et des idées* 4 (1960): 335–9. For a discussion of Spinelli's vision of European unity, see P. Murray, 'Spinelli and the European Union', in

connections below and above nation-states creating a mosaic of overlapping differences, which he elegantly called an 'archipelago of spaces'.[8] However, for the majority of European politicians, integration was, in the words of Alan Milward, intended to 'rescue' nation states, and not to merge (or unite) them into something novel.[9] In a 1995 article, Milward argued that there were four explanations for European integration, which could not be reduced to a single cause.[10] Integration was to alter the conflictual nature of power politics with its 'zero-sum-game' rationale; it was not about giving up national ambitions or dissolving them in a mosaic of overlapping differences. The 1950 Schuman Plan and the subsequent 1952 Treaty of Paris establishing the European Coal and Steel Community (ECSC) effectively reconciled former enemies, while helping France to control Germany, albeit through a European framework. One of the architects of the Maastricht Treaty, Pieter Dankert, argued in 1982 that 'Franco-German reconciliation was the driving force behind the ECSC plan and formed the basis of European unification. As a result of the ECSC Treaty, the control of the Ruhr and other vital German resources was now put into the hands of the High Authority established by the six signatory countries.'[11] According to Tony Judt, it was 'a European solution to a – the – French problem'.[12] The unification of Germany and France, plus Italy and the Benelux countries, was not on the agenda. Neither was the enlargement of the newly born Community. The 'Protestant north' of the continent was not involved in this project, and when the United Kingdom (UK), together with Ireland and Denmark, applied for membership of the EEC in 1961, its application was vetoed by France.[13] Teija Tiilikainen also pointed to religious traditions as a factor shaping attitudes towards European integration, in particular in order to explain the weak propensity

---

P. Murray and P. Rich (eds.), *Visions of European Unity* (London and New York, Routledge, 2019). See also P. Anderson, 'Ever Closer Union?' *London Review of Books* 43, no. 1 (2021), www.lrb.co.uk/the-paper/v43/no1/perry-anderson/ever-closer-union.

8 M. Cacciari, *L'Arcipelago* (Milan, Adelphi, 1997). See also M. Castells, 'The Unification of Europe', in M. Castells (ed.), *End of Millenium*, vol. III: *The Information Age* (Oxford, Blackwell, 1998), pp. 342–70.

9 A. S. Milward, *The European Rescue of the Nation State* (Berkeley, CA, and Los Angeles, CA, University of California Press, 1992).

10 A. S. Milward, 'Allegiance. The Past and the Future', *Journal of European Integration History* 1 (1995): 11–12.

11 P. Dankert, 'The European Community – Past, Present, and Future', *Journal of Common Market Studies* 21, no. 1 (1982): 1–18, 5.

12 Judt, *Postwar*, p. 156.

13 For a discussion of Catholic and Protestant perspectives, see L. van Middelaar, *The Passage to Europe* (New Haven, CT, Yale University Press, 2013), pp. 245–6.

of the Lutheran Finnish state to participate in European integration.[14] This alone speaks volumes about the (lack of) political will to unite the entirety of 'free' Europe, let alone the entire continent, in the early years of integration.

The 1957 Treaty Establishing the EC contained the objective of an 'ever closer union', but only six European states signed this treaty, which in any case was chiefly about trade and agriculture rather than politics and culture. (The objective of an 'ever closer union' was retained in the 1992 Maastricht Treaty and the 2009 Lisbon Treaty.) For a long time, any reference to European peoples and their will remained elusive. The 1983 'Solemn Declaration' proclaimed the birth of the EU 'among Member States, as well as the peoples of Europe'; however, only ten European governments featured on this declaration and the will of their respective peoples was assumed, rather than actively sought or politically tested. Most importantly, this remained a quintessentially western European project. With a large part of Europe still under the Soviet Union's grip, it is hard to identify a single European official able to foresee a continent destined to become 'whole and free' in the coming years.

The fall of the Berlin Wall and the subsequent dissolution of the Soviet Union therefore came as a huge surprise to Europe's decision-makers, both those in the West and those in the East. In contrast, millions of eastern European citizens resisting Soviet rule in the 1980s had been much more farsighted. 'Return to Europe' had been their key political slogan, one that, as Václav Havel put it, explicitly evoked the idea of the continent's reunification through the overcoming of the arbitrary divisions of the Cold War. Havel developed the argument further in the introduction to one of the most comprehensive analyses of the eastern enlargement: 'This enlargement has [also] been perceived as something other than a "joining of the club" by a few (or even many) more members. It has immense political and even psychological significance as a "return to Europe" by the central and eastern European states, a reunification of Europe following the end of the divisions of the Cold War, and with the significant (problematic) potential for redrawing the boundaries of – and within – Europe.'[15] East central Europe was 'culturally Western', argued a much-cited essay by the Czech writer Milan

14 T. Tiilikainen, *Europe and Finland: Defining the Political Identity of Finland in Western Europe* (Aldershot, Ashgate, 1998).
15 Václav Havel quoted in M. Cremona, 'Introduction', in M. Cremona (ed.), *The Enlargement of the European Union* (Oxford, Oxford University Press, 2003), p. 2.

Kundera, albeit 'politically in the east and geographically in the centre'.[16] He was echoed by a plethora of dissidents in central and eastern Europe demanding their countries 'return to a place they always belonged to, a "native Europe"', to use Adam Michnik's words.[17] When these dissidents became parliamentarians and ministers, the 'return to Europe' dictum was put on the continent's diplomatic menu.[18] For central and eastern Europeans, however, reunification did not imply unity. No evidence suggests that the new candidate states intended to give up their recently regained sovereignty and swap the Soviet Union for another union. For eastern and central Europeans, returning to Europe meant returning to a zone of peace and prosperity, and rejoining a core European culture after years of Soviet-inspired or -imposed 'real socialism'. The problem was that the EU was more about thousands of laws and regulations than about culture, while the promise of prosperity required painful economic reforms, sacrifices and patience.[19] While the EU could help to create an environment conducive to peace, security proper had to be provided by the North Atlantic Treaty Organization (NATO) under US leadership. The notion of returning to Europe had been an important political tool in the struggles against communist regimes, but was, nevertheless, a notion steeped in idealisation of a mythical past. The dream of returning to Europe assumed the existence of a peaceful common home that never existed in reality, and downplayed the dark years of wars, pogroms and authoritarian rule that marked the history of the continent, nowhere with greater ferocity than in its east-central lands.[20]

While the fall of communism encouraged the beginning of a process of rethinking the past, the narrative of reunification remained highly popular throughout the late 1980s and early 1990s, also among many western European intellectuals. For some of them, Europe's reunification was a way to arrest the rise of xenophobic nationalism in central and eastern Europe. For others, it was a means of deterring Soviet and later Russian interference in the domestic politics of European states. And for yet more it was a means to make the German reunification complete and legitimate. At least initially, EU officials embraced this rhetoric half-heartedly, as they

---

16 M. Kundera, 'Un occident kidnappé ou la tragédie de l'Europe centrale', *Le Débat* 27 (1983): 3–23. See also A. Michnik, *Letters from Prison* (Berkeley, CA, California University Press, 1998), p. 150.

17 Michnik, *Letters from Prison*, p. 150.   18 Judt, *Postwar*, pp. 717–23.

19 B. Greskovits, *The Political Economy of Protest and Patience* (Budapest, Central European Press, 1998).

20 On the legacy of war in east-central Europe, see T. Snyder, *Bloodlands: Europe between Hitler and Stalin* (New York, NY, Basic Books, 2010).

seemed to have other priorities, with the completion of the single market and the creation of the European currency first among them. To put it differently, unifying rather than reunifying was the priority; to use the language of EU studies, deepening rather than widening should drive European integration, at least until the signing of the Maastricht Treaty.[21] We will return to the interplay of widening and deepening after scrutinising the successive waves of enlargement.

The Pre-2004 Enlargements

The EC/EU enlarged several times prior to 2004. First, the UK, Denmark and Ireland joined the original six member states of the EEC in 1973. Greece joined in 1981, while Portugal and Spain did so in 1986. In 1995, the European Free Trade Association (EFTA) members Austria, Finland and Sweden were admitted to the Union. This means that in the first four decades of its existence, the EC/EU more than doubled its membership from the original six to fifteen states.

Individual states' access to the EC/EU has often been interlinked. The accession and exit of the UK has determined Ireland's and to some extent Denmark's relationship with the EU because of these countries' close economic links to the UK. Ireland and Denmark applied for EC membership in 1961, followed by Norway in 1962, but both withdrew when de Gaulle vetoed the first British application. When the UK reapplied in 1967, all three states renewed their applications too. Denmark and Ireland joined the EC together with the UK in 1971, while Norway decided to remain outside for the time being. Portugal's accession to the EC/EU was linked to the Spanish accession. The fourth enlargement also created a link between Austria, Finland and Sweden, with Norway again failing to convince the public of the merits of joining the EC/EU.[22] In 1990, the German reunification moved the EU borders further east. Although representing a special case and as such difficult to compare with the enlargements before and after 1989, the impact of

---

21 On the origins of the widening versus deepening debate, see H. Wallace, 'Widening and Deepening: The European Community and the New European Agenda', RIIA Discussion Paper no. 23 (London, Royal Institute of International Relations, Chatham House, 1989).

22 For a recent examination of the complex relationship between Britain and the Nordic countries, see M. Broad, 'Keeping Your Friends Close: British Foreign Policy and the Nordic Economic Community, 1968–1972', *Journal of Contemporary European History* 25 (2016): 459–80.

German reunification on the process of European integration cannot be doubted.

It has been claimed that enlargement has 'always been part of the EC/EU's "historic mission"', but the evidence for this claim is mixed.[23] Indeed, the Treaty of Rome anticipated the enlargement of the EC and set up a seemingly straightforward criterion for admission: 'Any European state may apply to become a member.' The amended wording of the Treaty (Article 49 of the Treaty on the European Union (TEU)) added that candidates must respect and promote European values: 'Any European State which respects the values referred to in Article 2 and is committed to promoting them may apply to become a member of the Union.'[24] As the subsequent years showed, however, each enlargement was contested. Some were vetoed by member states or rejected in referendums by the citizens of applicant states; some dragged on for many decades without reaching completion, as in the case of Turkey. Having signed the (Ankara) Association Agreement with the EEC in 1963, the country officially applied for EEC membership in 1987 and a decade later was declared eligible to join the EU. The accession negotiations started in 2005; they remain uncompleted.

It is unclear whether the conflict-ridden history of the first enlargements was caused by the absence of a plausible, widely shared unification project or by the practical challenges experienced in each successive accession. Some of the frustrations and controversies emerged from the enlargement method adopted during the first enlargement and then replicated with all successive cases. The EC/EU always demanded that the candidate states adopt the entire body of European laws, with little if any space left for bargaining. In fact, the term 'accession negotiations' used in the diplomatic language was a misnomer, because in genuine negotiations each party has to compromise to some extent. This was not the case with EC/EU enlargements. For instance, the UK government believed that its extensive global trade links with the Commonwealth merited special considerations, Ireland wanted to protect its regional industrial incentives, Finland sought special treatment for its unique forests and Austria did so for its Alpine passes. In all these cases, applicants had to give in in some respects, although outcomes differed

23 C. Preston, *The Enlargement and Integration of the European Union* (London, Routledge, 1997), p. 3.
24 See 'Consolidated Version of the Treaty on European Union, Title VI – Final Provisions, Article 49 (ex Article 49 TEU)', https://eur-lex.europa.eu/legal-content/ EN/TXT/?uri=CELEX%3A12016M049. The original (Dutch) version of the treaty is available at https://eur-lex.europa.eu/legal-content/NL/TXT/PDF/?uri=CELE X:11957E/TXT&from=EN.

depending on the bargaining power of the candidates. Whereas EFTA countries were able to secure a number of their demands, this was not the case for Portugal, Greece and Spain.[25]

The EC/EU was prepared to agree on transition periods lasting a few years and to help applicant states to meet the criteria for entry. However, adjusting the *acquis communautaire* to successive enlargements was not up for negotiation. According to the EC/EU, it was up to the candidate states to demonstrate how they would adapt to the Community law and to justify the slightest temporary deviation from the *acquis communautaire*.[26] The fact that the EC/EU negotiated with all candidates separately produced a huge discrepancy of power between the two parties and allowed the EC/EU to play one candidate against another. For instance, the completion of negotiations with Austria, Finland and Sweden in March 1994 put pressure on the Norwegian government to reluctantly accept the deal on fisheries proposed by the EC/EU. The deal was later rejected by Norwegian citizens in a referendum.

The enlargement method adopted was not just a manifestation of the use or misuse of the EC/EU's power. The *acquis communautaire* reflected a series of difficult compromises emerging from complex negotiations; the EC/EU could not afford to reopen all these negotiations each time it was about to enlarge, hence the insistence that the candidate states simply joined the already existing arrangement. This method probably streamlined and sped up the enlargement 'negotiations', but it has also fuelled resentment in the candidate states. Some of them, like Norway, did not end up as EC/EU members, while others, such as Spain and the UK, tried to renegotiate their membership terms after entering the organisation. In both situations, the vision of a unified Europe has been undermined if not shattered.

The objectives behind the decision to enter and enlarge have varied through time on both sides of the negotiating table. Diplomatic historians have emphasised strategic motivations for the successive enlargements. The

25 M. Jorna, 'The Accession Negotiations with Austria, Sweden, Finland and Norway', *European Law Review* 10, no. 2 (1995): 131–58; F. Granell, 'The European Union's Enlargement Negotiations with Austria, Finland, Norway and Sweden', *Journal of Common Market Studies* 33, no. 1 (1995): 117–41; A. Tovias, *EEC Enlargement: The Southern Neighbors* (Brighton, European Research Centre, 1979).

26 On the realities and impact of the asymmetrical negotiations between applicant states and the EC, see Ludlow's examination of the first British application, N. P. Ludlow, *Dealing with Britain: The Six and the First UK Application to the EEC* (Cambridge, Cambridge University Press, 1997). For a recent discussion of how that early experience could apply to the Brexit situation, see N. P. Ludlow, 'When Britain First Applied to Join the EU: What Can Macmillan's Predicament Teach Us?' (2016), https://blogs.lse.ac.uk/brexit/2016/04/15/when-britain-first-applied-to-join-the-eu-what-can-macmillans-predicament-teach-us.

British accession has often been portrayed as an attempt by the UK to maintain its geopolitical significance while faced with the decline of the Commonwealth.[27] (Records show that conversations between Macmillan and de Gaulle were chiefly about geopolitics and foreign policy.)[28] In the words of Piers Ludlow, the UK's 'return to Europe' was seen by many as 'a recognition of weakness, a gesture of resignation, rather than a welcome escape from enforced marginalisation'.[29] Such a downcast perception of the UK's accession, argued Ludlow, helped to explain the 'awkward partner' narrative that dominated the UK's EC/EU membership.

Geopolitical considerations figured prominently also in other cases. The Greek accession was described as a geopolitical move aimed at preventing a communist take-over in this strategically important country.[30] According to Varsori, not only the Greek Communist Party, but also the 'radical, neutralist' Socialist Party, PASOK, opposing the 'pro-Western' Karamanlis government appeared as a geopolitical threat to President Chirac and other conservative EC/EU politicians. Loukas Tsoukalis points out that the EEC was denounced by the Greek radical left as 'a plot of revanchist Germany and imperialists'.[31] Leading up to the fifth enlargement, the neutrality of Austria, Finland and Sweden had represented a forced consequence of the Cold War. The demise of the Soviet Union eliminated the strategic reasons for remaining outside a militarily benign 'Western club' such as the EC/EU. Still, their accession to the EU received mixed evaluations. Several member states feared that the neutral status of Finland, Austria and Sweden would weaken the effort to strengthen the EC's common foreign and security policy.[32] For others, the accession of EFTA countries that remained outside NATO (in the case of Finland and Sweden) seemed to bring new links with Russia and eastern Europe, augmenting the EU's geopolitical grip.[33]

---

27 See J. W. Young, *Britain and European Unity, 1945–1992* (London, Macmillan, 1993), pp. 53–81; S. Ward, 'Anglo-Commonwealth Relations and EEC Membership: The Problem of the Old Dominions', in G. Wilkes (ed.), *Britain's Failure to Enter the European Community, 1961–63: The Enlargement Negotiations and Crises in European, Atlantic, and Commonwealth Relations* (London, Frank Cass, 1997), pp. 93–107.

28 A. Horne, *Macmillan*, vol. II: *1957–86* (London, Macmillan, 1989).

29 N. P. Ludlow, 'The Historical Roots of the "Awkward Partner" Narrative', *Contemporary European History* 28 (2019): 35–6.

30 A. Varsori, 'Crisis and Stabilization in Southern Europe during the 1970s: Western Strategy, European Instruments', *Journal of European Integration History* 15 (2009): 5–14.

31 Tsoukalis, *The European Community*, p. 29.

32 H. Wallace, 'Pan-European Integration: A Real or Imagined Community?', *Government and Opposition* 32, no. 2 (1997): 215–33.

33 F. Granell, 'The European Union's Enlargement Negotiations with Austria, Finland, Norway and Sweden', *Journal of Common Market Studies* 33, no. 1 (1995): 117–41, 137. See

Consolidation of democracy after the fall of fascist regimes was one of the key objectives in the Mediterranean (second and third) enlargements. As Sebastián Royo and Paul Christopher Manuel put it: 'Political considerations were the main motivation behind Portugal's and Spain's application to join the European Community . . . Portugal and Spain both wanted to strengthen their new democratic regimes, and they both held the desire to end the relative isolation they had experienced during the authoritarian years.'[34] Loukas Tsoukalis argued the same in the case of Greece: 'Entry into Europe was clearly a high political decision. It meant a choice of a political and economic regime and a framework within which the foreign policy of each country would be exercised.'[35] This observation concerned Spain and Portugal as well as Greece. The nine EC states were also keen to strengthen democracy in Greece, Portugal and Spain, which probably explains why they became reconciled to the challenges presented by the candidate states' agricultural production.

The issue of democracy entered the debate on enlargement even before the fall of fascist regimes in southern Europe. In 1962, Spain, under General Franco, attempted to sign an association agreement with the EC; its application was put on hold, despite the economic benefits that Spain's accession would have entailed for the EC.[36] Only a few years earlier, the French Foreign Affairs Minister Georges Bidault had forcefully argued, during a debate over the 'Spanish question' held in the French National Assembly, that 'il n'y a pas d'oranges fascistes; il n'y a que des oranges' ('there are no fascist oranges; there are just oranges').[37] However, the EC found itself under pressure from the European Parliamentary Assembly and several vocal non-govermental organisations, which argued against the establishment of formal links with the Franco regime on purely democratic grounds. In 1961, a report

also P.-H. Laurent, 'Widening Europe: The Dilemma of Community Success', *The Annals of the American Academy of Political and Social Sciences* 531, no. 1 (1994): 124–40, 133.

34 S. Royo and P. C. Manuel, 'Some Lessons from the Fifteenth Anniversary of the Accession of Portugal and Spain to the European Union', *South European Society and Politics* 8, no. 1–2 (2003): 1–30, 16. See also S. Royo and P. C. Manuel (eds.), *Spain and Portugal in the European Union: The First Fifteen Years* (London, Frank Cass, 2003).

35 Tsoukalis, *The European Community*, p. 128.

36 C. Powell, 'The Long Road to Europe: Spain and the European Community, 1957–1986' (2015), https://media.realinstitutoelcano.org/wp-content/uploads/2021/11/dt9-2015-powell-long-road-europe-spain-european-community-1957-1986.pdf. See also C. Powell, 'Spain's External Relations, 1898–1975', in R. Gillespie, F. Rodrigo and J. Story (eds.), *Democratic Spain: Reshaping External Relations in a Changing World* (London and New York, NY, Routledge, 1995), pp. 16–20.

37 P. A. Martínez Lillo, 'Las relaciones hispano-francesas entre 1948 y 1952', in J. R. de Urquijo and J.-P. Etienvre (eds.), *España, Francia y la Comunidad Europea* (Madrid, CSIC, 1989), pp. 145–7.

drawn up for the European Parliamentary Assembly by the German social democrat Willi Birkelbach, himself a political prisoner under the Nazis, argued that 'the guaranteed existence of a democratic form of state, in the sense of a free political order' should be 'a condition for membership'. According to the report,

> The guaranteed existence of a democratic form of state, in the sense of a liberal political organisation, is a condition for membership. States whose governments do not have democratic legitimacy and whose people do not participate in government decisions, either directly or via freely elected representatives, cannot seek to be admitted to the circle of nations that make up the EC.[38]

Powell has described the impact of the Birkelbach Report. He also refers to the 1962 Congress of the European Movement in Munich, which came to the conclusion that 'integration of any country with Europe, whether in the form of full membership or of association, requires democratic institutions' and produced a catalogue of prerequisites for Spanish membership largely borrowed from the European Convention on Human Rights.[39] Royo and Manuel emphasise the role of newspapers, such as the *Nieuwe Rotterdamsche Courant*, in pressing the EC to refuse Spain's access to the EC on democratic grounds.[40]

By the late 1970s and early 1980s, this had become an accepted norm, superseding earlier dilemmas. As Nuno Severiano Teixeira observed, 'Democratic consolidation and European integration [had become] inseparable.'[41]

Economic historians and political economists underline agriculture, finance and trade as the principal objectives of joining and enlarging the

---

38 W. Birkelbach, *Rapport fait au nom de la commission politique sur les aspects politiques et institutionnels de l'adhésion ou de l'association à la Communauté*, Services des publications des Communautés européennes, 15.01.1962, Assemblée parlementaire européenne, Documents de séance 1961–1962, Document 122, II, 3, 25 (our translation).
39 Powell, 'Spain's External Relations', pp. 7–8. See also D. C. Thomas, 'Constitutionalization through Enlargement: The Contested Origins of the EU's Democratic Identity', *Journal of European Public Policy* 13 (2006): 1197–1201.
40 Royo and Manuel, 'Some Lessons', p. 9.
41 N. S. Teixeira, 'Portugal and European Integration, 1974–2010', in N. S. Teixeira and A. Costa Pinto (eds.), *The Europeanization of Portuguese Democracy* (New York, NY, Columbia University Press, 2012), p. 8. For a recent appraisal of the relationship between enlargement and democratisation, see E. De Angelis and E. Karamouzi, 'Enlargement and the Historical Origins of the European Community's Democratic Identity, 1961–1978', *Contemporary European History*, 25 (2016): 439–58.

EC/EU.[42] Enlargements were said to increase mutual trade, encourage investments, stimulate industrialisation, lower unemployment and spread economic know-how. These arguments were obviously more pronounced among pro-marketeers than among those concerned with inequalities and structural asymmetries between strong and weak economies on the continent, as well as between wealthier and poorer EU citizens. Records of the accession negotiations also highlight economic objectives and preoccupations. They show that discussions focused on specific issues, such as sugar, fish, fruit, vegetables, wine or textiles, as well as on financial issues, including those related to the EU budget. Agriculture (and fisheries), rather than 'high politics', even dominated the negotiations with the UK; in this case, what was at stake was primarily the British importation of agricultural products from the Commonwealth.[43] Spain may well have had political reasons to join the EC/EU, but economic considerations were equally important. For a country heavily relying on revenues from agricultural trade such as Spain, in fact, the possibility of joining the EC's Common Agricultural Policy was a tantalising prospect; this explains why even General Franco attempted to join the EC. Greece counted not only on stimulating the inflow of foreign investments by joining the EC, but also on being able to act as a commercial bridge between the EC, the Middle East and the Balkans. Portugal was also hoping to act as such a bridge between the EC and its former colonies in Africa and Asia. For Portugal, and even more so for Ireland, joining the EC was a way to retain free access to the British market on which they were heavily dependent, and from which they could well be cut off after the British entrance to the EC.

While geopolitical and economic interests appear clearly in the analysis of the first four enlargements, cultural motivations are much more difficult to identify. This is perhaps because the European credentials of the candidate states were hardly ever questioned, even when fascist regimes had kept their countries in relative isolation from the core of Europe for many years.[44] As Sebastián Royo put it: 'There was no dispute that the Iberian countries belonged to Europe. This was not just a geographical fact. Spain and

---

42 See A. Moravcsik, *The Choice for Europe: Social Purpose and State Power from Messina to Maastricht* (London, UCL Press, 1999); Milward, 'Allegiance'.

43 S. Wall, *The Official History of Britain and the European Community*, vol. II: *From Rejection to Referendum, 1963–1975* (London, Routledge, 2013) See also *Fisheries Negotiations. Summary*, prepared by UKRep, 28 June 1971, The National Archives. Foreign and Commonwealth Office 30/976.

44 For analysis of cultural aspects of European integration, see, for example, C. Shore, *Building Europe: The Cultural Politics of European Integration* (London, Routledge, 2000); G. Delanty and C. Rumford, *Rethinking Europe: Social Theory and the Implications of Europeanization* (London, Routledge, 2005), especially pp. 50–68.

Portugal shared their history, traditions, culture, religion, and their intellectual values with the rest of Europe, and both countries had contributed to the Christian occidental conceptions of mankind and society dominant in Europe. Their entry to the European Community was a reaffirmation of that fact.'[45] Loukas Tsoukalis was more modest in linking enlargement to European culture; he wrote that at times he would have liked to have believed that 'the Mediterranean enlargement confirm[ed] a shift in the centre of gravity towards the old cultures and civilisations of Europe rather than a process of incorporating three peripheral countries into the European core'.[46] Despite the satisfaction expressed by several observers regarding the return of southern European countries to democracy and their successful admission to the EC, the southward enlargement was not saluted as European 'reunification'.

This is only partly surprising. (Re)unification could well represent one of Europe's unstated (or undercurrent) objectives, but numerous examples of failed applications to the EC/EU show the relative value of this objective, at least in the first four decades of integration. The two French vetoes of the British applications should be considered first, since they constitute a powerful reminder of the limits posed to the ambition of including Europe's major actors in the integration process. Both geopolitical and commercial–economic interests have been invoked to explain de Gaulle's European policy, and several different reasons have been given for his vetoes of British entrance to the EC. From a geopolitical perspective, the UK's close relationship with the United States, effectively preventing a Franco-British rapprochement on nuclear issues, was seen by some as the main reason for the veto. From an economic perspective, France's interests in agriculture seemed the defining issue.[47] For some, it was de Gaulle's scepticism regarding

---

45 S. Royo, 'The 2004 Enlargement: Iberian Lessons for Post-Communist Europe', *South European Society and Politics* 8, no. 1 (2003): 287–313, 287. See also N. G. Monteiro and A. Costa Pinto, 'Cultural Myths and Portuguese National Identity', in A. Costa Pinto (ed.), *Modern Portugal* (Palo Alto, CA, The Society for the Promotion of Science and Scholarship, 1998), pp. 206–17.

46 Tsoukalis, *The European Community*, p. 9.

47 On the geopolitical front, see I. Clark, *Nuclear Diplomacy and the Special Relationship: Britain's Deterrent and America, 1957–1962* (Oxford, Oxford University Press, 1994), p. 418. See also G.-H. Soutou, 'The Linkage between European Integration and Détente: The Contrasting Approaches of de Gaulle and Pompidou, 1965 to 1974', in N. P. Ludlow (ed.), *European Integration and the Cold War: Ostpolitik–Westpolitik, 1965–1973* (London, Routledge, 2007), pp. 11–35; F. Bozo, *Two Strategies for Europe* (London, Rowman & Littlefield, 2001). On de Gaulle's commercial–economic concerns, see A. Moravcsik, 'De Gaulle between Grain and *Grandeur*: The Political Economy of French EC Policy, 1958–1970 (Part 1)', *Journal of Cold War Studies* 2, no. 2 (2000): 3–43; A. Moravcsik, 'De

the UK's ability and willingness to fully adopt the European body of laws that guided his action. For others, leadership in Europe was at stake.[48] As Gilbert Trausch put it: 'Leadership and integration are terms difficult to reconcile. If, in 1950, Jean Monnet believed that only a small integrated Europe could guarantee France a leading role, Charles de Gaulle and Harold Macmillan, on the contrary, counted on a Europe of States in order to ensure their country first place.'[49] More recent historiography has provided a needed revision of the image of 'de Gaulle's vicious opposition to the European communities'.[50] Mathieu Segers' analysis of the behind-the-scenes cooperation between de Gaulle and Monnet between 1958 and 1963 showed that significant grounds for agreements and pragmatic convergence on Europe had existed between the two men. The UK's application for full EEC membership, however, produced an irreversible opposition and in fact a dramatic hardening of de Gaulle's position on European integration.[51]

The UK eventually joined the EC/EU after General de Gaulle's death. In several other cases, however, the outcome was less successful. Norway applied and concluded accession negotiations twice (in 1972 and 1994), but failed to join, chiefly because its citizens were unhappy with the fisheries arrangements. In fact, Norway has applied for membership a total of four times. The first two applications were abandoned following de Gaulle's veto against the UK's application. The later two (in 1972 and 1994) were turned down by Norwegian citizens in popular referendums.[52]

Switzerland applied to the EU in 1992 and then suspended its application following the rejection of the European Economic Area in a referendum. In 2016, just a week before the Brexit referendum in the UK, the Swiss parliament formally withdrew its longstanding application. The freedom of labour movement was seen as the most contentious issue between the EU and

Gaulle between Grain and *Grandeur*: The Political Economy of French EC Policy, 1958–1970 (Part 2)', *Journal of Cold War Studies* 2, no. 3 (2000): 4–68.

48 Preston, *The Enlargement and Integration*, pp. 18, 28–29.

49 G. Trausch, 'Introductory Notes', *Journal of European Integration History* 1 (1995): 4.

50 M. Segers, 'Preparing Europe for the Unforeseen, 1958–63. De Gaulle, Monnet, and European Integration beyond the Cold War: From Co-operation to Discord in the Matter of the Future of the EEC', *The International History Review* 34, no. 2 (2012): 347–70, 348.

51 Segers, 'Preparing for the Unforeseen', pp. 360–3; M. Segers, 'De Gaulle's Race to the Bottom: The Netherlands, France and the Interwoven Problems of British EEC Membership and European Political Union, 1958–1963', *Contemporary European History* 19, no. 2 (2010): 111–32.

52 See J. E. Fossum, 'Norway and the European Union', in W. R. Thompson (ed.), *Oxford Research Encyclopaedia of Politics* (Oxford, Oxford University Press, 2019), https://doi.org/10.1093/acrefore/9780190228637.013.1043.

Switzerland at the time. In 2014, the Swiss voters approved through a referendum a proposal to limit the freedom of movement of foreign citizens to Switzerland, in contrast with the existing arrangement with the EU. In 2016, Switzerland and the EU concluded a new agreement whereby a new Swiss law (in response to the referendum) would require Swiss employers to take on any job seekers (whether Swiss nationals or non-Swiss citizens registered with Swiss job agencies) whilst continuing to observe the free movement of EU citizens into Switzerland, thus allowing them to work there.[53]

Iceland applied for EU membership in 2009 when faced with a severe financial crisis, but decided to drop its membership bid in 2015, considering that 'Iceland's interests [were] better served outside the European Union', to cite the country's then foreign minister Gunnar Bragi Sveinsson.[54] We have already mentioned the protracted and so far unsuccessful Turkish application. States that have eventually entered the EU after protracted 'negotiations' have seldom been entirely satisfied with their membership. After being admitted, the UK insisted on and received financial rebates and opt-outs from certain fields of integration. Despite all these successfully negotiated benefits and exceptions, the UK left the EU in 2020. Spain was unhappy with the accession terms for fisheries and agriculture. Unable to negotiate its accession to the EC/EU on equal terms, Spain tried hard to improve the terms for its agriculture after acquiring full voting rights. Moreover, together with Portugal and Greece, Spain insisted that both the ratification of the Maastricht Treaty and the negotiations on a new EC budget (with an envisaged increase in structural funds) should be completed before the EFTA enlargement of 1995 could go ahead.[55] In other words, Spain, Greece and Portugal sought to use their newly acquired leverage to influence a new enlargement round and consolidate their position within the EC.

In short, while the first enlargement may have been the most problematic one, each successive enlargement has created not only winners, but also

---

53 'Decision No. 2/2016 of the EU–Switzerland Joint Committee of 3 December 2015 Amending Protocol 3 to the Agreement between the European Economic Community and the Swiss Confederation Concerning the Definition of the Concept of "Originating Products" and Methods of Administrative Cooperation [2016/121]', https://eur-lex.europa.eu/legal-content/EN/TXT/?toc=OJ%3AL%3A2016%3A023%3ATOC&uri=uriserv%3AOJ.L_.2016.023.01.0079.01.ENG.

54 Quoted in AFP, 'Iceland Drops EU Membership Bid: "Interests Better Served Outside" Union', *The Guardian*, 12 March 2015, www.theguardian.com/world/2015/mar/12/iceland-drops-european-union-membership-bid.

55 L. Friis, '. . . And Then They Were 15: The EU's EFTA-Enlargement Negotiations', *Cooperation and Conflict* 33, no. 1 (1998): 81–107, 94.

economic losers. The latter have often contested the nature of the accession and the subsequent membership terms. As the conclusion of a comprehensive analysis of the first four enlargements summarised: 'The existing member states use the enlargement process to pursue their own interests and collectively to externalise internal problems.' The author cites the Common Fisheries Policy as the clearest example of the EC developing a new policy in anticipation of enlargement.[56] This proved very difficult for the UK and Spain, and impossible for Norway. This does not mean that applicant states regretted the decision to join the EC/EU. With the exception of the UK, public opinion polls showed that the majority of citizens in 'new' EC/EU member states seemed to believe that benefits of being an EC/EU member outweigh the burdens.[57] Most economic data confirm the benefits of the EC/EU too. For instance, in the first 15 years after accession, Portugal's average per capita income grew from 56 per cent of the EU average to about 74 per cent.[58] However, it would be wrong to assume that enlargement was always seen as a fair process leading to prosperity. Data regarding the balance of gains and losses related to Portugal's membership in the Eurozone are much less upbeat, and this also concerns other states considered in this section, such as Ireland, Spain and Greece.

Although the first four enlargements revealed limited ambition to reunite the continent, the overall outcome was just that. Between 1952 and 2004, ever more European states came to share one institutional roof, with common laws and procedures to mediate diverging interests and ambitions. Power politics played a role in each successive enlargement, but enlargement was not guided by the selfish interests of any one state and it was carried out through diplomatic means only. The enlargement method could not do away with inequalities among individual states or between the EC/EU and applicant countries. However, these first four enlargements showed that applicants were free to withdraw their application and find prosperity outside the

56 Preston, *The Enlargement and Integration*, p. 230.
57 For recent data on public opinion on EU membership, see www.europarl.europa.eu/ne ws/en/headlines/eu-affairs/20180522STO04020/eurobarometer-survey-highest-support-for-the-eu-in-35-years. Data assembled by the Pew Research Center in 2014 showed a drop in confidence in the EU as a result of the Euro crisis, 'Crisis of Confidence in the EU Ending?', in *A Fragile Rebound for EU Image on Eve of European Parliament Elections* (2014), www.pewresearchorg/global/2014/05/12/chapter-2-crisis-of-confidence-in-the-eu-ending. For specific data on public trust in the single currency and the European Central Bank (ECB), see F. Roth and L. Jonung, 'Public Support for the Euro and Trust in the ECB: The First Two Decades', *Vox-EU/CEPR* (2019), https://voxeu.org/article/public-support-euro-and-trust-ecb.
58 Royo and Manuel, 'Some Lessons from the Fifteenth Anniversary', p. 5.

EC/EU framework. This was not necessarily the case in the post-2004 enlargements.

The Big-Bang Enlargement

The first official document proclaiming the EU's ambition to reunite Europe was adopted on the Greek island of Rhodes in 1988. In it, the EU declared its commitment 'to overcome the division of our continent and to promote Western values and principles'.[59] This declaration may look prophetic in hindsight, but there is no evidence suggesting that the leaders assembled in Rhodes envisaged the accession of states from central and eastern Europe to the EU in their lifetime. In fact, the first EU statement after the fall of the Berlin Wall was already more cautious. The EU summit held in Strasbourg in December 1989 merely talked about 'openness and cooperation, particularly with other European states'. The priority was to 'become stronger and accelerate [its] progress towards European Union'.[60] Records of private conversations between EU leaders show more concern than delight at the prospect of Europe's (and Germany's) unification.[61] Timothy Garton Ash quotes the British Foreign Minister Douglas Hurd saying in December 1989 that the divided Europe agreed upon in Yalta was a system 'under which we've lived quite happily for forty years'.[62] In particular, they were determined to make sure that the ongoing geopolitical earthquake would not frustrate their efforts to create a single European currency and to deepen integration among the countries already inside the 'club'. This view was initially shared by the European Commission. As one of the insiders, Günter Verheugen, a leading German politician who was later put in charge of enlargement within the European Commission, put it: 'In the EU Commission of Jacques Delors there was a view in the early 1990s that in another 25 years it might perhaps be possible to start talking seriously about expansion eastwards.'[63]

---

59 The European Council in Rhodes, 2–3 December 1988, 'Conclusions of the Presidency', www.consilium.europa.eu/media/20597/1988_december_-_rhodes__eng_.pdf.

60 The European Council in Strasbourg, 8–9 December 1989, 'Conclusions of the Presidency', www.consilium.europa.eu/media/20580/1989_december_-_strasbourg__eng_.pdf.

61 See J. Attali, *Verbatim*, vol. III: *Chronique des années 1988–1991* (Paris, Fayard, 1995), p. 796; M. Thatcher, *The Downing Street Years* (London, Harper Press, 1993), pp. 768–815.

62 T. Garton Ash, *In Europe's Name: Germany and the Divided Continent* (London, Vintage, 1994), p. 2.

63 G. Verheugen, *Europa in der Krise: Für eine Neubegründung der europäischen Idee* (Cologne, Kiepenheuer und Witsch Verlag, 2005), pp. 72–3.

These cautious, if not reluctant, opinions regarding the eastward enlargement proved short-sighted in view of the successive developments. As one
communist regime fell after another across most of eastern Europe, and the
Soviet Union dissolved itself, the call for European reunification through the
EU's enlargement became hard to resist. In June 1993, after the second Danish
referendum cleared the way for the adoption of the Maastricht Treaty, the
European Council held in Copenhagen concluded that 'the associated countries in Central and Eastern Europe that so desire shall become members of
the European Union'.[64] The Council also spelled out a package of political,
economic and administrative criteria for accession. Some of them, such as
democracy or the capacity to absorb the *acquis*, had already been applied to
previous applicants; other conditions were specifically tailored to the situation in central and eastern Europe, among them the protection of minorities
and the existence of a functioning market economy. The Council responded
to concerns that an over-ambitious widening would paralyse the EU's institutional framework by stating that 'The Union's capacity to absorb new
members, while maintaining the momentum of European integration'
remained 'an important consideration in the general interest of both the
Union and the candidate countries'.[65]

The next decade was marked by the speedy (if sometimes forced) adoption
of some 20,000 European laws and regulations by the candidate states, and by
protracted negotiations between the EU and individual applicants. Matters
discussed ranged from major institutional issues to seemingly trivial details,
such as milk quotas and the export of strawberry jam. The negotiations
were concluded in May 2004 in Copenhagen, paving the way to EU membership for eight states from central and eastern Europe (the Czech Republic,
Estonia, Hungary, Latvia, Lithuania, Poland, Slovakia and Slovenia), plus
Malta and Cyprus. Bulgaria and Romania joined the EU 3 years later and
Croatia joined in 2013.

The chronology and procedures resembled those adopted in previous
accessions. In the case of Hungary and Poland, the accession negotiations
lasted for 4 years and 10 months, while the overall process (from application
to accession) took 10 years and 1 month. This is comparable to the southern
enlargement; the negotiations for Portugal and Spain took more than 6 years
and the overall process took nearly 9 years. The accession of Austria, Finland

---

64 The European Council in Copenhagen, 21–22 June 1993, 'Conclusions of the Presidency',
    www.consilium.europa.eu/media/21225/72921.pdf.
65 Ibid.

and Sweden was much quicker.[66] Although the eastward enlargement was marked by many dramatic moments, one should recall that none of the previous enlargements had been smooth and painless. Which is not to say that the enlargement to the east was like any other in the history of the EC/EU. To start with, the EU had never simultaneously negotiated with so many applicants before. Furthermore, the applicant states were poorer than any previous applicant, their democracy and even statehood were more fragile, and their economic, legal and administrative structures were less developed. The power of the EU vis-à-vis the candidate states was also more on display than in the case of previous enlargements. The EU's conditionality package had never been so extensive or intrusive, partly due to the discrepancies just mentioned, and partly because the EU's body of laws had been constantly growing during the preceding years. At the same time, geopolitical considerations behind enlargement had never been so salient and the political rhetoric accompanying the enlargement had never been so charged and ambitious.

The declared objectives of the eastward enlargement in the western and eastern parts of the continent were similar: the accession of the new candidate states would foster Europe's security, prosperity and democracy. As Tony Blair put it in November 2002: 'Enlargement will extend Europe's area of peace, democracy and prosperity. We will also be safer and more secure through better co-operation on border controls, asylum and immigration, joint efforts to tackle crossborder crime, and shared environmental standards.'[67] The President of the European Commission, Romano Prodi, argued in a similar vein: 'Enlargement is the fulfillment of the European project. This project has given us half a century of peace and prosperity, and it should be extended to the whole continent ... Enlargement is also a terrific opportunity to redefine our role in the world.'[68] The public seemed to share these objectives. According to a December 2002 poll conducted by the EU among its fifteen member states, 84 per cent expressed confidence that the enlargement would open up new markets for local products, 78 per cent believed that the EU would become culturally richer and 69 per cent

---

66 See G. Avery, 'The Enlargement Negotiations', in F. Cameron (ed.), *The Future of Europe: Enlargement and Negotiations* (London, Routledge, 2004), pp. 35–63.

67 T. Blair, *A Clear Course for Europe*, speech given in Cardiff, on 28 November 2002. On the views of candidate countries' official delegates to the EU, see A. Krok-Paszkowska and J. Zielonka, 'The EU's Next Big Enlargement: Empirical Data on the Candidates' Perceptions', EUI Working Papers, RSC No. 2000/54 (Florence, European University Institute, 2000).

68 R. Prodi, *Enlargement – the Final Lap*, Speech/02/463, European Parliament, Brussels, 9 October 2002, https://ec.europa.eu/commission/presscorner/detail/en/SPEECH_02_463.

estimated that the move would reduce the risk of war and conflicts.[69] The referendums over accession to the EU held in the applicant states also showed overwhelming public support.[70]

More critical observers argued that the eastward enlargement was chiefly guided by the neoliberal quest for cheap labour and new markets and that the move answered America's strategic rationale more than Europe's interests.[71] The call for a reunified Europe had already been made by President Bush in 1989 in Mainz: 'Let Europe be whole and free.'[72] A decade later, the Czech Republic, Hungary and Poland joined NATO. Yet others argued that the eastern enlargement did not take place because of 'the constellation of power and interests' among member states, but because of what Frank Schimmelfennig called a 'rhetorical entrapment'.[73] Member states fell victim to their vague rhetoric promising to overcome the continent's historical division by bringing under one institutional roof all European countries sharing their liberal values. Those who resisted enlargement were 'shamed' and compelled to follow policies that were consistent with their rhetoric about norms and values rather than with the rational calculation of their interests.

A Europe Whole and Free?

Although official public pronouncements should always be taken with some caution, historical records show that most EU leaders were fully aware of the political, security and economic benefits that would result from the enlargement. In other words, these interests could sound vague, but they were nonetheless seen as important and real not only by political leaders, but also by the public at large. A Union of democratic European states trying to create lasting peace among themselves and able to resist any form of authoritarianism was not just a 'founding myth of European integration', as Schimmelfennig argued. It was the very rationale for European integration. The fact that member states spent most of their time arguing about

---

69 European Commission, *Flash Eurobarometer 132/2: Enlargement of the European Union* (Brussels, European Commission, Directorate General, Enlargement, 2002), pp. 48, 62.
70 See, for example, M. Marczewska-Rytko, 'Accession Referenda in the Fifth EU Enlargement', *Annales Universitatis Mariae Curie-Skłodowska* 12 (2015): 73–88.
71 See P. Anderson, *The New Old World* (London, Verso, 2009), p. 55.
72 Bush, *Remarks to the Citizens*.
73 F. Schimmelfennig, 'The Community Trap: Liberal Norms, Rhetorical Action, and the Eastern Enlargement of the European Union', *International Organization* 55, no. 1 (2001): 47–80, 72.

agricultural subsidies and competition laws did not mean that they were paying only lip service to peace, liberal economics and democracy. The preservation of these very norms and values was always said to represent the key pillar of national and European interests.

In this respect, it is important to acknowledge that the fall of the Berlin Wall created not just a power vacuum, but also a sense of common destiny, however illusory. The words pronounced by Václav Havel in the European Parliament in 1994 were echoed by numerous politicians and commentators across the continent with remarkable confidence: 'The idea of two Europes living cheek by jowl, the idea of a democratic, stable, prosperous Europe on the road to integration and a less democratic, less stable and less prosperous Europe is, in my view, completely illusory. It sounds like the idea of sustainable coexistence in a room which is half flooded and half dry. Despite its differences, Europe is indivisible, and anything serious which happens to it will have repercussions on, and consequences for, the rest of the continent.'[74]

The fall of the Berlin Wall set the conditions for a reorientation of the narrative of integration. Although the notion of European reunification has been described by some observers in terms of bias, 'ideology', or 'rhetorical entrapment', it is difficult to underestimate the impact that the fall of communism had on the continent. The end of the Cold War transformed the narrative of European history, brought two parts of Europe together and created a new interdependence, which needed to be structured and institutionalised. The EU's laws and its mode of operation provided a convenient blueprint for the new arrangement. The EU had a system of setting its borders, a system of bargaining among diverse interests and a system for arriving at common decisions. The EU system was anything but perfect, but rejecting it would have meant a jump into the unknown with possibly grave implications. On the eve of the twenty-first century, Europe's leaders and their public were clearly not prepared to take such a risk, and so they settled for the available blueprint in tune with a noble, self-flattering rhetoric of making Europe whole and free.

Although the narrative of reunification provided a powerful tool in the early stages of the eastward enlargement, perceptions changed once the process of accession was completed. Access to the EU decision-making table gave new member states greater freedom to assert their partisan

74 Václav Havel's speech to the European Parliament, 16 March 1994, *Europe Documents*, 1874, 16 March 1994, Agence International d'Information pour la Presse, English ed., p. 3, www.europarl.europa.eu/doceo/document/CRE-5-2000-02-16-ITM-012_EN .html?redirect.

interests. Some governments in the region tolerated corruption, others ignored EU environmental regulations, yet others constrained media freedom. Venelin Ganev went as far as to identify a 'post-enlargement hooliganism' of some governments in the region.[75] The post-accession assertiveness of new members was not novel; its manifestation, however, differed from case to case.

The reunification narrative and the image of a Europe whole and free seemed to finally dissolve with the growing success of illiberal forces across the continent. Although populism, with its anti-European rhetoric, was not invented in central and eastern Europe, most governments in the region in the course of time ended up in the hands of politicians defying basic EU principles such as the rule of law, democracy and respect for minorities.[76] This could not but create conflicts between the liberal and illiberal politicians within the EU, as manifested most vividly during the 2015 refugee crisis and then during the 2020 rule of law crisis. These political squabbles, however, did not shake the public's trust in European integration in the new member states. While the politicians who have held power in Poland since 2015 have clashed with EU institutions time and again, public opinion polls have consistently showed remarkable support for membership of the EU. According to a poll conducted by the Polish Research Centre on Public Opinion in 2019, 91 per cent of respondents supported Poland's membership in the EU.[77] A similar pattern could be seen in other states in the region.[78]

Conclusions

The first conclusion stemming from this chapter relates to the interplay between the widening and deepening of European integration. For many years, students of Europe emphasised the institutional rather than spatial aspects of integration. The history of integration was not about the European

---

75 V. I. Ganev, 'Post-accession Hooliganism: Democratic Governance in Bulgaria and Romania after 2007', *East European Politics and Societies* 27 (2012): 26–44.
76 For a detailed review of the situation in 2020, see J. Rupnik and J. Zielonka, 'From Revolution to Counter-revolution: Democracy in Central and Eastern Europe 30 Years On', *Europe–Asia Studies* 72 (2020): 1073–99.
77 See Centrum Badania Opinii Społecznej, '15 lat członkostwa Polski w Unii Europejskiej', *Komunikat z Badań CBOS* 59 (2019): 1–2.
78 On the situation in 2020, see L. Silver, M. Fagan and N. Kent, 'Majorities in the European Union Have Favorable Views of the Bloc', Pew Research Center (2020), www.pewresearch.org/global/2020/11/17/majorities-in-the-european-union-have-favorable-views-of-the-bloc.

conquest of territory, but about the conquest of yet another field of public activity. It all started with the ECSC, followed by the Common Market, common currency, common external borders, common foreign and defence policy, justice and home affairs, and now it deliberates common health and energy policies. At the same time as the deepening process was taking place, the Union also enlarged several times. While the steady widening of the EC/ EU was duly noticed, its significance was not fully appreciated. After all, the proclaimed aim remained an 'ever closer' rather than an 'ever wider' Union. Scholars fiercely debated whether the EU's final aim was to build a European federation, but they hardly posed the question 'Where does Europe end?' Accessions by new countries were seen as a kind of cloning: candidate states were being asked to transform themselves into Euro-clones by adopting the entire body of European laws. Successive enlargements, however, proved this reasoning misguided. Each enlargement changed the EC/EU and the nature of integration to a remarkable degree. Despite all pre-accession conditionality, each enlargement implied an importation of diversity that required new institutional arrangements. Moreover, each enlargement shifted the EC/EU's borders, creating new neighbours and prompting Europe to revise its strategic thinking and adopt new external policies. Legal culture, societal attitudes, economic concerns and religious geography also changed with each enlargement. Southern and later central and eastern European countries brought within the EC/EU long histories of autocracy and complicated legal and institutional inheritances whose consequences would become fully evident in time. Each new member state brought also a different relationship between religious and political institutions, mismatched and sometimes antithetical historical memories and hugely diverging economic traditions. With the passing of the years, it became increasingly evident that widening rather than deepening determined the nature of European integration.

After decades of expansion, Brexit marked the first territorial shrinking of the EU. Will this help the EU to concentrate again on deepening? When we look at fields such as defence or financial services, the answer seems to be negative. Brexit is likely to hamper the EU's integrated capacities in these fields rather than strengthen them. Without London, the EU's financial global reach will be diminished, and without the British military capacity the prospect of a meaningful European army looks dim. The latter observation applies notwithstanding efforts to beef up military budgets in several member states, Germany most notably, following the Russian invasion of Ukraine.

The second conclusion concerns the nature of power politics observed with all successive enlargements. If unity is not Europe's natural condition, then the EC/EU's constant quest for expansion tends to resemble an imperial project. Although EU officials have fondly referred to Charlemagne's legacy in their speeches, the EU was not proclaimed an imperial project. That said, it is hard to deny that the ever-larger EU 'looked, walked and talked' like an empire of sorts.[79] This is because enlargements involved the application of power, however soft, vis-à-vis formally sovereign states in the periphery of Europe's metropolitan core. In essence, all the candidate states were asked to adopt the ever-larger body of European laws with hardly any space left for bargaining. Although empire building in this case progressed only by consent, few candidate states could afford to stay out of the common market (and those which chose to stay out of the integration project, such as Norway and Switzerland, ended up applying the EU's laws without the ability to shape them).[80] With each enlargement, the EU also looked ever more like an empire in structural terms; enlargements created fuzzy borders and multiplied cultural identities as well as political loyalties, and the gap between the centre and the periphery grew ever larger with each enlargement. Although the EU never had an emperor, the Franco-German alliance was able to steer the EU in the desired direction. This does not need to be interpreted in a sinister manner; without power and leadership it is hard to do any good. Unity spontaneously arising from the bottom has existed in Europe only as an intellectual project. An example of this was the long-distance intellectual European community that emerged in the Middle Ages and thrived in the age of Enlightenment, becoming known as the Republic of Letters.[81] The normative unity of the continent was advocated by philosophers such as Erasmus and Kant, but they never envisioned an institutional structure reminiscent of the EU. While the EU's noble vision of itself may well be deceiving, it is hard to deny that integration has brought about numerous benefits not just for the EU's core, but also for its periphery. States and their citizens usually feel better off within rather than outside the EU, which

---

79 For broader explorations of the Europe as empire argument, see J. Zielonka, *Europe as Empire: The Nature of the Enlarged European Union* (Oxford, Oxford University Press, 2006); G. Marks, 'Europe and Its Empires: From Rome to the European Union', *Journal of Common Market Studies* 50 (2012): 1028–41; R. Del Sarto, 'Normative Empire Europe: The European Union, Its Borderlands, and the "Arab Spring"', *Journal of Common Market Studies* 54 (2016): 215–32.

80 E. O. Eriksen and J. E. Fossum (eds.), *The European Union's Non-members: Independence under Hegemony?* (London, Routledge, 2015).

81 D. Goodman, *The Republic of Letters: A Cultural History of the French Enlightenment* (Ithaca, NY, Cornell University Press, 1994), pp. 12–52.

explains the successive waves of enlargement. It is too early to assume that Brexit contradicts this trend. It is also premature to assume that further enlargements will not take place.

The third conclusion relates to the interplay of geography and values. Although states acceding to the EU had to subscribe to a set of European values such as democracy, the rule of law and respect for minorities, the accession process was a technocratic exercise focusing on practical aspects of cross-border movement of goods, capital, labour and services. States were left free to shape their own judicial systems, constitutional orders and ethical issues such as abortion or lesbian, gay, bisexual, transgender, queer plus rights. In time, this could not but cause the type of conflicts witnessed during the December 2020 European summit in Brussels, when the illiberal governments of Hungary and Poland threatened to veto the post-pandemic recovery plan if it were linked to the rule of law conditionality. As Luuk van Middelaar put it: 'The rule-of-law fight has made obvious a painful tension at the heart of the EU project: between the EU's founding document, with its insistence on common values, and its geographic ambition; between its attachment to liberal democracy and its desire to encompass the entire Continent.'[82]

While for many central and eastern European citizens the EU and its founding document remain an essential point of reference and an instrument of political struggle, 'the tension between the constitution and the political project' remains. Not by chance, this has been felt most strongly in Germany. First of all, because of the crucial role that 'respect for fundamental rights' holds for contemporary German identity. Secondly, because what is at stake today is precisely the effort to overcome the Cold War divisions promised by the eastward enlargement. No European country more than Germany embodied both divided Europe and its aspiration to become whole again. As van Middelaar put it, 'overcoming Europe's geographical East–West divide [. . .] is state religion too. Whereas Paris or The Hague could perfectly conceive of an EU without Poland and Hungary, for Berlin this is unthinkable.'[83] This conflict showed that the European unity to which the EU aspires cannot digest all types of diversity, and hence some painful decisions ought to be made. The EU tried and failed to spell out common values in the aborted European Constitution. Efforts to define a common

---

82 L. van Middelaar, 'Europe's Existential Crisis', *Politico*, 10 December 2020, www.politico.eu /article/europe-existential-crisis-rule-of-law-hungary-poland.
83 Ibid.

European culture were equally disappointing.[84] This has left the notion of European unity and reunification ambiguous and incomplete. To paraphrase a pioneer of Italian unification, Massimo d'Azeglio, we have made Europe without creating Europeans. The institutional and cultural borders of Europe do not overlap, creating misinterpretations, pigeonholes and conflicts.

Recommended Reading

Landesmann, M. A. and I. P. Székely (eds.). *Does EU Membership Facilitate Convergence? The Experience of the EU's Eastern Enlargement* (Basingstoke, Palgrave Macmillan, 2021).

Mayhew, A. *Recreating Europe: The European Union's Policy towards Central and Eastern Europe* (Cambridge, Cambridge University Press, 1998).

Tsoukalis, L. *The European Community and Its Mediterranean Enlargement* (London, Allen & Unwin, 1981).

Young, H. *This Blessed Plot: Britain and Europe from Churchill to Blair* (London, Macmillan, 1998).

Zielonka, J. *Europe as Empire: The Nature of the Enlarged European Union* (Oxford, Oxford University Press, 2006).

---

84 Delanty and Rumford, *Rethinking Europe*, pp. 50–68. See also van Middelaar, *The Passage to Europe*, pp. 230–51.

6

Moderately Failing Forward: The EU in the Years 2004–2019

FERENC LACZÓ

Introduction

In the history of European integration, the years after 2004 have been characterised by three main processes: the dialectic of deepening and broadening, the unfolding and impact of major crises, and new types and levels of European politicisation. This chapter aims to develop a perspective on how these three contemporary historical processes relate to the longer-term process of European integration. I claim that the enlarged European Union (EU) of the early twenty-first century may have been moderately failing forward when managing its numerous crises, but it has been able neither to substantially counter the fallout from repeated crises, nor to meaningfully reverse internal processes of socio-economic and increasingly also political divergence.[1] In global comparison, the failings of the EU have clearly been relative rather than catastrophic. At the same time, the steps the EU has taken in these years – to counter crises, integrate and democratise – would need to be assessed as rather moderate precisely because internal challenges have been mounting amidst a worsening external environment.

Regarding the parallel processes of deepening and widening, the present chapter focuses primarily on the intertwined yet paradoxical phenomena of relegation, transformation and reproduction of Europe's east–west divide since 2004. The aim is to discuss tendencies towards both 'positive'

---

1 The argument about the EU 'failing forward' was articulated in connection with the Eurozone in E. Jones, R. D. Kelemen and S. Mounier, 'Failing Forward? The Euro Crisis and the Incomplete Nature of European Integration', *Comparative Political Studies* 49 (2016): 1010–34. The argument that such projects of integration might advance through cycles of crises was originally suggested by Philippe Schmitter in ground-breaking articles such as P. Schmitter, 'The Neo-functional Hypothesis about International Integration', *International Organization* 23 (1969): 161–6; P. Schmitter, 'A Revised Theory of Regional Integration', *International Organization* 24 (1970): 836–68.

and 'negative' convergence and expose new lines of division between core and more peripheral areas within the Union. The terms 'positive' and 'negative' may, of course, imply a value judgement. Here they are used, among other purposes, to assess phenomena in relation to the (presumed) future chances of European integration. The main argument I would like to suggest in this part is that the 'big-bang enlargement' into eastern Europe has created a strangely (mis)balanced Union, which in turn has generated negative as much as positive tendencies of convergence.

Secondly, the chapter explores the early twenty-first century as a 'post-post-historical' phase. It focuses on the way in which the rather slow, legalistic-consensual political order of the EU ('the politics of rules') has been, as explained by Luuk van Middelaar, increasingly overtaken by a new 'politics of events' – the urgent need to improvise responses which has clearly boosted the intergovernmental component of decision-making.[2] The major crises I would like to briefly examine are the failed attempt at European constitution-making and its consequences in 2005–7; the financial and ensuing economic and Eurozone crises that had their worst phase between 2008 and the mid 2010s; the so-called migrant and refugee crisis with its peak year in 2015; the shambles around Brexit in the years since the June 2016 referendum in the United Kingdom (UK); and the worsening challenge posed by the anti-liberal turn in member states and the resulting rule of law crisis for the Union. While the resilience of the EU in this veritable vortex of crises is worth emphasising and shows just how inadequate narratives of decline and imminent collapse have been, it is important to probe further how the EU has performed as an instrument of crisis management. As I shall aim to explicate below, the overall assessment needs to be more multilayered but also somewhat more critical than what was articulated in van Middelaar's path-breaking insider account *Alarums and Excursions*.[3] More specifically, I shall argue that the responses to and impact of the five main crises of the years 2004–19 have contradicted the EU's cherished self-image and preferred strategy of self-legitimation (which may be ideal-typically defined as a union of liberal democratic states based on the rule of law, in which these states are developing new forms of multilayered governance to reach beneficial compromises and workable solutions that are pooling elements of their sovereignty in a directional

---

2 L. van Middelaar, *Alarums and Excursions: Improvising Politics on the European Stage* (Newcastle upon Tyne, Agenda Publishing, 2019).
3 Ibid.

process, a union that is at the same time open to the world, respecting universal human rights and practising solidarity).

Such a 'politics of events', that is, repeated crises requiring speedy and robust responses within a wider and already deeply integrated EU, also raises another analytical – and eminently political – question with new urgency: on what bases of legitimacy is power being exercised within the Union and where does sovereign authority ultimately lie? These moot questions are directly connected to the third major concern of this chapter. As decisions taken at the EU level have started to matter much more directly and immediately in the everyday lives of citizens of member states,[4] not only has politics within the EU been somewhat more Europeanised (understood as the growing resemblance of politics on the EU level to politics within liberal democratic member states with their elections, parliaments, governments, public spheres, etc.), but also the European project as such has become increasingly politicised. Groups on the opposite end of the political spectrum, popularly if imprecisely called pro-Europeans and Eurosceptics, have come to perceive a new breakthrough in integration and a halting or even scaling back of integration, respectively, as preferable to the status quo. Both these forces have contributed to Europe's politicisation in the early twenty-first century, but such heightened polarisation around 'the EU question' has been observable at a time when a rather immobile political centre – which appears to have been preoccupied with crisis management also at the expense of showing greater foresight – has continued to dominate. This chapter thus argues that, rather than following up on what the realistic, if imperfect, compromises at the time of the EU's foundation in the early 1990s made look desirable, the EU has instead been moderately failing forward in the decade and a half after 2004.

The Promise of European Integration, the Threat of Europe's 'Easternisation'

When the Cold War came to a sudden end in Europe with the unexpected collapse of the Eastern bloc in 1989–91, political elites on the two halves of the continent declared in unison their intention to overcome the legacy of their post-war division.[5] Upon the foundation of the EU in the early 1990s (which

---

4 On the shift to EU member statehood, see C. Bickerton, *European Integration: From Nation-States to Member States* (Oxford, Oxford University Press, 2012).

5 For a more elaborate argument regarding this point, see the introduction to F. Laczó and L. Lisjak Gabrijelčič (eds.), *The Legacy of Division: East and West after 1989* (Budapest and Vienna, Central European University Press–Eurozine, 2020).

admittedly already included a part of the former Eastern bloc in the shape of what used to be called the German Democratic Republic),[6] and some hesitancy in western and southern European countries notwithstanding, the ambition was quickly formulated to extend to the 'former East' what had until then been a western European Union in all but name.[7] In other words, at a time of renewed self-confidence in the west and amidst the complex early post-communist transformation crisis in the east, a plan was developed to incorporate numerous eastern European countries on Western terms and thereby not only deepen but also broaden the Union.[8]

During what in retrospect must strike us as a moment of Western optimism, mutual ignorance and deep-seated misperceptions deriving from the then recent decades of confrontation between eastern and western Europe seemed merely a temporary hindrance on the path towards their integration – or even their 'unification', to cite an overambitious expression frequently employed at the time. During this unipolar moment when wild ambitions to 'democratise the world' were also vocally articulated, most consequentially among American neo-conservatives, the future expansion of the European Union eastwards appeared to lack a fixed endpoint.[9] What was turning into a truly continental project in the post-Cold War period for the first time thus also had universalistic pretentions. However, the enlarged Union, rather than uniting Europe (as often and wrongly asserted at the time and since) has in fact divided eastern Europe into members and 'non-members', with the two largest countries in geographical Europe (Russia and Ukraine) belonging to the latter category – not to mention that the European project never seriously considered going beyond those quasi-geographical borders of the continent.[10]

From a technical point of view, the challenge related to nearly doubling the number of member states within a few years could be conceived as rather straightforward: making post-communist countries, which were supposedly

6 A highly critical treatment of the subject can be found in I.-S. Kowalczuk, *Die Übernahme: Wie Ostdeutschland Teil der Bundesrepublik wurde* (Munich, C. H. Beck, 2019).
7 The diplomatic processes that led to the remaking of the international order at the end of the Cold War are explored in K. Spohr, *Post Wall, Post Square: How Bush, Gorbachev, Kohl, and Deng Shaped the World after 1989* (New Haven, CT, Yale University Press, 2020).
8 On the criteria's origins, evolution, and enforcement, see especially C. Hillion, 'The Copenhagen Criteria and Their Progeny', in C. Hillion (ed.), *EU Enlargement* (Oxford, Hart Publishing, 2004), pp. 1–23.
9 For a scathing critique of the misconceptions and failures of US foreign policy since the Cold War in particular, see A. Bacevich, *The Age of Illusions: How America Squandered Its Cold War Victory* (New York, NY, Henry Holt and Company, 2020).
10 See R. Sakwa, *Russia against the Rest: The Post-Cold War Crisis of World Order* (Cambridge, Cambridge University Press, 2017).

just 'transitioning' to democracy, the rule of law and the market economy, compatible with the EU via the Copenhagen criteria specified in 1993.[11] With the entry of eleven post-communist states in 2004–13, the shared plan of integration – which was admittedly desired for rather different reasons by different actors – was soon implemented with only a few, if any, serious candidates for membership being left out (with the largest 'western Balkan' state, Serbia, constituting only a partial exception).[12] It is worth recalling that the eleven post-communist states (Bulgaria, Croatia, the Czech Republic, Estonia, Hungary, Latvia, Lithuania, Poland, Romania, Slovakia and Slovenia) joined the EU under wide-ranging, if not necessarily strictly enforced, conditions.[13] The fact that they were asked to fulfil more ambitious requirements than previous entrants itself reflected the advancement of European integration and was meant to contribute to its further deepening.

The priority these countries assigned to their rapid EU accession has certainly helped them stay the course of 'transition'. At the same time, setting such a priority may have hindered their development of a more open and democratic culture of debate. After all, as Ivan Krastev and Stephen Holmes have recently highlighted, the new democracies that emerged in Europe with the end of the Cold War found themselves in the role of imitators.[14] As authors such as Karl Schlögel or Bálint Magyar and Bálint Madlovics have underlined in affinity with Krastev and Holmes' imitation thesis, adequate intellectual instruments to measure the unprecedented transformation in post-communist eastern Europe were sadly missing at the time.[15] The absence of more precise instruments in turn facilitated the dominance of a simple teleological vision – captured well in the concept of 'transition' – that projected these countries into a 'standard Western future'.[16] The goal towards which they were heading was assumed to be already known, the

---

11 The classic study of the process remains M. A. Vachudova, *Europe Undivided: Democracy, Leverage, and Integration after Communism* (Oxford, Oxford University Press, 2005).

12 See M. A. Vachudova, 'EU Enlargement and State Capture in the Western Balkans', in J. Džankić, S. Keil and M. Kmezić (eds.), *The Europeanisation of the Western Balkans: A Failure of EU Conditionality?* (London, Palgrave Macmillan, 2018), pp. 63–85.

13 See G. Noutcheva and D. Bechev, 'The Successful Laggards: Bulgaria and Romania's Accession to the EU', *East European Politics and Societies* 22 (2008): 114–44.

14 See I. Krastev and S. Holmes, *The Light That Failed: A Reckoning* (London, Penguin, 2019).

15 K. Schlögel, 'This Mess of Troubled Times', in Laczó and Lisjak Gabrijelčič (eds.), *The Legacy of Division*; B. Magyar and B. Madlovics, *The Anatomy of Post-Communist Regimes: A Conceptual Framework* (Budapest, Central European University Press, 2021), pp. 59–69.

16 For a recent discussion of this highly influential approach of the 1980s and 1990s, see L. Diamond, F. Fukuyama, D. L. Horowitz and M. F. Plattner, 'Reconsidering the Transition Paradigm', *Journal of Democracy* 25 (2014): 86–100.

main uncertainty regarding their journey supposedly concerned only its length.

However, what was understood prior to 2004 as a straightforward process of extending Western rules, standards and norms to areas that yearned to become part of the European project, and were at the same time expected to exert only limited impact on its overall course, has come to unleash momentous processes within the Union – processes that admittedly only rather few western Europeans, who tended to combine far-reaching ignorance regarding eastern European matters with occasional superiority complexes, have been particularly well-prepared to tackle.[17] It is therefore worth asking how the self-confident attempts of the post-1989 years to simultaneously deepen and widen the EU have interacted with each other since the EU's 'big-bang enlargement' of 2004–13 into eastern Europe.

The first transformation to highlight concerns the Federal Republic of Germany, the only country that could draw on relevant prior national experiences of trying to unite its 'former West' and 'former East', a country that, however, had in many ways mismanaged the socio-economic integration of its *neue Bundesländer*, with negative consequences until today. The enlarged Federal Republic had also largely ignored the policy lessons that it could have drawn from the experiences of its eastern neighbours after 1989.[18] Germany was key to Europe's post-Cold War transformation also since – even though the country's dominant political culture has remained sceptical of geopolitical ruminations – it stood to profit the most from the new shape the Union was taking: Germany has quietly come to occupy an advantageous *Mittellage* (central position) in an 'enlarged Europe'. The emergence of such a 'reunited' Federal Republic as Europe's 'reluctant hegemon'[19] in the early twenty-first century, a role which may be summed up as pre-eminence largely confined to the economic sphere, which remains politically contested

17 On the origins of the concept of eastern Europe, see L. Wolff, *Inventing Eastern Europe: The Map of Civilization on the Mind of the Enlightenment* (Stanford, CA, Stanford University Press, 1994). On its conceptual history in modern times, see F. B. Schenk, 'Eastern Europe', in D. Mishkova and B. Trencsényi (eds.), *European Regions and Boundaries: A Conceptual History* (London, Berghahn, 2017), pp. 188–209. On the contemporary sense of a gradient, see A. Melegh, *On the East–West Slope: Globalization, Nationalism, Racism and Discourses on Central and Eastern Europe* (Budapest, Central European University Press, 2005).

18 See P. Ther, 'The Cost of Unity: The Transformation of Germany and East Central Europe after 1989', in Laczó and Lisjak Gabrijelčič, *The Legacy of Division*, pp. 30–47, 38.

19 For a discussion, see S. Bulmer and W. E. Paterson, *Germany and the European Union: Europe's Reluctant Hegemon?* (London, Macmillan, 2018). On German foreign policy in recent decades, see S. Bierling, *Vormacht wider Willen: Deutsche Außenpolitik von der Wiedervereinigung bis zur Gegenwart* (Munich, C. H. Beck, 2014).

also for reasons internal to Germany, is clearly inseparable from the EU's big-bang enlargement – and the partial 'easternisation of Europe' that has followed through the deep incorporation of east European semi-peripheries into the broader European economy.[20] What made these developments a crucial bone of contention by the early twenty-first century is that what may have been a conscious strategy to avoid open self-assertion on the part of Germany could appear as hypocritical obfuscation in the eyes of citizens and political representatives in member states with a less agreeable bargain.

Beyond having such a 'reluctant hegemon', the enlarged Union proved strangely (dis)balanced in additional ways. Its new lack of proper balance had to do with the fact that requiring the qualified majorities or even unanimity of twenty-eight on a host of issues is doubtlessly a tall order and tends to push steps in integration towards their lowest common denominator – which is especially true when representatives of a number of member states tend to conceive of their Union membership and their national sovereignty as mutually reinforcing. Often cherishing a narrative of recently (re)gained national independence after Soviet imperial subjugation, partly in contrast to the EU's mantra of 'ever closer union',[21] representatives of east European countries in particular tended to be consciously in favour of a 'European rescue of the nation state'.[22]

A new, reluctant hegemon and such divergent historical narratives and national self-perceptions aside, the lack of balance in the post-2004 Union had other and arguably even more crucial sources. While nearly every second member state could be called 'post-Eastern' by 2013, in demographic terms the newest additions to the Union contained only about one-fifth of the overall population. There being notable economic disparities between the western and eastern 'halves' of the Union in the early decades of the twenty-first century, the overall economic contribution of the latter has in fact remained well below one-fifth.[23] Remarkably, while there are certain regional

---

20 See especially D. Bohle and B. Greskovits, *Capitalist Diversity on Europe's Periphery* (Ithaca, NY, Cornell University Press, 2012). On the specifics of the economic integration of Germany and central and eastern Europe, a key study remains K. Bluhm, *Experimentierfeld Ostmitteleuropa? Deutsche Unternehmen in Polen und der Tschechischen Republik* (Wiesbaden, VS-Verlag, 2007).

21 On the politics of memory in post-communist central and eastern Europe, see J. Mark, *The Unfinished Revolution: Making Sense of the Communist Past in Central-Eastern Europe* (New Haven, CT: Yale University Press, 2011).

22 The reference here is, of course, to the classic study by A. Milward, *The European Rescue of the Nation State* (London, Routledge, 1992).

23 On the persistence of such disparities, see A. C. Janos, *East Central Europe in the Modern World: The Politics of the Borderlands from Pre- to Post-Communism* (Stanford, CA, Stanford University Press, 2000).

and generational exceptions to the overall pattern, the Union's twenty least developed regions still all lie along its eastern borders today.

In other words, a still quite distinct and economically rather underdeveloped part of the continent containing numerous mostly smallish member states would come to play a disproportionately large political role on the European level since 2004 – being responsible, to take two important examples, for nearly every second Council vote and nearly every second European Commissioner. At the same time, the newer member states would come do so without their citizens acquiring anywhere near proportional representation within the EU's own elite.[24] The conclusion should be clear: the enlarged EU has been less well balanced across various areas and also in terms of its political elites than the Union of twelve founded at Maastricht or its Cold War-era precursors (when, as the almost proverbial summary goes, French political ambitions and German economic might were mutually dependent on and supportive of each other).

Beyond yielding such discrepancies, enlargement to the east has also transformed how the EU operates and with what social and political consequences. The perception that western member states continued to use certain double standards to disadvantage citizens of the newer member states has been difficult to escape at first: in the light of the fact that freedom of movement has been a key principle of the European project, the restriction of the labour markets of older member states beyond 2004, with Romanian and Bulgarian citizens still having to wait to access the Schengen zone more than a decade after their country's EU membership, is an obvious point in case. Such questionable practices point to an attempt to buffer the potentially negative consequences of enlargement in western Europe from a position of strength.

A partial easternisation of Europe nonetheless soon started to become evident. It is manifested in the spending of significant parts of the budget, with newer member states quickly emerging as the largest net beneficiaries in proportional or even absolute terms (as has been the case with Poland), not least via structural-compensatory funds. Such a new eastern complexion to the European project has also become evident through migratory patterns, despite the just mentioned extension of restrictions. In eastern European countries, outmigration of an unprecedented intensity could be observed, coming on top of already ageing societies. It quickly resulted in what some

---

24 For recent data, see L. Drounau 'Geographical Representation in EU Leadership Observatory 2021', European Democracy Consulting, https://eudemocracy.eu/geo graphical-representation-eu-leadership-observatory.

prefer to call 'demographic panics'.[25] Reaching its peak in Lithuania and Latvia, countries whose populations have contracted by some 20 per cent in the early twenty-first century due mainly to emigration, and Bulgaria and Romania, where natural decrease has approached 10 per cent,[26] the massive migratory asymmetry between eastern and western Europe was intimately connected to widely differing levels of development, the disproportionately large negative impact of the post-2008 economic crisis on the semi-peripheries within the EU[27] and a sociopolitical order that in many ways reinforced rather than mitigated the concentration of resources and opportunities. With millions arriving from eastern Europe in quick succession, the consequences of an internally open European space – which western Europeans, in contrast also to southern Europeans, used only rather rarely to move across national borders on a longer-term basis – were swiftly transformed.

If the EU's rather generous subsidies have reinforced local state capacity as well as networks of power, the disproportionate outmigration of the young and the educated from east European countries has tended to reinforce the basic conservatism of national societies. The combined impact of the two processes meant that the transnationalisation of east European societies and the renationalisation of local politics could go hand in hand. This combined impact may in turn have contributed to the rather moderate convergence in terms of political norms and values between much of eastern Europe and (internal differences notwithstanding) a significantly more liberal west.

While democratic standards have been in decline in various member states in different macro-regions, by the late 2010s the threat of de-democratisation within the EU was identified primarily with attempts at illiberal state building in east European member states, such as Hungary and Poland (discussed in the next section). These attempts represented a backlash against the fast-paced liberalisation and Westernisation pursued by a previous generation – as well as the perception and consequent resentment, apparently particularly widespread in what used to be some of the most developed corners of the Soviet empire, of not being sufficiently respected in a prestigious and highly

25 See especially Chapter 1 of Krastev and Holmes, *The Lights That Failed*.
26 From a plethora of literature, see R. Black, C. Pantiru, M. Okolski and G. Engbersen, *A Continent Moving West? EU Enlargement and Labour Migration from Central and Eastern Europe* (Amsterdam, Amsterdam University Press, 2010).
27 For the impact on central and eastern Europe, see especially Chapter 7 of P. Ther, *Europe since 1989: A History*, trans. C. Hughes-Kreutzmüller (Princeton, NJ: Princeton University Press, 2016).

developed Union. In Hungary and Poland in particular, illiberal political projects have been launched that right-wing populists further west tended to view as examples worth emulating, not least due to their combination of sociocultural conservatism and ethnonational radicalism. Putin's Russia has also been a much-discussed actor in such networks.[28]

A comparable 'threat of easternisation' could be detected when it comes to social standards. As Philipp Ther has argued through his concept of co-transformation,[29] once the second, more radical wave of neoliberalism began to be implemented in east European countries around the turn of the millennium, itself an effect of having to build capitalism without local capitalists and needing to rely on foreign direct investment,[30] labour market regulations and welfare provisions came under greater pressure further west too. In both these ways, the EU's eastern enlargement may have contributed to boosting the chances of right-wing populists.

Thinking about the dialectic of deepening and widening the European project in the early twenty-first century is a way of trying to answer a question akin to the one raised by Piedmontese-Italian statesman Massimo d'Azeglio back in the nineteenth century: how has the EU fared creating Europeans out of westerners and easterners once a large Union had been established? (The phrase 'L'Italia è fatta. Restano da fare gli italiani' ('Italy has been made. It remains to make Italians') is often associated with the name of Massimo d'Azeglio, who used it in his memoirs *I miei ricordi* first published (posthumously) in 1867.) Our preliminary answer needs to include references to moderate successes as well as unforeseen complications. Judging from the evidence of a short 15 years, EU enlargement into 'the east' has resulted in 'negative' as much as 'positive' forms of convergence. What is more, the decade and a half under examination may have reinforced pre-existing misperceptions and biases between the two halves of the continent as much as it alleviated them, with propagandistic discourses about 'Western decadence' and 'Eastern authoritarianism' making powerful comebacks in the 2010s – developments to which Russia's authoritarian turn under Vladimir Putin and newly confrontational relationship with the West have obviously been central.

28 See A. Shekhovtsov, *Russia and the Western Far Right: Tango Noir* (London, Routledge, 2018).
29 See Chapter 9 in particular in Ther, *Europe since 1989*.
30 The argument was elaborated in G. Eyal, I. Szelényi and E. Townsley, *Making Capitalism without Capitalists: Class Formation and Elite Struggles in Post-Communist Central Europe* (London, Verso, 1998).

This limited convergence in an enlarged Union has been taking place in a broader context of growing social and spatial inequality across Europe. Zooming in to observe the divergence of standards and opportunities in town and country, it is perhaps the relative strength of the former in the west versus the latter in the east that we should be considering. By the late 2010s, cities such as Warsaw and Budapest were in many ways more closely comparable and more intricately connected to Amsterdam or Paris than they were around 2004, with members of younger generations in particular resembling each other more than before. At the same time, it has apparently proven easier to outvote and dominate the aforementioned capital cities of Warsaw and Budapest within their respective countries, where urbanisation rates are currently around 60–70 per cent, than Amsterdam and Paris in their significantly more urbanized environments (countries in which urbanization has reached more than 80 per cent or even 90 per cent). This moot example may also illustrate one of the central paradoxes of European integration, namely that despite all the discussions around 'European unification' in recent decades, integration has produced a highly diversified space.[31]

Crises as Opportunities, Crises as Tests

Crisis, a notion evoking diverse associations, has been a key concept in the writing of European integration history. An influential strand in integration history has indeed viewed crises as an engine of further integration – a pattern of narrativisation on which the recent 'failing forward' thesis evoked in this chapter's title draws.[32] Accordingly, much analytical effort has been spent on distinguishing different types of crises and assessing their varied impact over time.[33] Approached in this broader historical context, a key novelty of the years since 2004 appears to be a certain densification of crises, a development closely connected to the more general acceleration of time observable in contemporary history.[34]

This part of the chapter discusses how crises unfolded and were employed in the years between 2004 and 2019. It focuses chiefly on internal crises or highlights the specifically European dimension of broader, more

---

31 On this point, see E. Hirsch Ballin, E. Ćerimović, H. Dijstelbloem and M. Segers, *European Variations as a Key to Cooperation* (The Hague, WRR and Springer, 2020).

32 See Jones et al., 'Failing Forward?'

33 See, for example, L. Kühnhardt (ed.), *Crises in European Integration: Challenge and Response, 1945–2005* (London, Berghahn, 2009).

34 See H. Rosa, *Beschleunigung: Die Veränderung der Zeitstrukturen in der Moderne* (Frankfurt am Main, Suhrkamp, 2005).

global ones to argue that these major crises of the years 2004–19 have indeed served as drivers of further European integration in an age defined by the 'politics of events' but have done so only to a limited extent. The crises to be explored below concern the failed attempt at European constitution-making and its consequences in 2005–7; the financial and ensuing economic and Eurozone crises that had their worst phase between 2008 and the mid 2010s; the so-called migrant and refugee crisis with its peak year in 2015; the shambles around Brexit in the years since the June 2016 referendum in the UK; and the worsening challenge posed by the anti-liberal turn in member states and the resulting rule of law crisis for the Union.

More specifically, I intend to explore how these five crises unfolding in quick succession or even overlapping with each other have, when taken together, put the ideal type of the EU as understood around the turn of the millennium to a serious test. The ideal-typical definition of the EU in question, close to the cherished self-image of the EU, might be summarised as a union of liberal democratic states based on the rule of law developing new forms of multilayered governance to reach beneficial compromises and workable solutions that are pooling elements of their sovereignty in a directional process, a union that is at the same time open to the world, respects universal human rights and practises solidarity. As I aim to show below, the responses to and impact of these main crises, approached here as major contemporary historical tests, have contradicted this ideal type on practically every point.

From the Failed Adoption of a European Constitution to the Lisbon Treaty

During the attempted adoption of a European constitution, national majorities against the idea expressed through referenda in France and the Netherlands in May and June 2005, respectively, suddenly posed an unforeseen obstacle. The common solution, in the shape of the Lisbon Treaty, reached in December 2007 and eventually coming into force by December 2009, was to substitute for the Constitutional Treaty while preserving much of its originally planned agenda.[35] Assessed in the light of national democratic wills in two key west European member states, the treaty's provisions might be viewed as issued by 'royal fiat', even if they were agreed by democratically elected national representatives. The notion

35 See J. Ziller, 'Lisbon Treaty', in W. R. Thompson (ed.), *Oxford Research Encyclopedias: Politics* (Oxford, Oxford University Press, 2019).

that the EU acts as a union of liberal democratic states, all of which exercise their discretionary powers without contravention of democratic mandates from their respective national populations to pool elements of their sovereignty, was thus tested and found to be too optimistic, if not downright naïve.

Asymmetric Shocks within the Eurozone

The idea that the Union advances through reasonable and beneficial, if unavoidably imperfect, compromises was soon challenged during the financial crisis that triggered a profound Eurozone crisis.[36] This crisis eventually resulted in a prolonged recession in multiple member states. It impacted southern European countries and members of younger generations particularly negatively – while even its nominal beneficiaries in northwest European societies had to deal with persistently suppressed wages.[37] Greece's profound indebtedness- and Eurozone-related troubles, repeatedly addressed in the first half of the 2010s, amounted to an unprecedented economic downturn outside times of war, pandemics or natural disasters. This much-debated case of a country has demonstrated how the belief that states would almost by default be able to reach mutually beneficial compromises during the deepening process of European integration needed to be reconsidered.[38] It turned out that shocks within the Eurozone could be highly asymmetrical, especially if not counteracted by meaningful fiscal transfers – which may have been arranged as an act of extraordinary European solidarity but also as a conventional instrument of Eurozone economic rationality. In the absence of such transfers, the prolonged economic crisis within the EU revealed basic shortcomings in the construction of the euro, a common currency without shared fiscal policies and a lender of last resort.[39]

Refugees, Migrants and the Crisis of European Solidarity

During the so-called migrant and refugee crisis, several EU member states opposed calls for European solidarity amidst a humanitarian emergency and some even came to question the very right to asylum.[40] While the EU had

36 See especially Part III of A. Tooze, *Crashed: How a Decade of Financial Crises Changed the World* (London, Allen Lane, 2018).
37 For a critical perspective, see M. Matthijs, 'Mediterranean Blues: The Crisis in Southern Europe', *Journal of Democracy* 25 (2014): 101–15.
38 See G. Karyotis and R. Gerodimos (eds.), *The Politics of Extreme Austerity: Greece in the Eurozone Crisis* (London, Palgrave Macmillan, 2015).
39 See A. Verdun (ed.), *The Euro: European Integration and Economic and Monetary Union* (Boulder, CO, Rowman and Littlefield, 2002).
40 On the unfolding of this crisis, see N. Thorpe, *The Road before Me Weeps: On the Refugee Route through Europe* (New Haven, CT, Yale University Press, 2019).

preferred to depict itself as open to the world, based on universal human rights and practising international solidarity, the response in multiple member states as well as on the European level to the third major crisis of the period attested to the prevalence of rather different values and attitudes. Significant expressions of human solidarity notwithstanding, the much-repeated and negatively loaded narrative of a 'migration crisis' contributed to the further shift of the European political and cultural mainstream in an ethnocentric and exclusivist direction. The new pragmatic-negative attitude found striking expression, for example, in the March 2016 refugee deal with Turkey,[41] which aimed to largely outsource the burning issue to a crucial immediate neighbour in exchange for various benefits – a controversial deal that even German Chancellor Angela Merkel, the 'moral hero' of previous months, came to openly endorse and explicitly defend.[42]

While the EU does not keep official count of those dying in attempts to enter its territory, according to the estimates we possess, the annual rates have risen to the thousands in recent years.[43] It is similarly undisputed that the peak of the migrant and refugee crisis in 2015, when over a million people attempted to flee across the Mediterranean and into the Union's territory, was followed by a further wave of securitisation of the EU's borders. By late 2019, the Union-level response to the global emergency induced by war, violence and worsening environmental breakdown – a crisis of international solidarity as much as control when it comes to the EU – would include a symbolical move to appoint Greek representative Margaritis Schinas to a newly created vice presidency of the European Commission. Schinas' portfolio, later renamed from 'Protecting Our European Way of Life' to 'Promoting the European Way of Life', explicitly considers questions of the rule of law, internal security and migration as part of the same package.

Ever Closer but Still Reversible

If the flattering image of an EU based on universal values, open to the world and solidaristic with those suffering from war, violence and acute forms of deprivation, got severely damaged in 2015–16, the idea that pooling sovereignty via joint decision making on the European level was the path forward

---

41 For a critical perspective by an insider, see L. Batalla Adam, 'The EU–Turkey Deal One Year On: A Delicate Balancing Act', *The International Spectator* 52 (2017), 44–58.

42 On Angela Merkel, see K. Marton, *The Chancellor: The Remarkable Odyssey of Angela Merkel* (New York, NY, Simon and Schuster, 2021).

43 See C. Heller and A. Pecoud, 'Counting Migrants' Deaths at the Border: From Civil Society Counterstatistics to (Inter)governmental Recuperation', *American Behavioral Scientist* 64 (2020): 480–500.

was subsequently frontally questioned by the UK. Such a drastic questioning was somewhat ironic given that the UK, indubitably a major force within European integration since it formally (and belatedly) joined the project at the beginning of 1973, was among those few member states that had opted out of several key steps of further integration in previous decades – the UK under Margaret Thatcher's neo-conservative and neoliberal rule in the 1980s may have been a major proponent of establishing the single European market, but decisive parts of the UK's political elite did not view further political integration as desirable, nor did it adopt the common currency or join Schengen.

If the surprise victory of the campaign for Brexit in the June 2016 referendum eventually led to the first ever departure of a (leading) member state from the Union,[44] the convoluted process of negotiating the details of departure – which still need to be followed by developing new forms of partnership at the time of writing – has clearly highlighted the complexity and depth European integration has reached. While the process of exiting certainly helped reopen the debate around political alternatives within the UK, if at a time of acrimonious polarisation,[45] the UK's prolonged inability to reach a 'Brexit deal' has also exposed the predictably high cost of reasserting state sovereignty in a context of advanced interdependences. Far from the finest hour of any of the parties to this negotiated divorce, the brusque suing for divorce on the part of the UK under Theresa May's premiership arguably amounted to the EU's finest tragedy: the EU of twenty-seven to be would remain united and firm in opposing unprincipled compromises with an increasingly 'awkward partner'. The awkward partner narrative was first developed by Stephen George.[46] N. Piers Ludlow, who is currently working on a relevant monograph, has already done much to alter such an understanding.

De-democratisation and Complacency

If the absence of an amount of pragmatic flexibility on the side of the EU might be viewed as part of the problem when it came to the unexpected departure of a leading member state, the crisis of de-democratisation and

---

44 As a detailed account of the year of Brexit, T. Shipman, *All Out War: The Full Story of Brexit* (London, William Collins, 2016) remains unsurpassed. For an argument that the exit of Algeria and Greenland might be compared to Brexit (and how), see Chapter 7 in K. K. Patel, *Project Europe: A History* (Cambridge, Cambridge University Press, 2020).

45 For sharp-eyed reflections on British political culture in these years, see F. O'Toole, *Heroic Failure: Brexit and the Politics of Pain* (London, Head of Zeus, 2018); F. O'Toole, *Three Years in Hell: The Brexit Chronicles* (London, Head of Zeus, 2020).

46 S. George, *An Awkward Partner: Britain in the European Community* (Oxford, Oxford University Press, 1990).

worsening challenges to the rule of law within the Union, especially acute in the case of Hungary throughout the 2010s and in Poland by the second half of the decade, has revealed close to the opposite: it has shown just how little European institutions could and would do to protect, let alone promote, liberal democracy in member states in these years.[47]

While scholars have demonstrated that the EU's capacity to transform countries is higher prior to their accession (and this is particularly true, somewhat paradoxically, when accession is promised in a credible way) and that building state capacity rather than promoting democracy was the EU's actual forte,[48] the meagreness of both existing instruments and newly developed dedication to protect liberal democracies nonetheless came as a negative surprise, especially for those east Europeans who had come to perceive the EU as a 'community of values' during the accession process and now had to experience de-democratisation first hand. Its insufficient and partly even rather naïve response throughout the 2010s has arguably exposed the EU as a Fukuyaman believer on the stage of post-post-history.[49]

With Poland and Hungary being among the major net beneficiaries of the European budget during their respective periods of de-democratisation and the most successful challenger of the liberal democratic script – the Hungarian Fidesz party under Viktor Orbán's leadership – remaining an influential member of the European People's Party throughout the years under examination, one could reasonably doubt whether the EU has really done more to constrain than to enable the rising illiberal regimes within its realm.[50] When it comes to the European People's Party, the contrast with the British Tories, whom David Cameron had withdrawn from the largest European party family back in 2009, may be instructive once more: whereas the issue with the British on the conservative-nationalist right was their all too quick and firm decision to depart, the conundrum with Orbán's Hungarian radicals rather derived from their self-interested intention to stay.

---

47 For a recent take, see R. D. Kelemen, 'The European Union's Authoritarian Equilibrium', *Journal of European Public Policy* 27 (2020): 481–99.
48 See T. A. Börzel and F. Schimmelfennig, 'Coming Together or Drifting Apart? The EU's Political Integration Capacity in Eastern Europe', *Journal of European Public Policy* 24 (2017): 278–96.
49 F. Fukuyama, *The End of History and the Last Man* (New York, Free Press, 1992).
50 For a balanced argument from a few years ago, see A. Bozóki and D. Hegedűs, 'An Externally Constrained Hybrid Regime: Hungary in the European Union', *Democratisation* 25 (2018): 1173–89.

The moot question is not whether the EU needed to act politically in the 'post-post-historical' era of the early twenty-first century (it certainly did), but what choices it made, with what effects, and how those choices and their effects reflected on its legitimacy. The brief examinations above allow us to draw a rather uncomfortable conclusion: practically every element in the ideal-typical definition of the EU was put to the test in the early twenty-first century and the EU's actual responses have contradicted the high – perhaps unrealistically high – expectations that had been raised towards this new type of entity. Put differently, the EU has indeed managed to be less post-historical when it needed to, but it has also revealed itself to be less different from conventional political actors than it had preferred to claim.

The responses of the Union admittedly had to be developed in an increasingly difficult or even downright hostile international environment in which the United States showed declining interest in and later also commitment to its transatlantic ties; in which China, Russia and Turkey all grew more authoritarian internally and more assertive on the international stage; in which the democratisation attempts within Arab countries have been largely suppressed, often in calamitous ways; and in which large democracies such as India and Brazil have also seen their regimes severely challenged from within towards the end of the period. Placed in such a global context of liberal democratic malaise and worsening international strife, the EU's overall record of keeping centrifugal tendencies largely at bay certainly appears more agreeable.

The crises outlined above may indeed be viewed as resulting in the EU moderately failing forward via imperfect compromises as well as in a somewhat improved common understanding of membership benefits and rule of law criteria. However, if – as we have seen above – by the 2010s the potential future convergence between eastern and western European members has increasingly often been viewed as a threat rather than a promise by those in favour of a liberal democratic and more integrated Europe, the just-discussed crises ultimately meant that, even if the universalistic pretentions of the EU based on its 'normative power' may not have declined,[51] they have been accompanied by a growing sense that such normativity is an aspiration rather than a reality within the Union today – and that, even so, Europe might be a fragile exception worth protecting from the growing threats posed by large global forces.

---

51 The argument was originally made in I. Manners, 'Normative Power Europe: A Contradiction in Terms?', *Journal of Common Market Studies* 40 (2002): 235–58.

Europe's Politicisation

Professional research on, and polyphonic writing of, European history have been pursued for generations, and various reflections on European values and traditions have been offered for much longer than that. However, significant recent advances notwithstanding,[52] the historiography of the EU has remained a surprisingly limited subfield until today. For an extended part of the postwar decades, European integration history tended, quite out of synch with innovative trends in European historiography, to devote disproportionate attention to high politics and legal developments, with a strong focus on just a few great powers, key individuals and major treaties.[53] At the same time, EU institutions have preferred rather sanitised versions of their own histories.[54] While such institutions have at times encouraged and may even have directly commissioned the work of 'organic intellectuals', independent historians have been rather hesitant to perform more thorough and critical examinations of the EU's history in its varied contexts, not least to explore the gap between *Realgeschichte* (real history) and the EU's preferred modes of self-presentation. Similarly, novelists have rarely felt inspired to depict the EU until now.[55] This has begun to change in the early twenty-first century, not least via the newly possible archival research-based reinterpretations of the 1970s and 1980s. These decades had frequently been depicted as a period of 'Eurosclerosis', but in fact they laid the groundwork for the foundation of the EU.[56]

Historians have arguably started to devote greater attention to European integration as a key part of contemporary European history also since mainstream discourses of the early twenty-first century have increasingly, if rather problematically, identified 'Europe' with the EU whereas in other – at least equally problematic – discourses 'Europe' has come to be employed as

---

52 See K. K. Patel, 'Widening and Deepening? Recent Advances in European Integration History', *Neue Politische Literatur* 64 (2019): 327–57.

53 For an important exception focusing on an important member state that has been studied much less than Germany, France or the United Kingdom, see M. Segers, *The Netherlands and European Integration, 1950 to Present* (Amsterdam, Amsterdam University Press, 2020).

54 For more on the mainstream narrative of contemporary European history, see F. Laczó, C. Erlichman and P. del Hierro, 'Reconceptualisation and Renewal. On Writing Contemporary European History Today', Why Europe, Which Europe? A Debate on Contemporary European History as a Field of Research (2021), https://europedebate.hypotheses.org/740.

55 As a key exception in recent years, see R. Menasse, *The Capital*, trans. J. Bulloch (New York, Liveright, 2019).

56 The best presentation of this 'revisionist' argument can be found in Patel, *Project Europe*.

a counter-concept to the current, liberal shape of the Union. Such attempts at conceptual identification and opposition have reflected a broader politicisation that this part aims to explore. I argue below that, while European integration has started to have a more tangible impact on the lives of citizens in recent decades, the question of the Union's legitimacy has also begun to be raised with new urgency. Popular participation in what has become a more polarised European political landscape has also started to grow towards the end of the years under examination, but the 'Europeanisation of politics' (understood here primarily as the growing resemblance of politics on the EU level to politics within liberal democratic member states) has visibly lagged behind the 'politicisation of Europe'.

It is something of a commonplace that the precursors to the EU, which had to share space and compete with several parallel and partly competing international organisations, were mainly launched by continental west European Christian democrats.[57] For our purposes, it is equally important to recall that the political agenda of the Christian democrats – rather similarly to that of their major counterparts, the social democrats, with their original base in a now dwindling working class and labour movement – entered a crisis of reproduction by the late twentieth century.[58] On a largely secularised continent, where debates about religious difference, especially those that concerned Islam, may have been widespread but where everyday religiosity was no longer a decisive sociocultural factor,[59] and where leftist-progressive coalitions capable of attracting majorities would have had to be rebuilt for a post-industrial age,[60] the comparable crises of Christian and social democrats have yielded a broadly centrist Union of predominantly liberal complexion. Around the turn of the millennium 'third way' leftist parties appeared ascendant in several member states, including some of the most influential ones, but they soon lost significant parts of their popularity.[61]

---

57 See W. Kaiser, *Christian Democracy and the Origins of European Union* (Cambridge, Cambridge University Press, 2007).

58 For an argument in this vein, see C. Invernizzi Accetti, *What Is Christian Democracy? Politics, Religion and Ideology* (Cambridge, Cambridge University Press, 2019).

59 For a sophisticated take on this issue, see J. Casanova, 'Rethinking Secularization: A Global Comparative Perspective', *Hedgehog Review* 8 (2006): 7–22.

60 For a history of de-industrialisation in western Europe, see L. Raphael, *Jenseits von Kohle und Stahl: Eine Gesellschaftsgeschichte Westeuropas nach dem Boom* (Berlin, Suhrkamp, 2019).

61 On the transformation of the left, see S. L. Mudge, *Leftism Reinvented: Western Parties from Socialism to Neoliberalism* (Cambridge, MA, Harvard University Press, 2018).

This broadly centrist and predominantly liberal Union has arguably contributed to the liberal democratic malaise of our age in specific ways. Yascha Mounk has recently reflected on the growing gap between individual rights and the popular-majoritarian will as a key part of this malaise. He identified the rise of new agendas and regimes of 'rights without democracy' and 'democracy without rights', a framework which may indeed be fruitfully applied to the EU.[62] With the mass parties of both the centre right and the centre left caught in relative decline, heightened electoral volatility and the ascendance of neoliberal policies across Europe, a new opposition has indeed started to structure much of the political debate within the Union, namely that between strands of an insufficiently democratic liberalism and challengers mostly of a right-wing populist variety. It is worth recalling in this context that Jan-Werner Müller has underlined how 'Western Europeans fashioned a highly *constrained* form of democracy, deeply imprinted with a distrust of popular sovereignty after 1945.'[63] There has been much scholarly and public discussion about the evolution and contemporary character of populism, illiberalism, nationalism and right-wing radicalism in the years under examination.[64] Reflections have also been offered, if less frequently, on what conceiving of such a key opposition – which revolves primarily around cultural values and political styles rather than around distinct institutional preferences and policy agendas – may reveal about the contemporary political mainstream and the socio-economic transformations behind its emergence.[65]

Fierce as the clashes between cultural value systems and political styles may have seemed, at least since the rise of Silvio Berlusconi in Italy during the 1990s, such an opposition between a liberal centre and its right-wing populist challengers was also internal to the European People's Party. And it

---

62 See Y. Mounk, *The People vs. Democracy: Why Our Freedom Is in Danger and How to Save It* (Cambridge, MA, Harvard University Press, 2018).

63 See J.-W. Müller, *Contesting Democracy: Political Ideas in Twentieth-Century Europe* (New Haven, CT, Yale University Press, 2011). See also M. Conway, *Western Europe's Democratic Age, 1945–1968* (Princeton, NJ: Princeton University Press, 2020).

64 From a vast amount of literature, see especially C. Rovira Kaltwasser and C. Mudde, *Populism: A Very Short Introduction* (Oxford, Oxford University Press, 2017); J.-W. Müller, *What Is Populism?* (London, Penguin, 2016); F. Finchelstein, *From Fascism to Populism in History* (Oakland, CA, University of California Press, 2017).

65 On the practical disappearance of references to material inequality from hegemonic political discourses at a time of increasing material inequality, see Laczó et al., 'Reconceptualisation and Renewal'. For an argument on what the seemingly opposed forces often labelled as populists and technocrats have in common and how that reflects on contemporary European politics, see C. Bickerton and C. Invernizzi Accetti, *Technopopulism: The New Logic of Democratic Politics* (Oxford, Oxford University Press, 2021).

was this post-Christian democratic amalgam that regained the main levers of political power within the EU in 2004 and has managed to hold onto them throughout the period. Angela Merkel and Viktor Orbán, arguably the two key actors in the crisis of control and solidarity that the Union experienced during the dramatic peak of the migrant and refugee crisis in 2015 and who tended to be depicted at the time as representing clear alternatives, were in fact political allies on the European stage. While Merkel and Orbán indeed articulated alternative visions for Europe, the former a more liberal and open one, which saw compassion as central to Christian democratic practice, and the latter a nationalistic-religious one, which defined Europe through exclusive markers and whose vision at times bordered on open racism, both of them were representatives of a European power bloc stretching from the liberal conservative centre to elements of the anti-democratic far right – a power bloc apparently without a clear political or moral compass. As both Germany's long-serving chancellor and Hungary's prime minister belonged to the same party family in the years under analysis, the de-democratisation- and rule of law-related crisis within individual member states that threatened the integrity of the Union by the end of the period was to a significant extent traceable to developments internal to mainstream European political forces.[66]

Another noteworthy political development of the period concerned the so-called Eurosceptic forces – and was largely the result of another seminal crisis of the 2010s. If European parliamentary elections had been considered 'second-order elections' practically ever since their introduction in 1979,[67] by the early 2010s right-wing populist parties and their voters, ironically enough, constituted a significant exception in several countries, with the result that a party like the United Kingdom Independence Party would finish first in the UK in 2014 and the Front National performed the same feat in France. However, the prolonged shambles around, and predictably high costs of, Brexit just a few years later meant that right-wing populist parties in the twenty-seven EU member states of the future tended to reconsider their options. They were still vocally critiquing the supposed 'ultraliberalism' and 'hyper-bureaucratisation' of the EU, but – despite the first explicitly anti-EU

---

66 See R. D. Kelemen, 'The European Union's Authoritarian Equilibrium', *Journal of European Public Policy* 27 (2020): 481–99.

67 The argument about European elections being 'second-order elections' was first made in K. Reif and H. Schmitt, 'Nine Second-Order National Elections. A Conceptual Framework for the Analysis of European Election Results', *European Journal of Political Research* 8 (1980): 3–44.

US President occupying the White House at the time – the idea of reasserting state sovereignty through a rapturous exit became less rather than more popular in the second half of the 2010s. Confronted with the damning realities of Brexit, right-wing populists would have newly preferred to change the system from within – a development that calls into question the appropriateness of the very label 'Eurosceptic'.

In their own ways, the pro-European, broadly liberal mainstream and their right-wing populist challengers have thus both contributed not only to a higher level of polarisation around the European project but also to a certain Europeanisation of politics. (My specific use of the concept of Europeanisation here admittedly diverges from several mainstream approaches in recent scholarship, which tend to refer primarily to the impact of the EU on nation-states.)[68] In an age of crises, this eventually led to the reversal of decades-old trends of decreasing engagement with what was a still insufficiently democratic political process on the European level. This reversal could be observed, for example, in the heightened participation at the 2019 European Parliamentary elections, which – bucking a declining trend of some four decades – reached a 20-year high.

Growing mass interest notwithstanding, polarisation did not have transformative consequences in the final year analysed in this chapter: the broad coalition led by a post-Christian democratic amalgam by and large held in 2019. How the EU might function according to a more inclusive logic of pluralism and a more democratic logic of contestation remained to be seen, however. After all, next to the increased share of both liberal and right-wing populist forces (deriving, at least partially, from the emergence of a key symbolic-political divide between them), the main victors of these much-anticipated elections still included Germany's liberal conservative Christian Democrats and Hungary's right-wing populist Fidesz – Hungarian Civic Alliance. The politicisation of Europe may have advanced, but a more substantial Europeanisation of political life and choices was lagging.

Conclusions

How does such a picture of contemporary EU history – a broad, highly integrated but still remarkably diverse and increasingly politicised Union in crisis management mode undermining its cherished self-image – fit into or

---

68 These approaches are aptly summarised in U. Sedelmeier, 'Europeanization', in E. Jones, A. Menon and S. Weatherill (eds.), *The Oxford Handbook of the European Union* (Oxford, Oxford University Press, 2012), pp. 825–39.

perhaps contradict the longer-term process of European integration? As Kiran Klaus Patel has recently emphasised, in the case of such questions much depends on our image of European integration in the post-war period.[69] The fact that the EU has by and large preferred sanitised and teleological narratives has meant that the recurrent crises of the early twenty-first century have often been contrasted with an imagined past and were seen as posing unprecedented challenges. In a more realistic perspective, the EU has been an exceptionally successful international organisation that has managed to accumulate an unusually wide range of competences. However, it is far from being a providential entity with a teleological story.[70] By the time of its 'post-post-historical' years in the early twenty-first century analysed in this article, the EU has arguably exhibited uneasy balances: there has been too much integration relative to the modest levels of democratic control on the European level; there are too many member states, without sufficiently high levels of convergence between them; and there are too many common issues in an age of crises, with too few truly equitable common solutions being found.

Analysing this historical moment of uneasy balance, this article has focused on three questions that are crucial to an understanding of the contemporary path of the EU, namely the dialectic of deepening and broadening, the unfolding and impact of major crises, and types and new levels of politicisation. I have argued that the lack of proper balance in a larger Union has contributed to a moderate level of political convergence between eastern and western Europe and even to the strengthening of some rather negative trends in both 'former halves' of the continent. The examination of five major crises has allowed me to consider the EU's responses in the light of its key principles of legitimation and conclude that the EU has been rather moderately failing forward at a turbulent time. However, its responses have directly contradicted the ideal type of this organisation that had been recurrently sketched and largely disappointed expectations the EU itself had raised about being a novel kind of actor on the stage of history. Such new evidence that challenged the EU's cherished self-image in turn contributed to the growing politicisation of the European future.

In the closing part, I have therefore argued that the opposition between a liberal centre and its right-wing populist challengers has emerged as a key symbolic-political divide in these years. While the centre by and large held,

---

69 See Patel, *Project Europe*.
70 See especially Chapter 1, 'Europe and European Integration', in Patel, *Project Europe*.

political volatility has clearly increased. At the same time, a 'Europeanisation of politics' was lagging the 'politicisation of Europe'. In such a historical moment, growing polarisation within the political culture of the EU may have primarily been manifested in debates about questions of culture, identity and political styles. However, a broader historical perspective on such at times rather fierce and often unconstructive debates allows us to perceive how closely they were connected to socio-economic divergence within Europe – a divergence that can be grasped only with reference to the increasingly plutocratic shape global economic integration has taken and the resulting crisis of the European combination of liberal democracy and welfarist capitalism.[71]

Recommended Reading

Jones, E., R. D. Kelemen and S. Mounier. 'Failing Forward? The Euro Crisis and the Incomplete Nature of European Integration', *Comparative Political Studies* 49 (2016): 1010–34.

Kelemen, R. D. 'The European Union's Authoritarian Equilibrium', *Journal of European Public Policy* 27 (2020): 481–99.

Laczó, F. and L. Lisjak Gabrijelčič. *The Legacy of Division: East and West after 1989* (Budapest and Vienna, Central European University Press–Eurozine, 2020).

Middelaar, L. van. *Alarums and Excursions: Improvising Politics on the European Stage* (Newcastle upon Tyne, Agenda Publishing, 2019).

Mounk, Y. *The People vs. Democracy: Why Our Freedom Is in Danger and How to Save It* (Cambridge, MA, Harvard University Press, 2018).

Ther, P. *Europe since 1989: A History*, trans. C. Hughes-Kreutzmüller (Princeton, NJ, Princeton University Press, 2016).

Tooze, A. *Crashed: How a Decade of Financial Crises Changed the World* (London, Allen Lane, 2018).

71 See T. Piketty, *Capital and Ideology*, trans. A. Goldhammer (Cambridge, MA, Harvard University Press, 2020).

PART II

*

MULTILATERALISM
AND GEOPOLITICS

7

A Pillar of the Golden Age? European Integration and the *Trente Glorieuses*

ANTONIO VARSORI AND LORENZO MECHI

Introduction

In 1979 the French economist Jean Fourastié, who had been a member of Jean Monnet's 'Commissariat au Plan' and an expert both in the Organisation for European Economic Co-operation (OEEC) and in the European Coal and Steel Community (ECSC), published the volume *Les Trente Glorieuses ou la révolution invisible de 1946 à 1975*.[1] The book analysed the development of the French economy after the Second World War until the aftermath of the oil shock which hit the Western world in late 1973, after the Yom Kippur War. When it was published, Western countries had already launched a number of initiatives to respond to the economic troubles caused by the oil shock. At the same time, they had begun to seek solutions to the monetary problems caused by the collapse of the Bretton Woods system in 1971, with the start of the Group of Seven meetings and the first attempts at monetary coordination among the European Economic Community (EEC) member countries.[2] The late 1970s, however, continued to be characterised by strong instability, fuelled by a second oil-price shock and by marked disagreements between the western European countries and the US administration on the most effective way to tackle global economic problems.[3]

Fourastié's study, which focused on a period of steady economic growth and optimistic views on the capitalist system's future, partly contrasted with

---

1 J. Fourastié, *Les Trente Glorieuses ou la révolution invisible de 1945 au 1975* (Paris, Fayard, 1979). For an important study on the concept of economic growth, see M. Schmelzer, *The Hegemony of Growth: The OECD and the Making of the Economic Growth Paradigm* (Cambridge, Cambridge University Press, 2016).
2 E. Mourlon-Druol, *A Europe Made of Money: The Emergence of the European Monetary System* (Ithaca, NY and London, Cornell University Press, 2012).
3 See, for example, the 'classic' W. C. Biven, *Jimmy Carter's Economy: Policy in an Age of Limits* (Chapel Hill, NC, University of North Carolina Press, 2002).

the widespread pessimism about the fate of capitalism in most Western circles during the 1970s. In 1972, for example, the Club of Rome, a well-known think-tank, had published the so-called Meadows Report on *The Limits to Growth*, which was perceived as a wake-up call about the possible structural collapse of Western capitalism.[4] But, at least since 1968, with the wave of student and worker protests, Western societies and the capitalist system had become the target of harsh criticism (in some cases of a truly revolutionary opposition) by social and political movements that had shaped the mood of different strata of public opinion.[5] In short, during the 1970s, relevant sectors of Western societies looked at the *Trente Glorieuses* as a negative period that would better be forgotten. However, this perception changed radically within a few years, paradoxically at the very time when the start of the globalisation process and the 'neoliberal revolution' reaffirmed the rules of the capitalist economy unchallenged on a world-wide level. Even today not only scholars, but also journalists and opinion-makers regard the period between the immediate post-war years and the early 1970s as a unique phase in western European history, a 'golden age' when most citizens could look to their future with strong optimism as their living conditions were materially improving and they enjoyed growing social protection. Among the countless works that have used the expression 'golden age' for the historical phase under consideration, the most famous is probably Hobsbawm's *Age of Extremes*.[6]

Many scholars of post-war Europe, including economic historians, have argued that European integration, although combined with other factors, played a major role in fostering the economic reconstruction and development of the continent during the *Trente Glorieuses*.[7] Historians of the European Union (EU) have in recent decades mainly focused on the 1970s and 1980s, from the first enlargement of the EEC to the Maastricht Treaty. The previous period was extensively dealt with in the past decades, albeit

4 D. H. Meadows, D. L. Meadows, J. Randers and W. W. Behrens III, *The Limits to Growth* (New York, NY, Universe Books, 1972).

5 R. Vinen, *1968 Radical Protest and Its Enemies* (New York, NY, HarperCollins, 2018).

6 See E. J. Hobsbawm, *Age of Extremes: The Short Twentieth Century, 1914–1991* (London, Abacus, 1995), pp. 257–86.

7 M. Mazower, *Dark Continent: Europe's Twentieth Century* (London, Penguin Books, 1998), pp. 290–331; S. Colarizi, *Novecento d'Europa: L'illusione, l'odio, la speranza, l'incertezza* (Rome and Bari, Laterza, 2015), pp. 357–80; T. Judt, *Postwar: A History of Europe since 1945* (London, Penguin Books, 2005), pp. 302–9. A critical view can be found in J. Gillingham, *European Integration 1950–2003: Superstate or New Market Economy?* (Cambridge, Cambridge University Press, 2003), pp. 34–72. For a fundamental economic analysis, see B. Eichengreen, *The European Economy since 1945: Coordinated Capitalism and Beyond* (Princeton, NJ and Oxford, Princeton University Press, 2008).

mainly through strictly national perspectives or with a traditional 'diplomatic history' approach that paid too little attention to economic and social phenomena, perhaps underestimating the close relationship between these and wider political dynamics.[8] This chapter aims to contribute to filling this gap by trying to highlight the different ways in which European integration actually played a role in fostering the 'golden age' of western Europe. K. K. Patel in his recent work argues as follows: 'So international cooperation did play a significant role in the *trente glorieuses*. But given that the boom began five years before the founding of the ECSC and a whole decade before the Treaties of Rome [...], it is impossible that the EC could have been exclusively responsible.'[9]

The General Characteristics of Western Europe's 'Golden Age'

At the end of the Second World War most western European governments were confronted with almost impossible challenges. Towns and villages were razed to the ground, large parts of the building stock and infrastructure were destroyed, flows of refugees, deportees and war prisoners had to be repatriated, and there was a severe shortage of basic necessities. Although the conditions were less severe than those prevailing in the eastern part of the continent, economic recovery and the reconstruction of a stable society appeared to be a prohibitively difficult task.[10] But the task of the new ruling classes was equally challenging from a strictly political point of view. Although democratic institutions were restored and new constitutions were drafted, the anti-fascist ruling classes needed to offer their citizens new hopes and ideals. Such projects had to represent a radical shift from the democratic systems of the inter-war period, which had shown serious contradictions and weaknesses, especially in the economic and social field.[11] In particular, the largely ineffective responses of many European governments to the economic crisis of the 1930s, and their

---

8 On the historiography of the construction of the EU, see W. Kaiser and A. Varsori (eds.), *European Union History: Themes and Debates* (Basingstoke, Palgrave Macmillan, 2010).

9 K. K. Patel, *Project Europe: A History* (Cambridge, Cambridge University Press, 2020), p. 89.

10 For a description of the European situation at the end of the war, see, for example, Judt, *Postwar*, pp. 13–40.

11 On the reconstruction of democracy in post-war Europe, see the recent contribution by M. Conway, *Western Europe's Democratic Age 1945–1968* (Princeton, NJ, Princeton University Press, 2020).

inability to contain its worst social consequences – above all in terms of unemployment and widespread poverty – had contributed to discrediting those political experiences in the popular imagination. This, during the war, had stimulated a broad debate among the elites on the necessary transformations of liberal democracy. The London government's plan, published in the 1942 Beveridge Report, to build a social security system that would protect every British citizen from similar suffering in the future was one of the most famous fruits of this process, which quickly became central to the political debate in all European countries.[12] It appeared in fact as a potential antidote to the much more radical transformations advocated by the communist left, whose promise to build a brighter and more just future – sometimes summarised in the idea of a 'workers' paradise' – represented a dangerous challenge to the weak European democracies. This was a promise, moreover, whose appeal to the masses had strongly increased during the war, thanks to the prestige gained by the communist parties and the Soviet Union from their preponderant role in the partisan struggle and in the victory against Nazism.[13]

However, this situation of difficulty, uncertainty and potential instability was destined to change rapidly. Within a few years reconstruction and recovery were under way, and by 1951 all western European economies had surpassed pre-war production levels.[14] Then, in the mid 1950s, the entire continent entered a phase of unprecedented growth, which would last, essentially uninterrupted, until the oil-price shock of 1973. To give an idea, between 1950 and 1969 the gross national product of western Europe as a whole grew at an average rate of 4.6 per cent per year, with peaks of 6.2 per cent in West Germany and 5.4 per cent in Italy, breaking all previous records.[15] For the first time in over a century, these rates far exceeded those of the US economy, narrowing the historical gap with the leading country. Such a trend was even more visible for European labour productivity, which in the same period rose from less than half to more than 70 per cent of the American average. After thirty more years, at the beginning of the new century, the gap would be substantially closed.[16] This was also due to a process of modernisation which, to varying degrees, affected industry in all western European countries, and helped to significantly improve its

12 W. Beveridge, *Social Insurance and Allied Services* (London, HMSO, 1942).
13 On the appeal of the communist ideal, see S. Pons, *La rivoluzione globale: Storia del comunismo internazionale 1917–1991* (Turin, Einaudi, 2012), pp. 177–85.
14 Eichengreen, *The European Economy since 1945*, pp. 52–85.
15 D. H. Aldcroft, *The European Economy 1914–2000*, 4th ed. (London, Routledge, 2001), pp. 128–31.
16 Eichengreen, *The European Economy since 1945*, pp. 18–19.

international competitiveness. One of the most striking aspects of the 'golden age' boom was indeed the staggering increase in international trade flows, which grew in the region at an average of more than 8 per cent per year.[17]

A direct consequence of economic growth was the dramatic increase in prosperity that characterised the area between the 1950s and the early 1970s. The acceleration of the trend towards urbanisation and the new great availability of consumer goods were among the most visible aspects of all this, and resulted in the transformation of western European countries into true 'consumer societies' along the model of the United States.[18] As British Prime Minister Harold Macmillan had epitomised in a speech delivered in 1957: 'most of our people have never had it so good'.[19] From this point of view, however, the most distinctive feature of the *Trente Glorieuses* in western Europe was the building of the richest and most pervasive social security mechanisms in history. In Maurizio Ferrera's words:

> The three decades between the end of the Second World War and the mid-1970s are primarily remembered as the 'golden age' of welfare state expansion, characterized by a widening coverage of social insurance, an increasing generosity of transfer payments, and the greater scope and quality of services. At the beginning of the 1950s social security expenditure was still below 10 per cent of GDP in most European countries. By the early 1970s many countries (such as Belgium, Denmark, France, Germany, Italy, the Netherlands, and Sweden) had passed the 20 per cent mark and most of the remaining ones had already surpassed 15 per cent. The vast majority, if not the totality, of the population was included in social protection schemes for all the standard risks: old age, disability, and bereavement; sickness, maternity, and work injuries; unemployment and family dependants.[20]

The strengthening of free education at all levels and the creation of sophisticated national health systems completed the range of social services available to Europeans. Besides, these were no longer provided on the basis of specific political or administrative decisions, but as rights deriving directly from citizenship status.[21]

---

17 N. Crafts and G. Toniolo, '"Les Trente Glorieuses": From the Marshall Plan to the Oil Crisis', in D. Stone (ed.), *The Oxford Handbook of Postwar European History* (Oxford, Oxford University Press, 2012), pp. 356–78.
18 On the social aspects of consumer society, see Judt, *Postwar*, pp. 324–59; Colarizi, *Novecento d'Europa*, pp. 357–74.
19 Hobsbawm, *Age of Extremes*, p. 257.
20 M. Ferrera, *The Boundaries of Welfare: European Integration and the New Spatial Politics of Social Protection* (Oxford, Oxford University Press, 2005), p. 77.
21 Ibid., pp. 73–4.

It is impossible to overestimate the importance of the welfare state in the political dynamics of post-war western Europe, which not surprisingly has been underlined by an endless array of authors. For its role of redistribution and consensus-building, for example, Geoff Eley has identified the welfare state as one of the three 'pillars' of that political season, together with the diffusion of practices of social dialogue (i.e., dialogue and cooperation between business and trade unions) and the unprecedented role of the state in the management of economic policy which characterised all the countries of the region.[22] The German *Mitbestimmung* (co-determination), the French *comités d'entreprise* (works councils) and the collective bargaining bodies set up by the British Labour government were all expressions of the second 'pillar', in partial continuity with the corporatist practices of the inter-war period. They resulted in a widespread containment of social conflict and a relative moderation of trade union demands, which in turn encouraged investment, fostered growth and allowed full employment to be achieved almost everywhere in the region.[23] Barry Eichengreen points out that even in Italy, where the situation was more conflictual and it was not possible to create formal institutions of social dialogue, wage moderation was nevertheless pursued at the government's instigation and through the moderate claims of non-communist trade unions.[24]

The third of the mentioned pillars, that Eley summarises with the term 'Keynesianism', was itself heir to the experiences of the 1930s, now adapted to the aim of consolidating liberal democracies and guaranteeing the new 'social pact'. Making full use of the levers at their disposal – monetary policy, fiscal policy, nationalisation of enterprises and their management – the European governments implemented countercyclical policies, promoted social peace, encouraged productive modernisation, financed the welfare states and actively pursued full employment. In other words, they put all their power behind the new order, contributing to the combination of capitalist prosperity and social reformism that pacified European societies and was the basis for the political stabilisation of the 'golden age'.[25]

While it is true that high levels of growth also occurred in other parts of the world during the *Trente Glorieuses* (such as the planned economies of

22 G. Eley, 'Corporatism and the Social Democratic Moment: The Postwar Settlement, 1945–1973', in Stone (ed.), *The Oxford Handbook*, pp. 37–59.
23 I. T. Berend, *An Economic History of Twentieth Century Europe: Economic Regimes from Laissez-Faire to Globalization* (Cambridge, Cambridge University Press, 2006), pp. 212–15.
24 See Eichengreen, *The European Economy since 1945*, p. 365.
25 Eley, 'Corporatism and the Social Democratic Moment'.

eastern Europe and Japan), and that the trade boom was basically a global phenomenon, in western Europe Keynesianism, the welfare state and 'neo-corporatism' played a peculiar role.[26] It is, therefore, also on these that we are now going to focus our attention, in order to measure the impact of European integration on the great transformations that took place in the 30 years following the end of the Second World War.

The Role of the Marshall Plan

During the war, members of socialist, Catholic and liberal resistance groups in various occupied countries drew up plans aimed at solving the problems that had led to the rise to power of dictatorships and the emergence of nationalist and aggressive foreign policies. Some of these plans, such as the 'Ventotene Manifesto', which were critical of the traditional European nation-state, envisaged the creation of forms of close European political cooperation or integration. This goal was advocated mainly by federalist groups, which focused their attention on the political and institutional aspects.[27] The economic aspects of the future European settlement were, however, at the heart of these projects, most of which explicitly rejected the protectionist policies of the 1930s and envisaged the creation of a European customs union.[28] In fact, the close link between economic growth and social justice was probably the most relevant aspect of the political debate on post-war Europe, as the economic and social crisis of the 1930s was seen as the main factor paving the way for Hitler and the unleashing of his imperialist policy.[29] This is why most of the projects for European unity, federation or integration drawn up during the war had strong reformist traits, often with explicit references to the experiences of Roosevelt's New Deal and to the Beveridge Report.[30]

At the end of the war, however, these plans did not immediately translate into concrete initiatives. On the contrary, the ruling classes in western Europe started the reconstruction on strictly national lines, basing any

---

26 Ibid.
27 See, for example, S. Pistone, *I movimenti per l'unità europea 1945–1954* (Milan, Jaca, 1992). On Altiero Spinelli, see P. Graglia, *Altiero Spinelli* (Bologna, Il Mulino, 2008).
28 W. Lipgens and W. Loth (eds.), *Documents on the History of European Integration*, 4 vols. (Berlin and New York, de Gruyter, 1982–91); M. Dumoulin (ed.), *Wartime Plans for Postwar Europe, 1940–1947* (Brussels, Bruylant, 1995).
29 On the 1930s, see, for example, P. Brendon, *The Dark Valley: A Panorama of the 1930s* (London, Vintage Books, 2000).
30 L. Mechi, *L'Organizzazione Internazionale del Lavoro e la ricostruzione europea: Le basi sociali dell'integrazione economica (1931–1957)* (Rome, Ediesse, 2012).

initiative of international cooperation almost exclusively on traditional bilateral agreements. As is well known, the first concrete stimulus to European integration came from the US administration, with the launch of the Marshall Plan in June 1947. In fact, the drafters of the Marshall Plan considered it crucial to induce their European partners to develop expansionist economic policies, aimed at promoting growth, improving living conditions and thereby undermining the appeal of the communist parties, whose strength in countries like France and Italy in the early phase of the Cold War was seen with great concern. Encouraged by the recent performance of the US economy, they believed that such policies would be more effective if pursued in a context of cooperation and gradual integration of the European economies. The US administration therefore made it a condition for the European countries' access to the Marshall Plan that they undertake to progressively abolish reciprocal trade barriers and to coordinate national economic policies. These goals were pursued within the OEEC and the European Payments Union (EPU), founded in 1948 and 1950, respectively.[31]

Thus, while historiography still disagrees in quantifying the specific contribution of Marshall aid to Europe's economic recovery, it is undeniable that the Marshall Plan played a fundamental role from other points of view.[32] First of all, it ensured that trade liberalisation progressed successfully, resulting in a substantial reduction of non-tariff barriers in most member countries within a few years. Italy, for example, traditionally one of the most protectionist European countries, thanks to the OEEC and EPU mechanisms dismantled more than 99 per cent of those barriers by the early 1950s.[33] Equally important, however, was the cultural role of the Marshall Plan, not only as a carrier of patterns of mass consumption, thus contributing to the 'Americanisation' of the European societies, but even more so as an

---

31 M. Leimgruber and M. Schmelzer (eds.), *The OECD and the International Political Economy since 1948* (London, Palgrave Macmillan, 2017); J. J. Kaplan and G. Schleiminger, *The European Payments Union: Financial Diplomacy in the 1950s* (Oxford, Clarendon Press, 1989).

32 For some well-known contrasting interpretations of the Marshall Plan, see A. S. Milward, *The Reconstruction of Western Europe, 1945–51* (London, Methuen, 1984); A. S. Milward, F. B. M. Lynch, F. Romero, R. Ranieri and V. Sørensen, *The Frontier of National Sovereignty: History and Theory* (London, Routledge, 1993); M. J. Hogan, *The Marshall Plan: America, Britain and the Reconstruction of Western Europe 1947–52* (Cambridge, Cambridge University Press, 1987). For two more recent studies, see F. Fauri and P. Tedeschi (eds.), *New Outlooks on the Marshall Plan: American Aid and European Re-industrialization* (Bern, Peter Lang, 2011); B. Steil, *Marshall Plan: Dawn of the Cold War* (New York, Simon & Schuster, 2018).

33 L. Mechi, *L'Europa di Ugo La Malfa: La via italiana alla modernizzazione 1942–1979* (Milan, Franco Angeli, 2003), pp. 45–78; R. Ventresca, *Prove tecniche d'integrazione: L'Italia, l'Oece e la ricostruzione economica internazionale (1947–1953)* (Milan, Franco Angeli, 2017).

active disseminator of a specific approach to socio-economic matters and industrial relations.[34] In fact, the Marshall Plan was the main vehicle for transmitting to western Europe the orientations that had emerged in the United States during the war, centred on a cooperation between workers and employers aimed at pursuing constant increases in productivity. These orientations – summarised by historiography in the term 'politics of productivity' – fitted perfectly with the political aims of the Marshall Plan, fostering growth and promoting social peace at the same time. For this reason, the European Recovery Programme (ERP), as the Marshall Plan was formally known, was accompanied by countless initiatives aimed at disseminating the basic elements of 'productivism' – social dialogue, the joint pursuit of productive efficiency, relative moderation in trade union demands – in European political, economic and social circles, an action that culminated in 1953 with the creation of the European Productivity Agency, an ad hoc body closely linked to the OEEC.[35]

The contribution of the Marshall Plan to the dissemination of the principles of the politics of productivity in Europe is well established in the literature, even if it was not a uniform process, as it had to deal with the situation in individual European countries, pre-existing practices and the different attitudes of national political and social forces.[36] In France and Italy, for example, the 'productivist' principles clashed with the hostility of the communist trade unions – namely the Confédération Générale du Travail (CGT) and Confederazione Generale Italiana del Lavoro (CGIL), the largest in the two countries – as well as with the most conservative industrial circles, but were enthusiastically supported by the other trade unions and the rest of the business community.[37] As a whole, however, the ERP undoubtedly

34 On the concept of 'Americanisation', see, for example, V. De Grazia, *Irresistible Empire: America's Advance through Twentieth-Century Europe* (New York, NY, The Belknap Press, 2005); D. W. Ellwood, *Una sfida per la modernità: Europa e America nel lungo Novecento* (Rome, Carocci, 2012).

35 C. S. Maier, 'The Politics of Productivity: Foundations of American International Economic Policy after World War II', *International Organization* 31 (1977): 607–33; A. Carew, *Labour under the Marshall Plan: The Politics of Productivity and the Marketing of Management Science* (Manchester, Manchester University Press, 1987); B. Boel, *The European Productivity Agency and Transatlantic Relations, 1953–61* (Copenhagen, Museum Tusculanum Press, 2003).

36 On the various forms of the politics of productivity in different European countries, see D. Barjot (ed.), *Catching Up with America: Productivity Missions and the Diffusion of American Economic and Technological Influence after the Second World War* (Paris, Presses de l'Université de Paris-Sorbonne, 2002).

37 On the attitude of the trade unions, with specific details on the Italian ones, see for example, M. Antonioli, M. Bergamaschi and F. Romero (eds.), *Le scissioni sindacali: Italia e Europa* (Pisa, BFS Edizioni, 1999); A. Ciampani (ed.), *L'altra via per l'Europa: Forze sociali*

contributed to the creation of the basic conditions of the 'golden age', all the more so if one takes into account the three 'pillars' identified by Eley. Social dialogue, as noted above, was in fact a basic component of the ERP's philosophy, while Keynesianism and the construction of welfare states were perfectly suited to its political aims, and fully in tune with the New Deal tradition that inspired it. More importantly, however, the 'productivist' principles had a profound influence on the bodies for European economic cooperation that were set up in the following years, especially those with the most incisive powers, which would rapidly gain a central position in the integration process and would then become major vectors of the same guidelines: the ECSC and, a few years later, the EEC.

The European Communities as Major Components of the 'Golden Age'

Similar considerations to those just made for the Marshall Plan apply to the two communities and their role in the overall framework of the *Trente Glorieuses*. Indeed, economic historiography has attempted to quantify the impact of the EEC and the European common market (much less that of the ECSC, given its limited sectoral character) on economic growth in those years, again with mixed results. According to the most generous estimates, however, the contribution of the European common market during the 1960s amounted to a remarkable 1 per cent per annum, as seems to be demonstrated by the higher average growth of the six member countries compared with the rest of the region. Even more relevant seems to have been its contribution to the development of intra-European trade, not only within the EEC but also between countries outside it, thanks to the trade liberalisation initiatives taken in reaction to the launch of the common market itself, such as the European Free Trade Association.[38]

At least as important, however, was the role played by both the ECSC and the EEC in encouraging some of the policies, approaches and practices that were later identified among the most typical features of the 'golden age', starting with the three 'pillars' highlighted by Eley: Keynesianism, the welfare state and social dialogue.

e organizzazione degli interessi nell'integrazione europea (1947–1957) (Milan, Franco Angeli, 1995). On the Italian industrial circles, see F. Petrini, *Il liberalismo a una dimensione: La Confindustria e l'integrazione europea 1947–1957* (Milan, Franco Angeli, 2005).

38 Crafts and Toniolo, 'Les Trente Glorieuses'.

The two communities, both of which were focused on the construction of a common market, were characterised by a liberal economic approach, which in the case of the EEC was made particularly evident by its rigid rules on competition.[39] However, neither of the two founding treaties had any elements that conflicted with the Keynesian policies pursued by the European governments at the time. In line with their 'productivist' approach, the treaties merely indicated the pursuit of efficiency and economic growth as the main tasks of the communities, which would automatically guarantee the gradual improvement of living conditions in the member countries.[40] Indeed, the literature has abundantly shown how the liberal stance of the Communities and the 'interventionist' practices of national governments worked in perfect synergy from the outset, with the common market generating growth and thus providing resources to fuel investments, pursue full employment and build the welfare states. A mechanism summed up by Robert Gilpin in his famous definition 'Smith abroad, Keynes at home'.[41]

It has just been said that the second of the three pillars of the 'golden age' identified by Eley – the development of national welfare systems – also benefited from the dynamics triggered by the common market, profiting directly from the growth it generated. It should be added that the relationship between the welfare state and economic integration was the subject of a specific debate, which affected relations between western European countries at least since the early 1950s and was concluded with the signing of the EEC Treaty in 1957. With the prospect of ever closer integration between European economies, the presence of complex and heterogeneous mechanisms of social security in the different countries raised fears in various groups of a potential competitive disadvantage. The French government in particular, prompted by a heated domestic debate, emphasised in all international fora that the disparities between the national 'social costs' were a serious obstacle to integration. Failing to achieve concrete results, Paris decided to intensify its action during the negotiations on the Rome treaties, making French participation in the EEC conditional on a formal commitment by all member countries to harmonise national social policies in order to equalise their costs. The dispute was settled only in the final weeks of the negotiations,

39 K. K. Patel and H. Schweitzer (eds.), *The Historical Foundations of EU Competition Law* (Oxford, Oxford University Press, 2013).
40 Treaty Establishing the European Coal and Steel Community (1951), preamble and Articles 2–3; Treaty Establishing the European Economic Community (1957), preamble and Article 2.
41 R. Gilpin, *The Political Economy of International Relations* (Princeton, NJ, Princeton University Press, 1987), p. 355.

when resistance from the other delegations persuaded the French representatives to give in and agree to include in the EEC Treaty only a general commitment to equal pay for men and women (which, moreover, remained largely ineffective for many years).[42] Particularly interesting, however, are the theoretical arguments used to oppose the French proposal, which found their clearest synthesis in the report *Social Aspects of European Economic Co-operation*, which was drawn up in the spring of 1956 by a group of renowned experts chaired by the Swedish liberal economist Bertil Ohlin. The 'Ohlin Report' flatly denied the need to harmonise social policies prior to the launch of the common market, as it would interfere with the delicate political, economic and social balances of each nation. On the contrary, the report argued that the opposite logic applied, whereby the virtuous circle triggered by economic integration would generate resources to enable broad advances in social standards. This mechanism, moreover, was expected to bring the greatest benefits to the poorest countries with the highest growth margins, promoting social harmonisation in this way, rather than by a political decision.[43] This was exactly the approach that was eventually included in the EEC Treaty, which explicitly identified the common market as the main driver for a progressive 'upward harmonisation' (the expression is a translation from the original French text of the treaty) of national social systems and living conditions.[44] In the words of Alan Milward, the common market would work as an 'external buttress to the welfare state'.[45]

Even more visible, however, was the support of the two Communities for the third 'pillar' of the 'golden age': the dialogue between the social partners and their involvement in decision-making processes. In fact, the two treaties set up bodies specifically dedicated to this purpose – the ECSC Consultative Committee and the Economic and Social Committee within the EEC – in which employers and trade unions were represented on an equal footing.[46] In the case of the ECSC, then, after the signing of the treaty the governments

42 L. R. Svartvatn, 'In Quest of Time, Protection and Approval: France and the Claims for Social Harmonization in the European Economic Community, 1955–56', *Journal of European Integration History* 8, no. 1 (2002): 85–102; L. Mechi, 'A Precondition for Economic Integration? European Debates on Social Harmonisation in the 1950s and 1960s', in L. Coppolaro and L. Mechi (eds.), *Free Trade and Social Welfare in Europe: Explorations in the Long 20th Century* (London, Routledge, 2020), pp. 71–89.
43 International Labour Organisation, *Social Aspects of European Economic Co-operation: Report by a Group of Experts* (Geneva, International Labour Organisation, 1956); Mechi, *L'Organizzazione Internazionale del Lavoro*, pp. 181–91.
44 Treaty Establishing the European Economic Community, Article 117.
45 A. S. Milward, *The European Rescue of the Nation-State* (London, Routledge, 2000), p. 216.
46 A. Varsori (ed.), *Il Comitato Economico e Sociale nella costruzione europea* (Venice, Marsilio, 2000).

decided to let the employers' and trade union organisations nominate each one of the nine members of the High Authority, the central executive body of that community. In the first composition of the body, a series of events led to the appointment of two trade unionists: Heinz Potthoff, a member of the German trade union federation (Deutscher Gewerkschaftsbund), and Paul Finet, former secretary-general of the Belgian Federation of Labour and then president of the International Confederation of Free Trade Unions.[47] This practice was not replicated in the EEC framework, where the social partners were nevertheless consulted regularly and sometimes involved in the management committees of some community policies, although usually in an exclusively consultative role.[48]

Although such practices, as mentioned above, were already widespread in the individual national contexts, sometimes in far more incisive forms and with far greater powers, their introduction in the framework of the communities helped to consolidate them further. This is also because in that context they accompanied other policies and initiatives that affected directly sensitive issues for the social partners, especially the trade unions. Other features of the 'productivist' approach of the two treaties, in fact, induced workers' organisations to look with interest at any form of involvement in the institutional life of the communities. The fact that the ECSC and EEC had the power to influence fundamental aspects of economic policy, with potential effects on employment, wages and working conditions, was in itself sufficient to alert the trade unions. This was evident from the very beginning of the negotiations on the Schuman Plan in 1950, when most of the unions of the participating countries (except for those of communist orientation, which were hostile to the project) demanded to be involved in the negotiations and that social norms be included in the future ECSC Treaty. The decision to create the Consultative Committee also arose from pressures of this kind, as well as from the need to secure the support of non-communist trade unions for the ERP, which was seen as essential in the most acute phase of the Cold War.[49]

---

47 D. Spierenburg and R. Poidevin, *The History of the High Authority of the European Coal and Steel Community: Supranationality in Operation* (London, Weidenfeld and Nicolson, 1994), pp. 50–5; M. Carbonell, *Des hommes à l'origine de l'Europe: Biographies des membres de la Haute Autorité de la CECA* (Aix-en-Provence, Publications de l'Université de Provence, 2008).
48 See, for example, yearly issues of EEC Commission, *General Report on the Activities of the Community* (Brussels, European Economic Community, 1958–66).
49 Spierenburg and Poidevin, *The History of the High Authority*, p. 46.

Similar reasons led to the creation of a fund to help the adaptation of workers who would lose their jobs due to the opening of the coal and steel common market. The fear, expressed during the negotiations by the French and Belgian governments, was that the end of protections from foreign competitors could create serious problems for the weakest producers, forcing them to reduce their workforce and thus creating new unemployment. The need to alleviate such situations, which would inevitably strengthen the communist opposition in the worst affected areas, led to the creation of the ECSC re-adaptation fund. The latter's task was to finance the retraining and possible transfer of workers who had lost their jobs as a result of the above-mentioned dynamics, thus facilitating their reintegration into the labour market. The fund soon proved to be a very effective instrument, and ended up being widely applied to the employment difficulties arising from the crisis of the coal sector, which entered its peak phase at the end of the 1950s. By 1967, 350,000 workers had benefited from its resources, in operations that, in the high economic cycle of those years, often enabled the rapid re-employment of the workforce concerned.[50] In the meantime, a new tool had been created within the EEC framework, this time under pressure from the Italian government, which during the negotiations had called for the creation of a fund to contribute to the development of the Mezzogiorno, with particular emphasis on fighting unemployment. The European Social Fund, which was in operation since 1960, had very similar features to the ECSC fund, aiming to promote employment by supporting geographical and professional mobility of labour. In its first decade, however, an inadequate budget made its action far less incisive than that of its predecessor, a situation that improved only in the 1970s after the reform of its mechanisms and a substantial increase in its resources.[51]

Another element of social relevance that the two treaties had in common was the establishment of free movement of labour throughout the territory of the member states. Although the liberalisation of the 'labour factor' was a natural component of the common market, in both negotiations it was fiercely debated, and in the end its rules were much more a product of the

50 L. Mechi, 'Le politiche sociali della CECA', in R. Ranieri and L. Tosi (eds.), *La Comunità Europea del Carbone e dell'Acciaio (1952–2002): Gli esiti del trattato in Europa e in Italia* (Padua, Cedam, 2004), pp. 105–26; European Commission, *First General Report on the Activities of the Communities* (Brussels and Luxembourg, European Commission, 1968), pp. 246–7.
51 L. Mechi, 'Les états membres, les institutions et les débuts du Fond Social Européen', in A. Varsori (ed.), *Inside the European Community: Actors and Policies in the European Integration (1957–1972)* (Baden-Baden, Nomos, 2006), pp. 95–116.

balance of power between the governments involved than of abstract theoretical principles. The fact that it was initially supported only by the Italian government, anxious to open the European labour markets to its surplus of unskilled workforce (especially from the 'Mezzogiorno'), explains the extremely restrictive mechanisms by which it was applied under the ECSC, where it had no significant impact. The need for labour that characterised the West German economy from the mid 1950s, on the eve of its *Wirtschaftswunder* (economic miracle), led instead to the inclusion of much broader rules in the EEC Treaty, which were gradually implemented in the following years, in a process that was completed in 1968 together with the official opening of the common market.[52] At the same time, new instruments were created to guarantee the social rights of migrant workers, an issue traditionally regulated by bilateral agreements, but regarding which the trade unions and the governments of the emigration countries (including Italy, of course) had always called for the adoption of an international instrument. Two EEC regulations, enacted in 1958 and 1971, allowed migrants to combine social security rights acquired in different member states, thus settling a decades-old issue through a permanent legal guarantee.[53]

Despite their limitations, the rules on the two funds and on free circulation addressed complex social problems with solutions that, at the same time, aimed at fostering general economic efficiency, by promoting labour mobility and its optimal allocation in the production system. This approach, as we have seen, stemmed from the 'productivist' inspiration of the two communities, and also inspired many of their other initiatives in the 1950s and 1960s, aimed, for example, at developing vocational training, improving safety at work or, only in the framework of the ECSC, supporting social housing.[54] All this could not fail to attract the interest of the social partners, which were regularly involved in the management of these policies through the

---

52 E. Comte, *The History of the European Migration Regime: Germany's Strategic Hegemony* (London, Routledge, 2018). On Italy's position during the 'European relaunch', see A. Varsori, *La Cenerentola d'Europa? L'Italia e l'integrazione europea dal 1947 a oggi* (Soveria Mannelli, Rubbettino, 2010), pp. 119–58. See also the important records in Ministero degli Affari Esteri e della Cooperazione Internazionale, *Documenti sulla politica internazionale dell'Italia, Serie A: Europa occidentale e Unione Europea, il 'rilancio dell'Europa' dalla Conferenza di Messina ai Trattati di Roma* (Rome, Istituto Poligrafico e Zecca della Stato, 2017).

53 S. A. W. Goedings, *Labor Migration in an Integrating Europe: National Migration Policies and the Free Movement of Workers, 1950–1968* (The Hague, SDU Uitgevers, 2005); F. Romero, *Emigrazione e integrazione europea (1945–1973)* (Rome, Edizioni Lavoro, 1991), pp. 102–11.

54 R. Leboutte, *Histoire économique et sociale de l'intégration européenne* (Brussels, Peter Lang, 2008), pp. 619–48.

establishment of special committees, practices of consultation or, in the case of the funds, their direct involvement in individual operations. Regardless of their varying effectiveness, on the whole these policies strengthened the 'loyalty' of the social forces – but most particularly the trade unions, the main stakeholders in those issues – to the communities. By consolidating their inclusion in a structurally non-conflictual and dialogue-driven institutional context, they thus made a further contribution to the social and political stabilisation of the 'golden age'. The most visible demonstration of all this was probably the political trajectory of the communist CGIL, Italy's major trade union.

In line with the other forces in its camp, the CGIL had taken a strongly hostile attitude towards the Marshall Plan and the ECSC. This began to be reconsidered with the birth of the EEC, in the belief that the potential impact of the common market on labour would require the coordination of all the trade unions of the community. Throughout the 1960s the CGIL constantly pursued this goal, even opening a representation office in Brussels (shared for a few years with its French sister organisation, the CGT), and repeatedly asking to be admitted to the Community's various tripartite bodies, from which, like the other communist forces, it had regularly been excluded. This path, which would lead in 1974 to its accession – as the only communist union – to the newly created European Trade Union Confederation, went hand in hand with attempts at promoting unity of action at a domestic level with the other two major Italian unions, the Confederazione Italiana Sindacati Lavoratori and the Unione Italiana del Lavoro. It is true that the motivations for the 'unità sindacale' (trade union unity) were mainly in the internal political and social balances, and that this project had its climax only in the early 1970s, fuelled by the great mobilisation of 1968–9. It is clear, however, that the European dimension, whose characteristics had attracted the attention of the CGIL since the mid 1950s, represented an important ground for discussion and dialogue, and therefore also played a role in paving the way to that process.[55]

Finally, it is worth mentioning one last aspect. While the 'golden age' was characterised by a great boom in industry, mass consumption and urbanisation, it also further accelerated the decline of the rural world. The exodus from the countryside, which started with the second industrial revolution at the end of the nineteenth century, had always worried the conservative

55 I. Del Biondo, *L'Europa Possibile. La CGT e la CGIL di Fronte al Processo d'Integrazione Europea (1957–1973)* (Rome, Ediesse, 2007).

ruling classes, who feared the erosion of their traditional electoral bases and the growth of those of the left due to the expansion of industrial labour. For this reason, policies to support the rural world had been implemented in many European countries, but they proved insufficient to respond to the acceleration of these processes after the Second World War. The Common Agricultural Policy (CAP) introduced by the EEC Treaty was a response to these fears, as the 1958 Stresa Conference made clear, when the agriculture ministers of the Six officially agreed on the objectives of safeguarding the agricultural sector by offering farmers higher incomes and better living conditions. Although in the following years the Common Market further strengthened industrial growth and the trend towards urbanization, the CAP helped to mitigate some of the most feared effects of the latter on rural areas. In France, for example, from 1954 to 1968 the rural population decreased from 44 to 33.8 per cent of the total.[56] With its generous support to farmers' incomes, in fact, it acted as a sort of European welfare mechanism, reassuring the most conservative political circles – the most known example is probably that of French President Charles de Gaulle's party – and making the transformations of the 'golden age' more acceptable to them as well.[57]

In this way, too, the EEC and its mechanisms made an important contribution to the general stability that characterised the whole period under consideration.

Conclusion

A well-known Italian poster on the signing of the Rome Treaties showed six young ladies, their skirts with the colours of the six national flags, hand in hand. In the background there was a map of the six member states without frontiers and a slogan that stressed the relevance of the 'European union' for social and economic progress and peace. It is difficult to say to what extent the peoples of the member countries shared these expectations about the effects of the common market, but it is certain that the manifesto perfectly symbolised the optimism about the future that characterised most western European societies at the end of the 1950s, as well as the hope in the two communities held by some of the ruling classes of the Six. The EEC in fact

---

56 S. Berstein, *La France de l'expansion, vol. 1: La République gaullienne, 1958–1969* (Paris, Éditions du Seuil, 1989), p. 186.

57 On the CAP, see K. K. Patel (ed.), *Fertile Ground for Europe? The History of European Integration and the Common Agricultural Policy since 1945* (Baden-Baden, Nomos, 2009); A.-C. L. Knudsen, *Farmers on Welfare: The Making of Europe's Common Agricultural Policy* (Ithaca, NY and London, Cornell University Press, 2009). Both works point out the political and social implications of the CAP.

fitted perfectly into a path of economic integration of western Europe which had started with the Marshall Plan, was already helping to generate growth and spread prosperity, and would continue to do so until the early 1970s. This chapter has shown how this contribution came partly in the economic sphere, which the liberalisations of the early 1950s and the common market helped to nurture, and partly in cultural and societal aspects relating to domestic policies, the construction of welfare states and a socio-economic approach based on class cooperation and the common pursuit of efficiency. This was a culture coming from the US experience, which was then fully embraced by the bodies of European cooperation.

The *Trente Glorieuses* ended with the energy and monetary shocks of the early 1970s, which undermined the conditions on which they were based. But their foundations had already been challenged by the students' and workers' protests of 1968, which were at least in part aimed precisely at the situation established during the 'golden age'. The rejection of American patterns of consumption, the demand for greater freedom in schools and universities, and the emergence of 'youth' as a new social category with its own ambitions and expectations were all offspring of the abundance of the previous decades and the resulting mass schooling. The same can be said for the demands coming from labour, which were the result of a situation of full employment that had given unusual strength to the workers' request for greater democracy in the factories or for effective gender equality in the employment relationship.

In many respects, in short, the 'golden age' generated its own crisis. And European integration, which had been one of its key components, also played a central role in the search for answers to the new political, economic and social challenges. This was the primary aim of the new 'European relaunch' started by the Hague summit conference of December 1969, when the leaders of the Six worked out a long-term ambitious strategy.[58] In the economic field the most important projects dealt with the creation of a common European budget aimed at stabilising the CAP, and the setting up of a monetary system (the 'snake'), which was doomed to failure but would be the reference for the more successful European Monetary System of the late 1970s. However, the new European relaunch was not limited to the economic and monetary dimensions, as the European leaders were conscious of the changing

---

58 M. E. Guasconi, *L'Europa tra continuità e cambiamento: Il vertice dell'Aja del 1969 e il rilancio della costruzione europea* (Florence, Polistampa, 2004); J. van der Harst (ed.), *Beyond the Customs Union: The European Community's Quest for Deepening, Widening and Completion, 1969–1975* (Baden-Baden, Nomos, 2007).

mentality that was shaping large sectors of their public opinions. Most decisions were taken at a national level also due to a shift to the left in some member states – the most significant case was West Germany, where the Sozialdemokratische Partei Deutschlands came to power in 1969 and maintained control of the chancellorship until the early 1980s. But some initiatives were launched as new European policies, which became part of the new agenda established in The Hague and aimed at 'deepening' the integration process. It is worth mentioning, for example, the launch of new policies in the social, regional and environmental fields, all as a direct reaction to the emergence of the new sensitivities mentioned above.[59] In a vague attempt to counter criticism of Western consumer societies, initiatives for dialogue between the European Community and the European youth were also discussed, although effective policies in this area would not be realised until many years later.[60]

The changes of the 1970s, however, paved the way for a debate on the future of European and Western capitalism that would soon lead to the affirmation of new orientations and balances.[61] In fact, if at the end of the 1970s the *Trente Glorieuses* were definitely over, within a few years the neoliberal revolution and the first globalisation would pave the way for a renewed confidence in the potential of Western economies. The new situation, however, characterised by stronger competition in a global free market, would be based on a much less inclusive and dialogue-focused approach than in the past, and would soon begin to erode the welfare state, a trend in which the European institutions would also be progressively involved. In short, the fruits of the new growth would be reaped only by those who were able to adapt to a rapidly changing society and a more volatile and risky economy.

---

59 A. Varsori, 'Alle origini di un modello sociale europeo: La Comunità europea e la nascita di una politica sociale (1969–1974)', *Ventunesimo Secolo* 5, no. 9 (2006): 17–47; A. Varsori, 'European Regional Policy: The Foundations of Solidarity', in M. Dumoulin (ed.), *The European Commission 1958–72: History and Memories* (Luxembourg, Office for Official Publications of the European Communities, 2007), pp. 411–26; L. Scichilone, *L'Europa e la sfida ecologica: Storia della politica ambientale europea (1969–1998)* (Bologna, Il Mulino, 2008).

60 S. Paoli, 'La nascita di una dimensione educativa comunitaria tra interessi nazionali e istanze di movimento (1969–1976)', in A. Varsori (ed.), *Alle origini del presente: L'Europa occidentale nella crisi degli anni Settanta* (Milan, Franco Angeli, 2007), pp. 221–50.

61 L. Warlouzet, *Governing Europe in a Globalizing World: Neoliberalism and Its Alternatives Following the 1973 Oil Crisis* (London, Routledge, 2019); M. Gehler and W. Loth (eds.), *Reshaping Europe: Towards a Political, Economic and Monetary Union, 1984–1989* (Baden-Baden, Nomos, 2020).

Recommended Reading

Eichengreen, B. *The European Economy since 1945: Coordinated Capitalism and Beyond* (Princeton, NJ and Oxford, Princeton University Press, 2008).

Ferrera, M. *The Boundaries of Welfare: European Integration and the New Spatial Politics of Social Protection* (Oxford, Oxford University Press, 2005).

Milward, A. S. *The European Rescue of the Nation-State* (London, Routledge, 2000).

Stone, D. (ed.). *The Oxford Handbook of Postwar European History* (Oxford, Oxford University Press, 2012).

Varsori, A. 'European Regional Policy: The Foundations of Solidarity', in M. Dumoulin (ed.), *The European Commission 1958–72: History and Memories* (Luxembourg, Office for Official Publications of the European Communities, 2007), pp. 411–26.

Varsori, A. 'The Emergence of a Social Europe', in M. Dumoulin (ed.), *The European Commission 1958–72: History and Memories* (Luxembourg, Office for Official Publications of the European Communities, 2007), pp. 427–41.

Varsori, A. and L. Mechi. 'At the Origins of the European Structural Policy: The Community's Social and Regional Policies from the late 1960s to the mid-1970s', in J. van der Harst (ed.), *Beyond the Customs Union: The European Community's Quest for Deepening, Widening and Completion, 1969–1975* (Baden-Baden, Nomos, 2007), pp. 223–50.

8

The End of Bretton Woods: Origins and European Consequences

MARTIN DAUNTON

In July 1944, delegations from forty-five nations gathered at the Mount Washington Hotel in Bretton Woods to devise a monetary regime for the post-war world that aimed to replace the currency warfare of the 1930s and to provide a firm basis for the restoration of a multilateral world economy. Between 1971 and 1973, this system fell apart – and during the fruitless attempts at reform, the European Economic Community (EEC) took initial steps to move from the customs union and Common Agricultural Policy (CAP) to monetary union. This shift in priorities is usually explained as an internal European process,[1] but this chapter indicates that it needs to be understood within a wider context of the design flaws of the Bretton Woods system, failed reform by the International Monetary Fund (IMF) and growing European criticism of the American response.

The existing literature on the Bretton Woods system interprets its evolution and dissolution through four interconnected heuristics. The first interpretative framework rests on a choice in a 'trilemma' or 'impossible trinity' – that is, the need to decide on two out of three possibilities. A choice had to be made between fixed or floating exchange rates, free or controlled capital exports and a passive or active domestic monetary policy.[2] Before 1914, fixed rates on the gold standard, with free international financial movements, removed the possibility of an active domestic monetary policy. If interest rates were raised or lowered to influence the domestic economy, funds would move in and out of the country, which would put the exchange rate under pressure and so impose tight constraints. On the other hand, if

---

1 See, for example, E. Mourlon-Druol, *A Europe Made of Money: The Emergence of the European Monetary System* (Ithaca, NY and London, Cornell University Press, 2012).

2 M. Obstfeld and A. M. Taylor, *Global Capital Markets: Integration, Crisis and Growth* (Cambridge, Cambridge University Press, 2004), pp. 29–33.

exchange rates were set by the market, an active domestic monetary policy could be combined with financial flows. A middle ground was adopted at Bretton Woods. The shift to floating in the 1930s was widely interpreted as leading to currency warfare and economic nationalism that disrupted trade and economic relationships. The dominant view at Bretton Woods was that rigidly fixed rates on the gold standard prevented autonomous domestic economic policies, so the solution was a regime of fixed rates with an element of flexibility. The dollar was pegged to gold at $35 an ounce and other currencies were linked to the dollar, with fluctuation around par of plus or minus 1 per cent, and a right to devalue if the balance of payments was in 'fundamental disequilibrium'. Countries could also impose controls on the international financial movements so that national governments could use interest rates to stimulate the economy or contain inflationary pressure. This 'embedded liberalism' combined restoration of the global economy with space for national policies.[3]

This choice is associated with a second trilemma: a choice between deepening economic globalisation, national determination and greater democracy. The Bretton Woods agreement rested on the ability of the nation-state to pursue its own policies with democratic oversight; the pursuit of globalisation was subordinated to the needs of domestic welfare. It was a 'shallow multilateralism' that allowed policy makers to focus on domestic welfare and permit a restoration of global trade. There was a social contract between capital and labour in which workers agreed to wage moderation and industrialists agreed to invest profits in higher productivity, underwritten by state provision of welfare and tax incentives for investment. This trade-off was undermined from the late 1960s and early 1970s with the onset of slower growth, unemployment and inflation – above all in the United States, which was the linchpin of the system. The ensuing crisis led to deep divisions within and between countries over the approach to be adopted – whether a stress on globalisation and free markets at the expense of domestic welfare, or a continued concern for national growth and employment.[4]

This raises a third interpretative framework: does a stable monetary regime require a hegemonic power? Charles Kindleberger argued that

3 J. G. Ruggie, 'International Regimes, Transactions and Change: Embedded Liberalism in the Postwar Economic Order', *International Organization* 36, no. 2 (1982): 379–415.
4 D. Rodrik, *The Globalization Paradox: Why Global Markets, States and Democracy Can't Coexist* (Oxford, Oxford University Press, 2011), pp. xvi–xix; C. S. Maier, 'The Politics of Productivity: Foundations of American International Economic Policy after World War II', *International Organization* 31, no. 4 (1977): 607–33.

Britain was hegemonic before 1914, which led to stability; the lack of a hegemon between the wars led to instability that was overcome after 1945 when the United States dominated – and instability re-emerged as its economic power was eroded, and the rising economic powers of Europe and Japan failed to respond.[5] The weakness of this interpretation is that the postwar order was not entirely as the Americans intended. They assumed that the new regime would emerge after a short transitional period, but in reality a longer period of reconstruction and recovery was needed before convertibility on current account was restored in Europe in 1958. Paradoxically, the dominance of the American economy after 1945 led to a serious weakness. The war-damaged economies of Europe needed American goods but lacked export capacity, so that any available dollars went to the United States and created a liquidity shortage or 'dollar gap' in the world economy. The United States did not expect to play a direct role in post-war Europe; it was European governments that invited them to take a major part, and in the process reshaped American plans for a liberal multilateral order into support for welfare states. The United States was 'drawn into a more direct role in Europe, defending a system that the Europeans themselves effectively redefined'.[6] A major element in solving the dollar gap was the European Payments Union of 1950: member states no longer needed to settle trade balances bilaterally and settled the outstanding net balance between all the members.[7] Implementation of the Bretton Woods system therefore involved initial steps towards European monetary cooperation rather than, as the Bretton Woods agreement assumed, a swift return to freely convertible currencies. When convertibility was restored, serious issue emerged: the dollar was hegemonic, but the American economy was weaker, which led to serious problems.

Finally, these interpretations can be combined in a cycle that explains the rise and fall of international monetary regimes. Eric Helleiner points to an initial legitimacy crisis (the collapse of the gold standard in the Great Depression); a period of formulation of new ideas in the 1930s; and their crystallisation into new institutions at Bretton Woods, followed by a period of implementation up to convertibility in 1958. A new crisis of legitimacy followed as strains appeared in the Bretton Woods regime, culminating in the

---

5 C. Kindleberger, *The World in Depression, 1829–1939* (London, Allen Lane, 1973).
6 G. J. Ikenberry, 'Rethinking the Origins of American Hegemony', *Political Science Quarterly* 104, no. 3 (1988): 375–400, 376.
7 J. J. Kaplan and G. Schleiminger, *The European Payments Union: Financial Diplomacy in the 1950s* (Oxford, Oxford University Press, 1989).

crisis of 1971–3 and the formulation of new ideas. The crisis involved a redefinition of trade-offs in both trilemmas. The crucial questions were whether there should be a move from pegged to floating exchange rates with liberalisation of capital flows; and whether greater weight should be given to globalisation in assessing national policy choices. It also entailed reassessment of the role of the United States and the dollar in the international currency regime.[8]

These interpretative frameworks provide the context for understanding the impact of the demise of the Bretton Woods system on European monetary integration, which cannot be explained through an internal, teleological process.

The Flaws of Bretton Woods

The Bretton Woods system faced problems as soon as implementation was completed. The emphasis was on fixity rather than flexibility, for changes in exchange rates were seen as evidence of failure. Consequently, rates were often out of line with economic fundamentals, which led to speculative flows of money and, eventually, a large adjustment in a state of crisis. The Bretton Woods system was also asymmetrical. Surplus countries such as West Germany had no obligation to revalue and were reluctant to harm export competitiveness. As confidence in weaker currencies declined, funds moved into the Deutsche Mark, whose rate was expected to appreciate. Central bankers and finance ministries with weak currencies engaged in desperate efforts to prop them up; and those with strong currencies tried to stem the inflow of funds that threatened inflation and revaluation. Rather than creating stability, the Bretton Woods system led to speculative pressures, misalignment between currencies and sudden, large changes of rates.[9]

The system's dependence on the dollar created further problems. In the 1960s, the 'dollar gap' was replaced by a 'dollar glut' as the United States lost its international competitiveness and paid for troops in Europe and war in Vietnam. The hegemony of the dollar was a source of difficulties. The American government could not devalue just by changing the dollar price of gold, for other currencies were fixed to the dollar and not to gold. Further, the dollar glut provided liquidity for an expanding world economy. Robert

8 E. Helleiner, 'A Bretton Woods Moment? The 2007–2008 Crisis and the Future of Global Governance', *International Affairs* 86, no. 3 (2010): 619–36.

9 H. James, *International Monetary Cooperation since Bretton Woods* (Oxford, Oxford University Press, 1996).

Triffin – a Belgian economist based in Yale – pointed out that the United States deficits fostered the liberalisation of exchanges and trade. The 'Triffin dilemma' was that liquidity relied on the weakness of the American economy, which could undermine confidence in the dollar on which the entire system relied.[10] The response to this dilemma led to mutual recriminations across the Atlantic, and to debates over European monetary integration.

Seeking Solutions

A solution favoured in Washington and London was to create a new form of international money issued by the IMF to supplement or replace gold – the special drawing rights (SDRs). The French disliked reliance on supranational, artificial money and urged the simple expedient of doubling the price of gold. The French obsession with gold was a source of bemusement to other governments, who argued that doubling the price of gold was not a solution. It would be an abrupt 'one-shot increase' that would create a sudden, inflationary rise in the money supply rather than a steady, long-run provision of liquidity. It would do nothing to remove imbalances by reducing the American deficit or the German surplus by realigning exchange rates. The distributional consequences would also be unfortunate, for countries holding dollars would lose; the beneficiaries would be gold producers (above all South Africa and the Soviet Union) whose policies were not compatible with civil rights in the United States or security abroad – and countries that held large gold reserves (above all France). When SDRs were eventually agreed by the IMF in 1967, they made only a trivial contribution to liquidity, in part because of French resistance. The French approach to international monetary reform created tensions within Europe with governments that were more willing to work with the IMF and to cooperate with the United States.

Above all, the French feared that reliance on the dollar could be exploited by the United States for its ends. In 1961, the French economist Jacques Rueff complained that the Americans had found the 'marvellous secret of a deficit without tears', and that the discipline of the gold standard was needed to restore price stability in support of free markets and enterprise. The plea was taken up by President Charles de Gaulle in 1965 with a different motivation: preservation of national sovereignty and hostility to American global power. Gold had a 'nature that does not change' and provided the 'unquestionable

---

10 R. Triffin, *Gold and the Dollar Crisis: The Future of Convertibility* (New Haven, CT, Yale University Press, 1960).

monetary basis which does not bear the mark of any individual country'. He accused Washington of using 'seigniorage' – the ability to issue dollars that formed the basis of the world monetary system. The United States could cover its balance of payments deficit and had less need to take corrective action or to worry about the loss of foreign exchange reserves. In his opinion, the Bretton Woods system was 'abusive and dangerous', leading to an 'exorbitant privilege' for the dollar that funded 'greenback imperialism'.[11]

Although the government of West Germany was more Atlanticist and wished to work with Washington, it was concerned that the Americans were exporting inflation through monetary expansion. Otmar Emminger, a member of the board of the Bundesbank, worried that 'Cost and price developments in the US economy, the world's largest producer and consumer, determine largely whether the world economy, in the longer run, moves in the direction of inflation, deflation or stability.' Any instability in the United States would have serious consequences for other countries, and 'pinning the European currencies to the Dollar through a fixed par value means pinning it to an anchor which may itself be carried off by a high tide of inflation'.[12] The riposte in Washington was that over-reliance on the dollar reflected the failure of Europeans to 'carry some of the burden of the currency' or to pay for their defence.[13] National self-interest was in tension with internationalism.

Tensions also arose as financial flows returned and challenged the choice made in 1944 of fixed rates with capital controls. The growing interdependence of markets, as trade recovered, economies grew and multinational corporations expanded, put pressure on capital controls that were a backstop of the Bretton Woods regime. Although many countries retained exchange controls on capital account after 1958, it was difficult to prevent 'leakages' through Hong Kong and other centres with a free market in foreign currencies, or through capital movements disguised as current account transactions. When the Kennedy and Johnson administrations attempted to reduce the American balance of payments deficit by controlling financial outflows, the result was to stimulate the 'Eurodollar market'. American corporations held foreign earnings of dollars outside the United

11 C. S. Chivvis, 'Charles de Gaulle, Jacques Rueff and French International Monetary Policy under Bretton Woods', *Journal of Contemporary History* 41, no. 4 (2006): 701–20.
12 LBJ Library, Bator papers, Box 9, 'The Dollar as Seen from Europe: Talk Delivered by Otmar Emminger, New York, 7 October 1965'.
13 JFK Library, George W. Ball papers, Box 1, telecon, Walter Lippmann-Ball, 22 September 1962, 9.25 am.

States, above all in London, which allowed large quantities of dollars to move quickly in response to interest rate differentials and speculative pressures – above all, into West Germany in the expectation that the dollar might devalue and the Deutsche Mark revalue. Interest in economic and monetary union was not only an internal European issue, for it was a response to these wider pressures.

A modest proposal to address the inflexibility of the Bretton Woods system was to increase the margin of variation around par from plus or minus 1 per cent. To Milton Friedman, this reform did nothing to resolve the basic problem that exchange rates were maintained by increasingly desperate interventions that required controls on capital flows, wages and prices, and so undermined free markets. His preference was to remove these controls and restore free markets by allowing rates to 'float'.[14] This was a major ideological division over the role of the state and the market that was played out on both sides of the Atlantic – though the ultimate decision to float was more a response to events than an intellectual conversion.

Both the modest proposal for wider margins and the radical idea of floating would cause problems for European economic integration. What was the point of removing internal tariff barriers if wider currency margins created new barriers to trade and complicated payments under the CAP? Above all, the United States was criticised for evading responsibility for resolving its balance of payments deficits by taking steps to restore competitiveness, control its budgets and contain inflation. De Gaulle focused on the misuse of the dollar for political reasons; Germany was more concerned about inflationary pressure caused by an inflow of dollars in the expectation of devaluation in the United States and revaluation of the Deutsche Mark. The question of how to respond led to political disagreement between France and Germany, and within Germany. The Germans did not share the French obsession with gold and rigidly fixed rates. But should the inflationary inflow of dollars into Germany be checked by the use of capital and exchange controls, or by removing the incentive by floating the Deutsche Mark, in contravention of the Bretton Woods agreement? As long as exchange rates were fixed, the Bundesbank was obliged to purchase the inflow of dollars to prevent the Deutsche Mark from appreciating. The result would be an

---

14 M. Friedman and R. Roosa, *The Balance of Payments: Free versus Fixed Exchange Rates* (Washington, DC, American Enterprise Institute, 1967); M. Friedman, 'A Proposal for Resolving the US Balance of Payments Problem: Confidential Memorandum to President-Elect Nixon', in L. Melamed (ed.), *The Merits of Flexible Exchange Rates: An Anthology* (Fairfax, VA, George Mason University Press, 1988), pp. 429–38.

increase in the money supply and inflation. If the Deutsche Mark floated, there would no longer be a need for the Bundesbank to buy dollars, which would reduce inflationary pressure; instead, the Deutsche Mark would appreciate. This debate set interests against each other, for savers were obsessed with controlling inflation by whatever means – but floating and appreciation would harm German exporters and European economic integration. Finding a compromise would not be easy either domestically or within the EEC.

Meanwhile, confidence in sterling remained low, despite a major devaluation in 1967 and support for its managed decline as a reserve currency. After the war, the British government was torn between support for a 'one world' dollar system or a 'two world' system of dollar and sterling blocs. The question which now arose was whether membership of a European monetary bloc was the better option, especially when the British government reapplied for membership of the EEC. In France, strikes and student protests in May 1968 led to expansionary fiscal and monetary policies and a flight from the franc. After steps were taken to support the franc, speculative pressure moved to Germany, with an inflow of funds in anticipation of revaluation. The German government refused to revalue and restricted capital inflows and imposed temporary border taxes. The crisis resumed in 1969, with renewed IMF support for sterling and devaluation of the franc. The influx of money into Germany led Karl Schiller, the economics minister, to a unilateral float of the Deutsche Mark prior to revaluation in September 1969. These pressures in 1968 and 1969 were putting the Bretton Woods system under intense pressure and it was increasingly doubtful that it could survive. The governments of both the United States and Europe needed to decide on their response.

The Crisis of Bretton Woods

When Richard Nixon took office in January 1969, Paul Volcker, the undersecretary for international monetary issues at the Treasury, took the lead in devising American policies. He favoured 'substantial evolutionary change' by a 'negotiated multilateral solution' that would activate SDRs, realign undervalued currencies and secure greater exchange rate flexibility in the hope of long-run equilibrium. He offered a modest adjustment to the Bretton Woods system of fixed but flexible exchange rates. Nevertheless, Volcker realised that evolution might fail, for the Europeans might reject both realignment that would hit competitiveness and wider margins that would create problems for integration. The alternative was a 'financial deterrent' of 'unilateral flouting of US power' by suspending convertibility of the dollar into gold. The strategy was to convince the Europeans that realignment of currencies and acceptance of wider margins were preferable to the uncertainty caused by use of the 'deterrent'. Once the reforms were made, Volcker hoped that Bretton Woods would survive – provided that the United States cured its deficit and followed the German principle of 'extremely high priority in resisting inflation'.[15] The issue was whether domestic action to improve the competitiveness of the American economy was politically feasible.

The chances of a negotiated multilateral settlement were minimal. Henry Kissinger, the National Security Adviser, realised that Germany would oppose further revaluation and that other European countries would resent the Germans taking a lead in reform. The initiative therefore had to come from France, where President Georges Pompidou, who succeeded de Gaulle in 1969, was less dogmatic – though a change in approach would take time. Kissinger wrote off Britain as 'financially prostrate'. He concluded, reasonably enough, that 'political realities ... suggest that it will be extremely difficult to reach a negotiated multilateral agreement on a sufficient scale within a relevant time period unless the alternative were clearly perceived as worse by the key Europeans'.[16] Little happened, and the policy was characterised as 'benign neglect'. Nixon was more concerned with Vietnam and China, and re-election. Furthermore, the IMF failed to take any initiative – and the alternative forum of leading economies, the Group of Ten (G10), both lacked authority and was mistrusted by the United States because its membership was dominated by Europe.

The EEC criticised Washington for failing to tackle its balance of payments deficit and restore confidence in the dollar, which punished others for American shortcomings. The EEC started to devise its own solutions to the weaknesses of the Bretton Woods regime. Discussion had started before the Treaty of Rome in the context of restoring convertibility between currencies by building on the European Payments Unions, but in 1958 the process was completed within the Bretton Woods system. Interest in the creation of

---

15 'Summary of a Possible US Approach to Improving International Monetary Arrangements, 17 March 1969', in *Foreign Relations of the United States* (henceforth *FRUS*) (1969–76), vol. III, p. 119.

16 'Action Memo from the President's Assistant for National Security Affairs (Kissinger) to President Nixon, 25 June 1969: Your Meeting on International Monetary Policy', in *FRUS* (1969–76), vol. III, p. 131.

a stable European monetary zone revived as a result of disillusionment with American monetary policy and tensions in the Bretton Woods regime, and in order to build on the customs union that was completed in 1968. The Commission looked to common economic policies designed to transform the customs territory into an economically organised continent: 'we must gradually replace the old national policies with Community policies, changing the European area into an organized European society, with a general economic policy thought out and built up to the scale of the continent'.[17]

At the end of the year, Raymond Barre – the Commissioner for Economic and Financial Affairs – produced a plan for a common monetary policy. He differed from Triffin, who argued for monetary unification ahead of economic convergence. Barre took a more pragmatic approach of complementary progress on economic convergence, with low inflation and the use of exchange rate targets to support domestic policies to control prices, with monetary union as the eventual outcome. He argued that a customs union without coordinated economic and monetary policies could not deal with monetary crises, handle balance of payments disequilibria or encourage convergence in growth and prices: 'only those ignorant of the true nature of modern economics can believe that a multinational community could be organized solely on the basis of a customs union for manufactures, a common agricultural policy, and some measures of harmonization'. Indeed, incompatibility between the economic policies of members might threaten the survival of the customs union.[18] As Valéry Giscard d'Estaing remarked, 'If no common monetary arrangement existed, the slightest domestic upset of a monetary, economic, social or political nature would be enough to force a country to take isolationist measures that ran counter to the objectives of the Common Market.'[19]

The developing crisis of the Bretton Woods regime led European heads of state and government meeting at The Hague in December 1969 to consider the next steps after the completion of the common market. This process would entail the development of an economic and monetary union,

---

17 'Declaration by the Commission on the Occasion of the Achievement of the Customs Union, 1968', *Bulletin of the European Communities* no. 7 (1968): 5–8.

18 'Commission Memorandum to the Council on the Coordination of Economic Policies and Monetary Cooperation within the Community, submitted on 12 February 1969', COM (69) 150, Supplement to *Bulletin of the European Communities* no. 3 (1969); D. Howarth, 'Raymond Barre: Modernizing France through European Monetary Cooperation', in K. Dyson and I. Maes (eds.), *Architects of the Euro: Intellectuals in the Making of European Monetary Union* (Oxford, Oxford University Press, 2016), pp. 75, 81–8.

19 V. Giscard d'Estaing, 'La monnaie unique pour l'Europe', *Communauté européenne* (April 1969): 17.

dependent on 'harmonisation of economic polices'.[20] In March 1970, the European Council appointed a committee under the chairmanship of Pierre Werner, the prime minister of Luxembourg, which proposed a three-stage plan for economic and monetary union in a decade. The committee was divided. The French 'monetarists' gave priority to monetary union ahead of economic convergence on the grounds that it would provide an impetus to economic integration. They also preferred intergovernmentalism to supra-nationalism. The German 'economists' argued that monetary union should be a 'crowning achievement' after harmonisation of economic policies and convergence of wages, prices, growth and productivity, with political cooperation and Community-wide decision-making. Werner was closer to the French position and wished to press ahead with monetary union, but saw a need to compromise by adopting a 'fundamentally dual approach' that combined the monetarists and economists: 'we need to encourage the economic and financial fields to interact with each other ... we need to tackle the problem from both ends and develop parallel initiatives'.[21]

The report set out a timetable towards monetary union. The first stage was to reduce margins of fluctuation between members' currencies. The second stage was to integrate financial and banking markets to create free movement of capital, eliminate exchange rate fluctuations, and coordin-ate economic policies. Thirdly, exchange rates would be fixed between participating national currencies, with convergence of economic policies and a Community system of central banks. The proposal entailed a funda-mental shift in the relationship between the Community and individual nation states, for 'economic and monetary union means that the principal decisions of economic policy will be taken at the Community level and therefore that the necessary powers will be transferred from the national plane to the Community plane'. It would lead to political union and to 'the adoption of a single currency which would guarantee the irreversibility of the undertaking'.[22] President Pompidou initially opposed the plan on the grounds that it was too supranational – and Chancellor Brandt worried that it did not give sufficient weight to economic convergence and the need to control inflation before monetary union. In March 1971, the Council agreed to

---

20 Final Communiqué from The Hague Summit, 2 December 1969.
21 P. Werner, 'Politique monétaire européenne', *Bulletin de Documentation* no. 6 (1969): 17–19.
22 'Report to the Council and the Commission on the Realisation by Stages of Economic and Monetary Union in the Community "Werner Report"', supplement to *Bulletin of the European Communities* no. 11 (1970): 26.

implement the proposals, but ambivalence remained about how much economic convergence was needed to achieve monetary union, and whether monetary union would itself create convergence.[23]

The British government realised that the German position was 'schizophrenic. She does not want to seem anti-European or anti-French and does set considerable store on the continued process of political unification. But equally she does not want to sign a blank cheque for the benefit of her partners.' The British were also uncertain how to respond. A ministerial committee favoured sterling membership of a 'functional' rather than 'federal' economic and monetary union, for there seemed little chance of avoiding a decline in financial power outside the Community. The British hoped to form an alliance with France to shift from price stability favoured by Germany to economic growth – and in return to weaken French hostility to sterling.[24] The British ambassador in Paris realised that the French government's aim was for Europe to control its monetary destiny, while stopping well short of supranationality: 'their main objective is to achieve maximum security of parities compatible with minimum loss of sovereignty which means a high degree of exchange control since this is the only way of achieving relatively resilient fixed parities without going in the direction of a centrally controlled European economic policy'.[25]

There was also British scepticism about the project. Might it work against rather than support the customs union, for a monetary union would benefit some countries more than others? Samuel Brittan, the *Financial Times* columnist, thought the Werner Report was heading for the 'worst of all worlds', for loss of control over exchange rates could only work with 'a common budget, political union, and some form of European government' as an alternative means of adjustment.[26]

23 'Report by the Commission to the Council 30 Oct 1970', *Bulletin of the European Communities* no. 11 (1970): 15–18; 'Resolution of the Council and the Representatives of the Governments of the Member States, 22 March 1971', in *Selection of Texts Concerning Institutional Matters of the Community 1950–1980* (Luxembourg, European Parliament, 1982), pp. 177–83.
24 The National Archives (henceforth TNA), CAB134/2602 AEO(F)(70)5, 9 November 1970 Cabinet, 'Official Committee on the Approach to Europe Sub-committee on Financial and Monetary Aspects. Economic and Monetary Union. Note by the Treasury'; Prem 15/53, 'Proposals Regarding United Kingdom Participation in a European Monetary System, August 1970'; T328/654, 'Ministerial Committee on the Approach to Europe, AE(70)41, Economic and Monetary Union', 19 November 1970.
25 TNA, Prem 15/813, Soames to Alan Neale, 'The EEC, International Monetary Reform and EMU', 18 July and 1 August 1972.
26 A. Mody, *Eurotragedy: A Drama in Nine Acts* (New York, NY, Oxford University Press, 2018), pp. 6–7, 48–9.

Although the Werner Report coincided with pressure on the international monetary system, it did not explicitly consider the wider context. The implications were clear in Washington: the European initiative would affect the role of the dollar as a reserve currency, with the possibility of a two-bloc system based on the dollar and European currencies, with exchange rates more or less fixed in each bloc but free to vary between them. The fear in Washington was that under the Werner plan the EEC might become 'more inward looking and adopt European rather than wider solutions to international economic problems. In order to avoid disturbing its own efforts in forming an economic and monetary union, the EEC may stall efforts to improve the international monetary system until the Community is well advanced in its process of unification.'[27] On this view, the Europeans were more concerned with their own integration than with an international initiative on monetary policy where they disagreed on the best approach. American recourse to the 'financial deterrent' of unilateral suspension of convertibility of the dollar was becoming more likely to force the Europeans to accept change.

The international monetary system had barely survived 1968–9, and a crisis of confidence in the dollar was possible at any time. Despite revaluation, dollars continued to flood into Germany to pre-empt devaluation of the dollar. A reduction in German interest rates in March 1971 did not stem the influx, and there were divisions over the best approach. A repeat of the unilateral float of the Deutsche Mark would contradict the commitment to the European monetary system. The president of the Bundesbank, Klaus Klasen, had the support of most members in wishing to retain fixed parities with the backing of capital and exchange controls. In contrast, the Organisation of German Savings Banks, with its 30 million savers, and five leading economics research institutes supported floating to limit inflationary pressure from inflows of dollars. The final decision rested with the government. Schiller floated in 1969, and he continued to argue that capital flows could not be controlled by bureaucratic means. He therefore proposed a joint float of the Deutsche Mark with other European currencies that would allow 'inward stability and outward elasticity'. Brandt agreed to the strategy as 'a decisive step on the path

27 NARA RG59 State, Bureau of European Affairs, Box 4, FNI, 'Working Party 3, Balance of Payments Adjustments. Some Possible Implications for the United States of the Proposed Monetary and Economic Union of the EEC', A. I. Bloomfield, January 1971.

towards European monetary union' – but if the proposal was rejected, Germany would float unilaterally.[28]

The French continued to argue that wider margins would create greater turmoil and pressed for fixed rates and exchange rate controls; they rejected what they saw as the fetish of free markets. Rejection of Schiller's plan led to a massive speculative inflow on 3–5 May 1971 and a unilateral float of the Deutsche Mark. Germany's action divided the EEC's monetary committee. In the end, it agreed that the Germans could float for a short time until the governors of the European central banks took steps to prevent large inflows of speculative funds. Brandt later told Edward Heath, the British prime minister from 1970 to 1974, that the decision came close to breaking the EEC. In retrospect, Emminger saw that Bretton Woods 'broke down because *the limit of tolerance for the inflationary effect* of such currency inflows had been reached'. The United States failed to deflate, and allowed inflationary wage settlements to paper over economic and social conflicts. The result was a flight of capital to surplus countries. The outcome was 'the most inflationary mixture imaginable. It has helped to pervert fixed parities from being an instrument of discipline on deficit countries to one forcing monetary debauchery on surplus countries.'[29]

The Bretton Woods system was moving to a major crisis. In June 1971, Henry Reuss, chair of the Congress Joint Committee's Sub-committee on International Exchange and Payments, introduced a resolution that unless an international monetary conference were called, America should end convertibility and allow the dollar to float until it returned to equilibrium. His warning was reinforced by a large balance of payments deficit. On 12 and 13 August 1971, heavy selling of dollars led to an emergency meeting at Camp David to discuss options. The outcome was to close the gold window and impose a border tax of 10 per cent. Secretary of the Treasury John Connally dismissed foreign criticism. 'So, the other countries don't like it. So what? . . . Why do we have to be "reasonable"?'[30] To Volcker's chagrin, neither

---

28 W. G. Gray, 'Floating the System: Germany, the United States, and the Breakdown of Bretton Woods, 1969–73', *Diplomatic History* 31 (2007): 295–323, 308–9.

29 NARA, RG56 Treasury monetary reform, Box 5, 'Inflation and the World Monetary System, Lecture at Per Jacobsson Foundation', 16 June 1973.

30 Ford Presidential Library, Burns Papers, Box K31, 'Note on Camp David Weekend, 13–15 August 1971', 16 August 1971; A. J. Matusow, *Nixon's Economy: Booms, Busts, Dollars and Votes* (Lawrence, KS, University Press of Kansas, 1998), pp. 149–54.

long-term reform of the monetary system nor working with other countries was discussed.[31]

The monetary crisis coincided with Britain's third application to join the EEC, with a need to choose between the dollar and the European currency bloc. Membership of the dollar bloc would help British exporters, who would be more competitive when other currencies revalued against the dollar, without having 'to make some more fundamental effort to deal with wages and prices'. The problem was that 'Our adherence to the EEC bloc would almost certainly be demanded as evidence of our fitness and readiness to join Europe.' Indeed, maintaining the value of sterling against other European currencies would provide an incentive to control wage inflation and to avoid easy solutions of currency depreciation.[32] After the closing of the gold window, Lord Cromer, the Governor of the Bank of England from 1961 to 1966 and British ambassador to Washington from 1971 to 1974, concluded that there was 'a need of a European monetary bloc of scale that signifies', and he warned John Connally, the Secretary of the Treasury in 1971–2, 'that it would not be in the US interest if a European monetary bloc came into being in a spirit of retaliation to the US. The present American attitude seems quite likely to result in exactly that.'[33] The question was whether the world would fracture into competing blocs or whether the Bretton Woods regime could be restored after appropriate realignment of rates and a greater element of flexibility.

Responding to the Crisis

Use of the 'financial deterrent' assumed that the United States would have proposals for reform after the suspension of convertibility. Nevertheless, Volcker informed representatives of Britain, Japan, Italy, Germany and France that 'the Administration had no specific programme or blueprint for reform in mind'. This absence of a plan would, he argued, allow open-minded consultation that should create an opportunity 'in some sense "to free the world's hands"' for new approaches. He gave no indication of what the new approaches might be, beyond insisting that a change in the dollar price of gold

31 P. Volcker and T. Gyohten, *Changing Fortunes: The World's Money and the Threat to American Leadership* (New York, NY, Times Books, 1992), p. 78.

32 TNA, Prem 15/53, 'Proposals Regarding United Kingdom Participation in a European Monetary System', August 1970 and 'Paper on "Proposals Regarding United Kingdom Participation in a European Monetary System"', W. S. Ryrie.

33 TNA, Prem 15/309, Cromer to Foreign secretary, 'International Monetary Situation', 15 August 1971.

was unacceptable to Congress. Indeed, 'it was basically now for the other main countries to consider what programme of measures, including parity changes, would bring about the necessary strengthening of the American payments position'.[34] In Connally's infamous words to the G10 finance ministers, 'The dollar may be our currency but it's your problem.'[35]

Volcker's announcement caused surprise that the United States was abdicating responsibility for its economic problems and for reform of the international monetary system. The dangers of Connally's bargaining strategy were apparent even to the Nixon administration. Europe might decide to 'go it alone' with the outcome of, at best, 'benign regionalism' based on open trade between blocs or, at worst, degeneration into 'uncooperative, protectionist blocs'.[36] The risk, as Cromer realised, was that 'Connally might find the domestic political impact of his present external stance so seductive that he might be reluctant to settle on terms which other G10 members and even others in the administration would regard as reasonable.'[37] Peter Peterson – Nixon's assistant on international economic affairs – opposed Connally's nationalistic stance and saw a need to compromise. 'So far, we have left it to others to adjust to the situation we have created. But soon we will have to clarify what we want multilaterally and what we want bilaterally from key countries. Most feel that having taken the essential but shock-producing moves of August 15, we should be prepared to propose some positive initiatives in the reasonably near future.'[38] There was a lack of agreement in Washington on the approach. Volcker and Arthur Burns, the chairman of the Federal Reserve, wished to restore Bretton Woods. In contrast, Shultz was sympathetic to floating exchanges and open capital markets. The trade-off made at Bretton Woods of pegged exchange rates and controls over capital flows was under intense scrutiny.

The absence of an American plan led to calls for a joint European approach. Mario Ferrari-Aggradi, the Italian minister of finance, stressed that 'the American move calls for a European initiative for an international

34 TNA, Prem 15/309, A. D. Neale, 'Note for the Record: Meeting with Mr Paul Volcker', 17 August 1971; 'Note of a Meeting in the Chancellor of the Exchequer's Room, Treasury', 16 August 1971; 'Memo of Conversation, 16 August 1971: President Nixon's New Economic Program', in FRUS (1969–76), vol. III, p. 170.
35 Volcker and Gyohten, Changing Fortunes, p. 81.
36 Ford Presidential Library, Burns Papers, Box B65, International monetary crisis 1971 (3), 'International Negotiations: Objectives, Issues and Conclusions', 18 August 1971.
37 TNA, Prem 15/310, Cromer, 'International Monetary Situation', 4 November 1971; Prem 15/1271, Cromer to Douglas Allen, Treasury, 9 November 1971.
38 NARA, RG59 Shultz, CIEP, 'Negotiating the New Economic Policy Abroad', Peter G. Peterson, 23 September 1971.

monetary system based on conditions of equality [. . .]. This is the moment for Europe to take an initiative: if Europe really exists, this is the time for it to present itself as a united community.'[39] The task of reaching a common position was not easy. Karl Otto Pöhl, an economic adviser in the German government and subsequently president of the Bundesbank, pointed out to Brandt that members of the European Community had fundamental differences. Pompidou and Giscard disliked Schiller's approach of a joint float and were sympathetic to capital controls. They feared that the Deutsche Mark would dominate any European system, which would lead to over-valued currencies that would threaten the competitiveness of French industry. The French argued that the burden of adjustment should be made to fall on the United States by devaluing and raising the price of gold.[40] Schiller was losing ground at home. The Deutsche Mark was appreciating faster than other currencies, whose central banks were holding down the rate. As a result, German exporters complained of loss of markets, and unions feared unemployment. The changed political dynamic forced Schiller to attempt – without much success – to hold down the Deutsche Mark.

The G10 ministers met in Washington on 26 September without reaching agreement. Connally calculated that time was on his side and that the market would establish an appropriate set of exchange rates. He was content for the crisis to continue and for other currencies to appreciate without making a commitment to change the gold price of the dollar. The Bank of International Settlements – the central bank of central bankers – criticised the American approach as irresponsible: 'the US, which had declared its currency to be in fundamental disequilibrium, was evading its responsibility under the IMF rules by being unwilling to devalue [. . .]. It was unlikely that adequate exchange rate adjustments could be brought about if countries in fundamental disequilibrium refused to adjust.'[41] In fact, a compromise was starting to emerge before G10 ministers met in Rome on 29 November to 1 December 1971.

In Washington, Volcker was instructed to start 'intense dialogue and work' on what kind of reformed monetary system should be adopted. Clearly, Connally's hard-line tactics were pointless unless he could go beyond forcing

---

39 TNA, Prem 15/309, telegram from Selby, 17 August 1971, 'International Currency Situation'.
40 Bundesarchiv, B136-11608 Pohl to Brandt 20 August 1971; B136-7355 Weinstock report, 9 September 1971, on debates over monetary policy; B136-3332 Results of Council of ministers meeting 19/20 August 1971; B136-7355 Results of Council of Ministers Meeting, 13 September 1971.
41 TNA, T267/36, 'Treasury Historical Memorandum', p. 41.

other countries to realign their currencies. Opinion in Washington coalesced on a basic approach to monetary reform: flexibility by prompt rate adjustments, orderly creation of reserves to reduce dependence on gold and key currencies, followed by talks on long-term trade liberalisation for both industry and agriculture, a more equitable sharing of the burdens of defence, and the restoration of a free flow of investment. The shift in the German government's attitude also allowed a compromise in the EEC. The German government agreed to French demands to devalue the dollar against gold, on condition that the French agreed to wider margins, more frequent changes in rates and the use of SDRs.[42] When the finance ministers of the EEC met on 4 November, they agreed to realignment of parities with wider margins and a narrower band within the Community. In Rome, Connally was willing to consider a change in the dollar price of gold and to devalue now that other currencies had appreciated, and to increase margins to plus or minus 3 per cent. The Americans offered to end the import surcharge, provided progress was made in removing restraints on American exports to Europe and on better sharing of defence burdens. Despite progress, agreement collapsed because of the American demands to cut agricultural protection and pay more for defence. The EEC's commitment to the CAP as a central element of its identity collided with American resentment on limits to its agricultural exports. European dominance of the G10 led to suspicion in Washington that American interests would be downplayed.

The G10 ministerial meeting was scheduled to resume in Washington on 17–18 December. In preparation, Nixon and Pompidou (in effect representing the EEC) met on the Azores on 13–14 December 1971 to settle monetary and trade issues as an 'integrated whole'. Kissinger later commented that 'the extraordinary aspect of the encounter was that France and the United States should have taken it upon themselves to work out the exchange rate for every one of the world's important currencies'. The agreement was designed to deal with immediate difficulties by realigning exchange rates and to look ahead to longer-term reform. Pompidou secured a reduction in margins to plus or minus 2.25 per cent and a commitment to fixed rates rather than the weaker American proposal of 'established' rates. He also inserted gold convertibility as a future – largely symbolic – topic of discussion. The Americans agreed to 'assist in the stability of the system and the defence of the newly fixed exchange rates in particular by vigorous implementation of

---

42 TNA, T318/403, 'The Federal Republic's Handling of the Dollar Crisis: Ambassador at Bonn to Secretary of State for Foreign and Commonwealth Affairs', 12 June 1972.

its efforts to restore price stability and productivity'.[43] The French obtained – so they hoped – discipline over the Americans in return for agreeing to recommend that the Commission undertake trade negotiations which Nixon needed in order to convince Congress to accept a change in the dollar price of gold. Discussion over the sharing of defence costs was handed to the North Atlantic Treaty Organization and dropped as a bargaining weapon.

The deal struck on the Azores was presented to the G10 meeting at the Smithsonian Institute in Washington. Germany agreed to revalue the Deutsche Mark by 13.57 per cent, and the dollar was devalued against other G10 currencies by 10 per cent. At the same time, the American import surcharge was removed. Although Connally's tactics seemed to have worked in forcing realignment, the Smithsonian agreement was only a short-term fix that remedied neither the defects of the Bretton Woods monetary system nor the underlying deficit in the American balance of payments. It was an uneasy compromise between two principles for setting exchange rates. In theory, governments continued to fix and maintain the rate; in practice, as Shultz pointed out, 'US officials had formed an alliance with the market itself to force a change in the behavior of foreign officials.'[44] The new rates were unlikely to hold, for Nixon was not committed to defending parities by deflating the American economy.

By February 1972, Pompidou complained to Nixon of his 'uneasiness with regard to the evolution of the international monetary situation' and that the administration's policies were not consistent with their agreement. He pointed to 'certain shortcomings which risk weakening the correct implementation of our agreements' as well as to 'my preoccupation over steps taken or of positions envisaged by your administration and which, at first glance, do not seem to me to be consistent with what we agreed'. Specifically, 'the combination of a large budgetary deficit and of a policy of systematically low interest rates' weakened confidence in the new dollar parity. Pompidou expressed surprise that Nixon was abandoning his commitment to maintain exchange rates within wider margins and apparently turning to greater flexibility.[45] Nixon claimed that he would defend the new rate by 'vigorous efforts to restore price stability and productivity to the United States economy ...

---

43 H. Kissinger, *White House Years* (Boston, MA, Little Brown, 1979), pp. 961–2; 'Paper Agreed by President Nixon and President Pompidou: Framework for Monetary and Trade Settlement', in *FRUS* (1969–76), vol. III, p. 220.

44 D. J. Sargent, *A Superpower Transformed: The Remaking of American Foreign Relations in the 1970s* (New York, NY, Oxford University Press, 2015), p. 118.

45 'Pompidou to Nixon, 4 February 1972', in *FRUS* (1969–72), vol. III, p. 223.

I assure you that these fundamental objectives remain the basis of our domestic policies.'[46] The reassurance was meaningless, for his priority was re-election later in the year.

The European Response to Failed Reform

The wider margins in the Smithsonian threatened European integration. If one currency rose to the top of the band and another dropped to the bottom, there would be a potential fluctuation of 6 per cent which would – so it was claimed – disrupt the internal market. In January 1972, the Commission proposed to narrow the band between members to plus or minus 1.25 per cent – the 'snake' in the 'tunnel' of the Smithsonian bands. The existing six members of the EEC agreed in April 1972, as did the four members that were due to join in 1973 – Britain, Ireland, Norway and Denmark.

Problems soon emerged, for weaker currencies had difficulties in remaining within the 'snake'. The lira almost dropped out, and the British government was torn over membership. The advantage was that European monetary union might create 'a more nearly symmetrical system in which the US dollar is just one more currency, and indeed the world will have proper control of the supply of international liquidity instead of being at the mercy of US policies'. Heath viewed membership of the snake as a sign of commitment to the EEC, and a means of regaining practical, shared, sovereignty in place of theoretical sovereignty. On the other hand, the snake caused domestic problems, for the obligation to keep exchange rates within narrow bands constrained policies to encourage growth. The Chancellor of the Exchequer, Anthony Barber, made his priorities clear in March 1972. He announced that 'it is neither necessary nor desirable to distort domestic economies to an unacceptable extent in order to retain unrealistic exchange rates [...]. I do not believe that there is any need for this country or any other, to be frustrated on this score in its determination to sustain economic growth and to reduce unemployment.'[47] Pressure on sterling as a result of a balance of payments deficit and high price and wage inflation meant that continued membership of the snake would require deflation, so alienating labour and provoking strikes. On 23 June 1972, sterling floated. It was, as Volcker later commented, 'the first formal break in the Smithsonian

---

46 'Nixon to Pompidou, 16 February 1972', in *FRUS* (1969–72), vol. III, p. 224.
47 House of Commons, 21 March 1972, col. 1354.

central rates'.[48] Pompidou expressed disquiet at the breach of the European monetary system:

> I am convinced that a regime of fixed rates of exchange, in addition to the fact that it will favour the development of trade and investment, also constitutes one of the indispensable conditions for the proper functioning of the Common Market . . . Such a regime also seems to me to constitute the foundation of all progress in European monetary cooperation and all development in the reform of the international monetary system whose necessity, as you yourself have observed, has been demonstrated by recent events.[49]

The flight of money from London created inflationary pressures in Germany. Schiller's hostility to capital controls was under renewed pressure from Klasen at the Bundesbank and within the cabinet. The Deutsche Mark had revalued by 20 per cent against the dollar since 1969 and a further rise would hit competitiveness so that controls might be needed to stop further inflows. Schiller resigned and was replaced by Helmut Schmidt, who was more willing to use controls to stem inflows of funds. Speculators then moved against the dollar in the expectation of devaluation. George Shultz, who replaced Connally as Secretary of the Treasury, was sympathetic to floating the dollar, but he realised that the Europeans were not in favour. He therefore presented a compromise to the IMF meeting in September 1972.

This Plan X was devised by Volcker, who had doubts about unregulated floating.[50] Countries should declare a 'central value' for their currency, which they should intervene to maintain within a margin of plus or minus 3 or 4 per cent. Floating would be permitted either as a transitional step to a new central rate, or indefinitely on condition that controls on capital were dropped and the currency was subject to surveillance to prevent manipulation of the rate. Hence the plan could permit floating in combination with free flows of capital – a reversal of the Bretton Woods trade-off. The outcome was a 'non-system' which gave countries latitude on its exchange rate regime. The problem, as Volcker realised, was how to balance 'the apparent "freedom" of the looser exchange rate regime, while keeping the advantages of a strong international consensus as to certain basic rules of good behavior'.[51] Good behaviour was not a defining feature of Nixon's administration, where

48 Volcker and Gyohten, *Changing Fortunes*, p. 105.
49 TNA T354/275, Pompidou to Heath, 7 July 1972.
50 'Paper Prepared in the Department of the Treasury, 31 July 1972: Major Elements of Plan X', in *FRUS* (1969–76), vol. III, p. 239.
51 NARA, RG56 Treasury Briefing books, international monetary issues, Box 8, 'Special Working Group. A Sketch of a World Monetary System', undated.

inflationary pressures were not contained by domestic monetary policy. Europeans were alarmed.

Schmidt worried about American 'passivity' and doubted that the United States wished to adhere to the Smithsonian agreement.[52] Claude-Pierre Brossolette of the French Treasury thought that the American proposal merely reflected 'the continuing bias of the United States that surplus countries should be the ones to make the adjustment when international payments get out of balance'.[53] Giscard favoured 'few rather than frequent parity changes ... the main technique of adjustment should be internal policies rather than exchange rates'.[54] By September 1972, European views converged on modest reform of 'stable but adaptable' rates, convertibility into gold, greater discipline on both surplus and deficit countries, and regulation of short-term capital movements – essentially, the French position. Such an approach required the United States to take a disciplined approach. It did not, and by February 1973 the system was again in crisis. Brandt urged Nixon to defend the exchange rate between the dollar and the Deutsche Mark, and he stressed that monetary instability was an existential threat to the West. Schmidt rejected Schiller's stratagem of unilateral floating of the Deutsche Mark to check the inflow of dollars, which had led to serious divisions in the EEC. He preferred to defend the rate by capital and exchange controls, and to develop a united European approach as a political and economic counterweight to the United States.[55]

Only 14 months after the Smithsonian agreement, Volcker embarked on frantic international diplomacy to negotiate a new set of parities. It was no more likely to last, for Volcker's efforts merely confirmed that periodic readjustment by economic diplomacy was not a long-term solution. Speculation continued against the dollar with an inflow of dollars into Europe – above all Germany – that threatened inflation. The German government turned to a European solution. Rather than a unilateral float of the Deutsche Mark, Schmidt proposed that European currencies remain within a narrow band internally and float externally against the dollar, so encouraging European integration and acting as a counterweight to the

---

52 'Telegram from the Embassy in Germany to the Department of State 1 August 1972: Conversation with Economics and Finance Minister Schmidt', in *FRUS* (1969–76), vol. III, p. 240.
53 NARA, RG56 Treasury monetary reform, Box 5 MR-5 France, Donald McGrew, US Treasury rep Paris, to Volcker, 18 December 1972.
54 'Memorandum of Conversation, 31 May 1973, Reykjavik: Trade and Monetary Issues', in *FRUS* (1969–76), vol. XXXI, p. 41.
55 Gray, 'Floating the System', 317–21.

United States. The risk for the French was that the collective float would become a Deutsche Mark zone which would lead to appreciation of the franc and hit exports. Brandt urged Pompidou that the choice was between 'further integration, or the danger of a collapse of the community into a mere customs union'.[56]

On 12 March 1973, Germany, France, Denmark and the Benelux countries agreed to a joint float; Britain, Ireland and Italy remained outside; and Norway and Sweden, which were not members of the EEC, joined. The collective float was therefore not identical with the EEC, but the Commission hoped it would lead to greater integration. Bonn thought it a good outcome. It had secured agreement from France; there was no need to support weak currencies that remained outside the collective float; and the Deutsche Mark was insulated from speculative inflows, which helped the Bundesbank control inflation. The problems were greater for currencies that were tied to the Deutsche Mark as it appreciated against the dollar.

The Nixon administration had to decide on its position for the G10 meeting. Shultz's preference was to float the dollar rather than continue to intervene. He realised that fixed rates were possible only when the United States was the dominant economic power, and he argued that 'I don't see how we have the muscle to so dominate the situation to make a real fixed rate system of the kind we had in the post-war period.'[57] American economic hegemony was threatened. Nixon, as always, was more interested in geopolitics than in economics, and he worried that growing integration in Europe would now threaten American interests. He assured Shultz that 'you can't think of this, basically, as an economist. The whole European relationship is in a state of, I think, very profound change at this point.' Above all, his concern was 'to keep the Europeans closer to us, rather than having them push away.'[58] Kissinger agreed: it was vital that European integration was part of an Atlantic partnership, with avoidance of unilateral decisions in Brussels. Nixon was concerned that 'European unity will not be in our interest ... We have to recognize the stark fact that a united Europe will

56 Ibid., 321.
57 'Conversation among President Nixon, the Chairman of the Federal Reserve System Board of Governors (Burns), the Director of the Office of Management and Budget (Ash), the Chairman of the Council of Economic Advisers (Stein), Secretary of the Treasury Shultz, and the Under-secretary of the Treasury for Monetary Affairs (Volcker), 3 March 1973', in FRUS (1969–76), vol. XXXI, p. 16.
58 'Conversation among President Nixon, the President's Assistant for National Security Affairs (Kissinger) and Secretary of the Treasury Shultz, 3 March 1973', in FRUS (1969–76), vol. XXXI, pp. 16–17.

be led primarily by Left-leaning or Socialist heads of government', who were more likely to confront the United States than form a united front against the Soviets. The solution was to build a bloc of the United States, Japan and the underdeveloped countries of Latin America, Asia and Africa. Kissinger saw that 'we couldn't bust the Common float without getting into a hell of a political fight', but it was possible to create conditions in which it would not work: 'from now on we have to throw our weight around to help ourselves. And then they'll start paying attention to us again.'[59] European monetary integration raised serious concerns in Washington about challenges to American global influence.

Conclusion

The meeting of the G10 in Paris on 13–16 March 1973 marked the effective end of the rules-based system of Bretton Woods. The Bretton Woods regime rested on the dollar, which became more important as the American economy became less competitive and less hegemonic. The result was a crisis of legitimacy. The Nixon administration failed to provide leadership in resolving the problems that arose. The result was a complex and tense shift to a new regime – or, more accurately, a 'non-system'. In March 1973, the G10 could only agree that intervention 'may be useful at appropriate times, to facilitate the maintenance of orderly conditions'; the decision was left to individual countries 'when necessary and desirable, acting in a flexible manner in the light of market conditions and in close consultation with the authorities of the nation whose currency may be bought or sold'.[60]

At the press conference after the meeting, Shultz was asked to explain the implications of the European collective float for America's domestic monetary policy. He deferred to the autonomy of the Federal Reserve, and Burns responded that 'American monetary policy is not made in Paris; it is made in Washington.' His answer had serious implications. At a time when America was experiencing inflation and the international monetary system was under threat, it seemed that American domestic interests were given priority. By defending the autonomy of the Federal Reserve, Burns gave the

---

59 'Draft Memo from President Nixon to the President's Assistant for National Security Affairs (Kissinger), 10 March 1973', in *FRUS* (1969–76), vol. XXXI, p. 31; 'Editorial Note, Quoting Kissinger, 14 March 1973', in *FRUS* (1969–76), vol. XXXI, p. 35.
60 Communiqué issued by the Group of Ten and the European Economic Community, Paris, 16 March 1973.

impression that he did not support the international role of the dollar.[61] Although Burns was not convinced that market rates offered an 'infallible indication' of the correct rate and preferred fixed, managed rates, his comment paved the way for floating the dollar. Shultz was delighted that the new 'market-based system' was 'a great improvement over the inflexible gold-based system that preceded Camp David'. For his part, Kissinger hoped that Shultz's refusal to intervene to support the dollar would 'create conditions in which the common float is as hard to work as possible'.[62]

The demise of the Bretton Woods system led to a major shift in the 'impossible trinity'. The Americans had moved from a stable price of gold and the dollar to floating, with a commitment to free movement of capital. Domestic policy autonomy was retained by the ability to change the exchange rate and adopt 'soft' monetary policies, with the risk – all too apparent in the United States and Britain – of inflation and failure to address competitiveness. Instead, the exchange rate was allowed to 'take the strain' by depreciation to make exports more competitive, and monetary policy could be 'softer' now that the rate did not need to be supported.

The new trade-off approach posed problems in the EEC, for floating rates between European currencies were a threat to the customs union and economic integration. The EEC turned to internal stability by attempting to keep exchange rates within narrower bands. Nevertheless, there were divergences, which reflected different national policies. France wished to push monetary union ahead of economic convergence, whereas Germany preferred to wait until economies were more closely aligned. France faced greater difficulties of remaining within the narrow band of the collective float than did Germany, with its commitment to stability. Meanwhile, the British government was torn between the external discipline of the narrow band of the European monetary system on inflation and the realisation that it would limit domestic policies for growth. Hence the choice between wider and narrow bands, or between fixed and floating rates, reflected political choices over the extent to which domestic policies should be sacrificed to economic integration.

The argument of this chapter is that the emergence of the European monetary union was not only an internal dynamic after the completion of the customs union. It was also a response to the perceived failings of the United States in the crisis of the Bretton Woods regime – whether it be the

---

61 Volcker and Gyohten, *Changing Fortunes*, pp. 113–14.
62 Sargent, *A Superpower Transformed*, p. 127.

'exorbitant privilege' of the dollar and its 'deficit without tears' stressed by France, or the influx of dollars into Germany that threatened inflation. The crisis of legitimacy of Bretton Woods led to a new monetary regime or 'non-system' which permitted floating currencies, with Europe as a zone of exchange rate stability. The risk, of course, was that individual nation-states in Europe would be surrendering a large element of domestic policy autonomy.

Recommended Reading

Dyson, K. and I. Maes (eds.). *Architects of the Euro: Intellectuals in the Making of the European Monetary Union* (Oxford, Oxford University Press, 2016).

Garten, J. E. *Three Days at Camp David: How a Secret Meeting in 1971 Transformed the Global Economy* (New York, NY, Harper, 2021).

Gray, W. G. 'Floating the System: Germany, the United States, and the Breakdown of Bretton Woods, 1969–1973', *Diplomatic History* 31 (2007): 295–323.

James, H. *International Monetary Cooperation since Bretton Woods* (Oxford, Oxford University Press, 1996).

Matusow, A. J. *Nixon's Economy: Booms, Busts, Dollars and Votes* (Lawrence, KS, University Press of Kansas, 1998).

Mourlon-Druol, E. *A Europe Made of Money: The Emergence of the European Monetary System* (Ithaca, NY and London, Cornell University Press, 2012).

Schenk, C. R. *The Decline of Sterling: Managing the Retreat of an International Currency, 1945– 1992* (Cambridge, Cambridge University Press, 2010).

9

The Vicissitudes of Market Europe

GILLES GRIN

Introduction

After a dozen years of Eurosclerosis, a European revival was ready in 1985 to transform the European Communities. With the aim of creating an internal (or single) market without internal frontiers by the end of 1992, the new Commission presided over by Frenchman Jacques Delors launched a very important legislative programme which was to be adopted in 8 years and which succeeded in convincing the member states to modify the founding treaties of the 1950s. Accordingly, the Single European Act (SEA) was signed in 1986 and entered into force in 1987. The single market programme (SMP) captivated the minds of Europeans and had a lasting influence on the construction of Europe. We will examine several crucial questions in this chapter. What did the SMP and the SEA consist of? What was the motivation behind the will to complete the internal market? What was the outcome? How and in what way has the SMP had a lasting influence on the construction of Europe? Where are we today, almost 30 years after the supposed completion of the internal market?

The scholarly literature on market Europe and the internal market since 1985 is very large. This subject of study can be approached via different scientific disciplines, including history, political science, law and economics. Each discipline has its specificities, its questions and its tools. The exploitation of public and private archives, which have recently been opened and will continue to be made available, allows a more detailed knowledge of the role of the actors and driving factors at work (especially regarding the launch of the SMP). They supplement the study of official documents and the conducting of interviews with relevant actors. The availability of new sources allows the enrichment of a large debate in political science, which is older, since it dates back to the end of the 1980s and the 1990s and deals with similar themes. Neo-functionalist theories existing since the 1950s have proposed a specific dynamic for the European integration process independent from the member states participating in it by invoking the influence of transnational actors and spillover mechanisms. These have been questioned by intergovernmentalist theories postulating that real power remains based in the hands of states, especially the most important ones. This intergovernmentalist school has itself been challenged by the subsequent study of European institutions and business interest groups. Another important field of investigation in political science is concerned with the theories and practices of regulation and to what extent the functioning of markets is based on ever more sophisticated public regulations which are implemented by public authorities at different levels (national, regional and local, but also continental and global), hence the concept of multilevel governance. Internal market law occupies a very important place within European Union (EU) law and covers multiple issues that it would be impossible to summarise here. Economics, both at the microeconomic and at the macroeconomic level, has investigated the economic effects of the process of establishing the internal market. Developments in European integration have provided economists with an agenda for research and case studies. Here, the European institutions themselves have played an important role in commissioning studies. We can think of the famous Cecchini report of 1988, which will be mentioned later, or of the Single Market Review of 1996. The debate between economists on market Europe was most intense in the years 1988–91, before being supplanted by the theme of monetary integration. More recently, the Commission and the European Parliament (EP) have continued to conduct their own investigations.

A New Look at the European Internal Market since 1985

We shall begin by presenting the main stages of the relaunch of the European internal market initiated in 1985. We will therefore ask ourselves *how* the idea of market Europe came to the forefront. Then we will analyse the explanatory factors of the recovery, that is, *why* the idea of market Europe could become so important. We will then proceed to an assessment of the SMP carried out between 1985 and the end of 1992. Finally, we will briefly present the main developments that have occurred after 1992.

Main Stages in the Revival
The New Delors Commission

By the end of May 1984, France and Germany had agreed on the name of Jacques Delors, French Minister of Economy and Finance, to head the next Commission of the European Communities.[1] The Franco-German tandem's proposal was accepted by the other member states at a meeting in Brussels in October 1984 and formalised during the Dublin summit in December.[2] One of the linchpins of the new Commission was to be the British Conservative Lord Arthur Cockfield. Delors accepted the British proposal that Lord Cockfield be allocated the internal market portfolio.[3]

During his tour of European capitals in the autumn of 1984, Jacques Delors submitted four proposals for a European revival to his interlocutors: a common defence policy, monetary union, institutional reform and, finally, the completion of the internal market.[4] As none of the first three proposals met with unanimous agreement among member states, Delors agreed to fall back on the fourth. The completion of the internal market aimed to conclude work situated at the heart of the 1957 Treaty of Rome, while responding to contemporary concerns regarding liberalism and deregulation. The idea came at the right time. In the years preceding 1985, there had emerged a wide recognition that European companies were lagging behind their American and Japanese competitors, who in turn benefited from a large domestic market on which they could rely to conquer the still fragmented European market. The concept of the 'cost of non-Europe' had emerged in the early 1980s, calling for a unification of the European market to modernise the productive structures of the old continent.

The completion of the internal market was placed at the top of the European agenda from the autumn of 1984. The exact form of the project and its marketing remained to be defined. The idea of a project with the deadline of 1992 emerged during conversations between Delors and Cockfield before the new Commission took office on 6 January 1985.[5] In his first speech to the EP on 14 January, Jacques Delors asked the following question: 'Is it presumptuous to announce and then to carry out the decision

---

1 J. Attali, *Verbatim I: Deuxième partie, 1983–1986* (Paris, Fayard, 1993), p. 999.
2 Ibid., p. 1074.
3 A. Cockfield, *The European Union: Creating the Single Market* (London and New York, Wiley Chancery Law, 1994), pp. 19, 52.
4 J. Delors, *L'unité d'un homme: Entretiens avec Dominique Wolton* (Paris, Éditions Odile Jacob, 1994), p. 220; J. Delors, *Mémoires* (Paris, Plon, 2004), pp. 182–92.
5 Cockfield, *The European Union*, p. 33.

to remove all frontiers within Europe by 1992?'[6] Even if Delors' speech went well beyond the completion of the internal market, the reference to the abolition of internal borders was fundamental. It was to distinguish the Delors Commission's programme from previous efforts in the common market. The exact deadline for the completion of this programme was not definitively set until the end of winter: '1992' would mean 31 December 1992, and the programme would extend over the term of office of two successive Commissions.[7]

Mutual Recognition

The 'Cassis de Dijon' judgment of the Court of Justice, rendered in February 1979, had paved the way for the principle of mutual recognition, allowing a product legally manufactured and distributed in a member state to benefit from free access to the markets of the other member states insofar as it complied with legal objectives such as public safety or public health.[8] The Council of Ministers adopted on 7 May 1985 a resolution on a new approach to technical harmonisation and standards that was based on a Commission proposal of 31 January 1985.[9] The resolution was a political answer to an important set of technical issues to which a judiciary answer had already been given in 1979. Legislative harmonisation was becoming limited to the essential requirements (health, safety ...). Standards organisations would be responsible for establishing detailed technical specifications conforming to essential requirements determined by policy-makers. (These organisations are the European Committee for Standardization (CEN), European Committee for Electrotechnical Standardization (CENELEC) and European Telecommunications Standards Institute (ETSI).) These technical specifications, unlike the essential requirements, would not be binding for producers. A producer choosing not to comply with these technical specifications should, however, be prepared to prove that their products were conforming to the essential components specified by the Community. Finally, national authorities would be obliged to recognise that products in conformity with European standards (and, provisionally, national standards)

---

6 *Bulletin des Communautés européennes*, Supplément 1/85, 1985, p. 6.
7 Cockfield, *The European Union*, pp. 32–3.
8 Court of Justice of the European Communities, case 120/78 (20 February 1979).
9 *Bulletin des Communautés européennes* (no. 1, 1985), pp. 15–16; 'Council Resolution of 7 May 1985 on a New Approach to Technical Harmonization and Standards', in R. Bieber, R. Dehousse, J. Pinder and J. H. H. Weiler (eds.), *1992: One European Market? A Critical Analysis of the Commission's Internal Market Strategy* (Baden-Baden, Nomos, 1988), pp. 443–51.

would be presumed to comply with the essential requirements defined at political level. The new approach would focus mainly on neglected areas or on those where the traditional approach had been powerless. This approach would also influence the philosophy of the SMP being drawn up by the Commission between March and the beginning of June 1985, which would become the White Paper.[10]

The White Paper on Completing the Internal Market

This detailed programme of action was accepted by the Commission and was sent to senior national politicians a few days later, on 14 June.[11] The action was deliberate: it was a question of giving the heads of state and government enough time for them to be informed, but not enough to analyse it to the smallest detail and unravel the whole edifice.[12] The press coverage across Europe was excellent and the reactions to the document very favourable.[13] The question of the links between the completion of the internal market in the strict sense and the adoption of accompanying measures and policies had been discussed within the Commission. The opinion that the use of linkages was likely to delay or even threaten progress in each area prevailed very widely. The White Paper thus focused on the completion of the internal market, whereas accompanying policies would follow separately.

The White Paper was a formidable document which would set the Community's agenda for the internal market for the next 8 years, until the end of 1992. Given the novelty of the concept of removing all physical, technical and fiscal barriers in order to establish an area without internal frontiers, the preparation of the White Paper was logically a difficult exercise for the Commission services. Almost 60 per cent of the 300 or so proposals in the White Paper concerned the control and free movement of goods. The White Paper therefore was intended firstly to finish the work in this area. The idea was then to apply the concepts and methods of the free movement of goods to the field of services. Horizontal measures as well as the free movement of factors of production were also on the agenda. However, the

---

10 É. Bussière, 'Le Livre Blanc sur le marché intérieur objectif et instrument de la relance Delors', in M. Gehler and W. Loth (eds.), *Reshaping Europe: Towards a Political, Economic and Monetary Union, 1984–1989* (Baden-Baden, Nomos, 2020), pp. 227–45.

11 Commission of the European Communities, *Completing the Internal Market: White Paper from the Commission to the European Council (Milan, 28 and 29 June 1985)*, COM (85) 310 final, Brussels, 14 June 1985.

12 Cockfield, *The European Union*, pp. 48–9.

13 *Europe (Agence Europe)* (no. 4112, 19 June 1985), p. 1; Cockfield, *The European Union*, pp. 49–52.

free movement of people went beyond the strictly economic framework by displaying a civic ambition. The notions of abolishing internal frontiers and establishing free movement of citizens made the White Paper an ambitious programme going well beyond purely economic integration.

Alongside the White Paper, several major issues were on the agenda of the European Council meeting in Milan on 28 and 29 June 1985. There was notably the issue of institutional reform of the European Communities, which was particularly important for giving the proposals of the White Paper a chance to be adopted. Without such a reform, 90 per cent of its proposals would indeed have to be adopted unanimously by the Council of Ministers.[14] The question of how to improve political cooperation on foreign policy was also an important issue. The Milan summit began in a very busy atmosphere, described in the following words by British Foreign Secretary Geoffrey Howe: 'the Milan conference venue, when we finally did get there, gave a characteristically Italian impression of having been thrown together like some scene-stealing film-set. Prime Minister Craxi's briefing and chairmanship had something of the same quality. The Council was long and increasingly bad-tempered on all sides.'[15] It ended with a dramatic twist. After a vote had been called by Bettino Craxi, the member states, voting seven against three in favour, accepted the convening of an intergovernmental conference (IGC) to revise the founding treaties. As for the White Paper, it was welcomed and endorsed by heads of state and government.[16]

The Single European Act

The inaugural meeting of the IGC was held in Luxembourg on 9 September 1985. Jean De Ruyt participated in the intergovernmental conference as adviser to the chief of the Belgian delegation.[17] The Commission's recommendation to set up a single conference responsible for revising the treaties establishing the European Communities and dealing with the European Political Cooperation (EPC) had been followed. The aim of this single framework was to avoid the creation of a new political community from which the Commission would be excluded, and which would fragment European integration efforts. The United Kingdom, Denmark

14 W. De Clercq and L. Verhoef, *Europe Back to the Top* (Brussels, Roularta Books, 1990), p. 22.
15 G. Howe, *Conflict of Loyalty* (London and Basingstoke, Pan Books, 1995), p. 409.
16 Cockfield, *The European Union*, pp. 48–51.
17 Ibid., pp. 61–2; J. De Ruyt, *L'Acte unique européen: Commentaire*, 2nd ed. (Brussels, Éditions de l'Université de Bruxelles, 1989), pp. 67–8.

and Greece were present in Luxembourg even though they had voted against the convocation of the IGC.

The issues and challenges of the negotiations can be summed up as completing the internal market, codifying and developing flanking policies, dealing with the monetary dimension, solving institutional questions and formalising political cooperation on foreign affairs. Altogether, the most widely discussed ideas were those related to the internal market and to the powers of the EP.[18] The most significant obstacles facing the Luxembourg Summit were the internal market, the monetary dimension and research. Doubts had arisen about the possibility of reaching an agreement.[19]

The Commission played a major role in the intergovernmental negotiations. From the beginning, it emphasised the completion of the internal market and the associated required changes to decision-making procedures. Indeed, it was a wise strategy to start with the uncontroversial aim described in the White Paper on completing the internal market and to impose with it some institutional adjustments.[20] Discussions at the IGC were still controversial. Some countries were afraid of a decline in prevailing national norms regarding health, safety at work or protection of the environment.[21] Without saying so, many feared the encroachment of foreign firms on domestic markets. A key question was raised: to what extent should there be linkages between the completion of the internal market in a strict sense and flanking measures and policies? The debate was intense.[22]

The flanking policies under discussion for insertion into the treaty concerned technology, the environment, economic and social cohesion, and social policy. The most controversial was social policy: its inclusion had not been foreseen initially, but had been put on the table by Denmark and France. Modest ambitions were formulated during the first debates, and the disagreement of the British was overcome only at the end of the IGC.[23] The monetary dimension was also controversial. It was described as the

18 De Ruyt, L'Acte unique européen, pp. 74–6, 79–80.
19 Attali, Verbatim I, p. 1343; Delors, Mémoires, pp. 223–4; De Ruyt, L'Acte unique européen, pp. 74–8, 86.
20 De Ruyt, L'Acte unique européen, pp. 70–2.
21 Delors, Mémoires, pp. 224–5; De Ruyt, L'Acte unique européen, p. 74.
22 Europe (Agence Europe) (no. 4110, 15 June 1985), p. 11; Report Drawn up on Behalf of the Committee on Economic and Monetary Affairs and Industrial Policy on the White Paper from the Commission of the European Communities to the European Council (Milan, 28–29 June 1985) on 'Completing the Internal Market', European Parliament, PE 101.919/fin., 11 December 1985; Cockfield, The European Union, pp. 44–8.
23 Delors, Mémoires, p. 223; De Ruyt, L'Acte unique européen, pp. 73, 76–7, 80, 88.

'supreme battle' by Jacques Delors.[24] The greatest objections came from the United Kingdom and Germany. The Commission, Belgium, France and Italy were most in favour of it. Discussions started late on this question, in the middle of November.[25] The issue of the powers of the EP was difficult because it had no direct link with the completion of the internal market. Initial proposals were made by the Commission and the Luxembourgish presidency. As there was no consensus among member states to grant the power of legislative co-decision to the Parliament, the result had to be limited.[26]

Most discussions on the EPC took place at the Political Committee (composed of national ambassadors), and there were few debates among ministers. The discussions were based on a couple of national texts. The objective and the result were largely a codification of existing practices. France was at the forefront of the idea to create an EU with a General Secretariat in charge of the EPC. With this concept, an intergovernmental Union would encompass the supranational Communities. The Hexagon made such a proposal jointly with Germany before Milan (June) and brought it back before Luxembourg (December). But this controversial idea was not discussed at Luxembourg (it would return and be decided 6 years later at Maastricht).[27]

The most integrationist around the table were the Italians, Belgians, Dutch and Luxembourgers.[28] Leaders with ambitious integrationist objectives could adhere to the first aim of market integration insofar as it could pave the way for further progress. These personalities, particularly strongly represented within the European institutions and in several member states, did not see the integration of European markets as an end. They hoped that the 1992 objective could help progress flanking policies and institutional reforms. Integrationists, while adhering to the SMP, also wanted other developments to appear in the revision of the Treaty of Rome.[29] On the other end of the spectrum were the British and the Danes, who were very attached to their national sovereignty and were prepared only to make

---

24 Delors, *Mémoires*, p. 223.
25 Ibid., pp. 223–4; De Ruyt, *L'Acte unique européen*, pp. 73, 75, 77, 79.
26 Delors, *Mémoires*, p. 221; De Ruyt, *L'Acte unique européen*, pp. 79–80.
27 Delors, *Mémoires*, pp. 208–18; De Ruyt, *L'Acte unique européen*, pp. 77, 87. See also the archives of the Secretary General of the Commission, Émile Noël, held at the Historical Archives of the European Union in Florence, EN-1802, 1803 and 1804 (Acte unique européen: Coopération politique).
28 M. Thatcher, *The Downing Street Years* (London, HarperCollins Publishers, 1993), pp. 551–2; Attali, *Verbatim I*, p. 1345; De Ruyt, *L'Acte unique européen*, pp. 78–80, 83–4.
29 See Cockfield, *The European Union*, pp. 64–5, 182–3.

careful compromises to advance certain limited objectives.[30] The Franco-German tandem was rather integrationist, even if there were occasional differences between the two countries.[31] Finally, the main concern of Ireland and Greece was cohesion, which they saw as their best chance to face the significant liberalisation induced by the SMP. Spain and Portugal, which had observer status until the end of 1985 before accessing the Communities, shared this perspective.[32]

The negotiations were not easy, and many discussions were at an impasse on the eve of the European summit in Luxembourg on 2 and 3 December 1985. This meeting of heads of state and government was one of the longest in the history of the Communities, lasting more than 27 hours and ending at midnight on the second day. The chapter on the internal market was not completed until 10 p.m. on the second evening. It seemed for a long time that no agreement could be reached in Luxembourg, but eventually there was a result which might seem disappointing to some but was well balanced overall.[33]

French President François Mitterrand said that it was a compromise for progress and that an important part of the Milan agenda had been achieved. The other heads of state and government were generally satisfied with the compromise. Only the President of the Italian Council, Bettino Craxi, declared himself disappointed with the result obtained.[34] Jacques Delors expressed a degree of disappointment about what had been achieved. For him, the most disappointing part of the agreement concerned the powers of the EP.[35] Jacques Delors stated the following during a debate with Simone Veil on 4 December 1985 in Paris: 'Therefore, what happened last night, as I said before, does not respond to what I wanted. It corresponds to what I was reasonably hoping for. It is a compromise of progress. It will depend on many

30 Attali, *Verbatim I*, p. 1345; Delors, *L'unité d'un homme*, p. 245; Howe, *Conflict of Loyalty*, pp. 455–7; De Ruyt, *L'Acte unique européen*, p. 73; Thatcher, *The Downing Street Years*, pp. 551–7.
31 Attali, *Verbatim I*, pp. 1343–4; Delors, *L'unité d'un homme*, p. 222; Howe, *Conflict of Loyalty*, pp. 455–6; De Ruyt, *L'Acte unique européen*, pp. 77–9; Thatcher, *The Downing Street Years*, pp. 552–5.
32 De Ruyt, *L'Acte unique européen*, pp. 71, 73, 76, 79.
33 Howe, *Conflict of Loyalty*, p. 454; De Ruyt, *L'Acte unique européen*, pp. 77, 79.
34 *Europe (Agence Europe)* (no. 4218, 5 December 1985), pp. 3–6; Hans-Dietrich Genscher, *Erinnerungen* (Berlin, Siedler, 1995), p. 374; Helmut Kohl, *Erinnerungen 1982–1990* (Munich, Droemer, 2005), pp. 387–8, 439–40.
35 'Interview Jacques Delors', *L'Indépendant* (13 December 1985); Jacques Delors' archives (henceforth JD)-38 (interview de Jacques Delors, presse, 12/1985), p. 4, consulted at the Jean Monnet Foundation for Europe in Lausanne; 'Demain à la une', *Paris Match* (11 December 1985), JD-38, p. 8.

of us to turn it into a dynamic compromise.'[36] With more hindsight, though, Jacques Delors claimed in his memoirs that the SEA was his 'preferred treaty', arguing that 'with this text, the Commission had the political tool it needed, not only to put in place the internal market, but also to implement policies that would give to the Community the face of a European model of society, an equilibrium between market and regulation, a subtle dialectic between competition, cooperation and solidarity'.[37] As for the members of the EP, including its President Pierre Pflimlin and the federalist hero Altiero Spinelli, as well as members of the European Socialist Movement and the European Movement, they expressed their dissatisfaction with the results of the IGC. For them, the SEA would enable only a fraction of the path marked out by the draft treaty establishing the EU, voted for by the EP in February 1984, to be covered.[38]

What were the main results of the agreement?[39] The internal market received a definition referring to the area without internal frontiers, while certain protection mechanisms remained in the hands of states. The deadline of 31 December 1992 for completing the internal market had its place in the treaty, but it was a political commitment and not a legal one. The facets of some weaker economies were considered. The decision-making procedures were also modified, in particular to allow the completion of the internal market and to give more weight to the EP. Thanks to the agreement obtained, it can be estimated that the proportion of the measures contained in the White Paper that could be adopted by a qualified majority and no longer by unanimity of the member states would rise from 10 to 70 per cent.[40] Although the EP gained influence, it did not obtain the power of co-decision. Several new areas also found their place in the treaties. This mainly involved the codification of existing common policies. The SEA introduced a new chapter entitled 'Cooperation in Economic and Monetary Policy (Economic and Monetary Union)' into the treaty establishing the EEC. This chapter

36 JD-38, p. 22.   37 Delors, *Mémoires*, pp. 227–8.

38 *Europe (Agence Europe)* (no. 4218, 5 December 1985), pp. 3–6; *Europe (Agence Europe)* (no. 4220, 7 December 1985), pp. 3–3a; *Europe (Agence Europe)* (no. 4222, 12 December 1985), pp. 3–6; Pierre Pflimlin, *Itinéraires d'un Européen: Entretiens avec Jean-Louis English et Daniel Riot* (Strasbourg, La Nuée Bleue, 1989), pp. 324–5; Pierre Pflimlin, *Mémoires d'un Européen: De la IVe à la Ve République* (Paris, Fayard, 1991), pp. 351–2.

39 *Conseil européen des 2/3 décembre 1985 à Luxembourg* (Presidency Conclusions), DOC/85/3, 3 December 1985; *Bulletin des Communautés européennes*, Supplément 2/86, 1986. The following book contains the text of the Treaty Establishing the European Economic Community before and after the changes brought about by the SEA: S. Nelson (ed.), *Treaty Establishing the European Economic Community: Rome 1957* (Oxford, Nelson & Pollard Publishing, 1993).

40 De Clercq and Verhoef, *Europe Back to the Top*, p. 22.

merely codified the existing situation but could possibly be used by the proponents of a full economic and monetary union as a stepping stone for subsequent developments.

Some secondary points were still to be resolved after the Luxembourg summit. The SEA was signed by nine member states on 17 February 1986 in Luxembourg; Denmark, Greece and Italy signed it on 28 February in The Hague following a complication on the Danish side: the Danish parliament had in fact refused to ratify the treaty, as a result of which the people had to speak out in a referendum, in which the treaty was accepted by 56 per cent of the vote.[41] The ratification process encountered problems only in Ireland, where the government was compelled by legal recourse to hold a popular referendum, in which the 'yes' option triumphed with 70 per cent of the vote. The SEA could finally enter into force on 1 July 1987, 6 months later than scheduled.[42]

Europhoria

Until the spring of 1988, the pace of adoption of the measures contained in the White Paper was particularly disappointing. The main responsibility for this lay with the work of the Council. The Community's vigour was also depleted by the search for a multiannual budgetary agreement, at the centre of which were the financing of the common agricultural policy, the massive increase of the structural funds in favour of the regions which risked losing the most from the SMP and, finally, the creation of the Community's new financial resources of its own. It was at an extraordinary European Council meeting held in Brussels in February 1988 under the German presidency that the Twelve finally agreed on what had come to be known as the 'Delors I package'.[43] Given the fear of the polarising effects of the large internal market, Jacques Delors argued that without an agreement on this financial package doubling the structural funds in 5 years, the 1992 objective could not have been reached.[44]

The British magazine *The Economist* noted that the SMP was the 'European phenomenon of the spring of 1988', adding: 'now that most branches of European business are aware of it, 1992 has become a state of mind, a set of expectations that has political force, an obsession that amounts almost to

---

41 De Ruyt, *L'Acte unique européen*, pp. 88–90. 42 Ibid., pp. 91, 286.
43 *Note from the Presidency, Making a Success of the Single European Act. Consolidated Conclusions of the European Council (19 February 1988)*, SN 416/1/88.
44 Delors, *L'unité d'un homme*, pp. 230–7.

a new reality'.[45] The year 1988 indeed represented the shift towards 'Europhoria', a contraction of 'European euphoria', which would last for 4 years. European leaders first began to discuss the irreversible nature of the creation of a large internal market by the end of 1992. It was at this point that a broad awareness of the importance of the 1992 deadline had developed among economic and social actors in Europe. The media also entered the game. The United States, the main economic and strategic partner of the countries of western Europe, awakened at the same time to the project of a European internal market. The United States' initial attitude was generally positive, but at the same time imbued with scepticism and fears of discrimination against the United States. Seeing that the project was moving forward and that the latter was not the case, they became more and more positive, especially since the new administration of President George H. W. Bush, in power since January 1989, had an enhanced geostrategic prospect regarding the importance of transatlantic ties. The term 'fortress Europe', characteristic of early American fears, gradually ceased to be used between 1990 and 1992. Several hearings on 'Europe 1992' were organized by the American Congress between 1988 and 1992.[46]

Much ink was spilled over the expected economic effects of the SMP. In this regard, the Cecchini report played a crucial role.[47] This report, launched by the Commission and made public at the end of March 1988, was the result of 2 years of in-depth studies of the expected effects of the removal of non-tariff barriers provided for in the White Paper. At the time, a benchmark analysis of the economic consequences of market integration within the Community was missing.

From the publication of the reference works of economists Jacob Viner and James Meade in the first part of the 1950s introducing the concepts of trade creation, diversion and expansion pertaining to regional integration schemes,[48] economists had developed a line of enquiry, but they struggled for

45 N. Colchester, 'A Survey of Europe's Internal Market', The Economist 308, no. 7558 (1988): 1.
46 See G. Grin, The Battle of the Single European Market: Achievements and Economic Thought, 1985–2000 (London and New York, Kegan Paul, 2003), pp. 135–8.
47 Commission of the European Communities, Research on the 'Cost of Non-Europe', 16 vols. (Luxembourg, Office for Official Publications of the European Communities, 1988); P. Cecchini, with M. Catinat and A. Jacquemin, The European Challenge – 1992: The Benefits of a Single Market (Aldershot, Wildwood House, 1988).
48 J. Viner, The Customs Union Issue (New York, Carnegie Endowment for International Peace; London, Stevens & Sons, 1950); J. E. Meade, The Theory of Customs Unions (Amsterdam, North-Holland Publishing Company, 1955); J. E. Meade, The Theory of International Economic Policy, vol. II: Trade and Welfare (London and New York, Oxford University Press, 1955).

three decades to develop models allowing the quantification of the most important effects of regional integration, particularly taking into account the abolition of non-tariff barriers, economies of scale, imperfect competition and the surge of intra-industry trade. The Cecchini report forecast average expected gains of around 200 billion European Currency Units, representing around 5 per cent additional GDP. This study helped to mobilise economic circles in favour of the SMP. It created an agenda for research and gave rise to academic debates. Three themes going beyond the conclusions of the report were discussed specifically. First, how would the effects of the programme be distributed by region and by industrial sector? In particular, would the countries of the south be the main winners or losers? Secondly, would the SMP favour European companies on a global scale? Risks were mentioned: fears around a transposition of European free trade on a global level and fears that non-EU companies would use the internal market as a Trojan horse. Opportunities were also highlighted: the need to open the Community to the rest of the world, and the possibility of increasing the competitiveness of European companies on world markets. Thirdly, beyond the effects of static resource allocation as analysed in the Cecchini report, could the SMP sustainably increase the growth rate of Community Europe?[49]

The Rise of Contending Views for the Future

The European political choice of 1985, aimed at moving from the common market to the internal market, had identified a crucial bottleneck in the integration process. In the spirit of the Monnet method, it allowed action on a limited but decisive point. It was the prospect of its success, visible to all as early as the spring of 1988, which paved the way for new spillovers. The Europeans asked themselves new questions and opened the debate on the continuation of the integration process. These discussions and controversies arose at a time when the rest of Europe and the world were changing extraordinarily fast. The Soviet glacis in eastern Europe was dissolving, and the Cold War between East and West was coming to its end. Eventually, Germany would reunite, the Soviet Union would disappear, and Yugoslavia would disintegrate in fury and bloodshed. Some key questions confronted Community Europe. Should integration be limited to markets for goods, services and factors of production? Should the Community or the member states control social standards, taxation and currency? Should there be a common economic and social model? What place should be given to

---

49 Grin, *The Battle of the Single European Market*, pp. 73–105, 235–303.

private actors, to states and to the Community itself? Should the European integration project be limited to economic integration or would it be better to create a true political union?

It was becoming clear in 1988 that two opposing visions of the future of Community Europe were clashing, that of Margaret Thatcher and that of Jacques Delors. These two visions had been able to coexist for a while, but their opposition was growing stark. For the British Prime Minister, a supporter of a market Europe, it was necessary to establish regulatory competition between national standards. For her, the purpose of the SMP was to break down barriers in order to deregulate and promote free trade. The free movement of capital was to create tax competition and exercise control over states. The fact that capital would be able to flow freely would exert a constraint upon states. The latter would know that if the framework conditions that they offered were not competitive, capital would leave their country and strangle it. In this view, there was no need to develop accompanying policies or a political integration project. Mrs Thatcher was naturally opposed to developments in social policy, taxation, economic and monetary union, and political union. She believed that the Community institutions had acquired too much power. Her famous words from a speech in Bruges in September 1988 still resonate in our ears: 'We have not successfully rolled back the frontiers of the state in Britain, only to see them reimposed at a European level, with a European super-state exercising a new dominance from Brussels.'[50]

For the President of the European Commission, it was necessary to regulate the markets and prevent social and regional injustices due to market forces. Jacques Delors wanted to complement the SMP with the development of common policies, including social policy, and wanted to establish greater convergence of tax policies while economic, monetary and political union were on the horizon. In matters of tax policy there were fears of an under-taxation of capital caused by its free movement, which would strangle national treasuries or over-tax labour.

Monetary unification was clearly the new frontier of the European project. Even if the point was debated, many politicians and experts thought that there could not be a true internal market without monetary integration, especially since the free movement of capital had been introduced between

50 'Margaret Thatcher's Bruges Speech: Speech Given by British Prime Minister Margaret Thatcher at the College of Europe, on the State and Future of European Integration, Bruges, 20 September 1988', in A. G. Harryvan and J. van der Harst (eds.), *Documents on European Union* (Basingstoke and London, Macmillan, 1997), pp. 242–7.

1990 and 1992.[51] Stabilisation mechanisms such as the EMS worked less and less well in this context. The economist and future Nobel Prize winner Robert Mundell demonstrated that a country could simultaneously achieve only two of the following three objectives in relation to a group of other countries: free movement of capital, an autonomous monetary policy and a system of fixed exchange rates. As the first objective was part of the SMP, a choice had to be made between the two others. The Delors Committee, established by the European Council in June 1988, issued its report on the modalities for the creation of the Economic and Monetary Union (EMU) in April 1989.[52] The EMU project was at the heart of the Maastricht Treaty, which was signed in February 1992. This treaty was built on the achievements of the SMP and the SEA; apart from that, internal market issues were quite peripheral. The British had negotiated an exemption for both the EMU and the Protocol on Social Policy. The treaty experienced Homeric difficulties in its ratification: a negative result in an initial referendum in Denmark, subsequently rectified by a 'yes' vote after the country received opt-outs; a very small majority (51 per cent in favour) in the French referendum of 20 September 1992; the virtual collapse of the British government; and legal appeals in Germany. The Schengen Convention, which was signed in 1990 and entered into force 5 years later, was outside the Community's scope at that time. It aimed to extend the SMP by giving itself the means to get rid of all internal border controls within the Community.

A group of western European countries that did not want to belong to the European Communities at the time had created the European Free Trade Association (EFTA) in 1960 with the purpose of abolishing customs tariffs and quantitative restrictions on the trade of industrial goods. The EFTA model of a free trade area was thus less ambitious than the customs union model of the EEC with its common commercial policy. In the 1970s, free trade agreements entered into force between the EEC and EFTA countries. The success of the SMP in the second part of the 1980s was such that the EFTA member states feared the return of an economic division with the Community, where they would find themselves placed on the periphery of the economic integration process. Faced with this fear, the Community

---

51 For an analysis of the political and economic motivations behind the creation of the euro, see G. Grin, 'La création de l'euro: Motivations politiques et économiques', in G. Grin, F. Nicod and B. Altermatt (eds.), *Formes d'Europe: Union européenne et autres organisations/Forms of Europe: European Union and Other Organisations* (Lausanne, Fondation Jean Monnet pour l'Europe; Paris, Economica, 2018), pp. 57–81.

52 Committee for the Study of Economic and Monetary Union, *Report on Economic and Monetary Union in the European Community* (12 April 1989).

proposed the negotiation of the European Economic Area (EEA) project. After difficult negotiations, the Treaty of Porto was signed in May 1992.[53] It offered the EFTA countries access to the internal market by automatically adopting Community law as well as rules relating to the settlement of disputes. Contrary to what President Delors had initially hinted at, the EFTA states joining the EEA would not participate in decision-making within the Community. They avoided economic marginalisation at the cost of political subjugation.[54] The EEA entered into force on 1 January 1994. Austria, Finland and Sweden preferred to become full members of the Community, which became the EU. Iceland, Liechtenstein and Norway, on the other hand, opted for the EEA. Switzerland rejected the EEA in a referendum in December 1992, but did not want to join the EU. It can thus be concluded that the SMP enabled the European Community to win the battle for integration models in western Europe by supplanting the EFTA. The end of Soviet domination in eastern Europe, for its part, led to the dissolution of Comecon in 1991. The Community model thus became the compass of an entire continent.

Explanatory Factors of the Revival

The 1985 revival centred on the completion of the internal market corresponded to the 'art of the possible' of the time and to the needs perceived then. As we have seen, of the four stimulus ideas submitted by Jacques Delors to national capitals in the autumn of 1984, the completion of the single market was the only one to gain a consensus. At the same time, it was able to quickly develop in its wake the idea of institutional reforms, enshrined in the SEA.

The new Commission presided over by Jacques Delors was able to put forward an ambitious objective, that of a Community without internal frontiers by the end of 1992. It was able to rely on the legitimacy of the Treaty of Rome of 1957, which had fulfilled its objectives in terms of the abolition of internal quantitative restrictions and customs duties, but which one could hardly blame for the fight against non-tariff barriers other than the classic quantitative restrictions not having been carried on. Non-tariff barriers of this new type, which had been labelled as technical barriers to trade, did in fact develop a lot subsequently.

---

53 Agreement on the European Economic Area, 2 May 1992, Official Journal L 001, 03/01/1994.
54 P. G. Nell, *Suisse–Communauté européenne: Au cœur des négociations sur l'Espace économique européen* (Lausanne, Fondation Jean Monnet pour l'Europe; Paris, Economica, 2012), pp. 237–398.

At the same time, the 1992 objective contained in the SMP was not a simple reiteration of the ambition of the Treaty of Rome. Even if the latter contained the objective of the four freedoms (free movement of goods, services, persons and capital), the free movement of persons in fact concerned only economic actors. The SMP extended this free movement to all Community nationals, allowing the corresponding legislation to be adopted in 1990 and to constitute a milestone towards European citizenship and the Charter of Fundamental Rights. The Charter, which was proclaimed in 2000, became legally binding in 2009 with the entry into force of the Treaty of Lisbon. It guarantees a variety of rights pertaining to dignity, freedoms, equality, solidarity, citizens' rights and justice. The second crucial difference was that the common market of the Treaty of Rome could well be satisfied with the maintenance of internal borders. Here, the SMP shifted paradigm due to the consideration that the continuation of internal borders would inevitably lead to a pull in favour of the maintenance – even the development – of national controls. The internal market would therefore 'comprise an area without internal frontiers in which the free movement of goods, persons, services and capital is ensured in accordance with the provisions of this Treaty'.[55]

By proposing the SMP, the Delors Commission was able to address the two major economic concerns then faced by European states. The first was based on the observation that American and Japanese companies could take advantage of a large domestic market and thus amortise their production costs before setting off to attack foreign markets, including Europe. At the time, European companies in the automotive and mass electronics industries suffered the most from this competition. This explains why European industrial companies did intense lobbying work with European institutions. The European Round Table of Industrialists (ERT) in particular wielded considerable influence.[56] The second major economic concern was related to the change of economic paradigm. The 1970s and early 1980s had shown that the classical Keynesian view was not able to adequately explain the surge in

55 Article 8a of the Treaty Establishing the European Economic Community as modified by the Single European Act (now Article 26 of the Treaty on the Functioning of the European Union).

56 European Round Table of Industrialists (ERT), *Beating the Crisis: A Charter for Europe's Industrial Future* (Brussels, ERT, 1993), p. 10; M. G. Cowles, 'Setting the Agenda for a New Europe: The ERT and EC 1992', *Journal of Common Market Studies* 33 (1995): 501–26; A. G. Harryvan, 'The Single Market Project as a Response to Globalisation: The Role of the Round Table of European Industrialists and Other Non-state Actors in Launching the European Union's Internal Market (1983–1992)', in Gehler and Loth (eds.), *Reshaping Europe*, pp. 211–25.

stagflation, or to correctly prescribe the measures of economic and monetary policy to be taken. The rise of a new neoliberal economic vision, glorifying the market and the role of private economic actors, emphasising deregulation and the withdrawal of public power, could be seen as calling for the dismantling of barriers to trade. We may therefore argue that the SMP can be seen as a response to globalisation: that of economic actors and that of economic ideas.

The economic situation played a role in the European revival. As we have just seen, the difficult situation following the end of the post-war boom had greatly contributed to awareness. This is regarding the situation before 1985. Secondly, the economic situation from 1985 also played a favourable role, more as a lubricant than as a fuel. Community growth rates were highest in 1988 and 1989. Seven of the twelve member states also experienced their highest growth rate of the period in the same 2 years, while all the countries except for Denmark reached a peak between 1987 and 1990. The growth rates of the Community, that is, the annual variations of GDP in real terms, were as follows during the period 1985–92: 2.5 per cent in 1985; 2.9 per cent in 1986; 2.9 per cent in 1987; 4.3 per cent in 1988; 3.5 per cent in 1989; 2.9 per cent in 1990; 1.7 per cent in 1991; and 1.1 per cent in 1992. When we study the growth of twelve countries over 8 years, we get ninety-six positions. Of these positions, only five were negative, whereas forty-four were above 3 per cent.[57] We can therefore speak of an inverted U-curve. Unemployment rates, although they remained at a high level, followed a U-shaped curve with a lag in relation to the growth rates, reaching a minimum in 1990. Unemployment rates in the Community were as follows: 10.8 per cent in 1985; 10.7 per cent in 1986; 10.4 per cent in 1987; 9.8 per cent in 1988; 9.0 per cent in 1989; 8.4 per cent in 1990; 8.7 per cent in 1991; and 9.4 per cent in 1992.[58] This positive situation on the growth and, to a lesser extent, unemployment front undoubtedly facilitated the adoption of the White Paper measures. Europhoria, born in the spring of 1988, echoed a very positive situation in terms of growth (a parallel can be drawn with the very good economic situation of the 1960s within the EEC, which facilitated the establishment of the customs union).

At this stage, we can therefore say that the Delors Commission had succeeded in putting together a convincing European package with clear, innovative and ambitious objectives. It was a subtle blend of economics and

---

57 Commission européenne, 'Rapport économique annuel pour 1995', *Économie européenne* no. 59 (1995): 208.

58 Ibid., p. 201.

politics, echoing both historical ambition and contemporary concerns, aided throughout by the economic situation. The SMP was laser-focused on promoting market Europe, putting forward the principle of mutual recognition of national standards ahead of the development of European standards, while the SEA reintroduced the perspective with more cooperation and solidarity.

The final factor behind the revival was crucial: this was the extension of qualified majority voting in the Council of Ministers. Without this decisive contribution from the SEA, 90 per cent of the SMP measures would have had to be adopted unanimously by the member states, guaranteeing stagnation. Thanks to the SEA, 70 per cent could be adopted by a qualified majority.[59] This does not mean that member states systematically resorted to voting, but that the mere prospect of being outvoted made them more open to seeking compromise. The increase in the legislative power of the EP initiated by the SEA lengthened legislative procedures by just a few months on average, but in return brought better scrutiny of legal texts and greater democratic legitimacy.

Appraisal of the Single Market Programme (1985–1992)

Even though the Community achieved a lot during the period 1985–92 and the SMP was overall a great success, the work was in fact far from being completed. The benchmark of a Community without internal frontiers had not yet been reached. Of the 283 measures of the White Paper at the end of 1992, 258 had been adopted, meaning a success rate of 91 per cent (as opposed to the 100 per cent expected).[60] The main measures adopted between 1985 and 1992 concerned the mutual recognition of diplomas, the free movement of students as well as pensioners, easier access to the national civil service for nationals of another member state, facilitating the transfer of social security benefits from one country to another, the abolition (with rare exceptions) of customs controls at internal borders (while police controls still remained), a system of free circulation of medicines, an agreement on the approximation of value added tax rates and excise duties, the creation of a 'European passport' for financial institutions, measures concerning the

---

59 De Clercq and Verhoef, *Europe Back to the Top*, p. 22.
60 *Seventh Report of the Commission to the Council and the European Parliament Concerning the Implementation of the White Paper on the Completion of the Internal Market* (Brussels, Commission of the European Communities, COM (92) 383 final, 2 September 1992); *Le marché intérieur de la Communauté: Rapport 1993* (Brussels, Commission européenne, 1994).

opening of public procurement and the complete liberalisation of capital movements.[61] Beyond the White Paper, the Community had adopted a key regulation on the control of concentrations between undertakings, which gave the Commission the power to prevent mergers leading to the abuse of a dominant position.[62]

The twenty-five measures pending before the Council at the end of 1992 mainly concerned fiscal harmonisation, the statute for a European company, legislation on trademarks, the legal protection of biotechnological inventions and investment services.[63] Owing to national resistance, the SMP had also lost some very important proposals in connection with the free movement of persons along the way (these issues would be dealt with later in the framework of the third pillar of Maastricht). In contrast, the liberalisation of telecommunications had become part of the White Paper. The proportion of measures transposing the directives resulting from the White Paper, which were adopted at the end of 1992 by the member states, amounted to 75 per cent (as opposed to a target of 100 per cent). But only 39 per cent of the directives were then transposed in all the member states.[64]

The positive mood that had blossomed in the 1985 revival had faded. This difficult context explains why there was no exuberance associated with the imminent approach of the 1992 deadline. Indeed, 1992 was a very tumultuous year for the Community, but also for Europe more generally. The Treaty of Maastricht, signed in February 1992, experienced serious ratification difficulties, and these problems almost completely eclipsed the end of the implementation of the 1992 target. The greatest challenge then was to make the project of economic and monetary union a reality. Other problems further darkened the outlook: the end of an economic cycle, with falling growth and unemployment rising from an already high level, a monetary crisis with speculative attacks and forced departures from the EMS exchange rate mechanism, and a bleak climate in central and eastern Europe with the difficulty of reforms and war in the Balkans.

61 Délégation de l'Assemblée nationale pour les Communautés européennes, *L'état d'achèvement du marché intérieur* (Paris, Assemblée nationale, 1992), pp. 5–12, 43–4, 47–56.
62 Council Regulation (EEC) No. 4064/89 of 21 December 1989 (entry into force on 21 September 1990).
63 *Completing the Internal Market: White Paper from the Commission to the European Council (Milan, 28 and 29 June 1985)* (Brussels, Commission of the European Communities, COM (85) 310 final, 14 June 1985); *Seventh Report of the Commission to the Council and the European Parliament Concerning the Implementation of the White Paper on the Completion of the Internal Market. Le marché intérieur de la Communauté: Rapport 1993.*
64 *Seventh Report of the Commission to the Council and the European Parliament Concerning the Implementation of the White Paper on the Completion of the Internal Market*, p. 4.

Post-1992 Developments

At the end of 2022, the European internal market (or single European market) celebrated its thirtieth anniversary. It has remained at the heart of European economic integration, with many accompanying policies, in addition to the establishment of economic and monetary union. However, the internal market is not a static and immutable reality. It has been influenced by technological development and globalisation. The Union's geographical enlargements have also reshaped the internal market. The number of member states has grown from twelve at the end of 1992 to twenty-seven today. If we add the three EFTA member countries that joined the EEA when it was created in 1994 (Iceland, Liechtenstein and Norway), the number of states belonging to the internal market is now thirty. The integration of these many new states, in particular those of central and eastern Europe, was a draining challenge for Europeans during the 1990s and 2000s.

The management of the internal market requires the existence of numerous legal rules. An important part of the *acquis communautaire* thus constitutes the foundations of the internal market. This is not a state of nature and is not part of the natural order of things. On the contrary, in addition to legal rules, there must be the involvement of numerous institutions, at European, national, regional and local levels, with a corresponding political will. The internal market is clearly, both legally and materially, under the shared competence of the EU/EEA and member states. The problem of political will and its limits is most clearly demonstrated in the integration of services (representing 70 per cent of the Union's GDP), which lags far behind the integration of goods, but also of taxation and social policy, two areas where the unanimity rule continues to prevail within the Council.[65]

The internal market agenda is never-ending. The hurdles since 1993 have been the need to guarantee its proper functioning, to deepen it and to face the challenge of digitisation (let us not forget that the Internet saw the light of day only at the beginning of the 1990s and that many of the technological companies which are shaping the world today simply did not exist at the time). The internal market must also incorporate the imperative of energy transition and the decarbonisation of the economy (which the EU is now

---

65 European Commission, *The Single Market in a Changing World: A Unique Asset in Need of Renewed Political Commitment. Communication from the Commission to the European Parliament, the European Council, the Council, the European Economic and Social Committee and the Committee of the Regions*, COM (2018) 772 final, Brussels, 22 November 2018, p. 1.

taking in hand with its Green Deal).[66] There is a strong need to regularly update the existing rule book and to ensure that economic actors and European citizens are well informed of their rights and the opportunities created by the internal market.

Significant challenges continue to exist in the transposition of directives by member states and the implementation of EU law. The average deficit in the transposition by states of directives relating to the internal market was 25 per cent at the end of 1992. This rate was 9 per cent in October 1996, 6 per cent in November 1997 and 3 per cent in November 2000. During the 2000s, the rate fluctuated between 0.7 and 3.6 per cent, standing at 0.9 per cent in November 2010. During the 2010s, the rate fluctuated between 0.5 and 1.5 per cent, standing at 0.6 per cent in December 2019. The current average delay in transposing directives is almost a year.[67]

An interesting indicator of the fragmentation of the internal market is to consider the proportion of related directives which are not transposed simultaneously in all the member states. This rate was 61 per cent at the end of 1992,[68] then 46 per cent in October 1996, 27 per cent in November 1997 and 13 per cent in November 2000. During the 2000s, the rate fluctuated between 5 and 27 per cent, but clearly because of an enlargement effect: the rate was 9 per cent in November 2003, but jumped to 27 per cent in November 2004, 6 months after the great enlargement, and then fell back to 10 per cent in November 2005. The rate in November 2010 was 5 per cent. In the 2010s, it fluctuated between 4 and 7 per cent, standing at 4 per cent in December 2019. The most problematic areas of the internal market under this indicator at the end of 2019 were as follows: public procurement (a fragmentation rate of 27 per cent), intellectual property and copyright (19 per cent), financial information and company law (19 per cent) and financial services (12 per cent).[69]

Even if internal market directives are transposed by member states, they may be incorrectly transposed according to the European Commission, which will then open infringement proceedings against the member states

---

66 European Commission, *The European Green Deal. Communication from the Commission to the European Parliament, the European Council, the Council, the European Economic and Social Committee and the Committee of the Regions*, COM (2019) 640 final, Brussels, 11 December 2019.

67 European Commission, Single Market Scoreboard, Performance per governance tool, transposition.

68 *Seventh Report of the Commission to the Council and the European Parliament Concerning the Implementation of the White Paper on the Completion of the Internal Market*, p. 4.

69 European Commission, Single Market Scoreboard.

concerned. The relevant indicator, called the average conformity deficit, is 1.2 per cent. Given that 0.6 per cent of national transposition measures were missing at the end of 2019 and 1.2 per cent of measures were deemed incorrect by the Commission, in total almost 2 per cent of measures had actually not been transposed correctly.[70] Also, at the end of 2019, there were 800 cases pending for single market-related infringements, an average of twenty-nine cases per member state. The most problematic areas in terms of infringements are the environment (28 per cent), transport (17 per cent) and taxation (10 per cent).[71]

The EU's internal market regulatory policy became more complex after 1992. While, during the eight years of the SMP, the main objective was to adopt measures which enabled defragmentation of this market, it was more a question of articulating the promotion of free movement with the objectives of other community policies such as, for example, the protection of consumers, workers, the environment or data. The governance of the internal market has also become more complex since 1992 as there has been relatively less emphasis on adopting new rules (although this process has always continued) than on seeking greater efficiency of the normative framework. In addition, the development of new executive agencies and the process of enlargement have made the mapping of actors more complex.

The internal market has had to face several severe crises over the past 10 to 15 years: the great economic and financial crisis of 2008 (creating neoprotectionism and endangering the euro zone), Brexit (meaning the British withdrawal from the internal market and the customs union at the end of 2020) and Covid (the most serious health crisis for a century, with disastrous economic and social effects). Each time, the countries' first reflexes pushed them towards unilateralism. Then followed an awareness of their interdependence and the risks of acting alone, which paved the way for a rediscovery of the benefits of the internal market and awareness of the risks of letting it erode. Border controls and travel restrictions imposed by states in March 2020 due to the Covid epidemic have undermined the free movement of goods, services and people. The European Commission had to act over the following 3 months to lift around thirty restrictive measures, for example to ensure access to food, raw materials, medicines and protective

70 Ibid.
71 W. Weidenfeld and W. Wessels (eds.), *Jahrbuch der Europäischen Integration 2020* (Baden-Baden, Nomos, 2020), pp. 229–32.

equipment.[72] But member states continue to adopt recurrent border closure measures. The Commission is also active in preserving industrial supply chains as much as possible and in protecting strategic sectors. It risks being judged on the effectiveness of its action to promote rapid mass production and distribution of vaccines.

The reports of the European institutions clearly show that remaining barriers exist within the internal market. Here are some examples: it is difficult for companies to know all the regulatory requirements in force; there are complex administrative procedures in the member states; access to public procurement is not equal; member states sometimes add regulatory requirements in addition to European rules; there are problems for regulated professions (for example, engineers) and the retail trade; some cross-border purchases are rejected by suppliers; consumers have less confidence in cross-border online shopping; consumers are victims of cross-border fraud; differences between national tax systems create cumbersome procedures; the settlement of cross-border disputes creates complications; and registering an economic activity in other member states can be problematic. The root causes for these barriers are multifactorial: national rules that are too restrictive; complex European legislation; poor transposition of European directives; inadequate implementation of internal market law; insufficient or incompatible national administrative capacities; and insufficient coordination between the Commission and national administrations, as well as between the latter. Small and medium-sized enterprises (SMEs) and professionals (liberal professions) are the most penalised by the residual barriers existing in the internal market.[73]

Economic studies show that the internal market has helped increase the Union's GDP and foster job creation. Enlargement to include the countries of central and eastern Europe has been the main driver for further integration into the internal market, while the latter has helped the Union to cope better with economic crises. In a 2018 study, the European Commission estimated that the economic gains of the internal market amounted to around 8.5 per cent of the Union's GDP.[74] In a 2019

---

72 Discours du Commissaire Breton lors de l'échange de vues avec le Comité IMCO au Parlement européen (28 septembre 2020).

73 European Commission, *Identifying and Addressing Barriers to the Single Market. Communication from the Commission to the European Parliament, the Council, the European Economic and Social Committee and the Committee of the Regions*, COM (2020) 93 final, Brussels, 10 March 2020.

74 European Commission, *The Single Market in a Changing World: A Unique Asset in Need of Renewed Political Commitment*.

study on the 'cost of non-Europe' carried out by the services of the EP, the dividend of a fully realised internal market was estimated at 891 billion euros per year (pre-Brexit figure), or 5.8 per cent of the GDP of the Union.[75] If we synthesise the figures of the two preceding studies, we can conclude that the transition from a Europe without an internal market to a completely realised internal market would allow a gain in economic well-being of 15.6 per cent. On this path between a Europe without an internal market and a totally completed internal market, we can quantify the gains made thus far at 59 per cent of what could be achieved and the potential further gains at 41 per cent. Clearly, there is still a long way to go. In addition to the aforementioned figures, the internal market has also meant strengthened or new rights for European citizens. It is an area of freedom and not just of enhanced prosperity.

The internal market is at the heart of the European model of society. Even if it first abolished restrictions and barriers, it also meant regulatory activity and developed a solidarity dimension through legislative measures and redistributive policies, for example by protecting the interests of workers, consumers, SMEs, the environment and regions. For some, the neoliberal dimension at work during the 1990s and 2000s eclipsed the social dimension. However, too strict and rigid a competition policy would have weakened European industry in the fight against strong international competitors. The new importance that the EU seems to attach to its strategic autonomy and its capacity for resilience could mark a turning point in this regard. Clearly, the great debates around the internal market are crucial for the future of the continent and its place in the world.

Concluding Remarks

The history of the European internal market since 1985 has been rich and complex. This is clearly a success story in the process of the construction of Europe, even if there have been, still are and will remain in the future many challenges and crises to overcome. The existence of the internal market is not straightforward, and broad and constantly renewed political will is required in order to maintain smooth and effective functioning of the institutions

---

75 European Parliamentary Research Service, *Europe's Two Trillion Euro Dividend: Mapping the Cost of Non-Europe, 2019–24*, PE 631.745 (Brussels, European Parliament, 2019).

and the legal order. Economic actors and citizens must be aware of their rights and committed to the European project. The structural and cyclical economic situation in which European countries are living contributes to the reshaping of industrial structures and prevailing economic ideas, and this can help make the pursuit of the economic and political construction of Europe easier, or on the contrary more difficult. In this regard, a parallel may be drawn between the golden age of the common market (1958–69) and that of the internal market (1985–92). As we have seen, developments are the result of the combination of internal and external dynamics. The internal dynamics, in connection with the development of a process of economic and political construction on a continental scale, have undoubtedly been more widely studied over time.

However, the external dimension should not be neglected. Europe is in the middle of the vast world, and its interactions with this world are numerous. For example, at the level of the EU, the annual total of imports and exports of goods and services is around 6,000 billion euros for a GDP close to 14,000 billion euros.[76] There are three external drivers for change. The first is found on the side of globalisation and the competitive pressures it exerts on Europe. Globalisation does not only mean threats; it also grants Europeans the possibility to seize opportunities abroad. The second driver is technological progress, which is disrupting human societies and their economic activity in the broad sense. One of the striking examples of this is the 'information society'. Finally, the third external driver for change will increasingly shape the future of market Europe and the world in general: it concerns the challenges linked to the decarbonisation of human societies and the management of finite resources.

Recommended Reading

Commission of the European Communities. *Completing the Internal Market: White Paper from the Commission to the European Council (Milan, 28 and 29 June 1985)*, COM (85) 310 final, Brussels, 14 June 1985.

Cecchini, P. with M. Catinat and A. Jacquemin. *The European Challenge – 1992: The Benefits of a Single Market* (Aldershot, Wildwood House, 1988).

European Commission. *Identifying and Addressing Barriers to the Single Market. Communication from the Commission to the European Parliament, the Council, the European Economic and Social Committee and the Committee of the Regions*, COM (2020) 93 final, Brussels, 10 March 2020.

76 European Commission, *DG Trade Statistical Guide* (August 2020), pp. 17–18, 69.

European Commission. *The Single Market in a Changing World: A Unique Asset in Need of Renewed Political Commitment. Communication from the Commission to the European Parliament, the European Council, the Council, the European Economic and Social Committee and the Committee of the Regions*, COM (2018) 772 final, Brussels, 22 November 2018.

European Parliamentary Research Service. *Europe's Two Trillion Euro Dividend: Mapping the Cost of Non-Europe, 2019–24*, PE 631.745 (Brussels, European Parliament, 2019).

10

European Integration and the Challenges of Free Movement

MATHILDE UNGER

Introduction

According to the economist Amartya Sen, there are at least two 'moral' defences of the market. The first, and most common, is instrumental: we should protect the market because of the 'goodness of the results achieved'.[1] The market produces goods, contributes to collective utility and increases our freedom of choice. The second, less common, defence is based on fundamental rights: the right to property and the freedom to transact prevail and are valid notwithstanding the outcome they produce. Accordingly, the market derives its procedural value from rights, which exposes this second defence to significant criticism if, in reality, these rights are exercised only by the few.[2]

In the history of the European Union (EU), the market has served integration: the founding fathers expected it to ensure a rational distribution of goods and opportunities over a wide territory. However, from very early on, the free movement underpinning the market was referred to as 'fundamental principles' or 'fundamental freedoms'. Therefore, two views seem to coexist within the European construction: the market is valued for the prosperity and peace it provides,[3] but is based on the freedoms of movement which have acquired an autonomous status.

Several works have recently sought to trace the emergence of the term 'fundamental freedoms' for referring to the freedoms of movement in case law and doctrine.[4] From a critical perspective, Richard Bellamy has

---

1 A. Sen, 'The Moral Standing of the Market', *Social Philosophy and Policy* 2, no. 2 (1985): 1–19, 2.
2 Ibid., 5.   3 Preamble to the Treaty of Rome, 1957.
4 P. Caro de Sousa, 'Catch Me If You Can? The Market Freedoms' Ever-Expanding Outer Limits', *European Journal of Legal Studies* 4, no. 2 (2011): 162–91; T. Kingreen,

demonstrated the continuity between the 'Liberty of the Moderns', which Benjamin Constant defined as 'private' freedoms, and the 'market freedoms' which shape the EU.[5]

Nonetheless, it is unclear whether the 'freedoms of movement' should be defined as 'fundamental' freedoms or subjective rights, as they do not correspond to the lists of rights that characterise modern liberalism (e.g., the right to property, the right to choose an occupation and to exercise it, the freedom to come and go). In EU law, free movement has to be transnational in order to be protected. Moreover, it is doubtful whether these freedoms are of vital human interest.[6] The term 'freedom' could therefore be a misnomer.

But it would be hasty to arrive at such a conclusion. Indeed, the free movement of people within the EU has become the freedom of the EU citizen. And EU citizenship is a legal status[7] as well as a 'social fact'. That is, by travelling, by seeking a job in a neighbouring country or by shopping there, member states' nationals are behaving as citizens.[8] Moreover, these practices effect a 'shift in loyalty'[9] from the nation to the European entity. We cannot therefore immediately reject the idea that we are dealing with a freedom of the subject.

So does the introduction of European citizenship explain the shift from 'instrumental' to 'fundamental' freedoms? The first part of this chapter demonstrates that we cannot defend this hypothesis if the connection between fundamental freedoms and 'citizenship' is construed as signalling the progressive emancipation of freedoms from the market. While the four freedoms are fundamental freedoms of the subject, they are still essentially economic freedoms.

The second part of this chapter deepens this observation. Since the 2000s, market freedoms have been promoted to the rank of fundamental freedoms

---

'Fundamental Freedoms', in A. von Bogdandy and J. Bast (eds.), *Principles of European Constitutional Law*, 2nd revised ed. (Oxford and Portland, OR, Beck/Hart Publishing, 2011), pp. 515–50; L. Zevounou, 'Les libertés de circulation, des libertés fondamentales?', in L. Zevounou, A. Boujeka and T. H. Groud (eds.), *Les libertés européennes de circulation au-delà de l'économie* (Paris, Mare et Martin, 2019), pp. 165–95.

5 R. Bellamy, 'The Liberty of the Moderns: Market Freedom and Democracy within the EU', *Global Constitutionalism* 1, no. 1 (2012): 141–72.

6 V. Champeil-Desplats, 'La liberté d'entreprendre au pays des droits fondamentaux', *Revue de Droit du Travail* 1 (2007): 19–25.

7 A. Iliopoulou, *Libre-circulation et non-discrimination, éléments du statut de citoyen de l'Union européenne* (Brussels, Bruylant, 2007).

8 P. Magnette, *Le régime politique de l'Union européenne* (Paris, Presses de Sciences Po, 2009), p. 255.

9 Ibid.

to stand against the newly proclaimed 'fundamental rights'. The 'fundamental' dimension of economic freedoms can be strategically understood as a means of protecting the European market from potential barriers. In this context, the following question remains: are freedoms simply an instrument deployed by those wishing to protect the market for its own sake? This is a serious question, as the constitutionalisation of the freedoms of movement not only has the effect of legitimising integration, but is also a potential source of disintegration.

The Consecration of the Freedoms of Movement

The Freedoms of Movement in the Service of European Integration

The Alliance between the Freedoms of Movement and European Integration

'Free movement' refers to four distinct freedoms: the free movement of goods, persons, services and capital. While these objectives have existed since the advent of the Treaty of Rome,[10] the 'completion' of the internal market dates back to the Single European Act of 1986. Since 2004, a single directive[11] has also defined the movement and residence of European citizens within the EU, concerning not only workers and their families, but also students and jobseekers.[12] Its principle is the prohibition of nationality-based discrimination for citizens who legally reside in another member state, in matters covered by the Treaties.

Historically, freedoms have served the purpose of integration. Member states decided to open up their national markets in order to rationalise production and boost trade, without granting their nationals any new rights. The Court's activism has led to the gradual constitutionalisation of the principles of free movement. In challenging the Dutch import tariff on fertiliser, the transport company Van Gend en Loos asserted its rights under the treaties against national regulation. Legal experts see this as having given rise to 'direct effect', since individuals became the subjects of Community law. However, this recognition serves a separate purpose from

---

10 Treaty Establishing the European Economic Community.
11 Directive 2004/38/EC of the European Parliament and of the Council of 29 April 2004 on the right of citizens of the Union and their family members to move and reside freely within the territory of the member states.
12 Ibid.

these rights – that of 'establishing a common market'.[13] According to Robert Lecourt, former judge at the Court (1962–7), in asserting their rights, private individuals are undoubtedly acting in their own interest, but 'by this behaviour the individual becomes a type of auxiliary agent of the Community'.[14] The result is an ingenious 'alliance'[15] between the promotion of freedoms and the advancement of integration.

The link between the hopes expressed in the Preamble to the Treaty of Rome (peace, prosperity and social progress), the purpose of the treaty (to establish the common market) and the means used (the law, more specifically the prohibition of trade restrictions) is subtle. Initially, the freedoms are subordinated to the objectives of integration. This is consistent with the neo-functionalist approach that emerged following the signature of the Treaty of Rome to describe European progress despite the faltering of the federal project.[16] The first milestones set were intended to create a spillover that would spontaneously lead to individuals pursuing their economic interests in order to advance integration. This interpretation enables advocates of neo-functionalism to explain the Communities' successes without attributing them to the intergovernmental sphere. Once the course was set, integration in certain sectors would create a need for cooperation in other spheres. For example, according to the Spaak report, the free movement of labour must act as a driver of growth for member states and as a means of combating endemic unemployment in Europe. Its function is to serve the 'purpose' of the market, that is, to create a 'powerful unit of production',[17] a higher standard of living for Europeans and harmonious stability. Freedoms of movement were so little an end in themselves that the report anticipated the problems that would be caused if they were to be exercised extensively.[18]

This is reflected in the teleological method[19] used by the European Court of Justice (ECJ) to distinguish what does and what does not comply with the Treaties in terms of this purpose. Thus, for one former judge at the

---

13 European Court of Justice (ECJ), 5 February 1963, *Van Gend en Loos*, case 26/62, para. 22.
14 R. Lecourt, *L'Europe des juges* (Brussels, Bruylant, 2008), p. 260.
15 L. Azoulai, 'L'ordre concurrentiel et le droit communautaire', in L. Boy (ed.), *L'ordre concurrentiel: Mélanges en l'honneur d'Antoine Pirovano* (Paris, Éditions Frison-Roche, 2004), pp. 277–310, 285.
16 See E. B. Haas, *The Uniting of Europe: Political, Social, and Economic Forces, 1950–1957* (Notre Dame, IN, University of Notre Dame Press, 2004 [1958]).
17 P.-H. Spaak, 'The Brussels Report on the General Common Market' (1956), http://aei .pitt.edu/995 (henceforth Spaak Report), p. 13.
18 Ibid., pp. 88–91.
19 ECJ, 5 May 1982, *Gaston Schul Douane Expediteur BV v. Inspecteur des droits d'importation et des accises, de Roosendaal*, case C-15/81, para. 33.

Court (1967–80), the treaties' rules express 'an instrumentalist conception of economic liberalism'.[20] The Court's role is not to promote an economic model or to protect liberal rights, but to work towards the realisation of the common market, which in turn aims to bring nations closer.

Freedoms as 'Fundamental Principles'

Two developments initiated the association of free movement with fundamental freedoms, the first of which was the free movement of people and goods being recognised as occupying the rank of a 'fundamental' freedom in case law, and the second being the Court's use of fitness and proportionality tests.

First, a 1974 judgment held that by reserving certain jobs in the merchant navy for its nationals, France was evading 'fundamental rules' laid down by the treaties, namely the free movement of workers.[21] The expression was more commonly used at that time by Advocates General. This, as well as the free movement of goods, had more frequently been described as a 'fundamental principle'. In the 1974 *Van Duyn* case, the term was used to disallow the UK's refusal of a Dutch national entering the country to work for the Church of Scientology.[22] By using the term 'fundamental', the Court said nothing about the individual situation of potential workers. What matters is that movement is the rule and restriction the exception. Before the late 1980s, the term 'fundamental' was rarely attached to freedom itself. When it was, it referred to the free movement of both goods and people. The Court referred in 1984 to the free movement of people and goods, and to the freedom to provide services and the right of establishment as 'fundamental freedoms'.[23] The freedoms arising from the treaties must therefore be considered 'with caution'.[24] By protecting these freedoms, the Communities above all ensured the 'effectiveness of the objective of integration'.[25] From this perspective, the freedoms could at best form part of the benefits that legitimised the integration process.

---

20 J. Mertens de Wilmars, 'La jurisprudence de la Cour de justice comme instrument de l'intégration communautaire', *Cahiers de droit européen* no. 1 (1976): 1–10.

21 ECJ, 4 April 1974, *Commission of the European Communities v. French Republic*, Case 167/73, para. 359. See also ECJ, 22 November 1995, *Ioannis Vougioukas v. Idryma Koinonikon Asfalisseon (IKA)*, Case C-443/93.

22 ECJ, 4 December 1974, *Yvonne van Duyn v. Home Office*, Case C-41/74.

23 ECJ, 11 December 1984, *Criminal Proceedings against J. G. Abbink*, Case C-134/83. See Kingreen, 'Fundamental Freedoms'.

24 Azoulai, 'L'ordre concurrentiel et le droit communautaire', p. 285.   25 Ibid.

The term 'economic constitution', which is used in the doctrine, does not belie this observation. The distinctive feature of the European legal order is that it has constitutionalised its instruments (free movement, competition) but not its objectives.[26] This explains why the freedoms of movement are deemed 'fundamental'[27] by virtue of the rank they occupy in the legal order, without the interests they protect having any intrinsic value.[28] To reiterate the words of A. Sen, the moral defence of the market remains instrumental.

Secondly, the Court of Justice's assessment of the 'barriers' to the four freedoms can be likened to a method adopted by constitutional justice. The restrictions maintained by member states can be justified on grounds of public policy, public security or public health. The burden of proof for why a measure is justified on the basis of such interests lies with the member state. These justifications are contained in Articles 36 (concerning goods), 45 (concerning workers) and 52 (concerning the freedom to provide services and freedom of establishment) of the current Treaty on the Functioning of the European Union (TFEU). The Court has developed an additional list of justifications. In order to be accepted, the restrictive measures must be appropriate (adequate to attain the end) and necessary. The vocabulary of proportionality is traditionally associated with the judicial review of acts (laws, regulations) that violate fundamental rights. However, there is no basis to conclude that, because infringements of freedoms are reviewed in a similar way, these freedoms have a higher status in the Community order, or even that they constitute freedoms in a subjective sense.

The main reason for questioning this is the 'unity'[29] of the regime applied to freedoms, whether in relation to goods, persons or services. This unity was later challenged.[30] The definition of obstacles and proportionality review

---

26 L.-J. Constantinesco, 'La constitution économique de la C.E.E.', *Revue trimestrielle de droit européen* 13, no. 2 (1977): 252. On the uses of this notion, see also J. Drexl, 'La Constitution économique européenne – L'actualité du modèle ordolibéral', *Revue Internationale de Droit Economique* no. 4 (2011): 419–54; L. Azoulai, 'Constitution économique et citoyenneté de l'Union européenne', *Revue internationale de droit économique* 25, no. 4 (2012): 543–57; F. Martucci, 'Constitution économique, quelques fragments de doctrine française', in F. Martucci and C. Mongouachon (eds.), *La constitution économique: En hommage au professeur Guy Carcassonne* (Paris, Éditions La Mémoire du Droit, 2015), pp. 27–53.

27 S. A. de Vries, 'Balancing Fundamental Rights with Economic Freedoms According to the European Court of Justice', *Utrecht Law Review* 9, no. 1 (2013): 169–92.

28 Zevounou, 'Les libertés de circulation, des libertés fondamentales?'

29 É. Dubout and A. Maitrot de la Motte (eds.), *L'unité des libertés de circulation* (Brussels, Bruylant, 2013).

30 See, for example, J. Snell, 'And Then There Were Two: Products and Citizens in Community Law', in T. Tridimas and P. Nebbia (eds.), *European Union Law for the Twenty-First Century*, vol. II (Oxford, Hart Publishing, 2004).

operate in the same way for all freedoms. In a 1986 judgment concerning the *Lawrie-Blum* case, a British national was denied access to a teacher training course in Germany because she was not German. The applicant argued that the narrow definition of 'worker' (employee and not trainee) reduced the freedom of movement to a 'mere instrument of integration'.[31] The Court did not uphold this argument, instead simply reiterating that free movement is a 'fundamental rule' and that any derogation thereof must be strictly necessary to the interests raised by the member state. Despite the use of the term 'fundamental', the instrumental function of freedom was not called into question. All in all, in this emerging market, freedoms counted less as the liberal rights of individuals which were invocable against public authorities, but more as an intrinsic part of economic instruments providing peace and prosperity.

European Citizenship and the Subjective Turn of the Freedoms of Movement

Freedoms as the Attributes of European Citizens

Since European citizenship was introduced by the Maastricht Treaty in 1993, a new 'subject of law' has emerged.[32] The right to move and reside in the EU and the right to equal treatment, which had previously been attached to workers, became applicable to citizens. Citizenship furthermore became the 'fundamental status'[33] of member state nationals moving or residing in another member state.

Directive 2004/38 envisages the movement and residence of citizens according to several distinct categories: workers, their families, former workers, students and jobseekers. The residence of 'inactive persons' who have not acquired the right to permanent residence in another member state is subject to conditions, and the directive sets limits on member states' financial obligations towards them.[34] But the spirit of the directive is clear: to go beyond the sectoral and fragmentary approach to the freedom of

---

31 ECJ, 3 July 1986, *Deborah Lawrie-Blum v. Land Baden-Württemberg*, Case C-66/85, para. 12.
32 Loïc Azoulai discusses a 'subjective point of imputation', in L. Azoulai, 'Le sujet des libertés de circuler', in É. Dubout and A. Maitrot de la Motte (eds.), *L'unité des libertés de circulation: In varietate concordia?* (Brussels, Bruylant, 2013), pp. 385–411.
33 ECJ, 12 May 1998, *María Martínez Sala v. Freistaat Bayern*, case C-85/96; ECJ, 20 September 2001, *Rudy Grzelczyk v. Centre public d'aide sociale d'Ottignies-Louvain-la-Neuve*, case C-184/99; ECJ, 17 September 2002, *Baumbast and R v. Secretary of State for the Home Department*, case C-413/99.
34 Directive 2004/38, Articles 7 and 24.

movement.[35] At the same time, it affirms a 'fundamental and individual right to move and reside freely within the territory of the member states'.[36] While this wording is also found in one of the articles of the Charter of Fundamental Rights,[37] that is not the case for the free movement of goods and capital. There is therefore every reason to attribute the 'subjective' turn and the 'fundamental' dimension of freedoms to this new 'citizen' status.

This shift tends to be referred to as the transformation of the 'market citizen' into the 'EU citizen'. In the 1960s, 'market citizen' referred to membership based on the contribution of individuals to the common market.[38] The European citizen inherited the substance of the market citizen's rights, while being emancipated from the market citizen's solely economic purpose. This citizen now also had political rights (the right to elect and to be elected, the right of petition), which granted a public outlet for the exercise of private autonomy.[39] Above all, the new status of 'citizens' gave the Court the means to treat their benefits as fully fledged rights.

The Double Dimension of the Freedoms of Movement

Does the introduction of citizenship explain the more frequent use, in 1990s case law, of the term 'fundamental freedoms' for referring to the freedom of movement? Let us look at the freedom of establishment: citizens who exercise this freedom must not be discriminated against on the basis of their nationality when setting up or conducting business. EU law also ensures that there is only one set of applicable rules, so that the self-employed are not subject to multiple sets of rules at once. These prohibitions are always justified by the desire to strengthen intra-Community trade. It is unclear whether this is a fundamental right. Yet for some commentators, citizenship is a gamechanger.

One case illustrates this. In 1995, the Court ruled that the requirement to be a member of the Milan Bar Council in order to practise as a lawyer

---

35 On European citizenship, see Iliopoulou, *Libre-circulation et non-discrimination*; M. Benlolo Carabot, *Les fondements juridiques de la citoyenneté européenne* (Brussels, Bruylant, 2007); Azoulai, 'Constitution économique et citoyenneté de l'Union européenne'.

36 Directive 2004/38, recitals.   37 Article 45 TFEU.

38 C. Schönberger, 'European Citizenship as Federal Citizenship – Some Citizenship Lessons of Comparative Federalism', *European Review of Public Law* 19, no. 1 (2007), online, 21 pages; J. Barroche, 'La citoyenneté européenne victime de ses propres contradictions: De la nationalité étatique à la rationalité économique', *Jus Politicum* no. 19 (2018).

39 J. Habermas, 'The Crisis of the European Union in the Light of a Constitutionalization of International Law', *The European Journal of International Law* 23, no. 2 (2012): 335–48.

violated the right of establishment of a German lawyer settled in Rome. However, the requirement was not discriminatory since it applied equally to Italian and German nationals. The Court held, in keeping with the instrumental conception of the freedoms, that the purpose of establishment was to promote 'economic and social interpenetration within the Community'.[40] Additionally, the Court found that the Italian rule was likely to 'hinder' the exercise of 'fundamental freedoms'[41] or make exercising them 'less attractive'. But which freedom was hindered? In the case in point, the citizen's freedom of movement was not impeded. Indeed, the German national would have certainly been subject to similar constraints in his country of origin.

Therefore, the 'fundamental right' at stake was not the freedom of movement, but the right to pursue an economic activity in another member state.[42] From this point of view, the 'fundamental freedom' must be taken literally as one of those public freedoms not to be restrained without good reason, which are found in national constitutions.[43] Various authors thus attribute the subjective turn of freedoms to the introduction of citizenship. This development is considered 'liberal', not because the Court is hostile to all regulation, but because it is hostile to all 'excessive' regulation. Liberal freedom, which has become a 'community right', aims to protect individuals and their sphere of activity from government intervention.[44] The focus is no longer placed on the market alone, but on the 'individual', as national rules are deemed incompatible with the treaties while movement is unhindered.

The market is said to have given rise to freedoms in the liberal sense of the term. According to the opinion of Advocate General Maduro in 2006, the freedoms of movement are 'fundamental' because they are an element of the 'fundamental status of nationals of member states'. They derive from European citizenship and are not reducible to the 'promotion of trade between member states'.[45] To support this assertion, the Advocate General proposes adopting the dual perspective of opening up both markets' and

---

40 ECJ, 30 November 1995, *Reinhard Gebhard v. Consiglio dell'Ordine degli Avvocati e Procuratori di Milano*, Case C-55/94, pt 25.
41 Ibid., pt 37.
42 C. Barnard, *The Substantive Law of the EU* (Oxford, Oxford University Press, 2016), p. 228.
43 E. Spaventa, 'From Gebhard to Carpenter: Towards a (Non-)economic European Constitution', *Common Market Law Review* 41, no. 3 (2004): 743–73, 765.
44 Ibid.; Snell, 'And Then There Were Two'; N. Nic Shuibhne, 'The Outer Limits of EU Citizenship: Displacing Economic Free Movement Rights?', in C. Barnard and O. Odudu, *The Outer Limits of European Union Law* (Oxford and Portland, OR, 2009), pp. 167–95.
45 Opinion of Advocate General Maduro in Joined Cases C-158/04 and C-159/04, *Alfa Vita Vassilopoulos and Carrefour Marinopoulos*, 30 March 2006, para 40.

citizens' rights as producers or consumers.[46] This duality is useful in understanding why measures are prohibited, even if they are neither discriminatory nor unfavourable to movement. This is taken one step further when citizens' rights are conceived of independently of the freedom of movement. Citizens are said to have 'fundamental freedoms' that are detached from the market. Take, for example, the *Carpenter* case, in which the wife of an occasional service provider from a third country acquired a right of residence because of the potential damage that her departure would cause her husband's (partly transnational) business.[47] Here, the market serves as an instrument to protect citizens' rights.

The Specificity of Federal Citizenship

This progressive separation of rights relating to movement was advocated by Advocate General Sharpston. According to her, European citizenship must give rise to 'sedentary' rights, allowing nationals to challenge the rules of their member state *without* exercising their freedom of movement. A 2008 case[48] concerning health insurance initially reserved for workers residing in Flanders demonstrated the limits of citizenship based on free movement. The Court could only rule on the discriminatory effect on Dutch nationals, not on the discrimination suffered by workers residing in another region in Belgium. In the face of this 'reverse discrimination' inherited from the transnational logic of citizenship, Sharpston held that the enjoyment of EU citizenship rights must not be dependent on the crossing of borders.[49] Several cases concerning the right of residence of the family members of European citizens confirm this trend to detach citizens' rights both from cross-border movement and from the economic purposes of such movement.[50]

To attain pureness of form, European citizenship would have to leave the fold of the market.[51] According to the philosopher Habermas, citizens

---

46 Advocate General Maduro, quoted in Azoulai, 'Le sujet des libertés de circuler', p. 288.
47 ECJ, 11 July 2002, *Mary Carpenter v. Secretary of State for the Home Department*, Case 60/00.
48 ECJ, 1 April 2008, *Government of the French Community and Walloon Government v. Flemish Government, ECR [2008] ECR I-435*, Case C-212/06.
49 ECJ, 1 April 2008, *Government of the French Community and Walloon Government v. Flemish Government, ECR C-212/06, Opinion of Advocate General Eleanor Sharpston, 28 June 2007*, p. 144.
50 ECJ, 11 July 2002, *Mary Carpenter v. Secretary of State for the Home Department*, Case C-60/00; ECJ, 8 March 2011, *Gerardo Ruiz Zambrano v. National Employment Office (ONEm)*, Case C-34/09.
51 M. Everson, 'The Legacy of the Market Citizen', in J. Shaw and G. More (eds.), *New Legal Dynamics of European Union* (Oxford, Clarendon Press, 1995), pp. 73–89;

created by, but liberated from, economic freedoms may even act retro-spectively as 'constituting powers' for legitimising economic integration.[52] Yet, while this perspective heeds the signs of citizenship as a separate status, it says nothing of the substance of the fundamental freedoms enshrined by the Court. It merely suggests that the freedoms acquire a fundamental status once market citizens have become genuine citizens. This interpret-ation therefore implies linking the 'personal' dimension of freedom and its independence with regard to movement and economic ends. However, this connection is not obvious.

There is an alternative hypothesis, according to which the freedoms of movement form part of the rights conferred on individuals by 'emerging' federations.[53] In configurations where citizenship is derived from the nation-ality of a 'sister' state, this right even constitutes the main tool for enabling the unity of the federated entities. In this regard, Christoph Schönberger noted that the Articles of Confederation which united the thirteen American colonies in 1777 specifically included federative rights relating to free move-ment. The citizens of each state had to be able to freely enter and leave the other states. They were furthermore granted the same privileges of 'move-ment and trade' within them.

The aim of these Articles of Confederation was undoubtedly to build goodwill between the sister states, but the rights conferred nonetheless constituted a form of 'inter-state citizenship'. This citizenship was derivative, but not instrumental. The elimination of differences between foreigners and citizens within the states, which was permitted by the nascent Confederation and today corresponds to the principle of non-discrimination protected in Article 18 of the TFEU, certainly assumes movement. It is nevertheless a genuine right, which defines membership of the federal entity. The exclu-sion of indigent persons and vagrants remained in force until the Supreme Court's landmark ruling on *Edwards v. California* in 1941. Even so, the freedoms of movement, accompanied by the principle of non-discrimination on the basis of nationality, are civil liberties whose transnational character is neither transitory (i.e., applicable only until a true federal state is formed) nor

---

A. J. Menéndez, 'European Citizenship after Martínez Sala and Baumbast: Has European Law Become More Human but Less Social?', *ARENA Working Paper* no. 11 (Oslo: Centre for European Studies, University of Oslo, 2009); Azoulai, 'Constitution économique et citoyenneté de l'Union européenne'; Barroche, 'La citoyenneté européenne victime de ses propres contradictions'.

52 Habermas, 'The Crisis of the European Union'.
53 Schönberger, 'European Citizenship as Federal Citizenship'.

symptomatic of an imperfection. It is only on this basis that we can consider these freedoms of movement, which since the 1990s have been reimagined as citizens' freedoms, and understand the fundamental status that is now explicitly attached to them.

Market freedoms, which are sometimes referred to as 'modern freedoms' to distinguish them from citizens' participation in public affairs, are certainly far removed from the economic freedoms that appear in the declarations of rights of the Enlightenment. These freedoms, which are present in the treaties, are entirely distinct from the right to property, the freedom to conduct a business and the freedom to choose one's occupation, all of which are enshrined in the Charter of Fundamental Rights of the European Union.[54] It would therefore be difficult to try to conceive of them as 'human rights'.[55]

On the other hand, economic rights can be conceived of as citizens' rights, in the spirit of those guaranteed to individuals by the liberal declarations of the Enlightenment.[56] But, to defend this perspective, it should be added that these rights arise from a federal citizenship, enabled by movement. Thus, European citizenship may explain the subjective turn of freedoms, as long as this explanation does not underestimate their economic purpose. Moreover, since the 2000s, the commercial dimension of the four freedoms has been invoked by the Court to resolve potential conflicts between those freedoms and other rights. Hence, emancipation from the market is not a requirement for the subjectivation of freedoms. Nonetheless, the opportunistic use of the language of rights poses a challenge to the 'fundamental economic freedoms' hypothesis. There is always a risk that the interpretation of trade and the movement of capital as the exercise of a 'subjective right' serves to legitimise a neoliberal international order. Several studies have demonstrated how advocates of laissez-faire capitalism have tactically switched to the language of rights.[57]

The second part of this chapter considers this use of freedoms against other fundamental rights as a defence strategy.

---

54 On the equivalence of the right to property and the right to freely exercise one's professional activities, see ECJ, 14 May 1974, *J. Nold, Kohlen- und Baustoffgroßhandlung v. Commission of the European Communities*, Case C-4-73; ECJ, 13 December 1979, *Liselotte Hauer v. Land Rheinland-Pfalz*, Case 44/79.
55 On this issue, see Zevounou, 'Les libertés de circulation, des libertés fondamentales?'
56 Champeil-Desplats, 'La liberté d'entreprendre au pays des droits fondamentaux'.
57 Q. Slobodian, *Globalists: The End of Empire and the Birth of Neoliberalism* (Cambridge, MA, Harvard University Press, 2018), pp. 277–8.

The Freedoms of Movement: A Defence Strategy?

The Freedoms of Movement against Fundamental Rights

The Freedoms of Movement as a Challenge to Fundamental Rights

The first cases involving a conflict between the freedoms of movement and fundamental rights concerned the free movement of goods. In a *Schmidberger* judgment from 2003, the free movement of goods was invoked by a transport company after environmental protesters blocked the Brenner motorway in Austria. The obstruction arose as a result of the demonstrators exercising their freedom of expression and assembly. The Court recognised that the authorities' decision not to ban the rally was intended to protect the fundamental rights enshrined in the European Convention on Human Rights (ECHR) and the Austrian Constitution.[58] For the first time, the freedom of movement was 'balanced' with the interests of the demonstrators, who were entitled to be able to draw public attention to their cause.[59] The Court found that Austria had no other means of guaranteeing the freedom of expression, and that 'unauthorised demonstrations' would have caused much more serious disruption to the traffic on this major European main road.

The fundamental nature of freedom led the Court to seek to reconcile two norms of equal rank. The judgment is remarkable because it establishes a symmetry between economic freedoms (here the free movement of goods) and rights, in which freedoms may even be reduced to protect fundamental rights. It was an isolated case, as reconciliation usually takes a more classical form. In the 2004 *Omega* judgment,[60] the Court had to rule on the city of Bonn's prohibition of 'laser-sport' in a city establishment. According to the authorities and local residents, this 'death game' infringed human dignity. However, closing it down impeded the freedom to provide services of the British company Pulsar which marketed the game model. The Court held that, while this freedom to provide services was 'fundamental', it was not absolute: placing restrictions on it was acceptable if the safeguarding of dignity was at stake.[61]

---

58 ECJ, 12 June 2003, *Eugen Schmidberger, Internationale Transporte und Planzüge v. Republik Österreich*, Case C-112/00 (hereafter *Schmidberger*), para. 69.
59 Ibid., pt 90.
60 ECJ, 14 October 2004, *Omega Spielhallen- und Automatenaufstellung GmbH v. Oberbürgermeisterin der Bundesstadt Bonn*, Case C-36/02.
61 Ibid., pt 42.

The incorporation of 'fundamental rights' into the European legal order, which many were sorry not to have seen happen sooner,[62] might have resulted in the constitutionalisation of freedoms. In the case of conflict, freedoms must be defended in the same 'language'[63] as rights. The inclusion in the Charter of the freedom of movement of citizens and the freedom to conduct a business might indicate that the EU is now structured as a constitutional order in which conflicts of rights arise. There is a wealth of literature on this subject.[64] But let us avoid concluding that the freedoms lose their instrumental dimension as a result. Indeed, in the *Schmidberger* case, the Court held that the free movement of goods was an 'indispensable instrument' for achieving a market without borders.[65]

The Counter-attack in the Language of Rights

Since the enlargement of the EU in 2004, structural unemployment has amplified tensions between member states over the flow of workers, business and capital. It is in this context that the two landmark decisions on the current challenges to free movement were made.

In the *Viking* case, Rosella, a Finnish-registered ferry operating under Finnish law between Tallinn and Helsinki, came up against competition from Estonian ferries. Viking decided to register as a company in Estonia in order to be able to pay lower taxes and employ cheaper labour. The Financial Services Union, to which its employees belonged, opposed this decision, with the help of the international branch of the transport union, whose role included combatting flags of convenience. The collective action taken by the union resulted in Viking abandoning its plans. The dispute brought before the Court involved a conflict between the right to strike and the freedom of establishment.

The *Laval* case concerned the posting of workers on behalf of a Latvian company based in Riga for the execution of a construction project in Sweden. Laval refused to adhere to the collective agreements that apply to the construction sector in Sweden, which led the Swedish trade union to take collective action (blockade, picketing) to exert pressure. The freedom to provide services was invoked by the company to challenge the strike. The dispute pitted a 'fundamental freedom' against a 'fundamental right'.

---

62 J. Coppel and A. O'Neill, 'The European Court of Justice: Taking Rights Seriously?', *Legal Studies* 12, no. 2 (1992): 227–39.
63 G. de Búrca, 'The Language of Right and European Integration', in J. Shaw and G. More (eds.), *The New Legal Dynamics of European Union* (New York, Oxford University Press, 1996), pp. 29–54.
64 S. A. de Vries, "Balancing Fundamental Rights with Economic Freedoms'.
65 *Schmidberger*, para. 56–7.

This dispute was symptomatic of the tensions created when transnational movement is undertaken in order to reap the benefits of more advantageous national legislation. The market offers legal and natural persons the possibility of setting up business or working in other member states. However, the directive does contain several provisions intended to combat 'social dumping'.[66] Nonetheless, the legal form that the dispute takes is detrimental to the right to strike.

In both judgments, the Court held that exercising the right to strike acted as a restriction on one of the 'fundamental freedoms'[67] guaranteed by the Treaties. It held that nothing impeded movement, if not for the fact that striking made exercising those freedoms 'less attractive',[68] and made the freedom of establishment 'pointless'.[69] In line with *Schmidberger*, the Court recognised that the protection of fundamental rights may therefore constitute 'overriding requirements relating to the public interest' capable of justifying obstacles to fundamental freedoms. It even linked the two fundamental norms to two distinct purposes of the Communities: first, the creation of an internal market characterised by the abolition of obstacles to the free movement of goods, people, services and capital; and secondly, 'policy in the social sphere' and the promotion of a 'high level of employment and social protection'.[70] It is a question not of taking freedoms out of the economic sphere and giving them a fundamental status, but rather of promoting them in spite of their economic nature to a level where they can be reconciled with social objectives.

However, their reconciliation is not a symmetrical exercise. Indeed, collective action must be proportionate so as not to hinder the operations of businesses. Freedoms prevail, and review is unidirectional: it applies to social rights. In the *Laval* judgment, the Court concluded that the protection of workers was already guaranteed under the Directive. In *Viking*, the Court left it to the national court to judge the degree of this necessity. Despite the 'symmetry' sought between the norms, the burden of proof was placed on the trade unions, which were required to show that their action was not excessive with respect to the end sought. Yet, in relation to the exercise of rights, such as those at issue in *Viking* and *Laval*, proportionality tests are not appropriate. When the playing field is not level, the action must be

---

66 ECJ, 15 July 2010, *Commission v. Germany*, Case C-244/04.
67 ECJ, 18 December 2007, *Laval un Partneri Ltd v. Svenska Byggnadsarbetareförbundet, Svenska Byggnadsarbetareförbundets avdelning 1, Byggetan and Svenska Elektrikerförbundet*, Case C-341/05 (henceforth *Laval*), para. 103; ECJ, 11 December 2007, *International Transport Workers' Federation and Finnish Seamen's Union v. Viking Line ABP and OÜ Viking Line Eesti*, Case C-438/05 (henceforth *Viking*), pt 59.
68 *Laval*, para. 99.   69 *Viking*, para. 72.   70 *Laval*, para. 104.

detrimental to the employer in order for it to be successful. The deterrent effects of the proportionality test have been widely emphasised in the literature.[71]

The fundamentalisation of economic freedoms therefore takes place in a 'defensive' context in which the Court of Justice is required to restore the right hierarchy among norms that have, in principle, acquired the same rank. If true symmetry really existed, it would disrupt the legal architecture of the EU and give the Court of Justice the status of a constitutional court, with powers that it does not possess. It is not collective bargaining but economic freedom that connects the cases to EU law.

Danger of Disintegration?

Member States' Constitutional Identity under Threat

The recent success of the 'differentiated integration'[72] concept, which envisages an 'à la carte' Europe in which some member states gain access to the market without joining other parts of the construction (the euro, the Schengen area, security and justice, etc.), testifies to the persisting dogma that freedoms of movement are neutral and do not necessarily lead to a deeper cooperation between the member states. Yet, a jurisdiction that limits itself to removing trade barriers raises legitimacy issues. This led Gráinne de Búrca to consider, after the integrating potential of rights, the divisive effect of freedoms when single market freedoms clash with public policies that express different values. By doing away with national regulations, the Court is in fact encroaching on areas that fall within the jurisdiction of member states. This stems from harmonisation failures in many areas, when combined with the growing power of a Court acting as a 'guardian of freedoms'.

A 1991 judgment[73] illustrates the friction that can arise between the exercise of the freedoms of movement and the constitutional identity of member states. At the time, voluntary termination of pregnancy was deemed to contravene the right to life, which is protected under the Irish Constitution. Mr Grogan, a medical student, was the head of an association

---

71 A. C. L. Davies, 'One Step Forward, Two Steps Back? The Viking and Laval Cases in the ECJ', *Industrial Law Journal* 37, no. 2 (2008): 126–48; C. Barnard, 'A Proportionate Response to Proportionality in the Field of Collective Action', *European Law Review* no. 2 (2012): 117–35, 121.

72 R. Bellamy and S. Kröger, 'A Democratic Justification of Differentiated Integration in a Heterogeneous EU', *Journal of European Integration* 39, no. 5 (2017): 625–39.

73 ECJ, 4 October 1991, *The Society for the Protection of Unborn Children Ireland Ltd v. Stephen Grogan and Others*, Case C-159/90.

that published an annual list of clinics performing abortions in the UK. An anti-abortion association in Ireland was suing Mr Grogan and similar associations. A conflict touching on as significant an ethical and religious issue as how to interpret the right to life was brought before the ECJ because of its connection with free movement. Could abortion not, in fact, be deemed to be the free provision of services between two member states? The Court dismissed the moral question – what mattered was whether the provision of abortion, in exchange for payment, was a service within the meaning of the Treaties. Or, rather, whether advice on abortion clinics was a transnational 'service', protected by the Treaties. The Court found that it was not, since the link between a doctor's advice and the medical act of abortion is too tenuous.

However, for those who fear attacks on the constitutional identity of member states, the threat is real since, on the pretext of removing barriers to trade, the EU is in fact interfering with a political community's essential choices on the distinction between what is and is not lawful. The Court avoided ruling on a potential conflict between the fundamental economic freedom to provide or receive services and the national constitutional principle.[74] The issue was subsequently settled by Protocol 17 to the Maastricht Treaty, now Protocol 35 to the Lisbon Treaty. The decision is often criticised for viewing a fundamental right (to publish and receive information) through the prism of a fundamental economic freedom. However, as this is the only element that connects the case to EU law, it could not have been otherwise. Another concern is that the onus is now on the member state to justify its constitutional identity, if this identity constitutes an obstacle to the market.[75] In more recent cases concerning healthcare, the onus has even been placed on the member state to prove that the restrictions (e.g., restricting the sale of pharmaceuticals to pharmacists) are necessary for public health. These rulings respond, in terms of the freedom to provide services, to the questions raised by the opening of shops on Sundays in terms of the free movement of goods in the 1990s.[76]

The freedom to provide services was once again promoted to the rank of a 'fundamental principle' in order to protect it against fundamental rights. However, its fundamental status is not merely opportunistic, as according to many authors it is explicitly linked to the right to seize a broad spectrum of

74 S. O'Leary, 'The Court of Justice as a Reluctant Constitutional Adjudicator: An Examination of the Abortion Information Case', *European Law Review* 17 (1992): 138–57.
75 Coppel and O'Neill, 'The European Court of Justice', 242.
76 See, for example, ECJ, 26 September 2013, *Ottica New Line di Accardi Vincenzo v. Comune di Campobello di Mazara*, Case C-539/11.

opportunities which are thought to comprise liberal equality. It could even be a form of Rawls' freedom to enjoy equality of opportunity.[77] From this perspective, freedoms expand individuals' capacity to live according to their 'aspirations'[78] and pursue their economic activities as they see fit. Actually, the opportunities available to European citizens are no longer limited by the outcome of collective choices within each political structure. In short, EU law frees individuals from their political community and encourages them to realise their own version of the good life.[79]

In this interpretation, the freedoms of movement are actually the fundamental freedoms of the subject, because they concern vital interests and protect the sphere of individual autonomy against the power of the member state. Some conclude that this is the expression of genuine personal freedom, which prevails over the power of member states to be the final arbiter of any conflict of values. The destabilisation – in a field that is not purely economic – of the relationship of dependence of citizens on their member state is coming to light. Indeed, EU law offers jurisdictional protection for the movement and residence of European citizens in a member state where they will be subject to different, potentially more permissive, legislation.[80] Therefore, the freedoms of movement are the obvious vehicle for a modern form of freedom – that of making one's own way. Yet, this hypothesis does not preclude the effects of fragmentation or disaffiliation to which the resurgence of nationalism in Europe is attributed. This is especially true insofar as there is no intrinsic continuity between private autonomy (movement of students and tourists, setting up of companies, flow of ideas and information) and the development of Europeans' public autonomy.

A Risk of Social Disintegration?

The subjective turn of the freedoms of movement falls within this liberal tradition in the broad sense. However, a constitution cannot be built on the exercise of fundamental freedoms alone. What is more, these freedoms may

---

77 N. J. de Boer, 'Fundamental Rights and the EU Internal Market: Just How Fundamental Are the EU Treaty Freedoms? A Normative Enquiry Based on John Rawls' Political Philosophy', *Utrecht Law Review* 9, no. 1 (2013): 148–68.
78 F. De Witte, *Justice in the EU: The Emergence of Transnational Solidarity* (Oxford, Oxford University Press, 2015), p. 62.
79 Ibid.
80 J. Weiler and N. J. S. Lockhart, 'Taking Rights Seriously: The European Court and Its Fundamental Rights Jurisprudence: Part II', *Common Market Law Review* 32 (1995): 579–628, 605.

promote the disaffiliation and 'loneliness' of European citizens.[81] The effect of a legal order based on 'fundamental' economic freedoms ultimately raises a social issue.

The abstract language of economic freedoms conceived as human rights perpetuates the illusion that they benefit all citizens equally. This criticism has often been made in the Marxian tradition of property rights since Marx's famous diatribe against the Declaration of the Rights of Man and the Citizen, but it is also applicable to the freedoms of movement, which mainly benefit companies and individuals with economic and cultural capital.[82] Moreover, the consequences of this movement are neither identical in the different member states of the EU nor identical between the nationals in these member states.

Early on, the problem of reverse discrimination highlighted the specific advantages to be gained under EU law by nomadic Europeans. The privileged social status of moving citizens, in particular students, sufficiently demonstrates the inequity of money transfers between taxpayers in the member states and their mobile beneficiaries.[83] The same logic applies to health tourism, which, via the freedom to provide services, offers a premium to patients who have the means to move around within the EU.[84] Conversely, the idea of 'social tourism' for unemployed citizens is gaining ground. In several pre-Brexit decisions,[85] the Court applied to the letter the restrictions provided for under the 2004 Directive. It responded to the fear, voiced by the British, of the financial burden caused by free movement. However, a report commissioned by the Commission from the consultancy firm ICF-GHK found that economically inactive EU citizens living in another member state accounted for no more than 1 per cent of the total EU

81 A. Somek, *Individualism: An Essay on the Authority of the European Union* (Oxford and New York, Oxford University Press, 2008); É. Dubout, 'L'échec de la citoyenneté européenne? Les mutations d'une citoyenneté complexe en période de crise identitaire', *Jus Politicum* no. 18 (2017); Barroche, 'La citoyenneté européenne victime de ses propres contradictions'.

82 C. Barnard, *EU Employment Law* (Oxford, Oxford University Press, 2012), p. 39.

83 A. Somek, 'Solidarity Decomposed: Being and Time in European Citizenship', *European Law Review* 32 (2007): 787–818.

84 See in particular the debates generated by the 2006 *Watts* judgment: C. Newdick, 'Citizenship, Free Movement and Health Care: Cementing Individual Rights by Corroding Social Solidarity', *Common Market Law Review* 43, no. 6 (2006): 1645–68; O. Gerstenberg, 'The Justiciability of Socio-economic Rights, European Solidarity, and the Role of the Court of Justice of the EU', *Yearbook of European Law* 33, no. 1 (2014): 245–76.

85 Court of Justice of the European Union, 11 November 2014, *Elisabeta Dano, Florin Dano v. Jobcenter Leipzig*, Case C-333/13.

population in 2013.[86] The savings which Brexiters promised were largely inspired by this sentiment.[87] But it is hard to establish a balance sheet, because the savings are too interdependent to calculate the costs and benefits of EU membership for each member state.

The freedoms of movement do, however, crystallise a social critique of free movement in which 'access' to national markets and inclusion in the host society substitute for distributive justice as a collective principle.[88] The discourse in favour of freedoms defends the opening up of social spaces without concerning itself with the substance of the rights guaranteed within them. But, aside from their depoliticising effect (in breaking up political communities by proposing other modes of affiliation), the freedoms are accused of creating situations of transnational domination, as they bring together players with unequal economic power, and because they give companies powerful ammunition: the threat of setting up or hiring elsewhere. This has been described by several authors as a competitive federalism, marked by a competition of norms.[89] Recent studies on the horizontal effect of the freedoms of movement provide interesting insights into horizontal dominance.[90] Criticism no longer emanates solely from republicans or liberal nationalists, but also from a Marxian-inspired left that is sensitive to disparities between the elites and workers[91] and has more recently taken a critical view of the cultural presuppositions of EU law.

Damjan Kukovec, for example, challenges the language of general interest to which EU law claims to aspire. In his opinion, the position of peripheral member states is not represented in European legal discourse. In particular, he questions whether the institution of the market will result in the expected economic and social cohesion. The exercise of freedoms does not mean

---

86 ICF-GHK, *Fact Finding Analysis on the Impact on Member States' Social Security Systems of the Entitlements of Non Active Intra EU Migrants to Special Non Contributory Cash Benefits and Healthcare Granted on the Basis of Residence* (2013), p. 200.

87 A. Somek, 'Four Impious Points on Brexit', *German Law Journal* 17, no. S1 (2016): 105–8.

88 A. Iliopoulou, 'Le Brexit et les droits des citoyens', *Revue Française de Droit Administratif* no. 3 (2020): 420–6.

89 See Alain Supiot, *L'esprit de Philadelphie: La justice sociale face au marché total* (Paris, Éditions du Seuil, 2010), p. 66; F. W. Scharpf, 'The Asymmetry of European Integration, or Why the EU Cannot Be a "Social Market Economy"', *Socio-economic Review* 8, no. 2 (2010): 211–50.

90 E. Frantziou, *The Horizontal Effect of Fundamental Rights in the European Union* (Oxford, Oxford University Press, 2019).

91 A. Somek, 'From Workers to Migrants, from Distributive Justice to Inclusion: Exploring the Changing Social Democratic Imagination', *European Law Journal* 18, no. 5 (2012): 711–26; D. Kukovec, 'A Critique of the Rhetoric of Common Interest in the European Union Legal Discourse', *IGLP Working Papers*, Harvard Law School, Institute for Global Law & Policy, 2012.

the same thing to citizens in the centre of the EU as it does to those on the periphery. Indeed, for workers in the east, the freedom of movement is the main springboard for improving their living conditions.[92] Thus, the freedoms of movement become 'social' depending on whose perspective is adopted. Yet, these freedoms cannot be fundamental rights within the meaning of the declarations, as they provide benefits which vary depending on their holder.

The rhetoric of rights is therefore completely challenged in this critical discourse. When conceived as a fundamental freedom, free movement serves to protect abstract interests, disregarding unique social situations. According to Kukovec, the market does not have to justify itself through rights. On the contrary, it is a mode of governance based on permissions and prohibitions, the effects of which should be assessed according to regions and their citizens' standard of living. From this perspective, the conflict from which the fundamentalisation of the freedoms of movement stems is simply a smokescreen masking tensions which pose an even greater threat to the unity of the EU.

Conclusion

The bitter negotiations on Brexit demonstrated the integral character of the unity of the freedoms of movement. The UK wanted to escape its obligations arising from the citizenship articles, in particular the right of residence accompanied by the principle of non-discrimination, while continuing to benefit from the absence of customs duties and the free movement of services and capital. The 'Leave' camp campaigned on social tourism and the flow of migrant workers. In refusing to fragment freedoms, the EU's position was undoubtedly strategic; it was based on the idea that, after a series of opt-outs that benefited the UK, the agreement could not reserve the lion's share for the UK without any *quid pro quo*. It also revealed a deeply rooted philosophy in the history of European integration: one of a regime applying indiscriminately to all four freedoms of movement. Yet, this is not a sufficient basis on which to conclude that free movement is a subjective, fundamental freedom in the same way as the rights guaranteed by the declarations governing national and European legal orders.

Following the obvious instrumentalisation of the freedoms of movement for market purposes, they were presented as freedoms of subjects at two key moments of European integration: after the introduction of citizenship, and in conflicts pitting them against rights. In this chapter we have argued that, in

---

92 Kukovec, 'A Critique of the Rhetoric of Common Interest'.

both cases, it is hard to think of them as 'fundamental freedoms' by analogy with the freedoms guaranteed within member states. In the early 1990s, when they appeared as citizens' freedoms, they were accused of being incomplete, precisely because of their economic and federative nature. Yet the content of freedoms is very clearly economic and transnational. At the turn of the millennium, the so-called fundamental freedoms were much more distinctly economic freedoms, which came up against interests of a different order. Yet their 'ranking' has essentially proved to be a strategy to defend them against rights. The hopes placed in material and intellectual trade since the Enlightenment should lead us to think of freedoms as vehicles of liberal emancipation, in the wake of the other freedoms won. But the importance of this ever-fragile promise is lost if we are too quick to associate the constitutionalisation of free movement with moving beyond an economic Europe, when free movement remains its essence. Free movement thus calls into question the spirit of Europe itself, which is caught between the cosmopolitical ideal that thinkers such as Habermas are unable to relinquish and its flipside: economic deregulation, the erosion of public policies and the placement in competition of workers and standards.

Recommended Reading

Azoulai, L. 'Le sujet des libertés de circuler', in É. Dubout and A. Maitrot de la Motte (eds.), *L'unité des libertés de circulation: In varietate concordia?* (Brussels, Bruylant, 2013), pp. 385–411.

Bellamy, R. 'The Liberty of the Moderns: Market Freedom and Democracy within the EU', *Global Constitutionalism* 1, no. 1 (2012): 141–72.

de Búrca, G. 'The Language of Right and European Integration', in J. Shaw and G. More (eds.), *The New Legal Dynamics of European Union* (New York, Oxford University Press, 1996), pp. 29–54.

Everson, M. 'The Legacy of the Market Citizen', in J. Shaw and G. More (eds.), *The New Legal Dynamics of European Union* (New York, Oxford University Press, 1996), pp. 73–89.

Schönberger, C. 'European Citizenship as Federal Citizenship: Some Citizenship Lessons of Comparative Federalism', *European Review of Public Law* 19, no. 1 (2007), online, 21 pages.

Spaventa, E. 'From Gebhard to Carpenter: Towards a (Non-)economic European Constitution', *Common Market Law Review* 41, no. 3 (2004): 743–73.

11

The EU as a Global Trade Power

KOLJA RAUBE

Introduction

This chapter focuses on the development, practice and contestation of the European Communities (EC)/European Union (EU) as a global power in the light of ever-more advancing globalisation and European integration. It focuses particularly on the EU's Common Commercial Policy (CCP) or EU trade policy in the context of a larger set of external actions undertaken by the EU. Thus, this chapter concerns the development of the EC/EU as a global power in terms of its external actions, especially in trade. As this chapter will show, it is especially thanks to the EC/EU's so-called 'low' level of external action, especially its trade policy, that the EC/EU developed as a global power long before the EU contributed to global governance through the so-called 'high' foreign policy. At the same time, the ability to perform as a global power in trade – to harness the opportunities of globalisation, but also to answer the challenges of globalisation – has become increasingly dependent on four key dimensions: the EU's actorness,[1] the EU's effectiveness,[2] the EU's coherence[3] and the EU's democratic legitimacy.[4]

---

1 E. Drieskens, 'Actorness and the Study of the EU's External Action', in Gstöhl and S. Schunz (eds.), *The External Action of the European Union:Concepts, Approaches and Theories* (London, Macmillan International, 2021), pp. 27–40.

2 S. Schunz, 'Analyzing the Effectiveness of European Union External Action', in Gstöhl and Schunz (eds.), *The External Action of the European Union*, pp. 134–48.

3 M. Smith, 'The European Union's Commercial Policy: Between Coherence and Fragmentation', *Journal of European Public Policy* 8 (2001): 787–802; C. Portela, 'Conceptualizing Coherence in EU External Action', in Gstöhl and Schunz (eds.), *The External Action of the European Union*, pp. 87–101.

4 C. Lord, 'Legitimate and Democratic? The European Union's International Role', in C. Hill, M. Smith and S. Vanhoonacker (eds.), *International Relations and the EU* (Oxford, Oxford University Press, 2018), pp. 186–205; K. Raube and B. Tonra, 'From Internal-Input to External-Output: A Multi-tiered Understanding of Legitimacy in EU Foreign Policy', *Global Affairs* 4 (2018): 241–51.

The European Union as a Power in Global Governance

In the shadow of the Cold War conflict,[5] transnational connectivity grew ever more after the Second World War,[6] not least thanks to transnational cross-border cooperation and increasing international cooperation, and ever greater complex interdependences around the globe,[7] which led to the rise of globalisation and globalism.[8] In other words, while *Realpolitik* remained a major paradigm in post-war politics and informed systemic ideologically driven geostrategic rivalry,[9] globalisation brought into being another perspective on the functional necessity of cross-border cooperation and global problem-solving – a perspective that, next to rivalry and polarisation, underlined the coming together in search of collective answers to common global problems in global governance.[10]

Following Max Weber's classic definition of power ('Macht bedeutet jede Chance, innerhalb einer sozialen Beziehung den eigenen Willen auch gegen Widerstreben durchzusetzen, gleichviel worauf diese Chance beruht.'),[11] the EU's ability to act as a power in global governance would be defined by the EU's chance of enforcing its own preferences in global (social) relations and problem solving, even against opposition and irrespective of how great the chance is in the first place. In an effort to deepen globalisation, but also to answer challenges due to globalisation, the EU had to emerge as a power in global governance. To respond to the quest for global power and global problem solving, the EU underwent significant institutional changes from the Single European Act to the Lisbon Treaty, and beyond. Moreover, also in terms of actual policy output the EU became more ambitious in making strategic and comprehensive contributions to what later became called

5 W. Loth, 'States and the Changing Equation of Power', in A. Iriye (ed.), *Global Interdependence: The World after 1945* (Cambridge, MA, The Belknap Press, 2014), pp. 11–201, 72ff.

6 A. Iriye, 'The Making of a Transnational World', in Iriye (ed.), *Global Interdependence*, pp. 681–848.

7 R. O. Keohane and J. S. Nye, *Power and Interdependence*, 4th ed. (London, Longman, 2011).

8 R. O. Keohane and J. S. Nye, 'Globalization. What's New? What's Not? (So What?)', *Foreign Policy* 118 (2000): 104–19.

9 S. Duke, *Europe as a Stronger Global Actor: Challenges and Strategic Responses* (Houndmills, Palgrave Macmillan, 2017).

10 T. Weiss, *Global Governance: Why? What? Whither?* (Cambridge, Polity Press, 2013).

11 See M. Weber, *Wirtschaft und Gesellschaft*, 5th ed. (Tübingen, Mohr Siebeck, 1972), p. 28.

(global) 'governance'. ('Governance is the sum of many ways individuals and institutions, public and private, manage their common affairs. It is a continuing process through which conflicting or diverse interests may be accommodated and co-operative action taken. It includes formal institutions and regimes empowered to enforce compliance, as well as informal arrangements that people and institutions either have agreed to or perceive to be in their interest.')[12] In essence, the EU has become a global power over time, contributing to various global governance arenas, taking the chance to enforce EU preferences on the basis of historical legacy, economic necessity and universal values.[13] From the first years of European integration until today, the European Communities and later the EU have had a global reflex, even if they were primarily driven by domestic and regional concerns in the first place.

The emergence of the EU as a global power has been embedded in the environment of the post-war international system – with the EC/EU operating in the framework of other multilateral organisations, be it the General Agreement on Tariffs and Trade (GATT)/World Trade Organization (WTO), the United Nations (UN), the Organisation for Economic Co-operation and Development (OECD) or other international organisations.[14] Not surprisingly, the EC/EU's preferred working method in global governance has to this day been that of multilateralism.[15] From the early 2000s onwards, however, the idea of effective multilateralism has reached its limits, as multilateral channels, such as WTO reform, became blocked and the liberal international order showed signs of contestation.[16] Under these circumstances, the EU has had to rely on complementary ways of pushing its global agenda, not least in trade policy, where bilateral trade agreements with key strategic partners have become a key part of the EU's global power.

12 See Commission on Global Governance, *Our Global Neighbourhood* (Oxford, Oxford University Press, 1995), p. 4.

13 S. Meunier and K. Nicolaidis, 'The European Union as a Conflicted Trade Power', *Journal of European Public Policy* 13 (2006): 906–25; P. Pasture, 'The EC/EU between the Art of Forgetting and the Palimpsest of Empire', *European Review* 26 (2018): 545–81.

14 M. Smith, 'The European Union and International Order: European and Global Dimensions', *European Foreign Affairs Review* 12 (2007): 437–56.

15 Ibid.; K. Raube, A. Andrione-Moylan and J. Wouters, 'The EU's Commitment to Multilateralism in Times of Contestation: Reshaping EU–Japan Relations?', in E. Ogawa, K. Raube, D. Vanoverbeke and J. Wouters (eds.), *Japan, the European Union and Global Governance* (Cheltenham, Edward Elgar, 2021), pp. 20–43.

16 M. Zürn, *A Theory of Global Governance: Authority, Legitimacy and Contestation* (Oxford: Oxford University Press, 2018).

The EU as a Global Trade Power

To this day, trade stands out vis-à-vis other external action of the EU.[17] As the largest single and export-driven market, the EU's trade objective, namely to push for a deeper integration of the world economy and support for globalisation by means of market integration, does not come as a surprise; at the same time, the EU has always aimed to protect its citizens against the negative consequences of globalisation, especially through global and regional regulatory frameworks and protective measures. In general, the EU has aimed for a rules-based international order in trade.[18] In comparison, in the field of development cooperation, the EC/EU has also pushed for greater integration of developing countries into the world economy, on the one hand, while at the same time providing aid for transition processes, on the other. Often, the EU's policies to promote the access of developing countries to global markets clashed with the idea of protecting European markets from global competition – with the EU running the risk of being accused of neo-colonial policies.[19] In its Common Foreign and Security Policy (CFSP), too, the EU oversaw its integration into the larger multilateral framework of global security, especially the UN, while developing its own security structures 'at home'. The development of the EU's foreign and security policy not only led to the EU's own security capacities without 'supranational structures',[20] but also resulted in the emergence of questions regarding structural competition with other (already existing) security structures, such as those of the North Atlantic Treaty Organization (NATO) or the West European Union (WEU), or, indeed the UN.

Considered as 'low' in importance and not necessarily representative of European integration as a whole, trade was seen as specialised and

---

17 B. White, *Understanding European Foreign Policy* (Houndmills, Palgrave Macmillan, 2001); K. Pomorska and S. Vanhoonacker, 'Policy-Making in EU External Relations', in C. Hill, M. Smith and S. Vanhoonacker (eds.), *International Relations and the EU* (Oxford, Oxford University Press, 2017), pp. 97–122; S. Keukeleire and T. Delreux, *European Foreign Policy*, 3rd ed. (London, Bloomsbury, 2022), Chapter 8.

18 See also the EU's latest strategic reflections on globalisation and trade in 2017 and 2021: European Commission, 'Reflection Paper on Harnessing Globalization', COM(2017) 240, Brussels, 10 May 2017; European Commission, 'Communication from the Commission to the European Parliament, the Council, the European Parliament, the European Economic and Social Committee of the Regions: Trade Policy Review – An Open, Sustainable and Assertive Trade Policy', COM(2021) 66 final, Brussels, 18 February 2021.

19 Meunier and Nicolaidis, 'The European Union as a Conflicted Trade Power'.

20 C. Bickerton, 'Towards a Social Theory of EU Foreign and Security Policy', *Journal for Common Market Studies* 49 (2011): 171–90.

'bumpy' politics by intergovernmentalists.[21] And yet it became clear over time that trade would be a powerhouse of the EU's external action, providing tools to exert power that none of the other external action domains, especially the European Political Cooperation (EPC) and later the CFSP/ Common Security and Defence Policy (CSDP), had.[22] Trade policy did not work solely on the institutional basis of a larger set of competences of the Union, with the European Commission assuming an influential position in global trade negotiations – both in bilateral negotiations with third partners and in multilateral terms at the WTO in Geneva. In addition, substantively, trade policy is arguably of unrivalled importance to the EU's projection of global power. In a nutshell, as a global trade power, the EU would be able to use its power to support European preferences in world trade specifically, and global governance more generally. But how did the EU's global power evolve and push its trade interests over time? How could the EU get access to markets through reciprocal trade policies in multilateral and bilateral trade agreements,[23] contribute to liberalisation of global trade in the global trade regime of the GATT/WTO,[24] and foster non-reciprocal trade policies, including the prosecution of trade barriers and implementation of anti-dumping rules,[25] and – finally – how did the EU utilise trade and investment agreements to spread its own regional regulatory norms globally? Furthermore, how was the EU able to pair its interests and values, pushing for trade interests on the one hand as well as values on the other? How did the global trade power which rests not only on hard economic interests, but also on fundamental values,[26] bring the two together without compromising the values and principles of the EU, including the promotion of democracy, human rights and the rule of law[27] and the contribution to the progressive development of the Global South?

21 S. Hoffmann, 'Obstinate or Obsolete? The Fate of the Nation-State and the Case of Western Europe', *Daedalus* 95 (1966): 862–915, 886.
22 Smith, 'The European Union's Commercial Policy'.
23 A. R. Young and J. Peterson, *Parochial Global Europe* (Oxford, Oxford University Press, 2014), pp. 71ff.
24 S. Gstöhl and D. De Bièvre, *The Trade Policy of the European Union* (Houndmills, Palgrave Macmillan, 2018), pp. 109ff.
25 Young and Peterson, *Parochial Global Europe*, pp. 102ff.
26 N. Hachez and A. Marx, 'EU Trade Policy and Human Rights', in J. Wouters, M. Nowak, A.-L. Chané and N. Hachez (eds.), *The European Union and Human Rights: Law and Policy* (Oxford, Oxford University Press, 2020), pp. 365–85.
27 Gstöhl and De Bièvre, *The Trade Policy of the European Union*, pp. 188ff.

The EU as a Global Trade Power: Actorness, Effectiveness, Coherence and Democratic Legitimacy

To answer these questions, we will look into four dimensions that contribute to the EU as a global power: *actorness, effectiveness, coherence and legitimacy*. Overall, these four dimensions contribute to our understanding of the EU's external action (which 'can [...] be understood to include all types of engagement with non-EU interlocutors'[28]) in trade generally, especially when we assess the degree to which each of them shapes and amplifies the EU as a global power. In other words, by looking at each of these, we will get a sense of the kind of power that the EU has developed globally. By focusing on *actorness*, we are able to tease out conditions for the EU's action and generating power in terms of the concepts of the EU's global presence, opportunity and capability.[29] By focusing on *effectiveness* as a dimension of the EU's external action,[30] we are able to understand whether the EU's objectives are attained and whether power was exercised vis-à-vis third parties ('enforcing its own preferences in global (social) relations and problem solving').[31] By looking at *coherence*, we turn to one of the key concepts of the study of EU external action.[32] By focusing on the dimension of coherence in the EU's external action, we are able to focus on the effect that coherence (or rather incoherence) between policies, policy objectives and levels of governance has on the action outcomes and the generation of power. Certainly, an effective and coherent attainment of the EU's own objectives through trade policy as an external action has an impact on whether the EU is seen as legitimate. By looking at *democratic legitimacy* more specifically, we are not only able to focus on the EU's perception of output legitimacy,[33] but will also be able to investigate whether the EU's internal democratic input and throughput legitimacy has been changing and contributed to the generation of power in EU trade over time.[34]

---

28 S. Gstöhl and S. Schunz, 'Introduction: EU External Action and Tools to Study It', in Gstöhl and Schunz (eds.), *The External Action of the European Union*, pp. 3–6, 3.
29 Drieskens, 'Actorness and the Study of the EU's External Action', p. 30.
30 Schunz, 'Analyzing the Effectiveness of European Union External Action'.   31 Ibid.
32 Portela, 'Conceptualizing Coherence in EU External Action', pp. 87–8.   33 Ibid.
34 K. Raube and B. Tonra, 'From Internal-Input to External-Output'.

Actorness: Establishing Global Presence

The Treaty of Rome was a milestone in developing the global actorness of the EC/EU, especially with regard to trade. Ever since, trade has become the EC's 'oldest instrument for shaping its external relations'.[35] Through the common external tariff and the creation of a customs union by the 1960s, the Community gradually acquired global 'market power'.[36] The Treaty of Rome allowed integration, in order to push for internal economic convergence, which had an effect on external actorness: 'Because a customs union is a community of nations that liberalize trade internally while erecting common external barriers, it does require a common policy toward third countries.'[37] And as a consequence, the Commission had the right to lead bilateral and multilateral negotiations in trade (Article 113 of the Treaty of Rome), in other words to represent the EC in 'international economic fora'.[38] The Commission was expected to negotiate more efficiently on behalf of the Community, meaning that lengthy domestic debates would be avoided and, at the same time, third parties could trust that the negotiated and agreed issues were also acceptable inside the Community.[39] And yet, the Council of Ministers continued to play a pivotal role in trade as well, whereby national interests and protectionist measures were allowed to enter into consideration, which did indeed influence the EC's overall external position, especially in the 1970s and 1980s.[40]

Over time, trade policy has substantially been shaped by the idea of working in the larger confines of the US-led and Organisation for European Economic Co-operation world economy, while, at the same time, aiming at bringing down tariffs and protecting European national markets (especially in agriculture).[41] However, the making of the Common Commercial Policy (CCP) was a gradual and often difficult process.[42] On the one hand, the ability to speak with one voice in multilateral global trade rounds (Dillon Round 1960–2; Kennedy Round 1963–8; Tokyo Round 1973–9; Uruguay

---

35 K. K. Patel, *Project Europe: A History* (Cambridge, Cambridge University Press, 2020), p. 232.
36 S. Woolcock, *European Union Economic Diplomacy: The Role of the EU in External Economic Relations* (Farnham, Ashgate, 2012), p. 47.
37 S. Meunier, *Trading Voices: The European Union in International Commercial Negotiations* (Princeton, Princeton University Press, 2005), p. 6.
38 White, *Understanding European Foreign Policy*, p. 50; S. Gstöhl, '"Patchwork Power" Europe: The EU's Representation in International Institutions', *European Foreign Affairs Review* 14 (2009): 385–403, Gstöhl and De Bièvre, *The Trade Policy of the European Union*, pp. 123ff.
39 Meunier, *Trading Voices*, p. 7.
40 Woolcock, *European Union Economic Diplomacy*, p. 49.
41 Patel, *Project Europe*, pp. 240–2.
42 Young and Peterson, *Parochial Global Europe*, p. 52.

Round 1986–94) increased, not least because of the Single European Act and the European Single Market.[43] In short, 'As the acquis became stronger, member states' positions counted less, as the EC position was based more and more on the agreed EC policy.'[44] On the other hand, member states had difficulties in agreeing on the actual level of the common external tariff and eventually kept residual national quotas until the completion of the European Single Market. Moreover, member states wanted to keep for as long as possible the right to conduct bilateral agreements, while, thanks to the ruling of the European Court of Justice (Opinion 1/94), the competences of the Community in trade were expanded to areas where internal rules had been set by the Community.[45] It was, however, not until the Lisbon Treaty that EU trade policy formally became 'comprehensive', now also expanding to trade in services, trade-related areas of intellectual property and foreign direct investment.[46] Nevertheless, what emerged over time was the EC/EU as a global trade power, that was able to compete with other major actors, such as the United States.[47] EU trade policy had to be consistent with other policies and principles in order for the EU to speak with one voice in global governance.[48] The latter objective was legally fixed by the Maastricht Treaty and further confirmed by the Lisbon Treaty, underlining the need for consistency across policies and principles of overall EU action.[49]

The EC, being compartmentalised in nature, developed different forms of representation towards the world in various global governance fora and bilaterally with third actors. The EC gained presence internationally on the basis of either exclusive (trade) or shared (development) competence. At the same time, the European Commission developed a network of bilateral delegations towards third actors or representation at international organisations.[50] In other words, the internal coordination on matters related

---

43 Meunier, *Trading Voices*, p. 12.
44 Woolcock, *European Union Economic Diplomacy*, 49.
45 R. Leal-Arcas, *EU Trade Law* (Cheltenham, Edward Elgar, 2019), pp. 92ff.; Young and Peterson, *Parochial Global Europe*, p. 52.
46 Young and Peterson, *Parochial Global Europe*, p. 56.
47 For a more critical, intergovernmentalist account on whether the EC actually could compete with the United States, see Hoffmann, 'Obstinate or Obsolete?', p. 886.
48 E. da Conceição-Heldt and S. Meunier, 'Speaking with a Single Voice: Internal Cohesiveness and External Effectiveness of the EU in Global Governance', *Journal of European Public Policy*, 21 (2014): 961–79.
49 Portela, 'Conceptualizing Coherence in EU External Action', pp. 90ff.; A.-C. Marangoni and K. Raube, 'Virtue or Vice? The Coherence of the EU's External Policies', *Journal of European Integration*, 36 (2014): 473–89.
50 D. Spence, 'The EEAS and its Epistemic Communities: The Challenges of Diplomatic Hybridism', in D. Spence and J. Bátora (eds.), *The European External Action Service – European Diplomacy Post-Westphalia* (London, Palgrave Macmillan, 2015), pp. 43–64.

to exclusive and shared competence was matched by an active coordination and representation on external matters. Even with the Maastricht Treaty this system of diplomacy did not change. On the one hand, the European Commission would remain responsible for international representation in areas of exclusive and shared competence, while in the area of the CFSP, on the other hand, it was up to the presidency and the member states to coordinate and represent EU positions. By the same token, European Commission delegations would be primarily concerned with trade, economic and development matters, while political coordination towards third countries was in the hands of the Presidency and member states. It was, in fact, not until the Lisbon Treaty in 2009 that a new European diplomatic system was set in place on the basis of the EU's new international legal personality. With this move, the EU could (a) be represented on all matters which the EU covered (including the CFSP) and (b) coordinate these matters through a more unified delegation system. The new High Representative of the CFSP/Vice President of the European Commission (HR/VP) officially represented the EU on all external matters – next to the (intergovernmental) President of the European Council. Overall, the European External Action Service would function as the diplomatic headquarters of the EU in Brussels, while the European Commission's external Directorates General (DGs), especially DG Trade and DG for International Cooperation and Development (DEVCO, later renamed DG for International Partnerships), remained responsible for their respective external action, but had to coordinate it with the European External Action Service (EEAS). Outside Brussels, the Commission delegations were turned into EU delegations, which now could also represent the EU on all CFSP matters.

However, the Commission retained the ability to control trade-related matters in the delegations on the ground. In other words, trade-related matters were directly coordinated between DG Trade and respective trade desks in the delegations. In Geneva, the EU kept a separate delegation to the WTO. Thanks to a further compromise of the original act that established the EEAS, staff in Brussels and at the EU delegations would consist of both EU officials and delegated diplomatic staff of the member states. Moreover, systematic diplomatic cooperation between member states, which is also explicitly foreseen in the EU treaties, remains an essential part of EU diplomacy.

Overall, the new system has thus not become supranational in nature, but contains a mixture of supranational and intergovernmental elements. This hybridity or 'post-Westphalian system' has remained unchanged until today,-[51] which time and again makes a unified representation of Union preferences in global governance difficult. The evolving system of the EU was meant to push for greater actorness and effectiveness in the EU's external action, especially in the CFSP/CSDP, in order to arrive at a more coherent and coordinated foreign policy. Trade, however, retained a special place within this system, carved out to function under the premise of an exclusive competence and a Commission-led policy, which allowed it to maintain a global power status that other domains of the EU's external action still aim to achieve.

Effectiveness: Forcing Market Access and Regulatory Power

While trade has had a special position amongst other types of external action to exert European global power abroad, the question remains whether the EC/EU has been able to use this special capacity and translate it into tangible results. Focusing on the actual *effectiveness* as a dimension of EU trade policy,[52] we are able to understand whether the EU's objectives have been attained and whether power actually materialised vis-à-vis third parties through tangible results.

It is only in the mid 1990s that the EU set itself strategic objectives that can be used as benchmarks to assess the performance of the EU as a trade power.[53] As Young and Peterson accurately illustrate, while the EC/EU certainly became a trade power between the 1950s and the mid 1980s, the EC/EU policy activism was rather reactive to the initiatives of others (including the United States) and protective rather than liberal in its policy direction until the 1990s.[54] This changed in the 1990s in the aftermath of the Cold War, with the emergence of a political EU that would invest in strategising trade. The EC/EU's difficulty in finding a more active approach was often seen as being related to the preoccupation with internal market integration, the management of former colonies through bilateral trade agreements and the different positions member states had regarding a common trade position.[55]

Certainly, the Treaty of Rome foresaw the 'harmonious development of world trade, the progressive abolition of restrictions on trade and the lowering of customs barriers'. Article 110 of the Treaty of Rome reads:

> By establishing a customs union between themselves the Member States intend to contribute, in conformity with the common interest, to the

51 D. Spence and J. Bátora (eds.), *The European External Action Service: European Diplomacy Post-Westphalia* (London, Palgrave Macmillan, 2015).
52 Schunz, 'Analyzing the Effectiveness of European Union External Action'.
53 Young and Peterson, *Parochial Global Europe*, p. 57.   54 Ibid.   55 Ibid.

harmonious development of world trade, the progressive abolition of restrictions on international exchanges and the lowering of customs barriers.

The common commercial policy shall take into account the favourable incidence which the abolition of customs duties as between Member States may have on the increase of the competitive strength of the enterprises in those States.[56]

But the objectives of treaties and the action of the EC and member states which followed did not always match. The liberal rhetoric in the treaty was not translated into proactive and liberal trade policies. Also, Article 115 of the Treaty of Rome allowed member states to employ restrictive measures to protect domestic markets, and put into question the overall trade objective of the Treaty of Rome. Article 115 of the Treaty of Rome reads:

> In order to ensure that the execution of measures of commercial policy taken in conformity with this Treaty by any Member State shall not be prevented by diversions of commercial traffic, or where disparities between such measures lead to economic difficulties in one or more of the Member States, the Commission shall recommend the methods whereby the other Member States shall provide the necessary co-operation. Failing this, the Commission shall authorise the Member States to take the necessary protective measures of which it shall determine the conditions and particulars.
>
> In cases of emergency and during the transitional period, Member States may themselves take such necessary measures and shall notify them to the other Member States and also to the Commission which may decide that the State concerned shall amend or revoke such measures.
>
> In choosing such measures, priority shall be given to those which cause the least disturbance to the functioning of the Common Market and which take due account of the necessity for expediting, as far as possible, the introduction of the common customs tariff.[57]

Not only the early years of trade actorness, but also the 1960s and 1970s thereafter saw the EU rather as a protectionist power, due to the changing economic environment, with rising inflation and unemployment, and slowed economic growth. Market intervention and protectionist trade attitudes signalled the EU's overall objectives in trade, which focused more on retreat from liberal trade multilateralism rather than a push for it. Not surprisingly, the new protectionism in the 1970s led member states to use protectionist

---

56 'Treaty Establishing the European Economic Community (Rome, 25 March 1957)', www.cvce.eu/en/obj/treaty_establishing_the_european_economic_community_ro me_25_march_1957-en-cca6ba28-0bf3-4ce6-8a76-6b0b3252696e.html.
57 Ibid.

measures (e.g., national quotas on imports).[58] A more liberal course was, however, followed in the 1980s once Keynesian market interventionism had been put in question and the adoption of neoliberal economic thinking was on the rise. In the 1980s the Single European Market, which had itself been inspired by the neoliberal idea of market-driven economic growth and employment, led to a stricter liberal rules-based policy being pursued by the Commission, including compliance with the rules set by the multilateral trade system. Because of both domestic and international factors, the EU turned from a more reactive/protectionist posture to a proactive/liberal approach in the late 1980s/early 1990s.[59] First, the single market not only created opportunities for integration into a larger European market, which would make it easier to attract investment and goods from outside Europe, but also made it possible to promote rules and a regulatory framework globally in a more united fashion than before. Secondly, not only was the EU ready to compete globally with third actors, including the United States and Japan, due to the great leap forward which the EU undertook with the Single Market and subsequent European integration in the 1980s, but also the end of the Cold War led to a push for integration into global governance institutions, which underpinned not only universal values but also Western-based market capitalism and international competitiveness 'at the end of history' along the lines of the Washington Consensus.[60] Third, neo-functionalist and supranational governance approaches help us to understand why an alliance of influential trans-European business cooperations pushed not only for the single-market integration in the 1980s,[61] but also for a liberal approach in global trade in the 1990s, once European firms had, thanks to European market integration, gained competitive market size to attract foreign investment and to import goods and services from abroad.[62] In other words, European transnational businesses started to profit from globalisation, and the European Commission found an important ally in pushing the liberal agenda, even if a good number of member states still

58 Woolcock, *European Union Economic Diplomacy*, pp. 47–8.
59 Young and Peterson, *Parochial Global Europe*, pp. 59–60.
60 P. Ther, *Die Ordnung auf dem alten Kontinent: Eine Geschichte des neoliberalen Europa* (Frankfurt am Main, Suhrkamp, 2014), p. 122; F. Fukuyama, 'The End of History?', *The National Interest* 16 (1989): 3–18, 3–4; J. Williamson, 'A Short History of the Washington Consensus' (2004), www.piie.com/commentary/speeches-papers/short-history-washington-consensus.
61 A. Stone Sweet and W. Sandholtz, 'European Integration and Supranational Governance', *Journal of European Public Policy* 4 (1997): 297–317, 308.
62 See also Young and Peterson, *Parochial Global Europe*, p. 60.

preferred protectionist responses to globalisation. As the Commission remarked in its trade strategy of 1996:

> If European industry is to reap the full benefits of improved competitiveness policies at home and to take advantage of the economies of scale that operating in an increasingly integrated market would imply, the European Union must shape its approach to international economic relations with a view to improving the climate in which European firms operate.[63]

Not surprisingly, following this strategic outlook, over time the various global trade strategies of the EU have emphasised both domestic liberalisation and external market access.[64] In order to achieve *market access through global trade liberalisation*, the EU concentrated on three tools: dispute resolution, multilateral trade negotiations and bilateral trade negotiations. First, the EU was ready to use 'the shield and the sword'[65] by means of global trade disputes at the WTO in the name of the EU's interests. Indeed, especially in the 1990s the EU used this channel to gain market access. Once the Uruguay Round had strengthened the dispute settlement systems thanks to the EU's role in the negotiations, dispute-related market access and anti-dumping became a viable tool – especially in times of multilateral market access and limited existence of (alternative) bilateral trade agreements.[66] Overall, by pursuing the politics of 'shield' (anti-dumping) and 'sword' (market access), the EU was able to 'deliver protection while market access policy has been quite robust in challenging trade barriers'.[67] In other words, the EU's effectiveness as a trade power prevailed by opening up global markets for European business and simultaneously preventing non-reciprocal trade policy. Similarly, the EU showed long-term effectiveness in pursuing the politics of market access via bilateral trade and investment agreements in the absence of effective multilateral achievements in the Doha rounds. Of course, these agreements did not happen overnight. Developments started in the first decade of the twenty-first century with bilateral, often long-lasting, trade negotiations with Singapore (2005), the Association of Southeast Asian Nations (ASEAN, 2007), India (2007), South Korea (2007) and Canada (2009) and continued in the second decade with negotiations with the Mercado Común del Sur (Mercosur, 2010), Vietnam (2012), the United States (2013),

---

63 European Commission, 'The Global Challenge of International Trade: A Market Access Strategy for the European Union', COM (1996) 53, Brussels, 14 February 1996, pp. 2–3.
64 Young and Peterson, *Parochial Global Europe*, p. 65.   65 Ibid., pp. 102ff.
66 Ibid., p. 105ff.   67 Ibid., p. 123.

Japan (2013), Mexico (2016), Australia (2018) and New Zealand (2018). The EU was able to conclude agreements with Singapore (2013), South Korea (2013), Canada (2017), Mexico (2018), Vietnam (2019), Japan (2019) and Mercosur (2019) and a foreign investment deal with China (2020). Although some negotiations have not yet been ratified, are ongoing (India) or are even considered to be failing (United States), the EU pursued over several years a rather consistent global approach of winning market access externally – often causing contestation at home: consider, for example, the Transatlantic Trade and Investment Partnership (TTIP) with the United States and the Comprehensive Economic and Trade Agreement (CETA) with Canada. This is particularly so in view of the agreement's impact on regulatory cooperation and effects that its investment protection provisions would have, which broad sections of European societies were not able to accept.[68]

With the rise of a global trade strategy from the 1990s onwards, the EU increasingly became vocal in expanding the EU regulatory frameworks across borders. This 'market power Europe' and, in the words of Chad Damro, 'externalization of its market-related policies and regulatory measures',[69] has had an implicit 'Brussels effect'[70] over time: regulatory practice made in Brussels became 'one of the most powerful regulatory poles, if not the most powerful' in global governance.[71] In other words, the EU's strategic objectives then ('The elaboration and application of internationally agreed standards [. . .] to avoid difficulties arising from diverging technical regulations because of their wider impact')[72] and now ('to develop a more strategic approach to international regulatory cooperation [. . .] to adopt a more proactive stance when designing new regulations so as to be better equipped to promote EU regulatory approaches around the world)[73] have effectively been guiding the EU on its way to become, and further grow as, a global regulatory power. The ability to 'set norms globally allows the EU to prove to its critics that it remains relevant as a global economic power' and 'enhances the EU's global standing'.[74]

68 F. De Ville and G. Siles-Brügge, 'Why TTIP Is a Game-Changer and Its Critics Have a Point', *Journal of European Public Policy* 24 (2017): 1491–1505, 1501.
69 C. Damro, 'Market Power Europe', *Journal of European Public Policy* 19 (2012): 682–99, 695.
70 A. Bradford, *The Brussels Effect: How the European Union Rules the World* (Oxford, Oxford University Press, 2020), p. 24.
71 Young and Peterson, *Parochial Global Europe*, p. 176.
72 European Commission, 'The Global Challenge of International Trade', p. 6.
73 European Commission, 'Trade Policy Review – An Open, Sustainable and Assertive Trade Policy', Com (2021), Brussels, 18 February 2021, p. 16.
74 Bradford, *The Brussels Effect*, p. 24.

The Quest for Coherence: Trade Nexuses with Other External Action of the EU

The EU's effectiveness was also meant to be set in motion through a comprehensive trade policy. In the absence of hard power in the EU's other external action domains, the EU linked trade to other external dimensions, including development and foreign policy at large – not least to achieve objectives beyond trade, be it in the area of good governance, human rights, development cooperation, sustainable development or climate change.[75] Indeed, the EU can not only promote 'issue linkage' within trade policy, but also actively use trade policy *as foreign policy*. In other words, as Young and Peterson point out, 'trade policy is thus viewed as a core component of the EU's more general *foreign* policy' and the EU 'pursues its objectives primarily through non-military means, such as trade'.[76] For example, the 'General System of Preferences' underlines the link between trade and development cooperation.[77] Effectively linking the EU's other external action objectives to trade increases the EU's ability to perform as a global power, but it also raises the question of how coherent trade and other areas of the EU's external action actually can be, once they are paired. Coherence can be seen as the absence of inconsistencies and at a maximum policy synergy in EU external action – between different external actions (horizontal) and between the EU and its member states (vertical).[78] If the EU wants to appear as a credible global power, then the objectives not just of one of the EU's external actions, such as trade, but of all EU-related external actions need to be achieved in a complementary and non-contradictory manner. To this end, the Single European Act had already highlighted the need to coordinate between areas of Community competence, the EPC and member states. The Maastricht Treaty made consistency a key priority, too.[79] Only if the compartmentalised areas of the EU's external action could be linked through the objective of coherence would effectiveness and, therefore, output-driven legitimacy be enhanced. Also, the wording of the Lisbon

---

75 J. Wouters, A. Marx, D. Geraets and B. Natens (eds.), *Global Governance through Trade: EU Policies and Approaches* (Cheltenham, Edward Elgar, 2015).

76 Young and Peterson, *Parochial Global Europe*, p. 183. See also S. Keukeleire and T. Delreux, *European Foreign Policy*, 3rd ed. (London, Bloomsbury, 2022).

77 Regulation (EU) No 978/2012 applying a scheme of generalised tariff preferences and repealing Council Regulation (EC) No 732/2008, 25 October 2012, Official Journal of the European Union, L 303/1, 31 October 2012.

78 See C. Portela and K. Raube, 'The EU Polity and Foreign Policy Coherence', *Journal of Contemporary European Research* 8 (2012): 3–20.

79 See Article C Treaty of the European Union (Maastricht).

Treaty systematically juxtaposes coherence and effectiveness. (Article 13 TEU (Lisbon): 'The Union shall have an institutional framework which shall aim to promote its values, advance its objectives, serve its interests, those of its citizens and those of the Member States, and ensure the consistency, effectiveness and continuity of its policies and actions.') It stipulates: 'The [member states] shall work together to enhance and develop their mutual political solidarity. They shall refrain from any action which is contrary to the interests of the Union or likely to impair its effectiveness as a cohesive force in international relations (Article 24.3 [Treaty of the European Union (TEU)]).' And, finally, the Lisbon Treaty mentions that 'The Council and the High Representative of the Union for Foreign Affairs and Security Policy shall ensure the unity, consistency and effectiveness of action by the Union (Article 26.2 TEU).' Indeed, the established equation seemed to be simple: the more the EU was able to arrive at coherent action, the more effective its performance in global governance. In the case of trade, on the one hand, and development cooperation, on the other, coherence reflections took shape in the 'European Consensus on Development',[80] the Commission' s trade strategy paper 'Trade for All'[81] and a new set of European Commission reflection papers, including 'Harnessing Globalization'.[82] Finally, in an attempt to formulate an overarching perspective of all external policies, the EU's 'Global Strategy' laid out the idea of a comprehensive and integrated approach to the EU's external action.[83] Overall and over time, the idea of coherence envisioned linkage between the EU's areas of external action, in which at least two different policies would mutually enhance each other's effectiveness, such as the trade–development, trade–human rights and trade–sustainable development nexuses.[84] In this regard, the development objective of fostering growth through exports and access to (EU) markets

---

80 Joint statement by the Council and the representatives of the governments of the Member States meeting within the Council, the European Parliament and the Commission on European Union Development Policy, 'The European Consensus', Official Journal of the European Union, C 46/12, 4 February 2006.

81 European Commission, *Trade for All: Towards a More Responsible Trade and Investment Policy* (Luxembourg, Publications Office of the European Union, 2017).

82 European Commission, 'Reflection Paper on Harnessing Globalization', COM (2017) 240, Brussels, 10 May 2017.

83 European External Action Service, *Shared Vision, Common Action: A Stronger Europe* (Brussels, Publications Office of the European Union, 2016).

84 M. Carbone and J. Orbie, 'Beyond Economic Partnership Agreements: The European Union and the Trade–Development Nexus', *Contemporary Politics* 20 (2014): 1–9; P. Van Elsuwege, 'The Nexus between Common Commercial Policy and Human Rights: Implications of the Lisbon Treaty', in G. Van der Loo and M. Hahn (eds.), *The Law and Practice of the Common Commercial Policy: The First 10 Years after the Treaty of Lisbon* (The Hague, Brill and Martinus Nijhoff, 2021), pp. 416–43; L. Bartels, 'Human Rights and

has become a major incentive for the Economic and Partnership Agreements with African, Caribbean and Pacific (ACP) countries and for the EU's 'General System of Preferences', including its more specific preferential arrangements 'Everything but Arms' (towards least developed countries) and 'GSP (Generalized Scheme of Preferences) +' (towards non-ACP development countries), which treats a least developed country preferably if it has become a signatory to twenty-six international conventions in the context of sustainable development and good governance, including human rights.[85] Critical observers have pointed out that the EU often looks 'conflicted' between development, human rights and trade objectives,[86] and that often the EU seems to apply double standards depending on which trade partner it is dealing with.[87] Lately, the recently signed China Investment Agreement (CAI) was criticised for not paying enough attention to sustainable development standards in China, including on labour, climate and corporate social responsibility (CSR), and because no meaningful enforcement mechanisms were foreseen.[88]

Overall then, when projecting the EU's global power in trade, horizontal coherence and policy nexuses play an important role. The EU's use of trade *as foreign policy* has become a major asset of the EU's power projection abroad, but obviously questions of incoherence and double standards in the execution of EU trade policy remain important – these can be seen as caveats, especially in the context of the EU's perception as a credible global trade power.

Democratic Legitimacy: Empowering Parliaments in Times of Politicisation

The legitimacy of the EU as a global trade power contributes to its overall acceptance, both internally and externally. Given its sheer market power in the world, the EU has been widely accepted and recognised by external parties as a legitimate trade actor. By looking at *democratic legitimacy* more specifically, we will be able to investigate whether the EU's internal input and

---

Sustainable Development Obligations in EU Free Trade Agreements', in Wouters et al. (eds.), *Global Governance through Trade*, pp. 73–91.

85 For 'Everything but Arms', see Articles 17–18, Regulation (EU) No. 978/2012; for 'GSP +', see Articles 9–16, Regulation (EU) No. 978/2012.

86 Meunier and Nicolaidis, 'The European Union as a Conflicted Trade Power'; Carbone and Orbie, 'Beyond Economic Partnership Agreements', p. 5.

87 Hachez and Marx, 'EU Trade Policy and Human Rights', 382.

88 F. Godement, 'Wins and Losses in the EU China Investment Agreement (CAI)', Institut Montaigne, Policy Paper, January 2021. See also M. Burnay and K. Raube, 'Obstacles, Opportunities, and Red Lines in the European Union: Past and Future of the CAI in Times of (Geo)-politicisation', *Journal of World Investment & Trade* 23, no. 4 (2022): 675–99.

throughput legitimacy has been changing and contributed to the projection of trade power over time.[89] In other words, did the representation of citizens and democratically elected institutions (input legitimacy) in trade policy and the democratic process of making trade policy (throughput legitimacy) enhance the EU's global power, or was it rather detrimental to that end? Certainly, the sources of democratic legitimacy in the EU have been diverse. Depending on whether an area of the EU's external action was leaning towards supranationalism or intergovernmentalism, authority and sources of legitimacy have been allotted differently.[90] As a consequence, the compartmentalisation of the EU as a global power finds expression not just in the different competences which have been lent to different external actions of the EU, including trade, but also in the authority of actors in each of the areas and the accountability of their action. While member states until today remain key sources of legitimacy in each of the different policy areas, the degree to which supranational actors, including the European Parliament (EP), can lend additional legitimacy to the respective decision-making modes varies across policies. In this respect it is important to note that the role of the EP in the EU's external action was rather limited until the Lisbon Treaty.[91] Over time, arrangements such as the Luns–Westerterp Procedure (1964, extended in 1973), the Stuttgart Declaration (1983) and the 2005 and 2010 inter-institutional agreements between the EP and the European Commission led to an informally accepted increase of parliamentary influence in trade, and increased the ability to scrutinise trade policy.[92] Only with the Lisbon Treaty did the EP gain the formal right to be required to consent to all international agreements of the EU, including trade agreements, while in development cooperation its role remains fragmented, and in the CFSP/CSDP its formal role remains limited.[93] The EP was not shy when it

89 V. A. Schmidt, 'Democracy and Legitimacy in the European Union Revisited: Input, Output and "Throughput"', Political Studies 61, no. 1 (2012): 2–22; K. Raube and B. Tonra, 'From Internal-Input to External-Output', 242–3; J. Wouters and K. Raube, 'Rebels with a Cause? Parliaments and EU Trade Policy after the Lisbon Treaty', in J. Santos Vara and S. Rodríguez Sánchez-Tabernero (eds.), The Democratisation of EU International Relations through EU Law (Abingdon, Routledge, 2019), pp. 195–209.

90 Lord, 'Legitimate and Democratic?', pp. 196ff.

91 K. Raube and J. Wouters, 'The Many Facets of Parliamentary Involvement and Interaction in EU External Relations', in D. Jančić (ed.), National Parliaments after the Lisbon Treaty and the Euro Crisis: Resilience or Resignation? (Oxford, Oxford University Press, 2017), pp. 281–98, 285.

92 Ibid., p. 289.

93 Articles 207 and 218 TEU. See also A. Ripoll Servent, 'The Role of the European Parliament in International Negotiations after Lisbon', Journal of European Public Policy 21, no. 4 (2014): 568–86; G. Rosén, 'The Impact of Norms on Political Decision-Making:

came to using its newly won powers on several occasions in the case of the Anti-Counterfeiting Trade Agreement and the Society for Worldwide Interbank Financial Telecommunication. Thus, Lisbon became a game changer, as under the condition of a 'shadow of the future' the EP's involvement is no longer confined to that of a consenting body, 'but an institution that has to be fully informed at most stages of EU trade policy making'.[94] Similarly, national parliaments claimed their role in the making of bilateral trade agreements over the last couple of years in cases in which trade agreements fell within the areas of competence both of the EU and of a member state and had to be signed as 'mixed agreements'.[95] Certainly, the politicisation and contestation of trade policy, such as in the cases of the TTIP and CETA, has empowered the view that the EP and national parliaments need to be involved and represent their respective constituencies.[96] While input legitimacy has been increased in the case of trade, new working relationships between parliaments and the Commission were established to provide greater exchange of information on trade negotiations and, thus, arrive at greater throughput-legitimacy.[97] Over time, the democratic legitimacy of trade, including procedures to strengthen transparency, has increased,[98] contributing to the provision of a support structure for the EU as a global power.

Conclusions and Outlook: Trade Power, Politicisation and Geopolitical Rivalry

This chapter aimed to assess the EU's ability to act as a power in global governance by defining power, following Max Weber's definition, as the EU's chance of enforcing its own preferences in global (social) relations and problem solving, even against opposition and irrespective of how great the

How to Account for the European Parliament's Empowerment in EU External Trade Policy', *Journal of European Public Policy* 24 (2017): 1450–70.
94 Wouters and Raube, 'Rebels with a Cause?', p. 199.
95 Ibid., pp. 202–5; C. Roederer-Rynning and M. Kallestrup, 'National Parliaments and the New Contentiousness of Trade', *Journal of European Integration* 39 (2017): 811–25.
96 C. Neuhold and G. Rosén, 'Introduction to "Out of the Shadows, Into the Limelight: Parliaments and Politicisation"', *Politics and Governance* 7, no. 3 (2019): 220–6.
97 B. Crum and A. Oleart, 'Accountability and Transparency in a Multilevel Polity: European Commissioners in National Parliaments', RECONNECT (2021), https://reconnect-europe.eu/wp-content/uploads/2021/01/D6.3.pdf, pp. 13–21.
98 G. Van der Loo and A. Marx, 'Democratic Legitimacy in EU Trade Policy: Assessing the Achievements and Challenges of Increased Transparency in EU Trade Policy', RECONNECT (2020), https://reconnect-europe.eu/wp-content/uploads/2020/06/D12.1.pdf, p. 41.

chance is in the first place.[99] To this end, the chapter focused specifically on trade and asked whether the EU has indeed evolved as a global trade power.

The chapter found that, given the EU's standing as a trading bloc in a globalised world, its trade policy has become a tool to serve policy objectives both within and outside the EU's trade policy. The EU has been able not only to impose its own preferences in global trade relations, but also to use its power through trade to achieve objectives beyond trade. Thus, the EU contributes to global governance through trade in several ways: by showing its presence and capacities on the international scene (actorness), by effectively contributing to the diminution of trade barriers, protecting European interests in ever more competitive globalised markets and influencing the regulation of transnational goods by establishing European standards as global benchmarks (effectiveness), by linking trade to the EU's other external action (coherence) and by building a trade policy that can be based sufficiently on democratically elected institutions and procedures (democratic legitimacy). While this chapter showed that the EU's trade power has not evolved all at once in any of these dimensions (in fact, the chapter showed that there have been many challenges on the way), it was in the EU's trade policy that the EU became a powerhouse and influenced the course of trade liberalisation, regulatory practice and other areas of the EU's external action. First, insofar as actorness is concerned, it could be shown that trade retained a special place within the overall system of external representation and diplomacy, as it carved out a function under the premise of exclusive competence and a Commission-led policy, which allowed trade to maintain a global power status that other domains of the EU's external action still aim to achieve. Secondly, studying the effectiveness of the EU as a global trade power underlined that the EU pursued over several years a rather consistent global approach of winning market access externally and that it effectively became a global regulatory power. Thirdly, our analysis showed that horizontal coherence and policy nexuses play an important role in utilising the EU's global trade power, with the consequence that trade as foreign policy has become a major asset of the EU's power projection abroad. Fourthly, we could see, by means of our analysis, that the democratic legitimacy in trade has increased and bears the potential of supporting the EU's standing as a global trade power.

Placing the findings of the EU as a global trade power in context, the chapter implicitly points to past and contemporary challenges, both

---

99 Weber, *Wirtschaft und Gesellschaft*, p.28.

internally and externally. First, given the differences among historical and current outlooks from one policy to another, the EC/EU can best be described as a 'compartmentalised' global power, as the EU's actorness, effectiveness, coherence and legitimacy differ from one policy to another.[100] For example, the EC/EU's authority has been asymmetrically distributed between member state and EC/EU competences, institutional actors and external representation, with trade policy developing not only on the basis of the EU's competence, but also as an important field of negotiation and external representation for the European Commission.[101] Similarly, accountability, as one tenet of the EU's legitimacy, has been evolving differently from one policy to another, showing that the EU as a global trade power has been evolving over time. Parliamentary accountability held by the EP and national parliaments has been on the rise over the last decade since the Treaty of Lisbon.[102] Overall then, the chapter implicitly showed that the conceptualisation that may best describe the EC/EU's development in terms of its substantial contribution to global governance is that of a global power with multiple trajectories: trade, development cooperation and foreign policy have been implemented differently, representing the great variety of overlapping, but also conflicting, ideas and interests of the EU.[103] While most observers – except perhaps realists[104] – agree that the EU itself has developed the status of a power in global governance, their main dividing points are related to how and in which of the EU's external actions the EU has achieved such a status, for which reasons and to what end. The multiple identities of the EU, whereby the EU appears sometimes altruistic and cosmopolitan in nature, sometimes interest-based and guided by domestic politics, represent the multitude of the EU's international objectives, as laid out in Article 21 of the TEU. In the attempt to bring together different

100 Pomorska and Vanhoonacker, 'Policy-Making in EU External Relations', pp. 101–4.
101 S. Meunier and K. Nicolaidis, 'The European Union as a Trade Power', in C. Hill, M. Smith and S. Vanhoonacker (eds.), *International Relations and the EU* (Oxford, Oxford University Press, 2017), pp. 209–34.
102 K. Raube and J. Wouters, 'The Many Facets of Parliamentary Involvement and Interaction in EU External Relations: A Multilevel Tale', in Jančić (ed.), *National Parliaments after the Lisbon Treaty and the Euro Crisis*, pp. 281–298.
103 Amongst the many concepts of the EU as a power, see M. D. Cross, 'Europe, a Smart Power?', *International Politics* 48 (2011): 691–706; Damro, 'Market Power Europe'; I. Manners, 'Normative Power Europe: A Contradiction in Terms?', *Journal of Common Market Studies* 40 (2002): 253–68; H. Sjursen, 'The EU as a "Normative" Power: How Can This Be?', *Journal of European Public Policy* 13 (2006): 235–51; W. Wagner, 'Liberal Power Europe', *Journal of Common Market Studies* 55 (2017): 1398–1414.
104 A. Hyde-Price, '"Normative" Power Europe: A Realist Critique', *Journal of European Public Policy* 13 (2006), 217–34; A. Hyde-Price, 'A "Tragic Actor"? A Realist Perspective on "Ethical Power Europe"', *International Affairs* 84 (2008): 29–44.

objectives, ideas and interests, the EU has often looked like a conflicted power, struggling with the tensions between universalism and Eurocentrism, multilateralism and bilateralism as well as geopolitics, on the one hand, and international cooperation, on the other.[105] These conflicts have led critical observers to conclude that the EU looks hypocritical, empire-like, centralised (rather than decentralised) and primarily economically driven.[106]

The second challenge is that of politicisation of trade policy, or rather, how to deal with trade politicisation. In essence, politicisation points to a growing salience, polarisation of opinion and expansion of the range of actors and audiences engaged in EU trade.[107] Bilateral trade negotiations, such as the TTIP and CETA, have been subjected to politicisation, generating a broad and ongoing academic debate.[108] Many different actors have been mobilised and organised around bilateral agreements, such as the TTIP and CETA. Relatedly, trade has often been in the limelight of contestation and polarisation.[109] Simply aiming for effectiveness and efficiency by means of achieving a permissive consensus in trade policy no longer seems to be an option in times of politicisation.[110] Rather, a more inclusive and transparent trade policy that considers pluralistic perspectives and polarisation would seem suitable. Arriving at such a shift, however, is a daunting task as long as EU trade needs to reflect the economic interests of market liberalisation alongside more specific societal needs and objectives.

The third challenge is that of rising geopolitical tensions and the 'geopoliticisation of trade'.[111] While *trade as foreign policy* has certainly become a well-established aspect of the EU's global trade power, it has recently been pointed

---

105 Meunier and Nicolaidis, 'The European Union as a Conflicted Trade Power'. See also S. Meunier and K. Nicolaidis, 'The Geopoliticization of European Trade and Investment Policy', *Journal of Common Market Studies* 57 (2019): 103–13.

106 Meunier and Nicolaidis, 'The European Union as a Conflicted Trade Power'; J. Zielonka, *Europe as Empire: The Nature of the Enlarged European Union* (Cambridge, Cambridge University Press, 2006); S. Keukeleire and S. Lecocq, 'Operationalizing the Decentring Agenda: Analysing European Foreign Policy in a Non-European and Post-Western World', *Cooperation and Conflict* 43 (2018): 277–95; Pasture, 'The EC/EU between the Art of Forgetting and the Palimpsest of Empire'.

107 P. De Wilde, A. Leupold and H. Schmidtke, 'Introduction: The Differentiated Politicisation of European Governance', *West European Politics* 39 (2016): 3–22.

108 D. De Bièvre, 'The Paradox of Weakness in European Trade Policy: Contestation and Resilience in CETA and TTIP Negotiations', *The International Spectator* 53 (2017): 70–85.

109 D. De Bièvre, P. Garcia-Duran, L. J. Eliasson and O. Costa, 'Editorial: Politicization of EU Trade Policy across Time and Space', *Politics and Governance* 8 (2020): 239–42.

110 Raube and Tonra, 'From Internal-Input to External-Output', 242.

111 Meunier and Nicolaidis, 'The Geopoliticization of European Trade and Investment Policy', 106.

out that various EU trade initiatives had a geopolitical background. The increasing contestation by the United States during the Trump administration, rivaling competition with China and the strategic rethinking during the Covid-19 crisis have prompted the EU recently to focus on geopolitics and strategic autonomy.[112] The recently signed EU–Japan agreement is targeted not only at trade relations between the EU and Japan, but also at the geopolitical competition with China. In essence, the EU–Japan Economic Partnership Agreement (EPA) can be seen as a consequence of the disruptive role the Trump administration played (by leaving the Trans-Pacific Partnership) and the trade tensions inflicted on the EU (by the US–EU trade war on tariffs).[113] Also, the investment screening mechanism recently established by the EU is an example[114] of a new approach that, amongst other things, tries to 'take a first step towards reining in investment with geostrategic motives – above all from China'.[115] With the latest EU trade strategy in place, it becomes evident that the strategic autonomy will be further expanded, for example into areas of digital trade.[116] The particular challenge that the EU is facing will be how the combination of defending domestic markets and geostrategy can go hand in hand with the long-term objectives of the EU as a global trade power.

Recommended Reading

Damro, C. 'Market Power Europe', *Journal of European Public Policy* 19 (2012): 682–99.
Gstöhl, S. and D. De Bièvre. *The Trade Policy of the European Union* (Houndmills, Palgrave Macmillan, 2018).
Gstöhl, S. and Schunz (eds.). *The External Action of the European Union: Concepts, Approaches and Theories* (London, Macmillan International, 2021).

---

112 European Council, 'Strategic Autonomy for Europe – the Aim of Our Generation', speech by President Charles Michel to the Bruegel think tank, 28 September 2020, Press Release, Speech 603/20, 28 September 2020; European Parliament, 'Speech by President-Elect von der Leyen in the European Parliament Plenary on the Occasion of the Presentation of Her College of Commissioners and Their Programme', 27 November 2019.

113 European Council, 'Strategic Autonomy for Europe'; European Parliament, 'Speech by President-Elect von der Leyen in the European Parliament Plenary'. See also Raube, Andrione-Moylan and Wouters, 'The EU's Commitment to Multilateralism', p. 38.

114 Regulation (EU) 2019/452 of the European Parliament and of the Council of 19 March 2019 establishing a framework for the screening of foreign direct investments into the Union, Official Journal of the European Union, 21 March 2019, L 79 I/1.

115 Meunier and Nicolaidis, 'The Geopoliticization of European Trade and Investment Policy', 106.

116 European Commission, 'Trade Policy Review', p. 16.

Meunier, S. and K. Nicolaidis. 'The European Union as a Conflicted Trade Power', *Journal of European Public Policy* 13 (2006): 906–25.

Smith, M. 'The European Union's Commercial Policy: Between Coherence and Fragmentation', *Journal of European Public Policy* 8 (2001): 787–802.

Young, A. R. and J. Peterson. *Parochial Global Europe* (Oxford, Oxford University Press, 2014).

Woolcock, S. *European Union Economic Diplomacy: The Role of the EU in External Economic Relations* (Farnham, Ashgate, 2012).

12

The Enduring Relationship between NATO and European Integration

LUCA RATTI

Introduction

This chapter assesses the enduring relationship between the military role of the United States in Europe, through its participation in the North Atlantic Treaty Organization (NATO), and European integration from the Cold War to the present. It argues that, during the Cold War, western European security cooperation was conceived as part of a wider endeavour, which also included the United States and Canada. Also after the end of the East–West division, diverging priorities among the European countries and their preference for intergovernmental rather than supranational cooperation, together with US determination to preserve the transatlantic alliance, bolstered NATO's role as the bedrock of European defence, while confining the role of European institutions to the range of peacekeeping and crisis management tasks. After reviewing the current state of the art of research on European security and defence, the chapter proceeds as follows. The first section focuses on the relationship between transatlantic and European security in the late 1940s, showing how western Europe's security initiatives, such as the Dunkirk Treaty and the Brussels Treaty Organization (BTO), endeavoured to secure a US pledge against the Soviet threat rather than to foster defence integration in Europe. The second section debates the project of a European Defence Community (EDC) in the early 1950s, emphasising diverging west European perceptions of the EDC and of West German rearmament. More specifically, France viewed the EDC mostly as an intergovernmental toolbox to control the Federal Republic of Germany (FRG), rather than a truly supranational organisation. This section also argues that the British declined to participate, dreading the prospect of undermining NATO. After the EDC's failure in 1954, the creation of the Western European Union (WEU) unequivocally left west European defence under the US umbrella. The next section analyses the tensions that developed between Washington and the west European allies during the late 1950s and early 1960s in the context of East–West détente and French President Charles de Gaulle's harsh criticism of the alliance. Then, the chapter reviews the endeavours to establish a European pillar within the alliance through the WEU's reactivation in the late 1970s and the early 1980s. The next section highlights how diverging perceptions among the west Europeans allowed the United States to preserve NATO as the linchpin of European security after Germany's unification and the demise of the East–West division. The concluding remarks suggest that the US-engineered adaptation of NATO after the Cold War and diverging priorities among west Europeans slowed down the deepening of European security cooperation, continuing to leave European defence under NATO's wing also in the twenty-first century.

State of the Art: The Role of the United States and NATO in European Defence

Scholarship on the evolution of security and defence policy in Europe during and after the Cold War and its relationship with NATO is extensive and manifold. This scholarship has focused on the institutional developments of European security and defence from the late 1940s and early 1950s until the formal establishment of the European Union's (EU's) Common Security and Defence Policy (CSDP) with the 2007 Lisbon Treaty. The role of member states within this process has also been widely debated.[1] However, the impact of US policy and NATO on more than 70 years of European security cooperation has not been sufficiently explored by international historiography and deserves more analytical and empirical analysis. The United States and NATO have deeply influenced European defence both during and after the Cold War. The Americans supported European initiatives in the fields of security and defence, including the EDC and the WEU in the early 1950s, the definition of the Petersberg tasks in the early 1990s and the development of the European Security and Defence Policy (ESDP) in the late 1990s and of

---

1 Some of the most recent contributions on the relationship between NATO and European integration are N. M. Ewers-Peters, *Understanding EU–NATO Cooperation: How Member States Matter* (Abingdon, Routledge, 2021); S. Duke, C. Gebhard and N. Graeger (eds.), *EU–NATO Relations: Running on the Fumes of Informed Deconfliction* (Abingdon, Routledge, 2020); P. Koutrakos, *The EU Common Security and Defence Policy* (Oxford, Oxford University Press, 2013); S. Rohan, *The Western European Union: International Politics between Alliance and Integration* (Oxford and New York, NY: Routledge, 2014); S. R. Sloan, *Defense of the West: NATO, the European Union and the Transatlantic Bargain* (Manchester, Manchester University Press, 2016).

the CSDP in the early 2000s. Nonetheless, they also made clear their opposition to any initiatives that threatened to decouple western Europe from North America or appeared to call into question NATO's role as the ultimate guarantor of the continent's security. While there is a rich literature on NATO's evolution and European security cooperation during and after the Cold War, historiographical analysis of the close interdependence between US and European initiatives has remained fragmented. Furthermore, scholarship on European security after the end of the Cold War relies on thin documentary evidence and is mostly anecdotal. Current issues, including the withdrawal of the United Kingdom (UK) from the EU, the US shift towards Asia and the impact of Russia's invasion of Ukraine on European security raise additional questions and provide a timely opportunity to reflect on the state of research on European defence. The chapter aims therefore to address this gap, assessing the evolution of European defence and its interaction with US policy both during and after the Cold War. While scholars of political science and international relations have long engaged with these issues and discussions, providing theoretical insights about the relationship between NATO and European security cooperation, only following the publication of documentary collections and the partial opening of archival sources in the United States and some west European countries, mainly the UK, Germany and France, have historians begun to address the evolution of European security and defence after the Cold War and its relationship with NATO. The chapter aims therefore to complement most recent analyses, taking stock of the growing availability of new primary and secondary sources in order to bring about a concise, yet comprehensive, explanation of the role of NATO in European integration.

The Cold War and the Origins of European Defence

'I am sure that the determination of the free countries of Europe to protect themselves will be matched by an equal determination on our part to help them.'[2] These words uttered by President Harry Truman before Congress on 17 March 1948 aptly captured the close relationship between the United States and European defence in the early days of the Cold War. In February 1946, a lengthy telegram from the deputy head of the US Mission

2 'Special Message to the Congress on the Threat to the Freedom of Europe', 17 March 1948, www.trumanlibrary.gov/library/public-papers/52/special-message-congress-threat-freedom-europe. Also as 'Address by the President of the United States to the Congress, March 17, 1948', in *Foreign Relations of the United States* (henceforth *FRUS*) (1948), vol. III, p. 55.

in Moscow, George F. Kennan, to the State Department had encouraged a firm American response to Soviet expansionism and imperialist designs. In the following years, the Truman administration decisively endorsed west European security cooperation as a means of overcoming US diffidence towards entangling arrangements and anchoring America to the defence of western Europe. Securing a US commitment to European security was a primary objective of both the UK and France. The UK had won the war but at a huge cost to its finances and resources. Faced with unprecedented economic and political difficulties, after the war Clement Attlee's new Labour government endeavoured to secure American support and promote cooperation among west Europeans against the Soviet threat.[3] As the British government hurried to enter technical arms talks with Washington, then leader of the opposition Winston Churchill's 19 September 1946 'Sinews of Peace' speech at the University of Zurich urged Europeans to turn their backs on the horrors of the past, advocating the construction of a 'kind of United States of Europe'.[4]

After the war also French decision-makers were deeply concerned with the threat posed by the Soviet Union and were keen to obtain a US commitment to the defence of western Europe. However, they were equally anxious about Germany and feared that the Americans and the British might move ahead too quickly in securing a German contribution to the defence of the West. Nonetheless, Prime Minister Robert Schuman and Foreign Minister George Bidault soon acknowledged that Germany's incorporation into the transatlantic bargain might be the best course of action, for France as for the West as a whole.[5] Faced with the prospect of having to underwrite the defence of western Europe with massive economic and military aid, the Truman administration encouraged the UK and France to cooperate with each other and other west European nations. US officials, such as Secretary of State George C. Marshall, soon betrayed a preference to make the area under American tutelage as broad, inclusive and cohesive as possible and to establish a framework for Germany's participation in the Western community. In this respect, the Truman administration carefully crafted a balance between US involvement in the defence of western Europe, American dislike of foreign entanglements and European fears of abandonment. Hence, the

---

3 *Documents on British Policy Overseas* (henceforth *DBPO*), Series I, *European Recovery and the Search for Western Security, 1946–1948*.

4 'Winston Churchill's Speech', http://aei.pitt.edu/14362/1/S2-1.pdf.

5 M. Creswell and M. Trachtenberg, 'France and the German Question, 1945–55', *Journal of Cold War Studies* 5, no. 3 (2003): 5–28.

United States pursued a strategy of dual containment, spearheading the defence of western Europe against the Soviet threat and endeavouring to encapsulate Germany into a broad political, economic, cultural and ultimately military framework. Nonetheless, there were serious differences between the Americans and the nations of western Europe as well as among western Europeans about how best to proceed.

The First Steps: The 'Dunkirk Model', the BTO, and the North Atlantic Treaty (1947–1949)

The Truman administration had made clear its preference for multilateral rather than bilateral arrangements already with the signing of the inter-American treaty of reciprocal assistance in September 1947 in Rio de Janeiro between the United States and the countries of Latin America. The administration regarded the inter-American treaty as a model for west European defence and as a stepping-stone towards the creation of a wider transatlantic security system. On this issue the US position was rather cautious. While the UK's objective was to 'entangle' the United States in the defence of western Europe, the Americans were reluctant to underwrite their commitment to an Atlantic pact. In the State Department, the Director of the Policy Planning Staff George Kennan and Soviet expert Charles E. Bohlen had genuine concerns about dragging the United States into a military alliance with west Europeans. The most contentious issue for Washington was the binding character of a mutual pledge of assistance. Hence, in the US view, the UK was expected to have a key role in this process, which would have also required France's restoration to a position of strength, although the latter was regarded in Washington as a less reliable partner.[6]

Nonetheless, while both the UK and France were keen to 'entangle' the United States in the defence of western Europe, there were important differences in the attitudes of London and Paris. These differences revolved especially around the role of Germany in transatlantic and European defence. British views about Germany were much more conciliatory than those prevailing in France. However, both nations were wary of rehabilitating the Germans and provoking the Soviets. In February 1947, the Treaty of Dunkirk between the UK and France pledged the signatories to assist one

---

6 *FRUS* (1948), vol. III, pp. 1091–2.

another in the case of a resurgent German threat rather than against Soviet or communist aggression.[7]

Bilateral security agreements, however, were not the solution favoured by the Truman administration. Although until the 1948 presidential elections the administration was held back by fears of a domestic backlash and reluctant to offer binding commitments to the west Europeans, the Americans regarded the Dunkirk Treaty – directed solely against Germany – as 'unreal and inadequate' and believed that any regional arrangements should be inserted within the framework of a wider initiative.[8] Other west European nations also held different views. Like the United States, the Benelux countries felt that the Dunkirk model was inappropriate. By the end of 1946, Belgian views about Germany had already shifted from a policy of vigorous control to rapprochement and gradual reintegration in Europe. Nonetheless, Belgium's prime minister, Paul Henry Spaak, believed that the United States was too far away to take on the role of leader of the West.[9] Only a few Christian Democrats, such as Paul Van Zeeland and Frans Van Cauwelaert, openly argued for an Atlantic union.[10]

After the London Council of Foreign Ministers in December 1947 between the Anglo-Americans, the French and the Soviets exposed the impossibility of reaching an agreement over Germany, US pressures upon western Europe increased in 1948, as relations with the USSR continued to deteriorate. At the Anglo-American discussions that were held in January in London, the Americans demanded a firm connection between Germany, European unity and the creation of a Western security system. Like the Americans, the British considered the German problem central for west European security and were determined 'to avoid the danger of a resurgent Germany itself, on the one hand, and the threat of a Germany on the wrong side in the Cold War, on the other'.[11] However, they viewed the Treaty of Dunkirk as a first step towards broader west European cooperation.[12] In the same month, in his

---

7 J. Baylis, *The Diplomacy of Pragmatism: Britain and the Formation of NATO, 1942–49* (Basingstoke, Palgrave Macmillan, 1993), p. 60.

8 The National Archives (henceforth TNA), Kew, NA: FO 371/73045, Inverchapel–Hickerson meeting, Telegram No. 324, 21 January 1948.

9 'Memorandum by the Director of the Office of European Affairs (Hickerson) to the Secretary of State', in *FRUS* (1948), vol. III, pp. 6–7.

10 R. Coolsaet, *Atlantic Loyalty, European Autonomy: Belgium and the Atlantic Alliance, 1949–2009* (Ghent, Academia Press; Brussels, Egmont Insititute, 2009), p. 9.

11 J. L. Gaddis, *We Now Know: Rethinking Cold War History* (New York, NY, Oxford University Press, 1997), p. 116.

12 J. Baylis, 'Britain and the Dunkirk Treaty: The Origins of NATO', *Journal of Strategic Studies* 5, no. 2 (1982): 236–47.

speech to the House of Commons, the UK's Foreign Secretary Ernest Bevin stressed the need to consolidate western Europe before rehabilitating Germany, referring to the Anglo-French Treaty of Dunkirk as a basis of cooperation.[13] He also indicated that similar agreements would be proposed to the Benelux countries.[14] On the contrary, according to American officials, the Dunkirk model, in the light of its anti-German character, was not the proper way to proceed, because it would make it harder to bring Germany into a broader multilateral system in the future.[15] Furthermore, the formula of bilateral agreements against Germany reflected the strategy employed by Moscow in eastern Europe in order to establish its own bloc. Hence, it was not adequate to promote genuine west European security cooperation.

It was Moscow's east European conduct that coalesced Western views. In early 1948 the coup in Czechoslovakia and Soviet pressure on Norway triggered highly secret negotiations at the Pentagon in Washington between the United States, the UK and Canada during which the North Atlantic Treaty was effectively conceived. The American position, however, was cautious and reflected undercurrents within the administration and the State Department about the mutual pledge of assistance and the right of each nation to decide what action to take in the case of aggression. The British were now particularly alarmed and thought it wise to exploit the momentum to convince the Americans about the soundness of their arguments. Bevin remarked that Moscow was 'actively preparing to extend its hold over the remaining part of continental Europe and subsequently, over the Middle East and no doubt the Balkans and the Far East as well'.[16] He also stressed that early March 1948 would be 'the last chance for saving the West'.[17] In March the UK, France and the Benelux countries entered into a mutual assistance pact that bonded them together for 50 years and established the BTO. This agreement provided for economic cooperation, a declaration of intention on social matters, the development of cultural exchanges and automatic assistance (Article IV) in the event of attack.[18]

13 TNA, Kew, NA: FO 271/64250.
14 'House of Commons, Parliamentary Debates', *Hansard* 5th series 446 (1947–8): col. 383ff.
15 'Kennan to Secretary of State, 20 January 1948', in *FRUS* (1948), vol. III, p. 8.
16 Quoted in V. Mastny, *The Cold War and Soviet Insecurity: The Stalin Years* (New York, NY, Oxford University Press, 1996), p. 43.
17 *FRUS* (1948), vol. III, pp. 32–3.
18 For the official text of the 'Brussels Treaty', see www.nato.int/cps/en/natohq/official_texts_17072.htm. See also *DBPO*, Series I, vol. X: *The Brussels and North Atlantic Treaties, 1947–1949.*

Nonetheless, there were some undercurrents among its signatories. Although the treaty was negotiated and signed within the very short period of just 2 months, each country had different expectations about the ultimate outcome. The French were very sensitive about Germany and preferred to proceed on the Dunkirk model, while the British viewed the treaty as part of a broader endeavour to organise Western defences. On the contrary, the Benelux countries were not keen on the Dunkirk model and preferred the model of the inter-American Rio Treaty as a more appropriate basis for the establishment of a regional pact. Benelux leaders went out of their way to reject the kind of references to Germany that had been contained in the Dunkirk Treaty and proposed a regional pact under Article 52 of the United Nations. This was also the position of the Americans, who considered French concerns about Germany 'outmoded and unrealistic'. Furthermore, neither the Scandinavians nor the Italians were willing to adhere to the treaty. The Italians feared the BTO's impact on their domestic politics: large sectors of Italy's public opinion opposed participation in military alliances. The Scandinavian countries held strong reservations about their adherence to the treaty and preferred the idea of a British–Scandinavian defence union. Other important differences revolved around the most appropriate military strategy to defend western Europe from a Soviet attack. France and the Benelux countries advocated a forward defence strategy as far to the east of the European continent as possible. In contrast, the UK backed the principle of peripheral defence, in other words falling back on the British Isles, Spain, Gibraltar and North Africa. This was also the predominant view among US defence planners.[19]

Ultimately the BTO proved more symbolic than substantial, lacking the capacity to counter the almost 3 million men that Moscow still maintained under arms. The most the BTO's handful of divisions could achieve in the face of a Soviet ground attack would be to buy time in the hope of an eventual US intervention. Nonetheless, the BTO's establishment partly reassured the Americans. On 30 April 1948, the defence ministers and military chiefs of staff of the five Treaty of Brussels countries began a series of meetings to study their military equipment needs and determine what supplementary aid they could request from Washington.[20] In the same month, Bevin urged the Americans to begin conversations with the BTO members, although there was continuing resistance in the United States to the prospect of a military alliance.

---

19 *FRUS* (1948), vol. III, pp. 1097–8.
20 D. A. Carter, *Forging the Shield: The U.S. Army in Europe 1951–1962* (Washington, DC, Center of Military History, United States Army, 2015), p. 6. See also *FRUS* (1948), vol. I, part 2, pp. 510–29.

Nonetheless, Western inability to win Moscow's agreement for economic reform in the occupied areas of Germany and Soviet intermittent interference with railroad traffic into Berlin soon allowed further progress towards an Atlantic pact. On 11 June, Congress passed Resolution 239, which endorsed the proposal of Republican Senator Arthur Vandenberg, recommending the progressive development of regional and collective arrangements for self-defence in accordance with the purposes, principles and provisions of the UN Charter.[21] After Congressional approval of the Vandenberg resolution and Soviet imposition of the Berlin blockade on 24 June, talks were extended to the French and other BTO members. In July, top-ranking American and Canadian defence officials attended in a non-member status the meetings of the defence ministers and military chiefs of staff of the five members of the Treaty of Brussels. Truman's surprise victory in the presidential elections in November set in motion the final round of talks that culminated in the signing of the North Atlantic Treaty in April 1949. While promising assistance against external aggression, Article 5 of the North Atlantic Treaty stopped short, however, of establishing an automatic military pledge among its signatories.[22] Furthermore, by stating that 'the Parties may, by unanimous agreement, invite any other European State . . . to contribute to the security of the North Atlantic area', Article 10 of the treaty betrayed the US purpose of securing a German contribution to European defence. In May of the same year the Western powers established the Federal Republic of Germany (FRG). The connection between the establishment of a provisional West German state and the formation of a Western military alliance emerged therefore as a key feature of the new transatlantic security architecture. Nonetheless, in the following years the handling of the FRG's rearmament and of the modalities to keep it under control risked undermining the whole transatlantic bargain.

The Elephant in the Room: West German Rearmament and the Korean War (1949–1950)

Following the signing of the North Atlantic Treaty and the FRG's establishment, West German rearmament rapidly gained centre stage in US defence strategy. After the war, rapid demobilisation had greatly reduced the number

---

21 For the text of the 'Vandenberg resolution', see www.nato.int/cps/en/natohq/offi cial_texts_17054.htm.
22 For the official text of the North Atlantic Treaty, see www.nato.int/cps/en/natolive/ official_texts_17120.htm.

of American forces in Germany. However, as the Cold War began to unravel, Washington swiftly began to push for a West German contribution to European defence. As early as in 1947 American military commanders in Germany first floated the prospect of exploiting German manpower for Western defences. In the same year, the US Army's Operations and Plans division began debating how to integrate Germany into the US strategic posture. In the following years the issue of how to secure a German military contribution to the defence of the West deeply shaped the delicate balance between Washington's fears of foreign entanglements and Western concerns about the Soviet Union, making West German rearmament a watershed for the relationship between European and transatlantic security.

However, the practical modalities of West German rearmament rapidly turned it into a source of friction between the Americans and west Europeans. Washington regarded the FRG's rapid reconstruction and integration into a broader Euro-Atlantic security system as a strategic priority. In contrast, despite having renounced demands for a separation of the Ruhr from West Germany and being increasingly inclined to accept the solution favoured by the United States, the French perceived German rearmament as premature and potentially threatening. In early April, the editor of the French magazine *Le Monde* had bitterly remarked that 'German rearmament is contained in the Atlantic Pact like the embryo in the egg.'[23]

The British, like the Americans, were keen to secure West German participation in the defence of the West. However, they were also cautious, fearing a Europe dominated politically and economically by the Germans.[24] London's preferred option was the FRG's alignment with the West in a non-military capacity through its admission into the Council of Europe. The subsequent step of this process should have been Germany's gradual association with subsidiary organisations, which would be set up under the North Atlantic Treaty. The UK's planners hoped that in this way the awkward questions connected with German adherence to the treaty itself could be avoided, at least for some time.[25] Furthermore, according to the British, it would have been unthinkable 'to rearm Germany until French strength had been greatly revived'.[26]

---

23 *Le Monde*, 6 April 1949. Quoted in J. Raflik, 'The Fourth Republic and NATO', in J. Hanhimäki, G.-H. Soutou and B. Germond (eds.), *The Routledge Handbook of Transatlantic Security* (Abingdon and New York, NY, Routledge, 2010), p. 51.
24 *DBPO*, Series II, vol. II, pp. 81–7.
25 *DBPO*, Series II, vol. II, pp. 95–106, quotation on p. 105.
26 *DBPO*, Series II, vol. II, pp. 115–20, quotation on p. 117.

The French were more cautious than their US and British counterparts. Although top-ranking French officials shared American views, most French political forces viewed the prospect of German rearmament as both out of place and premature. The powerful communist party, under the direct influence of the USSR, campaigned strenuously against it. In an attempt to break the deadlock and overcome French fears, the British campaigned for West Germany's adherence to the BTO as the obvious regional subsidiary of NATO. This was seen in London as a convenient compromise between the UK's initial preference for the FRG's participation in the Council of Europe and US pressures for Bonn's immediate rearmament. West European uncertainties about how to proceed with German rearmament, however, caused widespread irritation in the United States. Already at the end of January 1950, President Truman had instructed the State and Defence Departments to undertake a re-examination of US strategic plans in Europe. The report 'National Security Council (NSC) 68' was submitted to the president by the study group headed by the Director of Policy Planning Paul Nitze. It emphasised the need to strengthen the West, calling for a division of duties between the Americans and their European allies and ruling out the prospect of Germany's neutrality.[27] In May the US Joint Chiefs of Staff noted that the 'early rearming of Western Germany is of fundamental importance to the defence of Western Europe against the USSR'.[28] Also West German decision-makers favoured rearmament, viewing it as an opportunity to strengthen their country's association with the West. However, the FRG's government expected the UK to play a marginal role in this process and sought to overcome French concerns. In March 1950, the FRG's first chancellor, Konrad Adenauer, suggested the formation of a Franco-German union as a foundation for a 'United States of Europe' in an attempt to reassure the French and secure a partial restoration of German sovereignty over the Saar.[29]

The White House was keen to step up pressure on the British and the French, but was also aware that rearmament might cause potential problems, as 'once the power balance was upset it may be impossible to constrain the forces of German expansion through legal bonds and limitations'.[30] By late spring 1950, France's prime minister, Georges Bidault, and his foreign minister, Robert Schuman, accepted the principle of a West German contribution to Western defence. However, they demanded as a precondition the creation of a highly integrated NATO structure, including the appointment of

27 FRUS (1950), vol. I, pp. 237–92.   28 FRUS (1950), vol. IV, p. 687.
29 K. Adenauer, Memoirs 1945–53 (London, Weidenfeld & Nicholson, 1966), pp. 244–8.
30 FRUS (1952–4), vol. VII, pp. 356–61, quotation on p. 358.

a supreme commander and the establishment of a combined military staff.[31] Furthermore, French officials also advocated economic integration between the FRG and France. In May 1950 Schuman proposed the pooling of Franco-German coal and steel production under the joint supervision of a European High Authority.

It was the eruption of the Korean War in June 1950 which, shocking Western leaders and exposing the military imbalance of conventional forces in Europe, decisively broke the deadlock. The outbreak of the conflict in the Far East, following Moscow's first nuclear test at the end of August 1949 and the signing of a Sino-Soviet treaty of alliance in February 1950, prompted Washington to commit several divisions to the UN command in Korea. At the same time, it strengthened in the eyes of American decision-makers the need to secure an immediate German contribution to NATO's ground forces in Europe. In the administration's view and in the light of the UK's feeble commitment to European integration, however, Germany's attraction into the Western security system should have occurred under the leadership of France or, if necessary, under the US lead.[32]

Anglo-American differences were exposed by their contrasting reactions to Schuman's proposal. While the British were wary of its supranational aspects, the Americans saw it as an opportunity to bring Germany into the transatlantic fold. Secretary of State Dean Acheson was dubious at first, fearing a cartelisation of heavy industry and arms production, but Secretary of State John Foster Dulles and US High Commissioner for Germany John McCloy were supportive of Schuman's plan and petitioned the FRG's government, industrialists and trade union officials to support it. Ultimately, Adenauer's warm reception of the plan, with its promise of permanently ending Franco-German animosity over the Ruhr, was far more than the Americans could have possibly hoped for.[33] In September, with US forces struggling to hold their lines in Korea, President Truman announced that he had approved substantial increases in the strength of American forces in Europe. In the same month, at the New York meeting of the North Atlantic Council (NAC), Acheson put forward a package deal that linked the feasibility of US troops' commitments to the FRG's rapid rearmament.

---

31 Creswell and Trachtenberg, 'France and the German Question'.

32 A. Deighton, 'Three Ministers and the World They Made: Acheson, Bevin and Schuman, and the North Atlantic Treaty, March–April 1949', in Hanhimäki, Soutou and Germond (eds.), *The Routledge Handbook of Transatlantic Security*, pp. 10–12.

33 J. McAllister, *No Exit: America and the German Problem 1943–1954* (Ithaca, NY, Cornell University Press, 2002), p. 183.

Nonetheless, there were still problems. London endorsed Acheson's proposal and greeted the stationing of additional US forces on the continent as a demonstration of commitment far bigger 'than we could have ever hoped for'.[34] However, Acheson's proposal had failed to convince the French to make a public endorsement of West German rearmament.[35] The government, now led by René Pleven, was particularly sceptical that the Anglo-Americans would be able to control Germany after it was rearmed and feared that acceptance of rearmament would trigger a domestic backlash. Despite being sympathetic to Acheson's arguments, Foreign Minister Schuman responded that no French government could remain in power if it agreed to Germany's rearmament, and suggested that the question be postponed until French public opinion could be swayed. He concluded that, if the French government were forced to take a stand on this issue before French public opinion was ready, 'everything might go wrong'.[36]

The Pleven Plan and the European Defence Community (1950–1954)

Only in the autumn of 1950 did American pressures elicit a more constructive French response. In October, Prime Minister René Pleven called for the establishment of an integrated European army, consisting of small national battalions to be merged into international army corps. No corps would include more than two divisions of the same nationality. The European force would be endowed with a common budget and placed under the command of NATO. All participating countries would be allowed to maintain their defence ministries, general staff and certain independent armed forces. West Germany, being permitted to establish only battalion-level units of 800–1,200 soldiers, would be the only and obvious exception. Furthermore, the FRG would remain outside the Atlantic alliance. While publicly signalling French acceptance of the principle of German rearmament, the Pleven Plan triggered, however, an unenthusiastic response in Washington and London. To Secretary of Defence George Marshall it appeared as a 'miasmic cloud', while Churchill dismissed it as a 'sludgy amalgam'.[37] Reactions in the FRG

34 *DBPO*, Series II, vol. III, p. 178.
35 D. Acheson, *Present at the Creation: My Years in the State Department* (New York, NY, W. W. Norton, 1969), pp. 437–40.
36 For Schuman's arguments against German rearmament, see *FRUS* (1950), vol. III, pp. 296, 299–300, 312, 342.
37 Both quoted in M. Trachtenberg, *A Constructed Peace: The Making of the European Settlement, 1945–1963* (Princeton, NJ, Princeton University Press, 1999), p. 110.

were also negative; Adenauer was very disappointed with the discrimination against the Germans, lamented the lack of American participation and stressed that German rearmament could not be postponed until the institutional framework for a united Europe was in place.[38] In a speech to the Bundestag on 8 November, he suggested that discussions about the French proposal should not be allowed to stand in the way of more immediate measures aimed at improving Western defences against the USSR.[39]

Nonetheless, a deteriorating situation in Korea, following the entry into the war of the People's Republic of China's (PRC) in November 1950, convinced the US government to work out an acceptable compromise with the French. In the same month the 7th US Army was reactivated in Europe, while in December Dwight D. Eisenhower was appointed Supreme Allied Commander in Europe (SACEUR).[40] In exchange for France's acceptance of German rearmament, the US government also promised to support French efforts to organise a European army conference in Paris.[41] Unlike the Americans, the British remained cautious, regarding a European army as a threat to Western unity and a potential 'cancer on the Atlantic body'.[42] However, they were also aware that it was highly unlikely that the French could be successful in their efforts.[43] Also the Germans remained sceptical about the merits of a European army. The chancellor insisted on political and military equality for Germany and excluded any solution based on the formation of small regimental combat teams and the entire concept of a European army, as the French understood it.[44]

The ensuing debate crudely exposed persisting undercurrents between the United States and the west Europeans. The Pleven Plan had sealed French acceptance of a German role in transatlantic security, while providing Paris with a tool 'of self-protection against American pressure' and an opportunity to prevent the formation of a national German army and defence cadres. However, with the conflict in Korea delaying the dispatch of US reinforcements to Europe, for Washington there was no plausible alternative to a German contribution to the defence of western Europe.[45]

When negotiations on the Pleven Plan began in Paris in February 1951 there were deep nuances also among west Europeans on the modalities of

38 H. Blankenhorn, *Verständnis und Verständigung: Blätter eines Politischen Tagebuchs 1949 bis 1979* (Frankfurt am Main, Propyläen Verlag, 1980), pp. 115–16.
39 K. Adenauer, 'Regierungserklärung des Bundeskanzlers Adenauer in der 98. Sitzung des Deutschen Bundestages' (1950), www.konrad-adenauer.de/seite/8-november-1950.
40 McAllister, *No Exit*, p. 198.   41 *FRUS* (1950), vol. III, pp. 457–64.
42 *DBPO*, Series II, vol. III, pp. 291–6, quotation on p. 293.   43 Ibid., vol. III, p. 272.
44 Ibid., vol. III, pp. 354–5.   45 Ibid., vol. III, calendar 84i.

Germany's contribution. Beyond the FRG only Belgium, Luxembourg and Italy had accepted France's invitation. The Dutch and the British – alongside other alliance partners – participated as observers. Although London did not stand in the way of the Pleven Plan, Whitehall feared the federalist leanings of the French proposal and its impact on NATO. Already in 1950 Bevin had promptly highlighted British concerns, stating in the House of Commons, 'Europe is not enough; it is not big enough, it is not strong enough, and it is not able to stand by itself. It is this great conception of an Atlantic Community that we want to build up.'[46] In a report to the Defence Committee in November 1950 the Foreign Secretary had explained that the UK could not afford to allow 'the European federal concept to gain a foothold within NATO and thus weaken instead of strengthen the ties between the countries on the two sides of the Atlantic. We must nip it in the bud.'[47] The UK's reservations about the French proposal further increased following the Conservative Party's return to power in October 1951. The third Churchill Ministry regarded Pleven's project as impracticable and drew a clear distinction between cooperation within Europe and a European federation. At the end of November, Foreign Secretary Anthony Eden announced at a press conference in Rome that British troops would not participate in a European defence force. The UK's refusal to play an active role in plans for European military integration caused much disappointment across the Atlantic: Eisenhower later remarked that he used 'every resource, including argument, cajolery and sheer prayer to get Winston to say a single kind word about EDC'.[48]

Other west European governments were also cautious, fearing a strengthening of French influence and the shifting of resources from economic reconstruction to defence. Italy's Prime Minister Alcide De Gasperi, fearful of French hegemonic ambitions and aware of Italian public opinion's distrust of military alliances, proposed the creation of a European political authority, advocating the merging of the European Coal and Steel Community and the EDC through the establishment of a European 'federal' structure. The Americans were very supportive of the Italian plan, but the other five governments were sceptical about the further development of the political

---

46 Quoted in C. Gifford, *The Making of Eurosceptic Britain: Identity and Economy in a Post-imperial State* (Aldershot, Ashgate, 2008), pp. 32–3.
47 S. Rohan, *The Western European Union: International Politics between Alliance and Integration* (Oxford and New York, NY, Routledge, 2014), p. 31.
48 Quoted in D. Gowland and A. Turner, *Reluctant Europeans: Britain and European Integration 1945–1998* (Harlow, Longman, 2000), p. 60.

community. Nonetheless, at the end of December it was agreed that the Parliamentary assembly of the future defence community should present proposals towards the establishment of a political community to be reviewed at a governmental conference. This agreement and the project of a political community were then incorporated as Article 38 of the EDC.

However, there were still difficulties. First, west Europeans did not share new US President Eisenhower's basic assumption that the presence of American forces on the continent should be seen only as a temporary solution. Secondly, American officials doubted whether a western European army would be strong enough to balance Soviet power.[49] Thirdly, France did not favour a supranational solution, which would guarantee the Germans a status of equality. Only a persisting conventional imbalance and fears of Germany's neutralization convinced the United States and the west Europeans to sideline their differences. In February 1952 NATO's Lisbon Conference reaffirmed the need for West German rearmament, calling for 96 divisions and 7,000 combat aircraft to be available at 30-day notice for deployment in Europe by 1954.[50]

In March the Western powers, fearing a stratagem to prevent the FRG's incorporation into the EDC, formally rejected Stalin's last offer of a draft peace treaty and of a united but neutralised Germany. In April, also as a result of US insistence, London agreed to enter technical association with the EDC and to sign agreements providing for the inclusion of British army and air force units in European formations under SACEUR command. In May the United States, the UK, France and the FRG went ahead with the signing in Bonn of the Convention on Relations between the Three Powers and the FRG, which ended the occupation status and restored German sovereignty. On the following day, the treaty establishing the EDC between France, the FRG, Italy and the Benelux countries and a protocol for mutual military assistance between the UK and the EDC were signed in Paris.[51] However, the EDC proved not to be a durable solution in the search for a more equitable share of the burden of Western defence. Furthermore, in 1953 Stalin's death, Moscow's new peace offensive and the ceasefire in Korea softened perceptions of the Soviet political and military threat. As a result of the new détente in East–West relations and the breakthrough in atomic weaponry, through the development of thermonuclear bombs, the urgency

---

49 Trachtenberg, *A Constructed Peace*, p. 119.
50 NATO Military Committee, 'Force Goals for 1952, 1953 and 1954', https://archives
.nato.int/uploads/r/null/1/2/121172/SGM-0545-52_ENG_PDP.pdf.
51 *FRUS* (1952–4), vol. v, p. 685.

to secure an immediate West German contribution to NATO's conventional forces partly faded away.

The WEU and West German Rearmament within NATO (1954–1955)

The signing of the Paris agreements and the beginning of East–West détente had not erased, however, west European concerns about the modalities of West German rearmament. On the contrary, these concerns quickly resurfaced in the first months of the ratification debate. In France there were a tide of objections to the loss of national sovereignty and fears that the deal would not provide a sufficient degree of control over the FRG. The elections of January 1953 were followed by the formation of a new coalition in which Bidault replaced Schuman as foreign minister. Unlike his predecessor, Bidault feared that European integration might weaken France's position in the international pecking order. The new government delayed action on ratification of the treaty until 1954.

The Americans were irked by French hesitations. However, France's failure to ratify the EDC had not come as a complete surprise to the British.[52] The Foreign Office had already been working towards designing an alternative solution, and in March 1952 Eden had proposed that the various western European communities come together under the umbrella of the Council of Europe.[53] The EDC's members endorsed the British plan in principle, but the Eisenhower administration was frustrated by the sluggish pace of west European initiatives. In a speech to the North Atlantic Council on 14 December 1953 Secretary of State John Foster Dulles had already hinted at the risk of an 'agonising reappraisal' of US policy, if the question of Germany's contribution to European defence remained unsolved, warning Europeans that the United States might reconsider its commitment to west European security.[54] While many in western Europe dismissed the Secretary of State's threat as a 'calculated bluff', London viewed it as an opportunity to play upon American fears. At the Bermuda Conference from 4 to 8 December, which had been requested by the British – the first tripartite

---

52 For the text of the EDC treaty, see US Department of State, *American Foreign Policy 1950–1955: Basic Documents*, 2 vols. (Washington, DC: Department of State, 1957), pp. 1107–50.

53 'House of Commons Debate, 24 March 1952', *Hansard* 498 (1952): col. 32–4, https://api.parliament.uk/historic-hansard/commons/1952/mar/24/council-of-europe-united-kingdom.

54 For the text of Dulles' speech, see *FRUS* (1952–4), vol. v, pp. 461–8.

summit between the Anglo-Americans and the French since the end of the war – the UK's Prime Minister Winston Churchill complained to the US president that, as a result of French uncertainties, 'the West had wasted three years in futile negotiations' and suggested that the allies should reconsider the idea of rearming the FRG and incorporating it into NATO.[55]

Lack of US support for a diplomatic settlement over Vietnam at the Geneva Conference and the defeat of French forces at Dien Bien Phu in June further complicated matters, triggering the collapse of the government of Joseph Laniel and the formation of a new executive with communist support led by Pierre Mendès France. The new government was under significant domestic pressure to bury the EDC in order to win honourable terms from Moscow over Indochina. France's failure to ratify the EDC provided the UK with the opportunity to devise an alternative solution to the integrationist approach and shape the transatlantic security structure at a critical juncture for the relationship between NATO and European integration. During a visit to the White House in June 1954, the UK's prime minister and his foreign secretary stressed the need to act with the 'real elements of strength in the West', as there was a risk that – if measures were not taken soon to restore West German sovereignty – the Soviets might be able 'to pull the Germans across the line'.[56]

The West Germans supported the UK's initiative, as ultimately the FRG's direct inclusion into NATO was also Bonn's favourite option. On 30 July the US Senate voted unanimously – by an 88 to 0 vote – to restore West German sovereignty, even without a French ratification of the EDC. Thirty days later, on 30 August the French National Assembly's decision to put off further debate on the subject allowed the UK to propose at the nine-power conference between the five members of the BTO, West Germany, Italy, the United States and Canada, which was held in London between the end of September and early October 1954, an enlargement of the BTO to include the FRG and Italy and its transformation into the WEU. The UK's proposal provided a convenient compromise between American requests for a fast-track path to Germany's rearmament and French concerns about the FRG, without raising, however, all of the supranational complications posed by the EDC. Once Dulles had indicated a willingness to restate the same assurances that the United States had provided for the EDC, London agreed to station

---

55 S. Dockrill, *Britain's Policy for West German Rearmament 1950–1955* (New York, NY, Cambridge University Press, 1991), pp. 130–1.

56 Quoted from TNA, Kew, Eden. NA, PREM 11/618 and *FRUS* (1952–4), vol. v, p. 986.

a British army and a tactical air force in Germany for 50 years, as requested by the French.[57]

On 23 October 1954, the signing of the Paris accords, by amending the 1952 convention on relations between the FRG and the three Western powers, created a treaty basis for the continued, long-term presence of Western forces in Germany.[58] At the same time, the new arrangements modified and completed the Brussels Treaty, allowing the accession of the FRG and Italy to the WEU. They entered into force on 5 May 1955, formally ending West Germany's occupation status. On the following day, the FRG was incorporated into the alliance.[59] While Dulles regretted the lack of a supranational provision in Eden's solution, the framework proposed by the UK had proved an effective compromise between French and German expectations. Adenauer's acceptance of the same restrictions and force levels within NATO, which had been originally envisioned under the EDC, made it much easier for the government of Pierre Mendès France to consent to direct West German membership of the Western alliance and for the British to construct a transatlantic security structure that was at its core intergovernmental.[60]

Frictions in US–West European Relations and de Gaulle's Challenge to the Transatlantic Architecture (1956–1968)

The establishment of the WEU and the FRG's rapid integration into NATO had durable repercussions on the relationship between the alliance and European integration. The new institution was tasked with the objective of 'promoting the unity and encouraging the progressive integration of Europe'. However, the WEU was strictly intergovernmental: its primary organ – the Council of Foreign Ministers – would act, with only a few exceptions, mostly on the principle of unanimity. On paper, Article V of the 1954 Paris Treaty, which had been retained from the original Article IV of the BTO, bound the WEU's members by a commitment that was more far

---

57 A. Deighton, 'The Last Piece of the Jigsaw: Britain and the Creation of the Western European Union, 1954', *Contemporary European History* 7, no. 2 (1998): 181–96.

58 For the official text of the Paris protocol modifying and completing the Brussels Treaty, see www.nato.int/cps/en/natohq/official_texts_17408.htm?selectedLocale=en.

59 *Documents on Germany, 1944–1959: Background Documents on Germany, 1944–1959, and a Chronology of Political Developments Affecting Berlin, 1945–1956* (Washington, DC, US Government Printing Office, 1959), pp. 124–41.

60 D. C. Large, *Germans to the Front: West German Rearmament in the Adenauer Era* (Chapel Hill, NC, University of North Carolina Press, 1996), pp. 213–20.

reaching than that of NATO. Nonetheless, its signatories acknowledged NATO's premier role as well as the need to avoid any duplication of the alliance. The WEU's military command structure was integrated into that of NATO. Furthermore, the WEU was assigned hardly any military assets and relied on the alliance for information and advice on military matters.[61]

As confirmation of the WEU's implicit subordination to NATO, the NAC was recognised as the appropriate place to discuss strategic planning and defence policy. When, in November 1954, NATO's Military Committee revised the alliance's first strategic concept, it made no mention of the WEU.[62] Moreover, the Eisenhower administration's 'New Look', epitomised by the strategy of massive retaliation, and the NAC's adoption of the report M.C. 48, placing greater emphasis on the use of nuclear weapons and shifting the focus of military planning from defence to deterrence, further augmented western Europe's dependence upon the United States.[63] In the following years, although the WEU prompted a degree of foreign policy cooperation, particularly during the 1956 Suez Canal crisis, it failed to promote closer defence ties among its members, and after 1957 its role in the areas of economic, social and cultural cooperation was largely taken over by the European Economic Community (EEC).

The risks posed by the WEU's weaknesses and western Europe's excessive dependence upon the United States became crudely apparent in the second half of the 1950s, fuelling anxiety about overreliance on US nuclear weapons. In late 1957 the governments of France, Italy and the FRG, building upon the successful conclusion a few months earlier of the negotiations on the European Atomic Energy Community, reached a landmark agreement on the joint production of advanced military equipment, including atomic weaponry, with the purpose of reducing their dependence upon the United States. European apprehensions about the threshold of American resolve to use force in defence of western European interests climaxed in the early 1960s after French President Charles de Gaulle's demands for the creation of a three-power 'political–military directorate' at the head of the alliance of the Americans, the British and the French was firmly rebuffed by Washington.

---

61 For the text of the 1954 Paris Treaty, see www.cvce.eu/content/publication/2003/11/26/7d182408-0ff6-432e-b793-0d1065ebe695/publishable_en.pdf.
62 Military Committee 48, 'Report on the Most Effective Pattern of NATO Military Strength for the Next Few Years', www.nato.int/docu/stratdoc/eng/a541122a.pdf.
63 'NSC 162/2, Basic National Security Policy, 30 October 1953', FRUS (1952–4), vol. 11, pp. 585–6, 593.

Following US Defence Secretary Robert McNamara's announcement in 1961 of a shift from massive retaliation to flexible response in the American strategy, de Gaulle's verbal attacks against the United States plunged the alliance into a divisive crisis. In the same year, through the first Fouchet Plan, the French president called for the incorporation of defence into the EEC on an intergovernmental basis. However, he also categorically ruled out any forms of supranational cooperation among the Six, thereby proving unable to win support from France's European partners. While the Netherlands and Belgium expressed unequivocal hostility to the French proposal, the Italians were diffident and doubted de Gaulle's ultimate intentions, fearing the potential dominance of France in a defence union in which Paris would be the only nuclear power.

The West Germans also were at best ambivalent about the French plan. Adenauer agreed with the French president that one could not regard America as committed forever to the idea of defending Europe and that west Europeans should not fall into a position of being entirely dependent on America for their defence. Nonetheless, despite Bonn's apprehensions about the shift in the US strategy to flexible response and cautious reaction to the construction of the Berlin Wall in 1961, the FRG's decision-makers were reluctant to face the risk of a transatlantic decoupling. They feared that the French president's vision of a European 'Third Force' based on the Franco-German axis – which General de Gaulle put forward after the failure of the second Fouchet Plan in 1962 – was motivated more by a desire to thwart the FRG than to promote effective bilateral cooperation. Furthermore, France would be unable to secure the defence of the FRG's eastern frontier against a Warsaw Pact ground attack or to protect West Berlin against East German pressures. In 1963 France and the FRG signed a bilateral treaty in Paris, which entailed a secret military clause.[64] However, at the time of its ratification, the Bundestag firmly restated the FRG's commitment to NATO, swiftly putting to rest the prospect of bilateral Franco-German military cooperation.

It was the Americans, however, who had feared the most the divisive impact of de Gaulle's policies. In order to neutralise the French president's initiatives, which Washington perceived as disruptive and incompatible with Western unity, the United States took steps to reassure its west European allies. Between 1961 and 1963 the Kennedy administration repeatedly cajoled

---

64 The text of the treaty is available at https://www.assemblee-nationale.fr/12/dossiers/traite-franco-allemand.pdf.

the UK to apply for EEC membership. France's opposition, however, epit-omised by de Gaulle's vetoes in 1963 and 1967, added additional complexity. Kennedy's successor in the White House, Lyndon B. Johnson, also proposed the establishment of a NATO Multilateral Nuclear Force.[65] As the US president explained to the UK's Prime Minister Harold Wilson in December 1964, this would 'keep the Germans with us and keep their hand off the trigger'.[66] However, the administration soon became anxious about the FRG's nuclear aspirations and opted to bury this proposal, establishing in December 1966 the Nuclear Planning Group within NATO as well as pursu-ing dialogue with the USSR to negotiate the Treaty on the Non-proliferation of Nuclear Weapons.[67]

Although de Gaulle portrayed his efforts – including his decision in 1966 to withdraw from the alliance's military structure – as aimed at emancipat-ing France and western Europe from Washington, the other west European countries continued to privilege NATO as the landmark of their security. Nonetheless, in the late 1960s relations between Washington and its west European partners also suffered as a result of the United States' growing involvement in Vietnam and of the west European refusal to commit troops to Indochina. The UK was no exception to these dynamics. Johnson's decision to escalate the war contrasted with Wilson's determination to keep the UK out of the conflict, much to the disquiet of the White House. The president was enraged that the British could not even send 'a platoon of bagpipers'. Secretary of Defence Robert McNamara at one time remarked that the UK should send troops to Vietnam as part of 'the unwritten terms of the special relationship', while Secretary of State Dean Rusk even threatened that Britain should not expect any US assistance in the future, stating at one point: 'they can invade Sussex and we wouldn't do a damn thing about it'.[68]

Furthermore, as west Europeans, particularly the West Germans, began to pursue their own bilateral détente with the Soviet Union, in the late 1960s defence spending turned into a serious source of transatlantic friction, leading

---

65 Lyndon Baines Johnson Library, Papers of Lyndon Baines Johnson, National Security Files, Country File, France, Box 177, Extract of February 6, 1965 cable from Ambassador Kohler, 9 February 1965.

66 Quoted in Alan Dobson, *US Economic Statecraft for Survival, 1933–1991: Of Sanctions, Embargoes, and Economic Warfare* (New York: Routledge, 2002), p. 159.

67 *FRUS, 1964–68*, Vol. XIII, pp. 280–1.

68 Peter Jones, *America and the British Labour Party: The Special Relationship at Work* (London: Tauris, 1997), p. 150.

to repeated calls in the US Congress, particularly by Democratic majority leader Mike Mansfield, for substantial reductions in US troop levels.[69] Nonetheless, the White House, fearing that unilateral reductions in American forces might undermine Western defences, continued to press its allies to work together. From 1968 onwards, ten west European members of the alliance began to hold regular meetings of their defence ministers on the eve of the semi-annual conferences of NATO's Defence Planning Committee. As a result, the WEU's activities were reduced to a minimum, and in the 1970s also some of the SACEUR's responsibilities were gradually transferred to the newly established Independent European Programme Group (EUROGROUP) within the alliance.

The Revival of European Security Cooperation after de Gaulle (1969–1987)

Tensions among the allies continued to deepen following Richard Nixon's election to the White House in November 1968. The new administration's paramount priorities were to extricate US troops from Vietnam and avert an excessive shift in the global balance of strength. This objective was pursued through Henry Kissinger's triangular diplomacy and overtures to the People's Republic of China (PRC). The enunciation of the Guam doctrine in 1969 exposed Washington's frustration with west Europeans for failing to commit troops to Vietnam and increase defence spending. US pressures spearheaded new European initiatives in the security field. In 1970 the EUROGROUP countries adopted a special European Defence Improvement Programme with the aim of strengthening cooperation in order to improve allied capabilities. Nonetheless, fears of a transatlantic decoupling were rekindled by the amendment which Senator Mansfield introduced in 1971, requiring that US troop deployment in Europe be reduced by 50 per cent – roughly 150,000 men – by the end of 1971. The administration reassured its allies that it would not reduce the number of its troops in Europe, except in the context of reciprocal East–West action. Furthermore, in May 1971, the Senate defeated the Mansfield resolution. However, the melting down of the Bretton Woods system in 1971 and 2 years later the Arab embargo on oil exports during the Yom Kippur War further highlighted the risks of western Europe's excessive dependence upon Washington.

---

69 See the Mike Mansfield Papers, https://scholarworks.umt.edu/mike_mansfield_papers.

The Nixon administration's demands for a more robust European role called into question the notion of extended deterrence, triggering a number of initiatives to strengthen European security cooperation. After the EEC's enlargement to include the UK, Ireland and Denmark, at their 1973 Copenhagen Summit, in the context of the Conference on Security and Cooperation in Europe negotiations, the EEC members affirmed a determination to introduce the concept of European identity into their foreign relations, and in 1975 the creation of the European Council (EC) marked an important step to strengthen foreign policy coordination. However, the new body was not assigned any competence in the security and defence fields. As a result, in the late 1970s, while under President Valéry Giscard d'Estaing France began to resume cooperation with the alliance in the context of deteriorating East–West relations, other EEC members, particularly Italy and the FRG, called for more effective cooperation. In 1981 the Italian and West German foreign ministers, Emilio Colombo and Hans-Dietrich Genscher, submitted to the other EEC members a Draft European Act, which called for closer European political cooperation and aimed to add a security and defence component to European foreign policy.[70]

However, in the early 1980s, as a result of the new surge in East–West tension, new French President François Mitterrand was hesitant to have European defence on the EEC agenda, thus effectively sealing the fate of the Genscher–Colombo initiative, which was brought to a conclusion in the form of the solemn declaration at the Stuttgart EC in June 1983.[71] Also the UK's conservative Prime Minister Margaret Thatcher, despite having benefited from the EEC's diplomatic support during Argentina's 1982 invasion of the Falklands and having signalled an interest in increased foreign policy cooperation, opposed the prospect of further institutional integration. The failure of the Genscher–Colombo plan confirmed Anglo-French preferences for intergovernmental rather than supranational cooperation. It also revealed France's willingness to repair transatlantic ties at a time of deepening East–West tension. Mitterrand's Bundestag speech in January 1983 at the peak of the Euro-missile crisis marked a significant shift in France's approach to European security after several years of Gaullist rhetoric. On this occasion, which coincided with the twentieth anniversary of the 1963 Franco-German treaty, the French president overtly called for the FRG to accept US Pershing

---

70 'Draft European Act. German–Italian Initiative Submitted to the European Council 26–27 November 1981', *Bulletin of the European Communities* no. 11 (1981): 87–91.
71 'Solemn Declaration on European Union, Stuttgart, 19 June 1983', *Bulletin of the European Communities* no. 6 (1983): 24–9.

II and cruise missiles and, hence, to reaffirm its commitment to the alliance, warning of the dangers of nuclear decoupling between the United States and Europe.[72]

Nonetheless, President Ronald Reagan's announcement in March of his intention to develop a defence system against potential intercontinental ballistic strikes – the Strategic Defence Initiative – rekindled European fears of decoupling. In January of the following year, France circulated a memorandum calling for a reactivation of the WEU. Reactions to the French proposal varied among France's European partners: the UK was initially cautious, fearing a strengthening of French influence and a weakening of the alliance, while the FRG's Chancellor Helmut Kohl was particularly supportive, hoping to get France more involved with NATO's military structure. The Italians saw an opportunity to provide a new lifeline for European integration, strengthen the European role within NATO and pursue dialogue with countries of central and southeast Europe, as well as to generate greater involvement in collaborative arms production.[73]

In 1987, Mitterrand's support for the formation of a Franco-German brigade and the creation of intergovernmental army units, the Eurocorps, to which all WEU member states were invited to contribute, created the embryo of a European military caucus within the alliance. Mitterrand's initiatives were compatible with the UK's preferences, as they did not call into question member states' sovereignty and headed off the attempts of other EEC members to incorporate the WEU into the EEC's structure. Both Mitterrand and Thatcher pressed hard for the exclusion of defence from the Community's competences in the 1986 Single European Act (SEA), despite repeated attempts by the European Parliament and the European Commission to garner support from member states for a more active European role. By then, all EEC members were also members of the alliance with the sole exception of Ireland, although France and Spain did not participate in NATO's military structure. The SEA set the long-term objective of a European foreign policy but acknowledged that defence remained a matter for NATO and the WEU. In the following years the new thaw in East–West relations triggered additional initiatives, such as French Prime

---

72 For the text of Mitterrand's speech in German and French, see https://dserver
.bundestag.de/btp/09/09142.pdf.

73 Italian Ministry of Foreign Affairs, 'Reactivation of UEO (Ideas and Factual Data)',
13 December 1984, Istituto Luigi Sturzo, Archivio Giulio Andreotti, NATO Series,
Box 170, Subseries 1, Folder 072, https://digitalarchive.wilsoncenter.org/document/
ministry-foreign-affairs-reactivation-ueo-ideas-and-factual-data.

Minister Jacques Chirac's address to the WEU's assembly in 1986, calling for a 'New Security Charter' for western Europe, and the WEU's adoption in 1987 of the 'Platform on European Security Interests'.[74] These initiatives too, however, betrayed a preference for intergovernmental rather than supranational cooperation. Moreover, in the light of the sudden unravelling of the certainties of the Cold War, they were guided more by a concern to preserve France's role at the centre of Europe than by a desire to deepen European cooperation.

NATO and European Security Cooperation at the Cold War's End: From German Unification to Maastricht (1988–1992)

In the second half of the 1980s, the crisis of the Soviet bloc and the beginning of the transition process in the countries of central and southeast Europe rekindled the debate about the relationship between NATO and European integration, adding, at the same time, more complexity to it. As early as 1986 the new Soviet leader, Mikhail Gorbachev, had called for the establishment of a 'common European home' and a Pan-European security system that would ultimately supersede both NATO and the Warsaw Pact. However, the new US president, George H. W. Bush, was adamant that the United States should retain its nuclear and conventional presence in Europe, viewed the Atlantic alliance as the bedrock of transatlantic security and was unwilling to question its role.[75] As the president himself put it to Thatcher in 1989, 'NATO was fundamental, indeed more important than ever', particularly against the risk of 'apathy and unpredictability'.[76]

The Americans were aware that keeping the alliance alive would entail significant adaptation. In the administration's view, the newly united Germany would become the alliance's European stronghold and main base of operations.[77] Already during his first trip to Europe as president, Bush had described the United States and Germany as 'partners in leadership'.[78] In

---

74 'Platform on European Security Interests. Meeting of the Foreign and Defense Ministers of the Western European Union. The Hague, 27 October 1987', http://aei .pitt.edu/43384/1/WEU.Platform.pdf.

75 P. Zelikow and C. Rice, *Germany Unified and Europe Transformed: A Study in Statecraft* (Cambridge, MA, Harvard University Press, 1995), pp. 169–70.

76 *DBPO*, Series III, vol. VII, *German Unification 1989–1990*, p. 313.

77 J. A. Engel, 'Bush, Germany, and the Power of Time: How History Makes History', *Diplomatic History* 37, no. 4 (2013): 639–63, 660.

78 G. Bush, 'A Europe Whole and Free' (1989), https://usa.usembassy.de/etexts/ga6-89 0531.htm.

December 1989, a few weeks after the Berlin Wall fell, Secretary of State James Baker emphasised the need to keep the United States firmly linked to Europe.[79] Later in the same month, in the West Indies, Bush reiterated to Mitterrand Washington's commitment to the alliance, stating 'I don't want to see us decoupled from Europe; I don't want to see us pull out of Europe.'[80] American endeavours to revamp NATO were welcomed by west Europeans, who feared that the end of the bipolar structure of European security might lead to denuclear-isation of the alliance and a renationalisation of defence in Europe. Thatcher's poignant remark in June 1990 that one does not cancel a 'home insurance policy just because there have been fewer burglaries in your street in the last twelve months' summarised a widespread view among west European governments.[81]

Nonetheless, there were also differences between US views and those of some of their allies, particularly France. Mitterrand agreed with the basic US objective of preserving NATO as the linchpin of Euro-Atlantic security. He also agreed with the Americans that the new united Germany should be a full member of the alliance. However, the French president was frustrated by the prospect of a continuing US hegemony over Europe. Hence, he favoured an increase in the WEU's strategic role and the EEC's acquisition of compe-tences in the areas of security and defence. Furthermore, France also believed that the alliance should take into due account the security interests of the USSR. The Bush administration, however, viewed Mitterrand's demands for increased west European autonomy and for closer ties with the Soviets as premature and potentially disruptive.

As well as provoking anxiety in the United States, Mitterrand's proposal to enlarge the powers of the EEC and turn the WEU into the EEC's defensive arm was problematic also for some of France's European partners. While the Italians endorsed the prospect of closer west European security cooper-ation and advocated an increase in the powers of the EEC, the Germans trod very cautiously. Kohl disliked the French president's narrative about

79 J. A. Baker, 'A New Europe, a New Atlanticism: Architecture for a New Era', *Berlin Press Club*, 12 December 1989, State Department Press Release, reprinted in V. Mastny, *The Helsinki Process and the Reintegration of Europe: Analysis and Documentation, 1986–1990* (New York, NY, New York University Press, 2008), doc. no. 59, pp. 196–7; J. A. Baker, 'Speech by US Secretary of State James Baker to Berlin Press Club', in L. Freedman (ed.), *Europe Transformed: Documents on the End of the Cold War – Key Treaties, Agreements, Statements, and Speeches* (New York, NY, St. Martin's Press, 1990), pp. 397–8.

80 G. H. W. Bush, 'Joint News Conference Following Discussions with French President Mitterrand in St. Martin, French West Indies, 16 December 1989', in Government Printing Office, *Public Papers: George Bush* (Washington, DC, Government Printing Office, 1989), vol. ii, p. 1714.

81 F. Bozo, '"I Feel More Comfortable with You": France, the Soviet Union, and German Reunification', *Journal of Cold War Studies* 17, no. 3 (2015): 116–58.

encapsulating Germany into a solid European framework but was unwilling to alienate the French. The UK and the Netherlands, in contrast, firmly opposed French ambitions to assign European institutions a more robust role. London was also determined to avoid any federalist drift or talks of common defence that could lead to the creation of an independent command structure and, hence, duplicate NATO.

France's inability to gather sufficient support from its European partners helped the Americans assert their views and reconfigure NATO as Europe's premier security institution. The administration's approval of National Security Directive 23 in September 1989, regarding the changing nature of US relations with Moscow and the end of containment, was followed by the US President's reassurance at NATO's Brussels summit in December that Washington would maintain significant military forces in Europe and seek closer ties with the EEC.[82] On this occasion, Bush also proposed that the alliance should promote greater freedom in the East in this historic moment of transition.[83] Seven months later, at the London summit of the alliance in July 1990, the Americans tabled plans for a radical reform of NATO. The US proposal foresaw an expanded role for the alliance and a partnership status for central and east European countries.

Although there was no formal link between the two sets of negotiations, the reconfiguration of NATO as Europe's premier security institution had a deep impact also on the EEC's intergovernmental conference (IGC) that at the end of 1991 led to the inclusion in Article v of the treaty of Maastricht of a specific pillar on the Common Foreign and Security Policy (CFSP). The Bush administration and some of the alliance's European members, particularly the UK, the Netherlands, Denmark and Portugal, were worried that France's initiatives, which had been floated in Europe's intergovernmental conference on political union and were supported by a number of the EEC's members, such as Belgium, Spain, Luxembourg and Greece, might undermine NATO. After Mitterrand and Kohl addressed a letter to their partners in December 1990, outlining their vision of the future political union, in February 1991 the first more elaborate proposal on the CFSP was launched by the Luxembourg presidency, envisioning the development of European security cooperation through the WEU.

82 The text of National Security Directive 23 is available at https://bush41library .tamu.edu/files/nsd/nsd23.pdf
83 'Outline of remarks at the North Atlantic Treaty Organization headquarters in Brussels', 4 December 1989, in *Public Papers: George Bush*, 1989, Book ii, pp. 1644–8.

The proposal triggered an immediate reaction from Washington. In the same month, US Undersecretary of State for Arms Control and International Security Reginald Bartholomew and Assistant Secretary of State for European Affairs James Dobbins drafted a memorandum for the EEC member states, stating the United States' opposition to any institutional development that might marginalise NATO or accentuate the separation and independence of the European pillar from the alliance, including the subordination of the WEU to the EEC.[84] The debate continued to unfold in the following months, under the new Dutch presidency, in an attempt to reach a compromise between the recognition that NATO remained indispensable for European security and the ambition to deepen European security cooperation. In early October a joint 'Anglo-Italian' declaration called for the preservation of NATO's premier role for transatlantic security.[85] A few days later in a new joint letter to President of the EC Ruud Lubbers and to the other EEC members, Mitterrand and Kohl expressed their wish for reinforced Franco-German military cooperation and a revival of the secret military clause of the 1963 Franco-German treaty, together with closer cooperation with other members of the WEU, which could increase Europe's strategic role.[86]

The Americans wasted no time in countering French initiatives. At its Rome summit in November, NATO formally approved the New Strategic Concept (NSC), which envisioned a broader approach to security and the alliance's involvement in crisis management operations. The NSC acknowledged the efforts under way to strengthen the alliance's European pillar through an enhancement of the WEU's role and the steps taken in this direction by the EEC member states, formally giving US blessing to the development of a European security identity. However, it also delimited the boundaries of European ambitions, firmly enshrining them within the alliance.[87] In February 1992 the Maastricht Treaty, although containing far-reaching goals and intentions in respect of a common European foreign and security policy, confirmed that even after the end of the East–West division, European security would remain under NATO's blanket. The treaty formalised the establishment of the EU's CFSP, laying the foundation for the

---

84 For the text of the 'Batholomew telegram' of 20 February 1991, see W. van Eekelen, *Debating European Security 1948–1998* (The Hague: SDU Uitgevers, 1998), pp. 340–4.
85 The 'Anglo-Italian Declaration on European Security and Defence' is reproduced in *European Documents* no. 1735, 5 October 1991.
86 For the text of the letter, see *Le Monde*, 17 October 1991, pp. 4–5.
87 For the text of NATO's 1991 NSC, see www.nato.int/cps/em/natohq/official_texts_23847.htm.

progressive framing of a common defence policy through the WEU, which was identified as an integral part of the EU's development. However, the treaty also acknowledged the specific national character of the security and defence policies of EEC member states. Moreover, it pledged to respect the obligations of those member states that were also members of NATO, while subjecting joint actions on foreign policy issues to unanimous approval. The subsequent Petersberg declaration, adopted by the WEU Ministerial Council in June 1992, confined Europe's operational role to the range of the Petersberg tasks, tasking the WEU with limited capability, to be used only when NATO decided not to get involved.[88]

NATO and European Defence in the Post-Cold War World

In the run-up to the preparations for the 1991 IGC and the approval of NATO's NSC, the Bush administration had expressed concerns about the development of a European security mechanism that might ultimately undermine NATO and its command structure. Nonetheless, there was no common strategic vision among the EEC's members, and how much autonomy European policy should enjoy from NATO was a matter of heated debate also among west Europeans. The UK, which felt a closer affinity with the United States, headed a number of EEC members, including Denmark, Portugal, Italy and the Netherlands, which viewed NATO's reform and the development of a European common foreign and security policy as complementary rather than alternative enterprises. In contrast, France, Belgium, Spain and, to some extent, Germany stressed the need for the WEU to play a more robust role in the continent's security. This was also the preference of the president of the European Commission, Jacques Delors, who feared that the pillar structure and the intergovernmental method might exclude security from the Commission's competences and proposed that all provisions relating to external aspects be brought together in one article of the treaty.

The unfolding of regional conflicts in the Persian Gulf and southeast Europe seemed to vindicate this view. The dispatch of US forces to the Gulf and the Arabian Peninsula to counter the Iraqi invasion of Kuwait, in their largest overseas campaign since the end of the Second World War, and concerns about a rapidly deteriorating situation in Yugoslavia rapidly

---

88 'Declaration by the WEU Council of Ministers, Bonn, 19 June 1992', in C. Hill and K. E. Smith (eds.), *European Foreign Policy: Key Documents* (London and New York, NY, Routledge, 2000), pp. 205–11.

strengthened calls for a more robust European role. In his speech at the International Institute for Strategic Studies on 7 March 1991, Delors remarked how the Gulf War had proved that the members of the Community possessed 'neither the institutional machinery nor the military force' which would have allowed them to act together, emphasising the need to move towards a political union embracing a common foreign and security policy and to incorporate the WEU's common defence clause in the EU's new treaty structure.[89]

At the end of June a delegation involving the foreign minister of Luxembourg and chair of the EEC's Foreign Affairs Council, Jacques Poos, and the previous and future holders of this post – the Dutch foreign minister, Hans van den Broek, and Italy's foreign minister, Gianni de Michelis – travelled to the Croatian island of Brijuni to negotiate a ceasefire in the conflict between Yugoslavia and the secessionist states Croatia and Slovenia. The apparent success of the mission rekindled enthusiasm among European leaders. On 29 June in an interview with the *New York Times*, Poos hailed the European mediation as a demonstration of the EEC's international agency and diplomatic clout, boldly stating: 'The hour of Europe has dawned. This is the hour of Europe – not the hour of the Americans [. . .]. If one problem can be solved by the Europeans, it is the Yugoslav problem. This is a European country and it is not up to the Americans. It is not up to anyone else.'[90]

In December 1992, US involvement in the context of Operation Restore Hope in the Horn of Africa further fuelled calls for the development of European agency and capabilities. Furthermore, under the pressure of an ailing domestic economy, the newly elected Clinton administration seemed willing to increase Europe's share in the burden of transatlantic defence. The new American stance was captured by the remarks of the Undersecretary of State for Political Affairs Peter Tarnoff, who in May 1993 publicly called for selective US disengagement from Europe and a larger role for the WEU in security and defence.[91]

Nonetheless, rather than showing Europe's diplomatic clout, Yugoslavia crudely exposed the cumbersome nature of the CFSP's decision-making process, revealing the WEU's inadequate resources and command structure

89 For the text of the speech, see https://ec.europa.eu/commission/presscorner/detail/en/SPEECH_91_22.
90 *The New York Times*, 29 June 1991. See also Richard Holbrooke, *To End a War* (New York: Random. House, 1998), p. 28.
91 Peter Tarnoff, 'Remarks to the Overseas Writers Club', 25 May 1993.

as well as a huge gap between European expectations and capabilities. The Adriatic blockade implemented by some of the WEU's member states in the context of Operation Sharp Guard and the WEU's assistance to Bulgaria, Hungary and Romania to help them patrol the waters of the Danube, in order to implement the sanctions regime against Yugoslavia, proved largely ineffective, while European contingents that were deployed as part of the UN Protection Force to protect designated 'safe-areas' in Bosnia-Herzegovina, lacking a strong political mandate and strategic leadership, were often the target of deliberate attacks by Yugoslav forces. Furthermore, the 1992 Petersberg Declaration, which had listed the new WEU's tasks and responsibilities, had failed to clarify its operational relationship with NATO. As a result of the ineffectual response of European institutions, in April 1993 the alliance began its involvement in Bosnia with Operation Deny Flight, continuing to step up its presence in the following years. In August 1995 – a month after Bosnian Serb forces had overrun the Dutch battalion tasked with protecting the city of Srebrenica – NATO officially launched Operation Deliberate Force, with air strikes and extensive bombing of Bosnian Serb armed forces and strategic targets.

The EU's diplomatic and military failure in Yugoslavia and the alliance's intervention had long-lasting repercussions, further strengthening NATO as the bedrock of transatlantic and European security also after the Cold War. The widening of the European integration process to three neutral states in 1995 gave Austria, Finland and Sweden observer status in the WEU as a natural implication of their accession to the EU without obliging them to sign up for its mutual defence arrangements. Furthermore, Finland and Sweden did not support the integration of the WEU into the Union. While bolstering NATO's role, the EU's failure in former Yugoslavia, however, also triggered new calls by some member states, mostly France, Italy and the Benelux countries, as well as by the European Parliament and the Commission, to reform the CFSP and provide the WEU with the resources to play a meaningful role in the continent's security. The United States and the UK did not oppose these calls, as long as NATO's command and capabilities were not duplicated.

At its 1994 Brussels Summit, the alliance and the WEU had already reached an agreement on the establishment of combined joint task forces and the creation of a European Security and Defence Identity. This arrangement was based on the concept of 'separable but not separate capabilities': NATO's assets and resources would be made available to the WEU, on a case-by-case basis, and upon the NAC's approval. After the 1995 Dayton peace agreement, which brought the Bosnian war to an end, France's participation in the NATO-led international peacekeeping and stabilisation force in Bosnia-Herzegovina bolstered expectations of closer European security cooperation without detracting from its transatlantic character. In 1997 the Treaty of Amsterdam introduced a number of innovations in the EU's common foreign and security policy and created the post of High Representative for the CFSP.[92]

A landmark step was taken in the following year, at the Anglo-French summit in St Malo. Then, French President Jacques Chirac's formal acceptance that the Atlantic alliance remained the foundation of the collective defence of its members and the UK's endorsement of an autonomous European role, 'backed up by credible military forces', paved the way for the creation of the ESDP. The Clinton administration endorsed the content of the St Malo declaration. However, US Secretary of State Madeleine Albright also raised a warning flag, presenting Europeans with three formal conditions that reasserted the content of the Bartholomew–Dobbins Memorandum: first, the ESDP shall not 'duplicate' NATO assets, secondly it shall not 'discriminate' against non-EU NATO members and, ultimately, it shall not undermine the indivisibility of Euro-Atlantic security and lead to a 'decoupling' of Europe from North America.[93] These conditions were fundamentally a plea to the Union, in crafting the ESDP, not to expend scarce resources on trying to establish a separate European caucus within the alliance through the creation of a second set of capabilities. The establishment of the ESDP was formalised at the 1999 Cologne EC and preceded the appointment of NATO's former Secretary General Javier Solana to the post of High Representative for the CFSP.[94]

In the early 2000s, negotiations on the establishment of a political and legal framework for NATO–EU cooperation began. In 2001, the Treaty of Nice transposed the ESDP into the EU treaty structure, adding it to the range of instruments at the Union's disposal for crisis management and conflict prevention. However, it also confirmed that the new policy would not infringe upon the specific character of the defence policies of its members and of the obligations of some of them towards NATO. Many of the WEU's activities, particularly the revisited and enlarged Petersberg tasks

---

92 For the text of the Treaty of Amsterdam Amending the Treaty on European Union, the Treaties Establishing the European Communities and Certain Related Acts, see www
.europarl.europa.eu/topics/treaty/pdf/amst-en.pdf.
93 See Secretary Albright's remarks to the North Atlantic Council ministerial meeting, Brussels, 8 December 1998, https://1997-2001.state.gov/statements/1998/981208.html.
94 'Conclusions of the Presidency, Cologne European Council, 3–4 June 1999', www
.europarl.europa.eu/summits/kol1_en.htm.

and responsibilities in the area of arms procurement policy, with the exception of the WEU's common defence clause, were gradually transferred to the EU. In 1999, NATO's former Secretary General Xavier Solana was appointed Secretary General of the WEU and tasked with a dual-hatted mandate in order to oversee the transfer of functions between the WEU and the EU.

Following the terrorist attacks of 9/11 and the beginning of the 'War on Terror', the United States stepped up its endorsement of the ESDP. However, the Americans continued to demand compliance with their conditions. Already in February 2001, Secretary of State Colin Powell had stated that 'the U.S. supports and welcomes the creation of a European defence facility ... as long as it will actually enhance and strengthen the alliance's capabilities'. Negotiations between the EU and the alliance were finalised in Berlin in December 2002. The final package of agreements established the principles for the use of NATO assets and capabilities by the EU and for the creation of the NATO–EU Strategic Partnership. Arrangements were also reached about the involvement of non-EU European allies in the ESDP's missions. In the same month, the NATO–EU declaration on the ESDP welcomed the strategic partnership established between the EU and NATO but also reaffirmed that the alliance remained the foundation of the collective defence of its members.[95]

These arrangements were confirmed in March 2003 by a formal exchange of letters between NATO's Secretary General and the CFSP's High Representative on the release of NATO assets and capabilities for EU military operations.[96] At the end of the same month, European boots went on the ground for the first time, as the EU deployed Operation Concordia in North Macedonia, taking over responsibilities from NATO's operation Allied Harmony. In the same year, as a response to the civil war in the Democratic Republic of Congo, the ESDP conducted Operation Artemis without assistance from NATO, largely relying on French assets and capabilities. One year later European forces replaced the alliance at the command of the peacekeeping operation in Bosnia, which was then renamed Operation Althea. The Union's Bosnian deployment had extensive recourse to NATO's assets and resources and was headquartered in NATO's Supreme Headquarters Allied Powers Europe. The UK's General and Deputy Supreme Allied Commander Europe John Reith was appointed EU Operation Commander for Althea, highlighting the ESDP's close relationship with NATO.

---

95 For the text of the NATO–EU Declaration, see www.nato.int/cps/en/natolive/offi cial_texts_19544.htm.

96 M. Smith, *Europe's Common Security and Defence Policy* (Cambridge and New York, NY, Cambridge University Press, 2017), p. 64.

In the following years, however, the ESDP's capabilities remained limited and never exceeded the range of the Petersberg tasks. Furthermore, in the early 2000s the UK and a number of other EU members reiterated their opposition to any process that might ultimately lead to duplicating NATO and to a decoupling of the United States from Europe. At the same time, the EU's eastern enlargement further slowed down plans for deeper integration in security and defence, exposing deep differences in strategic cultures between old and new members and providing the United States with new leeway to influence the further development of the ESDP. Different interpretations of Europe's strategic role had crudely emerged in the run up to the US invasion of Iraq in March 2003, when the leaders of France, Germany and Belgium met in Brussels threatening to set up separate European headquarters from NATO. While the summit did not produce durable results, eight European members of the alliance, including many former Soviet bloc states, were deeply critical of this initiative.[97]

The intra-European fracture over Iraq, exposing diverging strategic priorities among EU members, further slowed down in the following years the enhancement of European military capabilities, although the 2007 Lisbon Treaty formally ushered in the creation of the CSDP, introducing a common defence and solidarity clause and spearheading the WEU's formal disbandment in 2011. The advent of the global financial crisis in 2008, which hit European defence budgets hard, delayed additional progress towards the development of European capabilities. It also rekindled tension with the United States over burden sharing, despite France's formal reintegration into NATO's military structure in 2009.

The modalities of NATO's Operation Odyssey Protector against Libya in 2011 further exposed the persisting dependence of the European allies upon the United States, raising additional concerns in Washington about burden-sharing and prompting President Barack Obama to accuse publicly the European partners of behaving like 'free riders'.[98] Following Russia's annexation of Crimea in 2014, the 2016 and 2018 joint NATO–EU declarations restated the indivisibility of the transatlantic security relationship.[99]

97 *The Wall Street Journal*, 30 January 2003, www.wsj.com/articles/SB1043875470158445104.
98 For the text of President Obama's interview with Jeffrey Goldberg, see www .theatlantic.com/magazine/archive/2016/04/the-obama-doctrine/471525.
99 Declaration by the Heads of State and Government participating in the meeting of the North Atlantic Council in Brussels, 11–12 July 2018, www.nato.int/cps/en/natohq/offi cial_texts_156624.htm?selectedLocale=en; Joint Declaration on EU–NATO Cooperation by the President of the European Council, the President of the European Commission,

Nonetheless, the Trump administration's outspoken criticism of the allies confronted Europeans – 70 years after Dulles' famous warning – with the threat of another 'agonising reappraisal', triggering the House of Representatives to pass a bill in 2019 prohibiting the appropriation or use of funds to withdraw the United States from NATO.[100] Although in 2021 newly elected President Joe Biden defined the American commitment to NATO as 'sacrosanct', the shift in the US strategic focus towards Asia and Russia's invasion of Ukraine in 2022 have not only highlighted once more the need to strengthen European capabilities but also shown the dangers of overreliance on the United States.

Conclusions

This chapter reviewed the relationship between NATO and European defence from the establishment of the transatlantic bargain in the late 1940s until the Russian invasion of Ukraine in 2022. It argued that in the early days of the Cold War, alongside the Soviet threat, a commitment by the countries of western Europe to mutual security cooperation – enshrined in the 1948 Brussels Treaty – was instrumental to securing the transatlantic bargain and overcoming Washington's diffidence concerning entangling alliances. With the establishment of the North Atlantic Treaty in 1949, western Europe became part of a wider security area, which also included the broader north Atlantic region. This new transatlantic compact established a firm connection between the Atlantic alliance and European integration and was based on the mutual assumption of the indivisibility of Euro-Atlantic security. However, during the 1950s the outbreak of the Korean War, presenting the United States with the prospect of a global confrontation with the Soviet Union and its allies, prompted a number of endeavours to coax west Europeans into providing more for their own defence through a fast-track solution to the divisive issue of Germany's rearmament. In the following years the FRG's incorporation into the WEU and NATO in 1955 cemented the link between transatlantic and European security. However, despite the efforts of some nations, particularly Italy and the Benelux countries, to promote genuine security cooperation in Europe, the UK and France

and the Secretary General of the North Atlantic Treaty Organization, www.nato.int/c ps/en/natohq/official_texts_156626.htm.
100 For the text of House of Representatives 676, 116th Congress, see www.congress.gov /bill/116th-congress/house-bill/676/text?format=txt.

held deep reservations about a supranational European defence. As a result, during the Cold War, while the WEU became the formal venue for European security cooperation, NATO remained the undisputed – yet also the sole authentic – bedrock of European defence.

The end of the East–West division did not fundamentally affect the relationship between NATO and European defence. In the new transatlantic security architecture the alliance was reconfigured as Europe's premier security institution, while the WEU was charged with the ancillary role of conducting peacekeeping and crisis management tasks but left without adequate military resources. Only in December 1998 – after Europe's sluggish and largely ineffectual response to Yugoslavia's disintegration – did the UK and France formally acknowledge in their joint St Malo declaration the need for autonomous European capabilities. However, they also agreed that NATO remained the primary Euro-Atlantic security institution, thus paving the way in the early 2000s to the 'Berlin plus' arrangements between the alliance and the EU and to the first military operations conducted under a European flag. The next logical steps of this process were the transfer of the WEU's peacekeeping and crisis management responsibilities to the EU and the introduction in the 2007 Lisbon Treaty of a mutual defence and solidarity clause. However, as a result of diverging preferences among member states, of expansion to the countries of central and southeast Europe, and of the 2008 financial crisis, in the following years no significant steps were taken towards the establishment of a truly effective European defence. The outbreak in 2022 of the largest and most brutal European war since 1945 made it evident that the European countries remain heavily dependent on Washington both in terms of political leadership and insofar as military capabilities are concerned. In future years the EU's priority should be expanding the enduring relationship with NATO, while renewing efforts towards deepening institutional integration and centralisation of decision-making in security and defence.

Recommended Reading

Hofmann, S. C. *European Security in NATO's Shadow: Party Ideologies and Institution Building* (Cambridge, Cambridge University Press, 2013).

Moens, A., L. J. Cohen and A. G. Sens (eds.). *NATO and European Security: Alliance Politics from the End of the Cold War to the Age of Terrorism* (Westport, CN, Praeger, 2003).

Zyla, B. *The End of European Security Institutions? The EU's Common Foreign Security Policy and NATO after Brexit* (Cham, Springer, 2020).

GLOBAL CHALLENGES: INTERNATIONAL POLITICS, THE PLANET AND THE UNIVERSE

13

European Integration and the United Nations

EDITH DRIESKENS

Introduction

This chapter analyses how the United Nations (UN) as an intergovernmental organisation, has shaped the functioning of the European Union (EU) and its member states in global governance over the years. The EU is often seen, both by scholars and by practitioners, as a special, even unique actor in the UN context, characterised by high levels of support, cooperation, institutionalisation and formalisation.[1]

This chapter approaches uniqueness not as a mantra, but as a question of empirical validation, by zooming in on the UN General Assembly (UNGA). This organ embodies the principle of universality by bringing together all UN members and, in addition, allowing a wide variety of observers to participate in its work, including the EU.[2] While the latter's functioning is well-documented, there remain some blind spots to be addressed, such as the UNGA's decision to grant the European Economic Community (EEC) observer status in October 1974. For ease of reference, this chapter will

---

1 E. Drieskens, 'Golden or Gilded Jubilee? A Research Agenda for Actorness', *Journal of European Public Policy* 24 (2017): 1541–3; E. Drieskens, 'Actorness and the Study of the EU's External Action', in S. Gstöhl and S. Schunz (eds.), *Studying the European Union's External Action: Concepts, Approaches, Theories* (Basingstoke, Palgrave Macmillan, 2021), pp. 32–3.

2 U. Fastenrath, 'Article 4', in B. Simma, D.-E. Khan, G. Nolte, A. Paulus and N. Wessendorf (eds.), *The Charter of the United Nations*, 3rd ed. (Oxford, Oxford University Press, 2012), pp. 342–3.

consistently speak of the EU even when referring to its predecessors, except where the context demands a greater level of specificity.

The remainder of this chapter analyses that decision in two steps. Taking a long-term perspective, albeit in search of defining moments, the first part provides a historical overview of the principles, procedures and practices that have defined the EU's functioning at the UN, both in general and in relation to the UNGA specifically. Presenting original historical research (for which the author thanks the staff of the Dag Hammarskjöld Library in New York for making archive research possible in pandemic times), the second part discusses the importance of observer status in UN(GA) decision-making and reconstructs the UNGA's decision to grant the EEC this status.

Background: A Brief History of EU–UN Relations

Certainty in Uncertainty

The year 2020 brought unprecedented challenges for everyone, with Covid-19 creating the biggest health crisis in recent history. Countless plans, big and small, had to be adapted, postponed or simply cancelled. This was also the case for the UN, which commemorated the seventy-fifth anniversary of its founding on 24 October of that year. However, even before the coronavirus hit the world, the organisation understood that this landmark occasion would not necessarily be a happy one. For certain, it had outlived its predecessor by almost half a century and there had also been considerable achievements along the way. At the same time, high hopes had fizzled out on different occasions, or even resulted in delusion. Moreover, as it approached its seventy-fifth anniversary, the organisation, like the rules-based system it embodies, faced increasingly strong head-winds from a growing number of 'isms' – including unilateralism, protectionism, populism, isolationism and authoritarianism. And while it was not the first time that it had come under fire, these winds seemed to come together as a perfect storm. They made the UN's future look more precarious than ever before and, quite logically, clouded any plans for celebration.

Language is telling here, particularly the kind that is used during the General Debate of the UNGA. This meeting brings world leaders together in New York in the middle of September and, resultantly, is considered one of the most important moments in the annual diplomatic calendar. A closer look at the interventions made during the 2019 edition shows that the barometer clearly pointed to stormy weather for the UN's seventy-fifth anniversary year. The picture painted by António Guterres was particularly daunting. The UN's Secretary General stated that the possibility of a 'Great Fracture' – 'the world splitting in two' – was real.[3] While he did not mention countries by name, it was quite clear that he alluded to the growing tensions between Donald Trump's United States and Xi Jinping's China, which put the UN, like the idea of international organisation more generally, under great pressure. Guterres repeated this message in even more urgent language in his New Year address in early 2020. Using the four horsemen metaphor, he stated that four threats jeopardised the future of the world organisation, or even signalled the end of times as per Christian lore: 'epic geopolitical tensions', 'an existential climate crisis', 'deep and growing mistrust' and 'the dark side of the digital world'.[4] He took this analogy further on the occasion of the 2020 General Debate, which was held virtually for the first time in history. Suggesting that the situation had become even more dangerous, Guterres opened the proceedings by warning that an unexpected fifth horsemen had galloped in, 'adding to the fury of each' and resulting in 'a crisis unlike any . . . ever seen'.[5] That fifth horsemen, of course, was the Covid-19 pandemic, which had started as a local outbreak in the Chinese city of Wuhan in December 2019 but escalated into a global health crisis throughout 2020.

Iterating a wider pattern of crisis and catharsis, the pandemic did add to the gloominess, but it also strengthened calls for renewed cooperation, and even triggered a renewed sense of common purpose. This was tangible at the 2020 General Debate, when Guterres reminded his colleagues about their historical responsibility, stating that they faced their 'own 1945 moment'.[6] This message did not fall on deaf ears, particularly not within the EU, which participates in this meeting as an observer. This came as no surprise. While the EU has changed significantly over the years, both in terms of size and in terms of function, its message has been one of unwavering commitment to multilateralism in general and the UN in particular.[7]

---

3 UN Secretary-General, 'Address to the 74th Session of the UN General Assembly', 24 September 2019.
4 UN Secretary-General, 'Remarks to the General Assembly on the Secretary-General's Priorities for 2020', 22 January 2020.
5 UN Secretary-General, 'Address to the Opening of the General Debate of the 75th Session of the General Assembly', 22 September 2020.
6 Ibid.
7 S. Biscop and E. Drieskens, 'Effective Multilateralism and Collective Security: Empowering the UN', in K. V. Laatikainen and K. E. Smith (eds.), *Intersecting Multilateralisms: The European Union and the United Nations* (Houndmills, Palgrave Macmillan, 2006), pp. 115–32; S. Biscop and E. Drieskens, 'The European Security

The 2020 General Debate was no different in this sense. In his video message, Charles Michel, who represented the EU as president of the European Council, referred to the EU as 'a driving force for multilateralism and the rules-based international order' and as 'an unwavering supporter of the United Nations'.[8] And while reform was needed, the EU's support for the UN remained 'as strong as ever'.[9] This message was repeated by Joseph Borrell, the EU's High Representative for Foreign Affairs and Security Policy, in an op-ed that appeared in parallel with the online proceedings.[10] It was echoed by the wishes that were sent from the EU to the UN about a month later on the occasion of the UN's official birthday, as it was in the EU's participation in the #EuropeTurnsUNBlue initiative, with the Brussels headquarters of the European External Action Service, the European Commission and the European Council being lit up in blue – the official colour of the UN – to mark the occasion.

EU–UN Relations Inside-Out

As these recent examples show, the EU's message on UN milestones is usually one of continuing support and of longstanding partnership. Cooperation between the EU and the UN indeed dates to the early days of European integration. The Treaty Establishing the European Economic Community, which created the Common Market in 1957, identifies the principles of the UN Charter as guiding principles for the (development of) relations with third countries and provided that the Community establish relations with the UN, making the European Commission responsible for doing so. Mirroring the Community's (exclusive) competences, such relations were first established in the larger spheres of trade and agriculture.[11]

Strategy: Confirming the Choice for Collective and Comprehensive Security', in J. Wouters, F. Hoffmeister and T. Ruys (eds.), *The United Nations and the European Union: An Ever Stronger Partnership* (The Hague, TMC Asser Press, 2006), pp. 267–79.

8 President of the European Council, 'A Stronger and More Autonomous European Union Powering a Fairer World – Speech by President Charles Michel at the UN General Assembly', 25 September 2020.

9 Ibid.

10 High Representative of the Union for Foreign Affairs and Security Policy, 'The EU Stands with the UN', 22 September 2020.

11 M. Farrell, 'EU Representation and Coordination within the United Nations', in K. V. Laatikainen and K.E. Smith (eds.), *Intersecting Multilateralisms: The European Union and the United Nations* (Houndmills, Palgrave Macmillan, 2006), pp. 30–3.

Different working arrangements were introduced, including the status of observer. In the UN context, the EU was granted this status by the Food and Agricultural Organization in 1962, the United Nations Conference on Trade and Development (UNCTAD) in 1964 and the Economic and Social Council (ECOSOC) in 1967.[12]

The creation of European Political Cooperation (EPC) gave the EU's functioning at the UN a new dimension, extending it to the spheres of peace and security and, thus, bringing the EU member states and their cooperation to the forefront.[13] Like EPC more generally, UN-related (inter-)action between these member states – the group expanded from six to nine in 1973 – largely developed on the basis of declarations and reports. A specialised working group (Coordination Nations Unies) was established following the Luxembourg Report in 1970. Additional arrangements on consultation and coordination were agreed upon in the Copenhagen Report (1973), Dublin Report (1975) and London Report (1981). Importantly, while it was the EU's decision to take its first steps on the global scene, it was the UN that cleared an important hurdle, particularly for common representation, by granting the Federal Republic of Germany (West Germany), which had been accorded observer status in 1952, membership in September 1973 (see below).

This chapter explores the observer status that the EU obtained a year later at the UNGA, on 11 October 1974. This episode has received little scholarly attention, if any. It tends to be routinely mentioned in publications on the EU's functioning at the UN, creating at least the perception that this status was granted without much of a fight, or even without debate. The second part of this chapter shows that reality is more complex and, thus, that this case is relevant for answering the question of whether the EU's history at the UN should be considered unique or generic, and whether it can be understood in terms of change or continuity. Research does, however, give us a sense of the context in which this status was sought. It shows that the UN became a test case for EPC, even though it was largely in the background of the EEC's attempts to become an actor on the global scene during these years, particularly compared with the Conference on Security

12 Commission of the European Communities, *The European Community, International Organizations and Multilateral Agreements: Amending Supplement until 1 January 1980. Updated to 1977* (Luxembourg, Office for Official Publications of the European Communities, 1980).

13 P. Luif, *EU Cohesion in the UN General Assembly* (Paris, EU Institute for Security Studies, 2003), pp. 9–12; M. E. Smith, *Europe's Foreign and Security Policy: The Institutionalization of Cooperation* (Cambridge, Cambridge University Press, 2004), pp. 71–4.

and Cooperation in Europe (CSCE), which was negotiated between 1972 and 1975 (see below).[14] This was especially so for the UNGA, where voting cohesion between the member states increased significantly. Such cohesion, that is, the extent to which these countries vote similarly in UN settings, has been seen as an important marker of EU foreign policy success, by practitioners as well as analysts.

Indeed, a closer look at the available research shows that many have studied the issue of whether and how new steps in integration influence the capacity of the member states to speak with one voice at the UN, notably in the context of the UNGA.[15] This implies that research on EU–UN relations has come in waves, triggered by both widening and deepening of European integration. Consequently, and despite growing awareness that a solid understanding of EU–UN relations requires both inside-out (EU) and outside-in (UN) perspectives, knowledge has a strong European footprint.[16] However, seeing the EU–UN relations predominantly, even exclusively, from the inside out is almost always associated with risk or consequence. In fact, the EU experienced this first-hand when implementing the Lisbon Treaty in the UNGA.[17] Its under-appreciation of the sensitivities and specificities surrounding this context, fuelled by the mantra of uniqueness, made its first attempt to upgrade its observer status fail spectacularly in September 2010. It would see its request approved only in May 2011, following substantial rewriting and extensive outreach.

That said, the observation that this upgrade enabled the European Council president to address the General Debate on behalf of the EU makes it seem logical to frame this episode, as well as the Lisbon Treaty more generally, in

14 P. Keatinge, 'The Twelve, the United Nations and Somalia: The Mirage of Global Intervention', in E. Regelsberger, P. de Schoutheete de Tervarent and W. Wessels (eds.), *Foreign Policy of the European Union: From EPC to CFSP and Beyond* (London, Lynne Rienner Publishers, 1997), pp. 275–96, 276; E. Johansson-Nogués, *The Voting Practice of the Fifteen in the UN General Assembly: Convergence and Divergence* (Barcelona, Institut Universitari d'Estudis Europeus, 2004), p. 3.

15 C. Bouchard and E. Drieskens, 'The European Union in UN Politics', in K. E. Jørgensen and K. V. Laatikainen (eds.), *Routledge Handbook on the European Union and International Institutions: Performance, Policy, Power* (London, Routledge, 2013), pp. 122–3.

16 K. E. Jørgensen and K. V. Laatikainen, 'The Political Impact of the EU's Interaction with International Institutions. Towards a Two-Way Street – Both Inside-Out and Outside-In Perspectives', in R. A. Wessel and J. Odermatt (eds.), *Research Handbook on the European Union and International Organizations* (Cheltenham, Edward Elgar Publishing, 2019), pp. 628–43.

17 E. Drieskens, L. Van Dievel and Y. Reykers, 'The EU's Search for Effective Participation at the UN General Assembly and UN Security Council', in E. Drieskens and L. van Schaik (eds.), *The EU and Effective Multilateralism: Internal and External Reform Practices* (London, Routledge, 2014), pp. 15–32.

terms of change. Continuity, however, can also be witnessed. Building on policy practice, the provisions introduced by the Single European Act (SEA) and the Maastricht Treaty illustrate just that. The SEA of 1986 establishes that the EU's common positions should be upheld in international settings by the participating member states. The Treaty on European Union, as signed in Maastricht in 1992, adds the obligation to inform the non-participating member states about matters of common interest. Also, it introduces a disclaimer clause for the UN Security Council (UNSC).

Echoing Article 108 of the UN Charter, this disclaimer specifies that the member states with permanent membership at the UNSC must defend the positions and interest of the EU, though without prejudice to their responsibilities following from the UN Charter. Research has shown that it was introduced in reaction to Italy's demand for coordination within this context, which, in itself, was a watered-down version of its plea for an EU seat at the UNSC.[18] The Commission too thought along such maximalist lines.[19] Such proposals were doomed from the start, as they crossed a red line for France and the United Kingdom (UK), the two member states with a permanent seat. Whereas the first drafts explicitly mentioned these countries by name, the final wording does not. This should be seen against the background of German unification and the foreign policy ambitions arising therefrom.

The Lisbon Treaty amended these provisions for the first time, introducing the new EU foreign minister – officially the High Representative of the Union for Foreign Affairs and Security Policy – to the UNSC. Research has shown, however, that these amendments are best read in terms of continuity.[20] Tellingly, the Lisbon Treaty puts in black and white that membership of the UNSC should be seen as a national matter. More change can certainly be found at the UNGA. This entails the yearly General Debate, but also day-to-day decision-making, with the new Delegation of the European Union to the UN – in other words, the EU's embassy in New York – growing considerably in its role as EU representative (see below).[21] Yet here too, it is important to stress that these innovations build upon past practice.

18 E. Drieskens, 'Beyond Chapter VIII: Limits and Opportunities for Regional Representation at the UN Security Council', *International Organizations Law Review* 7 (2010): 158–63.

19 R. Corbett, *The Treaty of Maastricht: From Conception to Ratification* (London, Longman, 1993), p. 219.

20 E. Drieskens, 'EU Actorness at the UN Security Council: A Principal-Agent Comparison of the Legal Situation before and after Lisbon', *European Journal of Law Reform* 10 (2008): 575–94.

21 E. Drieskens, 'What's in a Name? Challenges to the Creation of EU Delegations', *The Hague Journal of Diplomacy* 7 (2012): 61–3.

This past is also present in the Lisbon Treaty's affirmation of the EU's commitment to the UN specifically and multilateralism more generally. Tipping the balance further towards continuity, it repeats that the principles of the UN Charter should be respected and that cooperation with the UN should be established. In addition, it calls for the promotion of multilateral solutions to common problems, particularly in the UN framework. By way of this addition, the EU confirmed the strategic course that was set with the European Security Strategy in 2003.[22] As has been widely noted, this document called for an international order based on 'effective multilateralism' and defined the UN as the main framework for international relations. It has since been revised twice, by the Report on the Implementation of the European Security Strategy in 2008 and the EU Global Strategy in 2016. While there are significant differences between these documents, both suggest that the EU's choice in favour of multilateralism and the UN holds true even in times of challenge and change. By means of the first document, the EU responded to the emergence of new powers on the international scene, thus the shift towards multipolarity. It stipulates that the UN is the reference point for the EU's international relations as well as the organising framework for its relations with third countries and regional organisations. The second document was adopted in response to the more recent trend towards power politics, which was briefly touched upon at the beginning of this chapter. The document, while shifting the narrative to 'principled pragmatism', confirms that the EU remains committed to a rules-based multilateral international order with the UN at its core.

EU–UN Relations Inside-Out

The previous part has shown that the EU's engagement with the UN is firmly anchored in its core documents and, thus, rightfully seen as 'constitutional'.[23] But is the opposite true as well? There should be no doubt that the UN sees the EU as an important partner. Not only does the EU share the UN's founding values, but also, taken as a whole, the EU is its largest financial

---

22 Biscop and Drieskens, 'Effective Multilateralism and Collective Security', pp. 115–32; Biscop and Drieskens, 'The European Security Strategy', pp. 267–79; E. Drieskens and L. Van Dievel, 'The Multilateral System', in K. E. Jørgensen, Å. K. Aarstad, E. Drieskens, K. V. Laatikainen and B. Tonra (eds.), *The Sage Handbook of European Foreign Policy* (London, Sage, 2015), pp. 1029–42.

23 E. Paasivirta and T. Ramopoulos, 'UN General Assembly, UN Security Council and UN Human Rights Council', in R. A. Wessel and J. Odermatt (eds.), *Research Handbook on the European Union and International Organizations* (Cheltenham, Edward Elgar, 2019), p. 58.

contributor. However, as a regional organisation, the EU has been a difficult fit for the UN, which remains in essence structured in terms of a world of states. Indeed, while there is certainly room for regional organisations, UN membership remains reserved for sovereign states. The negative experience with group dynamics during the war years, as well as the reality that regional organisations were just starting to emerge at that time, can explain this choice.[24] In fact, only two such organisations participated in the San Francisco Conference which resulted in the creation of the UN: the League of Arab States (LAS) and the Pan-American Union. It was not until the 1960s, after the process of decolonisation gained momentum, that this type of organisation became more visible and vocal in UN politics, particularly in relation to (economic) development.[25] This development was given an important impetus by the creation of the Organisation of African Unity (OAU) – the predecessor of the African Union (AU) – in 1963 and the Association of Southeast Asian Nations in 1967.

The participation of the two aforementioned organisations, but also the ambition of the great powers to maintain authority in their respective regional spheres of influence, can explain why regional cooperation was included in the final rounds of negotiation.[26] As a result, the UN Charter includes a provision allowing for collective self-defence and a separate chapter on cooperation between the UNSC and regional organisations. Notably, practice has been giving even more importance to regional cooperation, particularly since the end of the Cold War, when the UNSC resumed its activity. Meanwhile, in a somewhat parallel development, the EU has taken important steps to strengthen its foreign, security and defence policies. These coinciding developments explain why the EU has, on the one hand, been able to establish itself as an important actor within this context and, on the other hand, also come to be known as an actor that sees itself as very different from most other (regional) organisations operating in the UN context. Within the UN, the EU is perceived as a unique regional

24 S. C. Schlesinger, *Act of Creation: The Founding of the United Nations* (Cambridge, MA, Westview, 2004), pp. 175–92; W. P. S. Sidhu, 'Regional Organizations', in T. G. Weiss and S. Daws (eds.), *The Oxford Handbook on the United Nations*, 2nd ed. (Oxford, Oxford University Press, 2018), pp. 314–17.
25 C. Schreuer, 'Regionalism v. Universalism', *The European Journal of International Law* 6, no. 3 (1995): 477–99, 480.
26 Sidhu, 'Regional Organizations', pp. 314–17.

actor, characterised by high levels of institutionalisation and formalisation. But there is also agreement that the EU laws and rules surrounding this functioning are internal matters, rather than demands on the UN to adapt itself.[27] In fact, the EU can expect a strong response from the UN members when this understanding is violated, as has been the case with the observer status upgrade following the entry into force of the Lisbon Treaty. While this upgrade attracted a great deal of scholarly attention, little is known about the UNGA's original decision to grant the EU – more specifically, the EEC – observer status in 1974. The following part sheds light on this decision and reconstructs the discussions surrounding it.

Research: The EEC's Observer Status

Regulations and Trends

Not only officials, but also scholars have taken the UN's seventy-fifth anniversary as an opportunity to look forward and back. Unsurprisingly, some have used this volume's overarching themes to organise their reflections on past, present and future practice. Weiss and Daws, for instance, conclude that the UN's history should be read in terms of 'fundamental continuity' and 'substantial change'.[28] As editors of the newest edition of the *Oxford Handbook on the United Nations*, they find numerous examples to substantiate the claim that both elements have defined practice, including the identity of the actors involved. Indeed, while state actors have been the key players, others have left their mark as well. Business, media and non-governmental organisations are mentioned here, including the more recent emergence of 'uncivil' actors such as belligerents, warlords and criminals.[29]

Even though they are certainly not the easiest group to define, observers would have deserved a spot on this list as well. More than 100 actors have this status today. The group includes regional organisations such as the EU and AU, but also bodies such as Interpol, the Holy See, the Sovereign Order of Malta, the New Development Bank, the Indian Ocean Rim Association and the Hague Conference on Private International Law. It is a complicating factor that these guests come with both different competences and different rights. Complicating things even further, these differences manifest

---

27 F. Hoffmeister and P.-J. Kuijper, 'The Status of the EU at the United Nations: Institutional Ambiguities and Political Realities', in Wouters et al., *The UN and the EU*, p. 15.

28 T. G. Weiss and S. Daws, 'World Politics: Continuity and Change since 1945', in Weiss and Daws (eds.), *The Oxford Handbook on the United Nations*, p. 4.

29 Weiss and Daws, 'World Politics: Continuity and Change', p. 6.

themselves both within and between organisations.[30] As a rule, however, observers do not enjoy full participatory rights. Most often, they have access to meetings and documents, but are seated apart and do not have voting rights. This is also the default mode in the setting that is the central focus of this chapter, namely the UNGA.

While hosting familiar names, observers remain something of a mystery. Some of them, like the EU, have generated quite a lot of scholarly attention. But this is not the case for all of them or for this group more generally. In fact, only a small body of literature is available.[31] Moreover, writings are mostly dated and often anecdotal. Because knowledge is fragmented, action seems disjointed. Admittedly, as the above list illustrates, this group is difficult to grasp. But the invitation of observers has been a constant feature of the UN's history. Moreover, the importance of observers in UN decision-making has increased over time. Not only has the group grown; it has also seen its rights expand over the years. Finally, following a shift towards informal decision-making, the context has become more receptive to the involvement of observers.[32] It is therefore important not to overlook these actors and their practices.

As noted, the observation that the EU is among the best studied observers in the UNGA needs some qualification. The EU's upgrade in 2011 certainly has been studied extensively, but the same does not hold true for when it was originally granted the status of an observer in 1974. The literature, does, however, provide some relevant insights into the structural and contextual factors shaping the background against which this development should be seen. More specifically, when combined with archival research, these insights shed light on two questions. First, why was a collective actor like the EU given this status, which was originally reserved for states? Secondly, why was the EU given this status only in 1974, whereas the Organization of American States (OAS) received it in 1948, the LAS in 1950 and the OAU – the AU's predecessor– in 1964? Why did the EU have to wait for another decade while it was increasingly seen as an actor in its own right, even as a model for integration?

30 J. Klabbers, *An Introduction to International Organizations Law*, 3rd ed. (Cambridge, Cambridge University Press, 2009), pp. 100–2.
31 N. Sybesma-Knol, 'The Continuing Relevance of the Participation of Observers in the Work of the United Nations', in K. Wellens (ed.), *International Law: Theory and Practice: Essays in Honour of Eric Suy* (The Hague, Kluwer Law International, 1998), pp. 371–2; H. G. Schermers and N. Blokker, *International Institutional Law: Unity within Diversity*, 5th revised ed. (Leiden and Boston, MA, Martinus Nijhoff, 2011), p. 132.
32 M. J. Peterson, *The UN General Assembly* (London, Routledge, 2006), p. 55.

The literature shows that the UN Charter regulates the status of observer both in letter and in spirit even though it does not include a specific reference to it. Insofar as the former is concerned, it allows any state which is not a member of the UN to bring to the attention of the UNGA and UNSC any dispute to which it is a party. Insofar as the latter is concerned, universalism has been the UN's key ambition ever since the early days, yet it is still not a reality. While 193 states currently have UN membership, only 50 countries signed the UN Charter in San Francisco. This means that, certainly in the early decades, issues were discussed in relation to non-member countries. The status of observer – which was pioneered by the United States in the League of Nations – was introduced to involve these countries. It increased the legitimacy of decision-making, and facilitated leveraging of relevant knowledge and expertise.

The literature also shows that the increase in membership did not make the observer status irrelevant. There are two reasons why, in fact, the opposite is true. First, membership had grown over the years, but applications were often affected by Cold War dynamics, particularly by the great powers' practice of 'mutual rejection'.[33] The high frequency of this stalling practice made some even argue that the 'single most impelling factor giving rise to observer status ... has been necessity, born of the politics of the Cold War'.[34] Secondly, the demand to involve other kinds of actors increased in the 1960s and 1970s. Reflecting the process of decolonisation, national liberation movements were invited as observers. Regional organisations were welcomed as well, echoing their growing importance in international politics. The OAU was given this status in 1965, bringing it on a par with the OAS and LAS, which had obtained this status in 1948 and 1950, respectively.

The fourth organisation – the EEC – had to wait for nearly ten more years. While understandable in the light of West Germany's late membership of the UN, this relative tardiness appears to stand in contradiction to the fact that the EEC was increasingly seen as an international actor as the 1960s went by, particularly, but not exclusively, within the context of the General Agreement on Tariffs and Trade (GATT) negotiations. This is illustrated by its close association with the notion of actorness.[35] Mentioned first in 1970, this notion echoed the growing awareness that nation-states, even if still

33 A. G. Mower, Jr, 'Observer Countries: Quasi Members of the United Nations', *International Organization* 20, no. 2 (1966): 266–83, 272.
34 Ibid., 271–2.
35 Drieskens, 'Golden or Gilded Jubilee?', 1541–3; Drieskens, 'Actorness and the Study of the EU's External Action', pp. 32–3.

predominant, were no longer the only actors in international politics. More specifically, scholars introduced this notion to assess the extent to which emerging collectives could be regarded as international actors. The UN and EEC were seen as front-runners, easily surpassing others such as the OAU. In fact, the use of actorness suggests that this was particularly so for the EEC: it did not take long for the concept to become almost exclusively associated with European integration.

The wider context in which European integration was achieved makes this timing more understandable, though. The Cold War not only prevented an early start of the implementation of EPC at the UN, but also delayed the achievement of the EEC's observer status ambitions in the UNGA. Apparently, this status was not granted to 'European organisations' until the mid 1970s because of 'the difficult political situation in Europe (the division between a "Western" and a Communist Europe)', but little detail or explanation is provided.[36] To validate and substantiate this claim, the remainder of this chapter reconstructs the discussions and decisions underlying the UNGA's approval of Resolution 3208(XXIX), through which the EEC was awarded observer status.[37] It will be shown that, even though this resolution was adopted without a vote, thus by consensus, the Cold War did cast its shadow over it. To make a long story short: the EEC and the Council for Mutual Economic Assistance (CMEA, also known as Comecon) were given, as some kind of package deal, the same observer rights at the same time. To understand the course of events that generated this outcome, detailed knowledge of the CMEA is not required. It is sufficient to know that this organisation, which ceased to exist in 1991, was created in 1949 as a counterweight to the Marshall Plan with the aim of coordinating the economic development of the Soviet-controlled eastern European countries. The following ten countries were members when the observer status question played out: Albania, Bulgaria, Cuba, Czechoslovakia, East Germany, Hungary, Mongolia, Poland, Romania and the Soviet Union. As a reminder, the EEC's membership had grown to a similar size, from six to nine countries, following the accession of Denmark, Ireland and the UK.

Discussions and Outcomes

Archival research suggests that it should have been no real surprise that the EU did not receive additional observer rights in 2011 without discussion or debate. In fact, the EU itself has known for a very long time that such an

---

36 Sybesma-Knol, 'The Continuing Relevance of the Participation of Observers', p. 375.
37 UN General Assembly, 'Status of the European Economic Community in the General Assembly, A/RES/3208, 11 October 1974'.

upgrade is seldom smooth sailing. Tellingly, when reflecting on the situation in the late 1970s, the European Commission concluded that the emergence of 'groupings exercising certain powers transferred to them by their members' resulted in 'problems of "recognition"'.[38] This was particularly so for the EEC, which 'should in theory be given a status higher than that of observer when the international organization in question is discussing matters falling within the jurisdiction of the Community, even if only partially' but experienced that 'in practice, an approach along those lines often runs into difficulties'.[39] Meeting records show that the difficulties encountered by the EEC in 1974 were much smaller than the ones its successor faced in implementing the Lisbon Treaty in New York, but also that it would be a mistake to portray the 1974 granting of observer status as an uneventful episode in the history of EU–UN relations. The discussions, which spanned a 10-week period between 31 July and 11 October, are reconstructed below as a four-step process. Holding the EEC presidency, France took the lead in all four steps.

Application (31 July 1974)

The first step was taken on 31 July, when the EEC formally requested, by letter from the Permanent Representative of France to the UN, that its status be included as a supplementary item in the agenda of the twenty-ninth session of the UNGA, which would start a few weeks later, in the middle of September.[40] The EEC's argumentation, so the accompanying memorandum reveals, centred around the idea of 'a widening of the sphere of common interest' between itself and the UNGA.[41] More specifically, the EEC framed its request as a logical consequence of the convergence of two parallel developments, namely itself playing 'an increasingly important role in the development of international economic relations' (as a result of which it had 'gradually made its presence felt in the organizations that deal with such problems, particularly in certain organs of the United Nations') and the UNGA paying 'increasing attention to economic problems'.[42]

---

38 Commission of the European Communities, *The European Community*, p. 3.   39 Ibid., p. 7.
40 UN General Assembly, 'Request for the Inclusion of a Supplementary Item in the Agenda of the Twenty-Ninth Session. Status of the European Economic Community in the General Assembly. Letter dated 31 July 1974 from the Permanent Representative of France to the United Nations Addressed to the Secretary-General, A/9701, 1 August 1974'.
41 Ibid., para. 3.   42 Ibid., paras. 1–2.

The EEC asserted the obviousness of its request not only by pointing to the convergence of interests and priorities between itself and the UNGA, but also by recalling that it enjoyed similar rights in both ECOSOC and UNCTAD (see above). Just as in those settings, the requested observer rights would allow the EEC to participate in the work of the UNGA, though only in the committees and for matters within its competence. Unsurprisingly, considering the integration process sketched in the previous part of this chapter, the main, but not exclusive, aim was access to the UNGA's Second Committee, which concentrates on economic and financial matters.

Prioritisation (19 September 1974)

In a second step, France requested that the EEC's wish for observer status be directly considered, even as a matter of high priority.[43] It did so on 19 September, at a meeting of the UNGA's General Committee, which has an important agenda-setting function. Proceeding with urgency would allow the EEC to participate as an observer in the upcoming session. This request was granted without further ado. However, when addressing the General Debate four days later, on 23 September, France once again took the opportunity to draw attention to the EEC's application, stressing the potential benefits for the wider UN membership. Though speaking in a national capacity, the French representative reflected upon the status quo on the European continent, particularly in relation to European integration. Providing a positive outlook, France argued that the EEC was becoming 'a coherent entity . . . capable of confronting the problems of our time' and, in doing so, would even 'serve as a model'.[44] As a consequence, the UN membership would 'hear the voice of the European Economic Community becoming more and more distinct'.[45]

A closer look at the UNGA agenda and the wider political context explains why, despite this apparent confidence and optimism, a speedy approval was deemed important. It shows that the EEC had to make its voice heard in an increasingly polarised context. The UN, and the UNGA in particular, were increasingly seen, and used, as arenas for confrontation between North and South.[46] The Yom Kippur War of October 1973, and the

---

43 UN General Assembly, 219th meeting, A/BUR/SR.219, 19 September 1974.
44 UN General Assembly, 2238th Plenary Meeting, A/PV.2238, 23 September 1974, para. 118.
45 Ibid.
46 B. Lindemann, 'Europe and the Third World: The Nine at the United Nations', *World Today* 32, no. 7 (1976): 260–9, 260.

subsequent discussion on raw materials, but also the more long-term trend towards decolonisation, should be mentioned here.[47] Three UNGA decisions of 1974 highlighted this changing balance of power between North and South and the extent to which the latter 'in a relatively short space of time made the United Nations its tool': the adoption of the Declaration on the Establishment of a New International Economic Order (May 1974), the decision to grant the Palestine Liberation Organization observer status (November 1974) and the adoption of the Charter of Economic Rights and Duties of States (December 1974) (see below).[48]

Imitation (8 October 1974)

The third step in the reconstruction shows, however, that it was not the emerging North–South divide, but the older East–West divide that hampered the EEC's request for observer status, more specifically the decision of the CMEA to mirror itself with the EEC, tabling a request for similar rights and privileges. Bulgaria, as the CMEA's spokesperson, launched this plan at the General Committee meeting of 8 October, requesting the inclusion of an additional item – the status of the CMEA at the UNGA – in the UNGA's agenda. While the CMEA demanded that its request be treated 'on a par' with that of the EEC, its ambitions went further, eying plenary meetings as well.[49] This envisaged scope, as well as the late timing of the request, made France ask some clarification questions. CMEA members reacted to these questions with irritation, stressing that the organisation merely asked for similar treatment, not for 'the slightest advantage ... over and above that which might be enjoyed by the EEC'.[50]

The fundamental, almost existential, nature of these questions did not hamper swift decision-making. On the contrary: the General Committee's meeting lasted only a little over an hour. Insofar as planning was concerned, it recommended that the UNGA would consider the two status requests successively 'for the purposes of rational procedure'.[51] Insofar as scope was concerned, it agreed to pass on this decision to the UNGA, considering the question of whether the rights would be applicable in plenary meetings a matter of substance. At the same time, the diplomatic bickering between France and the USSR which ended the meeting suggests that the EEC's request, and the underlying perception of uniqueness, remained a sensitive

47 Schreuer, 'Regionalism v. Universalism', 480.
48 Lindemann, 'Europe and the Third World', 260.
49 UN General Assembly, 221st meeting, A/BUR/SR.221, 8 October 1974, para. 3.
50 Ibid., para. 16.   51 Ibid., para. 27.

matter. Reflecting on how the meeting proceeded, France stated that it was 'interesting to note ... that in all aspects of the discussion, including the question of priority and the nature of the status, EEC was held up as a model to be emulated by CMEA'.[52] In a somewhat witty answer, the USSR said that it was rather 'surprising to note the extent to which the States members of EEC were concerned to ensure that the socialist countries did not enjoy the slightest advantage over them'.[53]

Approval (11 October 1974)

In the fourth and final step, the UNGA granted the EEC observer status through the adoption of Resolution 3208(XXIX). This was done at its plenary meeting of 11 October. Again, the main role was reserved for France, which framed the EEC's request in terms of 'progress', 'peace' and 'cooperation'.[54] As for progress, France pointed at the high degree of economic integration, including delegation of both jurisdiction and competence to common institutions, that had been achieved, particularly in the domains of trade, agriculture and development aid. As for peace, France reminded everyone that this integration 'serves to maintain peace and international equilibrium', which in itself should be no surprise, as 'the constructive attitude of the EEC is clearly expressed in the preamble of the Treaty of Rome, the signatories to which have proclaimed that they will abide by the principles of the Charter of the United Nations'.[55] Finally, insofar as cooperation was concerned, France pointed out the EEC's orientation, as witnessed at the Kingston conference, which had brought together the nine EEC member states and forty-four African, Caribbean and Pacific (ACP) countries in Jamaica in July within the context of association, but also within the context of food aid.

In terms of procedure, France stressed the precedent value of ECOSOC and UNCTAD, but also clarified, in a clear reference to the CMEA discussion, that the EU's request was limited to working bodies. There was a simple reason for this: 'The rules and customs of the UN have clearly determined what observer status is: observers do not speak in the Assembly itself, but can ask to speak in its committees, conferences and working groups.'[56] The CMEA remained silent during the meeting, but others did not. The questions and concerns that were formulated had nothing to do with the draft submitted by the EEC, but everything with the broader political context, notably the

---

52 Ibid., para. 33.   53 Ibid., para. 34.
54 UN General Assembly, 2266th Plenary Meeting, A/PV.2266, 11 October 1974, para. 9.
55 Ibid., para. 8.   56 Ibid., para. 12.

question of apartheid. While not affecting the outcome (or even trying to), they serve as a reminder that the North–South divide, as noted, increasingly affected UN(GA) decision-making in the early 1970s, particularly after the Yom Kippur War and the subsequent oil-price crisis (see above). As Lindeman wrote in 1976: 'The United Nations Organization is today the international forum where the industrialized nations and the developing countries confront each other in their entirety: here the West faces the united front of the Third World on all questions affecting their relations.'[57]

Nigeria, as chair of the Special Committee on Apartheid, acted as a spokesperson. Making it immediately clear that he did not intend to oppose the draft resolution that was on the table, the Nigerian representative took the opportunity to remind the EEC member states of the implications, namely 'that the Community will ensure strict compliance with all – and I repeat, all – United Nations resolutions'.[58] Meeting records show that two specific issues were mentioned here. First, there had been rumours that the South African mission in Brussels was entering into negotiations with the Community to obtain trade concessions. This was, according to the Nigerian representative, a violation of the obligations that the EEC member states had under the UN Charter. Secondly, he expressed the hope that the EEC would facilitate, 'in the spirit of the desirability of evolving a new economic order which has pervaded the United Nations' the early conclusion of the agreement resulting from the negotiations with the ACP countries.[59] In response to the first remark, France said that there were no negotiations scheduled with South Africa and that the EEC and its member states would do nothing that would advance the policy of apartheid. In response to the second remark, the French representative reminded his Nigerian colleague of the Kingston discussions.

With this fear taken away and this hope confirmed, the way was wide open for the unanimous approval of the EEC's observer status. Brief in nature, but typical for documents of this kind, the adopted resolution specifies that the EEC, in order 'to promote co-operation between the United Nations and the European Economic Community', would be invited 'to participate in the sessions and work of the General Assembly in the capacity of observer'.[60] The CMEA resolution, which mirrored this text, was subsequently approved

---

57 Lindemann, 'Europe and the Third World', 260.
58 UN General Assembly, '2266th Plenary Meeting, para. 13.   59 Ibid., para. 15.
60 UN General Assembly, 'Status of the European Economic Community'.

without vote, even without discussion.[61] In fact, the job was done after just over 2 hours, including the election of five new non-permanent members for the UNSC.

Curiously, while the issue was settled through twin resolutions, the CMEA was not mentioned in the reflections on the EEC's observer status, nor did its members intervene in the discussion. The other way around, it was just the same; the EEC was not mentioned in the reflections on the CMEA's status, and its members did not participate in the discussion. These decisions were brought together only by the United States after both had been adopted. Clarifying its position, the United States specified that it found the 'developments in Europe towards greater integration, especially in the economic field' both 'important and useful'. It said further that both status requests 'related to the special nature of these developments' were 'tailored to the specific relevant areas' and were 'fully in accord with the past practice and customs of the United Nations with regard to observers'.[62] Putting these requests on an equal footing, it stressed that this related 'equally' to both of the resolutions which had been adopted.[63]

Representation

While the consultation of archive materials challenges the idea, as implied by its absence in the literature, that the EEC was granted observer status in 1974 without opposition or confrontation, it does confirm that the UN, or at least the discussion in New York, has not always been at the top of the EU's priority list (see above). Numbers often tell only half the story, but a comparison of the EEC's and EU's presence in the UN's capital provides a clear illustration in point. Today, a decade after the observer status upgrade, the EU's representation in New York includes more than sixty staff members. By comparison, when the EEC was granted observer status in 1974, it was represented by a very small team, less than a handful of officials. Moreover, so documents reveal, this team was not installed because of the UN's presence in New York. Rather, it was a direct consequence of the importance that the EEC attached to its relations with the United States more generally.

More specifically, the story behind the EU's representation in New York starts in 1954, when the EEC opened a press and communications office in Washington. In 1963, it decided that this office would benefit from the

61 UN General Assembly, 'Status of the Council for Mutual Economic Assistance in the General Assembly, A/RES/3209, 11 October 1974'.
62 UN General Assembly, '2266th Plenary Meeting', para. 43.   63 Ibid., para. 43.

establishment of 'une "antenne"' (antenna) in New York.[64] This decision was inspired by the broader observation that European integration generated little enthusiasm among the public at large. It also rested on the growing need, resulting from accession and association, to provide information abroad. The United States was seen as particularly important here because of the GATT negotiations (see above). A representation in New York, so the Commission argued, would make it easier to reach 'une grande partie des correspondants de presse et des divers milieux qui exercent une influence sur l'opinion publique mondiale' ('a large part of the press correspondents and of the various circles that exert an influence on world public opinion').[65] Tellingly, the UN was not even mentioned here.

Weeks before the EEC was granted observer status, it was decided that it would have double representation, of both the Commission and the Presidency.[66] As a result of this decision, the Commission's staff in New York doubled: from one to two officials. The extra staff member would allow the Commission to expand its activities beyond information and communication. According to the job description, this entailed, first of all, the development and maintenance of good relations both with the business community (the banking sector in particular) and with think tank communities (such as the Council on Foreign Relations and the Ford Foundation); and secondly, acting as liaison with the UN (and assisting the member states with this task).[67] Further nuancing the role that the UN in New York played in the EEC's external relations at the time, this upgrade was part of a broader package by which the Washington delegation was significantly expanded. It was, indeed, 'not until West Germany joined the United Nations on 18 September 1973 and all the Nine were represented there, that the UN became ... one of the most important areas for European Political Co-operation (EPC)' (see above).[68]

Conclusion

Sketching the history of EU–UN relations in broad strokes, but providing a more detailed account of the origins and development of these relations at the UNGA in New York, this chapter has underscored the importance of

64 Communauté économique Européenne Commission, 'Mémorandum sur la politique des Communautés en matière d'information à l'attention des conseils', COM(63) 242, 26 June 1963, p. 11.
65 Ibid.   66 Hoffmeister and Kuijper, 'The Status of the EU', p. 11.
67 Commission des Communautés Européennes, 'Renforcement de la représentation extérieure dans certains pays tiers. Communication de la Commission au Conseil', SEC(73) 2055 final, 25 July 1973.
68 Lindemann, 'Europe and the Third World', 261.

understanding the EU's functioning at the UN as a 'two-way street' and, thus, of combining the traditional inside-out perspective with an outside-in one: this functioning cannot be understood – or changed, for that matter – without taking into account the written and unwritten rules and routines defining this context.[69] This awareness came suddenly when the implementation of the Lisbon Treaty, and the upgrade of the EU's observer status at the UNGA in particular, proved much more difficult than anticipated. In some EU circles, these difficulties even hit like a bolt from the blue.

Shining the light of history on these challenges and going back to the early days of EU–UN relations, this chapter suggests that they could have been handled more effectively, even avoided, with the right mindset. Indeed, while the UNGA's decision to grant the EU this status in the mid 1970s caused much less commotion than the aforementioned upgrade, these privileges were not granted without discussion or debate. With both East–West and North–South sensitivities defining the course of events, this decision could have served as a reminder that talking without listening and taking without giving is the privilege of few in UN politics. Within this context, few have questioned or will question that the EU is a unique actor, characterised by high degrees of formalisation and institutionalisation. But there is also little doubt that uniqueness, by itself, does not establish an automatic right, even monopoly, on the acquisition of rights and privileges. These parallels between past and present confirm, once more, that even if history never repeats itself, it does, indeed, often rhyme.[70]

Recommended Reading

Bourantonis, D. and S. Blavoukos (eds.). *The EU in UN Politics* (London, Palgrave Macmillan, 2017).

Drieskens, E. 'The United Nations', MOOC lecture (2023), https://youtu.be/WGtnHE73Abk.

EUN-NET eLearning Portal on EU–UN Relations, https://wb-ilias.uni-freiburg.de/goto.php?target=crs_122050&client_id=unifreiburgwb.

Hoffmeister, F., T. Ruys and J. Wouters (eds.). *The United Nations and the European Union: An Ever Stronger Partnership* (The Hague, TMC Asser Press, 2006).

Laatikainen, K. V. and K. E. Smith (eds.). *The European Union at the United Nations: Intersecting Multilateralisms* (London, Palgrave Macmillan, 2006).

69 Jørgensen and Laatikainen, 'The Political Impact of the EU's Interaction with International Institutions', p. 628.
70 C. C. Doyle, W. Mieder and F. R. Shapiro, *The Dictionary of Modern Proverbs* (New Haven, CT, Yale University Press, 2012), p. 121.

14

The European Nuclear Dimension: From Cold War to Post-Cold War

LEOPOLDO NUTI

Introduction

Studying the relationship between the process of European integration and nuclear energy means coming to grips with two of the central issues of the international system that emerged from the Second World War. Ever since the fateful dropping of two nuclear weapons on Hiroshima and Nagasaki, one of the key questions of international politics has been whether the power of the atom is compatible with a world of nation states or whether its immense destructiveness needs a radical rethinking of the international system and the creation of some form of supranational framework to manage it. But is the atom really shareable, or – as General de Gaulle supposedly said – *le nucléaire ne se partage pas?* Such a question is obviously linked to the second issue, namely what can be achieved by the experiment of European integration. How far can it go? How much of their traditional powers are European nation states willing to abandon, and how far are they willing to go in sharing some of their most jealously guarded national secrets and prerogatives? Can Europe *truly* share the management of nuclear energy, in all its scientific, civilian and military applications? And if so, to what purpose? Is the ultimate goal of European integration the restoration of a *Europe puissance* or something else?

This chapter tries to provide a historical analysis of how Europe has grappled with these crucial questions. Predictably, it concludes that the development of a common nuclear policy by the European Community (EC)/European Union (EU) has been made extremely difficult by the fact that managing the atom poses some truly fundamental questions about state power. The management of nuclear energy, in other words, epitomises – and to a certain extent magnifies – all the aspirations, limits and contradictions of the process of European integration, both *during* and *after* the Cold War. A common European nuclear policy has often been possible only by reducing to the lowest common denominator any expectations of what may be achieved in a *supranational* context, or alternatively by acting *outside* of the EC/EU framework, as well as by resorting to a certain amount of opacity either to paper over the most substantive differences among the member states or to conceal their aspirations. By looking at what Europe was – or wasn't – able to achieve in the nuclear field, therefore, one gets a better sense of the structural issues of the integration process.

Literature Review

The nuclear dimension of European integration has been the ugly duckling of the historiography on the making of the EC/EU. This is partly due to the fact that nuclear histories have been tackled predominantly from a national perspective, but it is above all the consequence of the comparison with the success story that – at least until 2008 – was the economic dimension of European integration. It is the latter which undoubtedly attracted the attention of the largest part of the historical and theoretical research on Europe, relegating the European Atomic Energy Community (Euratom) and the nuclear aspirations of European integration to the fringes of mainstream historiography. Alan Milward is perhaps the exception, with an in-depth analysis of the origins of Euratom.[1] With the exception of Bertrand Goldschmidt, in the memoirs of the protagonists Euratom often occupies a very limited space.[2] Similarly, most histories of European integration mention its nuclear dimension only with the inevitable reference to the 1955–7 negotiations and then quietly let the matter drop.

A number of scholars, however, have focused on specific aspects of the nuclear history of Europe. John Krige led a pathbreaking multinational research effort to investigate the creation of the Centre for European Nuclear Research (CERN) and then provided a superb account of how the United States used Euratom to both foster *and* control the evolution of

---

1 A. Milward, *The European Rescue of the Nation State* (London and New York, NY, Taylor & Francis, 2000), pp. 179–91.
2 M. Vaisse, 'La cooperation nucleaire en Europe (1955–1958): État de l'historiographie', *Storia delle relazioni internazionali* 8, no. 1–2 (1992): 201–13.

nuclear science and nuclear research in Europe.[3] Gunnar Skogmar has also explored the role of the United States in shaping nuclear Europe by providing a detailed account of the negotiations of the mid 1950s.[4] Of key importance are also some specific studies on the history of the main multinational European enrichment and reprocessing plants, namely Jean-Pierre Daviet's work on the European Gaseous Diffusion Uranium Enrichment Consortium (Eurodif), R. B. Kehoe's on Urenco, and Jean-Marc Wolff's on the European Company for the Chemical Processing of Irradiated Fuels (Eurochemic).[5] The edited volume by Michel Dumoulin, Pierre Guillen and Maurice Vaïsse canvassed the early post-war years from a variety of national perspectives.[6] Insofar as Euratom is concerned, scholars have emphasised how from the very beginning the project ran up against a number of obstacles.[7] In his pioneering work, Lawrence Scheinman emphasised what he called *nuclear nationalisms* as the main cause of the difficulties that prevented Euratom from achieving the goals envisaged by its promoters.[8] The origins are also covered by Peter Weilemann, Lawrence Droutman and Laurence Hubert.[9] Only one major study, however, covers the entire span of Euratom's first 30 years, namely the collective volume edited by Olivier Pirotte.[10]

Grégoire Mallard and Anna Södersten have renewed the field with original interdisciplinary approaches. The former has proposed an imaginative

3 A. Hermann, L. Belloni, U. Mersits, D. Pestre and J. Krige, *History of CERN*, vol. i: *Launching the European Organization for Nuclear Research* (Amsterdam, North Holland, 1987); J. Krige, *Sharing Knowledge, Shaping Europe: US Technological Collaboration and Nonproliferation* (Cambridge, MA, MIT Press, 2016).
4 G. Skogmar, *The United States and the Nuclear Dimension of European Integration* (New York, NY, Palgrave Macmillan, 2004).
5 J.-P. Daviet, *Eurodif: Histoire de l'enrichissement de l'uranium, 1973–1993* (Anvers, Fonds Mercator, 1993); R. B. Kehoe, *The Enriching Troika: A History of Urenco to the Year 2000* (Marlow, Urenco, 2002); J.-M. Wolff, *Eurochemic 1956–1990: Thirty-Five Years of International Cooperation in the Field of Nuclear Engineering: The Chemical Processing of Irradiated Fuels and the Management of Radioactive Wastes* (Paris, OECD Nuclear Energy Agency, 1996).
6 M. Dumoulin, P. Guillen and M. Vaïsse (eds.), *L'énergie nucléaire en Europe: Des origines à Euratom* (Bern, Peter Lang, 1994).
7 J. G. Polach, *EURATOM: Its Background, Issues, and Economic Implications* (Dobbs Ferry, NY, Oceana, 1964).
8 L. Scheinman, *Euratom: Nuclear Integration in Europe* (New York, NY, Carnegie Endowment for International Peace, 1967).
9 P. R. Weilemann, *Die Anfänge der Europäischen Atomgemeinschaft: Zur Gründungsgeschichte von EURATOM 1955–1957* (Baden-Baden, Nomos, 1982); L. J. Droutman, 'Nuclear Integration: The Failure of Euratom' (PhD dissertation, Columbia University, 1973); L. Hubert, 'La politique nucléaire de la Communaté européenne (1956–1968). Une tentative de définition à travers les archives de la Commission européenne', *Journal of European Integration History* 6, no. 1 (2000): 129–53.
10 O. Pirotte, P. Girerd, P. Marnal and S. Morson, *Trente ans d'expérience Euratom: La naissance d'une Europe nucléaire* (Brussels, Bruylant, 1988).

reading of the crucial years of the formation of Euratom, highlighting how a network of Eurofederalists on both sides of the Atlantic tried to surreptitiously foster a rather different agenda from the one officially presented by the treaty. They failed to make Europe a full-fledged nuclear power but, Mallard argues, they managed to carve out for it a special place in the global non-proliferation regime through the creation of a special safeguard system between the International Agency for Atomic Energy and Euratom – a topic which was also analysed from a more technical perspective by Darryl Howlett.[11] Södersten, on the other hand, has scrutinised the complex legal relationship of Euratom with the rest of the EU institutions.[12]

Diplomatic historians have investigated the interconnection between national and international nuclear trajectories. It is not possible to discuss here the large amount of work on the history of *national* European nuclear programmes. Suffice it to say that almost all of those who have written about the French nuclear programme have highlighted the centrality of France in any history of nuclear Europe. The complex relationship between the UK and Euratom has been investigated by Stuart Butler, Mauro Elli and Martin Theaker, focusing in particular on the different positions taken by the UK Atomic Energy Authority vis-à-vis the European project.[13]

On the military side, Colette Barbier, Eckart Conze, Leopoldo Nuti and Georges-Henri Soutou have explored the short-lived attempt to establish a military cooperation of France, Italy and Germany in 1957–8.[14] Beatrice Heuser has offered an in-depth analysis of the strategic cultures of three key European countries, France, Britain and the Federal Republic of Germany (FRG), as well as of the European ambitions of Franz-Joseph Strauss.[15]

---

11 G. Mallard, *Fallout: Nuclear Diplomacy in an Age of Global Fracture* (Chicago, IL, University of Chicago Press, 2014); D. A. Howlett, *Euratom and Nuclear Safeguards*, Southampton Studies in International Policy (Basingstoke, Macmillan and the Centre for International Policy Studies, University of Southampton, 1990).

12 A. Södersten, *Euratom at the Crossroads* (Northampton, Edward Elgar, 2018).

13 M. Theaker, *Britain, Europe and Civil Nuclear Energy, 1945–62: Power Politics, Britain and the World* (London, Palgrave Macmillan, 2018); S. A. Butler, 'The Struggle for Power: Britain and Euratom 1955–63', *The International History Review* 36, no. 2 (2014): 105–24; M. Elli, 'A Politically-Tinted Rationality: Britain vs. Euratom, 1955–63', *Journal of European Integration History* 12, no. 1 (2006): 324–41.

14 See the special issue of the *Revue d'histoire diplomatique* 104, no. 1–2 (1990); G.-H. Soutou, *L'alliance incertaine: Les rapports politico-stratégiques Franco-Allemands, 1954–1996* (Paris, Fayard, 1996).

15 B. Heuser, *Nuclear Mentalities? Strategies and Beliefs in Britain, France, and the FRG* (Basingstoke, Macmillan, 1998); B. Heuser, 'European Strategists and European Identity. The Quest for a European Nuclear Force', *Journal of European Integration History* 1, no. 2 (1995): 61–80; B. Heuser, 'The European Dream of Franz Joseph Strauss', *Journal of European Integration History* 3, no. 1 (1998): 75–103.

Frédéric Bozo has analysed the nuclear dimension of the Franco-German strategic dialogue in the 1980s, and Stuart Croft has examined Franco-British cooperation in the 1990s.[16] The evolution of non-proliferation in western Europe in the 1980s and the early 1990s has been inspected by a multinational research team led by Harald Müller.[17] A host of research reports and working papers have investigated the role that the EC / EU has developed in this field, with particular attention to the negotiations with Iran at the beginning of the twenty-first century.[18]

The Early Years, 1945–1954

During the Second World War the construction of the atomic bomb was to a large extent a collegial transnational effort, in which a number of countries and an international team of scientists played a role. By the end of 1945, however, the Truman administration was quickly moving in the direction of reversing the wartime cooperation with its allies.[19] With the approval of the 1946 McMahon Act, the United States actually stopped the circulation of *any* classified information related to its nuclear activities, while at the same time the United Nations (UN) negotiations failed to place nuclear weapons under the control of an international agency. Some key European countries also moved towards a national approach: the United Kingdom (UK) set up its nuclear research establishment at Harwell in October 1945, and formally decided to develop a national nuclear deterrent in January 1947. France, whose scientists had also played a role in the Manhattan Project, felt marginalised by its wartime allies and set up its own Commissariat à l'énergie atomique in October 1945. Other European countries followed suit: in late 1945 Sweden set up its Atomic Committee and authorised research on the

---

16 F. Bozo, 'The Sanctuary and the Glacis. France, the Federal Republic of Germany, and Nuclear Weapons in the 1980s (Part 1)', *Journal of Cold War Studies* 22, no. 3 (2020): 119–79; S. Croft, 'European Integration, Nuclear Deterrence and Franco-British Nuclear Cooperation', *International Affairs* 72, no. 4 (1996): 771–87.

17 H. Müller (ed.), *How Western European Nuclear Policy Is Made: Deciding on the Atom* (Basingstoke, Macmillan, 1991); H. Müller (ed.), *A Survey of European Nuclear Policy, 1985–87* (Basingstoke, Macmillan, 1989); H. Müller (ed.), *European Non-proliferation Policy, 1988–1992* (Lausanne, Peter Lang, 1999).

18 C. Grand, *The European Union and the Non-proliferation of Nuclear Weapons* (Paris, Institute for Security Studies, Western European Union, 2000); A. Viaud, *L'union européenne face à la crise du nucléaire iranien (2003–2017)* (Louvain, Presses universitaires de Louvain, 2017); C. Portela, *The EU's Evolving Responses to Nuclear Proliferation Crises: From Incentives to Sanctions* (Brussels, EU Non-proliferation Consortium, 2015).

19 S. J. Maddock, *Nuclear Apartheid: The Quest for American Atomic Supremacy from World War II to the Present* (Chapel Hill, NC: University of North Carolina Press, 2010), pp. 38–9.

military aspects of nuclear fission inside its national research organisation, the Försvarets forskningsanstalt.[20] In the western zones of occupation in Germany, on the other hand, Allied Law 25, issued in early 1946, strictly forbade any form of nuclear research except at a very theoretical level.

Yet the devastation wrought by the Second World War across western Europe limited the resources which states could channel into the development of an adequate scientific knowledge at the national level, let alone allocate to building the technical infrastructure to implement any theoretical achievement. As western Europe moved towards multilateral cooperation with the Marshall Plan and the Council of Europe, scientific collaboration was increasingly seen as a way to promote economic reconstruction and bridge the scientific and organisational gap with the United States. By late 1949, the idea of a European centre for atomic research began to circulate: initially imagined as a rather ambitious super-laboratory, the project was gradually downsized to the creation of a powerful particle accelerator, 'to be seen', as John Krige wrote, 'as contributing to the reconstruction of European physics without directly reinforcing the industrial or military strength of the collaborating nations'.[21] It was set up in 1954 as CERN in Geneva.

A theoretical research centre with no direct civilian or military implications would also provide a less threatening framework for the rehabilitation of German science, harnessing its impressive potential to the reconstruction of Europe without any form of discrimination against German physicists – even those, like Werner Heisenberg, who had played a role in the Nazi nuclear programme. The issue of German nuclear research, however, emerged with force during the negotiation of a treaty for the creation of a European Defence Community (EDC) in 1951–2, which made increasingly clear the centrality of this problem for *any* European security project. If the EDC was to be a partnership of equals, the FRG should perhaps be allowed the theoretical right to carry out unrestricted research on nuclear energy – and perhaps even manufacture nuclear weapons to be placed at the disposal of the Community itself. A fragile compromise was eventually found with Article 107 of the treaty, which stated that 'production, import and export of war materials [. . .], and technical research' had to be allowed by a licence from the Community's Commissariat. Besides, weapons of particular importance (as described in Annex I of the article) should not be manufactured in 'strategically exposed areas', a definition that basically applied to all the

20 T. Jonter, *The Key to Nuclear Restraint: The Swedish Plans to Acquire Nuclear Weapons during the Cold War* (London, Palgrave Macmillan, 2016).
21 J. Krige, 'I. I. Rabi and the Birth of CERN', *Physics Today* 57, no. 9 (2004): 44.

territory of the FRG, unless authorised by 'a unanimous decision in the Council of Ministers'.[22]

By the time the EDC debate reached its critical moment in 1953–4, nuclear energy had acquired a central relevance for the international system. In October 1953 the new Eisenhower administration adopted the strategic posture of massive retaliation, thereby making nuclear weapons the centre-piece of US – and transatlantic – security, and in December it launched Atoms for Peace, a major international initiative to promote the civilian use of nuclear power. By August 1954 the US Congress had approved a first revision of the McMahon act – the 1954 Atomic Energy Act – which allowed a limited dissemination of classified information, and in November 1954 the North Atlantic Military Committee formally approved MC-48, the report which integrated nuclear weapons into North Atlantic Treaty Organization (NATO) strategy.[23]

Such an increasing relevance meant that, after the failure of the EDC, any next step in European integration would have to address *both* the problem of including the FRG in any nuclear security arrangement *and* the relevance of nuclear power for the future of Europe. Some of the solutions envisaged during the EDC negotiations provided the basis for the compromises which led in the autumn of 1954 to the creation of the Western European Union (WEU) and later to the FRG's entry into NATO:[24] the FRG would *voluntarily* abstain from *producing* nuclear weapons *inside its own territory*, as Chancellor Adenauer pledged at the London Conference of 28–30 September 1954; a European armaments agency would supervise and control the production of weapons inside the new alliance; and a possible European arms pool might be open to an eventual German contribution.[25] The Paris Agreements of 23 October 1954, however, failed to set any limitations on what Germany could do in the *civilian* nuclear sector, nor did they manage to set any controls on what France could do in the *military* one. Shortly after the conclusion of the Paris Agreements, the FRG initiated its civilian nuclear project, and in

22 Skogmar, *The United States and the Nuclear Dimension*, p. 39.
23 On MacMahon, see A. Quist, *Security Classification of Information*, vol. 1: *Introduction, History, and Adverse Impacts* (Oak Ridge, TN, Oak Ridge National Laboratories, 2002), Chapter 4. On MC-48, see D. A. Carter, *Forging the Shield: The U.S. Army in Europe, 1951–1962* (Waashington, DC, Center of Military History, United States Army, 2015), p. 102; M. Trachtenberg, *A Constructed Peace: The Making of the European Settlement, 1958–1963* (Princeton, NJ, Princeton University Press, 1999).
24 Skogmar, *The United States and the Nuclear Dimension*, pp. 49–52.
25 Ibid., p. 80. For Adenauer's declaration, see pp. 83–5.

December 1954 the government of Pierre Mendès France formally embarked on a military one.[26]

A Defining Moment? The Difficult Birth of Euratom

At around the same time the UK, Belgium, Italy, the FRG and other western European countries all stepped up the tempo of their nuclear programmes. This flurry of national initiatives was accompanied by a growing number of bilateral contacts between each of these countries and the United States, as well as by bilateral interactions among the western Europeans themselves. At the multilateral level, an International Conference on the Peaceful Uses of Atomic Energy, convened in Geneva in August 1955 under UN auspices, called for the establishment of an International Atomic Energy Agency. Simultaneously, the Organisation for European Economic Co-operation (OEEC) Council of Ministers agreed to set up a working party to examine European cooperation in the field of peaceful uses of nuclear energy.[27]

The effervescence of nuclear initiatives in the mid 1950s had a major impact on the construction of Europe. The president of the European Coal and Steel Community (ECSC) Commission, Jean Monnet, and the Belgian Foreign Minister, Paul-Henri Spaak, envisaged a major role for nuclear energy in their debate about the relaunching of European integration. Nuclear power was regarded as a field with great economic and technological potential, unencumbered by the presence of consolidated national structures.[28] It also looked ideal as a means to face the looming energy shortage that threatened the future of the post-war economic recovery, and it was widely perceived as a 'new and a more potent symbol of modernization'.[29] A joint effort in the civilian field also had potential ramifications for European security. According to the French historian Pierre Guillen, by the summer of 1954 the French Chiefs of Staff were already thinking about 'la creation dans le cadre d'un pool atomique atlantique, d'une force atomique européenne integrée (avec si possible la participation de l'Angleterre)' ('the creation within the framework of an Atlantic atomic pool of an integrated European atomic force (if possible with the participation of England)'), with each

26 Ibid., p. 113.
27 L. Armand, 'Some Aspects of the European Energy Problem: Suggestions for Collective Action', pp. 7, 25–51, www.cvce.eu/obj/louis_armand_some_aspects_of_the_europea n_energy_problem-en-6761172f-1f18-45b0-a247-e50faedb0e5d.html.
28 J. Monnet, *Mémoires* (Paris, Fayard, 1976), pp. 588–91; P.-H. Spaak, *Combats Inachevés*, vol. ii: *De l'espoir aux déceptions* (Paris, Fayard, 1969), pp. 61–5; P. Winand, *Eisenhower, Kennedy, and the United States of Europe* (New York, NY, St Martin's Press, 1993), pp. 72–3.
29 Milward, *The European Rescue*, p. 180.

country contributing according to its capacities.[30] By early 1955 the idea of a European uranium enrichment plant, which would benefit *both* a European civilian agency *and* a French military programme, began to take shape.[31]

A joint European nuclear endeavour eventually became a central part of the Benelux memorandum that led to the Messina Conference in early June 1955. The creation of a European atomic community was perceived by the Foreign Ministers of the ECSC as central to their plan for *le relance européen* (European revival), but the project was hampered by widely conflicting visions. Besides the implicit tensions between the civilian and military aspirations of its proponents, a major challenge lay in the format of the new organisation. A new supranational European nuclear community *within the framework of the Six* implied the exclusion of the UK, which had the most advanced nuclear programme in Europe. A looser form of association within the OEEC, on the other hand, offered the attractive alternative of including Great Britain.[32]

The supranational approach eventually gained the upper hand. In May 1956 the Venice conference of the Six formally adopted the report produced by the Spaak committee in April, which introduced a number of compromises on the most controversial issues and turned down Jean Monnet's suggestion that member states renounce any military activity. It also deferred any decision about the creation of a joint enrichment plant to a *Syndicat d'études*.

A final text was approved only after some difficult compromises. Euratom was given only 'a limited power of coordination of national research programs', to be supplemented with the activities of Euratom's own Joint Nuclear Research Centre. In the field of nuclear industry its function was *both* 'regulatory' and 'promotional',[33] but full control of investments remained in the hands of national governments or private firms. Euratom's 'rights of ownership' over its fissile materials were almost purely nominal, while controls over the materials were limited to 'controls of conformity' with the declared goal (military or peaceful) of the national institution using them.[34] This rather

---

30 P. Guillen, 'Les chefs militaires français, le réarmement de l'Allemagne et la CED (1950–1954)', *Revue d'histoire de la Deuxième Guerre mondiale et des conflits contemporains* 33, no. 129 (1983): 3–33, 33.

31 Skogmar, *The United States and the Nuclear Dimension*, p. 102; Soutou, *L'alliance incertaine*, pp. 38–40.

32 Theaker, *Britain, Europe and Civil Nuclear Energy*, pp. 148–9; M. O'Driscoll, 'Missing the Nuclear Boat? British Policy and French Military Nuclear Ambitions during the Euratom Foundation Negotiations, 1955–56', *Diplomacy & Statecraft* 9, no. 1 (1998): 144–9.

33 Droutman, 'Nuclear Integration'.   34 Mallard, *Fallout*, pp. 138–9.

opaque and ambiguous terminology not only allowed a member country to develop its own military programme, should it wish to do so, but also allowed all dual-use activities short of weaponisation – such as enrichment or reprocessing – as long as they were openly declared. Finally, member countries could purchase whatever fissile materials they wanted as long as their acquisition did not harm Euratom.

Even after this massive watering down of its powers, however, Euratom might not have seen the light of day without the Anglo-French debacle at Suez. The crisis reinvigorated in both the French and the German governments the ambition to achieve a degree of strategic autonomy from the United States and strengthened their strategic dialogue in the autumn of 1956.[35] In January 1957 the signing of the Colomb-Béchar agreement between the German Defence Minister Franz-Joseph Strauss and the French one, Maurice Bourgès-Maunoury, hinted at a closer cooperation between the two countries and facilitated the papering over of the remaining obstacles in the Euratom negotiations.

The US role in the the coming into being of Euratom, however, was more complex than frustrating the Europeans at Suez. Inside the Eisenhower administration the Atomic Energy Commission (AEC) and the State Department held quite divergent views about the European nuclear projects, but the close relationship between Secretary of State Dulles and Monnet gradually tilted the balance towards supporting Euratom's supranational approach.[36] The United States agreed to proceed with bilateral agreements with some European states before Euratom was created, but it made clear 'that these bilateral arrangements [. . .] would be of an interim nature' and that, once Euratom came into being, the member countries 'would look towards the transfer to the Community of rights and obligations contained' in those agreements.[37] President Eisenhower also declared that the United States was willing to offer on the international market 20,000 kg of enriched uranium for peaceful purposes, making available to the Europeans a large quantity of U-235 at a much lower price than any future European enrichment plant might offer – thereby encouraging the development of a European

---

35 Skogmar, *The United States and the Nuclear Dimension*, pp. 220–1, provides an excellent synthesis of the issue.
36 See, for instance, Memo for Mr Merchant and Mr Smith, March 5, 1956, 'European Atomic Problems', in https://nsarchive.gwu.edu/document/20486-national-security-archive-doc-05-robert-g-barnes.
37 Gerard Smith to Admiral L. Strauss, 6 February 1957, in NARA, RG 59, lot file General Records relating to Atomic Energy Matters 1944–1962, Box 439, f. regional programs EURATOM, d. Bilaterals 1957; Krige, *Sharing Knowledge*, p. 57.

nuclear industry but also reducing the attractiveness of creating an independent enrichment plant.[38] Finally, the Eisenhower administration gave a very warm welcome to the 'Three Wise Men' – Louis Armand, Fritz Ertel and Armando Giordani – appointed by the Six to prepare a report on the use of nuclear energy in the development of Europe, laying the basis for future cooperation between Euratom and the United States. In short, the Eisenhower administration accompanied the development of Euratom with a number of initiatives which encouraged its creation but also made sure to steer it in a direction which was compatible with US interests.

The treaty signed in Rome on 25 March 1957 gave life to an organisation whose nature, purpose and structure were still very uncertain. All the compromises of the previous months had made possible the conclusion of an agreement, but they had somewhat emptied the original Euratom vision of its initial ambitions.[39] Nor did the Rome Treaty solve the issue of a European enrichment plant, which was only mentioned in an annex as a possible 'joint enterprise'.[40] The *Syndicat d'études* for the creation of a European plant extended its work until the end of 1957, but by the end of the year it had failed to achieve any satisfactory conclusions, possibly because of the influence of the Three Wise Men's report, 'A Target for Euratom', whose programme relied almost entirely on the supply of US enriched uranium.[41] In the last months of 1957, however, the issue of a joint enrichment plant became entangled with the controversial attempt of the French, German and Italian defence ministers – Chaban-Délmas, Franz-Josef Strauss and Paolo Emilio Taviani – to extend the cooperation among their countries to the realm of 'modern weapons production'. On 28 November 1957, the three defence ministers signed a protocol which committed their countries to cooperate in the field of modern weapons, including 'military applications of nuclear energy', and in April 1958 they concluded an agreement to limit their nuclear cooperation to the joint financing of a European enrichment plant, thereby resurrecting the old Euratom idea.[42] Marred by a number of ambiguities about its ultimate goal and by the perplexed reaction of the United

---

38 Winand, *Eisenhower, Kennedy, and the United States of Europe*, p. 89.
39 R. Schaetzel to D. Linebaugh, 3 January 1957, in NARA, RG 59, lot file General Records relating to Atomic Energy Matters 1944–1962, B. 439, f. regional programs EURATOM, d. Bilaterals 1957.
40 Daviet, *Eurodif*, p. 317.
41 L. Armand, F. Etzel and F. Giordani, 'A Target for Euratom' (1957), pp. 32–3, http://aei .pitt.edu/35730.
42 Doc. 380, Documents Diplomatiques Français, vol. XI, part II, 1 July–31 December 1957.

States, the half-hearted project faltered until the return to power of General de Gaulle in France seems to have dealt it a final blow in June 1958.

The failure of this key element of the initial Euratom vision must also be gauged against the contemporary success of the OEEC joint plutonium reprocessing plant, given that the negotiations regarding the OEEC plant were conducted in strict interrelation with those concerning Euratom. While more ambitious initiatives were eventually sidelined, the OEEC study groups on nuclear cooperation did lead to the creation of the European Nuclear Energy Agency (ENEA), whose statute was adopted by the OEEC Council in December 1957. In turn, the ENEA coordinated two important initiatives, namely a project on the joint operation of a number of experimental reactors and, above all, the convention signed on 20 December 1957 to develop Eurochemic, which would eventually lead to the creation of a spent-fuel-reprocessing plant at Mol, in Belgium.[43]

A Difficult Start

From its very beginning the new Community was marred by a number of challenges. Rather than the expected dramatic shortage of energy, Euratom faced an excess of production of both coal and gas, which made the heavy investments required to develop an advanced nuclear industry much less attractive. Simultaneously, the return to power of General de Gaulle had a strong influence on France's nuclear policy and its attitude towards European integration, accelerating the process that led to the nuclear tests in the French Sahara in 1960, and resisting any attempt to reinforce the supranational features of Euratom.[44] A first British attempt to enter the European communities was also turned down by de Gaulle in January 1963, even if the Macmillan government cautiously hinted at a closer cooperation with France in both the military and the civilian nuclear sectors.[45]

Still, a widespread feeling lingered that a European framework of some kind might provide a suitable solution to the Europeans' nuclear aspirations, and that the French bomb might somehow be Europeanised.[46] The French government did display some interest in promoting European independence

---

43 Wolff, *Eurochemic*, 89–110.
44 Mallard, *Fallout*, p. 186; L. Guzzetti, *A Brief History of European Union Research Policy* (Brussels and Luxembourg, European Commission Directorate General XII, 1995), p. 25.
45 W. Kaiser, 'The Bomb and Europe. Britain, France, and the EEC Entry Negotiations, 1961–1963', *Journal of European Integration History* 1, no. 1 (1995): 65–85.
46 Heuser, 'European Strategists and European Identity', in particular 65–70.

in the civilian and military application of the atom, but it was not ready to do so 'at the price of an increased supranational system in Europe'.[47] The task of coordinating the nuclear activities of Euratom members, therefore, became increasingly difficult, as each member developed a strongly national approach to its own nuclear projects ('organizational, political and economic-commercial').[48] The result was that, by the mid 1960s, the budget of the Community was almost completely dedicated to promoting research projects – either its own or those of the member states. As Guzzetti wrote, 'from seeking to become the cornerstone of a new technological revolution', Euratom was becoming 'a simple research agency to which member states entrusted [. . .] their most uncertain projects'.[49]

The United States continued to support Euratom but it wavered between encouraging civilian cooperation and worrying about its potential proliferation implications.[50] After the US Congress had passed the Euratom cooperation act in August 1958, an agreement on an ambitious joint US–Euratom programme was concluded in November, but it failed to revamp the fledgling European effort: the Europeans remained reluctant to finance their part of the deal, and by the early sixties only one of the six power plants envisaged by the programme was being built. The joint programme's main impact was on what kind of power reactor should be adopted by the Community, as the Commission confirmed US pressurised/boiling water reactors as its standard model, discarding the gas–graphite model proposed by France.[51]

The transatlantic interconnection was even more pronounced in the military dimension. After the December 1957 NATO Summit in Paris, the United States moved ahead with a number of initiatives that strengthened nuclear sharing inside the alliance, somewhat bypassing de facto the limited amendment of the MacMahon Act approved by the US Congress in 1958. By December 1960, the Eisenhower administration had proposed to make NATO a fourth nuclear power through the creation of a NATO multilateral nuclear force (MLF). Powerful personalities on both sides of the Atlantic –the 'Eurofederalists' – tried to use this project to promote an increased level of nuclear sharing and perhaps eventually the creation of an autonomous European deterrent by suggesting that the United States should relinquish its veto over the use of the MLF's nuclear arsenal if a federated Europe were created.[52]

---

47 Scheinman, *Euratom*, p. 35.   48 Ibid., p. 36.   49 Guzzetti, *A Brief History*, pp. 11–12.
50 Krige, *Sharing Knowledge*, p. 60.
51 L. Hubert,. 'La politique nucléaire de la Communauté européenne', *Journal of European Integration History* 6, no. 1 (2000), 142–3.
52 Mallard, *Fallout*, 163.

Each step the United States took in its nuclear policy towards Europe, however, was the result of difficult internal compromises.[53] In 1961 the arrival of a new administration in Washington added a new layer of complexity to the puzzle. While presenting the customary array of different points of view, the Kennedy administration was strongly committed to limiting the risks of a nuclear confrontation with the Soviet Union. Interested as he might have been in the idea of European integration, Kennedy was above all very cautious about NATO nuclear sharing, particularly after the dramatic risks of the Cuban missile crisis in October 1962. This ambiguity was reflected in the half-hearted effort with which in early 1963 the United States renewed the proposal to create a NATO MLF equipped with the new US Polaris medium-range ballistic missiles and manned by crews of different NATO countries.[54]

New Directions

By the mid 1960s, Euratom was in such disarray that by December 1967 the EC Council failed to approve the budget for a new 5-year plan. It limited itself to adopting an interim annual budget of $40 million for 1968 (against an annual average of $80–85 million for the previous 5 years). In the same meeting, however, the Council discussed a proposal of the Commission to investigate a number of other options to revitalise the Community, including the creation of a European enrichment plant.[55]

This time the initiative might have fared better than its ill-fated predecessors. By the late 1960s, there was a widespread feeling across western Europe of a growing technological gap with the United States that could be filled only by coordinating European efforts, possibly with the support of the UK if the new negotiations for a British entry into the EC were to succeed.[56] The expectation of a world-wide rapid growth of the nuclear sector also led to an intensification of the global search for uranium-enrichment capacities. In turn this led to a growing concern (reinforced by the first oil-price shock of 1967) about a possible bottleneck in supplies of highly enriched uranium, for which Europe depended almost entirely on the US Atomic Energy Agency. The concern was particularly acute in France, where there was a strong interest in

53 Krige, *Sharing Knowledge*, p. 77; Mallard, *Fallout*, pp. 180–1.
54 Mallard, *Fallout*, pp. 201–9.
55 Doc. CNEN (68)37, EURATOM – Terzo Programma Pluriennale, Istituto Luigi Sturzo (ISL), Archivio Giulio Andreotti (AGA), serie EURATOM, b. 425, f. 6.
56 Guzzetti, *A Brief History*, pp. 35–8.

the country's energy independence.[57] Over the horizon was also looming a major technological breakthrough, as centrifugal enrichment seemed about to overtake the huge gaseous diffusion plants which had dominated the field until then; and in the more distant future loomed the dizzying prospect of the myth of perpetual energy – the so-called 'plutonium economy' – to be achieved with fast breeder reactors (FBRs).[58]

As in the 1950s, however, Euratom's supranational approach to a joint plant was just one among many options. While the Commission set up a Special Study Group on enrichment,[59] the German, Dutch and British governments were debating a possible *trilateral* initiative in this field, and on 4 March 1970, they signed the treaty of Almelo for the development of the gas centrifuge process for uranium enrichment. It entered into force on 19 July 1971.[60] Simultaneously, the French government carried out a number of studies to strengthen its existing gaseous diffusion enrichment capacities *outside* the EC framework.[61] By the end of 1973, this led to the creation of a multinational joint stock company – Eurodif – which would be tasked with the actual construction of the plant, its stocks to be divided among five partners: France (47.5 per cent), Italy (22.5 per cent) and Belgium, Spain and Sweden in equal parts (10 per cent each). Faced with the alternative projects of Eurodif and Urenco, the Commission quietly abandoned the project of its own Euratom plant. The Special Study Group's final report, released in November 1973,[62] instead saw as promising the promotion of a policy of *concertation* between the producers of nuclear energy, with the EC creating a 'favourable framework' and perhaps even buying the excess production of the two plants. The result was that 'nuclear cooperation in Europe blossomed, *outside* [my emphasis] of EURATOM'.[63] Nor was the United States able to steer these efforts in a different direction: as in the past, Washington

57 Y. Bouvier, 'Les rythmes européens du nucléaire français. Accélérations et décélération aux temps des chocs pétroliers', in A. Beltran, E. Bussière and G. Garavini (eds.), *L'Europe et la question énergétique: Les années 1960–1980* (Brussels: Peter Lang, 2016), pp. 220–2; J.-P. Daviet, 'Les débuts du nucléaire en France', in Beltran et al. (eds.), *L'Europe et la question énergétique*, pp. 128–30.

58 US AEC, 'Annual Report to Congress of the Atomic Energy Commission for 1967', pp. 75–6, www.osti.gov/biblio/1364395.

59 Rapport du Groupe d'études speciales du CCRN, 30 May 1972, Archivio Achille Albonetti (henceforth AA), b. 17; Daviet, 'Les débuts du nucléaire en France', p. 130.

60 S. Schrafstetter and S. Twigge, 'Spinning into Europe: Britain, West Germany and the Netherlands: Uranium Enrichment and the Development of the Gas Centrifuge 1964–1970', *Contemporary European History* 11, no. 2 (2002): 253–72.

61 Daviet, 'Les débuts du nucléaire en France', p. 132

62 Propositions de la Commission au Conseil et projet de resolution du Conseil (enrichissement de l'uranium), 29 November 1973, AA, b. 18, f. 1.

63 Södersten, *Euratom at the Crossroads*, p. 24.

vacillated between outright obstructionism and a more supportive attitude, but eventually had to reconcile itself with the construction of two major enrichment plants in Europe.

The scramble for an autonomous European enrichment capacity must be gauged against the background of the impending entry into force of the Treaty on the Non-proliferation of Nuclear Weapons (NPT), which marked a significant watershed in the nuclear dimension of the transatlantic relationship. By late 1966, the Johnson administration had decided that concluding a non-proliferation treaty was worth sacrificing some of the most ambitious NATO nuclear sharing schemes, and accepted the Soviet position that they would not be compatible with a treaty. The full implications of this reversal came as a shock to the non-nuclear-weapon states in western Europe, particularly Italy and the FRG, which had redirected their nuclear ambitions towards the evolution of NATO nuclear sharing and were also worried about the repercussions of the new treaty on their civilian programmes.[64] Their frustrations were only partially mitigated by the substitution of the MLF with a reinforced form of consultation on strategic and nuclear affairs inside the alliance, namely the Nuclear Planning Group, which the USSR was willing to accept. Both governments, in any case, attached to their NPT ratifications a statement which somewhat resuscitated the 'European clause' of the MLF – namely that, if a European federal state were created, it would inherit the status of its military nuclear members without this being considered a case of proliferation.[65] Perhaps more importantly, the NPT was crafted in such a way as to allow the United States to continue to quietly deploy its own tactical nuclear weapons in the territory of its European allies, provided that Washington retained full control of its warheads. Together with the creation of the Nuclear Planning Group, this arrangement granted NATO's European allies a special nuclear status in the regime that the NPT was creating.

---

64 A. Lutsch, 'In Favor of "Effective" and "Non-discriminatory" Non-dissemination Policy: The FRG and the NPT Negotiations Process (1962–1966)', in R. Popp, L. Horovitz and A. Wegner (eds.), Negotiating the Nuclear Non-proliferation Treaty: Origins of the Nuclear Order (London, Routledge, 2017), pp. 36–58; L. Nuti, '"A Turning Point in Postwar Foreign Policy": Italy and the NPT Negotiations, 1967–1969', in Popp et al. (eds.), Negotiating the Nuclear Non-proliferation Treaty, pp. 77–97. On Germany, see also the different view of O. Bange, 'Nato as a Framework for Nuclear Nonproliferation: The West German Case, 1954–2008', International Journal 64, no. 2 (2009): 361–82.

65 H. Brands, 'Non-Proliferation and the Dynamics of the Middle Cold War: The Superpowers, the MLF, and the NPT', Cold War History 7, no. 3 (2007): 389–423; F. Dehousse, 'La non-prolifération des armes nucléaires', Chronique de politique étrangère 20, no. 6 (1967): 621–44.

Equally important was the result that Euratom was able to achieve within the NPT safeguards regime. Euratom members refused to accept the draft NPT Artcle III, which asked them to submit 'all their sources and fissionable materials' to the safeguards and inspections regime of the International Atomic Energy Authority (IAEA).[66] Instead, Article III was eventually crafted in such a way as to give Euratom the option to negotiate its own peculiar safeguards arrangement with the IAEA. The agreement, INFCIRC-193, established that the Agency shall 'make full use of the Community's system of safeguards' (Article 31). The Agency, in turn, was given the right to verify 'the effectiveness' of this system as well as to run joint inspections.[67]

This remarkable success aside, the period between 1968 and 1973 saw a veritable stalemate in Euratom's development. The merger treaty between the Communities, which came into effect in 1967, further dispersed Euratom's specific competences across 'separate administrative bodies, leaving to the Joint Research Center the management of nuclear projects'.[68] No new 4-year programmes were approved until the end of 1972, when the EC Paris Summit accepted the principle that the Joint Research Centre would reorient its activities mostly towards fundamental research and the safety of reactors, and away from supporting industrial development. Furthermore, the Centre would be allowed to expand its research beyond the nuclear domain.[69]

The competition about the different European enrichment projects and Euratom's cooperation in the NPT negotiations should also be assessed against the background of a renewed, if feeble, debate about the possibility of closer nuclear cooperation in the military field. The British accession to the EC in 1973 coincided with a major rethinking of some of the premises on which the integration process had developed, all the more so because the new Conservative Prime Minister Edward Heath made no mystery of his interest in sponsoring closer European coordination in the foreign policy field. In turn, this could be extended to defence policy, and perhaps to the nuclear sector, since the British entry into the EC meant that the Community

66 G. Mallard, 'Crafting the Nuclear Regime Complex (1950–1975): Dynamics of Harmonization of Opaque Treaty Rules', *European Journal of International Law* 25, no. 2 (2014): 445–72, 460ff.
67 Howlett, *Euratom and Nuclear Safeguards*, p. 168. See also www.iaea.org/sites/default/files/infcirc193.pdf.
68 'Second General Report on the Activities of the Communities 1968' (1969), http://aei.pitt.edu/31346.
69 Guzzetti, *A Brief History*, pp. 45–7.

would now include two full-fledged nuclear powers. Eventually, and perhaps inevitably, Heath's vague idea of a Franco-British nuclear 'trusteeship' to protect the security of the other European countries gradually petered out after the British entry into the EEC, meeting the same fate as that of the Euratom enrichment plant.[70]

Into the 1970s: Europe Becomes a Civilian Nuclear Superpower

In the following years, Europe increasingly took on an important role in the global nuclear order that was being crafted in the 1970s – but it did so mostly *outside* its supranational structures. The Commission acknowledged that nuclear power would remain 'one of the key elements in the Community's energy strategy', but without being able to do much more than trying to coordinate the outburst of activities of the 1970s.[71]

By 1983, the EC countries boasted two major *multinational* uranium enrichment centres, Eurodif and Urenco, with an annual production respectively of 10.8 million separative working units (SWU) for Eurodif's Tricastin plant, while Urenco's Capenhurst and Almelo plants produced 500,000 SWU each.[72] By 1976 there were 13 reprocessing plants in the EC and an impressive overall number of power (71) and research (117) reactors, a growth that was all the more remarkable in France and the FRG.[73] Significant research progress was achieved in some cutting-edge technologies, particularly in the field of FBRs, which were soon to be exploited at the commercial level through a Franco-Italo-German multinational project, which in July 1974 led to the creation of the Centrale Nucléaire Européenne à Neutrons Rapides SA[74] to finance and manage the construction of the SuperPhoenix sodium-cooled FBR, 'the first

70 E. Heath, 'Realism in British Foreign Policy', *Foreign Affairs* 48, no. 1 (1969): 39–50.
71 É. Bussière, 'At the Centre of a Web of Interdependence: Energy', in M. Dumoulin, É. Palmero, V. Dujardin, É. Bussière, P. Ludlow and J. Brouwer (eds.), *The European Commission 1973–86: History and Memories of an Institution* (Brussels, European Commission Publications Office, 2014), pp. 377–84, 380.
72 J. Goens, 'The Opportunities and Limits of European Co-operation in the Area of Non-proliferation', in S. Aga Khan (ed.), *Nuclear War, Nuclear Proliferation and Their Consequences* (Oxford, Clarendon Press, 1986), pp. 31–70, 34.
73 'The EURATOM Safeguards System', *European Communities Information* no. 9 (1977).
74 O. Keck, *Policymaking in a Nuclear Program: The Case for the West German Fast-Breeder Reactor* (Lexington, KT, D. C. Heath and Company, 1981), p. 175.

commercial-size plutonium-fueled fast breeder reactor in the world'.[75] By the mid 1980s, western Europe had 145 nuclear power stations.[76]

As a result of this rapid growth, the share of nuclear-energy-generated electricity in the EC jumped from 5.4 per cent in 1973 to 31.9 per cent in 1985.[77] By the end of the decade, Europe had transformed its position in the field of energy production, ending the quasi-monopoly of the United States in the export of enriched uranium on the world market, and it was ready to project its newly acquired capabilities on a global scale. The huge investments required to launch the nuclear industry, in fact, could not be compensated for by a production limited to European markets, which could not absorb the production capacity of the new plants. The requirements of the new European nuclear industry, however, had to be reconciled with the renewed US efforts to bolster the non-proliferation regime after the Indian 'peaceful' nuclear explosion of May 1974. In 1975 the United States convened a conference of the Nuclear Suppliers Group, which approved a set of guidelines as a first attempt to coordinate the export of sensitive dual-use technologies. In 1977 the new US president, Jimmy Carter, launched the idea of an International Nuclear Fuel Cycle Evaluation (INFCE) programme to assess the proliferation risks of the fuel cycle, and in 1978 the US Congress approved the Nuclear Non-proliferation Act, which imposed much tighter measures of control on US nuclear exports.

All these US initiatives found the European countries reluctant to abandon the prospect of a number of lucrative exports, and the EC had to be careful to protect the commercial exploitation of the nuclear capacities of its members.[78] In 1978 the Commission turned down a request by the US Congress to renegotiate the 1958 US–Euratom agreement. It also took an active part in the INFCE negotiations, partially harmonising the responses of its members. The Europeans criticised the US intention to delegitimise some features of the so-called 'plutonium economy', such as FBRs and

75 M. Schneider, 'Fast Breeder Reactors in France', in T. B. Cochran, H. A. Feiveson, W. Patterson et al., *Fast Breeder Reactor Programs: History and Status*, Research Report no. 8, International Panel on Fissile Materials (2010), https://fissilematerials.org/library/r r08.pdf, pp. 17–35, 19. See also J. A. Camilleri, *The State and Nuclear Power: Conflict and Control in the Western World* (Thetford, Harvester Press, 1984), pp. 151–2.

76 'Opinion of the Economic and Social Committee on the Consequences of the Chernobyl Nuclear Accident' (87/C 232/18), in *Official Journal of the European Communities* (1987).

77 Goens, 'The Opportunities and Limits of European Co-operation', pp. 31–2.

78 Pirotte et al. (eds.), *Trente ans d'expériénce Euratom*, pp. 212–15; W. Burr, 'A 'Scheme of "Control": The United States and the Origins of the Nuclear Suppliers' Group, 1974–1976', *The International History Review* 36, no. 2 (2014): 252–76.

reprocessing plants. When INFCE reached the conclusion that there was no quick technical fix in terms of prohibiting one kind of fuel cycle as more dangerous than the other, the Commission expressed its satisfaction regarding the 'Community cooperation, under the Council presidency'.[79]

By the early 1980s, the EC was becoming increasingly aware of the political importance of proliferation as well as of the need to coordinate the nuclear activities of its members. In 1981 the Political Committee of European Political Cooperation set up a Working Group on non-proliferation,[80] and Euratom negotiated two major agreements for uranium imports with Canada and Australia.[81] Another important step was the Dublin declaration by the ten foreign ministers of the Community on the need to endorse the 'London guidelines' on non-proliferation, on 20 November 1984.[82] Yet some member states initially contested the Commission's right to establish its own non-proliferation policy and, by the mid 1980s, this confrontation was taking the familiar lines of the attempt to prevent the Commission 'from obtaining any power of initiative' in order to maintain non-proliferation at the intergovernmental 'level of EPC'.[83] In the following years, the Twelve took a number of public steps to demonstrate a united front, but some of their strong differences remained.[84]

At the same time, the stunning growth of the European civilian nuclear sector was gradually slowing down, altering the course of the previous 15 years and the expectation that nuclear power was a technology 'strategic to Western Europe's future economic welfare and competitiveness'.[85] While the cost of oil remained low for most of the decade, the price of uranium remained relatively stable, making highly expensive investments in plutonium-fuelled FBRs much less attractive.[86] It was against this background that in April 1986 the dramatic incident at Chernobyl took place, forcing a number of countries to reassess their nuclear programmes and dramatically altering their perception in public opinion in those countries. Within about a year, the Netherlands, Belgium, Finland, Italy and Spain blocked existing plans 'to build more nuclear power

79 'Report of the Commission to the Council – International Nuclear Fuel Cycle Evaluation', COM_(80)_316_final, 11 June 1980.
80 H. Müller, 'European Nuclear Non-proliferation after the NPT Extension', EUISS Report (1996), p. 6.
81 Goens, 'The Opportunities and Limits of European Co-operation', pp. 42–3.
82 J. Goens, 'Current Events Related to Non-proliferation in the EEC', in H. Müller (ed.), A Survey of European Nuclear Policy, 1985–1987 (Basingstoke, Macmillan, 1989), pp. 11–20, 11.
83 Goens, 'The Opportunities and Limits of European Co-operation', p. 43.
84 Müller, 'European Nuclear Non-proliferation', p. 8.
85 W. Walker, 'The European Nuclear Industry in 1986', in H. Müller (ed.), A Surevy of European Nuclear Policy, 1985–1987 (New York, NY, St Martin's Press, 1989), pp. 21–39, 21–3.
86 T. B. Cochran, H. A. Feiveson, W. Patterson et al., Fast Breeder Reactor Programs: History and Status (Princeton, NJ, International Panel on Fissile Materials, 2010), pp. 8–10.

stations'.[87] In 1987, a referendum in Italy voted for completely phasing out the national nuclear programme. Chernobyl also forced the Commission to act on a variety of fronts: the Director General for Energy, Sir Christopher Audland, developed a closer cooperation with the IAEA and was later appointed special representative of the Commission to the Agency, while the Commission monitored the evolution of the situation in order to define 'the levels of radio-activity to be permitted in different foodstuffs'.[88]

Europe as the Virtual Battlefield of the Last Cold War Confrontation

At the military level, western Europe remained largely dependent on US extended deterrence. Throughout the Euromissiles crisis, the last great nuclear confrontation of the Cold War, the European states tried to shape a common position in order to influence the US decision-making process.[89] Their collaboration played a role in the adoption of the Atlantic alliance's dual-track decision in December 1979, and continued throughout the early 1980s as the Europeans tried to balance the more intransigent attitude of the new Ronald Reagan administration by promoting a more flexible attitude in the negotiations with Moscow. At the same time, they tried to promote a renewed intra-European security dialogue, which led to the attempt to revitalise the WEU at an extraordinary session of the WEU foreign and defence ministers in October 1984.[90] At a *bilateral* level, it also led to protracted and in-depth consultations between the French and German governments in which the Mitterrand administration opened up an unprecedented strategic dialogue with the FRG, in order to reduce 'as much as possible the consequences of the nuclear gap [between the two countries], a goal that was at least partly reached by the end of the decade'.[91] Then, in the final phase of the crisis, the European governments were somewhat puzzled by the sudden US–Soviet rapprochement and the swift conclusion of the Intermediate-Range Nuclear

87 Walker, 'The European Nuclear Industry in 1986', p. 21.
88 'Abstract', in CA.01.01, Chernobyl Disaster, Papers of Sir Christopher Audland, Historical Archives of the EU; J.-H. Meyer, 'Environmental Policy', in Dumoulin et al. (eds.), *The European Commission 1986–2000*, p. 374.
89 M. Gala, '"The Essential Weaknesses of the December 1979 'Agreement'": The White House and the Implementing of the Dual-Track Decision', *Cold War History* 19, no. 1 (2019): 21–38, 25.
90 Declaration by the WEU Foreign and Defence Ministers (Rome, 27 October 1984), www.cvce.eu/content/publication/2003/7/11/c44c134c-aca3-45d1-9e0b-04d4d9974ddf/publishable_en.pdf.
91 Bozo, 'The Sanctuary and the Glacis', 227.

Forces Treaty in 1987. The US allies welcomed the resumption of arms control negotiations, but they also displayed their customary concerns about a complete denuclearisation of western European security, best exemplified by the horrified reaction of Margaret Thatcher, who feared that 'the whole system of nuclear deterrence that had kept the peace for forty years was close to being abandoned'.[92] In the end, these worries – as well as all the previous consultations – never went beyond the generation of 'a disorderly effervescence in favor of European defense' which involved once again the theoretical reconsideration of the role of the French nuclear arsenal in case the bilateral arms control process might lead to a more isolationist US attitude.[93]

This low-key debate about a possible European military cooperation was overcome by the radical transformation of the strategic landscape, as the unravelling of the Cold War order opened the possibility of a structural rethinking of European security. Between 1989 and 1991 the western Europeans were forced to reassess their strategic posture and reconsider their reliance on extended deterrence as the central pillar of their own security: NATO accepted a massive denuclearisation of European security, best exemplified by the declaration at the Rome session of the North Atlantic Council, which defined nuclear weapons as 'truly weapons of last resort'. Even this radical restructuration, however, was limited by the French and British desire to hold onto their own national arsenals as well as by the willingness of some of the other NATO members to continue to host a limited number of US warheads. The New Strategic Concept, which NATO adopted in 1991, openly mentioned the important role of French and British nuclear forces and restated the 'essential political and military linkage provided by the US sub-strategic nuclear forces deployed in Europe'.

The European Nuclear Dilemmas after Maastricht

Reducing the importance of deterrence in its strategic posture was but one of the many steps through which Europe adapted its complex set of nuclear governance tools to a new international system. The creation of the EU and of its Common Foreign and Security Policy (CFSP) also required closer cooperation among the member states. The two EU nuclear weapon states, Britain and France, tried to coordinate their defence and security policies, in spite of their rather different views about what the CFSP should be. As early

---

92 M. Thatcher, *The Downing Street Years* (London: HarperCollins, 1993), pp. 470–1.
93 Bozo, 'The Sanctuary and the Glacis', 186.

as 1990, Paris and London sought a tighter coordination both at a conceptual/strategic level and in terms of weapons procurement, and by late 1992 this bilateral nuclear entente led to the creation of a Joint Nuclear Weapons Commission. This limited dialogue was sometimes described as a first step towards a possible Europeanisation of the two countries' nuclear deterrents – or maybe even a future common EU nuclear policy.[94] As the CFSP evolved into the European Security and Defence Policy and was reinforced by the adoption of the Lisbon Treaty in the new century, the entente progressed, and it was strengthened by the bilateral Lancaster House Treaties in November 2010, which had an important nuclear component. The evolution towards a vague European nuclear identity, however, remained a rather elusive goal: not only was it clearly dealt a serious blow by Brexit in 2016,[95] but also the EU member states continued to hold very different positions towards nuclear deterrence. All of NATO formally remains under the guarantee of the US nuclear umbrella, two European NATO members possess their own nuclear arsenals and five NATO members still host some 150–200 American warheads (Italy, Germany, the Netherlands and Belgium – and Turkey outside the EU). Across NATO, however, there is a growing amount of public hostility to the continuation of the practice of nuclear sharing, and some EU members such as Austria and Ireland have actually been among the promoters and signatories of the Treaty on the Prohibition of Nuclear Weapons, which NATO has steadily opposed.[96] The difficulty of managing 'la différence de statut nucléaire au sein de l'Union européenne' ('the difference of nuclear status within the European Union') still remains a serious challenge 30 years after President Mitterrand underlined it.[97]

The EU has been more successful in crafting a common non-proliferation policy, particularly after the French decision to sign and ratify the NPT in 1992. One of the first and more successful initiatives of the new CFSP was indeed the Council's adoption of its first joint action to support the indefinite extension of the NPT at the 1995 Review Conference of the Treaty.[98] Additional success in setting up a structured control regime on

---

94 Croft, 'European Integration'.
95 C. Jurgensen, 'L'Europe, la France et la dissuasion nucléaire', *Revue Défense Nationale* 821, no. 6 (2019): 56–68; K. Egeland and B. Pelopidas, 'European Nuclear Weapons? Zombie Debates and Nuclear Realities', *European Security* 30, no. 2 (2021): 237–58.
96 S. Hill, *Nato and the Treaty on the Prohibition of Nuclear Weapons* (London, Chatham House, 2021).
97 Jurgensen, 'L'Europe, la France et la dissuasion nucléaire', 61.
98 Council of the European Union, 'Joint Action Regarding Preparation for the 1995 Conference of the States Parties to the Treaty on the Non-proliferation of Nuclear Weapons' (1994), https://digitalarchive.wilsoncenter.org/document/175915.pdf?v=25d8f6d84217c1b2c04963c8ce69a55f.

nuclear exports,[99] however, was accompanied by some difficulties in adopting a common position towards the IAEA's efforts to extend its safeguards regime.[100] But the most divisive issue was the French resumption of atmospheric tests in the Pacific between 1994 and 1995. When, on 12 December 1995, the UN General Assembly passed a resolution against the tests, the EU members took very different positions.[101]

The events of 11 September 2001 helped mend these differences and had a deep impact on the EU's non-proliferation policy.[102] In December 2003 the Council adopted the EU Strategy against the Proliferation of Weapons of Mass Destruction, which was quickly developed into one of the key areas of the CFSP, leading to the creation of the EU Weapons of Mass Destruction (WMD) Monitoring Centre.[103] The new strategy was still in its infancy when it was tested in one of the most serious crises of the new century, namely the development of the Iranian nuclear programme. After France, the UK and the FRG had tried to open a dialogue with the Iranian government outside the EU in the summer of 2003, the EU High Representative Javier Solana joined the negotiations. Ever since then, the EU has played an important role in the process that led to the final 2015 agreement, the Joint Comprehensive Plan of Action.[104]

On the civilian front, nuclear power has continued to play a major role in the EC/EU's energy policy, but the curve of its general growth flattened at the level of about 25–30 per cent of the total energy consumption of the Union: in November 2020 there were '109 nuclear power reactors (107 GWe) operating in 15 of the 27 EU member states' accounting 'for over one-quarter of the electricity generated in the whole of the EU', with a large percentage of it developed in France.[105] The process of enlargement, moreover, created additional problems, as some of the new members use older-generation reactors with all sorts of environmental and safety consequences. As Figure 14.1 shows, while some countries continue to rely on nuclear reactors for a substantial amount of their energy, many others have phased out nuclear power altogether.

99 Södersten, *Euratom at the Crossroads*, pp. 213–14.
100 M.-H. Labbé, 'Y a-t-il une politique européenne de non-prolifération nucléaire?', *Politique étrangère* 62, no. 3 (1997): 307–19, 310–11.
101 Ibid., 316.
102 P. Van Ham, 'The European Union's WMD Strategy and the CFSP: A Critical Analysis', *EU Non-proliferation Consortium Non-proliferation Papers*, no. 2 (2011).
103 'EU Strategy against the Proliferation of WMD: Monitoring and Enhancing Consistent Application' (2006), https://data.consilium.europa.eu/doc/document/S T-16694-2006-INIT/en/pdf.
104 Viaud, *L'union européenne face à la crise du nucléaire iranien*; C. Adebahr, *Europe and Iran: The Nuclear Deal and Beyond* (Abingdon and New York, NY, Routledge, 2017).
105 'Nuclear Power in the European Union', www.world-nuclear.org/information-library/country-profiles/others/european-union.aspx.

EU member states with nuclear power plants operating and/or under construction (as of July 2022)
EU member states without nuclear power plants
Non-EU countries with nuclear power plants operating and/or under construction
Non-EU countries without nuclear power plants

Figure 14.1 EU member states and non-EU nations operating nuclear plants. Source: www.world-nuclear.org/information-library/country-profiles/others/european-union.aspx.

This gradual reduction of the salience of the civilian sector has also been affected by the EU's efforts to promote an energy policy which has increasingly prioritised renewable forms of energy, by the growing public opposition to nuclear power and by the impact of the 2011 Fukushima accident in Japan. After Fukushima, Germany and Belgium accelerated the planned phasing out of their nuclear industries, which they planned to complete by 2022 (Germany) and 2025 (Belgium), but in October 2022 German Chancellor Olaf Scholz ordered that the three remaining nuclear plants in the FRG continue to operate until April 2023 in order to prevent an energy crunch as a possible consequence of the Russian aggression in Ukraine. Sweden and France, on the other hand, continue to assign a high priority to the nuclear sector in their national energy policies.[106]

In this very fragmented landscape, the role of Euratom has remained important, but it has been somewhat sidelined when compared with the progress of other European institutions. From a legal point of view, the relationship between Euratom and the other EU institutions has never been fully streamlined, as Anna Södersten has highlighted, as this would imply raising a number of controversial political issues. Retaining its separate legal identity from the EU, and yet continuing to share most of the same institutions, Euratom has carved out for itself a special niche role by developing a number of important activities in the fields of radiation protection, nuclear safety and non-proliferation, in particular in cooperation with the IAEA for the enforcement of safeguards.[107]

Conclusions

Europe has made remarkable progress in developing a broad set of tools to coordinate its policies in the nuclear field, but they still fall short of a coherent and cohesive form of governance. The wide diversity of positions of the member countries – ranging across the full spectrum from a full-fledged nuclear weapons state to those hosting US warheads to neutral countries – has made it impossible to achieve a unified security posture, while the different degrees of importance attached to nuclear power by the member countries' energy policies replicated this difficulty – albeit to a lesser extent – in the civilian sector. The consequence is that the EU has assumed a contradictory nuclear identity both in the civilian and in the military field. Nevertheless, if one takes into account the large variety of military and civilian nuclear activities across the Union, it is clear that in an overall perspective Europe occupies a very special place in the global nuclear order, enjoying a number of privileges which not many other countries have. The very special safeguard system that Euratom has been able to carve out for its members, in other words, mirrors the unique opportunities which NATO countries enjoy by hosting US nuclear weapons on their territories or by participating in the activities of the Nuclear Planning Group. On a global scale, the cumulative effect of these exceptions, coupled

106 'Impacts of the Fukushima Daiichi Accident on Nuclear Development Policies' (2017), p. 38, www.oecd-nea.org/jcms/pl_14922/impacts-of-the-fukushima-daiichi-accident-on-nuclear-development-policies?details=true.
107 Södersten, *Euratom at the Crossroads*, Chapter 2.

with the presence on European soil of a bewildering array of enrichment and reprocessing facilities, gives Europe a very peculiar nuclear identity.[108]

It must be stressed, however, that not many of these features were achieved through the integration process – many of them actually were the results of projects and initiatives that unfolded *outside* the community framework. This special status must also be assessed in terms of its transatlantic perspective: it is undeniable that, for at least the first 25 years after the end of the Second World War, what Europe could and could not do in the nuclear field was heavily influenced by the US attitude. Through a mix of cooperation and control, as John Krige has demonstrated, the United States managed to frame the development of a nuclear Europe both in the civilian and in the military sector. While Europe subsequently managed to achieve an independent nuclear status in the civilian, economic and research fields, its military nuclear status has remained inextricably intertwined with the United States, given the important, if highly controversial, role that US extended deterrence played – and continues to play – for European security.

Recommended Reading

Daviet, J.-P. *Eurodif: Histoire de l'enrichissement de l'uranium, 1973–1993* (Antwerp, Fonds Mercator, 1993).

Hermann, A., L. Belloni, U. Mersits, D. Pestre and J. Krige. *History of CERN*, vol. I: *Launching the European Organization for Nuclear Research* (Amsterdam, North Holland, 1987).

Kehoe, R. B. *The Enriching Troika: A History of Urenco to the Year 2000* (Marlow, Urenco, 2002).

Krige, J. *Sharing Knowledge, Shaping Europe: US Technological Collaboration and Nonproliferation* (Cambridge, MA, MIT Press, 2016).

Mallard, G. *Fallout: Nuclear Diplomacy in an Age of Global Fracture* (Chicago, IL, University of Chicago Press, 2014).

Müller, H. *European Non-proliferation Policy, 1988–1992* (Lausanne, Peter Lang, 1999).

Pirotte, O., P. Girerd, P. Marsal and S. Morson, *Trente ans d'expérience Euratom: La naissance d'une Europe nucléaire* (Brussels, Bruylant, 1988).

Skogmar, G. *The United States and the Nuclear Dimension of European Integration* (New York, NY, Palgrave Macmillan, 2004).

Södersten, A. *Euratom at the Crossroads* (Northampton, Edward Elgar, 2018).

---

108 'Nuclear Power in the European Union' (2022), www.world-nuclear.org/informa tion-library/country-profiles/others/european-union.aspx.

15

From 'Helsinki' and Development Aid to Multipolar Hard Ball

ANGELA ROMANO

Introduction

This chapter argues that the European Communities (EC) and then the European Union (EU) rapidly became an international *political* actor which, despite the lack of military tools, did not limit its actions to the exercise of soft or civilian power.

Since the 1990s, numerous political scientists have debated the nature of the EU as an international actor, proposing the similar concepts of civilian power,[1] quiet superpower,[2] normative power,[3] transformative power[4] and liberal power.[5] Many debated and reappraised these definitions.[6] In the last 20 years, several historians have added their contributions to studies about the international political role of the EC/EU, revealing how the EC polity increasingly asserted itself as more than just an international economic

---

1 M. Telò, *Europe: A Civilian Power? European Union, Global Governance, World Order* (Basingstoke, Palgrave Macmillan, 2006). The concept appeared first in F. Duchêne, 'Europe's Role in World Peace', in R. Mayne (ed.), *Europe Tomorrow: Sixteen Europeans Look Ahead* (London, Fontana, 1972), pp. 32–47.
2 A. Moravcsik, 'Europe: The Quiet Superpower', *French Politics* 7, no. 3–4 (2009): 403–22.
3 I. Manners, 'Normative Power Europe: A Contradiction in Terms?', *Journal of Common Market Studies* 40, no. 2 (2002): 235–58.
4 M. Leonard, 'Ascent of Europe', *Prospect* 108 (March 2005): 34–7.
5 W. Wagner, 'Liberal Power Europe', *Journal of Common Market Studies* 55 (2017): 1398–414.
6 C. Hill, 'European Foreign Policy: Power Bloc, Civilian Model or Flop?', in R. Rummel (ed.), *The Evolution of an International Actor* (Boulder, CO, Westview Press, 1990), pp. 31–55; T. Diez, 'Constructing the Self and Changing Others: Reconsidering "Normative Power Europe"', *Millennium* 33, no. 3 (2005): 613–36; K. E. Smith, 'Beyond the Civilian Power EU Debate', *Politique Européenne* 17, no. 1 (2005): 63–82; J. Orbie, 'Civilian Power Europe: Review of the Original and Current Debates', *Cooperation and Conflict* 41, no. 1 (2006): 123–8; S. Lucarelli and I. Manners (eds.), *Values and Principles in European Foreign Policy* (London and New York, NY, Routledge, 2006); M. Loriaux, 'Many Europes and the Problem of Power', *Comparative European Politics* 14, no. 4 (2016): 417–34.

heavyweight, with some successes, some failures and several limitations.[7] This chapter intends to offer a critical historical overview of the EC/EU's international political role focused on what the EC/EU actually did, how and why it did it, and how it was perceived by its interlocutors.

It is necessary to first clarify the meanings of the terms that will be used. Joseph S. Nye conceptualised 'soft power' as the ability of a country to persuade – not coerce – other countries to adopt the actions or behaviours it wants. The soft-power toolkit would include cultural exchange and public diplomacy, but no instruments that either (threaten to) punish or (promise to) reward.[8] Soft power is one extreme in a continuum of ways in which an international actor can influence others' behaviours; at the opposite extreme is the use of force and in the middle are the promise or use of rewards (e.g., aid) as well as non-violent punishment (e.g., economic sanctions).[9] Some foreign policy instruments have a dual nature: conditionality, for example, can be an inducement (benefits will be granted if certain conditions are met) or a coercion tool (benefits will be cut if conditions are violated).[10] Nye considers coercion and inducement in the category of hard power, as both are used to command or control others' behaviour.[11] Civilian powers rely on soft power (persuasion and attraction) and pursue 'civilian ends', that is, international cooperation, solidarity and the strengthening of international law; whereas power blocs use inducement and coercion (carrots and sticks) to achieve their goals.[12]

Upon its first enlargement in 1973, the EC became the largest and richest trading bloc and aid donor in the world. It could thus exercise much leverage

---

7 See, for example, G. Bossuat (ed.), *L'Europe et la mondialisation* (Paris, Soleb, 2006); A. Deighton and G. Bossuat (eds.), *The EC/EU: A World Security Actor?* (Paris, Soleb, 2007); A. Romano, *From Détente in Europe to European Détente: How the West Shaped the Helsinki CSCE* (Brussels, Peter Lang, 2009); A. Varsori and G. Migani (eds.), *Europe in the International Arena during the 1970s: Entering a Different World* (Brussels, Peter Lang, 2011); M. Gainar, *Aux origines de la diplomatie européenne: Les Neuf et la coopération politique européenne de 1973 à 1980* (Brussels, Peter Lang, 2012); C. Hiepel (ed.), *Europe in a Globalizing World 1970–1985* (Baden-Baden, Nomos, 2014); L. Ferrari, *Sometimes Speaking with a Single Voice: The European Community as an International Actor, 1969–1979* (Brussels, Peter Lang, 2016); U. Krotz, K. K. Patel and F. Romero (eds.), *Europe's Cold War Relations: The EC towards a Global Role* (New York, NY, Bloomsbury Academic, 2019).
8 J. S. Nye, Jr, 'Soft Power', *Foreign Policy* 80 (1990): 153–71.
9 K. J. Holsti, *International Politics: A Framework for Analyisis*, 7th ed. (Hoboken, NY, Prentice Hall, 1995), pp. 125–6.
10 Smith, 'Beyond the Civilian Power EU Debate', 67.
11 J. S. Nye, Jr, *Soft Power: The Means to Success in World Politics* (New York, NY, Public Affairs, 2004), p. 7.
12 Hill, 'European Foreign Policy'; Smith, 'Beyond the Civilian Power EU Debate', 67–9.

in its external relations, and it seems quite implausible that it would have limited its methods to soft power. Moreover, when the persuading actor interacts with much less powerful states, the latter may perceive its intent as not being mere persuasion. Accordingly, this chapter does not consider the EC/EU a civilian power; it rather agrees with Smith that the EU is a hybrid of civilian power and power bloc and applies this interpretation to the EC's experience during the Cold War.[13]

This chapter explores the foreign policy of the EC polity from the mid 1960s to the mid 1990s, focusing on the Conference on Security and Cooperation in Europe (CSCE) and the ensuing Helsinki process, East–West relations and the political use of development aid.[14] The expression 'EC polity' encompasses both the Community and the member states acting collectively. The focus is on the pursuit of aims that were explicitly political and/or related to security, whereas foreign economic policy (where both objectives and means are economic) is covered by other chapters in this volume.

The chapter is organised in three chronological sections with similar structure. After a summary of the international situation in which the EC polity operated, each section describes the foreign policy apparatus and presents EC foreign policy objectives as set in declarations or internal meetings. Each section then reports cases that elucidate the EC polity's exercise of power in the areas under scrutiny and its impact. The conclusion appraises the trends regarding the use of inducement and coercion (hard power) in the EC/EU's foreign policy and discusses some central questions common to the *CHEU* – continuity versus change; 'Maastricht' as a turning point; and the impact of enlargements on EC/EU power in terms of capabilities, motivation and effectiveness.

From the Mid 1960s to 1975: The Stepping Stones

The International Environment

The environment in which the EC operated between the mid 1960s and the mid 1970s was characterised by the struggle of developing countries to redesign relations with the rich states and by the relaxation of

---

13 K. E. Smith, *European Union Foreign Policy in a Changing World*, 2nd ed. (Cambridge, MA, Polity Press, 2008), p. 22.
14 On the EC's development policy and relations with African, Caribbean and Pacific countries, see Guia Migani's Chapter 3 in this volume.

tensions – known as *détente* – between the two Cold War blocs. Détente had been initiated by French President Charles de Gaulle and then pursued by all western European governments, with the Federal Republic of Germany the latecomer yet fundamental player. Western European détente aimed at making life more liveable for Europeans in the short term and overcoming the Cold War divide of the continent in the long run. This transformative goal was pursued through the proliferation of contacts at all levels and cooperation in many fields, with the idea that socialisation would ultimately effect the desired change.[15] In January 1969 new US President Richard Nixon called for both an era of negotiations with the Soviets and partnership with the European allies.

Yet the keynote of the Nixon presidency was the pursuit of US national interests. Superpower détente was meant to reduce the costs of confrontation and consolidate superpower (con)dominium, while partnership with the Europeans was rather a call to burden sharing. Economically, western Europe was considered a strong competitor – summarised by Nixon with 'European leaders want to "screw" us and we want to "screw" them in the economic area.'[16] Politically, European détente's transformative nature disturbed superpower détente, and Nixon and National Adviser Henry A. Kissinger proved anything but supportive of it. Likewise, the Kremlin's peaceful coexistence (the Soviet version of détente) aimed at consolidating the USSR's international status and strengthening the socialist bloc, promoting economic cooperation while continuing ideological competition. In March 1969, the Warsaw Pact called for a pan-European security conference encompassing an economic cooperation component aimed at overcoming discriminatory blocs. The entire EC polity read it as a worrisome reference to the Community, which the socialist countries did not recognise. Overall, the perception of an opening window of opportunity and concerns for both US and Soviet challenges prompted the EC polity to elaborate a common foreign policy to advance core EC political interests and goals.

---

15 See, for example, W. Loth and G.-H. Soutou (eds.), *The Making of Détente: Eastern and Western Europe in the Cold War, 1965–75* (London and New York, NY, Routledge, 2008); F. Bozo, M.-P. Rey, N. P. Ludlow and B. Rother (eds.), *Overcoming the Iron Curtain: Visions of the End of the Cold War in Europe, 1945–1990* (Oxford, Berghahn Books, 2012); O. Bange and P. Villaume (eds.), *The Long Détente: Changing Concepts of Security and Cooperation in Europe, 1950s–1980s* (Budapest, Central European University Press, 2017).

16 *Foreign Relations of the United States, 1969–1976*, vol. III: *Foreign Economic Policy; International Monetary Policy, 1969–1972*, Doc. No. 100, Memorandum of Conversation, 11 September 1972, p. 264.

The (Creation of a) Foreign Policy Machinery

The 1960s saw several proposals for political cooperation; ultimately the summit at The Hague in December 1969 recorded consensus for European Political Cooperation (EPC).[17] The ensuing Luxembourg – or 'Davignon' – Report, drafted by the EC foreign ministers and approved on 27 October 1970, established EPC as an intergovernmental mechanism for foreign policy cooperation. It consisted of meetings of the foreign ministers (every 6 months); meetings of political directors (at least four times per year); ad hoc working groups of experts; and meetings of the heads of state and government if serious issues so required. The Commission could be invited to share its views when discussions affected EC activities. The mechanism worked on the principle of informality, with a commitment to consult and attempt to create a common view, but no legal obligation to agree one.[18]

The first EPC meeting on 19 November 1970 endorsed the Belgian proposal to collectively engage with the pan-European security conference proposal (the future CSCE). EPC also developed specific procedures to coordinate the EC states' stance within the North Atlantic Treaty Organization (NATO), where the CSCE was already being discussed; the EC states did not mean to undermine NATO, yet were determined to assert their common vision and defend EC interests.[19] The Copenhagen report on EPC (1973) described the EC as a 'distinct entity' that would bring its 'original contribution to the international equilibrium'.[20] Then the Paris Summit of December 1974 – which launched the European Council – sanctioned the first link between EPC and the Community, with the EC President-in-Office identified as the spokesman for the group in international diplomacy.[21] With the member states' top political level now steering both Community integration and foreign policy cooperation, the foundations were laid for a power bloc building on the economic might of the Community and guided by the political vision of its members. With the first enlargement to the UK,

---

17 M. E. Guasconi, *L'Europa tra continuità e cambiamento: Il vertice dell'Aja del 1969 e il rilancio della costruzione europea* (Florence, Polistampa, 2004), p. 174.

18 'Davignon Report (Luxembourg, 27 October 1970)', *Bulletin of the European Communities* no. 11 (1970): 9–14.

19 A. Romano, 'A Single European Voice Can Speak Louder to the World: Rationales, Ways and Means of EPC in the CSCE Experience', in M. Rasmussen and A. Knudsen (eds.), *The Road to a United Europe: Interpretations of the Process of European Integration* (Brussels, Peter Lang, 2009), pp. 257–70.

20 'Second Report on European Political Cooperation on Foreign Policy', *Bulletin of the European Communities* no. 9 (1973): 14–21.

21 'Final Communiqué of the Meeting of Heads of Government of the Community (Paris, 9 and 10 December 1974)', *Bulletin of the European Communities* no. 12 (1974): 6–13.

Denmark and Ireland on 1 January 1973, the EC had become the first trade power in the world, and this large economic weight entailed a clear political opportunity.

EC Rationales and Goals

The Davignon Report identified the promotion of détente 'first and foremost' in Europe as a key responsibility of the EC.[22] Speaking before the European Parliament on 8 June 1971, EC Commission President Franco Maria Malfatti declared, 'the Seventies should see the consolidation of a new atmosphere between us and the countries of the East'.[23] This goal ensued from the willingness to join national détente efforts but also from the need to safeguard the Community. The reference to the elimination of discriminatory blocs made in the Warsaw Pact proposal for a CSCE was perceived as threatening due to the socialist regimes' non-recognition of the EC. The situation became more problematic due to the forthcoming extension of the EC's Common Commercial Policy (CCP) to those countries, which would forbid bilateral trade agreements between them and the EC states. The positive international juncture and the implementation of the CCP on 1 January 1973 created the political necessity and possibility of a common détente policy.

The Commission was vocal about the urgency of the matter, and the first EPC ministerial meeting agreed that a collective eastern policy was required. In May 1971 EPC set the guidelines for it: cooperation with socialist countries should not prejudice the EC and its development; priority should be given to establishing relations between the Community and each socialist country; any agreement likely to strengthen the Soviet hold on its allies should be rejected. Thus there was explicit opposition to the idea of a trade deal with the Council for Mutual Economic Assistance (CMEA), which would contradict the last two of the three guidelines.[24] Trade was an end in itself, but also a means to political ends. First of all, EC trade agreements with socialist countries would signal their recognition and thus enhance the EC's international reach. Secondly, member states' national détente policies largely relied on economic means to improve political relations with socialist countries, and so could an EC collective policy.

22 'Davignon Report'.
23 Quoted in A. Romano, 'Untying Cold War Knots: The EEC and Eastern Europe in the Long 1970s', *Cold War History* 14, no. 2 (2013): 153–73, 160.
24 Ibid., 160.

The CSCE was an integral part of this emerging eastern policy; EC governments were the driving force behind NATO's conditional acceptance, in December 1969, of the pan-European conference idea vis-à-vis a sceptical US administration.[25] At the Paris Summit of 1972, the EC states affirmed 'their determination to pursue their policy of détente and of peace with the countries of eastern Europe, notably on the occasion of the Conference on Security and Cooperation in Europe, and the establishment of a sound basis for a wider economic and human cooperation'.[26]

EC Foreign Policy Action

The Final Act of the CSCE signed on 1 August 1975 called for balanced progress in three areas: questions of security in Europe, including principles guiding relations among participating states and confidence-building measures (so-called Basket I); cooperation in the fields of economics, science, technology and the environment (Basket II); and cooperation in humanitarian and other fields (Basket III). The 1975 European Councils in Dublin (March) and Brussels (July) praised the EC states' unitary action at the CSCE and emphasised their common vision of détente as a dynamic process.[27] In this respect, the CSCE represented a tool for the exercise of soft power and the pursuit of civilian ends: its provisions strengthened international law, promoted international cooperation in various fields and encouraged the facilitation of people-to-people contacts.

Yet the way the EC polity conducted the negotiations distinguished the EC group as playing diplomatic hardball. On the one hand, the EC group engaged in consultations with NATO allies as well as neutral and non-aligned countries; it also offered socialist countries genuine openings on economic cooperation. On the other hand, the EC polity set non-negotiable goals and pursued them determinedly until it had achieved their satisfaction. For a start, Basket III provisions on the freer circulation of ideas, people and information were the epitome of western European détente. The EC polity resisted all attempts of the socialist countries to scrap, contain or weaken Basket III. It also proved impervious to Kissinger's numerous statements about the pointlessness of provisions facilitating human contacts and to the

---

25 Romano, *From Détente in Europe to European Détente*, pp. 71–8.
26 'Déclaration du sommet de Paris', *Bulletin des Communautés européennes* no. 10 (1972): 15–16.
27 'The European Council [Dublin Summit 1975], Dublin, 10–11 March 1975', http://aei .pitt.edu/1921; 'The European Council [Brussels Summit 1975], Brussels, 16–17 July 1975', http://aei.pitt.edu/1427.

US administration's intensifying pressure to give the Soviets 'the short snappy conference with little substance' they wanted.[28] Indeed, the CSCE provisions represented a formidable challenge to the stability and legitimacy of the socialist regimes.[29] The EC delegations stuck to their requests, slowed down work in the other baskets to prevent negotiations in Basket III from being hastened to an end, refused to agree to a top-level final phase until concrete results had been reached on human contacts and eventually threatened to quit should the Soviets still refuse concessions. Thirty years after Helsinki, former Soviet ambassador Yuri Kashlev, who negotiated in Basket III, admitted that results therein came from the pressure that western European governments put on the Soviets, even at the highest level.[30]

The EC polity also carefully planned how to push recognition of the Community. Challenging the basic fact that the CSCE was convened among *states*, EC members operated to make the EC *as such* part of the negotiations. First, as states had the right to compose their delegations freely, Commission representatives joined the delegation of the state holding the EC presidency and expressed the official position of the Community when its competence so required. EC states resisted protests from the socialist delegates, and negotiations in Basket II eventually proceeded with socialist acquiescence. Secondly, the EC polity insisted that the EC as such should sign the Final Act. As this encountered vigorous socialist opposition, the EC governments declared it a non-negotiable condition for their assent to closing the CSCE at the summit level. Facing this intransigent position, the Soviets gave in, because Brezhnev had associated his name with the CSCE and could not risk failure. The signature of Italian Prime Minister Aldo Moro as president of the EC Council formally engaged the EC *as such* in the CSCE process.[31] Carefully prepared, acting as a unitary front and playing hardball, the EC group established itself as a force to be reckoned with. The Nixon administration was annoyed with the EC's determination to pursue its own goals; the Soviets complained repeatedly about the EC's attitude during bilateral meetings with Nixon and Kissinger as well as with western European leaders. Such complaints amounted to another form of recognition that the EC had proven to be a tough political player.

28 Quoted in A. Romano, 'Détente, Entente or Linkage? The Helsinki Conference on Security and Cooperation in Europe in U.S. Relations with the Soviet Union', *Diplomatic History* 33, no. 4 (2009): 703–22, 714.
29 D. Selvage and W. Süß, *Staatssicherheit und KSZE-Prozess: MfS zwischen SED und KGB (1972–1989)* (Göttingen, Vandenhoeck & Ruprecht, 2019).
30 Romano, *From Détente in Europe to European Détente*, pp. 212–13.   31 Ibid., pp. 206–12.

The policy towards the socialist countries is a full example of the EC acting as a power bloc, doling out economic rewards or withholding benefits to induce change in its interlocutors' behaviour. The EC polity had repeatedly stated that it had no interest in an EC–CMEA trade agreement, and that socialist countries should each establish relations with the Community to regulate trade. The EC members used the CCP implementation to pressure the socialist regimes into this. Mandated by the EC Council, in November 1974 the Commission sent each socialist government a letter explaining that as of 1 January 1975 bilateral trade agreements with EC states would no longer be possible, as trade competence was transferred to the Community. The Commission invited the recipient to open comprehensive negotiations, for which it enclosed a draft agreement; the latter addressed most of the socialist concerns, namely import quotas, most favoured nation treatment, safeguard mechanisms and payment problems. The promise of continued (and better) access to the EC wide(ning) market was clearly an inducement to move them to recognition. At the same time, the EC showed what refusal to deal with the EC entailed: the Council of Ministers set up a common import regime as of 1 January 1975 and then unilaterally established the annual import quotas for the socialist countries; pending recognition, it would continue to act unilaterally.[32] The EC knew from previous years that this was no minor problem for the European socialist regimes, whose economic strategy relied heavily on exports to western European markets; the EC's protectionist common agricultural policy had severely impacted on socialist exports, leading Poland, Czechoslovakia, Hungary and Romania between 1964 and 1968 to informally approach the Commission and negotiate tariffs and quotas.[33] By 1974, the combined effect of the EC's first enlargement, the Western recession following the oil-price shock and the forthcoming CCP further narrowed the door also to socialist manufactured goods, which represented half of their exports to western Europe. As recent historiography has demonstrated, EC enlargement and policies caused major predicaments for the socialist regimes, spurred an intense debate within the bloc and progressively modified their strategies; the EC was recognised as a power bloc aware of its interests and determined to defend them.[34] Moreover, socialist

---

32 Romano, 'Untying Cold War Knots', 163–4.   33 Ibid., 160.

34 S. Kansikas, *Socialist Countries Face the European Community: Soviet-Bloc Controversies over East–West Trade* (New York, NY, Peter Lang, 2014); A. Romano and F. Romero (eds.), *European Socialist Regimes' Fateful Engagement with the West: National Strategy in the Long 1970s* (London and New York, NY, Routledge, 2020).

regimes noticed that the EC rewarded those among them which, while paying lip service to the bloc's non-recognition policy, were willing to deal with the Commission. For instance, Romania, more autonomous than the rest, requested and got access to the Community's Generalized Scheme of Preferences as of 1 January 1974.[35]

The Period 1975–1985: Consolidation and Boldness

The International Situation

In the immediate aftermath of the CSCE, international détente started to be questioned, particularly in the US Congress. Some Soviet actions – interference in the Horn of Africa; support for left-wing liberation movements in Angola and Mozambique; and deployment of a new generation of intermediate-range ballistic missiles (SS-20s) targeting western Europe – were interpreted as contrary to détente and openly aggressive. The Carter presidency remained committed to continuing superpower strategic negotiations, though the president's uncompromising stance on human rights did not help to relieve general tensions and contributed to jeopardising the Belgrade CSCE follow-up meeting (1977–8). At the turn of the decade, the Soviet invasion of Afghanistan spurred general condemnation in the West and sanctions from Washington. Then, new US President Ronald Reagan fully adopted a confrontational policy towards the Soviet Union, made of harsh rhetoric, economic warfare and an arms race. Unsurprisingly, following the imposition of martial law in Poland, the Reagan administration imposed economic sanctions against the Soviet Union, which it considered as bearing a heavy and direct responsibility for the repression in Poland. Reagan's Cold Warrior approach also applied to central America, the troubles of which were read through the lenses of superpower competition. The growing tension between the superpowers and the crisis in the heart of Europe challenged the new-born EC détente policy. At the same time, they offered the EC polity the opportunity to prove its autonomous role and capacity to speak with one voice and to advance its own interests and vision.

A More Coherent Foreign Policy Machinery

Foreign policy became a regular chapter of the European Council's agenda, and EPC quickly grew beyond the practice recommended in the Copenhagen Report of 1973. Foreign ministers met far more frequently and discussed

---

35 E. Dragomir, 'Breaking the CMEA Hold: Romania in Search of a "Strategy" towards the European Economic Community, 1958–1974', *European Review of History* 27, no. 4 (2020): 494–526.

matters of political cooperation also during EC Council meetings; the Political Committee met on average once a month; expert working groups multiplied; and the Commission was increasingly involved.[36] The 1981 London Report on EPC established that the Commission should participate in all EPC meetings regardless of the topic, recognising that a collective foreign policy would benefit from joint EPC–EC action, especially in those situations where political and economic factors were closely interrelated. In other words, it invited the use of EC economic means to pursue political goals agreed in EPC. Moreover, the report officially extended the EPC's mandate to the 'political aspects of security questions'.[37]

In 1988, Pijpers estimated that three-quarters of the approximately 300 EPC declarations to date related to developing countries or regions.[38] Yet political considerations – or conditionality – would not become an element of EC development aid until November 1991; assessment of the domestic policy of the government receiving aid related solely to its developmental plans. Nonetheless, the Community made some exceptions for gross human rights violations.

EC Foreign Policy Views

As Soviet activities in Africa raised security concerns, the question of using economic sanctions to induce change in Soviet foreign policy emerged in transatlantic discussions. During the Rambouillet Summit of the Group of Six in November 1975, Italian Prime Minister Aldo Moro maintained that East–West trade was an important part of the process of détente that had been confirmed by the Helsinki Final Act; West German Chancellor Helmut Schmidt and French President Valéry Giscard d'Estaing expressed similar views.[39]

The events at the turn of the decade did not change the views of the EC polity. The West unanimously denounced the Soviet invasion of Afghanistan as incompatible both with the Charter of the United Nations and with

---

36 'External Political Relations of the European Community, Directorate General for Research and Documentation, No. 79/79, 1979', http://aei.pitt.edu/4537.

37 'Report on European Political Cooperation (London, 13 October 1981)', *Bulletin of the European Communities* suppl. 3 (1981): 14–17.

38 A. Pijpers, 'The Twelve Out-of-Area: A Civilian Power in an Uncivil World?', in A. Pijpers, E. Regelsberger and W. Wessels (eds.), *European Political Cooperation in the 1980s: A Common Foreign Policy for Western Europe?* (Dordrecht, Boston, MA and London, Martinus Nijhoff, 1988), pp. 143–65, 153–4.

39 A. Romano, 'G-7s, European Councils and East–West Economic Relations, 1975–1982', in E. Mourlon-Druol and F. Romero (eds.), *International Summitry and Global Governance: The Rise of the G-7 and the European Council, 1974–1991* (London and New York, NY, Routledge, 2014), pp. 198–222, 205.

détente and called for complete Soviet withdrawal, yet western Europe did not adopt sanctions.[40] The worsening crisis in Poland, which culminated in the declaration of martial law in December 1981, seriously threatened détente in Europe, yet the EC polity still avoided confrontational tones and punitive tools. As the EC polity had dreaded a possible Soviet intervention in reply to the worsening Polish crisis, it did not see the imposition of martial law by the Polish authorities as a fatal blow to détente and was determined to avoid adding to tensions. Consequently, the ad hoc EPC ministerial meeting on 4 January 1982 condemned the Soviets for putting serious external pressure on Poland but did not attribute to them direct responsibility for the repression; it rather requested the Polish government 'to end as soon as possible the state of martial law, to release those arrested and to restore a general dialogue with the church and Solidarity'.[41] The NATO extraordinary ministerial meeting on 11 January did not change EC states' views, and the final communiqué could only mention 'potential' measures.[42]

Unlike the US administrations, western European governments still 'recognised the role which economic and commercial contacts and cooperation have played in the stabilisation and the development of East–West relations as a whole and which [we] wish to see continue on the basis of a genuine mutual interest', as stated by the European Council of 29–30 March 1982.[43] The fundamental view behind the EC polity's approach was that trade and economic ties could reduce military threats in Europe, whereas economic warfare could incentivise the Soviet leadership to increase its military build-up.[44]

The EC polity was also concerned with Reagan's muscular policy in central America, which they saw as driven by the same Cold War confrontational rationales. The EC polity considered the Reagan administration's attempts at overthrowing the Sandinista regime in Nicaragua by military means as not only legally unacceptable but also as worsening regional instability; nor was US military aid to the right-wing government in El

40 Declaration of the Seven Heads of State and Government and Representatives of the European Communities, Venice, 23 June 1980, www.g8.utoronto.ca/summit/1980venice/political.html.
41 'Statements of the Foreign Ministers and Other Documents, European Political Cooperation, 1982', http://aei.pitt.edu/5584.
42 NATO Ministerial Communiqué, 'Declaration on Events in Poland', 11 January 1982, www.nato.int/docu/comm/49-95/c820111a.htm.
43 'The European Council [Brussels Summit 1982], Brussels, 29–30 March 1982', p. 182, http://aei.pitt.edu/id/eprint/1431.
44 H.-D. Genscher, 'Toward an Overall Western Strategy for Peace, Freedom and Progress', Foreign Affairs 61, no. 1 (1982): 42–66.

Salvador against leftist guerrillas taken lightly. At the above-mentioned March 1982 meeting, the European Council discussed the situation in central America and noted that grave economic problems and social inequalities were at the root of conflicts in the region and therefore the best means to help stabilise the area were development aid and regional cooperation, not military interventions.[45]

EC Action

The Helsinki Process

The determination of the EC polity to pursue its own vision and interests was very visible at the CSCE follow-up meetings in Belgrade (1977–8) and Madrid (1980–3). The first follow-up meeting was crucial to confirm the participation of the EC as such. The EC states insisted on presenting the matter as a fact deriving from the existence of the Community, the ensuing obligations of its member states, the EC president's signature of the Final Act and his accompanying statement. More strikingly, the EC states agreed that, should protests be made by the socialist countries, they would make it clear that their participation in negotiations would be seriously hampered. This was no inconsequential threat, as economic cooperation was of great interest to the socialist bloc. The EC states' delegations thus engaged in constantly underscoring the EC's presence as embodied by the Commission representatives, with their competence to negotiate on specific matters and express the EC viewpoint. More formally, the proposals on matters of EC competence were tabled with the heading 'European Communities'. The determination of the EC polity was a major factor in winning the socialist delegations over, but so was the pragmatic approach of the EC Commission officials within Basket II and their capacity to present the Community as a constructive partner. As a result, not only did the socialist delegates negotiate directly with Commission representatives, but also the latter intervened on matters beyond the EC's exclusive competence and fully participated in all working bodies, including drafting and informal contact groups.[46]

From a civilian power perspective, one would expect the EC polity to seek the expansion of the CSCE agenda a priori, yet the EC polity used its diplomatic weight to prevent the adoption of proposals within the

45 'The European Council [Brussels Summit 1982]', p. 183.
46 A. Romano, 'The European Community and the Belgrade CSCE', in V. Bilandzic, D. Dahlmann and M. Kosanovic (eds.), *From Helsinki to Belgrade: The First CSCE Follow-up Meeting and the Crisis of Détente* (Göttingen, Vandenhoeck & Ruprecht, 2012), pp. 219–21 and 224.

Mediterranean chapter of the Final Act that were likely to interfere with the EC's Mediterranean policy. The Belgrade Concluding Document convened an expert meeting on Mediterranean issues, but its mandate was limited to exploring ways to promote cooperation in 'economic, scientific and cultural fields, *in addition to* other initiatives relating to the above subjects already under way'.[47]

The Madrid follow-up meeting saw the EC polity standing up to the Reagan administration, which was interested in using the CSCE as a stick. Despite an unprecedented show of Western cohesion – with NATO foreign ministers flying into Madrid to denounce the imposition of martial law in Poland – the allies clashed on the question of recess as well as on matters of substance. After 9 months of intense transatlantic arm-twisting the EC successfully killed off the US idea of a 2- or 3-year recess which, they argued, would end the Helsinki process and seriously damage European détente. Moreover, the EC states' diplomats operated within and outwith NATO to overcome Reagan's prioritisation of maximalist human rights provisions – which blocked progress in the CSCE – in order to secure the convening of a Conference on Disarmament in Europe (CDE).[48] This was a major initiative of the EC polity to add a military dimension to the CSCE security chapter; it highlighted the importance which EC members attributed to the CSCE in strengthening European security at a time when disarmament talks between the superpowers and between the blocs were going nowhere and western European public opinion protested against the NATO-agreed deployment of US Pershing and cruise missiles in their countries.[49] The diplomatic manoeuvring put in place to secure acceptance of the CDE also signalled the EC polity's self-confidence in venturing into NATO's preserve.[50] The CDE was convened in Stockholm (1983–6) and adopted measures of the desired kind, including – for the first time during the Cold War – the right to conduct on-site inspections of military forces in the field.[51]

---

47 Ibid., p. 222.
48 A. Romano, 'More Cohesive, Still Divergent: Western Europe, the US and the Madrid CSCE Follow-Up Meeting', in K. K. Patel and K. Weisbrode (eds.), *European Integration and the Atlantic Community in the 1980s* (Cambridge, Cambridge University Press), pp. 39–58.
49 On NATO, see Luca Ratti's Chapter 12 in this volume.
50 A. Romano, 'Re-designing Military Security in Europe: Cooperation and Competition between the European Community and NATO during the Early 1980s', *European Review of History* 24, no. 3 (2017): 445–71.
51 J. Freeman, *Security and the CSCE Process: The Stockholm Conference and Beyond* (London, Macmillan, 1991).

East–West Relations

The EC polity firmly resisted continual US pressure to impose sanctions against the Soviet Union. In a nutshell, the Reagan administration saw the EC polity's positions as acts of self-Finlandisation, based on a dangerous dependence on trade with the East.[52] Yet political goals and a specific vision for the continent were the strong rationales driving the EC polity's choices. The EC's response to the Soviet invasion of Afghanistan was a typical use of soft power – persuasion and diplomacy – to pursue civilian ends, namely international cooperation and strengthening of international law. Initially, the strong condemnation of the invasion was followed by European Council statements (Venice, 13 June 1980; Maastricht, 24 March 1981) in support of resolutions by the United Nations, the Islamic Conference and the New Delhi Conference of the Non-aligned Movement for a political solution to the crisis. Then the European Council of Luxembourg (29–30 June 1981) presented its first coordinated action: it called for a two-stage international conference to be convened in October or November and tasked with agreeing international arrangements to end external interventions in Afghanistan, establish safeguards to prevent future ones, and ensure the country's independence and non-alignment. The permanent members of the UN Security Council, together with Pakistan, Iran and India (as neighbouring countries), the UN Secretary-General and the Secretary-General of the Islamic Conference, would be invited to participate in stage one of the conference; stage two would also involve 'representatives of the Afghan people' to agree on the implementation of such arrangements.[53]

The Polish crisis was different; while refusing to join US sanctions against the Soviets, the EC polity adopted its own hard power approach, made of a carrot and a (mild) stick, using the EC's economic weight for entirely foreign policy goals. The EC Council of Ministers in March 1982 adopted some restrictions on Soviet goods within the scope of the CCP to give the Kremlin a warning while avoiding the open hostility of sanctions.[54] At the same time, the Brussels European Council in the same month stressed the positive political value of East–West economic relations, sending a clear 'carrot' message. Additional evidence that the restrictions on Soviet goods

52 See, for instance, A. Chiampan, 'Those European Chicken Littles: Reagan, NATO and the Polish Crisis, 1981–2', *International History Review* 37, no. 4 (2015): 682–99.
53 'Conclusions of the Luxembourg European Council: Excerpt on Afghanistan (29 and 30 June 1981)', *Bulletin of the European Communities* no. 6 (1981): 9.
54 K. E. Smith, *The Making of EU Foreign Policy: The Case of Eastern Europe* (New York, NY, St Martin's Press, 1998), pp. 40–1.

were a political tool is the fact that they were not renewed the next year, as the Polish government lifted martial law and released political prisoners.

By avoiding escalation into confrontation, the EC polity was acting coherently with its interests. After the Helsinki CSCE, the EC saw an improvement in its relations with Eastern Europe and hoped to extend the Community's economic and political influence in the area.[55] The mix of carrots and a veiled threat of economic sticks served precisely the now 15-year-old policy of developing the EC's bilateral relations with socialist countries. The EC polity continued to reject any proposal of EC–CMEA trade deal and, aware of the importance of the EC market for the socialist economies, clearly used conditionality: socialist countries which dealt with the Community directly were rewarded with better access to the EC market, while the others continued to face unilaterally adopted EC quotas in more and more sectors, some of which – agriculture, textiles and steel – were crucial for their exports. The EC approach was so evident that the Hungarian representatives bitterly noticed that their country, which featured quite liberal socio-economic reforms, received fewer rewards than did Romania, a brutal dictatorship. The reason was that the Romanian authorities had immediately rejected the idea of a possible CMEA trade policy, advocated recognition of the EC and, pending the latter, proven willing to deal directly and quite openly with the Community.[56] Confronted with an assertive EC and facing the severe economic impact of its policies, most of the socialist regimes accepted direct relations with the Community, short of recognition.[57]

Development Aid

The first case of the EC using development aid as a hard power tool was in relation to Uganda. In response to the human rights atrocities committed by the government of Idi Amin, the Community, prompted by the UK government and the European Parliament, massively delayed aid. On 21 June 1977, the Council approved the so-called Uganda Guidelines, which, though not officially suspending development cooperation, allowed the retention of all financial means except those related to the Système de Stabilisation des Recettes d'Exportation (System for the Stabilisation of Export Earnings,

---

55 Historical Archives of the EU, EN 1569, DG I, Brief, 'Relations between the Community and Eastern Europe', 1 April 1977; EN 1989, Commission, Note by Crispin Tickell for the Record, 14 December 1977.

56 Romano, 'Untying Cold War Knots', 164–71.

57 For details, see Romano and Romero (eds.), *European Socialist Regimes' Fateful Engagement.*

STABEX). Human rights violations also prompted the Community to suspend the disbursement of funds to Equatorial Guinea in 1978 for projects and programmes other than STABEX, and to suspend aid to the Central African Republic in 1979 and Liberia in 1980.[58]

The use of aid also took the form of inducement (carrots), most visibly in central America. As explained above, the EC polity was concerned about US military interventions in the region, thought that the East–West dimension should be minimised and believed that the existing harsh socio-economic conditions were the actual roots of instability in the region. Recognising the latter, the European Council of March 1982 agreed to increase both national and EC aid to the region.[59] Aid was further used to reward the multilateral talks initiative that the Contadora group – Mexico, Venezuela, Panama and Colombia – launched in January 1983 to discuss regional problems without external interference. In June, the European Council of Stuttgart declared EC member states' support of the talks, specifically stating that they were 'convinced that the problems of Central America cannot be solved by military means, but only by a political solution springing from the region itself'; it also declared their readiness to further contribute to central America's economic development.[60] The EC polity's approach made it a main sought-after partner for the region. On invitation by the Costa Rican government, the foreign ministers of central American countries – including Nicaragua – and of the EC states convened in San José on 28–29 September 1984 to discuss dialogue and cooperation. A second conference, held in Luxembourg on 11–12 November 1985, formalised the political and economic dialogue between the EC and central America via a political Final Act and a framework cooperation agreement. Significantly, the EC made a commitment to substantially increase the total volume of aid to the region during the initial period of the agreement.[61] Again, the stark contrast with the approach and the actions of the United States highlights the willingness and capacity of the EC polity to pursue its own vision and

58 K. Urbanski, *The European Union and International Sanctions: A Model of Emerging Actorness* (Northampton, Edward Elgar, 2020), pp. 117–18. On STABEX, see Migani's Chapter 3 in this volume.
59 'The European Council [Brussels Summit 1982]', p. 183.
60 'The European Council [Stuttgart Summit 1983], Stuttgart, 17–19 June 1983', http://aei.pitt.edu/id/eprint/1396.
61 S. Nuttall, 'European Political Co-operation', *Yearbook of European Law* 5, no. 1 (1985): 325–40, 328; S. Nuttall, 'Interaction between European Political Co-operation and the European Community', *Yearbook of European Law* 7, no. 1 (1987): 211–49, 242.

goals. Moreover, the involvement in central America, which the United States considered its own preserve and where EC trade was not substantial, testifies to the EC's self-confidence.

From 1985 to the Mid 1990s: Embracing Full Political Conditionality

The International Environment

The appointment of Mikhail Gorbachev as secretary-general of the Soviet Communist Party dramatically changed the international environment in which the EC came to operate. Reagan found in Gorbachev the leader with whom to open superpower dialogue for disarmament and change. Their regular annual summits (Geneva 1985, Reykjavík 1986, Washington 1987 and Moscow 1988) are a testament to the political and human encounter that led to key disarmament treaties and to discussion of human rights and humanitarian matters as well as the settlement of regional conflicts. The Valletta Summit of December 1989 (with George H. Bush) featured a symbolic declaration on the end of the Cold War.

At the European level, Gorbachev's approach and actions brought massive changes. The new leader espoused the idea of pan-European relations as enshrined in the CSCE process in full; both his famous vision of a European Common Home and the Sinatra Doctrine, according to which Moscow would no longer keep in check Eastern European countries' domestic and foreign policies, implemented the principles and the spirit of the Final Act. Gorbachev increasingly shared the vision for the continent that the EC polity had vigorously promoted for more than a decade. This also included accepting the EC's views on relations with the socialist countries. Before Gorbachev, the Soviet Union had blocked socialist official recognition of the EC and had pursued, in vain, a comprehensive EC–CMEA agreement that would control socialist countries' bilateral relations with the EC. Gorbachev, unconvinced of the need to enforce bloc cohesion and not fearful of the EC's appeal, unequivocally changed the Soviet stance. First, in May 1985, he told Italy's Prime Minister Bettino Craxi, then president of the European Council, that he wanted to seek a common language on *political* matters to the extent that EC member states acted as a political entity. Secondly, in September 1986, EC–CMEA negotiations started on establishing relations according to their respective competences; the joint declaration signed in Luxembourg on 25 June 1988 unlocked the door to full recognition of the Community by each socialist country and their individual trade agreements with it. Gorbachev's approach towards the EC, the Sinatra Doctrine and his constructive reaction to the 1989 revolutions all aimed at building a partnership between the Soviet Union and a (forthcoming) united Europe.[62]

This idea of contributing to shaping a Common European Home is mostly visible in the adoption of the Paris Charter on New Europe, which was signed at the summit of the CSCE participating countries in November 1990. In the charter's opening paragraph, the signatories declared that 'The era of confrontation and division of Europe has ended' and they recognised the peoples' hopes and expectations for 'steadfast commitment to democracy based on human rights and fundamental freedoms; prosperity through economic liberty and social justice; and equal security for all our countries'. The first provision of the charter unequivocally declared, 'We undertake to build, consolidate and strengthen democracy as the only system of government of our nations.' The charter also established the Office for Free Elections, symbolically set in Warsaw. Reversing the order of the CSCE Final Act, the Paris Charter places the human dimension before all other fields for cooperation.[63] In a nutshell, the EC's vision had become the one shaping post-Cold War Europe and must have emboldened the EC polity to fully embrace conditionality in its foreign policy.

The EC/EU's Foreign Policy Tools and Goals: The Formalisation of Conditionality

Both the Single European Act (SEA) of 1987 and then the Treaty on the European Union – or Maastricht Treaty (1993) – were major steps towards a common foreign policy. The SEA formalised and strengthened what had been in place: it brought EPC into the treaty framework; confirmed the participation of the Commission in EPC; and improved close coordination between EPC actions and the Community's instruments of external economic policy. Then the Maastricht Treaty repealed the provisions on EPC and introduced the Common Foreign and Security Policy (CFSP). The latter, though, remained an intergovernmental exercise where decision-making was based on unanimity. Among the objectives of the CFSP was 'to develop and consolidate democracy and human rights'.[64]

---

62 V. Zubok, 'The Soviet Union and European Integration from Stalin to Gorbachev', *Journal of European Integration History* 2, no. 1 (1996): 85–98.

63 'Charter of Paris for a New Europe' (1990), www.osce.org/files/f/documents/o/6/3 9516.pdf.

64 'Treaty on European Union', http://data.europa.eu/eli/treaty/teu/sign.

Yet democracy and human rights had already been mentioned among the objectives set out in the preamble of the SEA and in several EC statements. In December 1988, the Rhodes European Council issued the Statement on the International Role of the European Community, which also asserted the commitment to 'work to overcome the division of Europe and to promote the Western values and principles that the member states have in common'.[65] The Madrid European Council of 26–27 June 1989 affirmed the determination of the EC polity to encourage reforms in eastern Europe.[66] In other words, conditionality became the essential feature of the EC's new eastern policy well before the enlargement.

On 28 November 1991, the Council of the EC took the first step towards formalising political conditionality also for development aid. The Council's Resolution on Human Rights, Democracy and Development listed several initiatives that the EC could take in support of the promotion of human rights and democracy; envisaged the possibility of adopting measures to respond to 'grave and persistent human rights violations or the serious interruption of democratic processes'; and emphasised that 'human rights clauses will be inserted in future cooperation agreements'.[67] The Maastricht Treaty incorporated conditionality, requiring that the Community should take into account the objectives of developing and consolidating democracy, the rule of law and respect for human rights and fundamental freedoms 'in the policies that it implements which are likely to affect developing countries'.[68] On December 1994, the Council included conditionality in the new Generalised Scheme of Preferences (GSP): the EU could withdraw GSP benefits from a country in response to the practice of any form of forced labour; export of goods made by prison labour; failure to prevent drug trafficking; fraud on certificates of origin; and unfair trading practices.[69] In May 1995 the Council decided that respect for human rights and democratic principles should be considered essential elements of all EC agreements (including the revised

65 'Declaration by the European Council on the International Role of the European Community', Rhodes, 3 December 1988, document no. 2/17, in C. Hill and K. E. Smith (eds.), *European Foreign Policy: Key Documents* (London and New York, NY, Routledge, 2000), pp. 149–51.
66 'The European Council [Madrid Summit 1989], Madrid, 26–27 June 1989', http://aei .pitt.edu/id/eprint/1453.
67 'Resolution on Human Rights, Democracy and Development', *Bulletin of the European Communities* 24, no. 11 (1991): 122–3.
68 'Treaty on the European Union', Article 130v.
69 'Council Regulation (EC) No 3281/94 of 19 December 1994 Applying a Four-Year Scheme of Generalized Tariff Preferences (1995 to 1998) in Respect of Certain Industrial Products Originating in Developing Countries', https://eur-lex.europa.e u/legal-content/EN/TXT/?uri=CELEX%3A31994R3281&qid=1637866144104.

Lomé Convention) and that the disbursement of funds could be suspended in response to violations.[70]

EC/EU Action

In the new era of conditionality, progress in trade and cooperation agreements with eastern European countries (1989–90) was used to steer and control the pace of democratisation. For instance, the Community suspended negotiations with the Bulgarian government from May 1989 to March 1990 because the latter violated the Turkish minority's rights. It also frequently interrupted negotiations with the Romanian authorities as a punishment for the slow pace of reforms and frequent violence in the country.[71] After the collapse of the socialist regimes, and facing requests for membership, the EC polity agreed to prioritise deeper integration over enlargement for the near future. Yet it offered central and eastern European countries a series of programmes and agreements that would allow them to establish closer ties and ensure that their reforms would succeed. Indeed, the whole of the EC's new eastern policy was based on political conditionality, which has led to some recent accusations of imperialism.[72]

The Group of Seven summit in Paris on 14–16 July 1989 recognised aid as an appropriate instrument to facilitate economic reforms in former socialist countries and help them integrate into the world economy, and acknowledged the EC's special responsibility for the region. The EC's conditionality, though, also placed strong emphasis on democratisation. The Community's aid programme titled Poland and Hungary: Assistance for Restructuring Their Economies, approved in December 1989, was conceived to assist the reform process in Poland and Hungary; within a year it was extended to the other countries. The EC also offered each central and eastern European country a comprehensive association agreement, a so-called 'Europe agreement'. In August 1990, the Commission established that the agreement would be signed upon receipt of evidence of the country's commitment to five criteria: rule of law, human rights, a multiparty system, free and fair elections, and a market economy. The preamble of each Europe agreement identified EC membership as the final objective; the promise of entering the sought-after club of rich democratic European nations was a powerful

---

70 Urbanski, *The European Union*, p. 120.
71 J. Pinder, *The European Community and Eastern Europe* (London, Pinter, 1991), p. 33.
72 G. Morgan, 'Is the European Union Imperialist?', *Journal of European Public Policy* 27, no. 9 (2020): 1424–40.

inducement and a tool to control the regime transition in those countries – a hard power tool. The Community was also the key maker of the European Bank for Reconstruction and Development (EBRD), which was meant to promote private investments. Approved by the Strasbourg European Council in December 1989, the foundation of the EBRD was negotiated with the Group of Twenty-Four countries, the seven eastern European states, the Soviet Union, Cyprus and Malta, and it started operating in 1991. It was the first multilateral organisation obliged to grant loans according to political criteria: only countries implementing multiparty democracy, pluralism and market economics would be eligible for loans. Unsurprisingly, the Community and its member states held 51 per cent of the EBRD's capital.[73]

The EU also denied access to its market to convey disapproval. In 1994, the EU and Russia finalised the partnership and cooperation agreement, which would initiate crucial commercial relations and establish a framework for political consultations; an interim agreement would precede its entry into force. In response to the Kremlin's violent handling of the crisis in Chechnya in 1994–5, the EU postponed the signing of the interim agreement. Only on 17 July 1995 was it signed, to reward the Russian authorities for cooperation in Bosnia and Herzegovina and to induce an ending of the crisis in Chechnya.[74]

In accord with the 28 November 1991 resolution, the Community suspended aid to Sudan, Haiti, Togo, Zaire, Malawi and Nigeria. Even before the resolution was adopted, the Commission decided not to embark on the Lomé IV indicative programming exercise with Sudan due to human rights violations, which also meant freezing STABEX transfers. On 3 October 1991, EPC condemned the military coup carried out 3 days earlier against the democratically elected President Aristide in Haiti, called for his reinstatement and an immediate return to the rule of law and suspended EC development aid, including all Lomé IV financial and technical cooperation.[75] In December 1991, the Community suspended aid to Togo,

---

73 Smith, *The Making of EU Foreign Policy*, pp. 48–9, 80–2.
74 T. de Wilde d'Estmael, 'The European Commission and the Transition to the Common Foreign and Security Policy', in É. Bussière, P. Ludlow, F. Romero, D. Schlenker, V. Dujardin and A. Varsori (eds.), *The European Commission 1986–2000: History and Memories of an Institution* (Luxembourg, Publications Office of the European Union, 2019), pp. 599–601.
75 'Report on the Implementation of the Resolution of the Council and of the Member States Meeting in the Council on Human Rights, Democracy and Development, Adopted on 28 November 1991, Communication from the Commission to the Council and the European Parliament. SEC (92) 1915 final, 21 October 1992', http://aei.pitt.edu/5443.

where five attempted military coups had taken place within 4 months.[76] On 22 January 1992, the Community and its members suspended their aid programme to Zaire, with the exception of humanitarian aid, following the suspension of the Zairean National Conference. In May, the Community suspended new projects for Malawi, where the government had made no progress on human rights and good governance.[77] In June 1993, EPC decided that the Community and its member states would suspend development aid to Nigeria following the cancellation of presidential elections.[78]

Finally, moving beyond Africa, in 1996–7 the EU imposed diplomatic sanctions and an arms embargo on Burma/Myanmar over its lack of democracy and cut off its GSP tariff preferences because of the widespread use of forced labour in the country. Moreover, following the country's entry into the Association of Southeast Asian Nations (ASEAN), the EU refused Burma/Myanmar access to the EC–ASEAN cooperation agreement.[79]

Conclusion

This chapter has argued that the EC/EU showed increasing determination to play an international political role from the late 1960s onwards and did not act simply as a civilian power. While the promotion of multilateralism and international law was a stable element of its foreign policy, the EC/EU did not limit itself to pursuing civilian ends and using soft power tools. It is often argued that the EC preferred cooperation because it lacked (the capacity to flex) any military muscles. It should be noted that history offers plenty of examples in which the use of force by either superpower proved counterproductive or ended in failure. Rather than arising from weakness, the EC's policy preference for using carrots rather than sticks in East–West relations during the Cold War ensued from the awareness that only in a pan-European space for cooperation could the EC advance its economic and political influence. The EC/EU had diverse means to pressure several of its interlocutors into the desired behaviour.

The EC polity used carrots and sticks to change other countries' behaviour whenever it considered that its interests and goals required that this be

76 *Bulletin of the European Communities* 24, no. 12 (1991), https://op.europa.eu/s/u4xi.
77 'Report on the Implementation ... SEC (92) 1915 final'.
78 *Bulletin of the European Communities* 26, no. 7–8 (1993), https://op.europa.eu/s/u4xZ.
79 Hill and Smith (eds.), *European Foreign Policy*, pp. 437–40; ASEAN–EC Cooperation Agreement (1980), https://asean.org/cooperation-agreement-between-member-countries-of-asean-and-european-community-kuala-lumpur-7-march-1980.

done. This becomes even more visible when the perceptions of the countries at the receiving end are appraised. From refusal to compromise during negotiations (e.g., on the CSCE) to granting (privileged) access to its rich market, from withdrawal of preferences to suspension of aid and loans, the image of a multipolar player of hardball comes closer to describing how developing countries, socialist regimes and even the two superpowers often came to see the EC/EU. While this chapter is intended only to ascertain the EC polity's use of hard power and not its effectiveness, it is worth noticing some successes. The Soviets' opposition to the EC's eastern policy proved in vain; one by one, all of the socialist countries forged relations with the EC on the EC's terms. Eventually the Kremlin came to accept the Community's way of reorganising relations within the continent and, following the 1989 revolutions, the White House recognised the EC's special responsibility for shaping the region's future.

In terms of machinery, we can notice more continuity than change over the period under scrutiny. Reports and treaties, though taking steps towards closer coordination – especially between Community means and intergovernmental decision making – mostly consolidated practices that had previously been tried out. The Maastricht Treaty, which supplanted EPC with the CFSP, did not represent a turning point, as it maintained the intergovernmental nature of foreign policy coordination and the unanimity rule in its decision-making.

Conversely, a major change is visible in the use of conditionality from the late 1980s. For two decades, the EC's eastern policy did not reward socialist regimes for their internal reforms, but did so for their readiness to deal with the Community. Only in the Gorbachev era did the EC polity start to dole out loans and agreements to steer the process, turning to full use of conditionality in the 1990s. The early 1990s was also the moment when democracy, rule of law and respect for human rights were officially established as conditions for access to development aid. The few cases of suspension of disbursement of funds to African countries in the late 1970s due to gross human rights violations were meaningful examples of hard power, but not yet the tools of a new approach. Also in this respect, the Maastricht Treaty seems to have been not a turning point but rather a consolidation of a recently acquired boldness and determination to shape the political, social and economic features of other countries, regardless of the possibility of their becoming members.

Finally, it is here possible to present some considerations on the impact of enlargements. The process leading to southern enlargement in the 1980s specifically contributed to building the EC's identity as a democratising force and may have opened the road to fully espousing conditionality in all external relations agreements a few years later.[80] Certainly, all of the enlargements caused shifts in the trade patterns of outsider countries, making access to the EC market either necessary or more appealing; this was one of the main motivations for European socialist regimes to deal with the Community despite Moscow's pressure not to do so. By augmenting the economic weight of the Community, each enlargement added more power to influence third countries' attitudes via the use of economic carrots and sticks.

Recommended Reading

Ferrari, L. *Sometimes Speaking with a Single Voice: The European Community as an International Actor, 1969–1979* (Brussels, Peter Lang, 2016).

Krotz, U., K. K. Patel and F. Romero (eds.). *Europe's Cold War Relations: The EC towards a Global Role* (New York, NY, Bloomsbury Academic, 2019).

Lucarelli, S. 'Seen from the Outside: The State of the Art on the External Image of the EU', *Journal of European Integration* 36, no. 1 (2014): 1–16.

Romano, A. *The European Community and Eastern Europe in the Long 1970s: Challenging the Cold War Order in Europe* (London and New York, NY, Routledge, 2024).

Romano, A. and F. Romero (eds.). *European Socialist Regimes' Fateful Engagement with the West: National Strategy in the Long 1970s* (London and New York, NY, Routledge, 2020).

Smith, K. E. 'Beyond the Civilian Power EU Debate', *Politique Européenne* 17, no. 1 (2005): 63–82.

Urbanski, K. *The European Union and International Sanctions: A Model of Emerging Actorness* (Northampton, Edward Elgar, 2020).

---

80 E. De Angelis and E. Karamouzi, 'Enlargement and the Historical Origins of the European Community's Democratic Identity, 1961–1978', *Contemporary European History* 25, no. 3 (2016): 439–58.

16

European Integration, the Environment and Climate Change

KATJA BIEDENKOPF AND TOM DELREUX

Introduction

Originally a mere side-product of economic integration in the first decades of European integration, European Union (EU) environmental and climate policy has evolved towards a comprehensive and dense regulatory framework. A complex set of rules, standards and procedures to protect the environment is in force in all major subfields of environmental policy, including water and air pollution, nature conservation, chemicals and the fight against climate change. Moreover, in environmental and climate policy, the EU prides itself on being an international leader.

This chapter traces and analyses the development and growth of EU environmental policy. Rather than presenting a chronological overview of the history of environmental policy,[1] we identify and examine the main trends of continuity and change in this policy field's evolution over time. The aim is to help the reader understand the broader historical evolution

The writing of this chapter was supported by the Erasmus+ Programme of the European Union (project number 611773-EPP-1-2019-1-BE-EPPJMO-MODULE) and by the Fonds de la Recherche Scientifique (FNRS) (Grant T.0064.19).
1 See T. Delreux and S. Happaerts, *Environmental Policy and Politics in the European Union* (London, Palgrave Macmillan, 2016); P. M. Hildebrand, 'The European Community's Environmental Policy, 1957 to "1992": From Incidental Measures to an International Regime?', in A. Jordan (ed.), *Environmental Policy in the EU: Actors, Institutions and Processes*, 2nd ed. (London, Routledge, 2005), pp. 19–42; C. Knill and D. Liefferink, *Environmental Politics in the European Union* (Manchester, Manchester University Press, 2014); C. Knill and D. Liefferink, 'The Establishment of EU Environmental Policy', in A. Jordan and V. Gravey (eds.), *Environmental Policy in the EU: Actors, Institutions and Processes*, 4th ed. (London, Routledge, 2021), pp. 11–31; H. Selin and S. D. VanDeveer, *European Union and Environmental Governance* (London, Routledge, 2015); A. R. Zito, 'Task Expansion: A Theoretical Overview', *Environment and Planning C: Politics and Space* 17, no. 1 (1999): 19–35; A. R. Zito, C. Burns and A. Lenschow, 'Is the Trajectory of European Union Environmental Policy Less Certain?', *Environmental Politics* 28, no. 2 (2019): 187–207.

over a number of decades. As a consequence, this chapter cannot provide a comprehensive overview of all environmental policy areas. It rather illustrates the trends with some examples. The chapter relies on primary documents, the extensive literature on EU environmental policy and the findings of several research projects we conducted on this policy field. Although the EU has changed its name over time – from the European Economic Community (EEC) that was created by the 1957 Rome Treaty and the European Community (EC), which was established by the 1986 Single European Act (SEA) to the EU introduced by the 1992 Maastricht Treaty – for simplicity's sake we use 'EU' for the Union's entire history.

The chapter is structured in two main parts, focusing, first, on continuity and, secondly, on change over time. The following section presents four continuities, which shaped European environmental policy, driven by logics of path dependence: (1) the steady expansion of the environmental *acquis*; (2) the increasing level of environmental ambition; (3) the link with the economy, first as an instrument serving the establishment of the common market and later as an economic growth engine; and (4) the lack of significant effects of enlargement waves on the scope and ambition of EU environmental policy.

The next section of the chapter discusses four critical junctures in the history of EU environmental policy, which were the main landmarks of change: (1) the entry into force of the SEA, which established legal competences on the environment, enabling an evolution from policies mostly based on the common market legal basis to more comprehensive environmental policies; (2) the attention paid to climate policy since the late 1990s and the subsequent increasing level of politicisation of climate change; (3) the shift from rigid regulatory policy instruments to a mix of more flexible instruments; and (4) the increased attention for environmental and climate policy integration and the mainstreaming of sustainability concerns in other policy areas.

Continuity in EU Environmental and Climate Policy

Continuity in the context of EU environmental and climate policy mostly means a continuous (upward) trend rather than a stable state of affairs. The history of EU environmental policy is characterised by the continuous development of an expanding environmental *acquis*, an increasing level of environmental ambition and a growing link between environmental and economic governance. One additional continuity is the limited impact of the EU's various enlargement waves.

Expansion of the Environmental acquis

Since the adoption of the first regulatory measures at the European level related to environmental protection at the end of the 1950s, both the quantity and the scope of EU environmental policy have progressively expanded.[2] The growth in the *number* of directives and regulations dealing with the environment particularly started to intensify in the 1980s, leading to several hundred directives and regulations being in force today.[3] Also the *scope* of the environmental *acquis* has expanded. The first environment-related policies serving internal market purposes primarily dealt with the harmonisation of product standards (see below), but more and more environmental subfields have been covered by EU policies since the 1970s. Transboundary air pollution was one of the first traditional sectors of environmental policies addressed, but water, chemicals and biodiversity policies followed soon. The last major expansion took place at the end of the 1990s, when the EU started to adopt climate policies (see below).

The continuous expansion of the *acquis*, both in quantity and in scope, has led to a mature and fully fledged policy field and a dense regulatory framework, covering most environmental challenges at the EU level. The maturity of the policy field and its broad coverage of all major environmental subfields is also exemplified by the fact that since the mid 1990s the number of pieces of legislation that covered previously unregulated issues has started to decline, and since the mid 2000s the majority of adopted environmental legislation consists of legislative acts that amend existing legislation and no longer regulate new environmental issues.[4] Indeed, current environmental policy-making is characterised by a 'continual process of amendment and revision'.[5]

The growth of the quantity and scope of the environmental *acquis* is the result of the changes in the evolution of environmental policy that will be

---

2 A. Jordan, R. Brouwer and E. Noble, 'Innovative and Responsive? A Longitudinal Analysis of the Speed of EU Environmental Policy-Making 1967–1997', *Journal of European Public Policy* 6, no. 3 (1999): 376–98.

3 Delreux and Happaerts, *Environmental Policy and Politics*.

4 T. A. Börzel and A. Buzogány, 'Compliance with EU Environmental Law. The Iceberg Is Melting', *Environmental Politics* 28, no. 2 (2019): 315–41.

5 R. Axelrod, M. A. Schreurs and N. J. Vig, 'Environmental Policy Making in the European Union', in R. S. Axelrod and S. D. VanDeveer (eds.), *The Global Environment: Institutions, Law and Policy* (Washington, DC, Congressional Quarterly Press, 2011), pp. 213–38, 224.

discussed in the next section of this chapter: the creation of a legal basis in the treaty; the increasing awareness of and attention to climate policy; the development of new policy instruments that go beyond a regulatory 'command and control' approach; and growing attention to environmental policy integration and the interlinkages between the environment and other policy domains. The expansion of the environmental *acquis* until the mid 1980s is particularly remarkable as there was no legal basis in the treaty on environmental policy in that period. It is only with the entry into force of the SEA in 1987 that member states formally attributed competences on the environment to the European level (see below). Yet, even in the absence of a legal basis and formal competences, the quantity and scope of environmental policy grew. The growth of the environmental policy field was then driven by a number of political and societal developments.

First, environmental concerns had risen on the political agenda, not only in Europe but also in other Western countries. The dominant post-Second World War socio-economic model led to improvements in living standards and well-being, but the production and consumption patterns also had a harmful impact on the environment. The increasing awareness of environmental pollution meant that the environment progressively became a political issue. Secondly, environmental movements and civil society organisations, followed later by green political parties, were established, mobilising around this increasing awareness. The organisation and institutionalisation – both societally and politically – of environmental interests increased the politicisation of environmental issues. Thirdly, this dynamic was catalysed by a number of industrial accidents with harmful effects on the environment and human health, such as the 'Seveso disaster', where dioxin was released from a chemical manufacturing plant in northern Italy in 1976, killing animals and injuring humans. Fourthly, cooperation on environmental matters at the European level was paralleled by the start of international cooperation at the global level, with the 1972 United Nations (UN) Stockholm Conference being considered the starting point of global environmental governance.

These four driving forces not only contributed to the expansion of environmental policies in the EU, but also had similar effects on environmental policy development at the national level in western European and other industrialised countries. Yet, the expansion of the environmental *acquis* at the European level in the period when there was no explicit legal basis was also prompted by two EU-specific dynamics. First, environmental legislation was adopted on the basis of common market competences and a generous reading of the treaty. Case law established by the European Court of Justice confirmed that such a broad interpretation of common market provisions could be used as the legal basis for environmental legislation. Secondly, certain member states such as the Netherlands and West Germany played a key role as 'leaders' or 'pioneers' by uploading the environmental standards that they had already adopted at the domestic level to the European level.

Together with the expansion of the environmental *acquis*, also the EU's institutional architecture evolved. For instance, in 1973, a task force on 'Environment and Consumer Protection Service' was established within the Directorate General (DG) Industry of the European Commission, which subsequently became the separate DG Environment in 1981. In 1994, the European Environmental Agency started its work in support of EU environmental policy-making and implementation. In 2010, climate policy was spun off DG Environment's responsibilities and moved to a newly created DG Climate Action.

EU environmental policy has evolved through experimentation and revisions of legislation so as to improve its functioning. One example is the EU greenhouse gas (GHG) emissions trading system (ETS). In 2003, the EU adopted a first iteration of the ETS and started with a pilot phase. Since establishing a GHG ETS requires introducing a trading system as well as measurement, reporting and verification procedures, among other things, and since the EU ETS was a pioneering effort, it was necessary to start with a learning-by-doing phase from 2005 to 2007.[6] Phase two (2008–12) was based on the experience and data generated during the pilot phase. Phase three ran from 2013 to 2020 and phase four started in 2021. Over time, various revisions have improved the EU ETS and ratcheted up its level of ambition, a trend that has marked EU environmental policy more broadly, as described in the following section.

Increasing Level of Environmental Ambition

Broadly speaking, the level of ambition of the EU's environmental policy has increased over time. Notwithstanding some exceptional individual pieces of legislation in which specific targets were lowered, the evolution in most environmental subfields – water, air, biodiversity, chemicals, climate – points to a strengthening of environmental ambition. Hence, the history of EU environmental policy is characterised not only by an expansion in the

---

6 J. B. Skjærseth and J. Wettestad, 'Making the EU Emissions Trading System: The European Commission as an Entrepreneurial Epistemic Leader', *Global Environmental Change* 20, no. 2 (2010): 314–21.

quantity and scope of the *acquis*, but also by an intensification of the main objective of this policy field, namely environmental protection.

Whereas gradually rising levels of ambition were rather evident and uncontested until the early 2000s, the financial and economic crisis at the end of that decade, and particularly the austerity policies that were put in place by European institutions and national governments alike, raised questions about the robustness of environmental policies and about the political and societal desirability of maintaining high levels of environmental standards. However, despite the concern of policy-makers and environmental groups that environmental ambition would suffer from the crisis and austerity policies, they ultimately did not lead to fundamental changes in the trajectory of EU environmental policy.[7] Indeed, the risk of policy dismantling – namely cutting, diminishing or removing existing policies – did not materialise, and no evidence of scaling back of environmental standards was found.[8] Burns, Eckersley and Tobin conclude that 'the picture that emerges is not one of a crisis ridden Union intent upon rolling back its environmental ambitions, but of a surprisingly resilient environmental policy actor that in the face of enormous challenges managed to keep the show on the road'.[9]

However, although there were no significant reductions in environmental rules and standards as a result of the financial–economic crisis, the level of ambition of the environmental *acquis* rather stagnated in several subfields, as there was less appetite for new and ambitious environmental policies, particularly in the period 2010–13.[10] Yet, that stagnation was not only the result of the financial and economic crisis and the subsequent austerity policies, but also reflected pre-existing preferences for reducing administrative and regulatory burdens ('red tape'), as well as the fact that most environmental issues

---

7 P. Slominski, 'Energy and Climate Policy: Does the Competitiveness Narrative Prevail in Times of Crisis?', *Journal of European Integration* 38, no. 3 (2016): 343–57.
8 V. Gravey and B. Moore, 'Full Steam Ahead or Dead in the Water? European Union Environmental Policy after the Economic Crisis', in C. Burns, S. Sewerin and P. Tobin (eds.), *The Impact of the Economic Crisis on European Environment Policy* (Oxford, Oxford University Press, 2018), pp. 19–41; V. Gravey and A. J. Jordan, 'Policy Dismantling at EU Level: Reaching the Limits of "an Ever-Closer Ecological Union"?', *Public Administration* 98, no. 2 (2020): 349–62; Y. Steinebach and C. Knill, 'Still an Entrepreneur? The Changing Role of the European Commission in EU Environmental Policy-Making', *Journal of European Public Policy* 24, no. 3 (2017): 429–46.
9 C. Burns, P. Eckersley and P. Tobin, 'EU Environmental Policy in Times of Crisis', *Journal of European Public Policy* 27, no.1 (2020): 1–19, 3.
10 C. Burns and P. Tobin, 'The Limits of Ambitious Environmental Policy in Terms of Crisis', in C. Adelle, K. Biedenkopf and D. Torney (eds.), *European Union External Environmental Policy: Rules, Regulations and Governance beyond Borders* (London, Palgrave Macmillan, 2017), pp. 319–37.

were already regulated by EU policies and that the environmental *acquis* had become a rather mature policy field.[11] Nonetheless, through a systematic operationalisation and measurement of ambition of environmental policies, combining several indicators, Gravey and Moore find that, overall, the ambition of environmental policies on industrial regulation, air quality and climate grew between 1995 and 2016 and that 'despite strong changes in discourses and policy framing, [EU environmental policies] appear to have withstood the economic crisis fairly well'.[12]

The rising ambition level of environmental policies is, however, not necessarily reflected in an equally improving state of the environment. On the one hand, EU environmental policy makes a difference as it has contributed to an improvement of the quality of ecosystems and of European citizens' health and living standards. On the other hand, important challenges remain. Whereas the targets that the EU has set for itself usually sound rather ambitious, the actual policies needed to reach these targets are often only partly implemented. In other words, many environmental policies are characterised by a gap between the actual policies in force and the policies that would be required to achieve the targets. For instance, whereas the EU's targets on biodiversity and nature protection look ambitious, the prospect of meeting these objectives looks gloomy. This makes the European Environment Agency conclude that 'viewed against Europe's long term vision and policy targets, Europe is not making enough progress in addressing environmental challenges' and 'despite the successes, persistent problems remain and the outlook for Europe's environment in the coming decades is discouraging'.[13]

There is also an increasing awareness that addressing fundamental environmental challenges requires systemic thinking and change, with policy changes and even paradigm shifts going beyond the traditional environmental domain. The acknowledgement that environmental challenges are strongly intertwined with other societal systems, as well as the announcement by the European Commission that such systemic thinking will be converted into actual policies, are key aspects of the 2019 European Green Deal (see below), which has the potential to be a game-changer when it comes to achieving the much-needed environmental ambition.

11 Burns et al., 'EU Environmental Policy'; Gravey and Moore, 'Full Steam Ahead or Dead in the Water?'.

12 Gravey and Moore, 'Full Steam Ahead or Dead in the Water?', p. 37

13 European Environment Agency, *The European Environment – State and Outlook 2020: Knowledge for Transition to a Sustainable Europe*, p. 11, www.eea.europa.eu/soer/2020.

A related recurring theme in the history of EU environmental policy is the challenge of difficult implementation and non-compliance.[14] Next to the gap between the policies and the EU's ambitions, there exists also a gap between the adopted policies and the extent to which member states actually comply with them. The implementation record of environmental policy is historically among the weakest and most problematic ones of all EU policy areas.[15] Environmental policy is indeed among those domains with the highest numbers of cases of infringement. Yet, considering non-compliance in relative terms, namely by taking into account the growing number of environmental acts in force and EU enlargement (see below), non-compliance started to decline in the mid 1990s.[16] Moreover, since about 2010, awareness of the large number of incidents of non-compliance has meant that more attention is being paid to 'better implementation' in the adoption and revision of environmental legislation. This is becoming clear in the avoidance of 'red tape', member states pushing for more realistically achievable targets, the choice of more flexible policy instruments and regulatory concepts that give member states more leeway in domestic implementation (see below) and the Commission adopting a more antici-patory behaviour towards non-complying member states.

The Link with the Economy

EU environmental policy has been linked to economic integration and prosperity throughout its history. Yet, the nature of the link has evolved. In the first decades, environmental policy served the purpose of market integration. Since the early 2000s, the EU has increasingly seen and tried to harness environmental and climate protection and related innovation as an economic growth engine. This was part of the EU's response to the financial–economic and Covid-19 crises that required investments to spur economic recovery. In this process, the paradigm of ecological modernisation – which postulates that environmental efficiency and

14 E. Bondarouk and E. Mastenbroek, 'Reconsidering EU Compliance: Implementation Performance in the Field of Environmental Policy', *Environmental Policy and Governance* 28, no. 1 (2017): 15–27; A. Zhelyazkova and E. Thomann, 'Policy Implementation', in A. Jordan and V. Gravey (eds.), *Environmental Policy in the EU*, 4th ed. (London, Routledge, 2021), pp. 220–41.

15 Delreux and Happaerts, *Environmental Policy and Politics*; C. Knill, 'Implementation', in J. Richardson (ed.), *European Union: Power and Policy-Making* (New York, NY, Routledge, 1996), pp. 351–75.

16 Börzel and Buzogány, 'Compliance with EU Environmental Law'.

related innovation can generate economic growth[17] – has dominated the EU's rhetoric and approach.

In the 1950s and 1960s, environmental concerns did not play a noteworthy role. The first directives that could possibly be attributed to the category of environmental policy pertained to the protection of workers and the general public against dangers arising from ionising radiation, which were adopted on the basis of the European Atomic Energy Community Treaty. In 1970, Directive 70/157/EEC on the approximation of member state laws relating to the permissible sound level and the exhaust system of motor vehicles was adopted on the basis of Article 100 of the EEC Treaty. This article allowed the Council to adopt 'directives for the approximation of such legislative and administrative provisions of the Member States as have a direct incidence on the establishment or functioning of the Common Market'. Until the adoption of the SEA, Article 100 of the EEC Treaty served as the legal basis of almost every environment-related EU law, in most cases in conjunction with Article 235 of the EEC Treaty, which stipulated: 'If any action by the Community appears necessary to achieve, in the functioning of the Common Market, one of the aims of the Community in cases where this Treaty has not provided for the requisite powers of action, the Council [. . .] shall enact the appropriate provisions.' Since the 1980s, several regulations pertaining to environmental matters have been adopted on the basis of Article 235 that pertained to external trade, such as Regulation 348/81 EEC on common rules for imports of whales or other cetacean products.

After the SEA's entry into force in 1987, Article 100 of the EEC Treaty continued to serve as the legal basis for several pieces of environmental legislation. Yet, the newly introduced Article 130 s – which together with Article 130 r built the new legal basis for environmental legislation – served as the legal basis for more than half of the EU's legislative acts on the environment adopted at the time. This trend of parts of EU environmental legislation being based on the internal market and other parts on the environmental legal basis has continued ever since. Ensuring the functioning of the internal market has thus transcended the history of EU environmental policy. In the 2010s, another trend that marries economic and environmental policy gained prominence. This relates to the paradigm of ecological modernisation and the harnessing of environmental innovation to generate economic prosperity.

---

17 A. P. J. Mol and G. Spaargaren, 'Ecological Modernisation Theory in Debate: A Review', *Environmental Politics* 9, no. 1 (2000): 17–49.

The 2000 Lisbon Strategy that aimed to make the EU 'the most competitive and dynamic knowledge-based economy in the world' by 2010[18] still focused on the economy, innovation and social aspects, while the Europe 2020 Strategy that aimed at 'smart, sustainable, inclusive growth'[19] already included some elements of the ecological modernisation paradigm. It included the EU's climate goals for 2020 of reducing GHG emissions by 20 per cent, increasing the renewable energy share to 20 per cent and improving energy efficiency by 20 per cent. In 2011, the European Commission presented a roadmap to achieve a competitive low-carbon EU by 2050. The reduction target at the time was 80–95 per cent by 2050 compared with 1990 levels. It clearly outlined investment needs but also economic opportunities of the low-carbon transition. The roadmap highlights the benefits of low-carbon investments, including reduced dependence on imported fuels and creating added value in the EU. The rhetoric stresses the stimulation of new sources of economic growth, in line with the ecological modernisation paradigm, which means that economic growth as such is not questioned.

The Commission's 2019 European Green Deal (EGD) Communication[20] continues and further enshrines the strong vision that environmental, economic and social goals need to be combined. The EGD is described as 'a new growth strategy that aims to transform the EU into a fair and prosperous society, with a modern, resource-efficient and competitive economy where there are no net emissions of greenhouse gases in 2050 and where economic growth is decoupled from resource use'. Again, economic growth is not questioned, rather the simultaneous harnessing of environmental protection and the economy are part of the rhetoric. The targets set by the EGD are more ambitious than previous ones, aiming at climate neutrality by 2050 (see below). Thus economic integration and environmental protection have been intertwined.

The Limited Impact of Waves of Enlargement

Although the EU has grown from originally six to twenty-seven member states, its environmental policy and ambition have not been negatively affected by the larger number and growing diversity of member countries.

18 European Council, 'Presidency Conclusions', www.europarl.europa.eu/summits/li s1_en.htm.
19 European Commission, 'Europe 2020: A European Strategy for Smart. Sustainable and Inclusive Growth', https://ec.europa.eu/eu2020/pdf/COMPLET%20EN%20BARR OSO%20%20%20007%20-%20Europe%202020%20-%20EN%20version.pdf.
20 European Commission, 'A European Green Deal', https://commission.europa.eu/st rategy-and-policy/priorities-2019-2024/european-green-deal_en.

As described above, the ambition and scope of EU environmental and climate policy have steadily grown. The EU's first enlargement wave in 1973 brought in the United Kingdom, Ireland and Denmark. Since EU environmental policy was only in its infancy at that time, the enlargement had little influence on the policy's development. The 1981 accession of Greece and the 1986 inclusion of Spain and Portugal brought into the EU countries that faced some challenges with regard to implementing the EU environmental *acquis* but, overall, this southern enlargement did not dent the upward trend of more (ambitious) environmental policy adoption. The 1995 enlargement with Austria, Sweden and Finland added environmentally ambitious countries. Especially Sweden has often acted as a leader pushing for higher environmental protection at the EU level. While each of these enlargement waves added few countries at a time, the 2004, 2007 and 2013 enlargement wave almost doubled the number of EU member states. This changed the dynamics, but has not triggered a reversal of EU environmental policy ambition.

The central and eastern European counties that joined in 2004, 2007 and 2013 had started transitioning out of inefficient and polluting economic structures since the end of the Cold War. Their environmental policy was developed over the course of the accession process when they had to implement the EU's entire *acquis communautaire*. Since they were not known as environmentally progressive – rather the opposite – some analysts feared that this enlargement wave would slow down the rise of EU environmental and climate policy.[21] As elaborated below, this has not noticeably happened so far.[22] Yet, the politics, especially of climate change, have become more controversial within and among the member states.

While the adoption of relatively ambitious environmental and climate policy has not been obstructed by central and eastern European member states, they had an impact on the agenda and substance of EU climate and energy policy.[23] Energy security has become a more salient issue on the EU agenda, driven by central and eastern European member states' dependence on Russian gas imports and the related security concerns. Moreover,

21 T. König and T. Bräuninger, 'Accession and Reform of the European Union: A Game-Theoretical Analysis of Eastern Enlargement and the Constitutional Reform', *European Union Politics* 5, no. 4 (2004): 419–39, 432.

22 M. Braun, *Europeanization of Environmental Policy in the New Europe: Beyond Conditionality* (London, Routledge, 2014).

23 P. Bocquillon and T. Maltby, 'The More the Merrier? Assessing the Impact of Enlargement on EU Performance in Energy and Climate Change Policies', *East European Politics* 33, no. 1 (2017): 88–105.

solidarity among member states has become more salient. In climate policy, 🌢
equitably sharing the efforts of reducing GHG emissions has become
a central element that inter alia gave rise to financial support mechanisms
such as the Just Transition Fund, which supports the regions most affected by
the challenges of transitioning to climate neutrality. Yet, central and eastern
European member states do not act as a homogeneous group, and the
political dynamics within the EU are more complex and issue-specific. The
lack of a common position among central and eastern European member
states could explain why they have not impeded the adoption of relatively
ambitious EU climate objectives.[24] Over time, some of the central and
eastern European countries have become more assertive. Especially Poland
has on numerous occasions objected or been reluctant to consent to EU
climate policy.[25]

In 2020, for the first time in the EU's history, a member state quit the EU.
The United Kingdom was, generally speaking, a proponent of ambitious
environmental – and in particular climate – policies and objectives, although
on a few topics such as renewables it advocated for lower standards. While
it is too early to evaluate the impact of Brexit, it is fair to say that the EU has
lost a climate-ambitious member state, together with the corresponding
diplomatic capabilities and experience.[26]

Change in EU Environmental and Climate Policy

Change in EU environmental and climate policy tends to consist of events
that built up over a few years or even longer and then were manifested in
a key act such as the revision of the EU Treaties or a decision by the European
Council or Commission. They respond to changing contexts such as the
rising urgency of addressing climate change. EU environmental history is
characterised by the seminal changes of providing an explicit legal basis for
environmental policy with the adoption of the SEA, the rising political
salience of climate policy, the broadened set of policy instruments providing
more flexible policy designs and mixes, and the shift towards environmental
and climate policy integration into other policy areas.

24 S. Ćetković and A. Buzogány, 'The Political Economy of EU Climate and Energy
Policies in Central and Eastern Europe Revisited: Shifting Coalitions and Prospects for
Clean Energy Transitions', *Politics and Governance* 7, no. 1 (2019): 124–38.

25 Bocquillon and Maltby, 'The More the Merrier?'; K. Biedenkopf, 'Polish Climate Policy
Narratives: Uniqueness, Alternative Pathways and Nascent Polarisation', *Politics and
Governance* 9, no. 3 (2021): 391–400.

26 Burns and Tobin, 'The Limits of Ambitious Environmental Policy', pp. 328–9.

The SEA and the Legal Basis

Legal competences on environmental issues were attributed to the EU only in 1987 with the entry into force of the SEA, which for the first time granted legal powers to adopt environmental protection measures. The 1957 Treaty of Rome did not include a legal basis for environmental policy. Yet, as discussed below, the absence of legal competences did not prevent the EEC from adopting legislation on environmental matters in the period 1957–87. The *acquis* that was adopted in the three decades before the SEA's entry into force was based on a generous reading of common market provisions, confirmed by case law by the Court of Justice. The attribution of environmental competences facilitated the evolution of European environmental policy from policies mainly related to product standards to a set of more comprehensive environmental policies that were no longer necessarily related to market integration. Although the evolution towards a broader and more comprehensive environmental policy had already started before the SEA's entry into force, the SEA did not merely codify an existing situation but also boosted the expansion of EU environmental policy.

Although the *legal* authorisation to act on environmental issues was delegated by the member states to the European level only in the SEA, member states had already in the early 1970s *politically* mandated the European institutions to conduct more comprehensive action on environmental protection. At the Paris Summit of October 1972, a meeting of the heads of state and government of the member states, the leaders 'emphasized the importance of a Community environmental policy. To this end they invited the Community Institutions to establish, before 31 July, 1973, a programme of action accompanied by a precise timetable.'[27] Given the absence of specific treaty provisions, this statement – adopted at the highest political level – can be considered as the first de facto authorisation by member states for European institutions to take action in the environmental field that is not necessarily linked to the common market. In April 1973, the Commission published its 'programme of action' in response to the Paris Summit's call.[28] It included a description of the actions the Commission intended to undertake, as well as references to some key principles that would later become cornerstones of EU environmental law, such as the

27 European Communities, 'Statement from the Paris Summit', www.cvce.eu/content/publication/1999/1/1/b1dd3d57-5f31-4796-85c3-cfd2210d6901/publishable_en.pdf.
28 Commission of the European Communities, 'Programme of Action (ECSC, Euratom, EEC) on the Environment, 1973–1976', https://cordis.europa.eu/programme/id/ENV-ENVAP-1C.

'polluter pays' principle. It turned out to be the first Environment Action Programme, which was from then onwards succeeded by a new programme every 7 years, laying out the priorities of European environmental policy for that period.

One of the rationales underlying the treaty modifications in the SEA was to progressively establish an internal market by 1992. As an internal market is above all an organised – and thus a regulated – market, that ambition required the EU to take action in a series of regulatory policy areas, such as environmental policy. In that sense, environmental policy was indeed 'a significant component of the single market agenda'.[29] It is in that context that a separate article on the environment was added to the treaties and that legal competences in this field were established by the SEA. This legally codified the political dynamic towards a more comprehensive environmental policy that was set in motion at the 1972 Paris Summit. The SEA not only provided an impetus to a further expansion of the environmental *acquis*, but also led to a further institutionalisation of the environmental policy field. Not only was the Commission's Directorate General (DG) Environment – which was established as a separate DG only in 1981 – gradually strengthened or did the importance of the European Parliament's Committee on Environment, Public Health and Food Safety grow, but also the European Environment Agency – tasked with gathering information on Europe's state of the environment – was created and the EU increasingly started to act as a single negotiation bloc in international environmental negotiations.[30]

The subsequent treaty amendments (Maastricht, Amsterdam, Nice and Lisbon) did not bring major *substantive* changes in the field of environmental policy. However, the introduction of the co-decision legislative procedure by the Maastricht Treaty (i.e., the 'ordinary legislative procedure' since Lisbon) had an important *procedural* impact on environmental policy-making. With a few notable exceptions, especially on environmental taxes and on policies affecting member states' choices regarding their national energy mix, most environmental legislation is nowadays adopted via the ordinary legislative procedure, which implies that the Council and the European Parliament have to agree upon the same version of the legislative act and that qualified majority voting is the decision-making rule in the Council. Overall, the SEA can be seen as a major change in EU environmental policy since it

29 Burns et al., 'EU Environmental Policy', 2.
30 T. Delreux, *The EU as International Environmental Negotiator* (London, Routledge, 2016).

provided an explicit legal basis, paving the way for environmental policy expansion. Other treaties heralded smaller changes.

Climate Change on the Political Agenda

Although today climate change is undoubtedly the most important and politicised issue on the EU's environmental agenda, it appeared only in the 1990s – at a time when policies on other environmental subfields such as water, air, biodiversity and chemicals were already in a rather developed stage.[31] EU-level policy development on climate change started with a call for action in this field by various EU institutions. In 1986, the European Parliament adopted a resolution, followed by a Commission Communication in 1988 and European Council Conclusions in 1990, urging that climate change should be addressed.[32] Non-legally binding in nature, these three documents called for stabilisation of GHG emissions at 1990 levels by 2000, but did not specify how that target should be reached and which policy instruments should be put in place.

These calls for action were followed by the adoption of several concrete policies in the first half of the 1990s. First, a number of traditional regulatory policies, albeit limited in scope, were adopted, for instance on technical standards for the energy efficiency of household appliances. The Commission applied the approach with which it was most familiar in other environmental subfields, namely regulation and standard setting.[33] Secondly, the Commission refrained from proposing binding rules on CO_2 emissions from cars, instead negotiating voluntary agreements with car manufacturers. The latter pledged to reduce emissions by 25 per cent, in return for a commitment by the Commission to refrain from proposing binding legislation. This approach

---

31 S. Oberthür and M. Pallemaerts, 'The EU's Internal and External Climate Policies: An Historical Overview', in S. Oberthür and M. Pallemaerts (eds.), *The New Climate Policies of the European Union: Internal Legislation and Climate Diplomacy* (Brussels, VUB Press, 2010), pp. 27–63.

32 European Parliament, 'Resolution on the Measures to Counteract the Rising Concentration of Carbon Dioxide in the Atmosphere (the "Greenhouse" Effect)' (1986), https://eur-lex.europa.eu/legal-content/EN/TXT/?uri=OJ:C:1986:255:TOC; European Commission, 'Communication to the Council. The Greenhouse Effect and the Community. Commission Work Programme concerning the Evaluation of Policy Options to Deal with the "Greenhouse" Effect' (1988), https://op.europa.eu/en/publi cation-detail/-/publication/0d100c41-1ec7-11e7-8932-01aa75ed71a1/language-en/for mat-PDF/source-search; European Council, 'Annex II: The Environmental Imperative. Declaration by the European Council' (1990), www.consilium.europa.e u/media/20562/1990_june_-_dublin__eng_.pdf.

33 A. Jordan, H. van Asselt, F. Berkhout, D. Huitema and T. Rayner, 'Understanding the Paradoxes of Multi-level Governing: Climate Change Policy in the European Union', *Global Environmental Politics* 12, no. 2 (2012): 43–66.

turned out to be largely ineffective, and binding legislation on emissions from cars was ultimately adopted in 2007. Thirdly, leaving the path of the regulatory policy approach, the Commission proposed an EU-wide carbon tax in the 1990s, yet that proposal was contested by the member states and it failed in the Council, where unanimity was required.

The main breakthrough in the development of EU climate policies took place at the end of the 1990s and early 2000s. It was driven by the adoption of the Kyoto Protocol at the international level. As the EU considered the 1997 Kyoto Protocol a diplomatic success of its external policies and aimed to corroborate its leadership role in international climate politics, delivering on its Kyoto commitments – reducing GHG emissions in the EU as a whole by 8 per cent by 2012 compared with 1990 levels – became an important incentive for the expansion of climate policies. At the EU level, the Kyoto Protocol was implemented through three sets of policies. First, in the 1998 Burden Sharing Agreement, the EU's joint 8 per cent target was distributed among the member states in a differentiated way so that each of the member states had its national emission reduction target, with richer member states having more stringent targets than poorer member states. Secondly, in 2003, the EU adopted what would become a cornerstone of its climate policies, the Emission Trading System (ETS), which establishes a market in which large-scale industrial installations and electricity utilities buy, sell and sometimes receive gratis allowances to emit GHGs (see below).[34] Thirdly, alongside the market-based instrument of the ETS, several other regulatory instruments were adopted, such as legislation on the energy performance of buildings, on biofuels and on fluorinated gases.

Developments in international climate policy continued to drive intra-EU climate policy. In the second half of the 2000s, international discussions focused on the so-called 'post-2012' climate regime, which was to succeed the Kyoto Protocol. The EU continued to aspire to play a leadership role in these negotiations. It therefore applied a 'leading by example' strategy. The European Council endorsed the 2020 climate and energy package with internal objectives on GHG emissions, energy efficiency and renewable energy to be achieved by 2020. Moreover, these ambitions were implemented in 2008 through a package of several pieces of legislation on a broad range of climate-related issues. This not only reinforced the EU's

---

34 J. Wettestad and T. Jevnaker, *Rescuing EU Emissions Trading: The Climate Policy Flagship* (London, Palgrave Macmillan, 2015).

climate *acquis*, but was also intended to show the EU's international partners that the EU was serious about achieving the announced objectives.

The 2009 UN climate conference in Copenhagen was nonetheless a major failure for the EU, as it was sidelined in the endgame of the negotiations and the outcome of the conference did not correspond to the EU's preferences. Together with the financial and economic crisis, which required that political attention be mainly concentrated on macroeconomic policies, the restraint in international climate politics diminished the importance of climate policies on the EU's political agenda. Yet, a new impetus came again from the international level, where negotiations on a new international climate regime resumed with the aim of adopting a new international climate treaty in Paris in 2015. On the one hand, the EU's approach to the negotiations on the Paris Agreement was similar to the way the EU had approached the negotiations in Copenhagen 6 years before. In 2014, the European Council adopted new objectives on emission reduction, energy efficiency and renewables, to be achieved by 2030. This set of objectives was again followed by the adoption of an implementation package of new and updated legislation. On the other hand, the EU had also learned lessons from its failure in Copenhagen, and it approached the negotiations not only with leadership ambitions, but also with more attention to coalition-building.[35] This ultimately contributed to the EU being rather successful in Paris and to a Paris Agreement that to a large extent corresponded to the EU's preferences.[36] The EU's more 'pragmatic' approach to international negotiations since the early 2010s is not limited to international climate negotiations, but is an evolution in the EU's external environmental diplomacy more broadly.[37]

The adoption of the Paris Agreement served as a catalyst for further developments in the EU's internal climate policy framework.[38] The post-Paris momentum, combined with an increasing salience of, and public attention to, the climate urgency, enabled considerable steps forward in the EU's climate *acquis*, with more ambitious policies including the ETS, national

35 K. Bäckstrand and O. Elgström, 'The EU's Role in Climate Change Negotiations: From Leader to "Leadiator"', *Journal of European Public Policy* 20, no. 10 (2013): 1369–86.

36 S. Oberthür and L. Groen, 'Explaining Goal Achievement in International Negotiations: The EU and the Paris Agreement on Climate Change', *Journal of European Public Policy* 25, no. 5 (2018): 708–27.

37 S. Schunz, 'The European Union's Environmental Foreign Policy: From Planning to a Strategy?', *International Politics* 56 (2019): 339–58.

38 J. Delbeke and P. Vis (eds.), *EU Climate Policy Explained* (London and New York, NY, Routledge, 2015); T. Delreux and F. Ohler, 'Climate Policy in European Union Politics', in F. Laursen (ed.), *The Oxford Encyclopedia of European Union Politics* (Oxford, Oxford University Press, 2019), online, unpaginated.

targets to be achieved in non-ETS sectors and strengthened regulatory frameworks on standard-setting. The Energy Union (under the Juncker Commission) and ultimately also the European Green Deal (under the von der Leyen Commission) were overarching strategies to link climate objectives to other policy fields and systemic change (see below).[39]

The rise of climate change on the political agenda leads to three final observations regarding this change in the history of EU environmental policy. First, internal and external EU climate policies are strongly intertwined. Major international milestones, such as the adoption of the Kyoto Protocol and the Paris Agreement, have not only incentivised a broader and more ambitious internal climate *acquis*, but also facilitated and legitimised changes in the governance structure of EU climate policy. For instance, the bottom-up and rather 'soft' governance approach of national climate plans that forms the basis of the Paris Agreement inspired the governance structure developed by the EU to implement its Paris commitments domestically, in which member states are required to submit their 'Integrated National Energy and Climate Plans' to the Commission, which then monitors the progress.[40] Secondly, climate change has quickly become the most politicised and salient issue in the environmental domain – and even beyond (see below). One of the manifestations of the high level of politicisation is the increased role of the European Council in EU climate policies.[41] Although the heads of state and government do not play a formal role in the legislative policy-making process, major steps in the development of climate policies can no longer be taken without the de facto consent of the European Council. Thirdly, the increased attention to climate change has led to its domination of the EU's environmental agenda. Although there are clear links between climate change and more traditional environmental subfields such as water or biodiversity policy, the high attention to climate policies might have come at the expense of decreased attention to questions of

39 C. Dupont, S. Oberthür and I. von Homeyer, 'The Covid-19 Crisis: A Critical Juncture for EU Climate Policy Development?', *Journal of European Integration* 42, no. 8 (2020): 1095–110.
40 K. Kulovesi and S. Oberthür, 'Assessing the EU's 2030 Climate and Energy Policy Framework: Incremental Change toward Radical Transformation?', *Review of European, Comparative & International Law* 29, no. 2 (2020): 151–66.
41 R. K. W. Wurzel, 'The Council, European Council and Member States', in Jordan and Gravey (eds.), *Environmental Policy in the EU*, pp. 75–93; R. K. W. Wurzel, D. Liefferink and M. Di Lullo, 'The European Council, the Council and the Member States: Changing Environmental Leadership Dynamics in the European Union', in A. R. Zito, C. Burns and A. Lenschow (eds.), *The Future of European Union Environmental Politics and Policy* (London, Routledge, 2020), pp. 62–85.

pollution and environmental protection and the equally urgent challenges in these areas in Europe and the world more widely.

More Flexibility

A third change that marks EU environmental and climate policy is the growing variety of policy instruments used to ensure environmental protection. Traditionally, EU environmental policy relied on command-and-control instruments, for example, setting binding quality targets for drinking water. In the 1990s, the EU began to broaden the set of policy instruments by adopting a few information-based instruments such as the 1992 Regulation establishing a European eco-label award scheme. In the 2000s, the EU additionally started using framework directives with, for example, the adoption of the 2000 Water Framework Directive. Roughly at the same time, the EU also began using market-based instruments, most notably the ETS that was adopted in 2003. Governing by goals has become a defining feature of EU climate policy with the 20–20–20 targets by 2020 mentioned above and more recent climate and energy targets for the years 2030 and 2050. Overall, the variety of policy instruments expanded, but this should not distract from the fact that the main approach remains regulatory command-and-control policies.

Information-based instruments aim to enable consumers and other actors to take informed decisions and shift demand. Probably the most prominent EU-level application is the eco-label, an EU-wide label that is awarded to products and services that meet certain criteria, which aim to ensure that they are environmentally friendly and adhere to circular economy principles. Companies are not obliged to adhere to the criteria and can choose not to apply for a label. The eco-label rather aims to highlight the best-performing products and services. Consumer demand is meant to steer production into a more sustainable direction. Rather than being the only instrument regulating the covered sectors, the EU uses information-based instruments to complement regulatory command-and-control instruments, which provide a baseline of environmental protection to be guaranteed by every actor.

Since 2000, the EU has used several framework directives that provide more flexibility for achieving the defined objectives. An illustrative example of this change is the Water Framework Directive. Rivers and lakes had already been regulated by command-and-control instruments since 1975, for example, setting standards for those rivers and lakes from which drinking water was taken. Over time, additional legislation was added, setting different quality standards and pollution control measures. Recognising that a more holistic approach was necessary, EU law-makers adopted the Water Framework Directive in 2000. It sets several objectives and requires the submission of river basin management plans that can involve several member states and actions. The Water Framework Directive aims to coordinate the application of different command-and-control directives such as the Urban Waste Water Treatment Directive and the Nitrates Directive. To a significant extent, this governance approach is modelled on the EU's open method of coordination, in which the member states jointly set objectives, and then each member state adopts measures to achieve these objectives, and reports on its achievements to the Commission, which takes stock of all accomplishments. If necessary, the joint objectives are revised and the cycle starts again. Variants of this flexible approach can be found not only in water governance but also in climate and energy governance as described below and other policy areas. While they have changed EU environmental and climate policy, command-and-control legislation approaches outnumber framework and target-setting approaches. This is, however, not surprising, since framework directives are overarching approaches, often bringing together numerous traditional legislative acts.

Apart from the EU ETS, elaborate market-based instruments are not frequently used at the EU level. Nonetheless, the EU ETS is significant, since it covers more than 40 per cent of the EU's GHG emissions. It is a single directive but with expansive coverage, whereas the other GHG emissions that stem from the so-called non-ETS sectors are covered by a plethora of measures. The Effort Sharing Regulation is an overarching piece of legislation covering all non-ETS sectors, but it is accompanied at the EU level by additional measures such as directives on renewable energy and energy efficiency.

A clear change to more flexible approaches in terms of information, framework, and market-based instruments in the 1990s and early 2000s is noticeable in EU environmental policy. Regulatory command-and-control instruments, however, are still more numerous than the flexible instruments. The flexible policy instruments tend to complement the traditional legislative acts by, for example, offering the opportunity to showcase higher levels of environmental ambition or providing an overarching layer on top of command-and-control instruments to ensure their consistent implementation.

Environmental and Climate Policy Integration

Over the first decades of EU integration, environmental policy developed into a separate policy area in its own right (see above). Initially, it often was considered an add-on that completed the common market, reducing non-tariff barriers to trade. In the 1980s, the fourth Environmental Action Programme initiated a change in this perception. It proposed an integrated approach looking at entire sectors and production processes with the aim of making them more efficient in terms of energy and material use but also pollution control. This can be seen as a shift towards sustainable development as the reference point[42] that led to an EU commitment to *environmental policy integration*. In 1998, the European Council adopted in Cardiff a requirement for the Council of the EU to integrate environmental considerations in other policy areas, launching the Cardiff process, which however faded away over time. With the rise of climate policy's political salience, *climate policy integration* has progressed faster and is more visible than environmental policy integration. Yet, the European Green Deal attempts to take integration a step further and proposes a more holistic approach.

Environmental policy integration describes the systematic inclusion of environmental considerations into other policy areas so as to achieve sustainable development. It has been included as a principle of EU environmental law in the EU's treaties since the SEA. Article 130 r(2) stated: 'Environmental protection requirements shall be a component of the Community's other policies.' Despite this early and clear commitment, environmental policy integration has resulted in a mix of promising changes and lack of implementation. On the one hand, there have been noteworthy institutional changes aiming to ensure policy integration through processes such as inter-service consultations among different DGs of the European Commission and restructured portfolios of European Commissioners. The then-European Commission President Jean-Claude Juncker introduced project teams and assigned various vice-presidents broad responsibilities that grouped multiple Commissioner portfolios into thematic teams. Commission President Ursula von der Leyen continued this structure in a slightly revised variant. Procedurally, policy integration has thus been translated into somewhat new structures that led to more effective horizontal coordination.[43] Also, clear changes have been made in some policy content, for example in the EU budget. The EU included for the first time in its 2014–20 Multiannual Financial Framework the commitment to make at least 20 per cent of its

---

42 C. Hey, 'EU Environmental Policies: A Short History of the Policy Strategies', in S. Scheur (ed.), *EU Environmental Policy Handbook*, pp. 17–30, 21, www.for.gov.bc.ca/h fd/library/documents/bib96347.pdf.

43 A. Bürgin, 'Intra- and Inter-institutional Leadership of the European Commission President: An Assessment of Juncker's Organizational Reforms', *Journal of Common Market Studies* 56, no. 4 (2018): 837–53.

expenditure climate-related. In the 2021–7 Multiannual Financial Framework this was increased to 30 per cent. This example illustrates, however, also that climate policy integration has become more prominent and superseded environmental policy integration.

On the other hand, although the shift towards policy integration was a clear paradigm change in the history of environmental and climate policy, its implementation has lagged behind the discourse. For example, the 'greening' of the Common Agricultural Policy (CAP) has been criticised for falling short of its aspirations to protect biodiversity and the climate. The revised CAP that is being implemented as from 1 January 2023 allocates at least 25 per cent of direct EU payments to environmentally friendly initiatives such as organic farming, but non-governmental organisations have criticised the fact that large parts of the member states' plans are likely not to achieve their stated environmental objectives.[44] When measuring environmental policy integration against the benchmark of generating a significant impact in terms of environmental protection, the EU's track record is less impressive than its rhetoric.

The 2019 European Green Deal represents a new level of political ambition to policy integration. It integrates economic, societal and ecological objectives and policies to a greater extent than previous strategies.[45] It aims 'to transform the EU into a fair and prosperous society, with a modern resource-efficient and competitive economy'.[46] It tries to deviate from a sectoral approach and focuses instead on challenges and transformations. The translation of the European Green Deal into concrete measures and actions is still in progress, and it remains to be seen to what extent the EU succeeds in better integrating policies to achieve sustainability.

Conclusion

Since the 1950s, EU environmental policy has changed tremendously. It did not even exist initially and was not included in the founding treaties. Over time, it has morphed into a strong policy area in which the EU strives to lead internally as well as internationally. While this stark contrast between the inception of European integration and today suggests drastic change, EU

44 WWF, EEB and BirdLife International, 'Will CAP Eco-schemes Be Worth Their Name? An Assessment of Draft Eco-schemes Proposed by Member States', www.wwf.eu/?531 2391/Joint-NGO-assessment-Will-CAP-eco-schemes-be-worth-their-name.
45 C. Dupont and A. Jordan, 'Policy Integration', in Jordan and Gravey (eds.), *Environmental Policy in the EU*, pp. 203–19.
46 European Commission, *A European Green Deal*, p. 2.

environmental policy actually is also characterised by four steady trends of continuity: the continuous expansion of the environmental *acquis*, the growing level of environmental ambition, the link with the economy and the limited impact of EU enlargement. These continuities do not equal an unchanged EU environmental policy; instead they describe long-term trends that have evolved in the same (upwards) direction over decades. EU environmental policy has, however, also been changed at some critical junctures: the adoption of the SEA, providing an explicit legal basis; the rise of climate policy to trump environmental policy in terms of political priority; the use of more varied flexible policy instruments; and the integration of environmental and climate concerns into other policy areas. These changes cannot be pinpointed to one specific day or even year since they built up before leading to monumental acts such as the adoption of the SEA. They nonetheless can be seen as turning points changing the nature and course of EU environmental policy. Thus, the interplay between the continuities and change can provide an overview of the historical evolution of EU environmental policy.

Some of the trends seem to be near to reaching a stage of maturity, whereas others are more likely to continue. The steady expansion of the environmental *acquis* is a trend that seems to have reached a certain degree of saturation. EU environmental policy covers all relevant areas and sectors, which has led to a growing number of revisions of existing laws instead of the adoption of completely new ones. The growing level of ambition received a new boost with the 2019 European Green Deal and seems to be a continuing trend. Similarly, the link between the economy and the environment has been strengthened by the European Green Deal and is likely to continue. The jury is still out on the long-term effect of EU enlargement. The initial decade after enlarging the EU with central and eastern European countries has not been marked by a significant impact on the other three continuity trends. Yet, especially Poland but also some other member states have developed a consistent track record of initially opposing ambitious EU climate policy. So far, they have come around in the end – often as a result of some sweetening of the deal in terms of financial transfers and exceptions.

The four changes have solidified EU environmental policy and somewhat changed its course. They constitute a change from previous situations and created new trends that are likely to continue for the foreseeable future. The European Green Deal has the potential to provide impetus for new change towards a new level of integrated policy and moving towards sustainability policy instead of distinct environmental, societal and economic policy. Future historians will need to judge whether this potential has been realised.

Recommended Reading

Adelle, C., K. Biedenkopf and D. Torney (eds.). *European Union External Environmental Policy: Rules, Regulation and Governance beyond Borders* (London, Palgrave Macmillan, 2018).

Burns, C., P. Eckersley and P. Tobin. 'EU Environmental Policy in Times of Crisis', *Journal of European Public Policy* 27, no. 1 (2020): 1–19.

Delreux, T. and S. Happaerts. *Environmental Policy and Politics in the European Union* (London, Palgrave Macmillan, 2016).

Jordan, A. and V. Gravey (eds.). *Environmental Policy in the EU: Actors, Institutions and Processes*, 4th ed. (Abingdon, Routledge, 2021).

Zito, A. R., C. Burns and A. Lenschow. 'Is the Trajectory of European Union Environmental Policy Less Certain?', *Environmental Politics* 28, no. 2 (2019): 187–207.

17

The Space Policy of the European Union

EMMANUEL SIGALAS

Introduction

The European Union's (EU's) space policy (EUSP) is one of the more interesting EU policy areas, even though it is one of the newer and lesser known ones. Officially, there is no EUSP, but rather a European Space Policy (ESP). Space became one of the EU's competence areas in 2009, when the Treaty on the Functioning of the EU (TFEU), also known as the Lisbon Treaty, was ratified. Satellite navigation and positioning have security dimensions and it is odd, to say the least, that the EU owns Galileo, a Global Navigation Satellite System (GNSS) comparable to the better-known Global Positioning System (GPS) owned by the US government.

The current chapter demonstrates that the birth and growth of the EUSP is a typical case of European integration going deeper. Nonetheless, the EU studies literature has largely ignored the EUSP. As a result, relatively little is known not only about the essentials of the EUSP, such as its main components and its origins, but also about the insights it can offer in relation to the European integration theories. This chapter aims to make a contribution in both respects. Rather than offering a typical history in the sense of merely narrating a sequence of events, the chapter tries to invest the development of the EUSP with meaning by relating it to neo-functionalism.

While the European Commission often uses the terms EUSP and ESP interchangeably, when scholars refer to the ESP, they often mean space policy at the European level, which includes the EU space programmes (what I call here the EUSP) but can go beyond them.[1] Since many of the

---

1 A. Kolovos, 'Why Europe Needs Space as Part of Its Security and Defence Policy', *Space Policy* 18 (2002): 257–61; K. Suzuki, *Policy Logics and Institutions of European Space*

European-level space initiatives started at the European Space Agency (ESA) or its preceding organisations, ELDO (European Launcher Development Organisation) and ESRO (European Space Research Organisation), the history of the ESP is to a large extent the history of the ESA (and ELDO and ESRO). However, the ESA (founded in 1975) is not an EU agency, but an independent international organisation, intergovernmental in its structure, with its own history.[2] Although all EU member states are in some form of cooperation with the ESA, only nineteen EU countries are full ESA members. Latvia and Slovenia are associate ESA members, while Bulgaria, Croatia, Cyprus, Lithuania, Malta and Slovakia have only cooperation agreements. Three more countries, Norway, Switzerland and the United Kingdom (UK), are ESA members, but not members of the EU. Finally, Canada, despite not being a European country, has a cooperation agreement with the ESA and a seat on its council. Thus, the full history of the ESP is beyond the scope of the present chapter. Instead, the chapter examines only the part of the ESP which has a clear EU imprint.

Drawing mainly on official EU documents from the late 1970s onwards, the analysis examines three aspects of the EUSP: (1) its current status and state of play, (2) its origins and (3) the milestones in its development that led to space being included in the Lisbon Treaty. Since the objective of the chapter is to provide a historical account that can relate to neo-functionalism, the focus is less on the technical details of the space programme and more on the official reasoning behind the birth and development of the EUSP. Relatively more attention is paid to Galileo, the biggest and most important EU space programme, while the relationship between the ESA and the EU deserves a separate study of its own.[3]

The next two sections look at the current state of the EUSP and its beginning. Following that, the chapter looks at the main developments in between. In the concluding section, I summarise the main findings and argue that neo-functionalism is a useful theory for explaining the development of the EUSP.

Collaboration (Aldershot, Ashgate, 2003); J. Krige, *Fifty Years of European Cooperation in Space* (Paris, Éditions Beauchesne, 2014).

2 For the history of the ESP as a whole, see Suzuki, *Policy Logics and Institutions of European Space Collaboration*; Krige, *Fifty Years of European Cooperation in Space*.

3 For more on this topic, see T. C. Hoerber, 'The European Space Agency and the European Union: The Next Step on the Road to the Stars', *Journal of Contemporary European Research* 5 (2009): 405–14; Krige *Fifty Years of European Cooperation in Space*.

Is There an EUSP?

At the time of writing, the latest EUSP document is the regulation 'establishing the space programme of the Union and the European Union Agency for the Space Programme'[4]. According to the Commission's press release,

> The Space Programme that the Commission proposes for 2021–2027 aims to ensure that the EU remains a global leader in the space domain. [...] It will consolidate all space-related activities of the EU into a single Regulation, namely:
>
> • Satellite navigation systems, with a budget of €9.7 billion: Galileo, Europe's own global satellite navigation system, provides accurate and reliable positioning and timing information [...]. The European Geostationary Navigation Overlay Service (EGNOS) provides 'safety of life' navigation services [...]. All services provided by EGNOS are already fully operational and the number of users is growing (already 350 airports using it). [...]
>
> • Earth observation, with a budget of €5.8 billion: Copernicus, a leading provider of Earth observation [...] covers six thematic areas: land monitoring, marine monitoring, atmosphere monitoring, climate change, emergency management response and security. Over 2021–2027 Copernicus will expand these existing services [...].
>
> • New security components, with a budget of €500 million: The new Governmental Satellite Communication (GOVSATCOM) initiative will provide Member States and EU security actors with guaranteed access to secure satellite communications. The Space Situational Awareness (SSA) initiative will support the long-term sustainability and security of space activities by ensuring protection against space hazards.[5]

As is often the case, the final budget deviates from the Commission's original proposal. Hence, the European Parliament (EP) and Council (2021) Regulation earmarks €9.02 billion for Galileo and EGNOS, €5.42 billion for Copernicus and €0.44 billion for SSA and GOVSATCOM.

The new regulation serves mainly the following purposes: putting all pre-existing EU space programmes under one legal roof, consolidating the older

---

4 European Parliament and Council, 'Regulation of the European Parliament and of the Council establishing the Union space programme and the European Union Agency for the Space Programme and repealing Regulations (EU) No 912/2012, (EU) No 1285/2013 and (EU) No 377/2014 and Decision No 541/2014/EU', *Official Journal of the EU* L 170 (2021): 69–148.
5 European Commission, 'Questions and Answers on the New EU Space Programme', https://ec.europa.eu/commission/presscorner/detail/en/MEMO_18_4023.

space programmes (Galileo, EGNOS and Copernicus) and introducing new ones (GOVSATCOM and SSA). Regarding the first aspect, it is obvious that grouping the different space programmes under one umbrella space programme is of great symbolic value and a step closer to owning an integrated and fully fledged EU space policy. As the Commission explains,

> The proposal for a Regulation significantly simplifies and streamlines the existing Union *acquis* by combining in a single text and harmonising almost all rules that were hitherto contained in separate Regulations or Decisions. This raises the profile of the Union space policy, which is in line with the major role that the Union intends to play in future as a global player in space.[6]

Regarding the second aspect, the consolidation of the pre-existing space programmes, it suffices to say that the EU currently has twenty-nine satellites in orbit (twenty-two for Galileo and seven for Copernicus) but more are planned. The full operational capacity of Galileo foresees thirty satellites, while for Galileo alone the Commission anticipates thirty additional satellites by 2033.[7] Even though in its earlier days Galileo was framed as being a 'civilian programme for civilian purposes',[8] Galileo has always had a security dimension. The Council of the EU was carefully not explicit about the security potential of Galileo, but did not rule it out either. According to a member of the GNSS panel of the Council, 'never was there a decision to exclude military use. You can have a military use of Galileo. It is not at all excluded. And it is one of the uses contemplated by the Member States.'[9] Its 'Public Regulated Service' offers more precise location and tracking information intended for governmental authorities, including the military.

The third aspect, which demonstrates that the scope of EU engagement in space affairs keeps growing, also has a security dimension. Having already invested billions of euros in the construction, deployment and maintenance of satellites, the critical infrastructure needs to be secured. Hence, SSA is supposed to deal with the threat posed by the increasing amount of space debris (it is estimated that there are about 780,000 pieces of space debris of

6 European Commission, 'Proposal for a Regulation of the European Parliament and of the Council Establishing the Space Programme of the Union and the European Union Agency for the Space Programme and Repealing Regulations (EU) No. 912/2010, (EU) No. 1285/2013, (EU) No. 377/2014 and Decision 541/2014/EU', COM (2018) 447 final, p. 2.
7 European Commission, 'Questions and Answers on the New EU Space Programme'.
8 Council of the EU, 'Regulation (EC) No 876/2002 of 21 May 2002 Setting Up the Galileo Joint Undertaking', *Official Journal of the European Communities* L 138 (2002): 1–8.
9 J. Feyerer, 'Lessons from Galileo for Future European Public–Private Partnerships in the Space Sector', in T. Hörber and P. Stephenson (eds.), *European Space Policy* (Abingdon, Routledge, 2016), pp. 211–23, 215.

diameter larger than 1 cm in Earth orbit)[10] and by space weather phenomena, while GOVSATCOM is expected to secure the satellite communications.

The aforementioned aspects suggest an EUSP, even if the term is sometimes avoided. The reason for hesitating to call the EUSP by its name is simple. The TFEU talks of a European, rather than EU, space policy. In particular, Article 3 states: 'In the areas of research, technological development and space, the Union shall have competence to carry out activities, in particular to define and implement programmes; however, the exercise of that competence shall not result in Member States being prevented from exercising theirs.'

Hence, the EU is enabled to have competences in space parallel to (and not just shared with) those of its member states. Furthermore, the formulation of another TFEU article is such that it allows the EU to develop its own independent space policy and still call it European. Paragraph 1 of Article 189 states that 'the *Union shall draw up a European space policy*. To this end, it *may* promote joint initiatives, support research and technological development and coordinate the efforts needed for the exploration and exploitation of space.' (emphasis added).

Thus, the EU has been granted the right not only to develop a space policy at the European level, but also to decide for itself whether to pursue any joint initiatives. Still, the reference to a *European* Space Policy is meant to reflect the fact there is another important space actor at the European level, namely the ESA. The ESA has been active in space far longer than the EU, and the gradual involvement of the Commission in space affairs raised questions about potential duplication of efforts and overlap of competences. Therefore, the idea behind the ESP is that the two entities, the ESA and the EU, will coordinate their efforts, in order to ensure a coherent approach, and that the Commission will be instrumental in coordinating all actors involved (see below, 'Space on the Road to Lisbon').

It is true that Paragraph 3 of Article 189 instructs the EU to establish 'any appropriate relations with the European Space Agency'. However, without, clarifying what kind of relations are appropriate, the treaty allows the European Commission a wide array of options ranging from minimal relations (i.e., effectively ignoring it) to integrating it into the EU. Thus, even though the TFEU is explicit about a European space policy, it does not prohibit the EU from pursuing an independent space policy, provided that national competences are not obstructed and that there is no legal harmonisation in this area (TFEU, Section 2 of Article 189).

---

10 European Commission, 'Proposal for a Regulation Establishing the Space Programme of the Union'.

Additional evidence that there are no tight boundaries between EU and European space policy can be found in non-legal texts of the Commission. For example, some webpages of the Directorate General (DG) responsible for space[11] refer explicitly to a space policy of the EU and so do several press releases.[12]

To sum up, using the Commission's own press release, 'the EU fully finances, owns and manages Copernicus, Galileo and EGNOS. The Commission is the programme manager of the EU Space programme and has overall responsibility for its implementation, including in the field of security. It determines the priorities and long-term evolution of the Programme and supervises its implementation.'[13] Note that the Commission refers to an EU space programme in the singular to underline that its space programmes now fall under one roof. However, I use the term here in the plural (programmes), as the Commission did until recently, in order to be able to distinguish between Galileo, Copernicus and so on.

Such assertiveness disperses any doubts that there is an EUSP, rather than simply an agglomeration of national space policies.[14] Given the formal treaty powers the EUSP now enjoys, and given that space falls under the ordinary legislative procedure (i.e., the Council and the EP co-decide, with the EP having veto powers), the EU has the legal foundations to pursue not only an EUSP in its present form, but an even more ambitious policy.

The Origins of the EUSP

Typically, the beginning of the EUSP is associated with the Commission's 1988 Communication titled 'The Community and Space: A Coherent Approach'.[15] Although this document marks a turning point in the development of the

---

11 DG GROWTH during the Juncker Commission and DG DEFIS (https://defence-industry-space.ec.europa.eu/eu-space-policy_en) during the Van Leyen Commission.

12 European Commission, 'Commission Launches Debate on a Space Policy for the EU', https://ec.europa.eu/commission/presscorner/detail/en/IP_03_82; European Commission, 'EU Space Policy Takes Off: EU Decision-Makers Discuss the Future of Space Technology', https://ec.europa.eu/commission/presscorner/detail/en/IP_03_720; European Commission, 'European Commissioner Busquin Tells European Economic and Social Committee That a Dramatic Increase in Funding Is Needed for EU Space Research and for a More Integrated EU Space Policy', https://ec.europa.eu/commission/presscorner/detail/en/CES_03_79.

13 European Commission, 'Questions and Answers on the New EU Space Programme'.

14 F. von der Dunk, 'Legal Challenges in the Context of the European Space Policy', in T. Hoerber and S. Lieberman (eds.), A European Space Policy (Abingdon, Routledge, 2019), pp. 75–95.

15 Suzuki, Policy Logics and Institutions of European Space Collaboration; Krige, Fifty Years of European Cooperation in Space.

EUSP, the first policy initiative came not from the Commission, but from the EP. All subsequent EU documents on space refer back to at least one pre-existing space-relevant document. The EP 1979 Resolution is the only one that does not refer to an earlier space-related EU document. Instead, the EP refers to a pre-existing Council resolution on an emerging science and technology policy which does not mention space at all.[16]

In 1979, the EP adopted a resolution 'on Community participation in space research'[17] based on the report of Camillo Ripamonti (1919–97), an Italian Member of the EP of the Christian Democratic party group. It is not clear why there was an EP report on space and who or what prompted it. A mechanical engineer by training with an interest in space engineering, Mr Ripamonti may have acted as rapporteur out of a genuine conviction that the European Communities' support of space activities would bring a number of benefits. We know that Mr Ripamonti kept books on space engineering in his library.[18] Of course, Italy counts among the countries with a space industry, but it is not possible to tell whether Mr Ripamonti's report was associated with specific national or industrial interests.

The resolution is just over one page long, almost frugal. It argues that the European Community (EC) will reap benefits from space activities already in the short term. It picks out the areas of telecommunications, air traffic and shipping control, earth observation, scientific research and even industry (benefits resulting from the dissemination of new technology). The long-term benefits, according to the report, concern material science (e.g., manufacturing new substances) and biological and medical research.

In addition to these benefits, there are other reasons for the EC to get involved in space. First and foremost, 'Europe cannot depend on outside sources to meet its own needs', the 1979 resolution argues, even though it is not obvious what these needs are. Secondly, the EC 'possesses the necessary intellectual and technological resources [...] to play an important role in space'. On the one hand, the EC has the brains (namely, its Joint Research Centre in Italy), the industrial basis and the financial means. On the other, European cooperation on space matters can be successful, as the example of the ESA proves. However, to 'play a decisive role in space', the resolution

---

16 European Parliament, 'Resolution of 14 January 1974 on an Initial Outline Programme of the European Communities in the Field of Science and Technology', *Official Journal of the European Communities* C 7 (1974): 6–7.

17 European Parliament, 'Resolution on Community Participation in Space Research', *Official Journal of the European Communities* C 127 (1979): 42–3.

18 See www.archiviocamilloripamonti.it/Biblioteca.html.

continues, it is necessary to have a space policy in place; one that sets out long-term objectives, secures funding and ensures that member states participate.

All this points to some very ambitious plans (or hopes) regarding the EC's future involvement in space. It is only towards the end of the resolution that the EP clarifies that it is referring to space research activities within the framework of an EC policy on science and technology. Similarly, it is not until the final paragraphs of the resolution that the EP acknowledges that the ESA has a role to play in the EC's space policy. In particular, the EP asks the Commission to establish 'relations with the ESA with a view to the coordination of space research programmes with Community projects'. The Commission is requested 'to assist the ESA in drawing up a comprehensive programme to meet the likely requirements of the Community Member States for the next 10 years'.

There are four important points to take from this parliamentary resolution. First, even with an only remotely relevant legal basis, the EP is pushing for an ambitious open-ended EC involvement in space, daring even to talk about a space policy. Secondly, the resolution was adopted 9 years before the first space-related initiative of the Commission showing that the EP was proactive rather than reactive to a Commission proposal. Thirdly, the resolution introduces a series of arguments in favour of an EU involvement in space which recur in many subsequent EP and Commission documents. The EU's involvement in space is regularly justified in terms of the benefits of space applications, industrial gains, economic growth and jobs and, more importantly, European independence.[19] Finally, the resolution contains the seeds of the EU space programmes on satellite navigation (Galileo) and earth observation (Copernicus) that would be born later.

It would be an exaggeration to say that the 1979 resolution caused the EUSP. After all, any EU policy is the result of a formal agreement that carries the input of several actors. However, to argue that the EP and its early resolutions on space were insignificant is also wrong. In the 1987 resolution,[20] for instance, the EP 'considers that the time has come for the European Community to work out a *coherent* policy on space activities' (my emphasis). It 'calls on the Commission to initiate the process by drafting a

---

19 E. Sigalas, 'Europe in Space: The European Parliament's Justification Arsenal', in T. Hörber and P. Stephenson (eds.), *European Space Policy* (Abingdon, Routledge, 2016), pp. 66–81.
20 European Parliament, 'Resolution on European Space Policy', *Official Journal of the European Communities* C 190 (1987): 78–80.

communication to the Council and the European Parliament'. In 1988, the Commission responded. Not only did it deliver a communication on space,[21] but also it partly adopted the EP's parlance. Keywords, such as 'coherence', 'coordination' and 'autonomy', amongst others, are found in both documents.

The call for coherence is particularly interesting. As has already been noted, it is a call for the ESA and the EC to coordinate their space initiatives, but it is also a call to the EC to make something more systematic out of space. This demand reappears in several subsequent documents,[22] suggesting not only persistent interest, but also a lack of progress in this respect and, therefore, the need for an overall space strategy. It is not an inconsequential demand, because, as will be shown in the next section, the eventual formation of a European space strategy was a stepping stone for gaining treaty powers on space. It is not clear whether the EP and the Commission were aware of the consequences of their repeated demands for coherence. If not, which appears to me as more likely, it is another case of a decision having unanticipated consequences, which is a premise of neo-functionalism (see Box 17.1 in the following section).

When a very similar argumentation and terminology is found both in a Commission communication and in an EP resolution, and when the EP resolution is published before the Commission communication, one can reasonably assume that the latter document has been influenced by the former. Formally, it is of course the Commission which is the agenda-setter, but when it wishes to propose something to a hesitant Council, then the EP's political support and its rhetoric can prove useful.

Of course, the EUSP would not have been possible without the consent of the Council and the cooperation of the ESA, but, insofar as the Council is concerned, there was not much on space to consent to in the 1970s and 1980s. The 1979 EP resolution makes its proposals on the basis of the legal foundation of a Council resolution that does not even mention space. Prior to the 1988 Commission communication,[23] space was mentioned only once and

---

21 European Commission, 'The Community and Space: A Coherent Approach', http://aei.pitt.edu/3821.
22 European Commission, *The European Community Crossroads in Space* (Luxembourg, Office for Official Publications of the EC, 1991); European Parliament, 'Resolution on the Commission Communication to the Council and the European Parliament "Towards a Trans-European Positioning and Navigation Network"', *Official Journal of the European Communities* C 104 (1999): 73–6.
23 European Commission, 'The Community and Space'.

in passing in a Council resolution.[24] Naturally, it was mentioned also in the Commission communication[25] that provided the foundation for the Council resolution. Out of eleven points which the Council recognises as 'major policy goals in the telecommunication policy', just one refers to space: 'the working out [of] a common position on satellite communications, so that this new information medium can develop in a favourable environment'.[26] Thus, although the Council was at the time far more powerful than the EP, the developments that triggered the EUSP did not come from within it.

Regarding the role of the ESA, the fact that both Galileo and Copernicus were conceived by the intergovernmental space agency speaks for itself.[27] Thus, all the early EC documents on space, roughly up to the mid 1990s, recognise an important, if not leading, role for the ESA. For example, the EP calls on the European Community to become a member of the ESA,[28] the EP and Commission praise the ESA for what it has achieved thus far[29] and the Commission recognises 'that thanks to the European Space Agency and complementary national programmes, Europe has developed a reputable technological and industrial capability in space'.[30] However, as the Community was gaining in self-confidence and its determination to play a greater role in space was growing, references to the ESA were becoming scarcer and/or more moderate. For example, a 1994 session of the EP mentions the ESA only once, when the Commission is called upon 'to reinforce its coordination and cooperation' with the ESA.[31] Actually, the EP mentions the ESA three times, but two references are merely formal statements where the EP 'instructs' its committee to promote with the ESA a conference on space and the EP president to forward the resolution to the ESA.

24 Council of the European Communities, 'Resolution of 30 June 1988 on the Development of the Common Market for Telecommunication Services and Equipment up to 1992', *Official Journal of the European Communities* C 257 (1988): 1–3.
25 European Commission, *Towards a Dynamic European Economy: Green Paper on the Development of the Common Market for Telecommunication Services and Equipment* (Brussels, Commission of the European Communities, 1987).
26 Council of the European Communities, 'Resolution of 30 June 1988 on the Development of the Common Market for Telecommunication Services', p. 3.
27 Krige, *Fifty Years of European Cooperation in Space*.
28 European Parliament, 'Resolution on European Space Policy' (1987).
29 European Parliament, 'Resolution on European Space Policy', *Official Journal of the European Communities* C 305 (1991): 26–7; European Commission, *The European Community Crossroads in Space*.
30 European Commission, *The European Community and Space: Challenges, Opportunities and New Actions* (Brussels, Publications Office of the European Union, 1992), p. 2.
31 European Parliament, 'Resolution on the Community and Space', *Official Journal of the European Communities* C 205 (1994): 467–8.

To sum up, the currently available evidence shows that the EUSP goes back as far as a 1979 EP resolution. In spite of lacking any formal legal powers, the EP set in motion a process that eventually led to the EUSP as we know it today.[32] As Laloux and Delreux[33] have shown, setting the agenda is a very important stage in the EU decision-making process. Therefore, the EP can claim credit for having initiated a process that, thanks to policy spillover and a few accidents (see below), resulted in the EU having fully fledged space programmes and formal competences in space.

Space on the Road to Lisbon: The Evolutionary Process

The European Commission responded to the EP's call to take action on space only after the Single European Act (SEA) was ratified in 1987. Although the first communication with space as its main topic was published in 1988,[34] a 1987 communication talks about the growing importance of satellite communication and the need for the EC to 'define a coherent European position'.[35] At this stage, the commission proposes nothing more than the 'review of regulatory arrangements',[36] and justifies its first space-related interventions as serving the SEA goal of establishing a common European market by 1992.

The 1988 Commission communication on 'Community and Space'[37] is also based on the then newly acquired mandates related to the completion of the internal market and to research and technological development (RTD). The communication starts with a bang: 'the era of the conquest of space has given way to an era of space exploitation'[38] – implying that the EC should show some interest in the latter.

In terms of scope, the Commission proposed initiatives related to RTD, telecommunications, earth observation, industrial development, the legal environment and training.[39] However, in terms of substance, the proposals

---

32 For a full account of the EP's role in the development of the EUSP, see E. Sigalas, 'The Role of the European Parliament in the Development of a European Union Space Policy', *Space Policy* 28 (2012): 110–17.

33 T. Laloux and T. Delreux, 'The Origins of EU Legislation: Agenda-Setting, Intra-institutional Decision-Making or Interinstitutional Negotiations?', *West European Politics* 44 (2020): 1–22.

34 European Commission, *The European Community and Space: A Coherent Approach*.

35 European Commission, *Towards a Dynamic European Economy*, p. 87.   36 Ibid., p. 86.

37 European Commission, *The European Community and Space: A Coherent Approach*.

38 Ibid., p. 1.   39 Ibid., p. 3.

Box 17.1 Defining Neo-functionalism

Neo-functionalism: a theory of regional integration that places major emphasis on the role of non-state actors – especially, the 'secretariat' [i.e., European Commission or EP] of the regional organization [i.e., the EU] involved and those interest associations and social movements that form at the level of the region – in providing the dynamic for further integration. Member states remain important actors in the process. They set the terms of the initial agreement, but they do not exclusively determine the direction and extent of subsequent change. Rather, regional bureaucrats [i.e., Commission or EP officials] in league with a shifting set of self-organized interests and passions seek to exploit the inevitable 'spill-overs' and 'unintended consequences' that occur when states agree to assign some degree of supra-national responsibility for accomplishing a limited task and then discover that satisfying that function has external effects upon other of their interdependent activities.

---

are not particularly impressive. To a large extent, they are about reviewing national regulations, impact assessments, training and cooperating with the ESA and national space agencies. Nevertheless, we notice that the seed for Galileo (satellite technology) and Copernicus (earth observation) is already there, and that the Commission justifies its proposals in terms of serving current policy priorities. In short, we discern the following argument. Because space applications are potentially important for the common market, industrial development, the environment, telecommunications and so on, space is important for the functioning of several Community policies. This, as we shall see below, becomes more pronounced in later EU policy documents, indicating that neo-functionalism (Box 17.1), one of the grand theories of European integration,[40] may be helpful for explaining the development of the EUSP.

A key premise of neo-functionalism is that the deepening of European integration can be explained in terms of competences spilling over from one policy area onto another.[41] This is the process of functional spillover, as

---

40 From P. C. Schmitter, 'Neo-functionalism', in A. Wiener and T. Diez (eds.), *European Integration Theory* (Oxford, Oxford University Press, 2004), pp. 45–74, 46.
41 E. B. Haas, *The Uniting of Europe* (Notre Dame, IN, University of Notre Dame Press, 2004).

opposed to political spillover, which refers to the gradual shifting of loyalties towards the EU. As Sandholtz and Stone Sweet argue, there is little evidence of political spillover.[42] Thus, they propose an updated form of neo-functionalism, to which the present chapter subscribes. This neo-neofunctionalism allows for functional spillover without it necessarily leading to new collective identities or political loyalties. According to neo-functionalism, this shift can be attributed to the national governments realising that the goals of a particular policy area are contingent on initiatives in another policy area, thus allowing the EU to expand its remit. Another premise of neo-functionalism is that sometimes EU-level decisions may have certain consequences that the national governments did not anticipate when they made the decision. Consequently, they may find themselves in a position where the best line of action is to concede even more powers or responsibilities to the EU and its institutions. Actually, neo-functionalism proposes a dynamic theory of integration. The more decisions are taken at EU level, the greater the chances for spillover and unanticipated consequences, prompting more European integration, which in turn increases further the chances for spillover and unanticipated consequences, resulting once again in more integration, and so on.

If neo-functionalism is right, we would expect to see the EU's supranational bodies, especially the Commission, pushing for more and more policy initiatives on space. These initiatives should be justified in terms of serving the existing EU policies, and we should also notice some decisions relating to unanticipated events that facilitated the emergence of space as an autonomous policy area.

Thus far, we have seen the Commission and the EP striving to make the European Community become active in space. Some evidence of the proposed space initiatives being linked to the needs of the pre-existing policy areas has already been presented and more can be found in later Community documents.

In 1990, the Commission published the 'Green Paper on a Common Approach in the Field of Satellite Communications in the EC'.[43] The communication, building on the Commission Green Paper on telecommunication

---

42 W. Sandholtz and A. Stone Sweet, 'Neo-functionalism and Supranational Governance', in E. Jones, A. Menon and S. Weatherill (eds.), *Oxford Handbook of the European Union* (Oxford, Oxford University Press, 2012), pp. 18–33.

43 European Commission, *Towards Europe-Wide Systems and Services – Green Paper on a Common Approach in the Field of Satellite Communication in the European Communities* (Brussels, Publications Office of the European Union, 1990).

policy,[44] stays within the objectives of the internal market and proposes the liberalisation of the satellite communications market. What is noteworthy is that now the Commission talks openly about a 'Community space policy', a term that was missing from the first space communication.[45]

To determine its role in space affairs, but also to legitimise its ambitions, the Commission set up a committee of independent experts that published the results of its work in 1991. The Commission clearly intended to appear to be engaging with all the relevant stakeholders and collecting a more or less representative sample of their views. This is apparent not only in the composition of the panel (eight experts from academia, the space industry and space agencies plus two senior officials of the ESA), but also in the methodology of the panel's work: 'A significant input to the Panel's deliberations came in the form of interviews between some of the Panel members and senior staff of several space-related international organisations and with some of the most influential figures in the European aerospace industry.'[46] 'The objective of the Panel [was] to provide a broad view of where European Community action could best contribute [...] to the successful further development of European space activities.'[47] Of the various proposals the expert panel made, two in particular stand out. First, the experts insisted on the Commission developing a long-term European space strategy. Secondly, this strategy should lead 'to the establishment of an operational earth observation capability for environmental protection purposes'.[48] The ESA, the experts argued, is a research and development organisation and as such unsuitable for operational systems focused on the end-user. In addition, participation in the ESA's earth observation programme is optional, meaning that only some ESA member states participated in it. The Commission should start discussions with all the stakeholders, in order to achieve a 'light and flexible European coordination'. Interestingly enough, the experts saw no problem in the fact that the EC had no space competences. 'The EC is clearly mandated to assume a central role in this,' they argued.[49]

In the meantime, the EP did what it could to promote the cause of the EC's involvement in space. In March 1991, it organised a hearing with various space policy stakeholders,[50] and in October of the same year it adopted a resolution on 'European space policy'.[51] The resolution called on the Commission to propose

44 European Commission, *Towards a Dynamic European Economy*.
45 European Commission, *The European Community and Space: A Coherent Approach*.
46 European Commission, *The European Community Crossroads in Space*, pp. 6–7.
47 Ibid., p. 6.   48 Ibid., p. 15.   49 Ibid.   50 Ibid., p. vi.
51 European Parliament, 'Resolution on European Space Policy' (1991).

a series of pilot programmes, 'to ensure the optimal development and utiliza-
tion of earth observation applications'.[52] Applications would be 'in support of
Community policies for agriculture, environment, regional development and
aid to developing countries'.[53] Moving away from the understanding that
a space policy could only be developed within the policy framework of RTD,
the EP asked the Commission 'in the context of its environmental policy [. . .] to
ensure a vigorous European participation in international programmes for the
study and monitoring of the environment [. . .] and to propose actions on the
issues of European interest [. . .]'.[54]

The publication of yet another Commission communication on space the
following year[55] indicates that the Commission was on full course to take
concrete action on space, as also the title of the communication suggests
('The EC and Space: Challenges, Opportunities and *New Actions*' (emphasis
added)). The Communication identified five objectives, of which the first,
and most important, was the 'development and exploitation of Earth observation applications [. . .] by initiatives contributing to the establishment of
a European operational system for the study and monitoring of the
environment'.[56] The other four objectives refer to (1) developing regulatory
conditions for the satellite communication services market, (2) developing
synergies between the EC and the ESA, (3) the growth of the space industry
and (4) 'international cooperation, particularly taking into account the new
opportunities for cooperation with the former Soviet republics and the
countries of Central and Eastern Europe'.[57]

Although coordination with the ESA and individual EC member states
would be one course of action, the Commission did not wish to stay in the
shadow of the ESA. The experts who had advised the Commission a year
earlier,[58] and had recommended a European earth observation programme,
proposed 'light and flexible coordination'. The Commission, on the other
hand, favoured 'the development of Earth observation applications and
new sensors within the Community Framework Programme for R&TD'.[59]
In other words, the Commission aspired to having a substantial part of any
European earth observation programme, especially the one concerned with
services to the end-user, belong to the EC rather than to the ESA.

---

52 Ibid., p. 27. 53 Ibid. 54 Ibid.
55 European Commission, *The European Community and Space: Challenges, Opportunities and New Actions*.
56 Ibid., p. 33. 57 Ibid., p. 34.
58 European Commission, *The European Community Crossroads in Space*.
59 European Commission, *The European Community and Space: Challenges, Opportunities and New Actions*, p. 34.

Like the first space communication,[60] the 1992 communication highlighted the interlinkage between space and several Community policies. Decisions concerning the internal market, trade, environmental policy, telecommunications policy, audio-visual policy and RTD, the Commission maintained, 'will increasingly impact on Europe's space effort. At the same time, space is making its impact felt on the implementation of Community policies'.[61] Thus, the official discourse suggests that once more the case for a functional spillover (see Box 17.1) was being made. To justify its space policy aspirations, the Commission tried to distinguish its role from that of the ESA and the national space agencies. According to the Commission, whereas the ESA and the space agencies concentrate on 'technology-push' matters (RTD, technological progress and industrial capacity), the 'demand-pull' aspect (space applications) has been left underdeveloped and this is where the EC should be taking the lead.[62]

The ratification of the Maastricht Treaty (Treaty on the EU, TEU) in 1993 marked a turning point in the evolution of the EU's initiatives on space. Article 3 of the TEU introduced a common transport policy and the 'encouragement for the establishment and development of trans-European networks [TEN]'.[63] Consequently, TEN fell under the co-decision procedure, where the Council decides on the basis of a qualified majority and the EP can exercise a veto. The Commission immediately took advantage of the opportunity and used TEN and transport policy as the new legal basis for its space proposals.

Once more we notice the spillover logic at play. In the first post-Maastricht communication, the Commission argued that, because 'the efficiency and security of the transport system' is a crucial part of TEN, 'a high quality standard radio navigation system for Europe, eventually based on satellites, will support the effective functioning of the network'.[64] Perhaps without realising the spillover potential, the Council had already accepted the Commission's rationale. In the 1993 meeting of research ministers, the

60 European Commission, *The European Community and Space: A Coherent Approach.*
61 European Commission, *The European Community and Space: Challenges, Opportunities and New Actions*, p. 2.
62 Ibid.
63 Council and Commission of the European Communities, *Treaty on European Union* (Luxembourg, Office for Official Publications of the European Communities, 1992).
64 European Commission, *Proposal for a European Parliament and Council Decision on Community Guidelines for the Development of the Trans-European Network* (Brussels, Publications Office of the European Union, 1994), p. 3.

Council[65] considered that the Commission should continue to develop its role as a user of space technology, in particular in the field of earth observation, with a view to contributing to the optimisation of the use of satellite data as well as to the *implementation of Community policies*.

In June 1994 the Commission put forward its proposal for a Council resolution that was the foundation of EGNOS and Galileo. 'The time has come', the Commission stated, not without some pomposity, 'for the European Union to show its determination to master one of the essential tools for its economic development'.[66] In short, the Commission proposed the development and implementation of GNSS 1 and GNSS 2, a first- and second-generation global navigation satellite system, respectively. GNSS 1 would include a European supplement (EGNOS) to the American GPS and possibly also to the Russian GLONASS (Global'naya Navigatsionnaya Sputnikovaya Sistema) satellite navigation system. GNSS 1 would offer more accurate positioning services than the GPS. However, relying on the GPS was a source of concern. The Commission was interested in an internationally controlled civilian system, but the GPS had been developed, and was owned, by the US military,[67] and there was always the possibility that its services would be interrupted if the American authorities chose to do so (a prospect that materialised during the NATO bombings in Serbia and Kosovo in 1999). Hence the need for GNSS 2, which was a longer-term project to be developed in parallel with GNSS 1.

Towards the end of 1994, the Council adopted the resolution on GNSS.[68] The Council endorsed the Commission's proposals for both GNSS 1 and GNSS 2. However, it was keen to engage also the private sector, not only because the Council believed that this would help the European (space) industry to grow, but also because it was mindful of the GNSS's financial implications. Keeping the costs down was particularly important to overcome the reservations of some EU member states.[69] The Council could not have known it at the time, but the strategic choice to involve the private sector would prove decisive. It would pave the way for the Galileo

65 European Council, '1657th Council Meeting 29 April 1993 – Research, Press Release' (1993) 6060/93, p. 9.
66 European Commission, *Satellite Navigation Services: A European Approach – Draft Council Resolution* (Brussels, Publications Office of the European Union, 1994), p. 17.
67 Krige, *Fifty Years of European Cooperation in Space*.
68 European Council, 'Council Resolution of 19 December 1994 on the European Contribution to the Development of a Global Navigation Satellite System', *Official Journal of the European Communities* C 379 (1994): 2–3.
69 E. Sigalas, 'The European Union Space Policy', *Oxford Research Encyclopedia of Politics* (Oxford, Oxford University Press, 2017), pp. 1–18.

public–private partnership (PPP), which would later collapse, thus prompting the EU to take full ownership of Galileo (see below).

Unlike the preceding period, the years 1995–7 were relatively quiet. The Commission did not publish any communications on space and progress on the GNSS was very slow. Early in 1998 the Commission was calling on the Council to reaffirm its commitment on the GNSS.[70] GNSS 2 was still in an early stage of development, the Commission warned,[71] but also EGNOS was in need of 'specific actions [...] to complete the programme successfully'.[72] Finally, an agreement between the EU, the ESA and the European Organisation for the Safety of Air Navigation was signed in mid 1998, adopting EGNOS and dividing tasks between the three organisations. The Commission reiterated the need to go beyond EGNOS, because of sovereignty and security concerns.[73] Even though the GPS's services were available gratis, thus acting as a counter-incentive to developing a European GNSS, Europe could not afford, the Commission argued, to be left behind or to be dependent on the decisions of the US authorities, which of course it could not influence. Thus, it identified three possibilities for the development of GNSS 2: (1) joint development by all 'major players', (2) development with the US and/or Russia or (3) an independent EU system of regional or global scope.

The same year, the then British Commissioner for Transport Neil Kinnock asked the Director of DG Transport, Matthias Rüte, to 'look at [GNSS] and either kill it or make something more substantive out of it'.[74] DG Transport went for the latter, and produced another communication in 1999, renaming GNSS 2 to Galileo.

The Director of DG Transport of the Commission came to the conclusion that it was worth making something of GNSS 2 following 'a large conference organised jointly by the Commission and the French space agency'.[75] The 'large conference' must have been the 'GNSS 2 Forum' which 'supported the Commission's thinking'[76] on institutional, technical, legal and financial matters and produced a final report in December 1998. France's interest playing a leading role in EUSP is clear, since it is a major European space power and

---

70 European Commission, *Towards a Trans-European Positioning and Navigation Network* (Brussels, Publications Office of the European Union, 1998).
71 Ibid., p. 7.   72 Ibid., p. 8   73 Ibid.
74 Quoted in Sigalas, 'The European Union Space Policy', p. 170.   75 Ibid.
76 European Commission, *Galileo: Involving Europe in a New Generation of Satellite Navigation Services* (Brussels, Publications Office of the European Union, 1999), p. 7, note 12.

was keen seeing the EU getting involved in space.[77] However, even in France certain reservations had to be overcome, in order to support Galileo. As Suzuki argues, the French Ministry of Defence was unwilling to finance Galileo, because of its own financial constraints and because it deemed GPS reliable.[78]

This time, the Commission was unequivocal. It was backing the third option, a fully independent European GNSS, even though it was a more costly option, compared with joint development with other space powers. The US authorities, the Commission explained, were not willing to share control of the GPS, which was vital if the EU wanted guarantees of continuous service, no excessive future charges and equal access to new technologies.[79] As had been foreshadowed in the 1994 communication, the Commission was now proposing the setting up of a PPP, to ensure that part of the funding came from private sources and to stimulate the private sector's interest in space applications, even though a freely available GPS created difficulties in raising revenues.[80] In a new resolution, the EP emphasised the importance of public funding and warned that the expectations from the private sector were too optimistic, but this did not change the course of events.[81]

As in previous communications, the Commission justified Galileo in terms of its usefulness and its contribution to other EU policy objectives. 'These systems will play a crucial role in creating the integrated European transport system that is crucial to support the single market,'[82] the Commission stated. Similarly, the EP argued that the EU must not be left behind, and that the GNSS would be essential for economic growth, competitiveness, job creation and transport safety, with applications also in the fishing, agriculture and leisure sectors.[83] The Council also adopted the Commission's justification when it endorsed its proposals for Galileo in 1999. 'Hence, we note in Council that Galileo will make a major contribution to an effective use of transport

---

77 Sigalas, 'The European Union Space Policy', p. 171.
78 Suzuki, *Policy Logics and Institutions of European Space Collaboration*, p. 195.
79 European Commission, *Galileo*.
80 Suzuki, *Policy Logics and Institutions of European Space Collaboration*.
81 European Parliament, 'Resolution on the Commission Communication to the Council and the European Parliament "The European Union and Space: Fostering Applications, Markets and Industrial Competitiveness"', *Official Journal of the European Communities* C 34 (1998): 27–30.
82 European Commission, *Galileo*, p. iv.
83 European Parliament, 'Resolution on the Commission Communication to the Council and the European Parliament "Towards a Trans-European Positioning and Navigation Network"', *Official Journal of the European Communities* C 104 (1999): 73–6.

infrastructure, to an increase in safety, to a reduction of environmental pollution and to the setting-up of an integrated transport system with crucial importance for the Single Market.'[84]

However, the most important consideration in the Council's decision is 'independence in one of the most important key technologies',[85] which features first in the list of reasons in favour of Galileo. During the 1999 NATO bombings of Yugoslavia, the GPS signal was downgraded, causing serious problems in the air traffic of the neighbouring regions and countries.[86] Consequently, the EU member state governments realised that the Commission was not exaggerating when it warned that dependence on the GPS compromised European 'security and sovereignty'.[87]

The Council's agreement to commence the definition phase of Galileo in 1999 did not guarantee that the EU would end up with its own functioning satellite constellation. The Council expected a cost–benefit analysis from the Commission to determine the viability of Galileo. As Krige has illustrated, a series of problems soon started appearing, bringing Galileo, and the Commission's space ambitions, close to a premature death.[88]

Even though the Council resolution[89] foresaw that a decision on the future of Galileo had to be taken by the end of 2000 at the latest, there was hesitation amongst the EU governments. Concerns about the cost, the contribution of the private sector and the temptation of an upgraded and freely available GPS made a decision difficult. For nearly 2 years Galileo was in limbo.[90]

Fearing that Galileo would be abandoned, the Commission tried harder. In an attempt to show that the Commission was backing Galileo at the highest level, Commission officials 'managed to drag in Romano Prodi', the Commission President at the time, to a session of the ESA Council meeting in Edinburgh in November 2001.[91] A month later, during the State of the Union address in Strasbourg, Prodi was calling on the EU member state governments to assume their responsibilities, while pressure from France,

---

84 Council of the EU, 'Resolution of 19 July 1999 on the Involvement of Europe in a New Generation of Satellite Navigation Services – Galileo – Definition Phase', *Official Journal of the European Communities* C 221 (1999): 1–3.

85 Ibid.

86 Sigalas, 'The Role of the European Parliament'; Krige, *Fifty Years of European Cooperation in Space*.

87 European Commission, *Towards a Trans-European Positioning and Navigation Network*, p. iv.

88 Krige, *Fifty Years of European Cooperation in Space*.

89 Council of the EU, 'Resolution of 19 July 1999'.

90 Krige, *Fifty Years of European Cooperation in Space*.

91 Sigalas, 'The European Union Space Policy', p. 169.

the European space industry and top national military officials grew.[92] Eventually, the Council consented to Galileo entering the development phase and the Galileo Joint Undertaking was established,[93] but it did not became operational until July 2003.[94]

Disagreements among Spain, Italy, France, Germany and the UK, about the share of each in the capital of the new joint undertaking and about the location of the satellite control centres and other facilities, caused delays in the handing out of industrial contracts. In addition, the private companies of the two consortia, which eventually merged to one to make up for the lost time and to satisfy national demands, found it difficult to agree on key decisions, such as nominating a commonly accepted director. The ESA argued for at least two consortia, in order to deal with the risk of a potential failure to deliver.[95]

The launch of the first Galileo satellite in 2005 was overshadowed by the significant delays and the cost overruns of the programme. By mid 2007 the situation had become untenable and the Commission issued a communication arguing for the termination of the PPP arrangement.[96] According to the Commission's new position, public funding should be provided not only for the definition and validation phases, as had originally been foreseen, but also for the deployment and operation phases. A new PPP could be examined in the future, once the full constellation was in place and Galileo was firmly in the exploitation phase. Hence, the Commission was inviting the Council and the EP to '[r]ecognise that the European GNSS programmes are defined, agreed, managed, and overseen at the level of the European Union'.[97] A year later, the Council and the EP accepted the Commission's proposals, and EGNOS and Galileo became the first infrastructure fully funded and owned by the EU.[98]

This crucial yet unanticipated consequence of the decision to embark on a European GNSS can be attributed to three factors. First, as the Commission admitted,[99] the EU miscalculated the costs, the difficulties and

92 Krige, *Fifty Years of European Cooperation in Space*, pp. 363–4. For Prodi's speech, see https://ec.europa.eu/commission/presscorner/detail/en/SPEECH_01_621.
93 Council of the EU, 'Regulation (EC) No. 876/2002 of 21 May 2002'.
94 Krige, *Fifty Years of European Cooperation in Space*, p. 374.   95 Ibid.
96 European Commission, *Galileo at a Cross-Road: The Implementation of the European GNSS Programmes* (Brussels, Publications Office of the European Union, 2007).
97 Ibid., p. 13.
98 European Parliament and Council, 'Regulation (EC) No 683/2008 of 9 July 2008 on the Further Implementation of the European Satellite Navigation Programmes (EGNOS and Galileo)', *Official Journal of the European Union* L 196 (2008): 1–10.
99 European Commission, *Galileo at a Cross-Road*.

the appropriateness of the given PPP. The consortium that was supposed to build and operate Galileo was reluctant to proceed without additional public funding, because of concerns about the profitability of Galileo. Krige attributes the reluctance to the 'immense difficulty of evaluating the commercial returns in a highly competitive market [where Galileo would have to compete with the GPS, the Russian GLONASS and the Chinese GNSS] so far upstream from implementation, the need to take out a substantial bank loan to finance construction, concerns about the cost of replacing the satellites that would be retired before the twenty-year concession expired'.[100]

> [T]he EU has taken an assumption that Galileo could be developed and deployed in a much shorter time and with considerably less public funding than it took the US for GPS. [...] the EU assumption may have been optimistic [...]. The current industrial organisations are neither efficient nor capable of reaching decisions [...]. In addition [...] the Merged Consortium has a composition with different focus, namely mostly the construction of the constellation whilst a PPP would ideally require a consortium led by service providers.[101]

Secondly, the Commission convinced the Council and the EP that European independence in satellite navigation was a strategic need, indispensable for meeting the EU's objectives in other policy areas. Adopting an abridged version of the Commission's[102] argumentation, the Council and EP regulation maintained that 'the development of satellite navigation is fully in line with the Lisbon Strategy and other Community policies, such as transport policy'.[103] Thirdly, given the investment already committed, backing away from EGNOS and Galileo would mean substantial net losses for the EU and its member states. Not to mention the blow to the EU's public image.

The late 1990s saw the birth not only of Galileo, but also of Global Monitoring for Environment and Security (GMES), which later became Copernicus, the EU's earth observation programme, and a European space strategy. There is not much new to be learned from Copernicus in relation to the process of functional spillover, so I will not explore the programme's development here. The foundations for Copernicus were laid in Baveno, Italy, where the Commission, the ESA, the European Organisation for the Exploitation of Meteorological Satellites and national space agencies agreed

---

100 Krige, *Fifty Years of European Cooperation in Space*, p. 376.
101 European Commission, *Galileo at a Cross-Road*, p. 5.   102 Ibid.
103 European Parliament and Council, 'Regulation (EC) No. 683/2008 of 9 July 2008 on the Further Implementation of the European Satellite Navigation Programmes (EGNOS and Galileo)'.

on a 'manifesto' for the development of a programme on earth observation.[104] The EU's official involvement started with the Council (2001) resolution urging the Commission to cooperate with the ESA to this end, and it culminated with the EP and Council regulation (2010) endorsing GMES's initial operation.[105] What is important is that Copernicus enriched the EU's space portfolio by adding a second space programme, thus raising the stakes for a successful space policy even further. (Originally, GMES stood for Global Monitoring for Environmental Security, but later it changed to Global Monitoring for Environment *and* Security to reflect the programme's potential contribution to the goals of the EU's foreign and security policies.) With two expensive programmes in the making, and with the Commission's and EP's systematic argumentation that Europe needed its own satellite constellation, which should prove useful for a number of EU policies and initiatives, the inclusion of space in the EU treaty was only a step away.

The EU's increasing involvement in space affairs inevitably raised two significant questions. First, what role exactly should the EU play in space and, secondly, what should its long-term objectives be? These are strategy questions that the EU could no longer avoid once Galileo entered the definition phase in 1999. Until then, space was mostly the playfield of national space agencies and the ESA. The entry of a new actor raised concerns about competence overlap, effort duplication and resource allocation at the European level. In short, the 'who does what?' question was pressing, and the need for a coherent approach on space was growing.

It is no accident that in 1999, the year the EU Council gave the go-ahead for Galileo, the Commission published a working document titled *Towards a Coherent European Approach for Space*.[106] As we saw above, the EP had long been asking for coherence in space activities, and finally the Commission tried to deliver. The various strategy-related communications that the Commission published between 1999 and 2004,[107] the year the framework

104 V. Reillon, *European Space Policy: Historical Perspective, Specific Aspects and Key Challenges* (Brussels, European Parliament Research Service, 2017).
105 For a detailed account of the EU–ESA cooperation on GMES, see Krige, *Fifty Years of European Cooperation in Space*.
106 European Commission, *Towards a Coherent European Approach for Space* (Brussels, Publications Office of the European Union, 1999).
107 European Commission, *Towards a Coherent European Approach for Space*; European Commission, *Europe and Space: Turning to a New Chapter* (Brussels, Publications Office of the European Union, 2000); European Commission, *Towards a European Space Policy* (Brussels, Publications Office of the European Union, 2001); European Commission, *Green Paper – European Space Policy* (Brussels, Publications Office of the European Union, 2003); European Commission, *Space: A New European Frontier for an Expanding Union* (Brussels, Publications Office of the European Union, 2003).

agreement with the ESA was signed, were meant to embed the EU's space actions in a separate policy framework. Two primary dimensions can be discerned in these communications. The first is about defining the relation of Galileo/EGNOS and GMES to the EU's strategic goals and to its existing policies and priorities. The analysis thus far has given a representative sample of the Commission's arsenal of arguments, so there is no need to repeat them. The second dimension is mainly about finding a balance between the Commission and the ESA and dividing the tasks accordingly.

Together with the ESA, the Commission devised a strategy for space that aimed at three objectives: (1) 'strengthening the foundation for space activities', (2) 'enhancing scientific knowledge' and (3) 'reaping the benefits [of space] through a demand-driven exploitation'.[108] The Commission's role would be establishing the appropriate regulatory conditions, animating research and development efforts, and 'bringing together all actors and competences around common political objectives in projects of a European-wide interest'.[109] In addition, the Commission would be leading the development of Galileo, in association with the ESA, while the ESA would 'remain the principal programming and funding agency'.[110] Of course, the latter aspect was partly compromised when Galileo/EGNOS became EU-funded programmes in 2008.

Thus, throughout the late 1990s and early 2000s the EU's space policy dynamic, initiated mainly through Galileo and Copernicus taking shape, but also through the emerging European space strategy, was gaining momentum. Although Galileo still had major obstacles to overcome and Copernicus was in a very early stage, the Commission was looking ahead. As one senior Commission official explained, 'What's the next step? Do we [the Commission] go for a fully-fledged space policy? [...] In those days we were entering the so-called [European constitutional] convention process [...] and of course the idea came quite naturally to seize this opportunity to say "well, why don't we try to put space in the EU treaty as an EU policy?"'[111]

Initially, part of the Commission apparatus was reluctant to include space in the new treaty, because of fears that it would complicate the negotiations process. However, eventually, after some successful lobbying, the leadership of the Convention for the Future of Europe, which led to the draft constitutional treaty and subsequently to the Lisbon Treaty, came to accept the proposal to include space policy as a new EU competence area. The

---

108 European Commission, *Europe and Space*, p. 3.   109 Ibid., p. 4.   110 Ibid.
111 Quoted in Sigalas, 'The European Union Space Policy', p. 171.

Convention was chaired by a Frenchman (Valéry Giscard d'Estaing) and one of its two vice-presidents was Belgian (Jean-Luc Dehaene) and both the French and the Belgians 'have a sensitivity on space. So, there are two key persons who were rather receptive to the issue of space'[112] according to the senior Commission official. The fact that the second vice-president (Giuliano Amato) came also from country with a space industry (Italy) might have made him equally receptive to the idea of a space article in the new EU treaty.

Conclusion

This chapter showed that confusion about whether the EU has an 'EU' or 'European' space policy is justified. The Lisbon Treaty may refer to an ESP, implying the involvement of actors other than the EU, especially the inter-governmental ESA, but the EU is free to go its own way. The ESP is the result of the evolving EU space policy, which is supposed to be part of the ESP. This not only adds to the confusion, but also suggests a tension between the EU and the ESA regarding who has the policy lead and what the relationship between the two should be. At some point, the Commission suggested that the ESA could even be integrated into the EU structure,[113] but for the time being the status quo of two independent organisations cooperating with each other remains intact. This is certainly an area where more research would be welcome.

The EUSP commenced thanks not to a Commission initiative, but to an EP resolution. This does not necessarily pin down its causation. In fact, a parliamentary resolution of 1979, long before the EP had any legislative powers, was the first EC institutional document calling for the EC to play a role in space. Even more interesting is the fact that many of the key arguments in favour of an EUSP, such as autonomy and benefits in several areas, can already be found in many of the subsequent EU documents on space. Whilst it would be going too far to say that the EUSP owes its existence to the EP, the latter certainly played a positive role, and its agenda-setting powers should not be underestimated.

The fact that the EU has its own satellite constellation in space is very interesting in itself. Galileo, the EU's GNSS, is already operational and it competes with the GPS and other satellite navigation and positioning

---

112 Quoted in Ibid., p. 172.
113 European Commission, *Establishing Appropriate Relations between the EU and the European Space Agency* (Brussels, Publications Office of the European Union, 2012).

systems. Similarly, the Commission has high hopes for Copernicus, the EU's earth observation and monitoring programme, which can certainly be put to good use. Copernicus has already started bearing fruit (data, to be more precise) useful for dealing with climate change and natural and manmade disasters, but also for aiding military missions or improving agricultural productivity.

What really stands out in the EU's space policy development is that it took place without the EU having any formal competences in space until only recently. Using as legal foundation limited competences on scientific cooperation, before the SEA, and RTD and the completion of the internal market, before the TEU, the Commission was preparing the ground. The Maastricht Treaty gave the EU competences on transport, which included telecommunications, and the environment. This brought space into the Community pillar of the EU and allowed the flow of more money into space programmes.

The analysis of several Commission and EP documents has shown that both supranational institutions were not only interested in space and systematically pushing the Council in this direction, but also justifying their arguments in terms of benefits for existing policy areas and priorities. In addition, important yet unexpected events played a crucial role in the birth of Galileo and its subsequent ownership by the EU. By choosing, first, to capitalise on the opportunity offered by international developments and, secondly, to fund Galileo on its own, the EU effectively decided to become a new player in outer space politics. This also meant that it was now easier to formally recognise space as an EU competence area. In parallel with Galileo, the Commission and the ESA were developing a European space strategy which contributed to the dynamic that led to the inclusion of space in the Lisbon Treaty.

All these findings indicate that neo-functionalism is useful for explaining European integration. The analysis has presented evidence of supranational activism, spillover and decisions with unintended consequences. Of course, neo-functionalism is not flawless. Scholars have already pointed out some weaknesses, such as poor evidence of political spillover[114] or difficulty in explaining disintegration.[115] Irrespective of whether the way forward is accepting that neo-functionalism can explain only some aspects of European

---

114 Sandholtz and Stone Sweet, 'Neo-functionalism and Supranational Governance'.
115 D. Webber, 'Trends in European Political (Dis)integration. An Analysis of Postfunctionalist and Other Explanations', *Journal of European Public Policy* 26 (2019): 1134–52.

integration, as Hooghe and Marks[116] propose, or refining the theory, the history of the birth and growth of the EUSP shows that neo-functionalism remains a relevant regional integration theory.

Recommended Reading

Krige, J. *Fifty Years of European Cooperation in Space* (Paris, Éditions Beauchesne, 2014).

Paladini, S. *The New Frontiers of Space* (Cham, Palgrave Macmillan, 2019).

Suzuki, K. *Policy Logics and Institutions of European Space Collaboration* (Aldershot, Ashgate, 2003).

Hoerber, T. C. and E. Sigalas (eds.). *Theorizing European Space Policy* (Lanham, MD, Lexington Books, 2017).

116 L. Hooghe and G. Marks, 'Grand Theories of European Integration in the Twenty-First Century', *Journal of European Public Policy* 26 (2019): 1113–33.

PART III

*

PERSPECTIVES AND IDEAS

18

Researching the Eurocrats

CRIS SHORE AND RENITA THEDVALL

Introduction: Integration Theory and the Dynamics of Europeanisation

It is 9 October 2001 and one of the authors, Thedvall, has been working for a month as a *stagiaire*/researcher at the Directorate General (DG) of Employment and Social Affairs (DG EMPL). It is morning, and she is taking part in an induction course at the DG EMPL to become familiarised with the European Commission, the DG, and their ways of working. Induction courses are frequently held at the DG and the European Commission in general. There is a constant influx of people starting to work as *fonctionnaires* with permanent positions or arriving as detached national experts (DNEs) or *stagiaires* staying for a few months or a few years. The influx is matched only by the constant stream of farewell parties and goodbye drinks. People move in and out of the city all the time. Brussels is a city where friends constantly leave. The room, a typical meeting room in the DG with grey/blueish chairs, tables, floors and walls, is filled with a mix of people of different nationalities, positions and levels, from directors to trainees/*stagiaires*. The day starts out with the Director General welcoming us and talking about the European Union (EU) project. As Director General of DG EMPL, he is particularly pleased that the EU project has expanded to include social issues, moving the EU closer towards a federation. He is convinced that, within this decade or the next, the EU will become a proper federal union with working political processes and a European Parliament as important as its member states' parliaments.

Today, his prediction might seem naïve, but at that time, when Thedvall was doing fieldwork in the European Commission, the EU was about to put into circulation its new euro banknotes and coins, and enlargement of the EU from fifteen to twenty-four countries was scheduled to happen within a few years. For European federalists there were reasons to be optimistic.

The current Director General is probably not as hopeful,[1] but for someone working as a *fonctionnaire* in the European Commission the 'European idea' needs to be on the agenda. For EU policy elites, the notion of a united Europe demands commitment and attention. This is also something that distinguishes the EU from national governments and intergovernmental organisations. There is always a tension in terms of loyalty and identity between the national and the supranational, or in this case, the European. This chapter is about the 'Eurocrats' – those officials and professional Europeans who work in, and for, the EU and its institutions – and how they navigate those tensions.

Dissolving the boundaries between the EU and its member states has often been described as an essential step towards 'Europeanisation'. By this term we do not mean just political and economic adaptation to the EU or the influence of its policies on nation states.[2] Rather, we define Europeanisation in a wider anthropological sense as the processes by which European citizens are exposed to – and enculturated by – the norms and values of the EU, particularly within its institutional habitus.[3] Writing over six decades ago Ernst B. Haas, the German-American political scientist and inventor of the 'neo-functionalist' theory of integration, defined European integration as the process whereby 'political actors in several distinct national settings are persuaded to shift their loyalties and activities towards a new centre, whose institutions possess or demand jurisdiction over the pre-existing national states'.[4] According to Haas and his supporters, the integration of national

---

1 D. Chalmers, M. Jachtenfuchs and C. Joerges, *The End of the Eurocrats' Dream: Adjusting to European Diversity* (Cambridge, Cambridge University Press, 2018).

2 U. Sedelmeier, 'Europeanization', in E. Jones and A. Menon (eds.), *The Oxford Handbook of the European Union* (Oxford, Oxford University Press, 2012), pp. 825–39.

3 M. Abélès, 'Political Anthropology of the Trans-national Institution: The European Parliament', *French Politics & Society* 11 (1993): 1–19; R. Harmsen and T. M. Wilson, 'Introduction: Approaches to Europeanization', in R. Harmsen and T. M. Wilson (eds.), *Europeanization: Institutions, Identities and Citizenship* (Leiden, Brill, 2000), pp. 13–26; C. Shore, 'La socialisation de l'administration de l'Union européenne: Une approache anthropologique des phénomènes d'européanisation et de supranationalisme', in H. Michel and C. Robert (eds.), *La fabrique des 'Européens': Processus de socialisation et construction européenne* (Strasbourg, Presses universitaires de Strasbourg, 2010), pp. 169–96; I. Bellier, 'A Europeanized Elite? An Anthropology of European Commission Officials', in R. Harmsen and T. M. Wilson (eds.), *Europeanization: Institutions, Identities and Citizenship* (Leiden, Brill, 2000), pp. 135–56; M. Kuus, *Geopolitics and Expertise: Knowledge and Authority in European Diplomacy* (Hoboken, NJ, John Wiley & Sons, 2013).

4 E. B. Haas, *The Uniting of Europe: Political, Social, and Economical Forces, 1950–1957* (London, Stevens, 1958).

elites would flow naturally from a steady process of 'political spillover'.[5] Like Haas, many scholars portray Europeanisation as the processes whereby member states' national policies, identities, beliefs, norms and institutional structures are increasingly influenced or 'domesticated' by their involvement with the EU's laws and institutions.[6] States become more Europeanised when the European dimension penetrates their national arenas of politics, policy and bureaucracy.[7] The idea of 'enhancing the European dimension' is often used by the EU institutions as a way to increase their power by redefining national ideas of peoplehood, territory and citizenship in terms of the EU and its federalist project.[8]

Europeanisation occurs at multiple levels, including both among member state nationals and among EU elites in Brussels. Within political science and EU studies, there is an extensive body of research that has sought to explain how officials working for the EU become 'socialised to Europe' or, in Jeffrey Checkel's words,[9] 'go native' within the EU's institutions. Much of this work draws on the neo-institutionalist methodologies that seek to understand how institutional rules, norms and 'cultures' shape the actions and orientation of individuals when they are part of a political institution. These approaches typically draw on organisational theories, political science models and psychological perspectives to measure cognitive shifts and loyalty transfer among European elites with the aim of identifying the 'scope conditions' that produce Europeanisation.[10] A key assumption that informs this work is that the habit of working together within the EU's institutions and continued exposure to the EU's norms and values has a transformative effect

5 S. George, *Politics and Policy in the European Community* (Oxford, Clarendon Press, 1985); P. Taylor, *The Limits of European Integration* (London, Croom Helm, 1983).

6 B. Jacobsson and U. Mörth, 'Europeiseringen och den svenska staten', in G. Ahrne (ed.), *Stater som organisationer* (Stockholm, Santérus Förlag, 1998), pp. 179–202; M. G. Cowles, J. Caporaso and T. Risse (eds.), *Transforming Europe: Europeanisation and Domestic Change* (London, Cornell University Press, 2001); K. Featherstone and C. M. Radaelli (eds.), *The Politics of Europeanisation* (Oxford, Oxford University Press, 2003); B. Jacobsson, P. Lægreid and O. K. Pedersen, *Europeanisation and Transnational States: Comparing Nordic Central Governments* (London, Routledge, 2004).

7 C. M. Radaelli, 'The Europeanisation of Public Policy', in K. Featherstone and C. M. Radaelli (eds.), *The Politics of Europeanization* (Oxford, Oxford University Press, 2003), pp. 27–56.

8 J. Borneman and N. Fowler, 'Europeanisation', *Annual Review of Anthropology* 26 (1997): 487–514.

9 J. Checkel, '"Going Native" in Europe?: Theorizing Social Interaction in European Institutions', *Comparative Political Studies* 36 (2003): 209–231.

10 J. Beyers, 'Multiple Embeddedness and Socialization in Europe: The Case of Council Officials', *International Organization* 59 (2005): 899–936; L. Hooghe, 'Several Roads Lead to International Norms, but Few via International Socialization: A Case Study of the European Commission', *International Organization* 59 (2005): 861–98.

on national and European civil servants; that over time this exposure generates supranational solidarities, European identity and a palpable sense of 'we-ness' among European officials. According to Jahl Trondal,[11] the EU's institutions are powerful agents in the re-socialisation of national civil servants and prime sites for incubating 'Europeanness', or what we might more accurately term 'EU-ropeanisation'. Even though it is increasingly recognised that Europeanisation is not as easily accomplished as some political scientists and integration theorists imagined, it is still assumed that Eurocrats take on a European identity and supranational solidarities accordingly.[12] But is this necessarily the case? As we argue below, the Europeanising/socialising effects of the EU's bureaucracy are not as straightforward or as predictable as these theorists assume.

These attempts to promote EU-ropeanisation, planned or unplanned, and how they are played out, responded to and navigated in relation to 'Eurocrats' are the focus of this chapter. By 'Eurocrats' we mean the senior officials (or *fonctionnaires*) with permanent positions in the European Commission, Parliament and Council, DNEs or trainees (*stagiaires*), who stay for a limited time working in the EU institutions; and representatives of member states in the EU's committees and working groups moving in and out of Brussels for a day or two every other month or so. These different positionings and responsibilities shape the way they act and how they are integrated within the institutions.[13] Eurocrats are typically viewed as the driving force of European integration and the embodiment of European identity.[14] Anthropologists have highlighted the active role that Eurocrats and national civil servants play in EU policy-making processes.[15] They have also shown how the EU civil service's supranational ethos and ideology influence the subjectivities of those who work for it.[16] Indeed, officials in

11 J. Trondal, 'Re-socializing Civil Servants: The Transformative Powers of EU Institutions', *Acta Politica* 39 (2004): 4–30.
12 Chalmers et al., *The End of the Eurocrats' Dream*.
13 A. Spinelli, *The Eurocrats: Conflict and Crisis in the European Community* (Baltimore, MD, Johns Hopkins University Press, 1966).
14 Trondal, 'Re-socializing Civil Servants'.
15 R. Thedvall, *Eurocrats at Work: Negotiating Transparency in Post-national Employment Policy* (Stockholm, Almqvist and Wiksell International, 2006); R. Thedvall, 'The EU's Nomads. National Eurocrats and European Policy-Making', in R. A. W. Rhodes, P. 't Hart and M. Noordegraaf (eds.), *Observing Government Elites: Up Close and Personal* (Basingstoke, Palgrave Macmillan, 2007), pp. 160–79; K. Geuijen, P. 't Hart, S. Princen and K. Yesilkagit, *The New Eurocrats: National Civil Servants in EU Policy-Making* (Amsterdam, Amsterdam University Press, 2008).
16 M. McDonald, 'Identities in the European Commission', in N. Nugent (ed.), *At the Heart of the Union: Studies of the European Commission* (Basingstoke, Macmillan, 1997), pp. 49–70; C. Shore, *Building Europe: The Cultural Politics of European Integration* (London, Routledge, 2000).

Brussels even had their own idiom for describing this process, which was often referred as '*engrenage*', a French term evoking the idea of 'enmeshing' or being caught in the cogs of a wheel.[17]

Ethnographic studies show that the everyday working life of Eurocrats involves not just a balancing act between the political and the technocratic, but also a complicated web of supranational and national ideals and practices where national identities are expressed through language, bureaucratic traditions and a tendency to interpret action through national stereotypes.[18] Georgakakis and Rowell[19] focus on the power relations and access to capital within what they describe as a Bourdieusian bureaucratic field of Eurocracy involving Eurocrats in all sorts of organisations involved in EU policy-making, including expert groups, the European Trade Union Confederation and European business leaders. They are concerned with the institutional and social construction of authority. We ask, what did 'Europeanisation' look like to the Eurocrats themselves and how did they navigate the national–supranational tensions between the interests of member states and those of the EU? In answering these questions, we will also illustrate why this issue remains relevant for understanding the challenges of administering the EU today.

Outline and Method: Returning to Field Notes

Our argument is set out in five parts. In the first we describe our method. The second describes the background and explains the types of Eurocrat dealt with in the chapter. In the third, we draw on empirical and ethnographic examples to examine more closely what the integration or socialisation of Eurocrats entails in practice. In the fourth, we elaborate on the deliberate attempts, planned or unplanned, to 'EU-ropeanise' Eurocrats and how they are played out, responded to and navigated in relation to the national and the European. Finally, the fifth section draws out some wider conclusions about the nature of socialisation or *engrenage* among EU elites.

Our aim is to provide an anthropological analysis of the EU on the basis of ethnographic research conducted within its institutional heartlands in

---

17 Shore, *Building Europe*, pp. 147–53.
18 M. Abélès, I. Bellier and M. McDonald, 'An Anthropological Approach to the European Commission', Report for the European Commission (1993), http://aei.pitt.edu/41765/1/A5783.pdf; McDonald, 'Identities in the European Commission'; Bellier, 'A Europeanized Elite?'; P. M. Lewicki, *EU-Space and the Euroclass: Modernity, Nationality, and Lifestyle among Eurocrats in Brussels* (Bielefeld, Transcript, 2017).
19 D. Georgakakis and J. Rowell (eds.), *The Field of Eurocracy: Mapping EU Actors and Professionals* (Berlin, Springer, 2013).

Brussels. This includes transcripts of interviews with Eurocrats, analysis of policy documents and grey literature, and field notes from participant observation carried out by both authors on the evolving administrative culture and internal dynamics of the European Commission during the 1990s and 2000s. There are reasons to believe that the administrative culture and internal dynamics today are similar to what they were then, but for an ethnographic study this is historical material and has to be treated as such. Except for our vignettes, we have therefore decided to use the past tense in the ethnographic material even though it is not unusual in ethnographic writings to use the 'ethnographic present'.

Shore carried out two periods of fieldwork in the Brussels headquarters of the European Commission (1993 and 1995–7) exploring the various ways in which the EU was seeking to expand its reach into the area of 'culture' (a previously national competence) and pursue its agenda for creating a 'people's Europe' and promoting European consciousness.[20] This entailed, among other things, following the activities of DG X, the DG responsible for culture, media, heritage, youth and sport. However, the research later shifted towards a study of DG 9 (Administration) and the administrative culture of the European Commission itself to explore whether EU civil servants embodied the supranational European identity that the EU claimed to be nurturing among European citizens. The focus on DG 9 was also prompted by advice from EU insiders that this was the place to look if one wanted to understand how the Commission works – and 'where the bodies are buried'.

Thedvall followed the Swedish as well as European Commission Eurocrats doing participant observation (2001 and 2002). First, she held a trainee position, a *stagiaire*, in DG EMPL in the European Commission during the autumn of 2001. Throughout 2002, she became an 'observer-member' of the Swedish delegation to the EU Employment Committee. She attended its preparatory meetings at the Swedish Ministry of Industry, Employment and Communication, went on its trips to Brussels and sat in on the Employment Committee meetings in Brussels.[21] The EU Employment Committee is the 'first' committee, in a hierarchy of committees, working groups and council meetings, where the member states and the Commission discuss and negotiate on EU employment issues which Thedvall was

20 C. Shore, 'Inventing the "People's Europe": Critical Perspectives on European Community Cultural Policy', *Man* 28 (1993): 779–800; Shore, *Building Europe*, pp. 26–32.
21 R. Thedvall, *Eurocrats at Work*; Thedvall, 'The EU's Nomads'; R. Thedvall, 'Negotiating Impartial Indicators: To Put Transparency into Practice in the EU', *Journal of the Royal Anthropological Institute* 18 (2012): 311–29.

studying. The EU Employment Committee was where most of the negotiations took place and, in practice, most decisions were made before the formal decision was taken in the Council of the EU. The European Commission has many of these committees and working groups preparing decisions.

We also briefly analyse what it is like to return to field notes from 20–25 years ago. Field notes are not just about what is going on. They are personal, and it has been a personal experience to return to them. Shore recalled the atmosphere of optimism and élan that still permeated the Commission following Jacques Delors' presidency and the huge strides that had been made towards widening and deepening the EU. The ideal of 'ever-closer union' proclaimed in the EU's founding treaties seemed to be coming to fruition. The Treaty on European Union, or Maastrich Treaty, which entered into force on 1 November 1993, represented a massive leap forward for the EU's project to construct a new European political order. The Maastricht Treaty established the EU, granted EU citizenship to every person who was a citizen of a member state and provided for the introduction of a central banking system and common currency (the euro). It also committed members to implementing common foreign and security policies and an 'area of freedom, justice and security'. EU officials and politicians were now speaking openly of the Commission as a future 'government of Europe' and the EU becoming a federal polity to rival the United States.[22] Yet, in contrast to this image of cohesion, dynamism and efficiency, Shore increasingly found evidence of a dysfunctional administration wracked by cleavages and contradictions. Far from being a streamlined, integrated and fully Europeanised civil service, the EU administration seemed to be an organisation riddled with factionalism, clientelism and networks, many of which were based on interest groups or nationality. As one insider commented, 'mafias' were everywhere in the EU. It had a thriving 'informal' system of administration that in many ways was more important and effective than its formal system.[23] Shore recalled the awkwardness of this situation and the dilemmas it posed for him, as an ethnographer trying to write about the EU's organisational culture.

22 C. Shore, '"Government without Statehood?": Anthropological Perspectives on Governance and Sovereignty in the European Union', *European Law Journal* 12 (2006): 709–24.
23 C. Shore, 'Culture and Corruption in the EU: Reflections on Fraud, Nepotism, and Cronyism in the European Commission', in D. Haller and C. Shore (eds.), *Corruption: Anthropological Perspectives* (London, Pluto, 2005), pp. 131–55; D. Spence and A. Stevens, 'Staff and Personnel Policy in the Commission', in D. Spence and G. Edwards (eds.), *The European Commission* (London, John Harper, 2006), pp. 173–208.

However, 2 years later, in March 1999, an independent committee produced a devastating report on fraud and mismanagement in the Commission which led to the resignation of the entire Santer Commission, paving the way for a major reform of the organisation.

Thedvall was reminded of her 30-year-old self in her field notes: her fast, not-thought-through, observations of the EU and its bureaucracy that had not yet benefited from her analysis in a PhD thesis; remembering friends she made, but with whom she had now lost contact; and remembering that her return ticket to Stockholm was with the airline Sabena, which went bankrupt (on 7 November 2001) during her fieldwork. She was also reminded that on her second day as a *stagiaire* terrorists flew hijacked airplanes into the World Trade Center towers in New York, and European Commission staff were told that they were allowed to go home if they felt unsafe. No one knew whether the EU might be under threat. Most of the people working in her building were not very worried. If the EU were to come under attack, which was highly unlikely, they thought it would be the European Parliament, or the buildings around Rond point Schuman: the Berlaymont housing the European Commission's headquarters or the Council of the EU. This might seem naïve today, as we have become more used to attacks of this type in Europe, but that was not the case in 2001. Still, it would continue to be a subject of discussion during the autumn, especially with the US-led wars against Afghanistan and Iraq that followed. It was also evident from field notes how life just went on. There was some more security when entering the Commission buildings for a few days, but then it was back to normal.

Background: The Eurocrats of the EU

The popular view of EU officials typically sees them as the epitome of what Herzfeld[24] identifies as the stereotypical bureaucrat: a rigid, inflexible, boring person working for his bureau rather than its clients or society at large. Eurocrats are frequently associated with forming useless, interventionist and regulatory policies, such as prescribing the size of a strawberry or banning curves in cucumbers and bananas. Moreover, like its national counterparts, the EU bureaucracy is held to be a hierarchical system akin to that envisaged by Max Weber[25] with its emphasis on rules, uniformity and compliance.

24 M. Herzfeld, *The Social Production of Indifference: Exploring the Symbolic Roots of Western Bureaucracy* (Chicago, IL, University of Chicago Press, 1992).
25 See H. H. Gerth and C. Wright Mills (eds.), *From Max Weber: Essays in Sociology* (Oxford, Oxford University Press, 1958 [1946]).

The bureaucratic stereotype only goes so far in describing the real world of EU policy-making processes. As one is drawn into that world, it becomes clear that the bureaucrats who populate it are complex, three-dimensional individuals; people of flesh and blood with different personalities and driven by different goals. Some of them are motivated by the urge to make the world a better place; some are just trying to do their job and perhaps climb the career ladder; some see themselves mainly as experts living up to the standards of their profession. Few of them match the stereotype of the bureaucrat strictly following the rules. Overwhelmingly, bureaucratic players in EU policy processes are, of necessity, flexible people.[26] They don't just apply rules. They take part in complex policy-making and organisational games. Broadly speaking, they are highly educated people with degrees in law, the social sciences and economics. They are not street-level bureaucrats[27] trying to implement policies. They are policy designers. As in classical bureaucratic theory, they offer advice to politicians, and their advice is based on technical, politically neutral expertise. In reality, the implied difference between 'politics' and 'administration' becomes blurred.[28] The notion of expertise becomes especially problematic in the context of the EU, because these Eurocrats have to act in the name of the EU or their member state when presenting 'EU' or 'national' positions and argue in the EU's or their member states' political interest.

Thus, the skills needed to do well in these games vary markedly from the classic role description of the bureaucrat, at least if you hold one of the higher grades, as a *fonctionnaire*, in the European Commission, or if you are one of those Eurocrats who have a position in the member state, but move in and out of EU meetings in Brussels representing your member state. Both these categories have to learn how to work in the EU context, but their processes of becoming integrated within the EU are different.

The ideal European Commission Eurocrats were the *fonctionnaires*. This is still the case, but as our knowledge about administrative levels, grades, taxes and 'Blue Books' (see below) is from our respective fieldworks, we will stick to the past tense. Most *fonctionnaires* enjoyed life-long employment in the Commission. Becoming a *fonctionnaire* started with a *concours*, or test. If

---

26 M. Albrow, *Do Organizations Have Feelings?* (London, Routledge, 1997).

27 M. Lipsky, *Street-Level Bureaucracy: Dilemmas of the Individual in Public Services* (New York, NY, Russel Sage Foundation, 1980).

28 G. Weiss and R. Wodak, 'Debating Europe: Globalization Rhetoric and European Union Unemployment Policies', in I. Bellier and T. M. Wilson (eds.), *An Anthropology of the European Union: Building, Imagining and Experiencing the New Europe* (Oxford, Berg, 2000), pp. 75–92.

one passed the test, one was called to an interview. The test differed depending on level and subject. There was a generalist *concours*, an economy *concours* and a lawyer's *concours*. The generalist *concours* might be directed to different areas like 'trade and development'. If one was accepted after the interview, it normally took 1–2 years (or longer) to get a position at the Commission, but once you had a job it was for life. As a *fonctionnaire*, you were one of the privileged at the Commission and in Brussels. You only paid a small tax to the Commission to cover your future pension and insurance, and the first year you did not have to pay any value-added tax.

There were A-, B-, C- and D-level *fonctionnaires*. A-level *fonctionnaires* were classified as 'conceptual' employees and had at a minimum a university degree, but many also had MAs and doctorates. B-level *fonctionnaires* had at a minimum a high-school diploma. A-level *fonctionnaires* were the people who handled their own areas and represented the Commission in meetings. These were the *fonctionnaires* who worked as policy designers. To become a Head of Unit or climb the Commission hierarchy, you had to be an A-level *fonctionnaire*. B-level *fonctionnaires* were generally assistants to A-level fonctionnaires. C-level *fonctionnaires* were mostly secretaries; and D-level *fonctionnaires* were security staff, porters and so on. If you had taken the B-level *concours* you could never be promoted to A-level: that required an A-level *concours*. Every level was divided into different wage and responsibility grades. Level A was divided into nine grades, starting at 9 and moving up the ladder. Every 2 years you were evaluated and then you also had the opportunity to move up a wage level. The first promotions were almost automatic, depending on how long you had worked in the Commission. However, few A-level *fonctionnaires* ever progressed automatically beyond A4 grade, as these senior positions were usually regarded as political appointments. To move up in the hierarchy, you had to become Head of Unit, Director, Deputy General Director or General Director, and that usually required intervention from national governments (typically, staff would comment that certain key senior posts had a 'national flag' over them). This effectively meant that the EU's civil service was only truly 'supranational' or independent up to the A4 level. Beyond that, you needed the political support of 'your' member state.

If you were not working as a *fonctionnaire* in the European Commission, you were either a DNE or a *stagiaire*. As the titles imply, you were only working temporarily in the European Commission. DNEs are national experts seconded by member state governments. They were supposed to learn how the Commission worked and take this knowledge back to their ministries. But this was also part of the Europeanisation process as the returning staff would, in theory, become emissaries for Europeanising the member states. DNEs were also an intermediate link between the Commission and the member states. DNEs usually stayed 2–3 years. They were paid both by the Commission and by their member state, and earned far higher salaries than the rate for an equivalent position in their home countries. DNEs had an interesting role. They might be high-ranking civil servants in their member state used to having major responsibilities, but when they arrived at the Commission they entered a very hierarchical system. DNEs complained that they did the job of A-level *fonctionnaires*, but they were not allowed to represent the Commission and were not always respected by lower-level *fonctionnaires*. DNEs from member states that have less hierarchical administrative systems than that of the Commission found it harder to adjust. The Commission hierarchy was built on the French civil servant model, and DNEs from, for example, the Nordic countries or the Netherlands and United Kingdom were used to a different style of organising.

There were also possibilities to become a *stagiaire*, or intern, in the European Commission. There were two main types of *stagiaire*; formal and informal. Formal *stagiaires* applied to have their name put in the 'Blue Book'. To become a Blue Book *stagiaire* you had to be of the right age (no older than twenty-seven) and have the right education. A degree in law, economics or political science and an MA in European Studies from the Collège d'Europe in Bruges or Johns Hopkins University in Bologna gave you a particular advantage. You then needed to be chosen from this book to become a *stagiaire*. Some Blue Book *stagiaires* were paid by the Commission, whereas others were not. Paid *stagiaires* were higher in ranking. If you wanted a *stagiaire* post you had to contact the place where you wanted to work and convince them to take you on. It was unlikely you would be picked from the book without making personal connections. Informal *stagiaires* were paid by their national government, university or some other organisation. They might be looking for a DNE post or they might not want to stay for as long as 2 years, which was the minimum for a DNE post. Candidate countries or countries outside the EU, such as Norway, would also send government *stagiaires*. When Thedvall enrolled in the induction course chronicled above, there was one *stagiaire* from Norway and two from Poland, which at the time of her fieldwork was still an accession state. Thedvall was a university *stagiaire*. There were usually several *stagiaires* doing research on the Commission itself, paid for by their universities or research centres. The standard duration of a *stage* is 6 months, but some do 3 months and others do a year.

A fourth type of Eurocrat was those working as member state representatives in the EU committees and working groups, travelling to Brussels for 1 or 2 days every other month. They were the 'occasional' Eurocrats, who often also had other areas of responsibility in their ministries in the member state in addition to the work connected to the EU arena. Finally, there was a fifth type of Eurocrat: those working for Commissioners as members of their cabinets. These were often individually hand-picked and trusted by Commissioners, but also included talented EU civil servants with expertise in a particular policy area.

The World(s) of Eurocrats

As anthropologists interested in culture and identity-formation within the European Commission, a key question for us was 'What does European integration look like at the heart of the EU?' The world of the Eurocrats in Brussels was surprisingly small and enclosed, and often characterised by considerable professional and social intimacy. Most of the EU buildings and offices were located within a small 2-kilometre square known as the 'European Quarter'. The Breydel building (where the Commission Presidency was located), the European Parliament and the Justus Lipsius building (the Council's headquarters) formed an even tighter triangle. Within this bounded area, EU *fonctionnaires*, seconded national experts, journalists, diplomats, lobbyists and politicians would mingle and interact on a daily basis. Local cafés and restaurants buzzed with 'Eurospeak', a curious blend of European languages often punctuated by foreign loan words and EU acronyms intelligible only to the initiated. Most EU staff, particularly those with children, tended to be concentrated in a handful of suburbs, typically the more affluent residential neighbourhoods such as Etterbeek, Ixelles/Elsene, Uccle and Woluwé Saint Lambert. Despite the oft-repeated claims about its multinational and multicultural character, what was striking about the Commission was its lack of ethnic diversity and the absence of women from senior posts. Indeed, despite conscious attempts to promote more gender equality, by 2002 the number of women 'A-grade' *fonctionnaires* was still only 22 per cent.[29] This enclosed geographical environment combined with the relative segregation of EU officials from the local *Bruxelloise* population created an extraordinary intensity of interaction among EU officials and

29 Spence and Stevens, 'Staff and Personnel Policy in the Commission'.

political actors. This was also something that Olivier Baisnée[30] noted in his study of the EU press corps in Brussels. Baisnée recounts the shock experienced by a journalist when first encountering this EU microcosm and the rules that govern it. This journalist speaks of

> a technocratic world that was obeying incomprehensible rules for the outsider; a conventional world; a world where I would say journalists, civil servants and diplomats were sleeping together. There was no distance at all, no objectivity. A European militant's world of people persuaded that they are working for the good of humanity. In short, I couldn't distinguish between who was a journalist, who was a civil servant and who was a diplomat. It's a bit strange, isn't it?[31]

Like the EU press corps, officials and lobbyists seemed to experience a real sense of community in the rituals of daily interaction, while the regular circuit of meetings and diplomatic engagements often gives the appearance of a 'traveling cocktail' party.[32] Shore recalls a dinner that seemed to capture many of the prevailing concerns shared by Eurocrats in this EU Brussels microcosm:

> It is March 1996, the 'European Year of Lifelong Learning' in the EU calendar, and three months into the Italian presidency of the Union. My partner and I have been invited to dinner by Geoff and Ingrid who live in Ixelles. Geoff is a British official who has worked for the European Parliament for two decades; his wife Ingrid is an interpreter at the Commission. The six guests are of mixed nationality (Philip is Spanish, Justine is French; others are Greek, German or South African). Over canapés and a glass of chilled Sancerre ('Santer's favourite', someone quips) we talk about how we know Geoff and Ingrid; everyone is connected with the EU: one is a lobbyist, another works for the Commission; the others are a journalist, translator and independent consultant, respectively. But apart from being expatriates, the key point of connection is that everyone has children at the European School. Over dinner the conversation moves quickly from a discussion of Britain's BSE beef crisis (everyone agrees that John Major is 'awful'), to the 'European Voice' newspaper that has just started a free distribution to all the EU offices, to Geoff's awful journey on the 'Eurostar' last week. I notice that direct references to people's nationality is studiously avoided (except when the conversation includes the topic of

---

30 O. Baisnée, 'Can Political Journalism Exist at the EU Level?', paper presented to the workshop on 'Political Journalism: New Challenges, New Practices', ECPR joint session, Copenhagen (2000).
31 Ibid., p. 5.   32 Ibid., p. 3.

Brussels or Belgian society: people feel safe to criticize the Belgians). As we progress through the main course an animated conversation ensues about the use of English in the EU. Ingrid insists that it is not simply that English is fast replacing French as the lingua franca of the EU, but 'the English language itself is being Europeanized'. English spoken inside the institutions is 'quite different' and 'unique'. Everyone agrees. But as we move to dessert, the main topic of conversation reverts back to the European School and gossip about particular teachers and the head of school. I ask the Greek and German couple what language their children speak at home: the answer is Greek with their mother and German with their father – and French or English at school and in the playground, depending on the company. Ingrid remarks on how cosmopolitan their children are – and how sad it must be 'to grow up as a monoglot'. I remember thinking: 'that's the first time I've ever heard that expression. Is this an example of the new Europeanized English I wonder?

(C. Shore, field notes 1996)

This combination of Brussels talk and awkwardness around national differences seemed typical of the way social groups interacted inside the EU's institutional milieu. More importantly, it was notable how much Eurocrats tended to mix and socialise with other EU-connected individuals in these expat enclaves within the Belgian capital.

In the Corridors of the Commission and EU Meeting Rooms

The professional world(s) of the Eurocrats we focus on here are played out in the corridors of the Commission and the EU meeting rooms. In what follows, we offer glimpses of the workings of these places.

While the Commissioner of a Directorate General makes the final decision in day-to-day policy-making, the decision-making process involved both permanent and temporary staff as well as national civil servants from the member states. Thedvall recalls the life of Eurocrats in the Directorate General of Employment and Social Affairs in the European Commission.

Shifting deadlines was a recurrent issue in the Commission. In this sense it was a rather whimsical organisation as those at the top were eager to have their hands on everything, which meant that issues were constantly moving up and down. An example of this was when Abigail and Thedvall were working on the articles for the member states' press releases that were to accompany the launch of the new Employment package. This included guidelines, national reports and comparisons between member states and recommendations to member states. The articles included some of those recommendations for the member states. Thedvall [Swedish] had been tasked to do Sweden and Finland and Abigail [British] was given the UK and Ireland. Bernard had left them with a model article that he had written about Italy. It was Friday and Bernard said it was okay if they were ready on Monday. However, after lunch Catherine, the Head of Unit, said that the Director and Director General required them that evening. By Monday, the articles had been run through the system and Abigail and Thedvall were asked to help with the changes. The Director General also wanted some changes in the general text. The Director's secretary called to make sure some changes were made in the Deputy Directors General's speech that Abigail and Bernard had been working on for a week.

(R. Thedvall, field notes 2001)

The hierarchical system of the Commission had its own workings, but as Commission Eurocrats they also had to handle the politics of the national.

Thom, a Detached National Expert [DNE] from the Netherlands, came into Abigail's [and Thedvall's] office to discuss a table that was in the document that compared the member states' labour markets. The document had been released a few days earlier and now complaints from the member states were starting to come to the Commission. As usual, Thom, speaking with a dry tone, said some of the member states didn't agree on the numbers. 'Everybody wants good numbers.' Abigail smiled and said ironically that we should have put the table in the supporting document, then they might not have seen it.

(R. Thedvall, field notes 2001)

The national civil servants were attentive to the way their member state was portrayed in the Commission document. Thom and Abigail, both seconded national civil servants, understood where this emphasis came from, but, as they were working for the European Commission, they had their Commission hat on and therefore privileged the EU perspective.

An important part of being a senior Eurocrat was taking part in various EU committees and working groups, especially on policy issues like employment and social protection which, with the 1997 Treaty of Amsterdam, had become a shared responsibility of the Commission and member states, along with jurisdiction over working conditions. There was a certain way of working in these committees that had to be mastered if members wanted to shape the arguments and influence the policy process. The members had to know when to speak, what to say and how to say it. As Schwartzman points out, a formal meeting needs, apart from rules about who starts and ends meetings, who has the right to call speakers and so forth, 'a series of rules and conventions for ordering and regulating talk'.[33] These rules included who

33 H. Schwartzman, *The Meeting: Gathering in Organizations and Communities* (New York, NY, Springer, 1989).

could be a member, voting systems and so forth. Other rules were not explicitly expressed or written down but had to be learnt by the members either through learning-by-doing or by someone explaining them. These were the rules that members had to know in order to put forward their positions in the group, such as asking for the floor by putting the member state sign on its end or having to speak into the microphone when presenting, so that the interpreter could translate. They also had to know what to present and how to present it. As a Commission representative in the meeting, they had to act and argue in the interest of the Commissioner. As a member state representative, they had to act and argue as their government expected. What this was had to be learnt.

> On the morning of a Committee meeting day, Anders, a senior Swedish representative, but also the President of the working group today, gave last-minute coaching to Annika and Marie, two new Swedish representatives in the Committee, on what they should say at the meeting. The expert on the issue of, in this case, 'gender equality' had not had time to prepare a Swedish position on the 'childcare' indicators beforehand, and now Anders informed Annika and Marie that this was an important question for Sweden, with high priority for the Swedish government. For this reason they must not only state the Swedish position but also emphasise its importance in the meeting. (R. Thedvall, field notes 2002)

Most decisions were made in the various working group and committee meetings among Eurocrats, even though the formal decision was taken by the Commissioners and Ministers in the Council of the European Union. It was therefore important to make allies if a certain issue was important.

> Catherine, the Head of Unit, Bernard, the Deputy Head of Unit, and Thedvall were walking out of the Council of the European Union building. We had taken part in one of the Council's working groups discussing the employment package as representatives of the Commission. We had been there for about an hour. Catherine and Bernard discussed strategy. Catherine said that if the Deputy Director General wanted to get through the issue of gender pay gap then the Commission needed to align themselves with some of the member states. We have to think about how we should play this, she said. A few weeks later when the issue was discussed in the COREPER [Council of Representatives to the European Union], the Commission asked for a cover note that they reserve themselves regarding the gender pay gap. The Commission had not been able to have a decision on this, because most of the member states were against it. (R. Thedvall, field notes 2001)

Thedvall recalled another time when making allies entailed one DG making friends with member states against another DG:

> The Swedish delegates to the Committee were in the lobby. It was evening and we were about to go to dinner. It had been the first day of two of the Committee meeting. One of the delegates had held a meeting with Svante, a Swede working in the Commission as a *fonctionnaire* in the Directorate General of Employment and Social Affairs. Svante wanted Sweden to support the proposal to introduce the Employment package in November. The Directorate General of Economy and Finance [DG ECFIN] wanted to present the package in February along with the EU's broad economic guidelines instead, but DG EMPL did not want this because it would mean that they would lose some of the agenda-setting power. It had moved all the way to the two Commissioners and they were set to meet with the President of the European Commission. (R. Thedvall, field notes 2002)

Negotiation, making allies and persuading others was a key part of committee and working group meeting life. Even if there was a possibility to decide by voting, the goal was to reach a consensus decision. Thedvall was following the policy process of developing indicators for measuring the quality of working life in national labour markets. The member states and the Commission had met several times already to discuss the indicators in the Employment Committee, made up of senior Eurocrats from the member states and the Commission. This was the last committee meeting before the issue would go to the Council of the EU and the committee had to make a decision.

> During a lunch break in one of the committee meeting, Thedvall went to lunch with one of her Commission colleagues, Manfred (20 November 2001). They took the lift to the top-floor restaurant. As they arrive they noticed that they were almost the only ones there from the Committee. Mark, one of the Secretaries in the Committee, once said that when the different delegations eat somewhere other than in the conference centre, he thought it was an indication that a difficult question was considered and that they had to discuss, in private, how to put their position across. This was certainly the case today because the discussions had been quite tough and members have encountered difficulties in agreeing on the indicators.
> (R. Thedvall, field notes 2001)

What these vignettes illustrate, besides the need to understand the invisible rules and unspoken norms of the Commission and master its meeting etiquette, is that a key part of the work of a Eurocrat entails learning how to reach consensus. These skills are essential features of what becoming a good Eurocrat means in practice.

The Presence of the National and the European
in the World of Eurocrats

In the world of Eurocrats, the national and the European are always present and in tension with each other, not just in the daily interaction or in the policy process, but also in the make up of the Commission. As Abélès et al. observed long ago,[34] the national is even encouraged by Commission leaders through its appointment of Director Generals, its *cabinet* system, the continuous secondment of DNEs, and the fast-track promotion of national appointees to top positions in the administration through what officials call *parachutage* ('parachuting'), although others denounce this as cronyism.[35] Interaction within the EU thus encourages member states to think according to the national. As Jacobsson and Mörth argue,[36] EU membership has, paradoxically, forced member states to adopt a 'national' position in areas where until now they did not feel the need for one.

At the same time the idea of a supranational civil service pioneering European integration is strong and, on taking up their post, each new Commission *fonctionnaire* is required to recite a 'solemn declaration' before the justices of the European court. A similar declaration is contained in the staff statutes which govern all EU officials. This is effectively an 'oath of allegiance' by which EU officials solemnly swear to carry out their duties independently of member states and refrain from taking instructions from any government, institution, body, office or entity.[37]

There are also more informal mechanisms that promote European solidarity and identity, including a certain kind of shared language. This 'Eurospeak', as officials sometimes called it, was made up of an abundance of acronyms, a lingua franca through French or English, or rather a pidginised French and English because most of the users did not have either language as their mother tongue. The French and English used was also often made up of a mix of both languages, spoken of as 'Franglais' or 'Frenglish', as the earlier dinner party vignette suggests. For Eurocrats living and working in Brussels, being conversant with the EU acronyms, local (i.e., institutional) gossip and jargon that pepper Eurospeak conversations is essential to operate effectively

---

34 Abélès, Bellier and McDonald, 'An Anthropological Approach to the European Commission'.

35 Shore, 'Culture and Corruption in the EU'.

36 Jacobsson and Mörth, 'Europeisering och den svenska staten', pp. 199–200.

37 European Commission, *Regulations of the Rules Applicable to Officials and Other Servants of the European Commission* (Luxembourg, Office of Official Publications of the European Commission, 1993).

within this bureaucratic milieu, as is the ability to move between languages mid-sentence.

Commission *fonctionnaires* were expected to master both French and English. The Commission was, however, made up of temporary staff in the form of DNEs and *stagiaires*, many of whom were more comfortable with English than French. Still, it was not unusual for French speakers to insist on speaking French during Commission meetings even though it meant that some staff did not completely understand, as Thedvall experienced many times. As a Eurocrat proper you should be fluent in French and English[38] and in the EU's plethora of acronyms. This shared Eurospeak was an important aspect of the EU's distinctiveness and identity. Even outside these formal office settings, it was an important marker of belonging to the EU. But the Eurocrat environment was also multilingual. Most formal meetings between member states and the Commission had interpreters present. Documents were translated into the member states' languages when a decision was made on a policy issue. Commission staff sometimes socialised among friends sharing the same language. The Director General of DG EMPL sent regular official invitations to fellow national staff members within the Commission to drinks. The *stagiaire* system even had clubs based on nationality and parties that involved showing off some peculiarity of their member state. The presence of the national was not only evident in the documents and the organisation of the DG with the national desks. It was also present through the presidency. The presidency moved between member states and changed every 6 months. The member state holding the presidency usually had an agenda it wanted to bring to a conclusion by the end of its presidency. During Thedvall's period doing fieldwork, this was in the area of employment issues and qualitative indicators on the member states' labour markets. This work had already started during the Portuguese presidency 18 months earlier, and had continued during France and Sweden's presidencies. The order of presidencies created (unexpected) alliances where the Portuguese, French, Swedes and Belgians were working together on this very issue.

The mix of the national and the European was particularly present in the negotiations in the EU's committee and working group meetings where member states and Eurocrats thrashed out the details ministers later ratified. This was evident when there were sensitive issues on the agenda, such as the 'quality in work' indicator noted earlier. The member states anticipated how

---

38 Abélès, Bellier and McDonald, 'An Anthropological Approach to the European Commission', pp. 32–8.

the indicators would play out when used and they wanted to make sure that they looked good in statistical tables, an important issue as the experience of Thom and Abigail showed. The committee working on these issues was asked, through its president, to make a statement in the Council of the EU on the progress on the indicators. It was a verbal report, but they anticipated that the Belgian presidency would request a written text, and written texts leave traces and affect policy. So, even if it was only a few paragraphs, the committee worked for 3 hours to write this statement together. As the president of the committee (from the UK) said at one point: 'Well, what fun this is. I meant what I said about not leaving the room until this is finished' (5 October 2001). The member states and the Commission had to negotiate their positions and formulate a common decision that was a mix of the Commission's European position and the national positions. This is how EU policy was made.

Conclusion: Eurocrats, Europeanisation and the EU Project

We began this chapter by asking what the 'EU-ropeanisation' of senior EU civil servants entails in practice; how they adapt to, or become socialised within, the EU's institutional habitus; and how they navigate the contradictions between the national and the supranational and the political and the technical. As we have argued, these tensions operate throughout the EU's administrative apparatus, and officials have learned to balance them in subtle ways. While the ideal of European cosmopolitanism is considered morally superior to nationalism or the selfish pursuit of national interests, the EU's project for European integration nevertheless requires that 'national perspectives' are recognised and accommodated in its policy process. EU *fonctionnaires* are, of course, 'professional Europeans' who have sworn an oath of allegiance to serve Europe and the European interest, but they also owe their livelihood, job security and careers to their position as EU employees. In one sense, these are arguably the most important 'scope conditions' for socialisation to Europe; that is, officials have a strong personal investment in the continuing success of the EU and its project. If the EU-ropeanisation of elites is measured by loyalty transfer and the extent to which officials come to identify with the EU's goals and acquire strong feelings of belonging to its institutions and values, then it stands to reason that Eurocrats both epitomise and embody European identity and consciousness in its most developed form. However, the vision entertained by Monnet, Halstein and other EU founding fathers, of an independent and autonomous European civil service acting as a 'higher' authority that stands beyond the influence of nation states and the logic of nationalism, is far from what exists in practice. If Eurocrats are the driving force of European integration and pioneers of European identity, as some claim,[39] this merely serves to highlight the composite, contingent and contradictory nature of the European Commission and the ways in which its core principles of independence and meritocracy have had to adapt to political realities and the interests and influence of its member states. This is another reason why learning to compromise is so important in the education and training of EU officials.

Our ethnographic studies also highlighted the performative dimensions of being a Eurocrat. Learning to become a competent EU official Eurocrat involved mastering a complex set of social, linguistic and bureaucratic skills and adapting to the often invisible and unspoken institutional rules of the game. Multilingualism, meeting etiquette, attention to hierarchy and protocol and the ability to shift register were all key elements in the socialisation of EU officials. These were defining features of what, to echo Bourdieu,[40] we might term the Eurocrat 'habitus'; that enduring set of structured dispositions through which the administrative culture of the EU is created and reproduced.

Anthropological research also revealed just how small, self-contained and insular the 'world' of EU officials in Brussels is. Beyond the exclusiveness of its institutional practices, this is partly a consequence of the residential locations, working patterns and affluent lifestyles that EU officials share; further 'scope conditions' for socialisation to Europe. This 'worlding' phenomenon is reinforced by the elite European School system, which is one of the perks of being a Eurocrat. Whether this was intentional or not, the rarefied expat lifestyle tends to insulate Eurocrats from contact with the harsher and more mundane realities of Belgian society. It also places Eurocrats in a world very different from that of other inhabitants of Brussels. In this respect, the EU-ropeanisation of Eurocrats does not provide a model or template for the EU's wider project for the Europeanisation of member state nationals. The integration of elites at the core is unlikely to spill over into shifting the loyalties of the European masses or forge a wider sense of 'We-ness' among the would-be European demos. This in turn raises the question about the depth and permanency of this sense of European identity

39 Trondal, 'Re-socializing Civil Servants'.
40 P. Bourdieu, *Outline of a Theory of Practice* (Cambridge, Cambridge University Press, 1977).

among Eurocrats. Put simply, is the EU-ropeanisation of Eurocrats more about 'fitting in' to the EU's institutional rules and ways of acting than any permanent shift in loyalty or changes to what, echoing Raymond Williams, we might call the 'structures of feeling'?[41]

As we have sought to illustrate, there are different ways of being a Eurocrat and different degrees to which EU employees become EU-ropeanised. European identity is situational, and the tensions between the European and the national play out differently for the various categories of Eurocrat. Europeanisation is both contingent and performative. From the perspective of the *fonctionnaires* themselves, it is also about belonging and having a sense of mission or purpose. The EU's narrative about itself is attractive and appealing as it places Eurocrats as pioneers at the vanguard of history; policy entrepreneurs working to promote the 'European idea' and serving the peoples of Europe. What the 'European interest' means in this narrative is typically undefined. Beyond a sense of being part of an elite project, the other appeals of being a Eurocrat include high status, excellent job security, high salaries and a comfortable lifestyle. The development of a distinct *esprit de corps* among staff working in the EU is therefore to be expected. However, as we discovered through our fieldwork, socialisation to Europe took different forms. While some officials were committed Eurocrats serving the European interest, others were politically networked and closely connected to their national government. That closeness to national government also related to the difference between the constant Eurocrats (*fonctionnaires*), who were supposed to be totally committed to the European project, and the occasional Eurocrats (DNEs, *stagiaires*, national representatives working in the EU) understood as somewhere in between. There were variations in how *fonctionnaires* understood their role and their relation to their national governments. We also met disillusioned time-serving Eurocrats caught in the EU's 'gilded cage' (i.e., unable to leave because the pay and conditions were too good to give up) and self-serving, entrepreneurial Eurocrats creatively building their own networks and bureaucratic empires.[42]

Playing the Brussels game, as some officials described it, is a useful metaphor for describing how EU-ropeanisation is understood by some officials. As an experiment in institution building, the European Commission now stands at a crossroads. The rise of populist nationalism across Europe has

41 R. Williams, *The Long Revolution* (New York, NY, Columbia University Press, 1961).
42 Shore, 'Culture and Corruption in the EU'.

once again drawn attention to the EU's so-called 'democratic deficit', prompting accusations that the EU is run by a ruling elite that is increasingly out of touch with the people it claims to serve. In this respect, and in a climate of growing Euroscepticism, the factors that produced successful integration among EU elites could also be the source of its greatest problem if the result is increasing distance between elites in Brussels and citizens in the rest of Europe.

Recommended Reading

Fligstein, N. *Euroclash: The EU, European Identity, and the Future of Europe* (New York, NY, Oxford University Press, 2009).

Georgakakis, D. *European Civil Service in (Times of) Crisis: A Political Sociology of the Changing Power of Eurocrats* (Cham, Springer, 2017).

Lewicki, P. M. *EU-Space and the Euroclass: Modernity, Nationality, and Lifestyle among Eurocrats in Brussels* (Bielefeld, Transcript, 2017).

Nugent, N. (ed.). *At the Heart of the Union: Studies of the European Commission* (Houndsmill, Macmillan, 2014).

Rhodes, R. A. W., P. 't Hart and M. Noordegraaf (eds.). *Observing Government Elites: Up Close and Personal* (Basingstoke, Palgrave Macmillan, 2007).

Shore, C. *Building Europe: The Cultural Politics of European Integration* (London, Routledge, 2000).

Thedvall, R. 'Negotiating Impartial Indicators: To Put Transparency into Practice in the EU', *Journal of the Royal Anthropological Institute* 18 (2012): 311–29.

Trondal, J. *An Emergent European Executive Order* (Oxford, Oxford University Press, 2010).

19

Elite Networks of Allegiance

GILES SCOTT-SMITH

Introduction

The narrative of European integration was long dominated by the role of the participating member states, as personified in their respective presidents and prime ministers, in forging an ever-expanding set of institutions and an increasingly dense legal framework. This orthodox view saw nation states at the centre of the process, gradually pooling sovereignty to construct an ever-closer union. Analyses have differed as to the driving forces behind these processes.[1] Debates in the 1990s between advocates of intergovernmentalism and supranationalism as the guiding explanatory frameworks still focused on an apparently self-contained European context, although the role of non-state actors did begin to feature more in the analysis.[2] In contrast, more recent scholarship has contested the way the history of European integration has generally been framed in isolation from wider social, economic and political developments. Repositioning the processes of European integration in a global context requires that Europe as an historical entity be 'provincialised'.

Very often, it does not suffice to study the internal institutional mechanisms of the European Community (EC)/European Union (EU) and their interplay with member states and external partners, such as candidate countries or the United States. Rather, one also needs to focus on the multiplicity of interconnections with other international organisations,

---

1 See, for instance, W. Lipgens, *A History of European Integration*, vol. 1: *1945–47* (Oxford, Clarendon, 1982); A. Milward, *The European Rescue of the Nation State* (London, Routledge, 1992).

2 D. Wincott, 'Institutional Interaction and European Integration: Towards an Everyday Critique of Liberal Intergovernmentalism', *Journal of Common Market Studies* 33, no. 4 (1995): 597–609; A. Moravcsik, *The Choice for Europe: Social Purpose and State Power from Messina to Maastricht* (London, Routledge, 1998).

with non-governmental platforms and with other actors crowding the international stage, which have energised, complemented or rivalled the efforts of the EC forum. Such an approach assesses the various routes of exchange and inserts the efforts of the EC into a broader history of European, transatlantic and global cooperation and often also into a longer chronological span. Accordingly, we have to move beyond an 'intrinsic' perspective.[3]

Taking this as its starting point, this chapter will examine how a focus on networks not so much provincialises as transcends our understanding of Europe. Networks, whether they have been based upon specific policy fields, political allegiance, or the esprit de corps of social 'elites' in general, have cut across 'nation-centric' interpretations of integration since the beginning. 'Europe', as an idea, a mission and a cultural teleology, connected many influential actors who fall outside the 'methodological nationalism' of the mainstream histories of European integration and its catalogue of heroic figures.[4] It is argued here that in order to grasp the full relevance of a network-based approach to the history of European integration it is necessary to decouple the consideration of networks from an assessment of their policy relevance. This opens up an understanding of networks as sites of socialisation, enabling the congregation and organisation of elite political interests that sought to shape European integration in particular directions.

As a case study to illustrate this, the chapter will examine the figure of Paul van Zeeland, a key 'Europe-builder' in the 1940s and 1950s, who blended his formal and informal diplomatic roles into a comprehensive strategy for Europe's future. Van Zeeland was Belgian prime minister twice during 1935–7, and foreign minister from 1949 to 1954. Alongside these official roles, van Zeeland occupied numerous positions in European and transatlantic non-state networks, such as the European League for Economic Cooperation (ELEC) and the Bilderberg meetings, that shared his aim of achieving an economically liberal form of integration based on the maintenance of national sovereignty. By analysing van Zeeland's role, it will be shown how membership of specific political networks enabled him to act out a two-level strategy both on the formal and on the informal level, arguing

---

3 K. K. Patel, 'Provincialising European Union: Co-operation and Integration in Europe in a Historical Perspective', *Contemporary European History* 22, no. 4 (2013): 649–73, 650–1.
4 See U. Beck, 'Toward a New Critical Theory with a Cosmopolitan Intent', *Constellations* 10 (2003): 453–68.

for national sovereignty while at the same time making use of transnational connections to bolster it.

After providing a brief general introduction to the value of networks for historical analysis, this chapter will look at the ways in which networks feature in the study of European integration. It will focus on the distinction between policy networks and political networks, and use this as the basis for the case study on Paul van Zeeland. The chapter will then conclude with some reflections on the place of networks in European integration history.

Analysing Networks

Historians have drawn on the approaches of network theories as devised in political science, anthropology and sociology to reinterpret how societies function, how ideas travel and how power has been diffused. This has involved reconsidering the connections between or through more established categories of analysis such as the family, the rural–urban divide or the nation itself. The term 'network' is in this sense generally used for 'loosely evoking the existence of a world of connections that go beyond taken-for-granted borderlines'.[5] However, connections in the form of social ties are a given in historical analysis. Identifying the existence of particular networks can illustrate more clearly how and why certain connections were more important over time than others. They can also tell us something about shared identities and belief systems, and how and why these were utilised to pursue political goals. Methodologically it is important not to read too much into the power of networks, in order to avoid 'strategic over-interpretations of network patterns' that assume a greater coherence and meaning to social ties than the actors themselves were aware of or making use of. If defined carefully, networks can be a useful tool 'to understand the patterns of precisely defined ties … to carefully consider their effects, their origins, their changes in response to external events and their consequences'.[6]

In the case of European integration studies, networks have been primarily investigated from the perspective of cross-border connections between policy-makers and how these have contributed to the direction and intensity of sectoral integration. Ernst Haas, the founder of neo-functionalism, had

5 E. Roldán Vera and T. Schupp, 'Network Analysis in Comparative Social Sciences', *Comparative Education* 42, no. 3 (2006): 405–29, 406.
6 C. Lemercier, 'Formal Network Methods in History: Why and How?', in G. Fertig (ed.), *Social Networks, Political Institutions, and Rural Societies* (Turnhout, Brepols, 2015), pp. 281–310, 284, 288.

posited the sequence of increasing interactions in one sector leading to a spillover effect in other related sectors, triggering the development of forms of regional institution to oversee the rules-based system that was emerging. Further down the line, this would lead to a transfer of allegiances as political and economic actors at the national level recognise the increasing importance of the regional (supranational) institutions. A crucial dimension to these processes was the socialisation of elites on a regional level as a precondition for concrete steps to integration, since a shared 'sympathy-feeling' for the outlook and behaviour of other groups was necessary in order to overcome national allegiances.[7] The use of constructivist theory and the identification of 'transnational policy communities' by Thomas Risse (formerly Risse-Kappen) later linked national circles of policy expertise, breaking open the notion of the nation-state as a unitary silo. Building on Haas, Risse laid the ground for exploring the transnational networks of experts, active both in the service of and outside of the state, who bridged national and European interests, in doing so transcending the more abstract approaches of neo-functionalism and intergovernmentalism by 'bringing people back in'.[8] This enabled further recognition of the input of individuals, their backgrounds and motivations, their connections and their images of integration, something that later neo-functionalist scholars have engaged with.[9]

Attention then shifted to patterns of governance that blended state and non-state actors in a wider, more informal, less hierarchical (and often less accountable) landscape of decision-making and political communication.[10] For most political scientists, these state/non-state linkages – generally termed policy networks – have stemmed from the relative decline of the nation-state as the primary administrative and regulatory body since the 1970s, caused by the increasing marketisation of public goods provision and the growing

---

7 E. B. Haas, 'The Challenge of Regionalism', *International Organization* 12, no. 4 (1958), 440–58, 443; K. W. Deutsch, S. A. Burrell, R. A. Kann et al., *Political Community and the North Atlantic Area: International Organization in the Light of Historical Experience* (Princeton, NJ, Princeton University Press, 1957).

8 T. Risse-Kappen (ed.), *Bringing Transnational Relations Back In: Non-state Actors, Domestic Structures and International Institutions* (Cambridge, Cambridge University Press, 1995); R. Keohane and J. Nye, *Transnational Relations and World Politics* (Cambridge, MA, Harvard University Press, 1972); W. Kaiser, 'Bringing People and Ideas Back In: Historical Research on the European Union', in D. Phinnemore and A. Warleigh (eds.), *Reflections on European Integration: 50 Years of the Treaty of Rome* (Basingstoke, Palgrave, 2009), pp. 22–41.

9 A. Niemann, *Explaining Decisions in the European Union* (Cambridge, Cambridge University Press, 2006).

10 R. A. W. Rhodes, 'Understanding Governance: Ten Years On', *Organization Studies* 28, no. 8 (2007): 1243–64.

competence of supranational regulatory institutions. For Rhodes, policy networks were 'sets of formal institutional and informal linkages between governmental and other actors structured around shared if endlessly negotiated beliefs and interests in public policy making and implementation'.[11] Extensive research in this field was pursued during the late 1990s and early 2000s, generally focusing on developments within specific isolated sectors that, cumulatively, would ideally provide an overview of European governance structures as a whole.[12] While most research adopted a presentist bias as if this governance turn were purely attuned to the forces of globalisation in the 1990s, there has been additional interest in the role of ideas, traditions and narratives in shaping the formation and direction of policy networks.[13] Historians countered the social scientific presentism by applying the same approach to the history of integration as a whole, raising the point that forms of state/non-state governance have been part of the processes of European integration since their formal beginnings after the Second World War.

In his history of the contribution of Christian Democracy to Europe's story, Wolfram Kaiser spelled out a clear agenda: 'It is vital therefore to move decisively beyond nation-state-centric approaches to understanding the increasingly integrated western Europe after 1945 and to connect it for the first time with the political and social history of (western) Europe more generally.'[14] For Kaiser, it makes no sense to write about the extensive impact of European institutions and rule-making on national political systems, economic behaviour and peoples' lives without acknowledging the full social, political and symbolic significance of transnational coalition-building.[15] This also meant taking aim at the tendency of political science research to focus only on policy-relevant fields, in order to trace the institutional rules and behavioural norms related to the making of European public policy. From this perspective, policy relevance has determined the extent to which

11 R. A. W. Rhodes, 'Policy Network Analysis', in M. Moran, M. Rein and R. Goodin (eds.), The Oxford Handbook of Public Policy (Oxford and New York, NY, Oxford University Press, 2008), pp. 425–47, 426.
12 H. Heinelt and R. Smith, Policy Networks and European Structural Funds (Aldershot, Avebury, 1996); E. Grande and A. Peschke, 'Transnational Cooperation and Policy Networks in European Science Policy-Making', Research Policy 28, no. 1 (1999): 43–61; A.-M. Bocse, 'Transnational Policy Networks and the European Union's Energy Policy', Contemporary Politics 21, no. 3 (2015): 294–307.
13 M. Bevir and R. A. W. Rhodes, Governance Stories (London, Routledge, 2006).
14 W. Kaiser, Christian Democracy and the Origins of the European Union (Cambridge, Cambridge University Press, 2007), p. 8.
15 W. Kaiser, 'From State to Society? The Historiography of European Integration', in M. Cini and A. Bourne (eds.), Palgrave Advances in European Union Studies (Basingstoke, Palgrave, 2006), pp. 190–208.

networks were addressed or not. Researchers analysing the field of multilevel governance regarded networks as relevant only to the extent that they contributed to our understanding of their 'multiple functions . . . within the EU policy process'.[16] In contrast, historians have expanded the field to focus on political and technical networks, escaping the policy-relevance criteria and loosening the bounds of the research to take in transnational connections beyond (and before) the EU.[17] This broader exploration of informal social ties and their importance for understanding and explaining the processes of European integration[18] has shifted attention to 'sets of actors not merely engaged in any kind of social communication, but forms of cooperation geared towards shaping the political organization of social life'.[19] This covers forms of social and political communication, socialisation, and the transfer of ideas *below* the supranational realm to escape the limitations of political science's fixation with policy outcomes in the EU alone. Actorness and agency have therefore been granted to a range of experts and protagonists, from political parties to churches to technicians to media, which have long been regarded as secondary or irrelevant from the perspective of government-based decision-making.[20]

This 'network turn' in the history of European integration has therefore removed the policy fixation, raised the profile of non-state actors, and decoupled a history of modern Europe from the history of EU institutions (while still necessarily arguing for their deep intertwining). It has embraced the non-binding 'informal realms' of European integration that function according to a 'lack of any legal or institutional base, or . . . off-the-record

16 T. A. Börzel and K. Heard-Lauréote, 'Networks in EU Multi-level Governance: Concepts and Contributions', *Journal of Public Policy* 29, no. 2 (2009): 135–52, 135.

17 J. Schot and V. Langendijk, 'Technocratic Internationalism in the Interwar Years: Building Europe on Motorways and Electricity Networks', *Journal of Modern European History* 6, no. 2 (2008): 196–217; W. Kaiser, B. Leucht and M. Gehler (eds.), *Transnational Networks in Regional Integration: Governing Europe 1945–83* (Basingstoke, Palgrave, 2010); R. Geven, 'Transnational Networks and the Common Market: Business Views on European Integration, 1950–1980' (PhD thesis, Maastricht University, 2014).

18 See K. Middlemas, *Orchestrating Europe: The Informal Politics of European Union 1973–1995* (London, Fontana, 1995).

19 W. Kaiser, B. Leucht and M. Gehler, 'Transnational Networks in European Integration Governance: Historical Perspectives on an Elusive Phenomenon,' in Kaiser, Leucht, and Gehler (eds.), *Transnational Networks*, pp. 1–17, 10. See also W. Kaiser, B. Leucht and M. Rasmussen (eds.), *The History of the European Union: Origins of a Trans- and Supranational Polity 1950–72* (London, Routledge, 2008).

20 See the following volumes in the *Making Europe* series led by Johan Schot and Phil Scranton : M. Kohlrausch and H. Trischler, *Building Europe on Expertise: Innovators, Organizers, Networkers* (Basingstoke, Palgrave Macmillan, 2014); P. Hogselius, A. Kaijser and E. van der Vleuten, *Europe's Infrastructure Transition: Economy, War, Nature* (Basingstoke, Palgrave Macmillan, 2016).

discussions behind closed doors that allowed for a free exchange of ideas'.[21] This cuts across our conception of the nation-state as a unitary actor, exposing alternative narratives that transcend the linear models of institution-building. The focus here lies more on broader *social processes* than on *policy outcomes* – on the multiple trajectories of state and non-state actors (be they acting in cooperation, in parallel or in conflict) and how they have interacted and collectively contributed to projecting images of future Europe.

The presence and role of prominent 'political networks' in shaping the contours of European social life is unquestionable. This does not make them the driving forces behind social change; instead, it acknowledges the influence that these networks can play in fusing interests at the intergovernmental or supranational levels. As Kaiser has noted, 'political networks ... cover dimensions of governing Europe that extend beyond decision-making at the EU level, especially processes of socialization and political transfer ... [which] mainly take place in trans-governmental and trans-national spaces'.[22] A good example would be the European Round Table of Industrialists (ERT), which was established in 1983 as a lobby group for transnational companies to promote a pan-European approach to infrastructure development and went on to become an officially recognised private-sector partner in shaping the single market.[23] The ERT was founded by the chairman of the Volvo group, Pehr Gyllenhammar, at a time when Sweden was not a member of the EU, an interesting example of transnational business interests overflowing institutional membership formalities. Yet, while the ERT represented 'wider Europe', it was still continental in its identity and interest. Analyses of it as a formation of the 'transnational capitalist class' undemocratically influencing the future of European socio-economic life have a point, but such criticism tends to reduce political networks to being driven by economic interests alone.[24] And while it has been regarded by some as the prime example of a non-state transnational network shaping the direction of European integration, such networks have always been an integral part of the process, if not the actual ferment out of which the official institution-building began.

21 L. van Heumen and M. Roos, 'Introduction', in L. van Heumen and M. Roos (eds.), *The Informal Construction of Europe* (London, Routledge, 2019), p. 8.
22 Kaiser, *Christian Democracy*, p. 2.
23 M. G. Cowles, 'Setting the Agenda for a New Europe: The ERT and EC 1992', *Journal of Common Market Studies* 33, no. 4 (1995): 501–26; B. van Apeldoorn, 'Transnational Class Agency and European Governance: The Case of the European Round Table of Industrialists', *New Political Economy* 5, no. 2 (2000): 157–81.
24 B. van Apeldoorn, *Transnational Capitalism and the Struggle over European Integration* (London, Routledge, 2002).

Transcending Europe

Moving the centre of gravity of research into the history of European integration away from the nation-state as prime actor means that the borders of 'Europe' become more porous. In other words, the circuits of social, political, economic and symbolic exchange that have contributed to the processes of making 'Europe' can be confined neither to the governments of those nation-states that became members nor even to their territories. The study of transnational networks and European integration necessarily situates the allegedly 'enclosed space' of Europe within wider circuits of exchange – a 'transnational transatlantic', where private, informal networks formed a shifting tapestry of interwoven political, economic and social connections.[25] These networks were predominantly transatlantic in orientation, reflecting the hegemonic role of the United States during the Cold War and its large-scale investment in shaping Europe's future. This was a fundamental part of the constant 'battle of ideas' that has been taking place regarding Europe's purpose, extent and identity. In charting the success of the 'community' model for Europe's future, Craig Parsons identified how the institution-building of this model effectively closed out alternative (intergovernmental or confederal) conceptions of Europe that lacked that foundation.[26] Political networks thus pursued rival plans for Europe's future, looking to utilise their respective political capital to turn their visions into reality.

US support for greater coordination between west European economies, to ensure a swift and efficient economic recovery following the Second World War and so contribute to Western defence against the Soviet threat, was clearly evident in the Marshall Plan of 1948–52.[27] US interest in the European Coal and Steel Community (ECSC) was a logical extension of this, and through the 1950s the Eisenhower administration supported the development of a stable European trading bloc within a wider transatlantic free trade space. Hence the United States did not support Britain's effort to bypass the European Economic Community (EEC) with its own European Free Trade Area, because the latter was divisive and undermining of the

---

25 G. Scott-Smith, 'The Transnational Transatlantic: Private Organizations and Governmentality', in C. Lerg, S. Lachenicht and M. Kimmage (eds.), *The Transatlantic Reconsidered* (Manchester, Manchester University Press, 2018), pp. 76–97.

26 C. Parsons, *A Certain Idea of Europe* (Ithaca, NY, Cornell University Press, 2003). See also J. Vanke, *Europeanism and European Union* (Palo Alto, CA, Academica Press, 2010).

27 D. Ellwood, *Rebuilding Europe: Western Europe, America, and Postwar Reconstruction* (London, Routledge, 1992).

purpose of the former. Neither was the United States in favour of the *'Europe des patries'* vision of Charles de Gaulle after he gained power in 1958, or the protectionist tendencies of the Common Agricultural Policy in the early 1960s.[28]

It is therefore not surprising that US internationalist elites also invested in and sometimes initiated political networks to influence the future of European integration. The American Committee on United Europe (ACUE) was founded in 1948 to provide political and above all financial support for the federalist European Movement (EM), and was led initially by the former head of the wartime Office of Strategic Services, William J. Donovan, and the future head of the Central Intelligence Agency, Allen Dulles. ACUE is an example of an 'informal and personal transatlantic network created by members of the intelligence and resistance community during the Second World War' in order to facilitate developments in the direction of US interests.[29] It demonstrated the ease with which European and American elites would join forces for apparently similar goals, with the impetus for ACUE coming originally from pan-Europeanist Richard Coudenhove-Kalergi and Winston Churchill. But it also signals how care needs to be taken when assessing the outcomes of political networks such as this. Despite US support, the federalists of the EM were never able to dominate the political debate. This does not remove their historical importance – returning to Kaiser, processes of 'socialization and political transfer' are of equal analytical relevance and should be taken as seriously as identifiable policy outcomes. The projection of a 'federal Europe' would continue to figure in elite conceptions of the continent's future.[30]

This is reflected in what was perhaps the most prominent European integration lobbying network during the 1950s and 1960s, Jean Monnet's Action Committee for a United States of Europe (ACUSE). In 1955 Monnet decided not to continue as president of the High Authority for the ECSC, instead establishing ACUSE as a transnational interest group. This move holds great significance for demonstrating how Monnet understood the potentially greater effectiveness of political networks in comparison with

28 P. Winand, *Eisenhower, Kennedy and the United States of Europe* (London, Macmillan, 1993); K. Weisbrode, *The Atlantic Century: Four Generations of Extraordinary Diplomats Who Forged America's Vital Alliance with Europe* (Cambridge, MA, Da Capo, 2009).
29 R. Aldrich, 'OSS, CIA and European Unity: The American Committee on United Europe 1948–60', *Diplomacy & Statecraft* 8, no. 1 (1997): 184–227, 186.
30 See, for instance, J. Fischer, 'From Confederacy to Federation: Thoughts on the Finality of European Integration', (2000), https://ec.europa.eu/dorie/fileDownload .do?docId=192161&cardId=192161.

formal institutions when it came to influencing the processes of integration.[31] Overall, ACUSE – which included American members to facilitate the transatlantic transfer of ideas and opinion – was important for acting as a pressure group to smoothe out ruptures in the processes of integration. ACUSE was carefully constructed to include members of the leading Christian democrat and socialist parties as well as trade unionists, since Monnet sought as much as possible to represent the major interest groups involved. In this way, he aimed to overcome the failure of the European Defence Community (EDC), pave the way for the Messina talks that led to the Treaties of Rome and Euratom, and even maintain constructive relations with Charles de Gaulle.[32]

The care Monnet took to keep the doors of the White House open for regular consultation illustrates how far the United States was a central player in influencing Europe's possible futures through the 1950s and 1960s. This is further confirmed by the 'blue chip' network of informal transatlantic diplomacy, the Bilderberg meetings, the inaugural gathering of which took place in the Netherlands in 1954. The status of its participants from the worlds of politics, business, media and academia places Bilderberg at the centre of what Thomas Gijswijt has termed the 'informal alliance', a 'group of private or semi-private transnational organisations engaged in fostering and promoting cooperation and understanding within the Western world'.[33] For some, Bilderberg has represented a meeting point for the 'Atlantic ruling class' and 'the testing ground for new initiatives for Atlantic unity'.[34] Others regard it as a typical evolution of 'thicker' solidarity between political and economic elites as the regulatory capabilities of the traditional state system have been overwhelmed by capital movements, technological communications and the rise of transnational corporations.[35] Those scholars who have examined the available records have concluded, like Gijswijt, that the group was not

---

31 F. Duchêne, *Jean Monnet: The First Statesman of Interdependence* (New York, NY, W. W. Norton, 1994); M.-G. Melchioni, 'Le Comité d'action pour les États-Unis d'Europe', in G. Bossuat and A. Wilkins (eds.), *Jean Monnet, l'Europe et les chemins de la Paix* (Paris, Presses de Sorbonne, 1997), pp. 221–51; F. Fransen, *The Supranational Politics of Jean Monnet: Ideas and Origins of the European Community* (Westport, CT, Greenwood Press, 2001); B. Szele, '"The European Lobby": The Action Committee for the United States of Europe', *European Integration Studies* 4, no. 2 (2005): 109–19.

32 M. Segers, 'Preparing Europe for the Unforeseen, 1958–63: De Gaulle, Monnet and European Integration beyond the Cold War: From Cooperation to Discord in the Matter of the Future of the EEC', *International History Review* 34, no. 2 (2012): 347–70.

33 T. Gijswijt, *Informal Alliance: The Bilderberg Group and Transatlantic Relations during the Cold War, 1952–1968* (London, Routledge, 2019), p. 2.

34 K. van der Pijl, *The Making of an Atlantic Ruling Class* (London, Verso, 1984), p. 183.

35 I. Richardson, A. Kakabadse and N. Kakabadse, *Bilderberg People: Elite Power and Consensus in World Affairs* (London, Routledge, 2011), pp. 16–20.

involved in decision-making, nor were any specific, actionable conclusions reached. However, the Bilderberg organisers did hope and expect that, through the agency of the Bilderberg participants, the discussions would have an impact on decision-makers and public opinion. They did not hesitate to bring the results of their discussions to the attention of government officials and political leaders, yet they had little control over what was done with this information.[36]

Others have further clarified this non-policy influence. Valerie Aubourg refers to several key functions: Bilderberg's contribution to 'transnational socialization' (particularly of social democrats) and the 'direct, private access to high-level Americans' for the Europeans; sharing information in a 'para-diplomatic' function to assist with the progress of formal relations; 'regulating tensions' such as the Suez crisis or the contest between the EEC and Britain's European Free Trade Area in the late 1950s; and integrating neutral and peripheral states such as Austria, Sweden and Turkey into wider Atlanticist discussions.[37] Elite socialisation, as Haas identified, was a key element of the network's *raison d'être*. Overall, Bilderberg has been a flexible, consensus-seeking body, geared more towards Parsons' 'confederal' idea of an open, liberal, expansive Atlantic community rather than the 'community' idea of a 'core Europe' represented by institution-building.

Paul van Zeeland: Meshing Formal and Informal Diplomacy

Of the many figures involved in the foundation of Bilderberg and active in the layered and overlapping networks of the 'transnational transatlantic', the Belgian Paul van Zeeland is an ideal figure through which to highlight the importance of elite socialisation and networks as 'forms of cooperation geared towards shaping the political organization of social life'.[38] Until now the studies of van Zeeland's role as a transnational organiser have rarely blended his official positions with his broader understanding of informal networks and political action, yet the two levels are inseparable throughout his career. It is also essential to appreciate how van Zeeland understood the role of a small state such as Belgium within the forcefields of international politics. For him, king and country remained paramount, yet

36 Gijswijt, *Informal Alliance*, p. 4.
37 V. Aubourg, 'The Bilderberg Group: Promoting European Governance inside an Atlantic Community of Values', in Kaiser, Leucht, and Gehler (eds.), *Transnational Networks*, pp. 48–55.
38 Kaiser, Leucht and Gehler, 'Transnational Networks in European Integration Governance', p. 10.

interdependence was not only unavoidable but also, in the interests of peace and prosperity, desirable. His activism in the post-war years therefore represented an attempt to maintain national sovereignty, block moves towards supranationality and yet solidify transnational solidarity and cooperation via border-transcending sectoral arrangements and informal encounters at the elite level. In this way he had a profound vision of both a national and a transnational system of order. The following section will explore how he pursued the construction of such an order along three overlapping, simultaneous pathways: European integration based on economic interdependence, which would be firmly situated within an Atlantic context and under US protection, and further cemented via a common Christian heritage.

A prisoner of war for most of the First World War, van Zeeland was one of the first beneficiaries of a post-war grant from the Belgian American Education Foundation to study in the United States. His time spent at Princeton under the tutelage of the economist Edwin Kemmerer was used to study the Federal Reserve and the functioning of Wall Street, providing him, after his return, with a PhD, a job at the Banque National de Belgique and a rapid rise through the financial establishment. Van Zeeland's views on Europe's future were very much framed by his US experience, and he soon became a central figure in the pro-business, free trade, market-orientated approach that eschewed supranational institution-building in favour of looser informal arrangements built on cultural affinities and beliefs as much as on economic interests. This was a Europe open to the Atlantic and accepting the United States as a 'local player' rather than as an outside hegemonic force. Writing on the Soviet Five-Year Plan as a relatively successful response to the Great Depression, van Zeeland nevertheless rejected its chauvinistic intent and considered instead that 'international cooperation in economic matters' was 'the only and necessary attitude to take' in order to secure 'a permanent international order' based on the free movement of goods and capital.[39] Soon becoming a *confidant* of the royal house, van Zeeland, influenced by the *dirigisme* of Henri de Man and Franklin Roosevelt's New Deal, attempted in 1935–6 to initiate a corporatist reform of the Belgian economy based on currency devaluation and Keynesian public spending.[40]

But van Zeeland always had the allure of an aloof technocrat, managing the necessities of party politics and government as a whole from a position on high. Embodying a Catholic sense of hierarchy and a royalist's belief in the

---

39 P. van Zeeland, *Regards sur l'Europe, 1932: Essai d'interprétation de certaines manifestations du nationalisme économique* (Brussels, Office de Publicité, 1933), pp. 101, 172.

40 G. Bombassei, 'Paul van Zeeland, un portrait (1921–1946)', unpublished paper (2019).

primacy of the nation-state, van Zeeland regarded informal networks as a vital channel for nurturing the interdependence of the state system, promoting the free market system, and overcoming autarkic tendencies. From the mid 1940s onwards, through the influence of elite 'groups de pressions' he sought to maintain national economic autonomy while at the same time overcoming the kind of inter-state fragmentation that occurred during the 1930s. For van Zeeland, both formal and informal diplomacy were therefore necessary to secure a peaceful international system. In this way he exemplified a diplomatic approach that sought to utilise and blend nationalism and internationalism, formal ministerial responsibility and informal transnational political networks.[41] Such a vision was 'European, liberal, technocratic, elitist, Atlanticist, anti-communist',[42] but not necessarily democratic – van Zeeland's attempts in the late 1930s to secure international agreement on open trade agreements and the ending of exchange controls included the hope that this would mollify Nazi Germany's expansionist drive.[43] It was, above all, geared to sustaining the position of small states such as Belgium within an international environment dominated by larger, competing great powers.

Residing in the United States as president of the Coordinating Foundation for Refugees during the war, van Zeeland joined the Belgian Commission pour l'étude des problems d'après-guerre, which was based in London. It was here that van Zeeland's informal contacts in the United States, particularly with the post-war planning groups of the Council on Foreign Relations, came to ensure his importance as a transatlantic liaison. It was also in this wartime period that he diverged from the pan-European designs of Count Coudenhove-Kalergi, which he found too unrealistic and disruptive of his own more practical designs.[44] Van Zeeland's ideas for European economic and financial integration were always situated within an Atlantic context, and in 1946, together with the Pole Joseph (Józef) Retinger, he formed the Independent League for European Cooperation, soon to become the European League for Economic Cooperation (ELEC), involving French, Belgian, Dutch, British and American representatives. ELEC was meant to promote the development of a European economy based on international

---

41 V. Dujardin and M. Dumoulin, *Paul van Zeeland 1893–1973* (Brussels, Éditions Racine, 1997), pp. 151–3.
42 Bombassei, 'Paul van Zeeland'.
43 P. Clavin, *Securing the World Economy: The Reinvention of the League of Nations 1920–1946* (Oxford, Oxford University Press, 2013), pp. 185–9.
44 Bombassei, 'Paul van Zeeland'.

agreements, free trade and financial stability, but without the ballast of formal institution-building. One of many integrationist initiatives that emerged from competing networks during and after the war, ELEC never achieved the kind of influence that van Zeeland hoped for.[45] Not only was he faced with competing visions for a federalist or supranationalist Europe, but also van Zeeland's initiative was opposed by socialists wary of the interests of transnational capital, and even by a rival Belgian business network, the Comité européen pour le progrès économique et social.[46]

As leader of ELEC, van Zeeland next joined the International Committee of the Movements for European Unity, which laid the groundwork for the seminal Congress of Europe in The Hague in May 1948. After this conference, the International Committee became the EM, tasked with pursuing The Hague's ambitious agenda of increased social, political, economic and legal integration. Van Zeeland was at the forefront of these developments as one of the vice-chairmen of the EM's International Council, focusing his attention mainly on the economic and cultural dimensions. The Council's meeting in Brussels in February 1949 expressed a point of view identical to van Zeeland's understanding of European affairs:

> In a world dominated by political and economic entities of continental dimensions, the nations of Europe cannot hope to survive as independent political or economic units. Europe must unite not only to safeguard the peace and freedom of its peoples and to restore and develop its material well-being, but also to reaffirm a certain set of values, which are now under threat, which it upholds, acts to preserve and revive by embodying them in a new structure.[47]

At the EM's European Cultural Conference in Lausanne in December 1949, van Zeeland again linked the two:

> The peoples of the West are ill at ease within the present frontiers of their States. A day will come when the various governments will grasp the fact that they must make better use of their national sovereignty.
> Europe can only raise its standard of living effectively and durably by recreating some form of economic unity.

45 Dujardin and Dumoulin, *Paul van Zeeland*, pp. 154–6.
46 S. M. Ramírez Pérez, 'The European Committee for Economic and Social Progress: Business Networks between Atlantic and European Communities', in Kaiser, Leucht and Gehler (eds.), *Transnational Networks*, pp. 61–84.
47 *Nouvelles de l'Europe, Le Congrès de Bruxelles: Organisation et Activités du Mouvement Européen* (Paris, Mouvement Européen, 1950) (translation by the author), www .cvce.eu/obj/declaration_de_politique_europeenne_du_mouvement_europeen_ bruxelles_25_28_fevrier_1949-fr-efc45451-b967-4589-89b1-81502a3de88c.html.

The battle of Europe, however, will be waged not only in economics or politics, but also in the cultural field.[48]

Lausanne laid the basis both for the European Centre for Culture under the leadership of Denis de Rougemont in Geneva and for the Collège d'Europe under Henri Brugmans in Bruges. The Swiss intellectual de Rougemont was a European federalist who saw the promotion of a distinct European culture through education and the wider public realm as an essential foundation for further political and economic integration.[49] To this end, he laid out an ambitious agenda at the conference, seeking to build 'Europe' as a single cultural entity through institutions devoted to that purpose:

> In the vanguard is a key institution, the European Cultural Centre. Among the innumerable 'cultural' organisations that the twentieth century saw the birth of, it is striking to note that there is not a single one whose object is Europe as a unit. Some want to embrace the whole world, while others are limited to a nation, a geographical region, or a particular discipline. However, it is indisputable that our countries form a whole, an organic complex of culture, easy to distinguish from its neighbours, and which in any case, the latter often distinguish from better than us. It is strange that this unit has not yet been studied as such, in a systematic way; and that there is no institution capable of providing information on Europe in general, on its present situation, on the state of its strengths and weaknesses, on its possibilities and its shortcomings.[50]

But the EM was an amalgamation of very different political forces, riven by disagreements between the 'unionists' promoting intergovernmentalism and the 'federalists' aiming for supranationalism. For van Zeeland, supranationalism would undermine the apparatus of national sovereignty and effectively erase the *raison d'être* of small states, something unthinkable for this Belgian patriot. At the same time, it was clear by 1950 that Britain was not going to play a leading role in the integration deliberations, instead becoming more of an obstacle to new initiatives. It is therefore significant that, while economic interdependence was a vital factor, for van Zeeland it had to be embedded within the conscious promotion of Europe as a single cultural community

---

48 'Message from Mr. Paul van Zeeland', 9 December 1949, Archives du Mouvement européen et sur les mouvements européens, BE A4006 FD CEHEC-B2, Dossier 4 File 13: Conférence européenne de la culture, University of Louvain.

49 N. Stenger, *Denis de Rougemont: Les intellectuels et l'Europe au XXe siècle* (Rennes, Presses universitaire de Rennes, 2015).

50 D. de Rougemont, 'Présentation de la conférence', *Fédération: Revue de l'ordre vivant*, 60 (January 1950), www.cvce.eu/obj/denis_de_rougemont_presentation_de_la_confer ence-fr-98be90da-11b1-4f6c-846b-391ff59f5b60.html.

with a mission. To pursue this, van Zeeland was again pivotal in founding the Comité International de Défense de la Civilisation Chrétienne (CIDCC) in March 1949, which sought to unite Protestants and Catholics in a common cause against the threat of atheistic communism. The CIDCC, a call to action triggered by the persecution of Cardinal Mindszenty in Hungary in 1948, was a creation of the Cold War, aiming to become the 'Christian internationale' in opposition to the 'communist and anti-Christian internationale' of the Soviet Union. Despite failing to secure the sought-after Christian unity in the Cold War struggle, the CIDCC would nevertheless function as a key elite network within trans-European anti-communism through the 1950s.[51]

From 1949 to 1954 van Zeeland was once again Belgian Foreign Minister and involved in the development of the North Atlantic Treaty Organization (NATO), ECSC, and EDC. This was the context for his most concerted effort of 'informal diplomacy' to secure alignment between the United States and western Europe: the Bilderberg meetings. By 1952, his ELEC and Bilderberg partner Joseph Retinger was also looking beyond the EM. The focus now would be on securing and maintaining the US commitment to European security and its political and economic future, especially with the Marshall Plan coming to an end in 1952. Van Zeeland was one of the select group that met with Retinger in Paris in September 1952 to discuss anti-Americanism in Europe and, equally, the danger that disillusionment with European plans might cause the United States to direct its attention elsewhere. Others present included Antoine Pinay, Guy Mollet, Hugh Gaitskell, Colin Gubbins, Paul Rijkens and Prince Bernhard of the Netherlands. Van Zeeland would be active in all discussions leading up to the first Bilderberg at the end of May 1954, hosting the final US–European preparatory meeting at his home, the Château Charle-Albert on the outskirts of Brussels, that February.[52]

Van Zeeland's support for Bilderberg as a necessary transatlantic communication channel, a kind of informal diplomatic 'safety net', went further than simply the exchange of ideas. In late 1955 he functioned as a go-between for a meeting of Prince Bernhard and the Comte Paul de Launoit in Brussels. De Launoit was a central figure of the Brussels socio-economic elite. From the

---

51 J. Großmann, *Die Internationale der Konservativen: Transnationale Elitenzirkel und private Außenpolitik in Westeuropa seit 1945* (Oldenbourg, De Gruyter, 2014); J. Großmann, 'The Comité International de Défense de la Civilisation Chrétienne and the Transnationalisation of Anti-Communist Propaganda in Western Europe after the Second World War', in L. van Dongen, S. Roulin and G. Scott-Smith (eds.), *Transnational Anti-Communism and the Cold War: Agents, Actions, and Networks* (Basingstoke, Palgrave Macmillan, 2014), pp. 251–63.
52 Gijswijt, *Informal Alliance*, pp. 33, 50.

mid 1930s, through the holding companies Cofinindus and Brufina and tight relations with the Banque de Bruxelles, he controlled a whole spectrum of industrial, mining and infrastructure operations. He was close to the royal house, and active in financing various anti-communist campaigns, including CIDCC and, more substantially, the Centre Européen de Documentation et d'Information, the 'Catholic internationale' of Otto von Habsburg.[53] He had known van Zeeland since at least the early 1930s, and had financed the latter's successful election campaign in 1937.[54] At the time, the prince was looking for a Belgian of stature to lead that country's section of his recently founded European Cultural Foundation (ECF), while de Launoit was keen to be involved both in the ECF and in Bilderberg.[55] The ECF, with a headquarters in Geneva, had been founded under the prince's sponsorship in 1954 to 'develop and maintain a feeling of mutual understanding and democratic solidarity between European populations by promoting cultural and educational activities of common interest'.[56]

The outcome was a lunch at Maison Flamande, Boitsfort, on 1 March 1956, with van Zeeland, the prince and de Launoit present.[57] The results of the discussion were meticulously recorded by van Zeeland: de Launoit agreed to join both the ECF and Bilderberg and 'decided to create a "fund" which would be endowed with a million for each of these operations'. Each organisation would then be able to draw on a maximum of 200,000 francs per year, guaranteeing a Belgian contribution to each 'for five or six years'. Van Zeeland, together with a representative chosen by the prince (this would be Unilever's Paul Rijkens), would oversee the accounts (at the time, 1 m Bfr. was equivalent to approximately $20,000).[58] Van Zeeland expressed his satisfaction at being able 'to help two initiatives whose action, for Europe, for its culture, and therefore, for Belgium as well as for Holland, is as useful as necessary'.[59] The prince's reply was 'This is an inspiring example that we will be sure to mention at the next opportunity, especially to our English

---

53 K. Schrijvers, '"L'Europe sera de droite ou ne sera pas!" De netwerking van een neo-aristocratische elite in de korte 20ste eeuw' (PhD thesis, University of Ghent, 2008); Großmann, *Die Internationale*, p. 195.

54 'Paul de Launoit op de slappe koord tussen patriottisme en kollaboratie', *De Tijd*, 13 February 1993.

55 Van Zeeland to Bernhard, 15 December 1955, Papers of Paul van Zeeland, 4.5, 926–7, GÉHEC University of Louvain (hereafter PvZ).

56 'Fondation Européenne de la Culture', PvZ.

57 Van Zeeland to F. A. de Graff (secretary to the prince), 22 February 1956, PvZ.

58 'Note résumant certaines décisions prises par le Président du Groupe [Brufina] à la suite d'une conversation avec le Prince Bernhard des Pays-Bas, le 1er mars 1956', 9 March 1956, PvZ.

59 Paul van Zeeland to Prince Bernhard, 10 March 1956, PvZ.

friends.'[60] Gijswijt has stated that 'it was a constant struggle to collect all the national contributions' for Bilderberg, and hence a guaranteed fund for 5 years or more was a major bonus, demonstrating a solid commitment.[61]

Setting up the funds proved more laborious than anticipated. The funds were deposited originally at Banque Nagelmakers in Brussels, but the wish to avoid Belgian inheritance tax and legal issues related to the ownership of the account led to a plan to establish them in a tax-free haven such as Vaduz, Liechtenstein. It took until September to finalise the paperwork, with van Zeeland then securely installed as 'chairman of the administrative council', the only other member of which was Rijkens.[62] It is significant that throughout this period the ECF had been requesting urgent access to the fund, with delegate-general Sir Terence Airey pleading of 'a financial crisis' in August. Van Zeeland's brother Marcel, a director with the Bank for International Settlements in Basel, who also happened to be treasurer of Denis de Rougemont's European Cultural Centre in Geneva, was also keen on gaining access.[63] After this episode, van Zeeland became more critical of the multiplicity of efforts being run for the cause of European (and transatlantic) unity. Reflecting on the situation in May 1958, he lamented the confusion caused by the existence of both a Centre and a Foundation for European Culture. De Rougemont, as 'the kingpin' of the Centre, was not up to the task: 'In my opinion, he conceived a plan that was far too ambitious, exceeding not only his strength but the means of any private institution.'[64] Despite the Centre flowing out of the EM's Cultural Committee, van Zeeland's sympathies did not lie with the Swiss intellectual. The Belgian was not a European federalist, preferring instead to use informal and formal political networks to knit states together yet still maintain the sovereign integrity of the (small) nation-state. But the landscape of 'political networks' was becoming too complicated:

> For quite some time now, I have personally taken a clear position, namely: the proliferation and dispersal of European propaganda works have reached such a point that no one can find their way and the situation is becoming chaotic. I make an exception for the Bilderberg Group which has a very definite role and which continues to play it cautiously and successfully.

---

60 Prince Bernhard to Paul van Zeeland, 17 March 1956, PvZ.
61 Gijswijt, *Informal Alliance*, p. 92.
62 F. Depireux (Banque Nagelmackers) to Paul van Zeeland, 27 August 1956; Dr A. Ritter, 'Fondation de Trusts', 7 September 1956, PvZ.
63 Marcel van Zeeland to Paul van Zeeland, 23 May 1956; Paul van Zeeland, 'Fondation Européenne de la Culture, Genève', 1 June 1956; Sir Terence Airey to Paul van Zeeland (then in Brazil), 23 August 1956, PvZ.
64 Paul van Zeeland, 'NOTE', 7 May 1958, PvZ.

As for the other European organisations, whether it is the Centre for Culture, the College of Bruges, the College of Strasbourg, Alpbach, Salzburg, Nancy, Bologna, what do I know? I believe that it is essential that all these institutions come together, distribute the tasks rationally and distribute among themselves, along the lines of a general budget approved by all, the public and private contributions intended to support the European idea.

At the moment, at least for a while, and for the reasons given above, I recommend abstaining from a financial point of view.[65]

In van Zeeland's view, the intervention of the Comte de Launoit had secured Bilderberg and the ECF for the foreseeable future, but the constant, increasing demands on limited funds led him to propose 'waiting until serious measures to coordinate efforts have been accepted by the various stakeholders'.[66] The impression this gives is one of fatigue – van Zeeland, who had himself initiated or supported multiple networks and organisations in pursuit of his particular understanding of European integration, was now surveying a situation where the multiplicity of activities was actually working against achieving the goal of greater unity of purpose. In 1965 the Vaduz trusts, by then almost empty, were wound up, and the remaining 60,400 Bfr. for Bilderberg were transferred to a bank in The Hague (by then the Dutchman Ernst van der Beugel had replaced Joseph Retinger as the European secretary).[67] Significantly, it was Rijkens who arranged this – van Zeeland had withdrawn from his role the year before due to declining health.

Despite the sombre note of his reflections from May 1958, van Zeeland did continue his efforts to coordinate and consolidate the field of non-state initiatives, this time on the transatlantic plane. During this decade various interest groups such as Clarence Streit's Atlantic Union Committee, the Atlantic Treaty Association and the NATO Parliamentarians Conference each put forward proposals for some kind of an Atlantic study centre to consider common issues of concern, and also to positively influence public opinion towards greater transatlantic cooperation. In June 1959, at the Atlantic Congress in London, a plan for a Studies Center for the Atlantic Community was put forward. Van Zeeland was one of its sponsors, and following the conference he led the steering committee that established the *raison d'être* and initial funding for what was now termed the Atlantic Institute (AI). When it was officially launched in 1961, van Zeeland was its chairman, and by the end of that year it had a start-up grant of $250,000 from the Ford Foundation and had set up operations in Paris under the

65 Ibid.   66 Ibid.   67 'Trust Bilderberg', 3 December 1964, PvZ.

directorship of Henry Cabot Lodge Jr.[68] But if van Zeeland saw this as a breakthrough in transatlantic coordination, his hopes were unfounded. The AI would certainly contribute towards fostering a new generation of intellectuals and officials who considered policy issues from a transatlantic rather than a national perspective, but it was never able to clearly define its role. A proposal from 1966 that the AI become an Institute for International Policy remarked that it was 'in constant difficulty for finding its right course of action, its proper organization as well as broadly balanced sources of finance'.[69] By the 1980s the AI was closely associated with the membership circles of Bilderberg and the Trilateral Commission, but was still looking to redefine itself to meet a clear need.[70] It closed in 1988, with its last Ford Foundation-funded project left incomplete.[71]

Conclusion

Both policy networks and political networks have been important features of the processes of European integration. Whereas policy networks illustrate the coalitions of interests that congregate around and push forward specific approaches to public policy, political networks – involving more informal forms of elite socialisation and social and political communication – have contributed to a broader sharing, shaping and projecting of ideas of Europe's future. Policy networks focus on outcomes – how they are reached, what they consist of, and what their consequences are once they have been formulated. Shifting attention from policy networks to political networks greatly increases the political environment deemed worthy of investigation. It addresses processes of socialisation and how like-minded elites congregate, accustom themselves to their differing cultural identities and interests, and normalise shared conceptions of Europe. It opens up the social dimension that embeds, maintains and propels the politics of integration.

68 V. Aubourg, 'Organising Atlanticism: The Bilderberg Group and the Atlantic Institute, 1952–1963', in G. Scott-Smith and H. Krabbendam (eds.), *The Cultural Cold War in Western Europe 1945–1960* (London, Frank Cass, 2002), pp. 92–105.
69 'A Proposal to Transform the Atlantic Institute into an Institute for International Policy', n.d. (1966?), Papers of Pierre Uri, Fonds PU-99, 1963–1978 Institut atlantique, Historical Archives of the European Union, EUI.
70 Andrew J. Pierre (AI Director General) to Enid Schoettle, 26 February 1988, File: Atlantic Institute, Ford Foundation Archives, Rockefeller Archives Center (henceforth RAC).
71 Enid Schoettle, 'Evaluation of PA850-0783 – The Atlantic Institute for International Affairs', 23 January 1991, File: Atlantic Institute, Ford Foundation Archives, RAC.

The study of Paul van Zeeland provides useful insights into these processes. Other individuals were equally astute at transnational networking in this regard, and there is a notable 'ego-study' subfield of European integration history that pays attention to the connectivity of these figures.[72] Throughout his career, van Zeeland operated on two simultaneous fronts, the formal and the informal, merging his official governmental and diplomatic duties with informal opportunities for continuing dialogue and exchange. Whereas the orthodox interpretations of political science tend to see the informal dimension as an add-on, a useful but ultimately indecisive element in the policy process, a study of van Zeeland demonstrates that it was the other way around. Maintaining a system of nation-states in a context of increasingly complex interdependence, coupled with the ideological and security-related tensions of the Cold War, required constant, determined efforts to ensure conciliation, agreement and compliance.

In between securing official agreements and treaties, the fabric of international relations could be held together only via elite networks of allegiance that connected through identity, values, beliefs and interests. These systems of exchange, with their overlapping agendas and regular meeting points, were vital for providing the social basis for political deliberation. Van Zeeland's investment in these networks was also directly related to his identity as a Belgian royalist and patriot – supranationalism was a threat to the integrity of the small state, and he pursued these alternative means to render it unnecessary. He was also attuned to the needs of modern communication. Elite planning still required popular support. It is notable that his political networking also involved several projects to persuade via the mass media, such as *L'Observateur catholique*, which was created to publicise the CIDCC, and *L'Occident*, which he established to promote the idea of an Atlantic community in the late 1950s. Ultimately, the 'community' model of institution-building seems to have won out over the looser 'confederal' model of informal ties supported by van Zeeland. The CIDCC or the AI, from an orthodox perspective, would be deemed irrelevant due to their lack of any substantial policy-related results. Yet these initiatives also formed part of the wider exchange of ideas over Europe's futures. In this sense, political

72 W. H. Weenink, *Bankier van de wereld. Bouwer van Europa: Johan Willem Beyen 1897–1976* (Amsterdam, Prometheus, 2005); M. B. B. Biskupski, *War and Diplomacy in East and West: A Biography of Józef Retinger* (London, Routledge, 2017); A. Bloemendal, *Reframing the Diplomat: Ernst van der Beugel and the Cold War Atlantic Community* (Leiden, Brill, 2018); P. Weller, *Alfred Mozer: Duitser, Nederlander, Europeaan (1905–1979)* (Utrecht, Stichting Matrijs, 2019).

networks can also represent paths not taken in the integration process, something that policy networks do not. The multiply varied career of Paul van Zeeland is therefore representative of the need for a more complex appreciation of networks in the multichannel history of European integration.

Recommended Reading

Dujardin, D. and M. Dumoulin. *Paul van Zeeland 1893–1973* (Brussels, Éditions Racine, 1997).

Gijswit, T. *Informal Alliance: The Bilderberg Group and Transatlantic Relations during the Cold War, 1952–1968* (London, Routledge, 2019).

Grande, E. and A. Peschke. 'Transnational Cooperation and Policy Networks in European Science Policy-Making', *Research Policy* 28, no. 1 (1999): 43–61.

Großmann, J. *Die Internationale der Konservatieven: Transnationale Elitenzirkel und private Außenpolitik in Westeuropa seit 1945* (Oldenbourg, De Gruyter, 2014).

Wolfram, K., B. Leucht and M. Gehler (eds.). *Transnational Networks in Regional Integration: Governing Europe 1945–83* (Basingstoke, Palgrave, 2010).

20

The Multidimensional Nature
of Public EU Attitudes

CLAES H. DE VREESE, ANDREAS C. GOLDBERG
AND ANNA BROSIUS

Introduction

It is a truism that not all citizens hold the same opinions when it comes to the European Union (EU), European collaboration, integration, the euro and more. That is rather logical. Why would they? The EU today covers a vast range of policy areas and it seems perfectly legitimate to support some initiatives more than others. Some citizens might be satisfied with how the EU operates, but do not feel that they reap the (economic) benefits, or vice versa.

In general terms, the past decades have seen a significant rise of Euroscepticism across many EU member countries. At the same time, support for pro-EU parties has also increased. This may seem contradictory, but it could also be a hint that EU attitudes can be mixed, ambivalent or multidimensional. We currently do not have a very good overview of how different dimensions of attitudes to the EU have developed over time. Most research was constrained to very limited indicators of public support in most public opinion surveys.

In this chapter, we have the opportunity to further unpack the multidimensional nature of public opinion vis-à-vis the EU. We show that citizens distinguish between satisfaction with the EU in terms of utilitarian considerations, the performance of EU institutions and their level of identification with the EU. We explore the multidimensional nature of EU attitudes using a ten-country study. We also explore how these different dimensions are represented in news media coverage. We know from previous research that news media can be an important antecedent for citizens' evaluations of and thoughts about the EU, but thus far it has not been ascertained whether news coverage also specifically addresses these different dimensions of public opinion.

Understanding the composition and development of attitudes to the EU is important at the very least for comprehending the legitimacy of the EU. Decisions made in the EU and integration in different policy fields hinge on the support of citizens. In the broad literature on this topic, a general picture is painted of public opinion about the EU moving from 'permissive consensus', where citizens by and large supported integration without discussing it, to integration being a topic of political contestation.

As noted by De Vreese et al., 'Euroscepticism' has become a buzzword which dominates the (public and political) discussion about EU attitudes, and media rely on the surge of this phenomenon (especially since the euro, refugee and Brexit crises).[1] Euroscepticism is a degree of public aversion towards European integration.[2] Previous research suggests that *specific* attitudes to the EU are more likely to fluctuate,[3] whereas *diffuse* support is more stable.[4] In previous studies of public opinion, the focus has been on general Euroscepticism,[5] instrumental and political Euroscepticism,[6] or support for enlargement of the EU.[7]

What We Think We Know about Public Opinion

As described before, the period of a 'permissive consensus' in which public opinion was quiescent and the European project mainly driven and dealt with by political elites is behind us.[8] The time since the Maastricht Treaty (1992) has been marked by an increasing politicisation of European issues. This

1 C. H. de Vreese, R. Azrout and H. G. Boomgaarden, 'One Size Fits All? Testing the Dimensional Structure of EU Attitudes in 21 Countries', *International Journal of Public Opinion Research* 31, no. 2 (2018): 195–219.

2 M. Lubbers and P. Scheepers, 'Political versus Instrumental Euro-scepticism: Mapping Scepticism in European Countries and Regions', *European Union Politics* 6, no. 2 (2005): 223–42; M. Lubbers and P. Scheepers, 'Divergent Trends of Euroscepticism in Countries and Regions of the European Union', *European Journal of Political Research* 49, no. 6 (2010): 787–817.

3 See also K. Armingeon and B. Ceka, 'The Loss of Trust in the European Union during the Great Recession since 2007: The Role of Heuristics from the National Political System', *European Union Politics* 15, no. 1 (2014): 82–107.

4 D. Easton, 'A Re-assessment of the Concept of Political Support', *British Journal of Political Science* 5, no. 4 (1975): 435–57.

5 L. Hooghe and G. Marks, 'A Postfunctionalist Theory of European Integration: From Permissive Consensus to Constraining Dissensus', *British Journal of Political Science* 39, no. 1 (2009): 1–23; M. Van Klingeren, H. G. Boomgaarden and C. H. De Vreese, 'Going Soft or Staying Soft: Have Identity Factors Become More Important Than Economic Rationale When Explaining Euroscepticism?', *Journal of European Integration* 35, no. 6 (2013): 689–704.

6 Lubbers and Scheepers, 'Political versus Instrumental Euro-scepticism'; Lubbers and Scheepers, 'Divergent Trends of Euroscepticism'.

7 S. B. Hobolt, 'Ever Closer or Ever Wider? Public Attitudes towards Further Enlargement and Integration in the European Union', *Journal of European Public Policy* 21, no. 5 (2014): 664–80; J. A. Karp and S. Bowler, 'Broadening *and* Deepening or Broadening *versus* Deepening: The Question of Enlargement and Europe's "Hesitant Europeans"', *European Journal of Political Research* 45, no. 3 (2006): 369–90.

8 I. Down and C. J. Wilson, 'From "Permissive Consensus" to "Constraining Dissensus": A Polarizing Union?', *Acta Politica* 43, no. 1 (2008): 26–49; Hooghe and Marks, 'A Postfunctionalist Theory of European Integration'.

means that decision-making on European integration is no longer reserved for political elites on the national and European levels, but increasingly involves European citizens.[9] In contrast to the previous elite consensus about European integration, nowadays European issues are surrounded by Euroscepticism, polarisation and conflict.[10] These trends are also reflected in public opinion surveys, most notably the Eurobarometer, which gives us an indication of how European citizens think about the EU over time.

Generally, public opinion tends to change around larger crises. For example, in the last decades, trust in the EU declined around the time of the 2010 Eurozone crisis as well as the 2015 migration crisis, but also recovered after each of these crises.[11] Nevertheless, levels of trust are low – there are more citizens who distrust the EU than who trust it, and the EU's overall image became more negative during the same crises. In addition to these fluctuations, there is a long-term trend of an increasing number of citizens holding a negative or neutral image of the EU, while the percentage of those with a positive image is going down over time. At the same time, the EU seems to be becoming less abstract and distant from its citizens. Whereas in the early 2000s, there were still many citizens who said they did not understand 'how the EU works', by 2020 a clear majority (60 per cent) said they do understand how it works.[12]

The Multidimensionality of Attitudes to the EU

A decade ago, Boomgaarden et al. investigated the configuration of attitudes to the EU in one country – the Netherlands.[13] Considering the multifaceted nature of the process of European integration and the theoretical notions

9 Hooghe and Marks, 'A Postfunctionalist Theory of European Integration'; G. Marks and M. Steenbergen, 'Understanding Political Contestation in the European Union', *Comparative Political Studies* 35, no. 8 (2002): 879–92.

10 H. Kriesi, 'The Politicization of European Integration', *Journal of Common Market Studies* 54, no. S1 (2016): 32–47; E. Grande and S. Hutter, 'Introduction: European Integration and the Challenge of Politicization', in S. Hutter and E. Grande (eds.), *Politicizing Europe: Integration and Mass Politics* (Cambridge, Cambridge University Press, 2016), pp. 3–31; S. Hutter and E. Grande, 'Politicizing Europe in the National Electoral Arena: A Comparative Analysis of Five West European Countries, 1970–2010', *Journal of Common Market Studies* 52, no. 5 (2014): 1002–18; A. C. Goldberg, E. J. van Elsas and C. H. de Vreese, 'Mismatch? Comparing Elite and Citizen Polarisation on EU Issues across Four Countries', *Journal of European Public Policy* 27, no. 2 (2020): 310–28.

11 European Commission, *Standard Eurobarometer 93* (2020), https://ec.europa.eu/comm frontoffice/publicopinion/index.cfm/Survey/getSurveyDetail/instruments/STAND ARD/surveyKy/2262.

12 Ibid.

13 H. G. Boomgaarden, A. R. T. Schuck, M. Elenbaas and C. H. de Vreese, 'Mapping EU Attitudes: Conceptual and Empirical Dimensions of Euroscepticism and EU support', *European Union Politics* 12, no. 2 (2011): 241–66.

mentioned above, they found that a more specific and fine-grained conceptualisation is needed when studying public opinion towards the EU. The
theoretical underpinnings of this multidimensional overview of EU attitudes
are explicated in their original article. Specifically, they identified the following
five dimensions: (1) EU affect, referring to feelings of fear of and threat from
the EU, which recognises the increasing role played by emotions in explaining
political evaluations; (2) European identity, indicating identification with the
EU, pride in being an EU citizen and feeling close to other Europeans and their
culture and history, but also adherence to EU symbols such as the flag; (3) EU
performance, pointing to the performance and democratic functioning of the
EU and its institutions, including considerations about the transparency of
decision-making and appropriate public expenditure; (4) utilitarian evaluations, consisting of the traditional general support measure, measures of
the country's and one's own personal benefit, and items that express a post-
materialist utilitarian approach to European integration in terms of the EU
helping to preserve peace, prosperity and the environment; and (5) strengthening of the EU, relating to the future of European integration and to
a process of further deepening and widening of the EU, such as support for
policy transfer and extended decision-making competences.

Moving from a single country study to a twenty-one-country test, de
Vreese et al. found that, generally speaking, we can confirm the multidimensional structure of five attitude dimensions cross-nationally as well.[14]
By and large, we find that, across the twenty-one EU member states in the
study, people consider different aspects of the EU and European integration
when responding to attitude questions, and hence show variability in terms
of their attitudes, distinguishing between emotional responses, utilitarian
considerations, matters of identity, performance and further strengthening
of the EU.

Moreover, we know that different dimensions matter for vote choice.
Goldberg and de Vreese have shown how negative affect can increase in an
EU referendum campaign and influence vote choice.[15] Van Elsas et al., for
example, found that attitudes to the EU matter both for voting for pro-EU
parties and for voting for anti-EU parties,[16] and van Spanje and de Vreese

---

14 De Vreese, Azrout, and Boomgaarden, 'One Size Fits All?', 213.
15 A. C. Goldberg and C. H. de Vreese, 'The Dynamics of EU Attitudes and Their Effects
on Voting', *Acta Politica* 53, no. 4 (2018): 542–68.
16 E. J. van Elsas, A. C. Goldberg and C. H. De Vreese, 'EU Issue Voting and the 2014
European Parliament Elections: A Dynamic Perspective', *Journal of Elections, Public
Opinion and Parties* 29, no. 3 (2019): 341–60.

showed that support for strengthening of the EU can affect voting in European Parliament (EP) elections.[17]

De Vreese et al. showed that citizens' evaluations of the EU's performance are in part a function of news media coverage.[18] What we do not know much about is whether media coverage can also be distinguished along the lines of the different dimensions of public opinion. In this chapter we provide a first entry point into both the configuration of public opinion and the media coverage which might be an impetus for this multidimensional opinion structure.

The (In)comparability of EU Attitudes: A Ten-Country Case Study

For our comparative analysis we consider ten EU member states: the Czech Republic (CZ), Denmark (DK), France (FR), Germany (DE), Greece (GR), Hungary (HU), the Netherlands (NL), Poland (PL), Spain (ES) and Sweden (SE). While not covering the whole EU-27, these countries are a representative sample of the EU, encompassing the variety of smaller and larger EU member states, geographically spread across the different regions of Europe and comprising both founding EU members and countries from various later rounds of enlargement. The countries furthermore differ in their experiences in and positions towards the EU. Additionally, the countries equally represent different media systems.[19] Belonging to the 'Polarised Pluralist' (or 'Mediterranean') model are France, Greece and Spain; representing the 'Democratic Corporatist' (or 'Northern European') model are Denmark, Germany, the Netherlands and Sweden; and finally there is a group of three central and eastern European countries (the Czech Republic, Hungary and Poland), none of which perfectly fits either of the aforementioned media models.

The manual content analysis was conducted within the EUROPINIONS project during the EP election campaign between April and June 2019. In order to cover the variety of news sources to which people may be exposed,

---

17 J. van Spanje and C. de Vreese, 'So What's Wrong with the EU? Motivations Underlying the Eurosceptic Vote in the 2009 European Elections', *European Union Politics* 12, no. 3 (2011): 405–29.

18 C. de Vreese, R. Azrout and J. Moeller, 'Cross Road Elections: Change in EU Performance Evaluations during the European Parliament Elections 2014', *Politics and Governance* 4, no. 1 (2016) online, unpaginated.

19 Following the classification in D. C. Hallin and P. Mancini, *Comparing Media Systems: Three Models of Media and Politics* (Cambridge, Cambridge University Press, 2004).

we aimed to code for each country the two most watched television news shows from public and private broadcasters, at least two newspapers (ideally a broadsheet and a tabloid) and at least two widely used online news websites. Owing to differences in media systems and restricted availability of some sources, these goals were not met for all countries. For some countries, we also included additional media sources.[20] For the relevant television news shows, every fourth episode was sampled and either recorded or sent to coders via a link to online databases. The coders subsequently identified each news item within a broadcast that related to the EU and coded them. Newspaper articles and online news articles related to the EU were identified using a search string, which was applied to the headlines and subtitles of each article. If the article contained one of the relevant keywords (see the documentation), it was archived; subsequently, every third article (in chronological order) was coded in order to make coding feasible but yield a sufficiently large sample size.

For this chapter, we document the results concerning a number of different variables; detailed descriptions of the coding instructions, examples and codes for these variables can be found in the codebook in the documentation. We first measured the general evaluation of the EU in the news item. The coders assessed a news item's evaluation of the EU, its institutions and its politicians by determining whether the news item merely mentioned the Union or evaluated it (rather) negatively, in a balanced/mixed tone or (rather) positively. We did not measure an equivalent of negative affect. The other four dimensions were measured as follows: for the dimension of strengthening, coders assessed whether news items mentioned any aspect related to future strengthening of the EU or its institutions; for identity, whether any aspect related to European identity is mentioned; for performance, whether the story mentioned that EU decision-making is (in)efficient or (in)adequate; and for utilitarianism, whether the story mentioned that the specific country has been affected by its EU membership or not. For all variables, coders had to distinguish between the dimensions being merely mentioned, evaluated positively, evaluated negatively or evaluated in a mixed tone. However, for the present analysis, we combined these four categories into a 'mentioned' category, which is contrasted to 'not mentioned at all', as case numbers are too low for one to draw meaningful conclusions

---

20 For an overview of all media sources sampled in each country, see A. Brosius, F. Marquart, D. C. de Boer, A. C. Goldberg, E. J. van Elsas and C. H. de Vreese, 'Europinions: Media Study' (2021), https://doi.org/10.4232/1.13796.

otherwise. This simplified coding still provides relevant insights as to how often different aspects of the EU are covered in the media.

In total, thirty-eight coders (mostly students at the University of Amsterdam) were trained by the project team to code news items in the ten countries. All coders were native in the language they coded in and received extensive training in three sessions over the course of a month before coding began. In line with the logic of three subprojects within the overall project, inter-coder reliability was determined in separate rounds for the Netherlands (subproject 1), Germany, Denmark, Spain and Hungary (subproject 2) and the Czech Republic, France, Greece, Poland and Sweden (subproject 3) by calculating Krippendorff's alpha. In addition, we assessed Fretwurst's (2015) Lotus as a chance-corrected coefficient, which assists in determining reliability for rare phenomena in the data (i.e., categories that rarely occur and hence give lower overall reliability for a variable). The lowest reliability score (Lotus) was at 0.40 for the overall evaluation of the EU (Krippendorf's alpha was 0.51 in this case) for a shorter period of coding in the Netherlands. Apart from this problematic case, inter-coder reliability (Lotus) scores were generally at least 0.73–0.81 for the overall EU evaluation in the ten countries, 0.64–0.80 for strengthening, 0.87–1 for identity, 0.49–0.86 for performance and 0.64–0.94 for utilitarianism. Since these reliability scores are not all within desirable ranges (values above 0.7), the data should be interpreted with caution. However, since it is very difficult to measure abstract concepts like the facets of attitudes to the EU in a content analysis with human coders at a higher level of reliability (and automated methods, at least until now, are not able to detect these concepts with high validity), the data can still give an indication of what media reporting around the EP elections looked like. Furthermore, it should be noted that, although coders had to distinguish between the valence for the four dimensions, we do not make this distinction for the analysis. This simplified coding is likely to have led to higher levels of inter-coder reliability.

In parallel to the media content analysis, we collected survey data in the same ten countries around the European elections in 2019.[21] All surveys were conducted by the company Kantar using computer-assisted web interviewing. The country samples slightly differ in terms of the databases from which they were drawn, that is, they stem from Kantar's own panels or partner panels such as TNS NIPO or Lightspeed. Light quotas were enforced in

21 A. C. Goldberg, E. J. van Elsas, F. Marquart, A. Brosius, D.C. de Boer and C. H. de Vreese, 'Europinions: Public Opinion Survey' (2021), https://doi.org/10.4232/1.13795.

sampling from these databases to ensure that the samples were representative according to age, gender, region and education (checked against information from the national statistics bureaus or governmental sources). The data collection followed a panel logic, with usually two to three waves collected in each country, including one or two pre-election waves and a post-election wave running from 27 May until 10 June in all countries. (The only exception to this rule is NL, for which we collected six waves to cover the longitudinal development in more detail; see below for more details about this.) For our analysis in this section, we exclusively focus on data from the post-election wave. The respective numbers of respondents per country are $N_{CZ} = 1{,}179$, $N_{DE} = 1{,}140$, $N_{DK} = 1{,}232$, $N_{ES} = 1{,}172$, $N_{FR} = 1{,}507$, $N_{GR} = 1{,}404$, $N_{HU} = 881$, $N_{NL} = 1{,}299$, $N_{PL} = 1{,}603$ and $N_{SE} = 971$.

For the measurement of the five EU attitude dimensions, we rely on the conceptualisation by Boomgaarden et al. cited above. Each of the five attitude dimensions (negative affect towards the EU, European identity, strengthening of the EU, utilitarianism towards the EU and performance of the EU) consists of three survey items (asked via seven-point Likert scales). These three items per dimension are combined to form a scale measure ranging from -3 to $+3$. The exact items per dimension and related reliability scores can be found in Table A20.1 in the appendix.

We begin with empirical patterns from the media coverage of the EU. The content analytical data show that the media mostly reports in a neutral tone about the EU (see Figure 20.1). However, if media reporting is valenced, it is typically negative, and only rarely positive. This is in line with general negativity biases of political news.[22] While country comparisons should be made with caution, some trends are noticeable. In some countries, such as France and Denmark, positive and negative evaluations are more balanced – even though the proportion of neutral articles is very different in those two countries. Denmark has one of the largest shares of items that contain evaluations, whereas in France, over 80 per cent of news items are neutral. A similar trend to the latter is found in Greece, Poland and Sweden. In some countries, negative evaluations are much more common than positive or neutral evaluations – this includes the Netherlands, Hungary and Spain. If we consider only news items that included an evaluation and compute the mean tone of these news items (a simplified calculation averaging the evaluations of the items with 1 being positive, 0 being balanced, and -1

---

22 S. Soroka and S. McAdams, 'News, Politics, and Negativity', *Political Communication* 32, no. 1 (2015): 1–22.

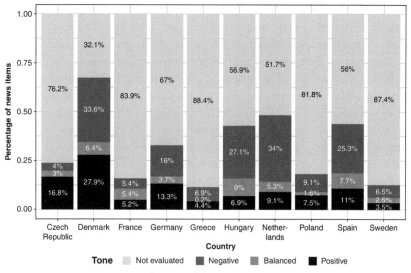

Figure 20.1 Evaluation of the EU in EU news coverage.

being negative, and neutral items excluded), the Czech Republic has the most positive media tone ($M = 0.54$), followed by France (-0.01), Germany (-0.08), Denmark (-0.08), Poland (-0.09), Greece (-0.22), Sweden (-0.24), Spain (-0.33), Hungary (-0.47) and finally the Netherlands (-0.51).

The four dimensions – identity, performance, utilitarianism and strengthening – appear in the media coverage of the EP election campaign period to different extents (Figure 20.2). In some countries (e.g., Greece, Sweden and Poland), none of the four dimensions is mentioned frequently, whereas media reporting in other countries is structured more around these dimensions. In general, aspects of European identity, or the lack thereof, are mentioned less often than the other dimensions – only in French news media coverage do identity-related issues emerge as the most common topic. When comparing the dimensions within each country, discussions of strengthening or weakening of the EU are most common in the Netherlands, Denmark and Sweden. Performance aspects are most commonly mentioned in Germany, Hungary and Spain, while utilitarian elements are most commonly found in the media of the Czech Republic and Greece. All country comparisons of news coverage should be interpreted cautiously, as media data are more likely to be impacted by methodological choices that impede country comparisons to some extent. Nevertheless, the content analysis shows that the mainstream media in different European countries cover

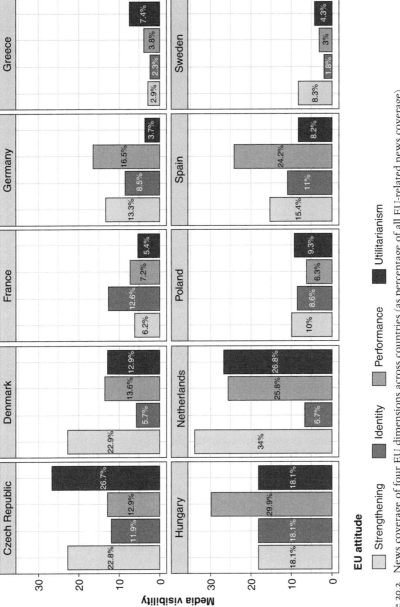

Figure 20.2 News coverage of four EU dimensions across countries (as percentage of all EU-related news coverage).

the EU quite differently, both in terms of general evaluations and in terms of topical focus points.

Turning to the public opinion in terms of multidimensional EU attitudes, the survey data equally show differences both within and between the ten countries. The vertical axis in Figure 20.3 represents mean attitudes of the respondents (on a −3 to +3 scale). Except for the negative affect dimension (which is negatively coded, i.e., negative values represent positive attitudes on that dimension), positive values stand for more positive attitudes on the respective dimension. As a first general pattern, in countries such as Poland or Spain and to some extent also in Hungary and Germany, the overall attitude towards the EU is generally positive, including positive attitudes across (almost) all five dimensions. In countries such as France, Greece and the Czech Republic, overall attitudes are rather balanced and neither very positive nor very negative (except the strengthening dimension). Finally, in countries such as Denmark, the Netherlands and Sweden, public opinion differs significantly across dimensions, thus comprising both (very) positive and (very) negative attitudes, depending on the specific dimension.

Zooming in on each of the five dimensions, public opinion is most positive when it comes to the emotional dimension of negative affect and the utilitarian dimension. On average, these two dimensions display positive attitudes in all of the ten countries. Citizens thus recognise the benefits the EU has brought for their country and Europe as a whole and overall they do not have negative feelings and emotions towards the EU. Notwithstanding the overall positive attitudes for both dimensions, there are also marked between-country differences, with the most positive attitudes among citizens living in Hungary, Poland and also Sweden.

The remaining three dimensions display more mixed patterns, which also vary more between countries. The greatest variation is present for the identity dimension, with values between −0.7 in the Netherlands and +0.7 in Poland. In roughly half of the countries, citizens on average tend to identify with the EU, while in the other half they do not. Attitudes towards strengthening of the EU also significantly differ, with values between −1 in Sweden and +0.4 in Spain. Yet, the positive attitude in Spain seems to be an outlier, as citizens in all other nine countries would prefer not to strengthen the EU any further, although they do not all as strongly oppose further strengthening as in Sweden. Attitudes to the EU are overall the most negative for the strengthening dimension. Finally, we observe both positive and negative evaluations

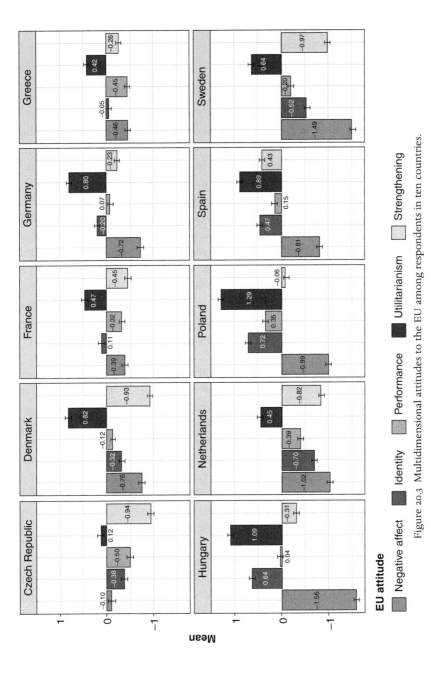

Figure 20.3 Multidimensional attitudes to the EU among respondents in ten countries.

EU attitude

Negative affect   Identity   Performance   Utilitarianism   Strengthening

527

by citizens for the performance of the EU, with an overall tendency to a slightly negative evaluation. However, in none of the ten countries are performance evaluations extremely good or bad, but instead rather close to the middle point of the scale.

The (In)stability of EU Attitudes over Time: A Case Study of the Netherlands

After the comparative analysis across ten countries, we now turn to the longitudinal development of attitudes to the EU. As discussed earlier, common data sources such as the Eurobarometer do not include multidimensional attitudes to the EU, and if they do include more specific attitudes, they are often not covered systematically across time. Ideally, for assessment of the real over-time development, one could rely on panel data including the same respondents over a long period of time. For this chapter, we aim to get as close as possible to such a panel set-up by combining three data sources from the Netherlands and examining the development of attitudes to the EU over 5 years. Given the general volatility of EU support over the last years – it has, as previously mentioned, been influenced by several crises – the time period under study provides a good starting point to uncover the (in)stability of multidimensional EU attitudes.

We focus on the Netherlands not only due to practical constraints of data availability, but also for three other reasons. First, the Netherlands is a long-standing EU member state and thus representative of countries with substantive experience in the EU. This implies the relative salience of attitudes to the EU among its citizens, in contrast to newer member states, where older generations were socialised in different political systems. Secondly, the Netherlands also represents a medium-sized country regarding its population, thus being neither one of the largest nor one of the smallest member states. Thirdly, as we have seen in the previous section, Dutch attitudes across the five dimensions are relatively representative of the pooled EU attitudes across the ten countries. Hence, the development of attitudes among Dutch citizens may give an indication of more general developments across the whole EU.

In order to cover a time span of just over 5 years, we combine three panel data sets. While we thus mainly examine within-respondent changes at the two time periods that connect the different data sources, changes may also be due to different panel compositions. Yet, the advantage of the three data sets is that all of them include detailed information about the five attitudes to the EU following the conceptualisation by Boomgaarden et al.[23] We first use data from the Netherlands stemming from the EUROPINIONS project. For the Netherlands, we collected data in six waves, starting in September 2017, until the aforementioned post-election wave for the European elections in May 2019. We complement these data with three waves from a panel study around the 2017 Dutch parliamentary elections collected between October 2016 and March 2017.[24] Finally, we link data from a panel study that started at the end of 2013 that includes three waves up to and including the EP elections in May 2014 and an additional four waves collected in 2016 around the Dutch Ukraine–EU Association Agreement referendum and the EU summit in Bratislava.[25] The combination of these three data sources results in seventeen time points over the 5 years under study.

To begin, Figure 20.4 displays the development of the five EU dimensions over time (including 95 per cent confidence intervals). While the solid black line connects data points within the same panel data, the dotted line represents changes in the data source and connects data points from two different panel data sets. Changes due to the latter should thus be interpreted with caution. We furthermore added two vertical lines indicating the beginning of the European migrant crisis and the date of the Brexit referendum, two events with potentially significant influence on attitudes to the EU. Fortunately, these two events occurred within the same panel data collection, so that potential changes around these events may be attributed to them without coinciding with a change in our data sources. In order to facilitate the comparison between more volatile or stable patterns across the five dimensions, we display a fixed vertical axis interval of 1.1 points on the −3 to +3 scale across all five graphs (yet starting at different overall attitude levels).

Following previous research, diffuse EU attitude dimensions should be more stable than more specific attitudes. This expectation is strongly confirmed by the negative affect pattern (a), which is very stable over the 5-year period under study. The overall mean value on this dimension is always around −1 and in fact is almost exactly the same value at the beginning and end of our time period under study. While the migrant crisis increased the feelings of negative affect to some extent, the observed change of around 0.2

23 Boomgaarden et al., 'Mapping EU attitudes'.
24 P. Van Praag and C. H. de Vreese, 'Dutch Election Campaign Voter Study' (2017), ASCoR-AISSR-de Volkskrant, Amsterdam.
25 C. H. de Vreese, R. Azrout and J. Möller, 'European Parliament Election Campaign Study: Data and Documentation', University of Amsterdam (2014).

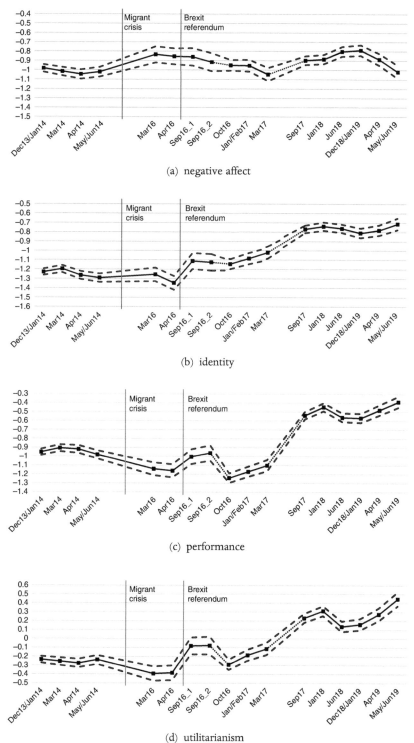

(a) negative affect

(b) identity

(c) performance

(d) utilitarianism

Figure 20.4 Development over time of five attitudes to the EU in the Netherlands.

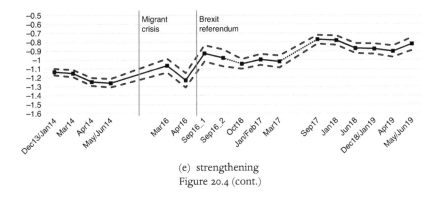

(e) strengthening

Figure 20.4 (cont.)

points on a 7-point scale is weaker than one could have expected. The Brexit referendum had no effect on negative affect.

Identity (b), a second diffuse dimension, is more volatile than negative affect, but still less so than the specific dimensions. The development around the Brexit referendum is particularly interesting, as Dutch citizens developed a more positive EU identity after Brexit took place. Although overall still on the negative side of the scale, the change of around 0.3 points towards the positive side is significant, also considering the otherwise rather stable identity pattern. This rise in the direct aftermath of Brexit matches findings in other studies, which have shown that (Dutch) citizens' EU support has gone up after Brexit, which, among other things, might have strengthened the shared feeling of being European.[26]

The two specific dimensions of performance (c) and utilitarianism (d) show the most volatile patterns, in line with expectations. As with the identity dimension, we observe a significant increase in both attitudes after Brexit. In the case of performance evaluations, this increase compensates for the decrease around the time of the migrant crisis. For utilitarianism, the increase after Brexit more than compensates for a previous decrease around the migrant crisis. The particularly strong effect on utilitarianism due to Brexit makes sense, given that citizens may have realised the value of their country's EU membership once the consequences of the Brexit referendum had been discussed more prominently. Yet, utilitarian attitudes were not only volatile

26 C. E. De Vries, 'Benchmarking Brexit: How the British Decision to Leave Shapes EU Public Opinion', *Journal of Common Market Studies* 55, no. S1 (2017): 38–53; S. van Kessel, N. Chelotti, H. Drake, J. Roch and P. Rodi, 'Eager to Leave? Populist Radical Right Parties' Responses to the UK's Brexit Vote', *The British Journal of Politics and International Relations* 22, no. 1 (2020): 65–84.

at the time, but also, for instance, more recently, as the respective attitudes increased to a similar extent in the year preceding the EP elections in 2019. Hence, it may be that both a significant event, such as Brexit, and a more prominent discussion of EU issues in the public debate – and particularly highlighting the advantages and accomplishments of the EU – may influence specific dimensions, and in particular the more specific ones.

Finally, attitudes to strengthening (e) are in between the more volatile and stable patterns, in line with the attitude dimension showing both more diffuse and more specific characteristics. Particularly noteworthy for attitudes to strengthening is the positive increase following both the migrant crisis and the Brexit vote, which is not the case for any of the other four dimensions. One potential reason behind the increase following both events might be that citizens perceive the need to increase the decision-making power of the EU in order to cope better with these and other crises. Having observed the struggles of the EU in dealing with the migration crisis on the one hand, or fearing 'contagion' effects of EU exit referendums in other countries on the other, citizens may aim to strengthen and improve the EU's political powers in order to stay on the (successful) path of European integration.

On a more methodological note, we would like to mention that the interpretation of aggregate changes such as those discussed in this chapter should be done cautiously. Although we discussed various aggregate developments and partly linked them to specific events, one has to be careful as there may be much more change at the individual level. For instance, the more stable aggregate pattern in negative affect may also represent similarly strong changes in the opposing positive and negative directions that ultimately cancel each other out, thus giving only an illusion of stability.[27]

Conclusion

Public opinion about the EU is no longer something that can be considered as being of secondary importance. Citizens' attitudes to the EU matter in their own right, as well as for voting behaviour in EP elections and EU referenda. Increasingly we understand that citizens' attitudes to the EU also differ, with variation across countries and in time. Additionally, attitudes to the EU also have different dimensions. In this chapter we unpacked the multidimensional nature of public opinion vis-à-vis the EU in ten EU countries. We integrate

27 For example, Goldberg and de Vreese, 'The Dynamics of EU Attitudes'.

this analysis of public opinion with an analysis of the media, as news media coverage is a key source for public opinion about the EU.

Our media content analysis shows that the media report about the EU differently in different countries. Not only is the EU evaluated both differently and to different extents, but the mainstream media in the ten countries we study also focus differently on varying aspects of EU public opinion. This means that the media, as primary sources for information about the EU, might provide similar factual information across Europe, but perhaps evaluate this information differently and focus on different aspects in interpretation and framing. Citizens of different European countries thus live – to some extent – in different information environments.

The unique survey data that we can report on showed that in some countries respondents are on average positive on all five attitude dimensions (e.g., Poland and Spain), while in others public opinion is more differentiated, with aggregate positive and negative attitudes depending on the dimensions (e.g., Denmark, the Netherlands or Sweden). In no country did we find exclusively negative attitudes. Comparing the five dimensions, attitudes are overall most positive for negative affect and utilitarianism, albeit still with marked between-country differences regarding the levels of these (positive) attitudes. The greatest variation between countries is present for identity, including aggregate negative and positive attitudes each being found in half of the countries. Overall, the most negative attitudes are found for the strengthening dimension.

In terms of the longitudinal perspective, the two diffuse dimensions of negative affect and identity are indeed more stable across time than more specific attitudes. Negative affect in particular is very stable, being affected neither by the migrant crisis nor by Brexit. Identity, in contrast, was affected by Brexit in the way that Dutch citizens felt more attached to the EU afterwards. Two dimensions, performance and utilitarianism, are most volatile over time and also influenced by external events. We observe particularly strong effects from Brexit on increased utilitarianism, that is, citizens may realise the value/benefits of being in the EU. Yet, scores for utilitarian attitudes also went up in the year preceding the EP elections in 2019. Thus, both a major event and a more prominent discussion of the EU may influence utilitarian attitudes.

Where do the findings of this chapter leave us? It is clear that public opinion about the EU is not a unidimensional entity. It is also clear that some aspects are more volatile than others. This matters in trying to understand the preferences of citizens, but it should also matter for the political debate and the 'political supply side'. European politics is not merely about pro- or anti-EU positions. This is one (almost meta) dimension, but far from being the only one. Political leaders are well served by talking politics when discussing matters in Europe, rather than reductionist pro/contra-EU arguments. Thus, as the process of European integration has never been a linear one, it is important to reflect choices in what is on offer in the political landscape. Since the Maastricht Treaty, the bandwidth of the EU has expanded, and with this comes an understanding of citizens' attitudes as multidimensional.

Appendix

Table A20.1 Operationalisation of five EU attitude dimensions in Europinions survey data

EU performance	*To what extent do you agree or disagree with the following statements:* (question and answer scales same for all EU attitudes)
	• The EU functions well as it is.
	• The EU functions according to democratic principles.
	• Leaders of member states work efficiently in taking decisions together.
	Combined variable with 7-point answer scale with labels for 1 (fully disagree), 4 (neither agree nor disagree) and 7 (fully agree). *Cronbach's Alpha: 0.83*
EU identity	• Being a citizen of the EU means a lot to me.
	• I share a common tradition, culture and history with other Europeans.
	• The European flag means a lot to me.
	Cronbach's Alpha: 0.80
EU utilitarianism	• [NATIONALITY] membership of the EU is a good thing.
	• [COUNTRY] has benefited from the membership in the EU.
	• The EU fosters peace and stability.
	Cronbach's Alpha: 0.88
EU negative affect	• I am angry about the EU.
	• I feel threatened by the EU.
	• I am disgusted with the EU.
	Cronbach's Alpha: 0.85

Table A20.1 (cont.)

EU strengthening	• European integration should go further.
	• The decision-making power of the EU should be extended.
	• The EU should be allowed to collect tax money.
	Cronbach's Alpha: 0.79

Recommended Reading

Boomgaarden, H. G., A. R. Schuck, M. Elenbaas and C. H. de Vreese. 'Mapping EU Attitudes: Conceptual and Empirical Dimensions of Euroscepticism and EU Support', *European Union Politics* 12, no. 2 (2011): 241–66.

De Vries, C. E. and S. B. Hobolt. *Political Entrepreneurs: The Rise of Challenger Parties in Europe* (Princeton, NJ, Princeton University Press, 2020).

Hameleers, M. and A. C. Goldberg. 'Europe against the People: Does Eurosceptic News Exposure Relate to Populist Attitudes? Evidence from a Linkage Study across Nine European Countries', *Political Research Exchange* 4, no. 1 (2022) online, unpaginated.

Hutter, S., E. Grande and H. Kriesi (eds.). *Politicising Europe: Integration and Mass Politics* (Cambridge, Cambridge University Press, 2016).

Gattermann, K. *The Personalization of Politics in the European Union* (Oxford, Oxford University Press, 2022).

Goldberg, A. C., E. J. van Elsas and C. H. De Vreese. 'Eurovisions: An Exploration and Explanation of Public Preferences for Future EU Scenarios', *Journal of Common Market Studies* 59, no. 2 (2021): 222–41.

21

Ideas of Europe: A View from Inside-Out, the 1880s to the 1910s (and Beyond)

MATTHEW D'AURIA

Introduction

In 1832, the Prussian novelist Gotthilf August von Maltitz published a curious epistolary novella, the *Journey among the Ruins of Old Europe in the Year 2830*. Telling of a journey of an American tourist to Europe to visit its ruins and learn about its past, von Maltitz meant this to be a 'serious and satirical' work. In it, Europe was a devastated land, invaded and despoiled by hordes from the East, the Russians first and foremost. Its peoples had been easily subdued because of their weakness after centuries of decadence, brought about by their materialism and individualism. In the novella, the comparison between Europe and the United States was a grim one indeed.[1] Von Maltitz's text, now a forgotten literary curiosity, was rather unusual in its day, and few of its readers would have seen in it a serious foreshadowing of European decline. In truth, the nineteenth century was an age of unprecedented economic, military and cultural expansion for Europe. Admittedly, Alexis de Tocqueville claimed that its nations had attained the acme of their power and that Russia and the United States, 'called by a secret design of Providence', would one day hold in their hands the destinies of the world.[2] Yet few others, at that time and for the best part of the century, were so prescient.

Things started to change in the 1890s. By then, the United States was clearly supplanting Great Britain as the world's leading economic power. In

My dear friend and colleague, Richard Deswarte, read this chapter in draft form and offered his precious advice. Very sadly and very unexpectedly, Richard passed away in July 2021. I dedicate this chapter to his memory.

1 G. A. von Maltitz, 'Reisen in der Ruinen des Alten Europa im Jahre 2830', in G. A. von Maltitz, *Pfefferkörner: Im Geschmack der Zeit; ernster und satyrischer Gattung* (Hamburg, Hoffmann und Campe, 1832), vol. II, pp. 99–203, especially 102, 186 and 194.

2 A. de Tocqueville, *De la Démocratie en Amérique* (Paris, Garnier, 1981 [1835]), vol. I, pp. 540–1.

1898, the *desastre*, Spain's defeat at the hand of the Americans, and the resulting loss of most of its empire, was one clear sign of the United States' increasing political and military might. In Africa, the defeat of the Italians by the Ethiopians at the Battle of Adwa (1896) and the difficulties the British met with in the Boer War (1899–1902) were both perceived to be signs of European weakness. And so too was the Russians' defeat in the war against the Japanese (1904–5), which had proven that European methods and technologies could be effectively adopted by others with devastating effects. More generally, an increasing loss of faith in an everlasting economic and social progress paved the way to discourses about European decadence which entwined with various (pseudo-)Nietzschean philosophies flourishing throughout the Old Continent. It was the Great War, that 'seminal catastrophe' of the twentieth century, that marked the definitive end of the global economic and political hegemony of the nations of Europe.[3] The year 1917 was the turning point. On the one hand, during that crucial year, and for the first time, the United States intervened militarily on the Old Continent itself to decide the future of its peoples. On the other, the Bolshevik Revolution, a new threat – or, depending on the perspective, an old threat in a new guise – represented for many contemporary observers the definitive sundering of Russia from Europe, which was now seemingly caught in between two real, potential or perceived enemies. Indeed, by the late 1910s, few among the readers of von Maltitz's novella would have seen its 'satirical' side.

This chapter considers the ways in which, from the late 1880s to the 1910s, discourses about Europe came to be shaped as a response to the threats and challenges posed by the United States on the one hand and by Russia on the other. The aim is to shed light on the intellectual foundations of those European unification projects that were to flourish in the ensuing decades. The following pages will consider the ideas of a number of more or less well-known scholars and intellectuals. The choice, of course, is not haphazard, for all of them considered issues that re-emerged, if in a different guise, when the political foundations of the integration process were in due course laid. Obviously, discourses about and ideas of Europe can be studied in a variety of ways. One way is by focusing on the 'internal' aspect, that is, on the concern to avoid war among the nations of Europe or overcome commercial barriers between them. Alternatively, attention might be drawn to the 'external' aspects, considering how notions about Europe developed as a response to challenges or threats

---

3 G. F. Kennan, *The Decline of Bismarck's European Order: Franco-Russian Relations, 1875–1890* (Princeton, NJ, Princeton University Press, 1979), p. 3.

posed by extra-European powers. The two kinds of issues that these different approaches conjure up are not mutually exclusive, as will become obvious in the following pages. Here, however, attention will be drawn to the external aspects alone and, from this angle, it might be useful to make two minor qualifications. First, when intellectuals, artists and political leaders wrote or spoke of America or Russia, they often used stereotypes, platitudes and myths. Clearly, these tell us much less about the Americans and the Russians themselves than about the men and women who produced them – and, because preconceptions act at a deeper level, they have much to tell. The second point to consider is that Russia was usually seen as closely tied to, and the United States even as a product of, European culture itself. This being the case, many observers saw in them images of a possible European future – one either to shun or to pursue. Therefore, the Othering process in play did not always lead simply to an outright rejection of the Other but featured several contradictions and much ambiguity that are particularly revealing for the historian.

The United States: A Model to Follow and a Threat to Avert

Diplomatic, Political and Economic Arguments and Concerns

In 1883, the English historian John Robert Seeley published a short book that was destined to become the 'bible of British imperialists'.[4] In his *Expansion of England*, Seeley offered a history of Britain's colonial expansion and pondered the ongoing struggle for global hegemony. The bedrock of his argument was that future world politics would be decided by a handful of great powers, each with enormous resources at its disposal. Such an understanding was predicated on what was to Seeley a clearly discernible tendency towards the creation of ever larger political units. His conclusion was that, should the United States and Russia continue steadily on their ascent, exploiting as best they could their vast resources, then they would 'surpass in power the states we now call great as much as the great country-states of the sixteenth century surpassed Florence'. In half a century, they would 'completely dwarf such old European states as France and Germany'.[5] Importantly, Seeley maintained that, although Britain too was running the same risk, thanks to the vastness of its empire it could avoid the fate of Europe's continental powers. Britain was at a crossroads, facing two courses of action, the one making of it a great

---

4 G. P. Gooch, *History and Historians in the Nineteenth Century* (Boston, MA, Beacon Press, 1959), p. 347.
5 J. R. Seeley, *The Expansion of England* (Chicago, IL, Chicago University Press, 1971), p. 62.

world power on a par with Russia and the United States, the other reducing it to a purely European state, a nation 'looking back, as Spain does now, to the great days when she pretended to be a world-state'.[6] The latter outcome would be attained by granting complete independence to its colonies; the former by turning its empire into a federation and giving birth to a Greater Britain, a 'world-state' with immense capacities and resources, a truly united polity no longer based on a single nationality.[7]

Interestingly, in a speech at the Peace Society in 1871, Seeley had advanced very different arguments, advocating the creation of the United States of Europe to avert the risk of war. This was to be a true federation, based on a new form of citizenship, and cemented by the strongest of bonds: 'We must cease to be mere English, Frenchmen, Germans and must begin to take as much pride in calling ourselves Europeans,' he claimed. The example to follow was that set by the United States of America, a political system that was 'gloriously successful as a federation'.[8] The differences between the stances adopted in the two texts are, of course, remarkable. In part, Seeley's change of mind mirrors a more general ambiguity towards Europe felt by British intellectuals and politicians, torn between the desire to play a major global role and the sense of being, culturally at least, part of Europe. It is an uncertainty that has accompanied British views about Europe ever since.[9] It is of yet more interest to note that two of the main assumptions undergirding Seeley's text – namely, that the struggle in the modern world could be faced only by large political units and that the United States was the model to follow – would later become key elements in discourses about European unification. For one, the Italian liberal economist and politician Luigi Einaudi formulated similar arguments in many of his works, starting with an article published in 1918.[10] From a different perspective, Count Richard Coudenhove-Kalergi too stated in his famous *Pan-Europa* (1923), in no uncertain terms, that the aim of his movement was 'the constitution of

6 Ibid., p. 237.
7 On the notion of 'Greater Britain', see D. Bell, *The Idea of Greater Britain: Empire and the Future of World Order, 1860–1900* (Princeton, NJ, Princeton University Press, 2007).
8 J. R. Seeley, 'The United States of Europe', *Macmillan's Magazine* 23 (1871): 442–3.
9 See, for example, Winston Churchill's famous speech at the University of Zurich, in 1946: W. Churchill, 'A "United States of Europe", 19 September 1946', in W. Churchill, *Never Give In! The Best of Winston Churchill's Speeches* (New York, NY, Hyperion, 2003), pp. 426–30.
10 On Einaudi's Europeanism, I take the liberty of referring to my own 'Junius and the "President Professor": Luigi Einaudi's European Federalism', in M. Hewitson and M. D'Auria (eds.), *Europe in Crisis: Intellectuals and the European Idea, 1917–1957* (New York, NY, Berghahn, 2012), pp. 289–322.

the *United States of Europe* following the example of the United States of America'.[11]

Seeley's assumption that the course of world politics would increasingly be decided by larger political entities, with ever greater resources at their disposal, was shared by one of the main precursors of geopolitics. Friedrich Ratzel is known today for having coined the term *Lebensraum*, a term infamously popularised by the Nazis three decades later.[12] *Lebensraum*, in Ratzel's definition, was the space within which a species, whether animal or human, lived and developed. In the case of modern nation-states, their vital space changed according to the needs of their people, cultural achievements, demographic growth and economic and military strength. History showed a tendency for larger nation-states to overwhelm and annex the smaller and weaker neighbouring polities. On the one hand, boundaries were then ever-changing, for they were determined by a nation-state's strength; on the other, nation-states themselves were a product of history and political contingency rather than an immutable fact of nature: they were simply a way in which people adapted to their environment. As for Europe, argued Ratzel, the global tendency towards the creation of larger political entities meant that its states were destined soon to become minor powers. Indeed, it was regrettable that in an age of 'large spaces and rapidly increasing and vivifying connections', the peoples of Europe still adhered to the narrow borders established in previous centuries. There, the development of an ever-expanding economy that transcended all boundaries was fettered by the fixed barriers posed by states, thus inevitably weakening the entire Old Continent.

Like many other observers, Ratzel too contrasted Europe and the United States. In particular, he was struck by the fact that, while the domestic market of the latter was every bit as large as the Old World, it was moreover endowed with 'a uniformity that Europe will never achieve'. As the largest and strongest economy in the world, the United States posed a threat to Europe's future, and against this Ratzel advocated the creation of *Mitteleuropa*. The latter he loosely defined as a form of 'European cooperation aiming at the division of labour and the saving of resources' on a continental

---

11 R. N. Coudenhove-Kalergi, *Pan-Europa* (Vienna, Pan-Europa Editions, 1923), p. 154; italics in the original text. On Coudenhove-Kalergi, see A. Ziegerhofer, *Botschafter Europas: Richard Nikolaus Coudenhove-Kalergi und die Paneuropa-Bewegung in den zwanziger und dreißiger Jahren* (Vienna, Böhlau, 2004).

12 M. Bassin, 'Race contra Space: Conflict between German *Geopolitik* and National Socialism', *Political Geography Quarterly* 6, no. 2 (1987): 115–45.

scale.[13] It would include Germany, Austria-Hungary, the Netherlands, Belgium, Switzerland and Italy too – which he saw at once as a central and a southern European country. In a previous work, penned in 1898, he even included France.[14] This aim he saw as within reach since, for Ratzel, these countries had already achieved a high level of economic integration. It is noteworthy that his assumption that the future would be dominated by larger states entailed two consequences. The first was the rejection of the nation as the main source of political legitimacy. In fact, Ratzel considered the principle of nationality to be outdated, in the face of the social, cultural and economic changes taking place in Europe. It was a regressive force since it depended on boundaries that were limited and fixed. Given the tendency towards greater political entities and towards increasing cooperation within ever greater spaces, nationalism was simply 'a step backward'.[15] The second consequence was Ratzel's belief, based on his own 'law of the expansion of space', that in the international arena some peoples would inevitably be conquerors and others were destined to be conquered and that, unavoidably, any future political space would be hierarchically ordered. Ratzel's *Mitteleuropa* would be dominated by the Germanic element, the most active and energetic of its components.

At the turn of the century, the idea that Europe should become a single economic space, with no state customs barriers, centred on Germany and Austria-Hungary, to counter the 'American danger' was espoused by many scholars and publicists. One of their number, the Austro-German politician, industrialist and intellectual Alexander von Peez, argued that only if its states were to form a single economic unit could the Triple Alliance withstand the competition of Russia, the United States and the British Empire. The historian Gustav Schmoller, who also feared the American threat, concurred. The Austrian-born economist Julius Wolf shared such concerns and advocated the adoption by the central European nations of common laws on trade and communications.[16] The views of these and other authors calling for the birth of *Mitteleuropa* differed in many ways, including the means to unite, the nature of the bond and, not least, which countries were to join. Usually, such

---

13 F. Ratzel, 'Der mitteleuropäische Wirtschaftsverein', *Die Grenzboten: Zeitschrift für Politik, Literatur und Kunst* 63 (1904): 255–7.

14 F. Ratzel, 'Mitteleuropa mit Frankreich', *Geographische Zeitschrift* 4 (1898): 143–56.

15 F. Ratzel, *Der Staat und sein Boden: Geographisch betrachtet* (Leipzig, Hirzel, 1896), p. 83.

16 A. von Peez, *Zur neuesten Handelspolitik* (Vienna, Szelinski, 1895), especially pp. 1–30; G. Schmoller, 'Die Wandlungen in der europäischen Handelspolitik des 19. Jahrhunderts', *Jahrbuch für Gesetzgebung, Verwaltung und Volkswirtschaft im Deutschen Reich* 24 (1900): 373–82; J. Wolf, *Das Deutsche Reich und der Weltmarkt* (Jena, Fischer, 1901). On the idea of *Mitteleuropa*, see H. C. Meyer, *Mitteleuropa in German Thought and Action: 1815–1945* (The Hague: Martinus Nijhoff, 1955).

plans included Italy, in some cases France, and, in a few instances, authors even debated whether Great Britain and Russia should be included. In most cases, such projects, economic in nature, were imagined as a step towards the United States of Europe. Yet, almost invariably, *Mitteleuropa*, howsoever conceived, was not a federation. The German industrialist and liberal politician Walter Rathenau, writing in 1913, did in fact suggest that economic integration would inevitably lead to political unification.[17] And yet, overall, political unification, if even envisaged, was left to a distant and hazy future.

In 1902, the Italian economist Federico Fiora argued that it was mainly to counter the American economic threat that politicians and scholars from across Europe and from different political standpoints were calling for the birth of a central European economic unity. Their projects, far from being 'idealistic and sentimental', were instead conceived for a 'specific material and economic' necessity. However, he noted bitterly, this movement of men and ideas was now meeting with unfavourable circumstances, and he foretold that Europe would soon witness once again the raising of high commercial barriers.[18] Fiora's prediction materialised in the ensuing years. Projects for economic unification, which had seemed to many more realistic than plans for a federation, were set aside. They did re-emerge during the First World War, thanks to Friedrich Naumann's famous *Mitteleuropa*, published in late 1915. Nevertheless, his notion was founded on an almost imperialistic design, foreseeing a united central Europe under German hegemony. The book raised suspicions right from the start, especially among members of the German Socialist Party. For one, Karl Kautsky accused Naumann of seeking German dominance over central Europe and proposed, instead, the birth of a federation of socialist European states.[19] Although Kautsky's criticism was not wholly justified, during the war the idea of *Mitteleuropa* undeniably acquired a more imperialistic hue. Eventually, in the 1930s, it became a key notion in the language of Nazi geopoliticians.[20]

Cultural Fears and Ideological Uncertainties

By 1900, the perception of an American economic threat pervaded scholarly and political circles alike. Works such as the *Péril américain* (1899), by the historian Octave Noël, *The Americanisation of the World* (1901), by the British

---

17 W. Rathenau, 'Deutsche Gefahren und neue Ziele', in W. Rathenau, *Gesammelte Schriften* (Berlin, Fischer, 1918), vol. i, p. 278.
18 F. Fiora, 'Il pericolo americano', *La riforma sociale* 9, no. 12 (1902): 467–8.
19 K. Kautsky, *Die Vereinigten Staaten Mitteleuropas* (Stuttgart, Dietz, 1916).
20 J. Brechtefeld, *Mitteleuropa and German Politics: 1848 to the Present* (Basingstoke, Palgrave, 1996), pp. 39–57.

newspaper editor W. T. Steed, and the *Amerikanischer Gefahr* (1902), by the German author Max Prager, testify, by their titles alone, to a sort of moral panic. Importantly, debates over economic issues became increasingly entwined with discussions regarding American society and culture as such. Many indulged in comparisons between the Old and the New World, and, in several cases, criticism of European values and ways of life was at least implicit. In 1889, the English novelist, journalist and poet Rudyard Kipling, after visiting the United States, wrote disparagingly about the Americans' 'massive vulgarity', and criticised their religion, which he saw as being devoid of any true spirituality: '[A] revelation of barbarism', as he put it. Kipling also had reservations regarding the Americans' notion of political freedom and disapproved of the 'despotic power of public opinion' over American society. In fact, his *Notes on America* were studded with references to the uncouthness of the Americans – in more than one way, a clear expression of his Eurocentrism. And yet he also believed that their simplicity made of the Americans the 'biggest, finest, and best people on the surface of the globe!'[21] The United States embodied, for Kipling as for many others, the energy and vitality that old Europe was now wanting.

Similar views emerge in Paul Bourget's *Outre-Mer* (1895), a travelogue of a journey on which he embarked, paradoxically enough, to learn about the Old World: 'What draws me to America is not America in itself, but Europe'. Like so many other observers, on reaching New York, Bourget was struck by the 'energy, the spirit of enterprise, manifested everywhere, and visibly without control'.[22] The contrast with the peoples of Europe was startling: if the Americans suffered an 'excess of energy, many Europeans suffer from the opposite ill', noted Bourget. Interestingly, the French novelist believed that the distinctive energy of the Americans was due to their turbulent past, which, so often denigrated by the Europeans, was in fact the story of an incessant struggle to subdue nature and to conquer the West, a struggle that had shaped a powerful civilisation of 'pioneers and hunters'. America was 'a nation that has lived more in its one hundred years than all Europe since the Renaissance'.[23] Dwelling on its history, Bourget compared the American Civil War with the Franco-Prussian War and considered their effects on America and Europe, respectively. Both conflicts he saw as clashes between

---

21 R. Kipling, *American Notes* (New York, NY, Arcadia, 1910 [1899]), citing pp. 185, 211, 227 and 185 again.
22 Paul Bourget, *Outre-Mer (Notes sur l'Amérique)* (Paris, Lemerre, 1895), vol. I, p. 6; vol. II, p. 317.
23 Ibid., vol. I, pp. iii, 200.

different 'races', between distinct peoples with contrasting values. However, while in Europe the war had produced 'wounds' that were still open, in the United States 'they have not only healed but have been forgotten'. Thanks to their vigour and strength, the people of America were now embarked on the task of 'finally mixing, blending, and amalgamating these two portions of a vast empire, this North and this South, so naturally, so radically antithetic'. Reconciliation seemed a more distant prospect in Europe. And yet, according to Bourget, once the 'crisis of acute militarism' caused by the Franco-Prussian War had been solved, 'either pacifically or otherwise', it would then become possible to build 'the United States of Europe, [. . .] the ideal of true civilisation, reconcilable with all forms of government and all local traditions'.[24]

Through comparisons drawn with the United States, by the late nineteenth century a growing number of authors were sketching a decidedly sombre portrait of Europe. In 1894, for one, Gustave Le Bon praised the Americans for their 'mental constitution, its features being perseverance, energy and strength of will'. While Americans were encouraged by their governments to give free rein to their vigour and initiative, the opposite was true of the peoples of Europe, oppressed by state rules and regulations in every aspect of their lives.[25] This was at once a cause and a symptom of decadence, and it particularly affected southern Europeans: '[D]ecadence threatens the vitality of the greatest part of the great European nations, especially the so-called Latin ones [. . .]. They lose each day their initiative, their energy, their will and their capacity to act. The fulfilment of ever-growing material needs tends to become their sole ideal.' Interestingly, Le Bon believed that America itself was now threatened by the immigration of 'inferior and non-assimilable elements' from southern and eastern Europe and this, in turn, could lead to divisions and wars such as those tormenting the Old Continent. But this, Le Bon believed, was a danger that lay in the distant future.[26]

The reference to the Latin nations of Europe in Le Bon's work is revealing of the complexity of the Othering process at play in the way the peoples of Europe saw themselves.[27] The relationship between notions of race and perceptions of decadence was also central to the works of the Italian historian

---

24 Ibid., vol. II, pp. 202, 327.
25 G. Le Bon, 'Lois psychologiques de l'évolution des peuples' (1894), in G. Le Bon, *Lois psychologiques de l'évolution des peuples; Aphorismes du temps présent; Les incertitudes de l'heure présente* (Paris, Les Amis de Gustave Le Bon, 1978), p. 93.
26 Ibid., citing pp. 130–1 and 93 n. 2.
27 See, on this, R. M. Dainotto, *Europe (in Theory)* (Durham, NC, Duke University Press, 2007).

Guglielmo Ferrero. In 1897, in his *L'Europa giovane*, he praised the northern countries of Europe for their vitality, thriving economies and liberal institutions, all of which he traced back to their industrious and enterprising middle classes. In particular, Ferrero believed that the reason why Great Britain and Germany were growing wealthier and stronger was that rather than 'some Plutarchian hero, like Giordano Bruno or Garibaldi, they give life to a great number of very humble heroes'. Conversely, the countries of southern Europe were dominated by 'classes that do not represent productive work' and that simply favoured soldiers and civil servants, to the detriment of the farmers. The contrast was between a commercial society, the northern one, nursery of modern capitalism and harbinger of solidarity and freedom – even though, Ferrero admitted, disinclined to great artistic achievements – and the southern world, completely engrossed in the pleasures of the 'senses and high intellectual and artistic gratifications, without degrading itself through the brutal employment of producing, with patience, anything'.[28] It is worth noting that this was a deep-rooted opinion – or, in fact, a prejudice – that would loom large in the history of discourses about Europe.

It was in 1908, when he visited the United States, that Ferrero started to consider the darker side of material progress which, until then, he had seen enshrined in the nations of northern Europe. In 1913 he wrote about his journey to America, depicting its society as the ultimate embodiment of industrialisation, capitalism and brute materialism. Ferrero's judgement was harsh. He wrote that America's rapid industrial development was creating a soulless society, concerned only with meeting material needs. By then, his views about Europe had changed. He had now come to argue that, in contrast to the United States, the northern countries of Europe had maintained a connection with their origins, the classical Mediterranean world. In Europe there was therefore still a balance between tradition and modernity, whereas American society was on the path to a complete mechanisation of life. Because of this, Ferrero saw in Europe and America the civilisations of 'quality' and 'quantity', respectively. Europe was still the land of moderation, he reasoned, because of its history and because of the southern element that was such an important part of it – a part that he had now come to appreciate. This notwithstanding, Ferrero feared that Europe, having engendered American civilisation, now risked falling prey to the logic of 'quantity', and

28 G. Ferrero, *L'Europa giovane* (Milan, Treves, 1897), pp. 187, 418.

saw rampant Americanism taking root in the Old World too.[29] In 1917 Ferrero once again changed his views about Europe and America.[30]

The First World War, that war of materials, in which the quantity of resources was to be the deciding factor, would soon lead to Ferrero's fears becoming more widespread. In the 1920s, and even more so in the 1930s, such concerns fuelled intense feelings of anti-Americanism in France, Italy, Germany and, albeit to a lesser degree, in Great Britain too. Excessive consumerism, hyper-capitalism and the standardisation of taste all became features of the feared Americanisation of European society. Inevitably, this dread became intertwined with the 'crisis of the European mind' of the inter-war years.[31] The historian Robert Aron and the essayist Arnaud Dandieu in 1931 wrote about the 'American cancer', that is, the 'supremacy of industry and the bank over the whole life of the age' and the 'hegemony of rational mechanisms' over those sentiments and feelings that 'are the profound motives of human progress'. Although the two authors conceded that the distant origins of such a malady lay in European history, they claimed nonetheless that it was now 'outside of Europe that the seat or the blooming of the evil that starts to gnaw Europe bare is to be found'.[32] Likewise, during a famous conference on the idea of Europe held in Rome in 1932, the Italian scholar Francesco Coppola depicted the United States as a profoundly 'anti-European power'. Its civilisation carried within itself the germs of a religious and moralising, fanatical and narrow-minded puritanism that merged with an 'exacerbated materialism'.[33] Even the great Dutch historian Johan Huizinga, while rejecting the most banal kind of anti-Americanism, was critical of the ways of life across the Atlantic.[34] Indeed, Americanism often embodied the coming of the age of the masses so feared by José Ortega y Gasset, D. H. Lawrence, Aldous Huxley, Lucien Romier and many others during the inter-war years – a fear that was partly tied to the rise of totalitarianisms across the Old Continent. For his part, Georges Duhamel argued in his *Scènes de la vie future* (1930) that Europe was following America on the path towards

---

29 G. Ferrero, *Fra i due mondi* (Milan, Treves, 1913).
30 G. Ferrero, *Le génie latin et le monde moderne* (Paris, Grasset, 1917).
31 On this, see R. Deswarte, 'Between East and West: Europe, the US and the USSR in the 1920s', in M. Hewitson and J. Vermeiren (eds.), *Europe and the East: Historical Ideas of Eastern and Southeast Europe, 1789–1989* (London, Routledge, 2023), pp. 235–50.
32 R. Aron and A. Dandieu, *Le cancer américain* (Lausanne, Age d'homme, 2008), pp. 18–19.
33 F. Coppola, 'La crisi dell'Europa e la sua "cattiva coscienza"', in Reale Accademia d'Italia (ed.), *Convegno di scienze morali e storiche – Tema: L'Europa* (Rome, Reale Accademia d'Italia, 1933), vol. I, pp. 256–8.
34 J. Huizinga, *America: A Dutch Historian's Vision, from Afar and Near* (New York, NY, Harper Torchbooks, 1972 [1918]), p. 312.

the uniformity of taste and the destruction of individuality. If the United States were the image of Europe's tomorrow, he argued, the future was indeed a cause for disquiet. It was an image that, with its censuring of the alleged vulgarity, shallowness and materialism of the American world, was destined to survive long after the inter-war years, offering us a glimpse of what Europeans thought of themselves. Behind it was an obvious form of Eurocentrism, one that would prove to be surprisingly resilient.[35]

Russia: Betwixt and between Europe and Asia

Political and Ideological Threats (Real or Perceived)

Between 1876 and 1894, the French geographer and anarchist Élisée Reclus published his nineteen-volume *Nouvelle géographie universelle*. It soon became one of the most widely known works of geography of the late nineteenth century. Remarkably, in an age of mounting nationalism, it was inspired by a strict rejection of chauvinism. In fact, Reclus strongly believed that people could truly understand the world they lived in only if they discarded that 'instinctive hatred between races, between nations, that often accustoms us to see men differently from what they are'. Cultural diversity itself he saw as beneficial, since the intermingling of different peoples hastened social and economic progress. Therein lay the springboard of civilisation, and Europe owed its greatness to its having been born on the shores of the Mediterranean, a sea that had brought together so many different peoples.[36] It was this sort of mixing that made progress possible. Emerging in Reclus' works was thus a very nuanced understanding of Othering processes, one plainly ahead of its time. He even recognised that, although the 'great drama of universal history is but the endless struggle between Europe and Asia', the roots of European civilisation itself were to be found in Asia, as the legends and myths of ancient Greeks and Romans had made clear.[37]

Be this as it may, Reclus accepted the notion that a hierarchy of civilisations existed, and while this was constantly changing, it was clear that, at the time, Europe was securely at its summit. In fact, in his *Hégémonie de l'Europe* (1894), Reclus celebrated the 'Europeanisation' of the world, claiming it had helped the peoples of Asia in their social, material and cultural progress. As he saw it, even colonialism had some merits, not least that of disseminating

---

35 See M. Wintle, *Eurocentrism: History, Identity, White Man's Burden* (London, Routledge, 2020).

36 É. Reclus, *Nouvelle géographie universelle* (Paris, Hachette, 1876–94), vol. I, pp. 5, 33.

37 Ibid., citing vol. VI, p. 41; vol. I, p. 10.

European values worldwide. It was within such a complex frame of reference that the French geographer pondered the destiny of the Old Continent, paying particular attention to the rise of the United States and Russia. These he saw both as the key actors of the history to come and, crucially, as embodying two opposite social and political models that could offer a glimpse of Europe's own future. Admittedly, having visited the southern states of the United States in the mid 1850s and having witnessed the brutality of slavery at first hand, he censured American society for it.[38] But he later came to admire its institutions and trusted in the might of its material progress. In the *Nouvelle géographie universelle*, he even came to argue that London, the centre of world trade and finance, would one day be replaced by one of the many ever-expanding American metropolises.[39] By the late nineteenth century, Reclus saw the United States as a model of economic growth and a beacon of freedom.

Even more interesting are Reclus' views regarding the other rising world power. In fact, as he saw it, if the United States constituted a 'republic, a protector of other republics', the Russian Empire enshrined the opposite values and political ideals. The one was a model of freedom and tolerance, the other exemplified conservativism and statism: '[T]he Russian Empire, the most powerful of all because of its vastness [. . .], most fully represents the conservative principles of ancient despotism.'[40] For Reclus, one explanation lay in its climate, monotonous countryside and immense steppes, that made of Russia a 'half-Asiatic nation', a civilisation attached intimately to the Orient 'through its races and its history'.[41] Deep within the Russian soul were the seeds of that oriental despotism that, at least from the sixteenth century onwards, had helped to shape a given image of Asia and, by contrast, a specific idea of Europe.[42] Remarkably for us, Reclus' use of oriental despotism had a twofold aim: on the one hand, it could be used to depict Europe as a place of freedom, right and democracy; on the other, it served as a warning to the peoples of Europe that the statism of the Russians might one day spread westwards. Indeed, the most hideous of tyrannies, one that history had 'bestowed on the man who is at once the heir of Genghis Khan and Ivan the Terrible', threatened the 'whole of western Europe' too. In fact,

---

38 See, in particular, É. Reclus, 'De l'esclavage aux États-Unis' (1860–1), in É. Reclus, *Les États-Unis et la guerre de Sécession* (Paris, CTHS, 2007), pp. 127–97.

39 Reclus, *Nouvelle géographie universelle*, vol. I, pp. 22–3.

40 É. Reclus, *L'homme et la terre* (Paris, Librarie Universelle, 1905–8), vol. V, p. 219.

41 Reclus, *Nouvelle géographie universelle*, vol. I, p. 13.

42 P. Bugge, 'Asia and the Idea of Europe – Europe and Its Others', *Kontur – Tidsskrift for Kulturstudier* 1, no. 2 (2000): 3–13.

although Reclus saw the yearning for strong rulers as a typically oriental trait, it was undeniable that in Europe too there were many 'base souls, happy to renounce themselves and to obey'.

But Russia was also, and undeniably, the place of transition, of cultural, social and political exchanges between Asia and Europe. According to the French geographer, through Russia 'Asia is Europeanised' – a desirable turn – while Europe 'tends to regress towards the Asiatic type' – a danger to be shunned. Thanks to Russia, European civilisation had taken root in the Caucasus, Turkmenistan and even in Mongolia and China; but, Reclus reminded his readers, 'nothing comes for free in this world, and the Asianisation of a part of the world corresponds to the Europeanisation of the other part'.[43] There was no clear and predetermined outcome in this struggle between Europe and Asia. One day, indeed, the former might fall prey to the heinous despotism arising from the latter, borne by Russian hordes. Reclus' fears were to be shared by intellectuals and the wider public alike in later years, finally appearing in a somewhat different guise after the 1917 Revolution. By then, many would have agreed with Oswald Spengler, the author of the famous *Untergang des Abendlandes* (1918), for whom the victory of Bolshevism meant that 'Asia has reconquered Russia, after Europe had annexed it thanks to Peter the Great'.[44]

Concerns of a cultural nature came into play among scholars also when pondering the political future of Europe. In 1900, in an essay on the 'États-Unis d'Europe', the French publicist and historian Henri Jean Baptiste Anatole Leroy-Beaulieu considered in some detail the boundaries of a possible European federation, dwelling in particular on the role of Great Britain and Russia, finally reaching the conclusion that neither of these could ever become part of the United States of Europe. In fact, while Great Britain was 'for its past, traditions and entire civilisation an essentially European country and one of the noblest representatives of European culture', because of its possessions scattered across the world it was 'global more than it was European'.[45] Even more interesting are Leroy-Beaulieu's thoughts on Russia. In this case, too, he denied that the Russian Empire could form part of a future federation. Not only did its size prevent it, but so too did its institutions and culture. In fact, in contrast to Great Britain, Russia had never been part of 'historical Europe'. Its traditions, institutions and national character made of

43 Reclus, *Nouvelle géographie universelle*, vol. v, citing pp. 485 and 484.
44 O. Spengler, *Jahre der Entscheidung: Deutschland und die weltgeschichtliche Entwicklung* (Berlin, Holzinger, 2016 [1933]), p. 45.
45 H. J. B. A. Leroy-Beaulieu, 'États-Unis d'Europe', *La revue des revues* 33 (April 1900): 450.

it a wholly different civilisation, somehow suspended between Europe and Asia. Consequently, argued Leroy-Beaulieu, any feeling of 'European solidarity' would never be felt by the Russians as strongly as it would be felt by the peoples of the 'Germanic or the neo-Latin countries'. Indeed, when facing Asia, Russia saw itself as part of Europe, but it was a different Europe 'from ours'. Its politicians, writers and thinkers endowed their country with 'another mind, another mission' than that of the western European polities, which they often considered to be 'old, if not decrepit'. Furthermore, most Russians believed their nation to be the champion of the Slavic and Orthodox cause and saw in it the future hegemon of the Old Continent. If, according to Leroy-Beaulieu, Russia would never feel the need to become part of a European federation, on the other hand its imposing might could spur on Europe in its anxiety to unite. In fact, it was unsurprising that several authors 'have even imagined the European federation directed against the Empire of the Tsars, aimed at curbing Muscovite ambitions'. Yet, at that date Leroy-Beaulieu considered these to be unwarranted fears. Russia was not a threat to Europe, he reckoned, but on the contrary a 'necessary element' in the global order and a counterweight to British and American power. He even predicted that, in the first half of the twentieth century, Russian and European mutual interest would bring their economies closer together, and that it was the dangers posed by the Anglo-Saxon nations that would be more likely to lead to the creation of a European federation.[46]

European Decadence and Rebirth

One of the most influential European philosophers of the late nineteenth century held very different views about Russia and its relationship with Europe. Writing in the 1880s, Friedrich Nietzsche famously claimed that the Old Continent lay in a state of decay and degeneration, its civilisation now 'moving towards a catastrophe'. It was like a 'river that restlessly, violently, headlong, wants to reach the end'.[47] The causes of Europe's decadence were to be sought in the very foundations of its civilisation, namely, post-Socratic philosophy, which had put an end to the tragic element in Greek thought, and Christianity, a religion that preached peace, praised meekness and despised all pleasures. Throughout its history Europe had been shaped by, and had drawn its might from, these values. However, Nietzsche wrote in Die fröhliche Wissenschaft, the 'good Europeans' had now 'outgrown

---

46 Leroy-Beaulieu, 'États-Unis d'Europe', pp. 452–3.
47 F. Nietzsche, Wille zur Macht: Eine Auslegung alles Geschehens (Stuttgart, Kröner, 1921), p. 1.

Christianity too, and are disinclined to it – and this precisely because we have grown out of it, because our forefathers were Christians, uncompromising in their Christian integrity'.[48] Now that faith in Christianity had been lost, Europe had reached the verge of the abyss. Reason and the sciences alone were unable to forge new values and, consequently, the European mind was now possessed by a sense of meaninglessness and futility. However, nihilism, this devaluation of all values, also meant that the people of Europe were finally free from the lies of metaphysics and Judaeo-Christian morality. On those free spirits, the 'good Europeans' who would grasp the chance offered to them, Nietzsche bestowed the duty of forging a new morality, one beyond good and evil.

In his reading of the course of European history, Nietzsche emphasised the oriental roots of its civilisation – for, after all, he noted, Christianity had been born in the East. In accordance with such an understanding, he claimed that the solution to Europe's plights lay in its re-orientalising.[49] In fact, in Asia one could still find the energy and strength that was now lacking in Europe. The barbarism of the East could rejuvenate the Old Continent: 'The disease of the will has spread unevenly across Europe. It appears greatest and most varied where the culture has been at home for the longest period of time; and it becomes increasingly faint to the extent that "the barbarian" still – or once again – asserts his rights under the loose robes of occidental cultivation.' Nietzsche turned to Russia, that 'vast intermediary zone where Europe flows back into Asia'. There, in this bridge between two worlds, a geographical and cultural meeting point, 'the strength to will has been laid aside and stored up over a long time; there, the will is waiting threateningly (uncertain whether as a will of negation or of affirmation), to be discharged'. More than other countries, Russia had maintained its immense strength and invigorating barbarism, not least because its Europeanisation had taken place only on the surface. However, having kept its original strength, Russia had now become a threat to a decrepit Europe, and therefore an incitement to its peoples to unite: the 'sort of increase in the menace Russia poses would force Europe into choosing to become equally threatening and, specifically, to acquire a single will by means of a new caste that would rule over Europe'. This new elite, asserting a 'terrible will of its own', would reject all humdrum politicking. It would end Europe's degeneration by setting out new values, giving 'itself millennia-long goals: so that the long, spun-out comedy of

---

48 F. Nietzsche, 'Die fröhliche Wissenschaft' (1882), in F. Nietzsche, *Idyllen aus Messina; Die fröhliche Wissenschaft; Nachgelassene Fragmente* (Berlin, de Gruyter, 1973), p. 313 (§ 377).
49 See D. Large, 'Nietzsche's Orientalism', *Nietzsche-Studien* 42, no. 1 (2013): 420–38.

Europe's petty provincialism and its dynastic as well as democratic fragmentation of the will could finally come to an end'.[50]

Another thinker who had a remarkable impact on the ways in which the relationship between Russia and Europe was conceived was Fyodor Dostoevsky. Like Nietzsche, the great Russian writer too believed that Europe was 'on the eve of a general and dreadful collapse' and argued that only the Russian mind could save it. Europe's 'moral principle is shaken loose from its foundations, lacking now any general and absolute notion'. The end was in sight, since the 'fourth estate' would soon rebel. Europe having renounced Christianity, once the source of its greatness and might, its peoples were now heading towards their downfall. Their sole hope lay in Russia, for only Russia had kept intact its profound mysticism.[51] In more ways than one, Dostoevsky's ideas served to reinforce the notion that Russia was a civilisation in between the East and the West, neither wholly European nor entirely Asian. It was a view that would eventually become influential among Panslavist thinkers in ensuing decades. But it also had an impact in western Europe, in particular among conservative intellectuals. For one, Arthur Moeller van der Bruck, the future leader of the conservative revolution during the Weimar Republic and the editor of Dostoevsky's complete works in German, saw in Russia a young nation that had yet to achieve its true potential. Partly following Dostoevsky's arguments, Moeller offered his readers the image of a Janus-faced Russia, a 'European' and a 'Siberian Russia'; the first, like western Europe, was artificial, decadent and materialistic; the other was active, young and mystical. In the latter, beneath the surface of the Europeanisation begun by Peter the Great, the Russians had remained pure, uncorrupted by the bourgeois shallowness of the West. Their deep-seated religiosity and their yearning for the infinite had been and still were in sharp contrast with the materialism of the peoples of Europe.[52] Furthermore, in maintaining their purity, the Russians had also retained their original communitarianism: they were, wrote Moeller, 'a people of number, a people characterised by massiveness and not by the principle of

---

50 F. Nietzsche, 'Jenseits von Gut und Böse' (1886), in F. Nietzsche, *Jenseits von Gut und Böse; Genealogie der Moral* (Berlin, de Gruyter, 1968), pp. 143–4 (§ 208).

51 F. Dostoevsky, *The Diary of a Writer* (New York, NY, Braziller, 1949), p. 1003 (August 1880).

52 A. Moeller van den Bruck, 'Zur Einführung: Bemerkungen über sibirische Möglichkeiten' (1908), in F. Dostoevsky, *Sämtliche Werke* (Munich, Piper, 1906–25), vol. XVIII, pp. ix–xiv; A. Moeller van den Bruck, 'Zur Einführung: Bemerkungen über Dostojewski als Dichter der Großstadt' (1907), in Dostoevsky, *Sämtliche Werke*, vol. XX, pp. ix–x.

individuality', in contrast to the Europeans, whose 'inner activity of will, initiative, energy, has formed in the weakest possible way'.[53] Importantly, during the inter-war years, Moeller's ideas would influence the views of authors such as Thomas Mann and Oswald Spengler on Europe and Russia.[54] Among those who came to share Moeller's arguments was Walter Schubart, who, in his remarkable *Europa und die Seele des Ostens* (1938), insisted that Russia was the only nation that could 'redeem Europe, since in the face of all crucial problems it assumes an attitude that is diametrically opposed to that of every European nation'. Because of the 'depth of its unique suffering', he went on, 'Russia can bring a deeper knowledge to mankind.' Interestingly, he believed this despite the fact that Russia found itself in 'the toils of Bolshevism' and was sure that the 'grey misery' of the Soviet period would soon pass and that the 'ancient saying *"ex oriente lux"* will prove true once again'.[55]

As was only to be expected, and despite the admiration of many conservatives for the Russian mind, during the First World War and at least up until the Treaty of Brest-Litovsk, the majority of German writers insisted on the risk that the whole of Europe could fall under the yoke of Russian despotism. Its failed westernisation was not a virtue, as Moeller had argued, but a curse for the entire continent. As the German Foreign Secretary Gottlieb von Jagow wrote in 1915, until then the Russian Empire, with its inexhaustible resources, had 'brooded over western Europe like a nightmare. Despite the veneer of Western civilisation given to it by Peter the Great and the German dynasty that followed him, its basically Byzantine–Oriental culture separates it from the Latin culture of the West, and the Russian race, part Slav, part Mongol, is foreign to the Germanic–Latin peoples of the West.'[56] Germany and its allies were a bulwark against the Asiatic barbarism of the Russians and the sole defence for Europe – a notion that, in a new guise, was to be restated by the Nazis a few years later in their (decidedly ambiguous) projects of

---

53 A. Moeller van den Bruck, 'Die Voraussetzungen Dostojewskis: Zur Einführung in die Ausgabe' (1908), in Dostoevsky, *Sämtliche Werke*, vol. I, p. xiii.

54 See M. Brolsma, 'Dostovesky: A Russian Panacea for Europe', in C. Reijnen and M. Rensen (eds.), *European Encounters: Intellectual Exchange and the Rethinking of Europe 1914–1945* (Amsterdam, Rodopi, 2014), pp. 189–203.

55 W. Schubart, *Europa und die Seele des Ostens* (Pfullingen, Neske, 1979), pp. 40–1.

56 F. Fischer, *Griff nach der Weltmacht: Die Kriegszielpolitik des kaiserlichen Deutschland 1914/ 18* (Düsseldorf, Droste, 1961), p. 243. On images of Russia and ideas of Europe during the First World War among German thinkers, see J. Vermeiren, 'In Defence of Europe: Russia in German Intellectual Discourse, 1914–1918', in M. D'Auria and J. Vermeiren (eds.), *Visions and Ideas of Europe during the First World War* (London, Routledge, 2019), pp. 43–61.

European unification.[57] Rather surprisingly, even authors who belonged to nations fighting against the Central Powers openly criticised the Russians' alleged barbarism. For one, the journalist, Norman Angell, the author of the famous *Great Illusion* (1913), which predicted the advent of a European federation, wondered whether a coalition of Slavs formed by Serbia and Russia, comprising '200,000,000 autocratically governed people, with a very rudimentary civilization, but heavily equipped for military aggression', was not a greater danger to Europe than 'a dominant Germany of 65,000,000 highly civilized [people] and mainly given to the arts of trade and commerce'.[58] It is important to note that in such views there emerged a clearly racialist undertone, one that was destined to remain long after the end of the war and which had deep roots in the history of discourses about Europe.

Post-1917 Reverberations and (Dis)continuities: Managing Decline

'Europe has become small', Karl Jaspers noted in 1946: 'The two great formations of the West, America and Russia, are taking over the world. If there were today the United States of Europe, they would perhaps be a power comparable to Russia and America.' He then went on to argue that Europe had to unite immediately, 'for the natural growth of the continental world powers makes Europe, which is already small, even smaller'.[59] Obviously, at the time this feeling of powerlessness was widespread among European intellectuals and politicians. A Europe that was completely shattered and materially and morally debased was being divided between the two great powers and on them its future now depended entirely. Fears that Europe would become a battlefield between the two contenders were also widespread: '[W]hether the sickle comes from the East or the West, the field to mow will always be [. . .] Europe', the Italian jurist Piero Calamandrei noted bitterly in 1950.[60] The need to unite was felt by many intellectuals and politicians – though, of course, the means were hotly debated. As we have seen, this perceived 'dwarfing of Europe' had deeper roots than is usually

57 See J. Elver, 'The "New European Order" of National Socialism: Some Remarks on Its Sources, Genesis and Nature', in D. Gosewinkel (ed.), *Anti-liberal Europe: A Neglected Story of Europeanization* (New York, NY, Berghahn, 2015), pp. 105–27.

58 N. Angell, 'The Menace of War: Dominance of Russia or Germany', *The Times*, 1 August 1914, 6.

59 K. Jaspers, *Vom europäischen Geist* (Munich, Piper, 1947), p. 17. (The text was first presented at a conference in Geneva, in 1946.)

60 P. Calamandrei, 'Appello all'unità europea', in P. Calamandrei, *Questa nostra Europa* (Gallarate, People, 2020), p. 99.

assumed and, equally importantly, it became entwined with changing perceptions about Europe shaped in response to the growing challenges posed by Russia and America well before 1917.[61] In particular, three aspects of the discourses on European unification seem worthy of attention here.

First, there was a shifting perception of European spatiality. This was a twofold process. On the one hand, from the late nineteenth century onwards it became increasingly clear that the distances between Berlin, London, Paris and Rome were 'shrinking' rapidly thanks to the ever-faster communication of goods and ideas. It was a process that many saw as irresistible, determined by economic and social necessities, and one that could hardly be controlled by individual nation states. In the face of the integration brought about by such changes, many started to view the boundaries between states as obsolete. As we have seen, this was a conviction shared by the advocates of *Mitteleuropa* as well as liberal thinkers such as Einaudi.[62] To manage economic integration, before as well as after 1917, they believed that the space of politics had to adapt to the space of economics. In the aftermath of the Second World War, it was the need to revive the European economies by removing fetters to trade that prompted many to campaign for a European federation. Frontiers were considered to be the main cause of Europe's economic difficulties, and, as some observers vividly put it, these artificial divisions, now obsolete, were 'the cause of the gangrene'.[63] On the other hand, equally important was the awareness that, to confront the threats posed by the United States in the west and Russia and then the Soviet Union in the east, the nations of Europe had to unite into a single continent-wide unit to muster more effectively their resources. While such a need was already felt at the turn of the twentieth century and though signs of it emerge in the writings of the authors considered above, it became especially urgent after the First World War. In 1930, the historian Charles Pomaret wrote of America's economic and financial 'conquest of Europe' and argued that the only way to counter such a threat was to create a single European market, one as vast as that on the other side of the

---

61 The expression is from A. Toynbee, *Civilization on Trial* (Oxford, Oxford University Press, 1948), pp. 97–125.

62 Other examples, in the inter-war years, are F. Delaisi, *Les contradictions du monde moderne* (Paris, Payot, 1925), pp. 468–71; F. S. Nitti, *La pace* (Turin, Gobetti Editore, 1925), pp. 205–6.

63 I. M. Lombardo and G. Caron, 'Raisons économiques de la Fédération Européenne', in Movimento Federalista Europeo (ed.), *Economie de la Fédération Européenne* (Rome, Union européenne des fédéralistes, 1952), p. 15.

Atlantic.[64] Arguments such as these, though laid out in a new context, echoed discussions surrounding the American peril of the early 1900s but, importantly, they were also felt after 1945. For one, the essayist and champion of European unification Altiero Spinelli in 1947 saw in the creation of a European federation the only way for its states to avoid 'turning into protectorates and instruments of American imperialistic politics'.[65] To the east, the threat had always been of a very different nature and, after 1917, fears of aggression increased as the capacity of the new-born Soviet Union to marshall its resources improved. In the years of the Weimar Republic, the jurist Carl Schmitt expressed his concerns about the ostensibly limitless resources of the Soviet Union and called for Europe to unite into a *Großraum* pivoting around *Mitteleuropa*.[66] After 1945, the might of the Russian army only heightened such fears among intellectuals and politicians. Jean Monnet and Konrad Adenauer, to name but two, were among them.[67] It is important to emphasise that, overall, from the late nineteenth century onwards, the increasingly urgent need to overcome the partition of Europe into several states was grounded on a realistic approach to politics. Unification was not only an aim pursued by idealists trying to attain 'perpetual peace'. It was also, and perhaps first and foremost, a question of sheer survival in a changing international scenario and in the face of the two new (and allegedly hostile) rising superpowers. Europe simply was a 'realist' project.

The latter point dovetails with our second aspect, since the concern to maintain a degree of independence from the United States and the Soviet Union entwined with the desire to preserve European values and ways of life – howsoever defined. At the dawn of the Cold War, the Soviet Union came to embody, for conservatives and liberals alike, a new kind of ancient despotism. Admittedly, Russia was now a modern and industrialised country, but beneath the surface little had changed. In fact, according to the Swiss historian Gonzague de Reynold, the USSR was the embodiment of 'eternal Russia' which, under Stalin, had now achieved its truest form. It was the opposite of everything that Europe stood for.[68] Of course, de Reynold was mainly repeating long-standing ideas, which had already been formulated by

---

64 C. Pomaret, *L'Amérique à la conquête de l'Europe* (Paris, Colin, 1931), pp. 209–84.

65 A. Spinelli, 'Discorso al Primo Congresso del Movimento Federalista Europeo', in L. Levi and S. Pistone (eds.), *Trent'anni di vita del Movimento Federalista Europeo* (Milan, Franco Angeli, 1973), p. 97.

66 C. Schmitt, 'Das Zeitalter der Neutralisierung und Entpolitisierung' (1929), in C. Schmitt, *Der Begriff des Politischen* (Berlin, Dunker and Humblot, 1991), pp. 79–95.

67 J. Monnet, *Mémoires* (Paris, Fayard, 2019), pp. 518–19; K. Adenauer, *Erinnerungen: 1945–1953* (Stuttgart, Deutsche Verlags-Anstalt, 1976), pp. 311–16 (March 1950).

68 G. de Reynold, *La Formation de l'Europe: VI – Le monde russe* (Paris, Librairie Plon, 1950), pp. 354–6.

the authors considered in the previous pages. To the west, the United States posed a threat of a different kind, and the anti-Americanism fomented by right-wing authors and now by left-wing intellectuals too did much to increase concerns. Even the two social theorists Theodor W. Adorno and Max Horkheimer, with their arguments on the dangers of mass society and by focusing on the United States, indirectly and unwittingly contributed to shaping an image of Europe as a place where individuality and freedom could be safeguarded and where people were more than their 'assets, income, position and prospects'.[69] While fears of a massification of everyday life could already be found in the texts of authors such as Ferrero, in the aftermath of the Second World War some authors were more explicit in their tying of projects of unification to the defence of European values. For one, the German historian Ludwig Dehio argued in 1953 that a 'federated Europe' would be 'a third force between the two Titans', the United States and the USSR, which would make it possible 'to maintain the superiority of the European way of life even against American civilisation'.[70]

Dehio's words bring us to our third and last noteworthy aspect, namely the persistence and even the exacerbation, from the late nineteenth century onwards, of Eurocentrism – and this despite Europe's obvious political decline. Indeed, as early as 1918, the novelist Hermann Hesse had satirised the feeling of European moral superiority in the face of the destruction caused by the war.[71] Yet few would have directed so disenchanted a gaze at Europe. Indeed, in the inter-war years, Eurocentrism was still strong, and it became even stronger as the political weight of the nations of the Old Continent waned. This emerged in a twofold manner. On the one hand, greater emphasis was placed on the role of Europe in world history. So, in 1919, Paul Valéry, while lamenting the political debasement of the Old Continent, was eager to remind his readers that 'everything has come to Europe and everything has come from Europe. At least, almost everything.'[72] Similarly, Ortega y Gasset portrayed the two world powers as both stemming from Europe and retaining some features of its civilisation. Both Soviet tyrannical Bolshevism and American aggressive capitalism, he argued, were but aberrations of ideas that had originally been European. However, severed

69 T. W. Adorno and M. Horkheimer, *Dialektik der Aufklärung* (Amsterdam, Querido, 1947 [1944]), p. 249.

70 L. Dehio, 'Das sterbende Staatensystem' (1953), in L. Dehio, *Deutschland und die Weltpolitik im 20. Jahrhundert* (Hamburg, Fischer, 1961), pp. 117–18.

71 H. Hesse, 'Der Europäer', in H. Hesse, *Der Europäer: Gesammelte Erzählungen*, vol. III: *1909–1918* (Frankfurt am Main, Suhrkamp, 1977), pp. 315–22.

72 P. Valéry, 'La crise de l'esprit', in P. Valéry, *Œuvres* (Paris, Gallimard, 1957), vol. I, p. 995.

from their roots, they had 'lost their meaning' and were now borne by civilisations threatening Europe and its culture.[73] A similar attitude was also shared by Thomas Mann in the immediate aftermath of the Second World War. Convinced that its nations would soon unite, he still believed that Europe had been and would remain 'the heart and the mind of the world'.[74] Such ideas were clearly rooted in the works of pre-1917 authors who were writing in a very different context – some of whom we have considered above.

One other way in which Eurocentrism took shape was by portraying both the USSR and the United States as civilisations with the same faults and flaws. For some writers, they were, beneath the surface, very much alike, both possessed by the demon of technicity and obsessed with the massification of production so characteristic of American Fordism – which, inevitably, also led to the massification of life itself. Arguably, while such a parallel had already been drawn in writings produced between the 1890s and 1917, it became widespread only from the 1920s onwards, mostly emerging in the works of conservative and right-wing authors, such as Spengler, Schmitt, the French novelist Pierre Drieu La Rochelle and the Italian jurist Sergio Panunzio.[75] But even the pacifist writer Georges Duhamel compared American and Soviet Russian societies and spoke of 'bourgeois communism' to emphasise the closeness between them.[76] And so too did the liberal journalist Alfred Fabre-Luce, for whom 'Bolshevik Russia was but a failed America'. Both societies held human life in the same contempt; in both, freedom was denied, in the one through laws, in the other by customs; both misleadingly equated technological progress with the moral advance of civilisation.[77] In many ways, the image of Europe, by implicit contrast, was flattering. Even more interesting are the remarks made by André Siegfried in the aftermath of the Second World War. As he maintained, the two super-powers, by then clearly destined to determine almost entirely the future of Europe, were both 'extra-European powers'. In fact, the structure of both the USSR and the United States was that 'of large spaces' and this 'predisposes

73 J. Ortega y Gasset, 'La rebelión de las masas' (1929), in J. Ortega y Gasset, *La rebelión de las masas y otros ensayos* (Madrid, Alianza, 2020), pp. 204–9.
74 T. Mann, '[Rückkehr nach Europa]', in *Essays VI: 1945–1950* (Frankfurt am Main, Fischer, 1997), vol. I, p. 246.
75 C. Schmitt, *Römischer Katholizismus und politische Form* (Stuttgart, Klett-Cotta, 2019 [1923]), pp. 21–3; Spengler, *Jahre der Entscheidung*, pp. 49–51; P. Drieu La Rochelle, *Genève ou Moscou* (Paris, Gallimard, 1928), pp. 168–9; S. Panunzio, 'La fine di un regno', *Critica Fascista* 15 (September 1932): 342–3.
76 G. Duhamel, *Scènes de la vie future* (Paris, Points, 2018), p. 114.
77 A. Fabre-Luce, *Russie: 1927* (Paris, Grasset, 1928), pp. 163–4.

them more towards mass than complexity. The maxim that man is the measure of all things has no meaning in the Russian steppe or the American prairie. We are far away, here, from the landscape of the Greek mind.' One could even wonder, Siegfried went on, whether under the guidance of 'such leaders, Western civilisation might not incline towards the colossal and hyper-organisation to the detriment of individualism, moderation, diversity'.[78] Considering the context in which Siegfried was writing, this is indeed a remarkable instance of the persistence of Eurocentrism.

Conclusion

As the Italian historian Federico Chabod noted in a course of lectures held in Nazi-occupied Milan between 1943 and 1944, the idea of Europe is formed 'by contrast, for there is something that is not Europe. [. . . T]he polemical foundation is essential.'[79] Since his lectures focused on the eighteenth century, the dichotomies that Chabod was interested in involved Asia (and the old notion of oriental despotism) on the one hand, and America (and the image of the noble savage) on the other. Yet his argument holds true when considering our time-span too – and for that matter, when pondering any identity formation process. In our case the ways in which Europe shaped its own self-representations acquired a very specific character when, from the late nineteenth century onwards, the contrast implied civilisations that were so intimately tied to and, in fact, even stemming from, European civilisation itself. This is by no means a negligible fact. The contrast and the comparison involved worlds that shared a common past but also implied, at least for many European observers, the possibility that the future of Europe might diverge from the paths both of the United States and of Russia/the USSR. In truth, if the Eurocentrism of our authors was often coupled with the hope of building a united Europe, this was not only to avert the risk of war between its nations but also, and perhaps mainly, to preserve the European ways of life and values. As to what these were, the intellectuals, politicians and activists we have briefly considered all offered their own answers – some, indeed, far more convincing than others. The question they posed was and still is fraught with difficulties. And yet it is still one worth asking, particularly now that peace among the nations belonging to the European Union (seems) an accomplished fact and the reasons for sharing a common future appear, to many, to be lacking.

78 A. Siegfried, 'Europe, Amérique, Occident?', *Hommes et mondes* 5, no. 18 (January 1948): 11.
79 F. Chabod, *Storia dell'idea d'Europa* (Bari, Laterza, 1998), p. 23.

Recommended Reading

D'Auria, M. and J. Vermeiren (eds.). *Visions and Ideas of Europe during the First World War* (London, Routledge, 2019).

Pagden, A. *The Pursuit of Europe: A History* (Oxford, Oxford University Press, 2022).

Pasture, P. *Imagining European Unity since 1000 AD* (Basingstoke, Palgrave Macmillan, 2015).

Spiering, M. and M. Wintle (eds.). *European Identity and the Second World War* (Basingstoke, Palgrave Macmillan, 2011).

Stirk, P. M. R. (ed.). *European Unity in Context: The Interwar Period* (London, Bloomsbury, 2016).

Weller, S. *The Idea of Europe: A Critical History* (Cambridge, Cambridge University Press, 2021).

Wintle, M. *Eurocentrism: History, Identity, White Man's Burden* (London, Routledge, 2020).

22

Beginning with Culture: A Certain Idea of Europe

JOEP LEERSSEN

The Community shall contribute to the flowering of the cultures of the Member States, while respecting their national and regional diversity and at the same time bringing the common cultural heritage to the fore.

Treaty of Maastricht (1992), Article 128

Beginning with Culture?

An Open Door

The 'European project' at first sight might seem a ploddingly pragmatic, even technocratic, instrument for achieving harmonisation between its member states. As such, it is habitually contrasted with the 'nation-states' which make up its members, and which, unlike the office blocks of Brussels and Strasbourg, are seen as historical communities ('nations') as well as states, united in their shared historical memories, language and culture. This unproblematic acceptance of the 'nation-state' makes for a skewed comparison when used in a problematisation of 'Europe'.[1] There seems to be little that Europe can offer by way of a common cultural bonding agent; at best, there is a notion of 'unity in diversity' (the official motto of the European Union (EU) since 2000). Indeed, the Treaty of Maastricht included a cultural paragraph which uneasily balanced the requirements of that cultural diversity and unity. The uncertainty concerning a common cultural basis is even seen as a characteristic weakness in the European project,

---

With thanks to Matthijs Lok and Arthur Mitzman. Arthur passed away as this chapter was being finished, after a long and fruitful life as a prominent historian. This chapter is dedicated to his memory.

1 For a problematisation of the nation-state, see my *National Thought in Europe: A Cultural History*, 3rd ed. (Amsterdam, Amsterdam University Press, 2018).

something that deprives it of a centripetal, cohesive force. Its absence means that the EU is perpetually and self-consumingly in quest of a self-definition and, in Cris Shore's formulation, lacks an identifying focus 'to capture the loyalty and allegiance of its would-be citizens; to transform nationals into self-recognising European subjects'.[2] Shore has also traced, in the mode of cultural anthropology, the corporate culture of the EU institutions, rather than analysing a cultural history or cultural agenda informing the European project.[3]

In that respect, Jean Monnet, father of the European project itself, is often quoted as saying that '*si c'était à refaire, je commencerais par la culture*' ('If we were to do it all over again, I would begin with culture'). Like most famous phrases, this one was never said in this form. The phrase was in fact hypothetically and ventriloquistically imputed to Monnet by Hélène Ahrweiler, who stated in a public speech that, were Monnet to return amongst us, he might well exclaim that, if we were to do it all over again, et cetera. Ahrweiler's imputation indicates at best that such cultural motivations as inspired the Monnet generation had been lost from sight 50 years after.[4] Nor indeed could Monnet ever seriously have said something like this; because, as I hope to show in this chapter, Europe had in fact started with culture. Culture, that is, not in the narrow sense (the aesthetically valorised comforts that enrich our material life), but more widely: as a conscience, a self-image framing people's reflections upon their actions and communications and rendering them meaningful.

Minimally, it could be asserted that the notorious European quest for a self-definition of its moral place in the world is itself an ongoing cultural praxis, and this at least would form an unquestionable manifestation of a European culture: being bothered by what it might amount to. In a Cartesian sense, the European starting point might be formulated as *dubito, ergo sum*.

Outline of This Chapter: Europe Reflecting on Europe's Reflections

In the next pages I aim to elaborate on the implications and manifestations of that minimalist starting point. My argument will be that older (Greek, Christian) discourses which evince, however intuitively, a sense of being

---

2 C. Shore, 'Inventing Homo Europaeus: The Cultural Politics of European Integration', *Ethnologia Europaea* 29, no. 2 (1998): 53–66. This issue of *Ethnologia Europaea* was reissued as P. Niedermuller and B. Stoklund (eds.), *Europe: Cultural Construction and Reality* (Copenhagen, Museum Tusculanum Press, 2001).

3 C. Shore, *Building Europe: The Cultural Politics of European Integration* (London, Routledge, 2000).

4 H. Ahrweiler, 'Jean Monnet et la culture', *Le Monde*, 21 June 1998.

separate from the rest of the world are re-articulated in a more conscious and self-aware form around the onset of modernity and are also increasingly relying on the self-identification 'European'. In tracing this development from an implicit European position towards an explicit idea of Europe, I follow Denys Hay's brief but masterful, and still authoritative, *Europe: The Emergence of an Idea*, which concludes with the observation that 'By the beginning of the eighteenth century, it is in terms of Europe that Europeans begin to view the world.'[5]

Hay's most important lesson lies in his history-of-ideas approach. He does not pretend to discuss 'Europe *an sich*', its geography and historical vicissitudes, or its purported 'character', 'spirit' or essence, but rather, at the meta-level, the history of how people conceptualised Europe: Europe as a subjectively held image rather than as an objective reality.

This European 'idea' – a European self-image consciously experienced and explicitly reflected upon – develops, then, out of an earlier, more intuitive position of implicit Eurocentrism. In its further development, that idea of Europe begins to see itself as a tradition: the discourse in which Europe reflects upon itself begins to develop a rearview mirror, a sense of its own historical track record.[6] The approach followed here and in my book *Spiegelpaleis Europa* is that of imagology, which studies the documentary record of ethnotypes (stereotyped characterisations of domestic and foreign cultures) in terms of their temperamental self/other juxtapositions, their textual rhetoric, intertextual conventions and historical (contextual) function.[7] At the core of it all, a primal Eurocentrism is perpetuated, but this is gradually wrapped up in an accumulation of reconsideration, reflection and self-reflection. By 1800 we can discern the crystallisation of historical narratives relating and reaffirming the plotlines of Europe-as-civilisation, Europe-as-morality or Europe-as-progress. Historical vicissitudes and turbulences (the rise and fall of Napoleon, the crises of empires, the rise of America, the rise of the nation-state) were increasingly experienced by something that was learning to call itself 'Europe'. From c. 1800 on, the notion of Europe as a 'concert' or political ecosystem takes hold, and this self-awareness also involves a historicist sense of sharing longstanding institutions, traditions,

---

5 D. Hay, *Europe: The Emergence of an Idea* (Edinburgh, University Press, 1957), p. 117.

6 I here draw on the more detailed approach in my *Spiegelpaleis Europa: Europese cultuur als mythe en beeldvorming*, 3rd ed. (Nijmegen, Vantilt, 2015), to which I refer the reader for additional sources and references.

7 On that method, see also M. Beller and J. Leerssen (eds.), *Imagology* (Amsterdam, Rodopi, 2007).

a history, things we now call 'culture'. That historicism and sense of inter-dependence developed from 'concert' diplomacy towards internationalism and an agenda of integration.

In the last 150 years, dominated though they have been by the rise of nationalism, that discourse of Europe was used to formulate an internation-alist political mission: to regenerate or preserve the continent thus named, to ensure its peace and prosperity and to maintain its achievements in a problematically modernising and globalising world. That was the mission of the internationalist intellectuals of the inter-war period. Their stance in turn inspired the decision-makers from the Hague Congress (1948) to the Treaty of Rome (1953) and beyond.

These later stages, which I shall follow more closely in the following pages, closely conform to the structure put forward in Stella Ghervas' recent book *Conquering Peace*,[8] that of a European self-image which arose through itera-tive cultural self-contemplations amidst emerging political challenges, solidi-fied to the point of inspiring an internationalist mission. Ghervas' view of European attempts to control international relations peacefully, first through a balance-of-power doctrine, then through a diplomatic system and finally in the form of pan-European political institutions, closely aligns with the approach taken here; and her view that these attempts bespeak an ethics (set of values) moves her analysis close to my view that they reflect Europe's implicit cultural self-image.

By the middle of the twentieth century, the European politicians of the Monnet–Schuman generation had a *certaine idée de l'Europe* (a particular idea of Europe) much as Charles de Gaulle had, famously, a *certaine idée de la France*. It was then that the standard works on the history of a European identity were written. We shall encounter often-quoted authors such as de Rougemont, Chabod and Duroselle at the end of this chapter, not the beginning, because their historical surveys are assertions of a belief in European culture at a time when that belief was inspiring the institutions of the European Economic Community (EEC) and the Council of Europe; they are (like the point where the Möbius strip folds over onto itself) both the endpoint of our primary documentation and the point of departure of an academic study of the historical record.

The iterative loops of self-reflection did not stop there: Europe has con-tinued since 1953 to question its mission, its identity, its character, its track

---

8 S. Ghervas, *Conquering Peace: From the Enlightenment to the European Union* (Cambridge, MA, Harvard University Press, 2021); it follows in the line of her earlier publications on the history of international peace-maintenance.

record and its position in the world. (Indeed, the present chapter is, at a yet more rarefied academic meta-level, a further reflection on all those reflections and reflections upon reflections.) At the heart of it all, however, there is still a set of attributes and characteristics which Europeans like to invoke to describe why they are special. Unreflective Euro-exceptionalism is the oldest, most deeply embedded stratum of the layered self-image of Europe, and, although it has been subjected to many reworkings and revisions, it was never forgotten or abandoned.

Run-Up

From Position to Idea

Many historians have traced the self-silhouetting of an intra-European space against the world outside. Some of these will be discussed in the closing pages of this chapter. Given the solid historiography, my outline of the pre-1800 stages of the European self-image will be brief and sketchy. The terms of that contrastive positioning were fluid both as regards the parties involved and as regards the operative distinction. Greek thinkers of the post-Herodotus centuries opposed a Hellenic world against the Persian Empire, thereby laying the basis for one of the most tenacious and protean stereotypes in European history: that of Oriental Despotism.[9] (While the concept is of long standing, the phrase is as recent as the Cold War, coined in a book fatally flawed by anachronistic determinism.[10] This should serve as a reminder of how prone we are to apply, unwittingly, lenses of very recent and shoddy manufacture when looking at ancient and long-term geopolitics.) Against this despotism of the East, the we-group (who were later folded into a 'European' aggregate) stressed their more civic, city-based (rather than court-based) society, based on the political participation of its stakeholders; words like civic and political all refer back to this municipal Graeco-Roman self-image, placing the twin concepts of private and public activity (domus/οἶκος and civitas/urbs/πόλις) in an ideal mid-way position between imperial court

9 E. Hall, *Inventing the Barbarians: Greek Self-Definition through Tragedy* (Oxford, Clarendon, 1989); F. Hartog, *Le miroir d'Hérodote: Essai sur la représentation de l'Autre* (Paris, Gallimard, 1980). For a modern approach, see G. Delanty, *Inventing Europe* (London, Palgrave Macmillan, 1995).

10 K. A. Wittfogel, *Oriental Despotism: A Comparative Study of Total Power* (New Haven, CT, Yale University Press, 1957). See also F. Venturi, 'Oriental Despotism', *Journal of the History of Ideas* 24, no. 1 (1968): 133–42.

and tribal encampment.[11] Even in the twelfth century, the Welsh cleric Giraldus Cambrensis, who invokes Ovid and Horace, propounds a stadialist civilisational ideal that moves from nomadism to agriculture, from forest to fields to villages and civil society ruled by laws. As the centuries passed, classical writings and attitudes remained, inculcated on the elite of Europe as in their formative educational years they were 'taught their letters' by means of Caesar, Livy and Xenophon.

An overlay in this East–West opposition came when in the Middle Ages the defining characteristic became that of religion: the internal order of the post-classical successor polities was defined as Christendom and opposed to the world of Islam, with which it saw itself confronted in Spain, around Constantinople and on the pilgrimage route to Jerusalem. As Denys Hay has shown, the world of Christendom came to be seen as a composite of different 'nations' at around the time of the closure of the Avignon Papacy (1376) and the Council of Constance (1417). When Mehmet II conquered Constantinople in 1453, the anxieties of the refined humanist Enea Silvio Piccolomini, who would soon become Pope Pius II, increasingly located Christendom in the territorial, classically derived geographical notion of 'Europe'. In a speech addressed to the Frankfurt Diet, he asserted that earlier confrontations and defeats had taken place 'in Asia and Africa, that is: in alien lands; but now we have been shaken and stricken in Europe, that is to say in our fatherland, in our own home, in our residence', going on to say that the conquest of Constantinople was much more grievous than previous incursions of the Turks into Greece, of the Tatars into the Don basin, or of the Saracens into Spain. (In the original: '[...] retroactis namque temporibus in Asia atque in Affrica, hoc est in alienis terris, vulnerati fuimus, nunc vero in Europa, id est in patria, in domo propria, in sede nostra percussi cesique sumus [...] et licet dicat aliquis ante plurimos annos ex Asia Turchos in Greciam transivisse, Tartaros citra Thanaim in Europa consedisse, Sarracenos Herculeo mari traiecto Hispanie portionem occupasse; numquam tamen aut urbem aut locum amisimus in Europa, qui Constantinopoli possit equari.')[12]

11 B. L. Sjöberg, 'The Greek oikos: A Space for Interaction, Revisited and Reconsidered', in L. Karlsson, S. Carlsson and J. Blid Kullberg (eds.), *Λαβρυς: Studies presented to Pontus Hellström* (Uppsala, Uppsala Universitet, 2014), pp. 315–28; J. Leerssen, 'The Camp and the Home: Europe as Myth and Metaphor', in J. Barkhoff and J. Leerssen (eds.), *National Stereotyping and Identity Politics in Times of European Crises* (Leiden, Brill, 2021), pp. 125–41.

12 E. S. Piccolomini, 'Constantinopolitana clades', in *Pii II orationes politicae et ecclesiasticae (1755–1759)*, as quoted in J. Helmrath, 'Enea Silvio Piccolomini (Pius II.). Ein Humanist als Vater des Europagedankens?' (2007), Themenportal Europäische Geschichte, www .europa.clio-online.de / essay / id / fdae-1327.

As religion met geopolitics, the Ottoman Sultan was also projected into the classical, pre-existing model of the 'oriental despot'. The clash with Islam is what turned Europe from an implied position into an explicit Idea, something foregrounded and specific.

As the overland Silk Route connections to the spices and riches of Asia collapsed, alternative routes were explored by sea, west of Gibraltar: around the cape of Good Hope and, in Columbus' misguided attempt at direct circumnavigation, westward across the Atlantic.[13] Thus the struggle with Islam fed into colonial expansion overseas, which in turn was aided by the scientific revolution: technological improvements involving gunpowder, the printing of maps, astronomically based navigational mathematics and technological tools ranging from the compass and the telescope to (by the early eighteenth century) the sextant and the chronometer. It is in these centuries that the self-image of Europe, linked as it is to economic dominance and technological superiority, becomes increasingly that of 'the continent that progresses'. Europe as Idea is expressed and outlined in many different forms, many of them visual: anthropomorphised amid other allegorised continents, or cartographically, in the maps of the world silhouetting the continent with a crisp coastal outline and a central position on the flattened globe (not to mention the allegorical figures that are such an important, but often-overlooked, presence embellishing the empty margins of baroque maps).[14]

The intellectuals involved in this freshly assertive Eurocentrism consider themselves to be co-inhabiting a united 'Republic of Letters' or 'Republic of Learning'. Although realms and churches may vie with each other and coerce the obedience of their subjects, intellectuals prize their open exchange of ideas, relying on the shared ambience of Latin, on a shared repertoire of erudition of Graeco-Roman vintage and on a university system which ranges from Coimbra to Prague and from Uppsala to Naples. These intellectuals project their own collective sense of identity back onto the European land-mass. If, in the later Middle Ages, 'Europe' was a fancy way of describing the world of Christendom, the word is now coterminous with that of a Republic of Learning, civilisation-as-such: Europe, henceforth, is the home of learning

---

13 E. O'Gorman, *La invención de América* (Mexico City, Fondo de cultura económica, 1995 [1958]).
14 M. Wintle, *The Image of Europe: Visualizing Europe in Cartography and Iconography throughout the Ages* (Cambridge, Cambridge University Press, 2006); M. Wintle, *Eurocentrism: History, Identity, White Man's Burden* (London, Routledge, 2020).

and refinement, and 'civilisation' is tantamount to European civilisation.[15] The Other against which Europe was silhouetted had been the 'Muslim infidel' or the 'cruel Turk', but he was now joined by another anti-European opposite. Alongside the Barbarian came the Savage, that is to say: any society considered backward for its lack of engineering, a manufacturing industry, a mercantile economy or a leisure-based public sphere. By contrast, Europe positioned itself implicitly as the continent of free inquiry and technical advance.[16]

There were, to be sure, a few developments towards greater relativism, culminating in the encounter with China and what Paul Hazard calls the *Crise de la conscience européenne* in the later seventeenth century. Montesquieu satirised Europe as he imagined how uncouth and silly it must look to Persian diplomats (in *Les lettres persanes*, 1721). Rousseau coined the idea of the 'noble savage' – a native of Tahiti or America, endowed with an instinctive moral integrity. The counterpart of his 'noble savage' was a new, intra-European hate-figure, the 'savage nobleman': the depraved aristocrats in *Clarissa Harlowe*, *Les liaisons dangéreuses* and *Le mariage de Figaro* or in the violent pornography of the Marquis de Sade. But these are nuances in the overall positioning that sees Europe, organically and naturally, as the continent that sets the world's standard. To be civilised means to be European, and to be European means to represent civilisation and progress on the world stage.

From Idea to Concert

If it had taken Mehmet II (so to speak) to propel 'Europe' from a tacitly implied position into an explicit home-ground, it took Napoleon to provoke the next stage, that of Europe as a forum, a formally regulated common space where historical identities and political developments were shaped and contextualised.

When Friedrich Schlegel in 1803 named a new, Romantic periodical *Europa*, he did not explain his choice of title, and it may be that he was merely evoking a classical–mythological icon (the princess abducted by Zeus in the guise of a bull), much as other periodicals at the time carried

---

15 For later Eurocentrism, see P. J. Marshall and G. Williams, *The Great Map of Mankind: Perceptions of New Worlds in the Age of Enlightenment* (Cambridge, MA, Harvard University Press, 1982); J. Fabian, *Time and the Other: How Anthropology Makes Its Object* (New York, NY, Columbia University Press, 2014 [1983]).

16 J. M. Blaut, *The Colonizer's Model of the World: Geographical Diffusionism and Eurocentric History* (New York, NY, Guildford, 1993); R. Nisbet, *History of the Idea of Progress*, 2nd ed. (London, Routledge, 1994).

mythological titles such as *Die Horen* or *Isis*. At best, like Schlegel's own *Athenäum* (which was named after the school founded by Emperor Hadrian – which was itself named after the Attic capital, centre of civilisation), Schlegel's *Europa* might connote a forum in which transnational dynamics occur. Indeed the first, long essay with which *Europa* opens evokes a journey from Germany to Paris, meditating on Germany's past and present, the differences between the two nations and their characters, and the problematic transition from one to the other across the Rhineland.

That indeed was precisely the way in which the intellectuals of this generation used the notion of Europe: as a framework balanced on a French–German polarity, and now upset in that balance by a disruptive shift between those two countries. From 1800 on, Napoleon's imperial rise was unhinging the established order of state relations. This process reached a climax in Napoleon's imperial self-coronation (1804) and the self-abolition of the Holy Roman Empire (1806). By 1803, Ernst Moritz Arndt, aghast at this unfolding upheaval, was already evoking a notion of Europe that was close to Schlegel's, in his tract *Germanien und Europa*. And both Arndt and Schlegel, in using the Europe-as-framework concept, adopted the view that Novalis (whose real name was Friedrich von Hardenberg) had developed in his *Die Christenheit oder Europa*. Novalis identified a crisis where the old model of continental cohesion, medieval Christendom, was under threat, this time from within. 'Europe' was now associated with notions of stability, tradition and rootedness in past institutions. As Burke had noted from his British vantage point, the chief danger of the French abolition of the monarchy and establishment of republican rule lay in its revolutionary character, in the powerlessness of ancient traditions and institutions to command the respect of the new politics. For the German onlookers, the power of tradition was associated with the medievally rooted Holy Roman Empire, itself a multi-state organisation and negotiation platform for local diversity. 'Europe' was, in this sense, both the antonym of French innovation and a wider synonym for the Christian successor states of the Roman Empire.[17]

The political application of this view was made obvious immediately after the fateful tipping-point year of 1806, when Friedrich Gentz, the German translator of Burke, wrote his *Fragmente aus der neuesten Geschichten des politischen Gleichgewichts in Europa* (1806), soon followed by A. H. Heeren and his Göttingen lecture series published as *Handbuch der Geschichte des*

---

17 Cf. my 'The Rise of the Charismatic Nation', in C. Carmichael, M. D'Auria and A. Roshwald (eds.), *The Cambridge History of Nationhood and Nationalism*, 2 vols. (Cambridge, Cambridge University Press, 2023), vol. I.

Europäischen Staatensystems und seiner Colonien (1809). This conservatism, and the emphasis on the need to maintain institutional continuity with the medieval roots of the European realms, was also propounded in the political science of Adam Müller.[18]

Before 1800, Europe had been seen loosely used as a framework for international politics or as a semi-poetical metaphor for 'the civilised modern world'; now, in these German responses to Napoleon's shifting of the power balance, it was beginning to obtain a more definite meaning. It was not only a forum for inter-state transactions, a common political and diplomatic playing field, but also something that provided a rootedness in traditions, a proper order of things, a self-stabilising balance of power; a political ecosystem.

The political ideal of a balance of power had been a century in the making.[19] It had emerged in full form when Louis XIV's ambitions were faced down by an international alliance around William III of the Netherlands. The tone is already present in the lengthy encomium on William III by his countryman, the Dutch poet Lukas Rotgans (1698), which repeatedly, even obsessively, hails that monarch as the 'restorer of Europe' ('Hersteller van Euroop', 'Heiland van Euroop', 'Luister van Euroop', in the service of "t uytgeteerde Euroop', "t worstelende Euroop', reversing "t bederf van gansch Euroop'). In later decades, David Hume wrote his *Essay on the Balance of Power* and Frederick the Great of Prussia his *Anti-Machiavel*, precursors both to that classic in the history of the European agenda, Kant's *Zum ewigen Frieden*. Something called 'Europe' was habitually being invoked as the forum within which this balance of power was to be calibrated. This view prepares the more explicit ideology of the counterrevolutionary poets and political thinkers of the post-1792 generation: Novalis, Schlegel, Arndt, Gentz. In the title of Gentz's book it is already a self-evident circumlocution that a balance of power means a European balance of power (*Gleichgewicht in Europa*). In poetical usage we also see a notion emerge that important political events play themselves out before Europe as a witness: 'before the eyes of astonished Europe' is a recurring phrase in the occasional verse of the period 1780–1850.[20] Metaphorically and poetically, Europe was becoming a sentient being.

18 M. Lok, *Europe against Revolution: Conservatism, Enlightenment, and the Making of the Past* (Oxford, Oxford University Press, 2023).
19 For an overview, see P. Maureth, 'Balance-of-Power Thinking from the Renaissance to the French Revolution', *Journal of Peace Research* 1, no. 2 (1964): 120–36.
20 For Rotgans' eight-canto encomium *Wilhem III* (1698), see www.dbnl.org/tekst/rot goo1wilho1_01. This resource also offers a good insight into the rhetorical and poetical use of the term *Euroop* (the poetically truncated form) in Dutch literature in the eighteenth and early nineteenth centuries. Its ngram viewer indicates usage peaks in

In the same process, Europe becomes an enveloping, moulding framework in which power relations form self-correcting, self-stabilising and interlocking elements. The self-applied term at the time was that of a 'concert', evoking both a concerted effort between like-minded, collaborating parties and the musical metaphor of each state playing its own part while being harmoniously embedded within the symphonic whole.[21] That metaphor, too, has a life of its own – it was dusted off in 1992 to serve as a title for Jacques Delors' collection *Le nouveau concert européen*.[22] But its life began around 1800, when it referred to an increasingly formalised collaborative framework ensuring a balance of power, and we should realise how deeply it was imbued with the traditionalist, even medievalist cultural outlook of the anti-Napoleonic intellectuals of the Romantic generation. Calling a European balance-of-power policy a 'concert' is usually traced back to a diplomatic contretemps of 1791, when the Austrian chancellor Kaunitz hinted that an aggressive unilateralism on the part of France would provoke a united anti-French alliance among the other European states. French diplomats for their part took umbrage at what was felt to be a 'concert européen' (i.e., a concerted anti-French stance). The term resurfaced in 1814 in the Treaty of Chaumont that established an anti-Napoleonic alliance; it is used three times in that sense. Under the Metternich system, the notion of a 'concert' was used most explicitly when defining a common policy vis-à-vis the Ottoman Empire.[23] The Porte, indeed, stood outside the Holy Alliance or the Congress System, but there were numerous areas of interaction or confrontation, and it is here that the powers chose to use the phraseology of acting 'in concert'. Pius II would have given a nod of approbation. It is in dealing with an outside partner (and after Napoleon, this once again involves the world of Islam) that a European self-image takes on a distinct outline.

the decades around 1700 and in the period 1800–50 – later occurrences are usually reprints of those original sources (www.dbnl.org/ngram-viewer).

21 S. Ghervas, 'Antidotes to Empire: From the Congress System to the European Union', in J. W. Boyer and B. Molden (eds.), *EUtROPEs: The Paradox of European Empire* (Chicago, IL, University of Chicago Press, 2014), pp. 49–81.

22 For the concept's Kissinger-inflected political afterlife, see also R. B. Elrod, 'The Concert of Europe: A Fresh Look at an International System', *World Politics* 28, no. 2 (1976): 159–74; K. Lascurettes, *The Concert of Europe and Great-Power Governance Today: What Can the Order of 19th-Century Europe Teach Policymakers about International Order in the 21st Century?* (2017), www.rand.org/content/dam/rand/pubs/perspectives/P E200/PE226/RAND_PE226.pdf).

23 See T. E. Holland, *The European Concert in the Eastern Question* (Oxford, Clarendon, 1885). This older study, with its significant date of appearance, is usefully complemented by R. Albrecht-Carrié, *The European Concert* (London, Palgrave Macmillan, 1968). J.-A. de Sédouy, *Le Concert européen: Aux origines de l'Europe (1814–1914)* (Paris, Fayard, 2009), p. 11 traces the phrase back to a mention by Metternich in 1830.

As we know, the concert foundered as a diplomatic–collaborative platform in the later part of the century; but in its deeply conservative and traditional-ist, quasi-chivalric outlook it did manage to add a new layer to the European self-image. Take, for example, the remarks by the diplomat Vincent (Count) Benedetti made in 1898. The Turks, he observes, have once again embarked on a course of vengeful and fanatical slaughter (with reference to the Armenian pogroms under Abdulhamid II), and Europe faces a new 'question d'Orient [...] avec ses dangers es ses complications éventuelles' ('eastern question [...] with its dangers and its possible complications'). To face these, he continues, the European powers will need to rescue a European concert from its ruins. That line of reasoning was not his alone. In 1876 the violent crises of the disintegrating Ottoman Empire had led the – much more radical – Victor Hugo to proclaim that 'What is happening in Serbia demon-strates the need for a United States of Europe.'[24]

Benedetti was no Victor Hugo, but an authoritative celebrity nonetheless. He had been the French ambassador to Berlin in 1870, when Bismarck had goaded French public opinion into the Franco-Prussian War. Benedetti represented the old guard of diplomatic custodians of the concert system, engineers of international relations dedicated to subtly not rocking the boat. Their Europe was the cautious playing field of finessed, noncommittal and circumspect diplomacy, where the national interest, represented abroad by gentlemen of discretion and refinement, is always tempered by their com-mon adherence to aristocratic honour and courtesy and a disinclination to destabilise the intricate skein of precarious sensibilities and niceties in inter-national relations.[25]

Thus the eighteenth-century notion of the balance of power was folded into a romantic-conservative nostalgia: the ideal of rootedness in the golden age of a chivalric Christendom; and there were very specific enemy figures against which this auto-image of European, chivalrically rooted civility could be offset: expansionist warmongers (be they Napoleon or Bismarck) or Turks perpetrating atrocities against Balkan or Armenian Christians.

24 Count Benedetti, 'Le concert européen', *Revue des Deux Mondes* 148, no 2 (1898): 497–547; V. Hugo, 'Pour la Serbie' (1876), in V. Hugo, *Actes et paroles*, https://fr.wikisource.org/wiki/Actes_et_paroles/Depuis_l%E2%80%99exil/1876, Section 7.

25 On the importance of diplomacy for the ecosystem of the Holy Alliance, see S. Ghervas, 'From the Balance of Power to a Balance of Diplomacy? Peace and Security in the Vienna Settlement', in B. de Graaf, I. de Haan and B. Vick (eds.), *Securing Europe after Napoleon: 1815 and the New European Security Culture* (Cambridge, Cambridge University Press, 2019), pp. 95–113.

As older self-images were wrapped up in new layers of self-reflection, this stratified, layered self-reflexivity was in turn bequeathed to a new century. The process was overshadowed by the very wars concert Europe had aimed to prevent, each more terrible than the last. Even so, amidst increasingly fervent national antagonisms, a self-image was kept alive allowing Europe to characterise itself culturally and morally as follows: a continent governed by law and morality; rooted in a long tradition of civilisation involving classical antiquity and medieval Christianity, but dynamically developing from these origins into a manageable, self-stabilising future; consisting of robustly established sovereign states, each with its own history, institutions and traditions, and requiring an international order so as to harmonise the interests of these states.

It was with this self-image that Europe moved into the calamitous twentieth century.

European Internationalism as a Moral Mission

Culture against Nationalism

Count Benedetti can be forgiven for yearning back to the days of a chivalrous concert Europe: by 1898, Europe had already taken the exit ramp towards Sarajevo. It is a contested issue among historians whether the process was one of sleepwalking, or the unavoidable outcome of an unsustainable incompatibility between French revanchism, the imperialism of Britain, Austria and Russia, and the mounting major-power (or world-power) ambitions of Germany. In any case, one is struck by the growing sense, around 1900, that Europe is bereft without an international order such as the concert system had provided, and that such an international order must be established one way or the other. Indeed, the fact that peace after 1918 and after 1945 was entrusted to bodies like the League of Nations or the United Nations should alert us to the fact that the Franco-Prussian War 1870–1, marking the final ruination of the European concert, had already been followed by a number of institutions dedicated to the peaceful arbitration of international conflicts.

The annexation of Alsace-Lorraine by victorious Prussia, on behalf of a reconstituted German *Reich*, followed what may have been the first war that had been dominated by public opinion as a 'home front'; and the propaganda campaigns of 1870 continued unabated after 1871. French and German intellectuals began a fervent debate over the justification (or not) of this annexation;[26] the debate would not be laid to rest until almost a century later. What is significant about these debates is that they were played out before a court of public opinion that was fundamentally international. Seen in this light, the drift towards 1914 was perhaps characterised not only by a growing unilateralism and national chauvinism in Europe, but also by a new international contextualisation, and even an internationalist response. The condition of unilateralism was opposed by a countermovement that stressed the need for a new multilateralism. This European internationalism had germinated mainly on the revolutionary left, as part of its general struggle against entrenched power structures mainly consolidated at the statist level of national sovereignty. It is here that we must situate Giuseppe Mazzini's 'Young Europe' initiative of 1834 and Victor Hugo's initial call for a 'United States of Europe', at a peace conference in Paris in 1849. In this utopian, continent-wide extension of various interlocking Risorgimento movements,[27] states were the target of international utopianism rather than actors in it, and the root system of that internationalism ramifies far and wide. It has been masterfully studied by F. S. L. Lyons.[28] Lyons surveys the many infrastructural, technological and economic developments that made international regulation a necessity (communications, transport, agriculture, trade, medicine); he also pays due heed to the border-crossing exiles and cooperation moments that were such a hallmark of socialism and the Labour movement; and to the moral universalism that inspired humanitarian issues such as abolitionism. But following this, Lyons draws attention especially to the humanitarian preoccupation with warfare. And it is here, in the field of armed conflict, that the state had a role to play; for, as Victor Hugo put it during the 1870–1 Franco-Prussian War, 'Une guerre entre européens est une guerre civile' ('A war between Europeans is a civil war').[29] The sentiment was, nonetheless, informed by anti-German bitterness. On the same page, Hugo exclaims, with his usual pathos, 'Je rentrerai dans la solitude, j'allumerai sur mon rocher d'exil la lumière de l'avenir, je crierai: États-Unis! République! et je montrerai, à l'Allemagne devenue Prusse, la

26 J. Leerssen, 'The Never-Ending Stream: Cultural Mobilization over the Rhine', in M. Beller and J. Leerssen (eds.), *The Rhine: National Tensions, Romantic Visions* (Leiden, Brill, 2017), pp. 224–61.

27 L. Bruying, 'The United States of Europe: An Italian Invention?', *Yearbook of European Studies* 3 (1990): 55–66 ably summarises the primary and secondary sources, highlighting the writings of Carlo Cattaneo. More generally, see my 'The Rise of the Charismatic Nation'.

28 F. S. L. Lyons, *Internationalism in Europe, 1815–1914* (Leyden, Sijthoff, 1963).

29 V. Hugo, *Œuvres complètes*, vol. XXVI: *Choses vues* (Paris, Ollendorf, 1913).

France devenue Europe.' ('I shall return to solitude, I shall set alight on my rock of exile the light of the future, I shall shout: United States! Republic! and I shall show, to a Germany that has become Prussia, a France that has become Europe.') As with Renan, French internationalism after 1871 was to a large extent fed by rancour and attempts to sublimate the nation's defeat into a higher edification. This mind-set fits Wolfgang Schivelbusch's analysis in *Die Kultur der Niederlage* and has direct relevance for our understanding of internationalism in post-1918 and post-1945 Germany.

The need for regulations transcending the sovereignty and interests of individual states had been impressed upon the public as journalists and photographers became witnesses on the battlefield; what they witnessed was not bravery and glory but blunders, carnage and suffering. The experiences of Florence Nightingale in the Crimean conflict and of Henri Dunant following the Battle of Solferino in the 1850s led to the development of the Red Cross and to the first Geneva Convention (1864); it was to be followed by additional ones in 1907, 1929 and 1947. Such conventions took over after the various congresses in the European concert had lapsed.

In the drafting of such conventions legal scholars found a new application for their academic expertise. They drew on earlier texts such as Schmalz's *Europäisches Völkerrecht* (1816), Klüber's *Droit des gens moderne* (1819) and Bluntschli's *Das moderne Völkerrecht* (1868). Mention should also be made of the influential German-American legal philosopher Franz/Francis Lieber (a former combatant at Waterloo and in the Greek War of Independence). He moved from Prussia to the United States by way of England in 1825–7, and in his new country formulated a pioneering and influential military code of conduct during the American Civil War (1861–6).[30] International law rose to prominence in the post-1871 decades, carrying the ideals of the reformist left into the political vacuum that had been left by the demise of the concert system.[31]

The point of incipience can be conveniently marked by the name of Frédéric Passy, whose Ligue Internationale et Permanente de la Paix of 1868 was an attempt to defuse the growing animosity between France and Prussia. Following the débâcle of 1871, Passy became a left-leaning parliamentarian in the Third Republic and rebooted his Ligue as a Société Française pour l'Arbitrage entre Nations (1889). The emphasis in international affairs was, meanwhile, shifting, with diplomats at a loss on how to curb high-handed

---

30 See B. Röben, *Johann Caspar Bluntschli, Francis Lieber und das moderne Völkerrecht 1861– 1881* (Baden-Baden, Nomos, 2003).

31 M. Koskenniemi, *The Gentle Civilizer of Nations: The Rise and Fall of International Law, 1870–1960* (Cambridge, Cambridge University Press, 2001).

unilateralism following the German annexation of Alsace-Lorraine. A permanent Court of Arbitration was established in The Hague in 1889, its mission buttressed by a first Hague convention in that same year, followed in 1907 by a second one. This second convention saw the involvement of a parallel foundation, the Institut de Droit International (founded in 1873). How the budding discipline of international law took the place of the diplomatic transactions of the European concert and consolidated itself in the new format of legal conventions and institutions is exemplified by M. Ernest Nys' 'Le concert européen et la notion du droit international' (1899).[32] The twinning of balance of power and European concert is structural, and worth noting.

Thus, as Europe slowly drifted towards the abyss of 1914, there was at the same time a growing internationalism aimed precisely at preventing war and regulating international affairs. It profited from wealthy donors such as Andrew Carnegie (who footed the bill for the Peace Palace in The Hague, 1907–13) and Alfred Nobel, who instituted his Peace Prize in 1901. Its first recipients in that year were Dunant and Passy; in 1904 the Nobel Peace Prize went to the Institut de Droit International.

These idealistic initiatives drew on Ernest Renan's aforementioned *Qu'est-ce qu'une nation?*, which stressed self-identification as lying at the heart of self-determination and called, metaphorically but by implication also literally, for referendums to establish preferential national self-identifications in disputed border regions. In so doing, Renan also implicitly entrusted the cause of national minorities to a multilateral, transnational oversight.

All these trends were part of the elitist utopianism of the decades around 1900, and badly out of touch with the growing grassroots nationalism that would feed into the Great War; but while those ideas failed to prevent the Great War, they nonetheless survived it. The cause for self-determination was taken up in Wilson's Fourteen Points; the newly empowered nation-states were placed into a League of Nations; Renan-style plebiscites became something of a fashion in post-1918 Europe.[33] Although, ironically,

---

32 See also M. E. Nys, 'La théorie de l'équilibre européen', *Revue de droit international et de législation comparée* 25 (1893): 34–57; M. E. Nys, 'Le Concert européen et la notion du droit international', *Revue de droit international et de législation comparée* 1, sér. 2 (1899): 273–317; C. Dupuis, *Le principe d'équilibre et le concert européen de la paix de Westphalie à l'acte d'Algésiras* (Paris, Perrin, 1909).

33 M. MacMillan, *Paris 1919: Six Months That Changed the World* (New York, NY, Random House, 2003). For a contemporary comment on the plebiscites, see P. de Auer, 'Plebiscites and the League of Nations Covenant', *Transactions of the Grotius Society* 6 (1920): 45–58. See also B. Conrad, 'Volksabstimmungen als ultima ratio? Die Plebiszite an Polens Grenzen nach dem Ende des Ersten Weltkriegs', *Zeitschrift für Ostmitteleuropa-Forschung* 64 (2015): 174–94.

Clémenceau re-annexed Alsace-Lorraine without bothering about the sort of plebiscite Renan had clamoured for, referendums about preferred state allocation were held in border areas reaching from Schleswig-Holstein to the Burgenland (on the new Austrian–Hungarian border), East Prussia, Upper Silesia, the Vorarlberg and Carinthia. The League of Nations had a special commission on minorities, which were the subject of treaties involving the victorious allied powers and the newly created states of Albania, Austria, Bulgaria, Czechoslovakia, Estonia, Greece, Hungary, Iraq, Latvia, Lithuania, Poland, Romania, Turkey and Yugoslavia.[34]

Such frameworks were not specifically European in scope or in self-understanding. Wilson's programme had a global impact and resonated also in the Asian portions of the former – now dismembered – Ottoman Empire, as well as in Europe's colonies in east Asia. Even so, it was within Europe that the salvage of international idealism from the ruins of the Great War, and under the looming clouds of totalitarianism, echoed with particular intensity. A French–German axis was tentatively set up by Aristide Briand's *Memorandum sur l'organisation d'un régime d'Union Fédérale européenne* (1929), which won League of Nations support but foundered in the 1930s. René Cassin, a war veteran and not yet the elder statesman he was to become after 1945, was working to ensure war prevention in these years as well.[35] The European message was continued by writers, artists and intellectuals.[36] Under the aegis of the League of Nations, Paul Valéry assembled a Société d'Esprits – including Johan Huizinga, Hermann von Keyserling, Julien Benda, Pál Teleki, Jean Cantacuzène and Jules Romains – to discuss perspectives for a freshly defined European identity in this darkening decade. At the Parisian World Fair of 1937, an International Institute for Intellectual Co-operation

---

34 H. Rosting, 'Protection of Minorities by the League of Nations', *American Journal of International Law* 17, no. 4 (1923): 641–60; E. Viefhaus, *Die Minderheitenfrage und die Entstehung der Minderheitenschutzverträge auf der Pariser Friedenskonferenz 1919* (Würzburg, Holzner, 1960); C. Fink, 'The League of Nations and the Minorities Question', *World Affairs* 157, no. 4 (1995): 197–205.

35 J.-F. Sirinelli, 'La France de l'entre-deux-guerres: Un trend pacifiste', in M. Vaïsse (ed.), *Le pacifisme en Europe des années 1920 aux années 1950* (Brussels, Bruylant, 1993), pp. 43–50. On Briand, see A. Elisha, *Aristide Briand, la paix mondiale et l'union européenne* (Paris, Ivoire-Clair, 2003); A. Fleury and L. Jilek (eds.), *Le Plan Briand d'Union fédérale européenne: Perspectives nationales et transnationales* (Bern, Lang, 1998). On Cassin, see J. Winter and A. Prost, *René Cassin and Human Rights: From the Great War to the Universal Declaration* (Cambridge, Cambridge University Press, 2013).

36 M. Hewitson and M. D'Auria (eds.), *Europe in Crisis: Intellectuals and the European Idea 1917–1957* (New York, NY, Berghahn, 2015); C. Reijnen and M. Rensen (eds.), *European Encounters: Intellectual Exchange and the Rethinking of Europe 1914–1945* (Leiden, Brill, 2014). An interesting roll-call of authors is also given in J.-B. Duroselle, *Europe: A History of Its Peoples* (London, Penguin Viking, 1990), pp. 366–9.

was launched, also under the auspices of the League of Nations. And the idea that all of Europe, ultimately, shared a common historical and cultural pedigree informed the more idealistic musings and initiatives of Richard Coudenhove-Kalergi. His vision was nothing if not cultural: it was Coudenhove-Kalergi and his Pan-European Movement[37] who proposed Beethoven's 'Ode to Joy' as a European anthem. The spirit of Count Benedetti survived in this cosmopolitan elitism, but in addition there was a greater sensitivity to the transnational connecting power of culture. Coudenhove-Kalergi, Hermann Graf Keyserling and Salvador de Madariaga, transnational also in their academic or aristocratic family background, effortlessly saw Europe as a cumulative inheritance of the old Republic of Letters and (by way of the Christendom of the chivalric Middle Ages and Charlemagne) of classical antiquity. This by now had become part of the accepted and unargued cultural baggage of the highly educated, who as yet had little or no reason to query their elitist Eurocentrism. 'Europe', as something threatened by national politics but united in an artistic and intellectual refinement transcending national prejudices, is what carried forward their vision, indeed their mission, of internationalism. It also carried, buried within its elitist pacifism, the legacies of Enlightenment and Romantic vintage: Europe as an ecosystem for a power-balanced *juste milieu* between the refined tyranny of the east and the raw uncouthness of the New World.

Even so, another, fresh layer was being added to this European self-image. It could hardly be otherwise, in a century that saw the bankruptcy of complacent colonialism, the carnage of total war and totalitarian dictatorship.

Culture after Auschwitz: Remorse as a Moral Imperative

Complacent, self-congratulatory Eurocentrism was a fond self-beguilement that was not easily abandoned. First came the shaming of colonialism. Its extortions and oppression had been camouflaged in the pious terms of a civilising mission (think Livingstone) bringing morality and progress to the colonies' benighted natives. Reports of humanitarian outrages on Stanley's voyages of exploration were among the first signs that things on the ground were far harsher than what the European public had fondly imagined; anti-colonial novels like Multatuli's *Max Havelaar* (1860) and, most of all, Joseph Conrad's *Heart of Darkness* (1899) put the case that

---

37 A. Ziegerhofer-Prettenthaler, *Botschafter Europas: Richard Nikolaus Coudenhove-Kalergi und die Paneuropa-Bewegung in den zwanziger und dreißiger Jahren* (Vienna, Böhlau, 2004); U. Wyrwa, 'Richard Nikolaus Graf Coudenhove-Kalergi (1894–1972) und die Paneuropa-Bewegung in den zwanziger Jahren', *Historische Zeitschrift* 283, no. 1 (2006): 103–22.

Europe in fact brought tyranny and barbarism to its colonies rather than Christianity and civilisation.[38] The colonial wars of the turn of the century (the repression of the Boxer Rebellion in China, the Aceh War in the Netherlands East Indies, the Boer Wars) marked both the acme of Eurocentric jingoism and the early signs of an anti-colonialist reaction among the radical pacifist intelligentsia. The inexorable process of decolonisation had begun, and with it the growing realisation that colonial rule had been a protracted infliction of bloody tyranny perpetrated by Europe. That process is still playing itself out in the reassessment of Europe's hegemonic role in world history.

From Stevenson's *Dr Jekyll and Mr Hyde* to Conrad's *Heart of Darkness*, the notion took hold that in the dark innermost recesses of the civilised European's soul there still lurked the atavistic, violent impulses of primitive savagery. The Savage was developing from Europe's Other to Europe's Inner. That view was amply borne out within Europe in the two world wars: the first one marking the apocalyptic derailment of Clausewitz's notion of 'cabinet wars' as brief military campaigns to settle a momentary failure of diplomacy; the second one targeting civilian populations more than belligerents and involving a totalitarian logic of mass internments, population transfers and extermination campaigns, coolly planned and technocratically implemented. Europe staggered out of 1945 with a sense that its vaunted civilisation had been nothing more than a thin veneer, easily stripped away at crisis moments to reveal the inner savagery.

Intellectuals came to terms with this ruinous fall from grace by associating evil with violent, totalitarian nationalism. The case was made with great force by Karl Popper, Jean-Paul Sartre, Karl Jaspers and Hannah Arendt. The remedy was sought in a strong commitment to human rights (memorably defined by Arendt as the one fundamental axiom from which all else followed: 'the right to have rights'); there was a widespread commitment to have these rights consolidated in the form of international organisations. The EU was one of these. International law, which had found its post-war continuation in the Nuremberg and Tokyo trials, was given a platform in various transnational courts and tribunals. This new world order was truly global, in a bipolar world under the competitive hegemony of the United States and the USSR.

---

38 I. R. Smith, *The Emin Pasha Relief Expedition, 1886–1890* (Oxford, Clarendon, 1972); P. E. Firchow, *Envisioning Africa: Racism and Imperialism in Conrad's Heart of Darkness* (Lexington, KT, University Press of Kentucky, 2000).

At the same time, the need was felt to create a specifically European international order within the bosom of the old continent; and this was first proclaimed at the Hague Congress of 1948. In the motivations of the European-minded intellectuals and politicians, the old self-image of Europe was now wrapped up in two additional moral layers. First, Europe was to embody an anti-totalitarian stance, a recoil from the mid-century dictatorships, explicitly endorsing the democratic values of human rights, the rule of law and the self-determination of peoples. This being the Cold War, these values were now seen in anti-communist, 'Western' terms: Europe was part of Western Democracy, allowing for a continued rejection of Oriental Despotism, its fundamental other. The incarnations of that Oriental Despotism were now the Communist Party leaders of the USSR and China, taking over from previous incarnations such as the Ottoman Sultan or the Tsar.[39] In this anti-orientalism, Europe could see itself as the home of individual freedom, asserting free inquiry against coercive authority, and conveniently directing the anti-totalitarian gaze away from its own dictatorial track record.

Secondly, a new master narrative took hold: that of a Europe rising from the physical and moral ruins of the past. Much as post-war Europe presented a stark contrast between its ancient glories and the ruins of its bombed cities, so too it embraced a need for a moral reconstruction after the spectre of the Nazi and fascist terrors. A new self-image projected Europe as the 'sadder and wiser' continent: the idea that all European nations have a history of bloody, deep fundamental divisions which, at some point, were overcome.[40]

Initially this post-dictatorial commitment to human rights was considered so self-evident as to derive directly fom fundamental logic and from categorical ethical imperatives, loosely referred to at the time as 'humanist' – a term ambivalently evoking both a historical lineage and a moral virtue. The term had been coined to identify the cultural climate of the early Renaissance in 1808, but carried a strong connotation of humane benevolence as promulgated in the late Enlightenment.[41] There was, however, a political

39 On the anti-communist, US-endorsed entanglements of the European project, see R. J. Aldrich, 'OSS, CIA and European Unity: The American Committee on United Europe, 1948–60', *Diplomacy & Statecraft* 8, no. 1 (1997): 184–227; G. Scott-Smith and H. Krabbendam, *The Cultural Cold War in Western Europe, 1945–1960* (London, Cass, 2003).
40 J. Fornäs, 'Symbols and Narratives of Europe: Three Tropes', *Punctum: International Journal of Semiotics* 6, no. 2 (2020): 85–100.
41 See V. Giustiniani, 'Homo, Humanus, and the Meanings of Humanism', *Journal of the History of Ideas* 46, no. 2 (1985): 167–95. For the invocation of humanism as a characteristic European source tradition, see C. J. Friedrich, 'Pan-humanism,

crystallisation process at work. In the historical force field of the period, such general invocations of heritage and morality became the anchoring points of a specific political agenda. That agenda, shared by the political centre ground (Christian democrats, social democrats, liberals), encompassed a rejection of the 'ideologies' of the far right and left in the name of a dedication to human rights and liberties, morally 'unpolitical' but firmly located in the 'Free West'. As, in the passing decades since 1945, the bourgeois doxa of the period is beginning to stand out more clearly, it also has become easier to discern its filiations and continuities across the decades. The legacy of the pre-1914 internationalists ultimately fed into the EU's Copenhagen Criteria established in 1993, which stipulate that prospective member states must be institutionally committed to democracy, the rule of law, human rights and respect for and protection of minorities. Historians such as Samuel Moyn have recently offered successful analyses of ethical notions like human rights as a political agency mobilising Christian democracy and the political centre in the post-1945 period.[42]

Bien-pensant Europe

The Hague Congress of 1948 and the Long Shadow of Denis de Rougemont

Held in the fluid transition years between the Second World War and the Cold War, the prestigious congress at The Hague in 1948 signalled the re-emergence of European ethical internationalism. The initiative had been taken by none other than Coudenhove-Kalergi, and it was on his invitation that Winston Churchill opened the proceedings and acted as honorary chairman. The Hague Congress is remarkable for bringing together an old European ideal (including its high-cultural, tradition-rooted self-image) and a young, post-war generation of politicians: among the delegates were Édouard Daladier, Anthony Eden and Alcide De Gasperi, but also François Mitterrand, Konrad Adenauer, Gustav Heinemann, Harold Macmillan and Altiero Spinelli. It contained three committees, a social–economic one chaired by Paul van Zeeland, a political one chaired by Paul Ramadier and a cultural one chaired by the anti-Franco stalwart Salvador de Madariaga, who successfully proposed the establishment of a 'College of Europe'. The

Culturism and the Federal Union of Europe', in L. S. Rouner (ed.), *Philosophy, Religion, and the Coming World Civilization* (The Hague, Martinus Nijhoff, 1966).

42 S. Moyn, *Christian Human Rights* (Philadelphia, PA, University of Pennsylvania Press, 2015).

Hague Congress also marked the debut of the new banner-bearer of the European movement, Denis de Rougemont; other representatives from the cultural field included the philosophers Raymond Aron and Bertrand Russell, the orchestral conductor Adrian Boult and the sculptor Paul Landowski. The fact that in these Cold War years their political orientation was heavily Atlanticist and 'Western' goes almost without saying. A perceived Americanisation of Europe had been frowned upon in the 1920s and 1930s, and would be frowned upon again from the mid 1960s onwards; but in these years the United States represented modernity and democracy *tout court*. And in any case, the European impetus came from the political centre, with a substantial conservative presence.

In the history of the EU, the Hague Congress is usually overshadowed by the Treaty of Paris (founding the European Coal and Steel Community), which was signed in 1951 and came into force in 1952. The direct consequences of the 1948 event did indeed lead in a slightly different direction. Besides establishing a College of Europe, the Hague Congress prepared the establishment of a Council of Europe with as its remit a Convention on Human Rights. Mooted by Madariaga and brought to fruition under its first rector, Henrik Brugmans, the College of Europe was intended to foster 'a spirit of solidarity and mutual understanding between all the nations of Western Europe and to provide elite training to individuals who will uphold these values'.[43] The Council of Europe has in its own way been as important in European affairs as the EEC/European Communities (EC)/EU, through a succession of conventions, commissions and charters and a proactive European Court of Human Rights, which in its formative years was chaired by no less a personality than René Cassin. In the person of Cassin we also see the strong continuity of the League of Nations internationalists of inter-war vintage. The heritage of Coudenhove-Kalergi, with its visceral elitism (Europe as the shared cosmopolitanism of the *bien-pensant* social and intellectual upper crust) was alive and well, and the emphasis on a shared inheritance of canonical culture was an automatic connotation of the idea of Europe. Certain symbols made their way from Coudenhove-Kalergi's Pan-Europa movement into the post-1945 years, despite a latter-day emphasis on coal and steel rather than Beethoven and Gothic cathedrals. When the Council of Europe officially established the blue twelve-starred flag (in 1955), and chose Beethoven's 'Ode to Joy' as the European national anthem (in 1972), they

---

43 See www.cvce.eu/en/recherche/unit-content/-/unit/04bfa990-86bc-402f-a633-11f39 c9247c4.

picked up on original recommendations of Coudenhove-Kalergi.[44] And the primacy accorded to culture in this European idealism was reflected in the fact that the drafting of the closing statement of the Hague Congress, the *Message aux européens* manifesto, was entrusted to its *cultural* committee.[45] This cultural–symbolical emphasis was adopted by the EC in 1985, as part of the recommendations for a 'People's Europe'.[46] The ad hoc committee 'A People's Europe', chaired by Pietro Andonnino, explicitly stated its adherence to the Council of Europe's chosen symbols in its report of 28–9 June 1985.

Personalism and the Ethics of the Political Centre

Among the post-1945 generation of intellectuals who were involved in the European project, a good few had affinities with personalism. Opposing itself to left-wing communism or socialism, to right-wing corporatism, and to liberal individualism, personalism in politics was associated with the emergence of Christian democracy from earlier, ultramontanist or traditionalist forms of Catholic activism. Philosophically (through Jacques Maritain, its most prominent representative), it was associated with a school of phenomenological thought that opposed the subordination of the sentient individual to corporatist, economic or class collectivities. (Philosophically speaking, liberalism was primarily inspired, in these years, by Karl Popper's *The Open Society and Its Enemies*. Since the 1970s, that liberal orientation appears to have drifted from Popper, by way of Edward Shils, to Milton Friedman; the drift is mirrored in the dwindling mutual affinity between political liberalism and the European project.) The gravitation towards Christian democracy and the more conservative wing of social democracy is unmistakable, albeit so discreet that it has only with hindsight become obvious. Denis de Rougemont, Coudenhove-Kalergi's successor as the mover and shaker of European integration, and a forceful presence at the Hague Congress, was strongly allied with this school of thought (witness his early *Politique de la personne*, 1934),[47] and many of the founding fathers of the European project

---

44 C. Curti Gialdina, *I simboli dell'Unione europea: Bandiera, inno, motto, moneta, giornata* (Rome, Libreria dello Stato, 2005).

45 D. de Rougemont, '35 Ans d'attentes déçues mais d'espoir invaincu: Le Conseil d'Europe', in D. de Rougemont, *Ecrits sur l'Europe*, ed. Christophe Calame, 2 vols. (Paris, La Différence, 1994), vol. ii, p. 808.

46 European Commission, 'A People's Europe', *Bulletin of the European Communities*, supplement 7/85 (Luxembourg, Office for Official Publications of the European Communities, 1985).

47 B. Ackermann, *Denis de Rougemont: De la personne à l'Europe. Essai biographique* (Paris, L'Âge d'Homme, 2000).

were sympathetic to it. As Samuel Moyn has pointed out, personalism provided a middle-class, centre-right anchorage for the post-1945 preoccupation with human rights and helped situate an image of Europe in what centrist politicians now invoked as the 'humanism' of Thomas More and Erasmus.[48] From de Rougemont to the posthumously popular writings of Jan Patočka (the intellectual mentor of Václav Havel), there has been a strong tradition of reflecting on Europe, including its political past and future, in personalist or phenomenological terms: as an experiential space (*Lebenswelt*) and a framework for moral choices.[49] The notion of *Lebenswelt* was developed in the late work of Edmund Husserl, which was published fragmentarily in the late 1930s. Seeing Europe as a moral *Lebenswelt* has also been a marked trend among thinkers who themselves hail from different philosophical traditions. Hans Magnus Enzensberger, for instance, even before the crisis year of 1989, already opposed a problematic political and bureacratic Europe with its true inner essence: that of a vibrant cultural diversity (*Ach Europa!*, 1987). Indeed the notion of a unity in diversity was taken on board by the European project, first implicitly acknowledged in the Maastricht Treaty's cultural paragraph of 1992, and officially proclaimed by the EU as its official motto (*In varietate concordia*) in 2000. What was lost from sight in this political gesture was that this very trope in fact drew on a longstanding source tradition in the European self-image. The Risorgimento historian Carlo Cattaneo, one of the early users of the notion of a United States of Europe, had around 1848 asserted that Europe, while it derived from Asia its unifying heritage of priesthood-religion, empires, scriptures and arts, differed from that greater continent by virtue of its characteristic pluriformity: 'Se v'è in Europa un elemento uniforme, il qualo certe ebbe radice in Asia, madre antica dei sacerdozii, degli imperii, delle scritture e delle arti, v'ha pur anco un elemento vario: e costituisce il principio delle singole nazionalità; [. . .] Le varie combinazioni fra l'avventizia unità e la varietà native si svolsero sulla terra d'Europa [. . .].' ('If there is an element of uniformity in Europe, it certainly had its root in Asia, ancient mother of priesthoods, of empires, of

48 S. Moyn, 'Jacques Maritain, Christian New Order, and the Birth of Human Rights', *SSRN* (2008), https://ssrn.com/abstract=1134345; S. Moyn, 'Personalism, Community, and the Origins of Human Rights', in S.-L. Hoffmann (ed.), *Human Rights in the Twentieth Century* (Cambridge, Cambridge University Press, 2010), pp. 85–106.
49 G. Marcelo, 'Ricœur and Patočka on the Idea of Europe and its Crisis', *META: Research in Hermeneutics, Phenomenology, and Practical Philosophy* 9, no. 2 (2017): 509–35; R. Gasché, 'European Memories: Jan Patočka and Jacques Derrida on Responsibility', in P. Cheah and S. Guerlac (eds.), *Derrida and the Time of the Political* (Durham, NC, Duke University Press, 2009).

writings and of the arts, yet there is an element of difference: and it constitutes the principle of the single nationalities; [. . .] the diverse combinations between fortuitous unity and the native diversity that occurred on European soil [. . .].')[50]

The European Construction of Europe's Cultural and Moral Foundations

Between them, names like Zygmunt Baumann, Jacques Derrida, Paul Ricœur and Tzvetan Todorov[51] indicate a corpus of reflections on Europe which are more than mere political commentary and which constitute for post-1950 Europe what the writings of the seventeenth-century *moralistes* were for ancien-régime France: a discursive, essayistic reflection on *mores*, the behavioural and ethical implications of participation in society.[52] The corpus is often read piecemeal, as separately individual reactions to different emerging and transitory political situations; but by now the contours of a literary history of such a *Moralisme européen* are beginning to come into focus, as are its intertextually shared assumptions of Europe as, precisely, a moral space.

'Moral' rather than historical. The growing corpus of histories of Europe which grew up almost in response to the topicality and the agenda-setting future of the European project (de Rougemont, Chabod, Duroselle) consists of texts that were similarly *moraliste*, presenting as a history of Europe what was in fact a chronologically arranged reflection on the meaning of Europeanness: showcasing the cultural characteristics that made people recognisably European across the ages. The past, in these histories, was the very opposite of 'a foreign country': it was calibrated to the anti-totalitarian–internationalist ideals of the present, and then presented as an inspiration.

50 Curti Gialdina, *I simboli dell'Unione europea*; Cattaneo, as quoted by L. Bruyning, 'The United States of Europe: An Italian Invention?', *Yearbook of Italian Studies* 3 (1990): 55–66, 60–1.

51 Z. Bauman, *Europe: An Unfinished Adventure* (Cambridge, MA, Polity, 2004); J. Derrida, *L'autre cap* (Paris, Éditions de Minuit, 1991); P. Ricœur, 'Quel éthos nouveau pour l'Europe?', in P. Koslowski (ed.), *Imaginer l'Europe: Le marché intérieur européen, tâche culturelle et économique* (Paris, Éditions du Cerf, 1992), pp. 107–16; T. Todorov, *Le Nouveau Désordre mondial: Réflexions d'un Européen* (Paris, Laffont, 2003).

52 L. Van Delft, *Le moraliste classique: Essai de définition et de typologie* (Geneva, Droz, 1982); L. Van Delft, *Les spectateurs de la vie: Généalogie du regard moraliste* (Montreal, Presses de l'Université Laval, 2005); B. Parmentier, *Le siècle des moralistes: De Montaigne à La Bruyère* (Paris, Éditions du Seuil, 2000); C. Le Meur, *Les moralistes français et la politique à la fin du XVIIIe siècle* (Paris, Champion, 2002).

The essays of de Rougemont, which from 1948 until 1986 formed a constant discursive ambience and amplifying sounding board for the developing EU, all draw on past centuries, constants and variables to deliver a strengths, weaknesses, opportunities and threats analysis for the European present and future. These writings amount to a major corpus.[53] Tellingly, the variables are always political, incidental and problematic, whereas the constants are cultural, permanent and reassuring. Similarly, the College of Europe distills a notion of European moral–cultural continuity from the political vicissitudes of the ages. It has established a canonical Hall of Fame by placing its successive academic years under the moral aegis of a Great European. It is worth considering the line-up of the most prominent patrons, as displayed in Wikipedia, since they constitute an informally assembled canon of European Greats and also exhibit a teleology that leads from Aristotle to the founding fathers of the European Project. Chronologically arranged, the most prominent patrons of the College of Europe form the following lineage: Aristotle, Virgil, Marcus Aurelius, Dante, Copernicus, Charles IV, Leonardo da Vinci, Columbus, Erasmus, Thomas More, Comenius, Rubens, Locke, Leibniz, Montesquieu, Voltaire, Saint Simon, Mozart, Wilhelm and Alexander von Humboldt, Ludwig van Beethoven, Mme de Staël, Alexis de Tocqueville, Fryderyk Chopin, Charles Darwin, Marie Skłodowska-Curie, Bertha von Suttner, Fridtjof Nansen, Tomáš Masaryk, Aristide Briand, Stefan Zweig, Antoine de Saint-Exupéry, Salvador de Madariaga, Richard Coudenhove-Kalergi, Hans and Sophie Scholl, Winston Churchill, Konrad Adenauer, Hannah Arendt, Jean Monnet, Robert Schuman, Altiero Spinelli and Denis de Rougemont. Thus the European project draws on, and in turn consolidates, a historical and cultural self-image. Not only do its institutions produce policy papers, political reflections and commentary, and even a meta-discourse on their workings and its history,[54] but also a non-institutional cultural historiography

---

53 In addition to his substantial history of Europe, *Vingt-huit siècles d'Europe: La conscience européenne à travers les textes d'Hésiode à nos jours* (Paris, Payot, 1961), there are 142 shorter essays filling the two substantial volumes of his *Écrits sur l'Europe*, vols. 2 and 3 of the *Œuvres complètes*, ed. C. Calame (Paris, La Différence, 1994).

54 Indicative counter-examples spanning a scale from in-house self-presentation to academic companion range from Birte Wassenberg, *History of the Council of Europe* (Council of Europe, 2013) by way of Giuliano Amati et al., *The History of the European Union: Constructing Utopia* (London, Bloomsbury, 2019) to Desmond Dinan (ed.), *Origins and Evolution of the European Union*, 2nd ed. (Oxford, Oxford University Press, 2014), with, notably, Dinan's own chapter on 'The Historiography of the European Integration', pp. 345–75.

has sprung up independently, discursively connected to the essayistic tradition of *moralisme européen*.

Federico Chabod's *History of the Idea of Europe* (1961) draws on the same cultural self-image and historical canon. Witness his conclusion, with its historicist, Euro-optimistic idealism:

> Perchè, identico rimanendo il principio della grande unità civile europea, negli uomini del Settecento come negli uomini della prima metà dell'Ottocento, identica rimane anche la conclusione: il senso della superiorità della civiltà europea su tutte le altre, passate e presenti, e la fiducia piena nell'avvenire, che dovrà vedere ulteriori progressi e nuovi splendori dell'Europa.
>
> (For that reason, much as the principle of the great unity of European civility persisted among the men of the eighteenth and of the first half of the nineteenth century, so too will persist its conclusion: a sense of the superiority of European civilisation over all others, past and present, and a full confidence in the future, which must witness the further progress and fresh glories of Europe.)[55]

As one may expect, de Rougemont's own *Vingt-huit siècles d'Europe* (also 1961), with its telling specification in the subtitle (*La conscience européenne à travers les textes d'Hésiode à nos jours*) folds the continent into this idealistic self-image. Of course, this was a history with an agenda, celebrating Europe much as Michelet's history writing had celebrated France or Treitschke's had celebrated Prussia; and among its merits must be reckoned the fact that it prepared the ground for a less politically instrumentalised European historiography (e.g., Norman Davies' *Europe: A History*, 1996; Peter Rietbergen's *Europe: A Cultural History*, 1998; the collection *Lieux d'Europe: Mythes et limites*, edited by Stella Ghervas and François Rosset, 2008; the *Europäische Erinnerungsorte* edited by Pim den Boer et al., 2012; or Antoine Arjakovsky's collection *Histoire de la conscience européenne*, 2016).

Many of these pan-European histories are, almost necessarily, kaleidoscopic in nature. But most of them rely on a historical core repertoire, a set of identifying concerns, which has found its clearest and most overtly programmatic expression in Jean-Baptiste Duroselle's *Europe: A History of Its Peoples*, published in 1990, in eight European languages simultaneously, and dedicated to Jean Monnet and his wife Silvia. Unabashedly Europhile, the book can be seen as a publicity production aimed at popularising and legitimising the European project.[56] This book was written on the initiative of

---

55 F. Chabod, *Storia dell'idea d'Europa* (Bari, Laterza, 1964 [1961]), p. 157.
56 Duroselle, *Europe* (further references by page number in the text).

the Euro-enthusiastic businessman Frédéric Delouche, who also sponsored a multi-authored school textbook on European history in 1992.[57] Duroselle's *Europe* celebrates the EU as the logical culmination of a bimillennial history, *à la* the College of Europe ancestral lineage from Aristotle to Denis de Rougemont. At the same time, it would be wrong to dismiss this as a mere public relations exercise written to serve the political needs of the moment. The European idealism that lies at the heart of Duroselle's book is itself the sincere and organic continuation of an 'Aristotle to de Rougemont' lineage, of an autonomous, longstanding discourse of reflections on Europe and what it stands for. The different layers of Duroselle's European self-identification all draw on old tropes that we have encountered as the previous pages surveyed earlier centuries, and these feed into an integrationist teleology. As in the College of Europe's self-selected line of descent, Duroselle's narrative template moves from Europe as the birthplace of humanism and of egalitarian individualism ('the decline of deference and the growth of compassion', pp. 21 and 230-3) to Enlightenment cosmopolitanism (pp. 237-9). It then turns to technological and industrial progress ('Inventive Europe', pp. 283-37 – notable are the echoes of older Eurocentrism in this chapter's conclusion: 'The Europeans [sic] were outdistanced in technology by the Chinese and the Arabs [sic] until the twelfth century; and they avidly took over the inventions made by these two great civilizations. In the fourteenth and especially the fifteenth century, they overtook their mentors [etc.]' (p. 307)), the threat of nationalism and Bismarck and the need for international balance (pp. 333-5). Then comes the moral crisis of totalitarianism, with an honourable mention for the personalist thinker Jacques Maritain and the 'optimists' around Coudenhove-Kalergi (pp. 367-8); the reboot of The Hague Congress in 1948 and a roll-call of the leaders of the European project (pp. 384ff.). Duroselle concludes that a united Europe, rather than 'an artificial creation *ex nihilo*', should rather be seen as 'the culmination of a long historical evolution which has given it a unique personality of its own, distinct from the other great regions of the world' (p. 409).

In addition, an afterword acknowledges the post-1989 situation: 'The strengths that grace every nation of Europe can only increase as they unite;

---

57 See J. van der Leeuw-Roord, 'Could the History of Europe Avoid the Traditional European Mirror of Pride and Pain? The Comparison of Two Different Versions of Frédéric Delouche's "History of Europe"', *Internationale Schulbuchforschung: Zeitschrift des Georg-Eckert-Instituts für Internationale Schulbuchforschung* (1996): 85-106; O. Calligaro, *Negotiating Europe: EU Promotion of Europeanness since the 1950s* (Basingstoke, Palgrave Macmillan, 2013), esp. pp. 57-67 ('A European History of Europe: The Duroselle/Delouche Project').

and developments in "the new Central Europe" will surely reinforce that trend. Europe has always been creative. European unity, when it comes, will be of a new kind, evolving as it progresses.' (p. 415). This pious flourish bespeaks the officially endorsed optimism of the moment. But it also evinces a *certaine idée de l'Europe* of long standing, which had initially served to provide a sense of place, had then been invoked so as to balance the continent's systemic inner relations, had subsequently asserted international-ism in the teeth of nationalism, and, having inspired the European project, has now become part of its official mission and rhetoric. In selecting and celebrating these inherited, much-recycled tropes and figures as the cultural and moral foundations of the European project, the *moralistes* and historians performed that enterprise which is now called an 'invention of tradition'.

This invention of tradition is itself a form of literature; indeed, a European literature. It is a literature that moves in the mode of learned disquisition rather than in the aesthetic genres of narrative, drama or lyricism; but it is literature nonetheless, addressed to a wider readership and to wider issues than to bureaucratic institutions and their business in hand. What is more, this literary production is not an ad hoc contrivance but has grown out of, and continues, a tradition of older writings that antedate the institutional establishment of the European project. That is, a literary tradition has emerged which has increasingly preoccupied itself with moral complexities that came, at the time, to be associated with a 'European' self-image, accompanying and echoing the developments traced here. One could fruit-fully re-read Goethe's *Die Wahlverwandschaften*, Stendhal's *La Chartreuse de Parme*, Turgenev's *Torrent of Spring*, Kurban Said's (Lev Nussimbaum's) *Ali and Nino* or Thomas Mann's *Der Zauberberg* from this perspective; or watch film productions from François Truffaut's *Jules et Jim* to Florian Henckel von Donnersmarck's *Das Leben der Anderen*. In sum: the European project has grown out of cultural reflections on Europe, rather than vice versa.

Recommended Reading

Arjakovsky, A. *Histoire de la conscience européenne* (Paris, Salvator, 2016).

Ghervas, S. *Conquering Peace: From the Enlightenment to the European Union* (Cambridge, MA, Harvard University Press, 2021).

Ghervas, S. and F. Rosset (eds.). *Lieux d'Europe: Mythes et limites* (Paris, Maison des sciences de l'homme, 2008).

Hewitson, M. and M. D'Auria (eds.). *Europe in Crisis: Intellectuals and the European Idea 1917–1957* (New York, NY, Berghahn, 2015).

Koskenniemi, M. *The Gentle Civilizer of Nations: The Rise and Fall of International Law, 1870–1960* (Cambridge, Cambridge University Press, 2001).

Reijnen, C. and M. Rensen (eds.). *European Encounters: Intellectual Exchange and the Rethinking of Europe 1914–1945* (Leiden, Brill, 2014).

Ziegerhofer-Prettenthaler, A. *Botschafter Europas: Richard Nikolaus Coudenhove-Kalergi und die Paneuropa-Bewegung in den zwanziger und dreißiger Jahren* (Vienna, Böhlau, 2004).

23

The European Union and Memory

ANA MILOŠEVIĆ

Introduction

This chapter engages with the under-explored knots of European memory politics both theoretically and empirically, linking theories of European Union (EU) integration with the study of collective memory at transnational, EU level. Collective memory[1] is a deeply political phenomenon: it is politically embedded, reflecting political visions, and enacting social and political worlds. Traditionally studied in Sociology and History, Nationalism and Cultural Studies, the politics of manifold memory practices has more recently emerged as an object of academic interest for International Relations (IR), International Law, Peace and Conflict Studies, Political Theory, Comparative Politics and the transdisciplinary field of Memory Studies proper. However, only recently has the study of collective memory overcome the boundaries of methodological nationalism[2] to question and analyse the impact the EU has had on nation-state memories, and vice versa.[3]

The past is central to the 'imagining of community'.[4] How people experience the past is intrinsic to their perception of the present[5] and their awareness of continuity with the past.[6] The scholars of nationalism

---

1 See M. Halbwachs, *Les cadres sociaux de la mémoire* (Paris, Félix Alcan, 1925).
2 C. De Cesari and A. Rigney (eds.), *Transnational Memory: Circulation, Articulation, Scales* (Berlin: De Gruyter 2014); A. Wimmer and N. Glick Schiller, 'Methodological Nationalism and Beyond: Nation-State Building, Migration and the Social Sciences', *Global Networks* 2, no. 4 (2002): 301–34.
3 A. Milošević and T. Trošt (eds.), *Europeanisation and Memory Politics in the Western Balkans* (New York, NY, Palgrave Macmillan, 2020).
4 B. Anderson, *Imagined Communities: Reflections on the Origin and Spread of Nationalism* (London, Verso, 1983).
5 P. Connerton, *How Societies Remember* (Cambridge,: Cambridge University Press, 1989).
6 E. J. Hobsbawm, *Nations and Nationalism since 1780: Programme, Myth, Reality* (Cambridge, Cambridge University Press, 1992); B. Misztal, *Theories of Social Remembering* (Maidenhead, Open University Press, 2003).

emphasise this quite strongly: shared territory, language, common experiences, memories and myths are unifying elements of nation-building.[7] The very coming into existence of the nation-state, at the turn of the twentieth century, 'depended on a process by which existing societies used representations to turn themselves into new wholes that would act immediately upon people's feelings, and upon which they could base their identities – in short, to make them into groups that individuals could identify with'.[8] Yet, if the nation-state is a 'natural' outlet for production and consumption of memory, what role did the past play in defining and narrating European unification?

Over time, the role assigned to the past in constructing the European project has changed dramatically: from a struggle to reconcile, to the making of consensus over the past (as a precondition for a future in togetherness), to transnational memory wars to defend national monopoly over interpretation of the past. The genesis of EU memory politics since its earliest days, how memory becomes a political question, who mobilises it and what effects Europeanisation of memory has, are the central queries underpinning this chapter. The EU has been relying on the existence of shared memories and identities as one of the key elements for fostering legitimacy. Similarly to the nation-building projects, at the EU level there were a number of policy attempts to craft and define what a European identity is and what it should entail. Yet, imagining Europe as a community of shared memory posed and continues to pose a significant challenge both for scientists and for policy-makers. In this chapter, I take a closer look at the key premises around which the EU politics of memory was built over time and the roads which were (not) taken.

Tracing the evolution of the use of the past across time, the chapter suggests that *EU memory politics* emerged gradually as a by-product of political attempts at hitting moving targets: from building self-legitimacy and European identity, to supporting restorative justice efforts. First, the chapter examines the emergence of the unification project, arguing that the past of the Second World War was imbued with transformative values. Thus, post-war Europe was constructed in antagonistic relationship with itself: the past and its violent ways were rejected, opening paths to a different future. Secondly, the gradual development of the Union and its own competences

7 A. D. Smith, *The Ethnic Origins of Nations* (Oxford, Blackwell, 1986).
8 D. Levy and N. Sznaider, 'Memory Unbound: The Holocaust and the Formation of Cosmopolitan Memory', *European Journal of Social Theory* 5, no. 1 (2002): 87–106, 90.

meant that its institutions grew powers diversifying their own roles and agendas. It is in this period of acute enthusiasm for an ever growing, deepening and widening Union after the Cold War that we can trace the first cross-institutional coordinated efforts at EU identity policy building. Facing the constant challenge of self-legitimacy and the primacy of the national over the European, significant efforts were invested in fostering a shared feeling of belonging to Europe. Thirdly, the chapter examines how the EU enlargement in the 2000s reactivated disagreements on the past by challenging and ultimately refuting the notion of EU identity defined on historical grounds. Before providing a conclusion, the chapter reflects upon amnesiac aspects of the historical narrative of Europe's past suggesting that EU memory politics, *a sine qua non* of the EU's future, is selective and deeply politicised.

A Future without a Past

Instead of the past, the future was the dominant time-category for the pioneers of the European Community (EC).[9] That future was based on consensus about the past Europeans had left behind. The foundational myth of the Community draws precisely on the consensus on rebuilding Europe from the ashes of the Second World War, best illustrated in the promise of 'never again'. Envisioning a future in which Germany regained trust, reconciliation became the main knot and strength of the European project – 'a victory of [that] time over history'[10] and its own *'mythe originaire'*.[11] Former enemies, now partners, would use the Community as a new learning platform to bridge their differences and overcome the past by tying their economies together, making 'war not only unthinkable but materially impossible'.[12] This was the future that the founding fathers such as Jean Monnet and Konrad Adenauer pleaded for: a future without the burdens of the past – a future in which reconciliation and solidarity, mutual trust and respect would prevent future cultures of violence.

9 O. Calligaro, 'Legitimation through Remembrance? The Changing Regimes of Historicity of European Integration', *Journal of Contemporary European Studies* 23, no. 3 (2015): 1–14.
10 H. C. Deutsch, 'The Impact of the Franco-German Entente', *The Annals of the American Academy of Political and Social Science* 348, no. 1 (1963): 82–94.
11 C. Guisan, *A Political Theory of Identity in European Integration: Memory and Policies* (New York, NY, Routledge, 2011).
12 'Schuman Declaration May 1950', https://europa.eu/european-union/about-eu/symbols/europe-day/schuman-declaration_en.

Just like the pioneers of the European project, the pioneers of scholarly research in post-war IR focused on the future of Europe, including the evolution of European identity. European integration theorists such as Ernst W. Haas[13] and Karl W. Deutsch,[14] despite articulating different theories in the 1960s, concurred that Europe's would-be polity was compatible with the reconsolidation of the nation-state after the horrors of the Second World War. While the argumentative lines between the neo-functionalist and communication theories of European integration were clearly drawn, neither view offered a well-developed perspective on the role of the past in building European identity and memory.[15] The question of what a European identity is and how it could be supportive of the Community's legitimacy building became salient only in the 1970s political discourse and in response to key challenges of that time: the economic crisis and the future of European integration. Following an Arab–Israeli war in October 1973, Middle East oil-producing nations imposed big price increases and restricted sales to certain European countries, which created economic problems throughout the Community.[16]

The initial success of political and economic integration needed to be reinforced with public support. At the Copenhagen European Summit in 1973, the heads of state and government of the nine member states affirmed their determination to introduce the concept of European identity into their common foreign relations. They affirmed that the Nine 'might have been pushed towards disunity by their history and by selfishly defending mis-judged interests. But they have overcome their past enmities and have decided that unity is a basic European necessity to ensure the survival of the civilization which they have in common.'[17] The main assumption of early research on European identity revolved around the question of a possible

---

13 E. B. Haas, *The Uniting of Europe: Political, Social and Economic Forces* (Stanford, CA, Stanford University Press, 1958); E. B. Haas, 'International Integration: The European and the Universal Process', *International Organization* 15, no. 3 (1961): 366–92.

14 K. W. Deutsch, *Nationalism and Social Communication* (Cambridge, MA, Technology Press, 1953); K. W. Deutsch, *France, Germany, and the Western Alliance: A Study of Elite Attitudes on European Integration and World Politics* (New York, NY, Scribner, 1967).

15 See, for example, J. T. Checkel and P. J. Katzenstein, *European Identity* (Cambridge, Cambridge University Press, 2009).

16 For a detailed analysis of the multifarious crises of the 1970s and their impact on the process of European integration, see, for example, S. M. Ramírez Pérez, 'Crises and Transformations of European Integration: European Business Circles during the Long 1970s', *European Review of History/Revue européenne d'histoire* 26, no. 4 (2019): 618–35.

17 'Declaration on European Identity', *Bulletin of the European Communities* no. 12 (1973): 118–22.

shifting of loyalties from the national to the supranational level, with particular attention accorded to the European political elites said to be the engines of transnationalism.[18] It is precisely in this period that we start to observe the diversification of EU actors and their divergent power roles in supporting a common agenda on EU identity, most notably in the case of the European Parliament (EP).

While the formal powers of the EP before the first direct elections (in 1979) were marginal,[19] the elected members of the EP (MEPs) became crucial activists for deeper political as well as institutional integration. Predominantly driven by pro-integrationist ideas of an 'ever closer union' – and of an ever-stronger EP, MEPs' convictions are clearly visible in their behaviour, which reflected their self-perception of being European rather than national delegates of a consultative assembly.[20] Their level of activity and involvement in Community policy-making significantly surpassed, at that time, quite narrow EP-related treaty provisions[21] to enlarge its powers. The success of this parliamentary quest for more powers is often analysed as a budgetary fight as well the result of the parliamentary bargain on the budget of key European policies such as the common agricultural policies and regional policies. Importantly, the legitimacy of the EP and the EC was also used to call for action in the framing of new narratives of Europe.

This early period of the EP is characterised by the proactive role taken by the MEPs and their visions of a united Europe. This was possible partially due to more direct forms of citizens' participation (elections), but also due to the opening towards new members. What narratives and underlying ideas drove the EP's activism? MEPs sought to involve young people in the project of ever closer integration, notably through attempts at creating a collective memory of the Communities as guarantor of peace and

---

18 Deutsch, *France, Germany, and the Western Alliance*; Haas, *The Uniting of Europe*; Haas, 'International Integration'; J. Caporaso, 'Fisher's Test of Deutsch's Sociocausal Paradigm of Political Integration: A Research Note', *International Organization* 25, no. 1 (1971): 120–31.

19 R. Corbett, *The European Parliament's Role in Closer EU Integration* (London, Palgrave Macmillan, 2001); R. Corbett, *The European Parliament*, 8th ed. (London, John Harper, 2011).

20 A. Milošević and P. Perchoc, 'Le Parlement européen et la politique de la mémoire: Explorer la constellation des acteurs', *Politique européenne* 71, no. 1 (2021): 6–27, 17–18.

21 A. Cohen, 'L'autonomisation du "Parlement européen": Interdépendance et différenciation des assemblées parlementaires supranationales (années 1950–années 1970)', *Cultures & Conflits*, no. 85–86 (2012): 13–33.

prosperity, and as a space of shared cultural heritage supposedly connecting – even if subconsciously – all citizens of the member states. This was particularly visible in the area of youth policy. Noticing a lack of public support for and identification with the Community project, MEPs invested considerable time and effort in creating a youth policy, hoping to forge pro-European generations willing to become actively involved in the pursuit of closer integration.[22] A major part of this endeavour was the creation of a collective memory of Europeanness: they invoked a common cultural heritage and built their appeals for young people's engagement in and identification with Europe on the member states' more recent collective memories of war, followed by a peace guaranteed by the Communities.[23]

For the promoters of a more politically integrated Community, it was necessary to find new *raisons d'être* for European integration, beyond economic growth. To this end, an increasing weight has been attributed to memory through heritage – a sign of the emergence of a new regime of historicity: presentism. In this regime, the official discourses and initiatives attempted to (re-)enact a common European past in the citizens' present. One such example is *European cultural policy*[24] that centred around heritage substantiating the efforts at enacting EU identity. The concept of *European cultural heritage* introduced in a resolution of the EP in 1974 was largely inspired by the Council of Europe's (CoE's) approach, strongly connecting heritage with values. European cultural heritage is a pivotal concept of the CoE's Cultural Convention (1954). The resolution addresses tangible and intangible aspects of heritage refering both to 'objects of European cultural value' and to 'language or languages, history and civilisation' of the different European nations that are part of the Convention.[25] As Calligaro[26] explains, in the 1970s, the EU integration process had lost its momentum. The economic crisis of the 1970s and the internal impact of the first enlargement of

22 M. Roos, 'The European Parliament's Youth Policy, 1952–1979: An Attempt to Create a Collective Memory of an Integrated Europe', *Politique européenne* 71, no. 1 (2021): 28–53.

23 Milošević and Perchoc, 'Le Parlement européen'.

24 For an analysis of the European policy on culture and an instrumental use of culture in the pursuit of broader objectives of economic development, intended to encourage social, or even democratic, development, see, for example, O. Calligaro and A. Vlassis, 'La politique européenne de la culture: Entre paradigme économique et rhétorique de l'exception', *Politique européenne* 56, no. 2 (2017): 8–28.

25 CoE, 'European Cultural Convention, December 1954', http://conventions.coe.int/ Treaty/EN/Treaties/Html/018.htm .

26 O. Calligaro, 'From "European Cultural Heritage" to "Cultural Diversity"? The Changing Core Values of European Cultural Policy', *Politique Européenne* 45, no. 3 (2014): 60–85.

the EC 'undermined this non-democratically rooted legitimacy and signifi-cantly decreased public support for European integration'.[27]

In the 1970s, the EU expanded from the original six to nine countries, and in the 1980s it expanded from nine to twelve countries. In the latter enlarge-ment the Community went Mediterranean, including Spain, Portugal and Greece – countries that had recently exited dictatorships. Spain's accession, for instance, was dictated by a domestic demand to consolidate democracy and the rule of law, as well as economic interests: the necessity of modern-isation and the attraction of foreign investments.[28] The position of the Community in relation to the membership of Spain was based exclusively on political reasons, namely the need for democratic reforms. The issues of past divisions in Spain, related to Franco's regime, were not a topic in the negotiations. Dealing with the past, transitional justice or truth-telling were, at best, regarded as national matters, and not treated as issues that concerned the whole of Europe. A source of commonalities, among old and newly welcomed members of the first enlargements, was their willingness to invest efforts in the future rather than in tackling issues of past divisions.

Only in 1986 did the European Commission, the Council and the EP issue a joint declaration on antisemitism, racism and xenophobia[29] that marked the turn in the EU's attitudes towards the past. Reactive rather than proactive, the birth of a joint approach towards the past as an educational tool and a negative template came amidst the trial of former Nazi Gestapo chief Klaus Barbie, 'the butcher of Lyon'. Jean-Marie Le Pen, leader of the Front National and an MEP, gave a shocking interview saying: 'I don't say that the gas chambers did not exist. I was not able to see them myself. But I believe this is a mere detail in the history of the Second World War.'[30] Le Pen was heavily criticised by his EP peers, who instantly adopted a declaration to condemn him.[31] Many of them, like Simone Veil – the first president of the directly elected EP, had suffered in and survived concentration camps, or had fought on the frontlines in the Second World War. They were outraged

---

27 Ibid., 65. See also D. H. Handley, 'Public Opinion and European Integration: The Crisis of the 1970s', *European Journal of Political Research* 9, no. 4 (1981): 335–64.

28 S. Royo and P. C. Manuel, 'Some Lessons from the Fifteenth Anniversary of the Accession of Portugal and Spain to the European Union', *South European Society and Politics* 8, no. 1–2 (2003): 1–30.

29 'Declaration against Racism and Xenophobia' (1986), pp. 1–3, https://eur-lex.europa .eu/legal-content/EN/TXT/?uri=CELEX%3A41986X0625.

30 As cited in K. S. Stern, *Holocaust Denial* (New York, NY, The American Jewish Committee, 2013), p. 34.

31 EP, 'Written Declaration on the Holocaust, the European Parliament and Le Pen' (1987), https://op.europa.eu/s/vKEU.

by his words, but also aware that the horrors from the past will continue to haunt Europe unless political leaders, in a united front, condemn and discourage statements like these. As one of the first instances of Holocaust denialism within the EU's own institutions, this example shows the reactiveness of the EP via soft laws and its determination 'that the lessons of the Holocaust should never be forgotten'.

Yet the recognition that the negative dimensions of European history are an integral part of European heritage was triggered only at the end of the Cold War when debates about the past became a salient issue. Until the collapse of communism across central and eastern Europe, the EU's joint approach towards remembering the past had been manifested through commemorating occasional anniversaries such as the end of the Second World War. In the 1990s, however, the EP took over institutional leadership in the role of fulfilling 'the duty of memory'[32] and intensified the use of soft laws – resolutions – in dealing with historical matters. Two major resolutions were adopted to include the negative heritage in the EU's identity: in 1993 the former Nazi concentration camps were designated European Historical Monuments and in 1995 the European Holocaust Remembrance Day was adopted.[33] The extension of European heritage began being reflected also in EU cultural programmes, guided by the European Commission, which since then has funded projects dealing with European wars and authoritarian regimes.[34]

As we can observe, between the 1950s and the 1990s, the role assigned to the past shifted multiple times, serving a wide variety of political purposes. Across multiple self-narrations, the past has served the EU as a 'negative template', a rationale for deeper and wider integration, and as an instrument to support general objectives such as legitimacy building. To this end, answering the question of what binds Europeans together and what kind of future the EU ought to have has been translated into addressing specific objectives: fostering citizens' ownership over the European project by promoting the notion of European identity based on cultural and historical heritage.

---

32 See O. Lalieu, 'The Invention of the "Duty of Memory"', *Vingtième Siècle. Revue d'histoire* 1, no. 69 (2001): 83–94.

33 See A. Wæhrens, 'Shared Memories? Politics of Memory and Holocaust Remembrance in the European Parliament after 1989–2009' (2011), DIIS working paper, http://subweb .diis.dk/graphics/Publications/WP2011/WP-2011-06_Anne-W%E6hrens_Shared%20 memories_web.pdf.

34 O. Calligaro and F. Foret, 'La mémoire européenne en action. Acteurs, enjeux et modalités de la mobilisation du passé comme ressource politique pour l'Union européenne', *Politique Européenne* 37, no. 2 (2012): 18–43.

Consensus-Making on the Past: Blurry Lines of History

Attempts at adding a transnational layer to existing national identities have been made by European political elites ever since the beginning of European integration. Yet, the single market (1993), completed with the 'four freedoms' – the free movement of goods, services, people and capital – radically transformed the Community – in particular with the 'Maastricht' Treaty (1993) and the Treaty of Amsterdam (1999). These developments induced the writing of a vibrant literature, particularly by historical institutionalists, who introduced a time dimension to theorising EU identity. Most of the early works, however, were more normative than empirical in orientation, drawing from several different theories, such as, for example, the social theory of Habermas, postulating an EU identity that is post-national and non-malignant.[35] Another group of scholars sketched the EU identity as a civilian and normative power.[36] What these various arguments on the nature of the EU identity have in common is not only the discrepancy between the normative ideal and empirical reality, but also the superficial consideration of the complexity of historical experiences and collective memories at EU level.

A case that supports the view of two realities – Europeanness as pursued by the EU and on-the-ground accepted forms of Europeanness – is the history of the EU's symbols themselves. As Bieber and Bieber point out, it is 'an illustration of the gap between their de facto acceptance over time based on their gradual introduction and the rejection of their formal and symbolic recognition, embodied by the failure of the 2005 'Constitution for Europe'.[37] The referendum was taking place a year after the 'big bang' enlargement when ten new members joined the EU. In the Maastricht Treaty an attempt was made to consolidate the formal symbols of the EU: the flag, the anthem, the motto, the currency and the EU Day. Except for the motto 'united in diversity', this provision did not contain anything novel or particularly formidable. The EP had already in 1983 adopted a flag for the European

---

35 See S. Susen, 'Jürgen Habermas', in P. Kivisto (ed.), *The Cambridge Handbook of Social Theory* (Cambridge, Cambridge University Press, 2020), pp. 369–94.

36 See I. Manners, 'Normative Power Europe: A Contradiction in Terms?', *Journal of Common Market Studies* 40, no. 2 (2002): 235–58; I. Manners, 'Symbolism in European Integration', *Comparative European Politics* 9, no. 3 (2011): 243–68.

37 F. Bieber and R. Bieber, *Negotiating Unity and Diversity in the European Union* (Berlin, Springer Nature, 2020), p. 137.

Community,[38] and the European Council was supportive of taking further steps at creating a visual identity of the EU. As confirmed by the heads of state and government in 1984, they strongly endorsed the need for a distinct EU symbolism – by 'adopting measures to strengthen and promote its identity and its image both for its citizens and for the rest of the world'.[39] The 2005 referenda showed that some member states did not, however, wish to constitutionally 'upgrade' the status of the EU symbols.

Ultimately, the rejection of the European Constitution suggested the primacy of national self over European self. In retrospect, we could safely argue that the enthusiasm of the unification of Germany, the fall of the Berlin Wall and the lifting of the Iron Curtain was met with underestimation of the importance that national self-affirmation on the international stage had for the eastern members. Importantly, such rejection signalled a challenge to the historical grounding used for further integration as it demonstrated the lack of understanding by European bureaucrats of the historical complexity and divisiveness of Europe's past.[40] The formerly communist countries from the Baltics to the Balkans sought to reaffirm their own national identities and histories. The interrupted continuity of the nation-state, due to authoritarian and totalitarian regimes in the post-war period, was perceived as one of the most important consequences, the other one being the high human loss due to gross violation of human rights. New members, returnees to Europe, brought their own interpretation of European history that suited their needs to come to terms with their respective communist pasts.[41]

The broad scholarly consensus is that before the EU's enlargement to the east, western Europe had little doubt about the nature of the past which had been left behind. Mass atrocities, gas chambers and the horrors of Nazi concentration camps became symbols of the Holocaust. However, after the Cold War, as Neumayer demonstrates,[42] a new constellation of

38 EP, 'Report Drawn Up on Behalf of the Political Affairs Committee on the Adoption of a Flag for the European Community' (1983), https://aei.pitt.edu/90617/1/1982-83.83.1194.pdf.
39 'European Council Fontainebleau, 25 and 26 June 1984, Conclusions', *Bulletin of the European Communities*, suppl. 7 (1985), p. 5
40 M. Pakier and B. Stråth, *A European Memory? Contested Histories and Politics of Remembrance* (New York, NY, Berghahn, 2010).
41 M. J. Prutsch, 'Research for CULT Committee – European Identity' (2017), www.europarl.europa.eu/RegData/etudes/STUD/2017/585921/IPOL_STU(2017)585921_EN.pdf.
42 L. Neumayer, 'Integrating the Central European Past into a Common Narrative: The Mobilizations around the "Crimes of Communism" in the European Parliament', *Journal of Contemporary European Studies* 23, no. 3 (2015): 344–63; L. Neumayer, *The Criminalisation of Communism in the European Political Space after the Cold War* (New York, NY, Routledge, 2018).

actors challenged the prevailing western European narrative constructed on the uniqueness of the Holocaust as 'the epitome of evil'.[43] The memory of Europe's past became an object of politicisation paving the path to intense policy-making at both national and EU level. To achieve pacification of tensions and reconciliation, the EU resorted to policy-building to find the lowest common denominator on historical experiences that bind Europeans together.

While the traditional Europeanisation theory has been applied practically on all levels of policy, from environmental to refugee issues, research has been hesitant to engage with the question of whether Europeanisation affects memory politics. Scholars of the past have situated Europeanisation of memory between transnationalisation and 'cosmopolitisation' of domestic discourses and remembrance practices.[44] Yet, an increasing number of studies explore and demonstrate the multitude of ways in which Europeanisation of memory is manifested, who its key actors are and what its effects are.[45]

The literature makes clear the causal relationship between the EU's enlargement policy and memory politics.[46] The ambitions of the Union for deepening and widening triggered the politicisation of memory, especially in the EP – which became the main 'memory entrepreneur'.[47] The process of Europeanisation of discourses on the past and their political use in the EP is carried out by a number of actors such as individual and like-minded MEPs, formal and informal political networks, committees and political parties.[48] For instance, the first informal group of MEPs that sought to find the lowest

---

43 See M. Kucia, 'The Europeanization of Holocaust Memory and Eastern Europe', *East European Politics and Societies* 30, no. 1 (2016): 97–119 for an in-depth analysis of the impact of transnationalisation of discourses on the Holocaust in eastern Europe.

44 Levy and Sznaider, 'Memory Unbound'; A. Assmann, 'Transnational Memories', *European Review* 22, no. 4 (2014): 546–56; M. Mälksoo, 'The Memory Politics of Becoming European: The East European Subalterns and the Collective Memory of Europe', *European Journal of International Relations* 15, no. 4 (2009): 653–80; S. Gensburger and M.-C. Lavabre, 'D'une "mémoire" européenne à l'européanisation de la "mémoire"', *Politique européenne* 37, no. 2 (2012): 9–17; A. Sierp, *History, Memory, and Trans-European Identity: Unifying Divisions* (New York, NY, Routledge, 2014); P. J. Verovšek, 'Expanding Europe through Memory: The Shifting Content of the Ever-Salient Past', *Millennium: Journal of International Studies* 43, no. 2 (2015): 531–50.

45 Kucia, 'The Europeanization of Holocaust Memory'; B. Törnquist-Plewa and K. Kowalski, *The Europeanization of Heritage and Memories in Poland and Sweden* (Kraków, Jagiellonian University Press, 2016); C. De Cesari and A. Kaya, *European Memory in Populism: Representations of Self and Other* (New York, NY, Routledge, 2020); Milošević and Trošt (eds.), *Europeanisation and Memory Politics*.

46 Milošević and Trošt (eds.), *Europeanisation and Memory Politics*, p. 13.

47 E. Jelin, *State Repression and the Labors of Memory* (Minnesota, MN, University of Minnesota Press, 2003).

48 Milošević and Perchoc, 'Le Parlement européen'.

common denominators of the past was 'Reconciliation of European Histories' (REH) – composed of members from both old and new member states. This group gave the initial impulse for policy-building on what have become key political answers to divergent views of the history of the Second World War and its aftermath.

These answers are to be found in EP resolutions, most notably in the proclamation of 23 August as a day of remembrance for victims of Stalinism and Nazism in 2008[49] and a 2009 resolution on 'European Conscience and Totalitarianism'.[50] Contrary to the 'multi-perspective history' advocated by European institutions, the REH group pursued a single 'historical truth' at the EU level: 'the task of true reunification of European history based on truth and remembrance is not completed. We have to continue work on converging the views of all the Europe about the history of the 20th century. [. . .] We aspire to develop a common approach regarding crimes of totalitarian regimes, inter alia totalitarian communist regime of the USSR, to ensure continuity of the process of evaluation of totalitarian crimes and equal treatment and non-discrimination of victims of all totalitarian regimes.'[51] REH – an informal group of MEPs – provided a platform for the MEPs to play an active role in bringing about a convergence of the European historical narratives.

Building upon joint commemorations and synchronising with regulations proposed by the European Commission, over the past two decades, the EP has contributed significantly to the emergence of EU memory politics. This is reflected in particular in the 'EU memory framework' – 'a number of legally non-binding, soft laws and decisions made by the EP – that delineates shared attitudes towards the past through the rejection of anti-semitism, xenophobia, racism and all forms of non-democratic, authoritarian regimes'.[52] While the Holocaust remains a key pillar of the EU's attitudes towards the past, the EU memory framework also communicates rather equivocal, blurry lines concerning otherwise quite different historical experiences of its member states, formulating an equivalence of red and black totalitarianisms. That the EU possess its own memory politics, however, is not merely reflected in its

---

49 EP, 'European Day of Remembrance for Victims of Stalinism and Nazism' (2008), www.europarl.europa.eu/doceo/document/TA-6-2008-0439_EN.html.

50 EP, 'European Conscience and Totalitarianism' (2009), www.europarl.europa.eu/doceo/document/TA-6-2009-0213_EN.html.

51 REH, https://eureconciliation.wordpress.com/about.

52 A. Milošević and H. Touquet, 'Unintended Consequences: The EU Memory Framework and the Politics of Memory in Serbia and Croatia', *Southeast European and Black Sea Studies* 18, no. 3 (2018): 381–99, 382.

ever-growing soft laws about the past. On a par with soft laws, new EU commemorative days were created, monuments built and European commemorations organised. The objective of this effort lies in 'political mobilisation of symbols and narratives, by the EU, to awaken and preserve beliefs and feelings about transnational past of Europe'.[53]

The post-2004 enlargement was followed by an important 'rupture' in the ways in which the past has been used at EU level. Integrating the negative aspects of the past into the self-narration became an objective in the post-enlargement period and a tool to achieve reconciliation in pursuit of an ever-closer Union. As the EP's 2009 resolution on 'European Conscience and Totalitarianism' suggests, there will be no unity – and hence no future – unless Europe 'is able to form a common view of its history, recognises Nazism, Stalinism and fascist and Communist regimes as a common legacy and brings about an honest and thorough debate on their crimes in the past century'.[54] Such a common view on the past – embodied in the EU's memory framework – became a *sine qua non* of the EU's future.

European Memory Wars

While for decades the informal model of Western democracies has been dialogue promotion and reconciliation as main vehicles to address the burdens of the past, the mid 2000s politically institutionalised European memory canons and therefore an *EU memory policy*. As the EP's memory framework continued to expand in relation to national histories of its member states, a significant effort has been invested also by the European Council in promoting and practising 'a common European history'.[55] A careful examination of the contents of the EU memory framework suggests that the Holocaust and anti-totalitarianism are at its core. Other elements such as 'Solidarność day'[56] or 'Holodomor remembrance'[57] are elevated only to the status of key dates of European history. A number of funding instruments, such as the European Commission's Europe for Citizens programme,

53 A. Milošević, 'European Commemoration of Vukovar: Shared Memory or Joint Remembrance?', in V. Pavlaković and D. Pauković (eds.), *Framing the Nation and Collective Identities* (New York, NY, Routledge, 2019), pp. 223–39.

54 EP, 'European Conscience and Totalitarianism', item K.

55 Council Regulation (EU) no. 390/2014 of 14 April 2014 establishing the 'Europe for Citizens' programme for the period 2014–20, OJ L 115, 17.4.2014, pp. 3–13.

56 EP, '25th Anniversary of Solidarity and Its Message for Europe' (2005), www.europarl .europa.eu/doceo/document/TA-6-2005-0357_EN.pdf.

57 EP, 'Commemoration of the Holodomor, the Artificial Famine in Ukraine (1932–1933)' (2008), www.europarl.europa.eu/doceo/document/TA-6-2008-0523_EN.html.

enabled EU memory policy to invest millions of euros in strengthening remembrance of recent European history. The Europe for Citizens programme 2014–20 had an overall budget of €167.2 million, of which 16 per cent has been allocated for projects on 'European Remembrance' whose annual call for proposals has identified key dates in European history reflecting the contents of the EU memory framework. By highlighting the Union's role in facilitating, sharing and promoting European memory politics, direct links between remembrance and European identity have been established.

The EU memory framework became a cornerstone of EU memory politics and an important anchor of many of the EU's other policies, strategies and programmes. This is particularly visible not only in subsidies for European remembrance, but also in the creation of European monuments such as a memorial for victims of totalitarianisms in Brussels and the House of European History (HEH) – the EP's own museum. The Platform of European Memory and Conscience, created through the EP 2009 resolution on 'European Conscience and Totalitarianism' is the main actor behind the Brussels monument, which has also been endorsed by the European Commission and the EP.[58] The project to establish the HEH was initiated by the former President of the EP Hans-Gert Pöttering – one of the main actors of the pivotal REH group. In the words of its creator, the HEH 'should be a place where a memory of European history and the work of European unification is jointly cultivated, and which at the same time is available as a locus for the European identity to go on being shaped by present and future citizens of the European Union'.[59] By the time of the official inauguration in 2017, however, the objective of 'European identity' building via historical reference had been abandoned in the political discourse and in conceptual documents of the HEH's curators. The permanent exhibition of the museum reflects the positionalities of the EU memory framework, accusing nationalism of being the root cause of conflicts and wars in Europe. 'With its strong focus on the similarities between National Socialism and Stalinism as regimes of oppression, moreover, it tells a story of Europeans as victims of abstract oppressive regimes,' as Kaiser argues.[60] Paradoxically, this suggests that the HEH employs the narrative tools of nationalism for overcoming nationalism.[61]

---

58 'Pan-European Memorial for the Victims of Totalitarianism in Brussels', https://memoryandconscience.eu/memorialbrussels.
59 H. G. Pöttering, interview with the author, 1 April 2014.
60 W. Kaiser, 'Victimizing Europeans: Narrating Shared History in the European Parliament's House of European History', *Politique européenne* 71, no. 1 (2021): 54–78, 54.
61 Ibid.

While the mid 2000s saw the revival of discourses on the past that have centred around competition in victimhood,[62] true 'memory wars'[63] were ignited by the proliferation of memory laws at both national and EU level.[64] The experience with the post-2004 enlargement suggests that the EP accommodated the historical experiences of new member states[65] and endorsed collective reinterpretation in older member states due to new historiographical debates or memory dynamics at the national level. In this process of 'uploading' national politics to the EU level, various memory entrepreneurs (political parties, formal and informal groups of MEPs, individuals, external actors) sought to influence the construction, institutionalisation and diffusion of EU memory politics. Although it is not legally binding, the EU memory framework is selectively 'downloaded' by (potential) members that seek to align with EU norms of remembrance, display their belonging to Europe, affirm their national narratives of the past at (trans)national level[66] or deploy memory as a foreign policy tool.

Importantly, the very existence of EU soft laws on memory prescribes a 'template' for dealing with the past – the model that has been emulated, copied and adopted in many non-EU countries – yet with different motivations. Each resolution of the EP ends with provisions / instructions on to whom the resolution is directed and who the direct recipients should be, for example, 'instructs its President to forward this resolution to the Council, the Commission, the Government and Parliament of Ukraine, the Secretary-General of the UN, the Secretary-General of the Organisation for Security and Cooperation in Europe and the Secretary-General of the Council of Europe'.[67] The major field of application of EU memory policy relates to the EU's anti-totalitarian stance towards history that often serves as a vocabulary to narrate and explain a wide variety of non-affiliated or

---

62 P. Vermeersch, 'Victimhood as Victory: The Role of Memory Politics in the Process of De-Europeanisation in East-Central Europe', *Global Discourse* 9, no. 1 (2019): 113–30.

63 J.-M. Chaumont, *La concurrence des victimes: Génocide, identité, reconnaissance* (Paris, La Découverte, 1997); P. Blanchard and I. Veyrat-Masson, *Les Guerres de mémoires: La France et son histoire: Enjeux politiques, controverses historiques, stratégies médiatiques* (Paris, La Découverte, 2008); G. Mink and L. Neumayer, *History, Memory and Politics in Central and Eastern Europe: Memory Games* (London, Palgrave Macmillan, 2013).

64 U. Belavusau and A. Gliszczyńska-Grabias, 'Memory Laws: Mapping a New Subject in Comparative Law and Transitional Justice', in U. Belavusau and A. Gliszczyńska-Grabias (eds.), *Law and Memory: Towards Legal Governance of History* (Cambridge, Cambridge University Press, 2017).

65 P. Perchoc, 'Les députés européens baltes et les débats mémoriels, entre stratégie politique et engagement personnel (2004–2009)', *Revue internationale de politique comparée* 22, no. 4 (2015): 477–503.

66 Milošević and Touquet, 'Unintended Consequences'.

67 EP, 'Commemoration of the Holodomor'.

non-related historical events. For instance, in the countries of former Yugoslavia the adoption or endorsement of the EP resolution on totalitarianism has sparked controversy and still ongoing political and scholarly debate on the nature of Yugoslav communism. As a result of this overarching stance towards red and black totalitarianisms, not only is a return to the past encouraged by political elites with the excuse of endeavouring to redress past injustices, but also efforts are made to symbolically paint the ideological divisions of the Second World War grey for the sake of present-day political objectives.[68]

Rather than promoting the initially advocated cosmopolitan forms of remembrance, the EU policy on the past inspires a partisan view of the past. Recent research suggests that the adoption of cosmopolitan memory cannot ensure positive outcomes for victims: its tenets are nationalised and its discourse distorted to assist the national interest.[69] Cosmopolitan memory, as Ryan argues in her study on Austria and Ireland,[70] is open to interpretation, semblances of adherence and, sometimes, outright manipulation. Mälksoo[71] argues that 'attempts to forge certain mnemonic consensus as a higher ideal of a cosmopolitan nature are not necessarily a more benign version of securitizing historical memory than the parochial nationalist variants' that exist/existed elsewhere. In other words, when the EU serves exclusively as a political opportunity structure to protect national monopoly over the past, national political elites transform themselves into transnational memory populists.

These instances go to show the divisive rather than uniting potential ascribed to collective memory on the transnational, EU level. The EP resolution in 2019 clearly prescribes the future of Europe's past: the shared European legacy of crimes committed by communist, Nazi and other dictatorships is of vital importance for the unity of Europe.[72] It follows from this that a common culture of remembrance based on shared values (respect for human dignity, freedom, democracy, equality, the rule of law and respect for

68 See J. Đureinović, *The Politics of Memory of the Second World War in Contemporary Serbia: Collaboration, Resistance and Retribution* (London, Routledge, 2020); J. Subotić, *Yellow Star, Red Star: Holocaust Remembrance after Communism* (Ithaca, NY, Cornell University Press, 2019).

69 L. Ryan, 'Cosmopolitan Memory and National Memory Conflicts: On the Dynamics of Their Interaction', *Journal of Sociology* 50, no. 4 (2014): 501–14.

70 Ibid.

71 M. Mälksoo, '"Memory Must Be Defended": Beyond the Politics of Mnemonical Security', *Security Dialogue* 46, no. 3 (2015): 221–37, 228.

72 EP, 'The Importance of European Remembrance for the Future of Europe' (2019), www.europarl.europa.eu/doceo/document/TA-9-2019-0021_EN.html.

human rights, including the rights of persons belonging to minorities) shall help EU citizens reject the crimes of fascist, Stalinist and other totalitarian and authoritarian regimes of the past as a way of fostering resilience against modern threats to democracy, particularly among the younger generation. This resolution, however, was primarily directed not at EU member states, but rather at Russia in its twofold role both as victim and as a perpetrator. The EP expressed concerns 'about the efforts of the current Russian leadership to distort historical facts and whitewash crimes committed by the Soviet totalitarian regime and considers them a dangerous component of the information war waged against democratic Europe that aims to divide Europe, and therefore calls on the Commission to decisively counteract these efforts'.[73] This suggests that the EP's memory laws are part of the mnemonic war via foreign policy that seeks to apply soft pressure and induce reactions from its recipients. In response, the Russian President Putin dismissed the resolution as utter 'nonsense', explaining national positionalities on the basis of Russian 'historical truth'.[74] In Russia, the revisions of the constitution carried out in 2020 have become a fight over history, suggesting that the state has the right and obligation to 'protect historical truth' from others, including the EU and individual member states of the EU.[75]

Given the complexity of history of the Second World War and its aftermath, it comes as no surprise that the most intensive memory work in the EP is carried out in (in)direct relation to Russia, with a prominent role being played by the countries that were once part of the Soviet Union. As early as in 2007, the EP intervened in the memory conflict between Estonia and Russia. The announcement of the Estonian government's plan to relocate the Soviet 'monument to the liberators of Tallinn' from the centre of the Estonian capital to a military cemetery a few kilometres away was followed by two nights of violence, which started with demonstrators attacking the police and resulted in widespread vandalism in the centre of Tallinn. The conflict over memory in Tallin not only became a diplomatic matter between Estonia and Russia but also placed the EP in a position to pass legislation and 'call on the Russian Government to engage in an open and unbiased dialogue with the Eastern and Central European democracies

---

73 Ibid., p. 16.
74 TASS, 'Putin Slams European Parliament Resolution on WWII Outbreak as "Complete Nonsense"' (2019), https://tass.com/politics/1103075.
75 Duma, 'What Changes Will Be in the Constitution of the Russian Federation?' (2020), http://duma.gov.ru/en/news/48039.

on the history of the 20th century and the crimes committed then against humanity, including by totalitarian Communism'.[76]

Roads Less Travelled

An examination of the role of history is vital in order to better understand why the grand design of a common memory for a united Europe – with a single market and a common foreign policy yet enough diversity to encompass cultural and social differences – posed and continues to pose challenges to its citizens. Collective memory on a transnational level is an amalgam of different and divergent views and experiences of the past. Given the volatile and often malleable character of such a collective memory, the collectivising potential of EU memory policy seems to be rather weak. Some member states effectively share a past, such as, for instance, Slovenia's and Croatia's post-1945 Yugoslav history. Yet, Spain and Portugal, while having been through ideologically similar dictatorial experiences, have had different historical trajectories. The blurring effect of EU memory politics in relation to the totalitarian and authoritarian history tends to wash out those differences and appears to have a stronger appeal and hence unifying potential only when constructed in relation to 'the Other'. These conflictual memory constellations at the European level explain why European memory politics is characterised by a sustained focus on specific time periods on the one hand and amnesia on the other.[77]

While the focus on the Holocaust and anti-totalitarianism remains central for some and a major knot of European memory for others, the EU's memory politics presents itself as a rather selective narrative of its own past. A retrospective gaze into the early days of EU integration is very valuable in understanding the origins of the amnesias in the EU's self-narrations and the ways in which memory canons continue to perpetuate such a narrow reflection of more than 70 years of unity. The founding fathers and reconciliation myths have turned out to be immutable and have remained unchallenged over the course of time and across the EU's various self-narrations and contours. Certainly related to the political reality of those times is the fact that the elitist, founding fathers myth has failed until recently to successfully integrate gender in the fundaments of the EU.

76 EP, 'Estonia' (2007), www.europarl.europa.eu/doceo/document/TA-6-2007-0215_EN .html.

77 A. Sierp, 'EU Memory Politics and Europe's Forgotten Colonial Past', *Interventions* 22, no. 6 (2020): 686–702, 686.

Women, invisible in this narration, worked in the shadows of the High Authority and the other institutions established since the 1950s. Despite this, Europe, an imagined community, has been narrated as an elite-led and elite-practised form of (men's) politics.[78] Gendering of EU memory politics and its practical application across related policies and programmes became a priority only recently.[79] The Citizens, Equality, Rights and Values programme (CERV) has as one of its key priorities raising awareness of the common European history while paying attention to equality between women and men.

The early days of the European Coal and Steel Community (ECSC) too can help us identify some of the other roads not taken in narrating EU history as they show the earliest proofs of truly entangled collective memories in Europe. The 15 years of independent existence of the ECSC illustrate the shortage of memory the EU continues to have in relation to the past. The first non-elite-led and -practised forms of Europeanness were made possible by the first border movers – the blue-collar labour force. Millions of workers and their families migrated during the first 5 years of the Common Market before the white-collar generations of 'Eurostars' were hatched in the Erasmus programme. During the years 1958–62, net emigration from Italy alone reached 716,000, with the greatest influx of foreign workers (as *Gastarbeiter*) in the Federal Republic of Germany. In the first 5 years of the Common Market, there was a net immigration of 1,600,000. These workers were largely citizens of Spain, Yugoslavia, Turkey and Greece.

Finally, while European integration was born after and in contrast to the Second World War, it was born during and in connection with the colonial experience. When the EC was first established, four of its six member states were still in control of colonial territories – which were regularly associated with the incoming common market, while Algeria was even made fully part of it.[80] Although it has largely been forgotten, the early association between colonialism and European integration has made it hard for the EC/EU to

---

78 A. Milošević, 'Does Europe Prefer Her Sons over Daughters? Adding the Gender Perspective to European Memory', LSE Engenderings (2018), http://blogs.lse.ac.uk/gender/2018/04/05/does-europe-prefer-her-sons-over-daughters-adding-the-gender-perspective-to-european-memory.

79 'Citizens, Equality, Rights and Values Programme (CERV)', https://ec.europa.eu/info/funding-tenders/opportunities/portal/screen/programmes/cerv.

80 L. Ferrari, 'Missing Memory: The European Parliament in Face of Europe's Imperial and Colonial Past' (2019), unpublished manuscript.

claim an anti-colonial character and to present itself as being in opposition to the European colonial powers.[81] Recent and very shy attempts at integrating those memories into the EU memory framework were carried out on the initiative of a group of like-minded MEPs and with the support of mediating (f)actors such as the European Network Against Racism and European Network of People of African Descent. In 2019 a resolution on 'Fundamental Rights of People of African Descent'[82] was adopted. While the attempts at addressing the colonial history of Europe have focused solely on the anti-discriminatory angle of people of African descent, citizens of Middle Eastern and Asian descent, who often suffer from discrimination as well, are not addressed by these mnemonic efforts.

These examples show the extent to which existing EU memory politics and accompanying policies have been shaping a rather selective narrative of Europe's past, omitting histories and memories that do not fit the classical East–West dichotomy. In other words, the emphasis on the significance of the Second World War has primacy over the pursuit of the EU's own history – the one that has been shared, although in different configurations, by nation-states, the members of the Union. The attempts at 'uploading' views, narratives and representations of the past to the EU memory framework that have been made reflect national positionalities. Yet, as, for instance, the experience with colonialism shows, even amnesia is part of the EU's memory politics. Ultimately, the evidence suggests that, even when resolutions are adopted in the name of all member states, such soft laws tend to be monopolised by those who effectively can identify with and benefit from them. For instance, the resolution installing the EU's 'Day of Remembrance for the Victims of Terrorism' (2004) was an important token of recognition for those who suffered such violence, either as individual victims or states proper. However, this EU remembrance day has weak reach as it is observed only in a handful of countries that suffered terror attacks, making this resolution and similar types of resolution 'European only by its name'.[83]

81 P. Hansen and S. Jonsson, *Eurafrica: The Untold History of European Integration and Colonialism* (London, Bloomsbury, 2014).

82 EP, 'Fundamental Rights of People of African Descent' (2019), www.europarl.europa .eu/doceo/document/TA-8-2019-0239_EN.html.

83 A. Milošević and G. Truc, '(Un)shared Memory: European Parliament and EU Remembrance Day for Victims of Terrorism', *Politique européenne* 71, no. 1 (2021): 142–69, 150.

Conclusion

The history of the EU is fundamentally a history of self-narrations that sought to underpin a number of shifting objectives over the decades: from self-legitimisation to foreign policy. A socio-historical analysis of the European institutions' attempts to promote a memory of European integration since the 1950s demonstrates how the European institutions and their representatives referred to and symbolised various pasts in order to historically ground the European project. The past has served as a 'negative template', as a rationale for deeper and wider integration and as an instrument to support general objectives such as legitimacy building. To this end, answering the question of what binds Europeans together and what kind of future the EU ought to have has been translated into addressing specific objectives: fostering citizens' ownership over the European project by promoting the notion of European identity based on cultural and historical heritage – including its dark sides. During the period between the end of the Cold War and the post-2004 enlargement there was an important 'rupture' in the ways in which the past has been used at EU level. Integrating the negative aspects of the past into the self-narration became an objective of the post-enlargement period and a tool to achieve reconciliation in pursuit of an ever-closer Union. Importantly, such mnemonic efforts have supported the emergence of proper EU memory politics, enabled through the intense memory work of the EP and its EU memory framework, supported by the European Council and made practically possible through the work of the European Commission. The intended effects and produced consequences of Europeanised forms of memory and its practices posed and continue to pose a significant challenge both for scientists and for policy-makers as 'memory wars' have made it increasingly difficult for Europe to have a proper conversation about the past, in particular of the Second World War.

Recommended Reading

De Cesari, C. and A. Kaya (eds.). *European Memory in Populism: Representations of Self and Other* (New York, NY, Routledge, 2020).

Neumayer, L. *The Criminalisation of Communism in the European Political Space after the Cold War* (New York, NY, Routledge, 2018).

Milošević, A. and T. Trošt (eds.). *Europeanisation and Memory Politics in the Western Balkans* (New York, NY, Palgrave Macmillan, 2020).

Pakier, M. and B. Stråth. *A European Memory? Contested Histories and Politics of Remembrance* (New York, NY, Berghahn, 2010).

Sierp, A. *History, Memory, and Trans-European Identity: Unifying Divisions* (New York, NY, Routledge, 2014).

24

European Culture(s)

MARKUS THIEL

Introduction

'Just as Rome opened up its Pantheon to gods of every race and put men with black skin on the imperial throne [. . .] Europe should declare itself ready, by virtue of these very roots, to include every other cultural and ethnic contribution, since openness is one of its most distinguished cultural features.'[1]

As in Umberto Eco's appeal to European cultural inclusivity on the basis of Roman history, Europe's narrative about its culture(s) is almost as rich as its past. And it is similarly complex and convoluted, with the European Union (EU) appropriating the idea of 'Europe' as a unifying signifier that awkwardly balances the EU's official motto 'unity in diversity', as it aims to be representative of the current twenty-seven constituent member states' cultures. Yet this conceptual framework leaves out, for instance, European countries that are not EU members, as well as tendentiously the non-European ethnic and cultural minorities that have found a home on the continent and have historically contributed to the region's culture and history. But the vague inclusivity of the term 'European culture' also seems to have contributed to more societal awareness and support. For one, there appears to be a relatively broad popular consensus on its value: three-quarters of Europeans are attached to the unifying idea of European culture according to Eurobarometer, the EU's public opinion instrument, although the attachment to its institutional embodiment, the EU, is markedly lower.[2] Moreover, national cultural heritage is valued outside of domestic borders as evidenced by the popularity of

1 U. Eco, *Chronicles of a Liquid Society* (Boston, MA, Houghton Mifflin Harcourt, 2017), p. 179.
2 European Commission, 'Special Eurobarometer 466: Cultural Heritage' (2017), https://data.europa.eu/data/datasets/s2150_88_1_466_eng?locale=en.

intra-European cultural travel. Thus the caring for distinct cultures that are often related because of common history and geography might be productive of a pan-European cultural heritage worth protecting. It should also be worth promoting, in the (EU's) interest of furthering the awareness of a common transnational pan-European identity. This is true despite the fact that 'culture', just like 'Europe', is an ambiguous term that has nationally specific connotations in each of the twenty-seven member states. Yet the recognition of a common European sociocultural heritage is theorised to enable Europeans to break free from an assumed national essentialism with its attendant problems of nationalism and the othering of other cultures. As Kristeva points out,[3] 'European nations are waiting for Europe to emerge, and Europe needs proud and valued national cultures that offer the world the cultural diversity that we have requested UNESCO to protect. National cultural diversity is the only antidote to the evil of banality.'

This post-war narrative of European identity/identities and culture(s) as 'protecting Europeans from each other' lost impetus in the contemporary peaceful re-fashioning of the region. As a result, a change in perception leading to a search for Europe's constitutive cultural elements is slowly taking hold. Part of the rationale to do so is to distinguish itself as a liberal utopia from other global powers in its often-posited European cultural exceptionalism or pre-eminence.[4] The common-culture narrative certainly had a political connotation when it became part of the EU's vocabulary in the post-war era, expressing the desire not only to encompass European national cultures in an attempt at reconciling former enemies, but also to create a new, modern and post-national identity.[5] Cultural policy as the manifestation of this ambition was added as an EU legal–political competence in the Maastricht Treaty of 1992, which also changed the name of the organisation from 'European Community' to 'European Union' to signal a closer collaboration. With the subsequent advancement of European integration and harmonisation, the governing EU institutions, as well as the scholarly community of European/EU Studies, have more recently embarked on a 'narrative turn', that is, they use narratives to advance policies, or, conversely, to analyse societal discourses on Europeanness.[6] Although scholars

---

3 J. Kristeva, 'Homo Europaeus: Does a "European Culture" Exist?' (2016), www .bbvaopenmind.com/wp-content/uploads/2016/01/BBVA-OpenMind-Julia-Kristeva-Homo-Europaeus-Does-a-European-Culture-Exist-1.pdf.

4 D. Sassoon, *The Culture of the Europeans* (New York, NY, HarperCollins, 2006).

5 Jan Berting, *Europe: A Heritage, a Challenge, a Promise* (Utrecht, Eburon Uitgeverij, 2006).

6 L. Bouza García, 'Introduction: A Narrative Turn in European Studies', *Journal of Contemporary European Studies* 25, no. 3 (2017): 285–90.

generally prioritise the investigation of the truth value of postulates advanced by the EU, there are likewise plenty of academic narratives that influenced EU policy-making – take Ian Manners' influential 'normative power Europe' concept foregrounding the EU's normative constitution, for example.[7] Hence this chapter aims to examine the congruence of cultural narratives surrounding Europe with its actual implementation in EU cultural policy. In doing so, it highlights a few challenges that may continue to impact on the gap between the narrative and the political reality in this regard. Such analysis is justified not only on analytical grounds, but also because unifying, politically advanced European cultural discourses are framed and constructed primarily on a narrative basis, similar to the 'imagined communities' of nations.[8]

Scholarly Literature and Trends

A joint identification based on common origin, history, philosophy, and societal and political developments, to name a few criteria, presupposes that the diversity of European cultures can seamlessly be enveloped in a broader European cultural frame, akin to perfectly fitting babushka dolls that can be placed inside each other. Yet, as the ubiquitous examples of wars and competition between European nations show, a common European culture, however vaguely defined, is just as much a product of tensions and conflict among Europeans over shared territories, symbols, identities and, ultimately, culture.[9] The European narrative then differs depending on the domestic lens or perspective through which 'Europeanness' is refracted according to national history and culture. Culture itself is notoriously difficult to define as a social phenomenon because it is manifested in a wide range of behavioural, historical, institutional, material and other sociopolitical ways.[10] One could further delineate it along the lines of intangible heritage, expressed in customs, knowledge and performative representations, or tangible material heritage that can consist of natural-environmental or man-made sites.[11] These manifestations and representations were historically somewhat fluid in

7 I. Manners, 'Normative Power Europe: A Contradiction in Terms?', *Journal of Common Market Studies* 40, no. 2 (2002): 235–58.
8 B. Anderson, *Imagined Communities: Reflections on the Origin and Spread of Nationalism* (London, Verso, 2006).
9 R. Halle, 'Introduction', *EuropeNow* no. 26 (2019), www.europenowjournal.org/2019/04/04/united-in-diversity.
10 M. Thiel and R. Friedman, *European Identity and Culture: Narratives of Transnational Belonging* (London, Routledge, 2012), p. 3.
11 S. Alves, 'Understanding Intangible Aspects of Cultural Heritage: The Role of Active Imagination', *The Historic Environment: Policy & Practice* 9, no. 3–4 (2018): 207–28.

terms of the narrative reference point under examination here: early transnational secular or religious empires that centred around religious communities, imperial courts and universities dotted around Europe gave way to
nationally circumscribed or imagined communities in the eighteenth and
nineteenth centuries. Around that time, colonialism and emerging globalisation added a regional cultural consciousness for Europe's elites that was more
or less self-reflective of a European cultural–historical distinctiveness. This
emerging trend was manifested in phenomena ranging from the often
expected 'grand tour of Europe' to broaden one's horizon to the cosmopolitan philosophies of the enlightenment era and the spread of popular coffee
or tea-houses as centres for intellectual exchange across European societies.
It also included the fetishisation and appropriation of extra-European cultural
artefacts that ironically today are often viewed as integral parts of European
cultural heritage. In the post-war history of European integration, a pan-
European cultural ideal has been politically advanced, although in reality it is
more precise to speak of a limited transnationalism for sub-regional cultural
formations, such as can be found on the Iberian peninsula, or in the Nordic
region, for instance. Hence 'European' culture emerged in a discontinuous
fashion and often without substantive penetration into broader public
spheres, and it was almost always superseded by more immediate socio-
spatial collective identities than a continental–regional one.

Narratives, then, help to frame, advance and reify the various meanings
contained in the notion of 'European culture(s)'. At the same time, they are
not always readily available and tend to be subtly engineered and manipu-
lated for a specific purpose. Hence the study of culture requires an analysis
of the way in which facts and fiction emerge, circulate and shape how social
communities develop.[12] Current examples abound, for instance the way in
which the EU institutions appropriate 'Europe' for themselves, or the manner in which conservative forces across Europe put forth a counter-narrative
of the impending end of European culture because of immigration or liberal
pluralism. Scholars thus pay more attention to the narrative quality of EU
politics, not only as fundamental for questions of transnational identity
formation,[13] but also because of its significance for competing visions of the
EU that circulate throughout the region.[14] These narratives are embedded in
'narrative networks' of people that create cohesion, but they also need to

12 A. Erll and R. Sommer, *Narrative in Culture* (Berlin, De Gruyter, 2019), p. 2.
13 M. Thiel, *The Limits of Transnationalism: Collective Identities and EU Integration* (Berlin,
Springer, 2011).
14 Bouza García, 'Introduction'.

have narrative resonance, meaning that they need to make sense in order for them to be adopted.[15] This precondition highlights some of the idiosyncrasies included in the narrative advancement of the concept of 'European culture' as propagated by European national as well as EU elites. These became more pronounced recently with the politicisation of the EU, the increasing ethno-cultural diversity in European societies, and the contestations emerging from post-colonial, Eurocentric memory politics, which will be detailed below.

Hence the complexity and broad reach of the notion of 'culture', especially in a European context, produce a number of issues that have been noted to increase the gap between expectations and actual performance in this area, such as different languages, historical perceptions, cultural differences, national administrative and management differences, and larger structural variations.[16] It is beyond the scope of this chapter to define culture as such, but analysts focusing on its role in Europe highlight how EU institutions have consistently excluded the power-laden and conflictual dimensions of con-necting 'Europe' to 'culture' in their top-down approach to cultural policies.[17] Only more recently have scholars attested to a more pluralistic development of European cultural policies through the inclusion of local actors and cultural professionals[18] – or 'multi-stakeholder governance', as it is termed in cultural policy jargon. Yet a more reflective and broad-based cultural policy is needed, as cultural heritage and the cultural sectors have come under threat with social changes (for instance through the loss of regional dialects or customs), armed conflicts and other external shocks (such as through civil wars or the Covid-19 pandemic), economic development and mass tourism (representing a threat to monuments across Europe), and, increasingly, climate change (exemplified by the changing Alpine or Danubian river environments). Importantly, most of Europe's cultural heri-tage faces a quadruple threat in the sense that all these factors tend to be linked and reinforce each other. As a result, it seems more important than ever to connect the various national heritage preservation systems to come

---

15 K. Eder, 'Europe as a Narrative Network: Taking the Social Embeddedness of Identity Constructions Seriously', in S. Lucarelli, F. Cerutti and V. A. Schmidt (eds.), *Debating Political Identity and Legitimacy in the European Union* (Abingdon, Routledge, 2011).

16 C. Gordon, 'Great Expectations – the European Union and Cultural Policy: Fact or Fiction?', *International Journal of Cultural Policy* 16, no. 2 (2010): 101–20.

17 C. Shore, *Building Europe: The Cultural Politics of European Integration* (London, Routledge, 2013); K. Xuereb, 'The New Agenda for Culture as a Tool for European Integration: A Critical Analysis', *The Arts Journal* (2020), https://theartsjournal.net/2020/03/03/xuereb-2.

18 K. K. Patel, *The Cultural Politics of Europe: European Capitals of Culture and European Union since the 1980s* (London, Routledge, 2013).

up with joint solutions to these urgent problems. National mandate holders for cultural policy, however, because of their regional or domestic focus, and the intention to preserve local control over cultural heritage, are at times difficult to convince of the advantages of European collaboration. This is the case even though their reliance on European funding, through the stipulation of transnational network building in EU guidelines, increasingly links domestic preservation specialists together in pan-European networks.

Hence the following sections probe the congruence of European narratives about culture with the reality found on the national and EU levels that is marked by contested historical memories, limited material support for the culture and arts sectors, and a commodifying EU cultural policy strategy. Finally, it offers recommendations that might address some issues in the future, such as the promotion of common European perspectives on culture, a conceptual reassessment of culture's value in and of itself, and a tackling of increasingly challenging environmental issues.

Contemporary European Cultural Policies between 'Solutionism' and Governmentality

In terms of how Europeans perceive the EU's investment in culture – an important legitimising factor as the EU regularly relies in its policy initiatives on European public opinion to justify its initiative – Europeans clearly support the EU's engagement in and support of European culture. As of 2017, over 80 per cent of sampled Europeans agreed that culture is important for the EU, and 84 per cent think that culture is important for them personally; 51 per cent declared that they are personally regularly accessing culture in one form or another, and 68 per cent stated that the presence of cultural heritage influences their choice of vacations.[19] Another special survey on European's access to culture 5 years earlier provides more detailed information on the dominant types of cultural activities: mass culture activities such as watching television or reading are more prevalent than 'high culture' outings to a theatre or museum, with lack of money, interest or time being cited as major impeding factors.[20] Thus culture in its broadest understanding, while almost representing an empty signifier, provides EU institutions and national governments with a potentially supportive, if diffuse, public backing to enact new policies and initiatives in this area. At the same time,

---

19 European Commission, 'Special Eurobarometer 466'.
20 European Commission, 'Special Eurobarometer 399: Cultural Access and Participation' (2013), https://data.europa.eu/data/datasets/s1115_79_2_399?locale=en.

a substantial number of Europeans are disengaged from culture, represented by the 49 per cent who do not want to participate in or access cultural activities, or may have limited opportunities to do. Hence the emphasis on culture as a means for social inclusion as expressed in the EU's latest 'New Agenda for Culture' on the occasion of the EU's 'European Year of Cultural Heritage' 2018[21] is relevant and ought to be emphasised in the next few years. In this sense, cultural inclusion needs to be conceived of vertically as well as horizontally, not only including various (native and migrant) cultures across space, but also cognisant of the socio-economic hierarchies and inequalities that prevent people from participating in public cultural life. Case studies highlighting de-industrialised urban spaces and the contributions of migrants towards revitalisation of those spaces through the European Cultural Capital programme illustrate the potential, as well as the simultaneous perpetuation of inequalities through the EU's action in this area.[22] Similarly, on national levels there is an increased discursive recognition of accessibility of 'culture for everyone', but I would suggest that moves to popularise such notions come from the civic and cultural professional sectors rather than from (inter)governmental actors.

Culture as a policy is a national competence, so that the EU is limited to supporting Europe's common heritage. In practice, that means that much of the financial support and working conditions remain in national hands. In the nineteenth and twentieth centuries, culture was largely perceived as having a national identity-building value for European elites. The national divisions after the world wars and the initial economic focus of European regional integration meant that culture was not viewed as a supranational area of activity. While individual auxiliary initiatives existed earlier, only with the expansion to political integration in the Maastricht Treaty of 1992 did a rudimentary EU cultural policy begin to take shape. In 2007, the EU developed for the first time a multi-year 'agenda for culture', which already clearly stipulated the role of culture for European diversity and exchange, as a catalyst for the creative industries and as a strategic element in the EU's international relations.[23] One can see how EU cultural policy morphed from supporting a common good to advancing specific solutions. This

21 European Commission, Directorate General (DG) Education and Culture, 'New European Agenda for Culture 2018' (2018), www.cultureinexternalrelations.eu/2018/06/01/new-european-agenda-for-culture.
22 A. Çağlar, 'Rescaling Cities, Cultural Diversity and Transnationalism: Migrants of Mardin and Essen', Ethnic and Racial Studies 30, no. 6 (2007): 1070–95.
23 EurLex, 'European Agenda for Culture' (2007), https://eur-lex.europa.eu/legal-content/EN/TXT/?uri=CELEX:32007G1129%2801%29.

transformation of purpose resulted in the 'instrumentalisation of culture through "solutionism"', that is, the prioritisation of strategies in service of often neoliberal goals, rather than valuing culture for its own sake.[24] Specifically, the EU's department in charge of this approach, the Directorate General for Culture, started to emphasise the commodification of culture in an attempt to become more policy-relevant and gain more resources: 'With the launch of the "creativity" frame, a clear paradigmatic change has taken place and economic concerns have become the core of the justification for the EU's cultural policy.'[25] This shift, as Littoz-Monnet points out, was possible because of the portrayal of culture as a potential solution to economic issues, and the added 'creativity' frame that eliminated opposition to purely economising narratives. Hence the 'New European Agenda for Culture' that was adopted by the European Commission updated the original one by emphasising the role of culture for economic growth and societal cohesion, including the integration of migrants. In its intercultural ambition, it extends the notion of 'cultural diversity' beyond European borders, and it is even cited as a means to bridge the increasing tensions among EU member states, from north to south or east to west. In its reformulation it is thus explicitly cognisant of the potential to mobilise citizens and to enable a more equitable citizenship across member states, but it also highlights the added value of the cultural/creative industries for prosperity and the vitality of labour markets. Lastly, it emphasises European culture's vital role as connector to other world regions,[26] which represents an aspirational but also lofty goal.

It becomes evident that two distinct poles are recognised in the latest reformulation of the EU's cultural agenda. On the one hand, culture is seen as a means to create more social cohesion and participation as well as possibly a common identity, among ever more diverse European societies.[27] On the other hand, the pragmatic ambition to use the EU's creative and cultural sectors to stimulate employment and economic growth becomes evident. Both respond in theory to contemporary regional challenges, but while the former societal narrative is more idealistic, the latter economic one appears more transactional. We shall return to the economising effects of European culture policy later, but a starting point for a more differentiated analysis

24 Xuereb, 'The New Agenda for Culture'.
25 A. Littoz-Monnet, 'Agenda-Setting Dynamics at the EU Level: The Case of the EU Cultural Policy', Journal of European Integration 34, no. 5 (2012): 505–22, 506.
26 European Commission, DG Education and Culture, 'New European Agenda for Culture 2018'.
27 T. Lähdesmäki, K. Mäkinen, V. L. A. Čeginskas and S. Kaasik-Krogerus, Europe from Below (Leiden, Brill, 2021).

necessitates the recognition that, aside from national variations in culture and policy, the performance of states as cultural actors has been quite mixed: central and northern European states provide more governmental support to their cultural sectors, whereas the south and central/east European states tend to rely more on private funding, with ensuing issues of clientelism. The latter generally have less robustly developed cultural policies and budgets, given their late democratic transitions and the lingering effects of economic–financial crises.[28] These governmental structures then condition the performance of national cultural policies, which consequently impact the EU's role in supplementing and integrating those policies regionally.

Searching for Solutions: Digitalisation and Narrative Engineering

Given the prevailing pressures of the neoliberal system and residual crises, one of the strongest interests and current investments from the side of the EU lies in the digitalisation of cultural heritage. This materialises in many ways, but the most prominent uses of this strategy can be found in the use of digital platforms and communications and the development of virtual reality/three-dimensional (3D) technology for monuments and museums.[29]

On the one hand, the EU's increasing focus on the digitalisation of cultural heritage, in order to preserve (in)tangible artefacts and monuments otherwise exposed to deterioration, can be considered a worthwhile undertaking. Moreover, digitalisation responds to the demands of an increasingly digitally informed society, which becomes even more reliant on these online platforms when crises such as the Covid-19 pandemic make it impossible to experience cultural sites at first hand. As highlighted by the European Cultural Heritage Conference 2020,[30] the digitalisation of artefacts is not merely intended to preserve or to make archives accessible online. There is also an increased emphasis on innovation in terms of the development of 3D imaging to access and preserve artefacts and monuments. Moreover, public accessibility as a cornerstone of public culture and as a pedagogical gateway to engage younger generations has become more important as well.

28 J. A. Rubio Arostegui and J. Rius-Ulldemolins, 'Cultural Policies in the South of Europe after the Global Economic Crisis: Is There a Southern Model within the Framework of European Convergence?', *International Journal of Cultural Policy* 26, no. 1 (2020): 16–30.
29 Cordis, 'How Digital Technologies Can Play a Vital Role for the Preservation of Europe's Cultural Heritage', https://cordis.europa.eu/article/id/413473-how-digital-technologies-can-play-a-vital-role-for-the-preservation-of-cultural-heritage.
30 Heritage 2020, Cultural Heritage Conference of the Croatian EU Presidency (2020), http://heritage.uniri.hr.

In this respect, probably the most prestigious EU-sponsored cultural digitalisation project is Europeana,[31] which was launched in 2008 and involves over forty European countries. More than 3,000 participating culture institutions have thus far digitised over 10 million artefacts and made them available online. Europeana consists of an enormous information and digitalisation portal whose ambition as a project that continually expands its capacity is, in its own words, to 'develop expertise, tools and policies to embrace digital change and encourage partnerships that foster innovation. We make it easier for people to use cultural heritage for education, research, creation and recreation. Our work contributes to an open, knowledgeable and creative society.'[32] As stated, the goals of Europeana are broader than just the insertion of technology into the cultural heritage sector. By linking it explicitly to policies regarding education, science and tourism, and a more diffuse societal transformation, it links Europe's cultural heritage to a number of tangible public policies and justifies investment and public funding in its operations. Hence it attempts to discursively move from a tangential sector to an essential one for the functioning of Europe's democracies through its public pedagogy.

One of Europe's exemplary pan-European projects that specifically aims to advance a novel narrative about European culture is the so-called 'time machine',[33] a digital history of localities across Europe, with over 14,000 institutional participants who digitise and trace Europe's history using specific sites, cities and regions. By doing so, they not only make local histories and artefacts accessible to the public, but also actually 'produce' a novel perspective on history (as the subtitle 'as common history *for* the continent' recalls) that connects the various historical sites. Hence they use innovative technology to create a forward-looking narrative about European history that may resonate better with audiences than just the backward-looking historical narratives that were dominant in the past.

On the other hand, aside from the preservation, public access and generative–innovative aspects, the drive towards digitalisation also appears to contain secondary economic motives. This becomes evident in the way the EU preferentially funds such technology-driven projects, as will be pointed out below.

Contrasting this venture to another one that explicitly localises pan-European culture and history for the purpose of generating an EU-supported

31 See www.europeana.eu/en. 32 https://pro.europeana.eu/about-us/mission.
33 www.timemachine.eu.

and EU-supportive narrative, the EU-funded House of European History in Brussels,[34] which was inaugurated in 2017, aims to be a place for critical reflection and learning through a specific transnational European viewpoint. According to its director, rather than simply presenting a historical European narrative in a positive light, its objective is to also illustrate how various perspectives and opinions on the same European events differ, or to what extent they are acknowledged at all, thus generating a meta-narrative on the role of 'Europe' for the EU's recent history.[35] Inevitably, questions of inclusiveness and narrative framing emerge in these projects. Hence, by materially supporting and even curating transnational initiatives, the EU has become an 'institutional memory entrepreneur', with the result that the new House of European History more closely resembles a pan-European narrative compromise, rather than being a genuinely innovative institution.[36] While all these endeavours are surely worthwhile, questions arise concerning what narratives about Europe they create or promote, and who ultimately profits from their establishment: European publics, the tech economy or the EU institutions?

EU Governmentality: What Should the Added Value of Cultural Policy Be?

As with almost every policy, the EU needs to justify its legal competence, but also the added value provided by its handling of a policy that otherwise could be managed by states themselves. In its own words, 'Culture is a specific domain characterised both by its business model, and its underlying nature of activity related to creativity, identity and self-expression.'[37] Hence the added value is stipulated often in terms of an increase in economic growth. This raises the question of what (non-material) value culture represents in and of itself, or does its value derive largely from its capacity to be commodified and generate wealth? As an example, the flagship 'European capital of culture' programme, whereby two or three European cities are annually highlighted and financially supported by the EU, narratively invokes pan-European cultural elements and connections beyond just showcasing local and regional

---

34 https://historia-europa.ep.eu.

35 European Memories, 'The House of European History: A Reservoir of the Diversity and Complexity of the Memories of Europe', https://europeanmemories.net/maga zine/the-house-of-european-history-a-reservoir-of-the-diversity-and-complexity-of-the -memories-of-europe.

36 W. Kaiser, 'Clash of Cultures: Two Milieus in the European Union's "A New Narrative for Europe" Project', *Journal of Contemporary European Studies* 23, no. 3 (2015): 364–77.

37 European Parliament Research Service, 'Employment in the Cultural and Creative Sectors' (2019), www.europarl.europa.eu/RegData/etudes/BRIE/2019/642264/EPR S_BRI(2019)642264_EN.pdf, p. 1.

culture. Discourse-analytical studies on European capitals of culture, how-ever, have found that the European dimension is only weakly present.[38] A strong, exclusive emphasis on Europe in EU cultural programmes would be short-sighted, however, as local and national perspectives admittedly are constitutive parts of a broader European culture. For instance, when Marseille-Provence was chosen in 2013, it linked up with north African artists in its symbolic embrace of the Mediterranean and connected to other European culture capitals by implementing similar actions, such as the 'in situ' Holocaust stumbling street stones found in several cities across the continent these days. Beyond this programmatic cultural vision, Marseille also highlighted its socio-economic transformation measured in reputational image gains and economic benefits by accounting for 15–20 per cent more visitors in following years despite the initial investment costs.[39] Moreover, the capitals programme was cited as fundamental for future ambitions, exemplified by Marseille's Olympic bid for 2024. Yet, beyond this flagship cultural showcase programme, which still is largely justified according to a narrow commodification of cultural impact or influence, the majority of the EU's cultural programmes, including the European heritage awards and music, architecture or literature prizes, do not reach a broader public or enter a wider pan-European societal discourse. In fact, Kaiser described the gap between the elite and popular culture narratives as a European 'clash of cultures'.[40] Rather, beyond the policy goal of transnationalising European culture, EU cultural programmes represent a means to support the cultural sector selectively, and to establish an identity or brand to justify expenditures in this volatile area.

More directly, regarding culture funding, the EU's regional cohesion policy centrally invokes the need to 'fully mobilise culture and creativity for regional development and job creation'.[41] Not only does this hint at the monetarisation of culture for socio-economic gains in the EU, but also the budgetary location within the cohesion policy is an indication of the EU's attempt to create transnational linkages by using budget headings such as 'regional convergence' or 'territorial cooperation'. For the 2007–13 period, it allocated €6 billion for cultural funding, including for preservation and the

---

38 C. Clopot and K. Strani, 'European Capitals of Culture: Discourses of Europeanness in Valletta, Plovdiv and Galway', in U. Kockel, C. Clopot, B. Tjarve and M. Nic Craith (eds.), *Heritage and Festivals in Europe* (London, Routledge, 2019), pp. 156–72.
39 U. Fulchs, presentation at European Cultural Heritage Conference, June 2020, unpublished.
40 Kaiser, 'Clash of Cultures'.
41 European Union, 'Cohesion Policy: Culture Funding' (2012), no longer available online.

creation of a 'cultural infrastructure'. This funding, directly tied to regional development and cohesion, is much larger than direct EU support for culture industries and heritage under the 'Creative Europe' programming line, which in the period 2014–20 received €1.46 billion and in 2021–7 has a budget of €2.44 billion. Despite the linking of culture to economic gains, and the ambition to create pan-European cultural networks, a report on the 2014–20 implementation comes to the conclusion that larger and older EU member states are able to profit more from EU cultural funding.[42]

This divergence in the utilisation of EU cultural funds and programmes evolved in part because of historically established policy patterns, in which countries such as France, Germany, Italy or the UK before Brexit put more state emphasis on cultural policy in order to facilitate domestic nation-building.[43] These also contained private donors and institutions that contributed to nationally specific variations of cultural policies. The UK's departure from the EU has affected both, in the sense that the EU has decreased political and financial leverage in culture policy, and the UK now lacks the transnational soft power channels it used to possess with EU membership. The aforementioned states are better able to exploit existing EU cultural instruments due to their longstanding, established national institutions and co-funding systems. The central and eastern European member states, while having been somewhat integrated through cultural Europeanisation and inclusion in existing EU programmes, still find it more challenging to compete with their western partners in obtaining project- or grant-based EU funding. This is despite the expansion of eligible funding to aspiring EU member states, for instance to Serbia, in upcoming European Capital of Culture selections. Such findings illustrate the incongruence between the EU's ambitious pan-European rhetoric and the practice of preferentially funding selected larger states' organisations. This selectivity is generally based on organisational capacity and the technical skills necessary to profit from EU funds, irrespective of the potential need for sub-regionally proportional funding opportunities.

Moreover, the preservation of cultural heritage may be a rather costly undertaking whose costs generally cannot be recouped through increased tourism revenues, and its protection can at times be in conflict with the need

42 A. Zygierewicz, 'Creative Europe Programme (2014 to 2020): European Implementation Assessment (Update)' (2018), www.europarl.europa.eu/RegData/etudes/STUD/2018/627127/EPRS_STU(2018)627127_EN.pdf.
43 V. Dubois, 'Cultural Policy Regimes in Western Europe' (2013), https://halshs.archives-ouvertes.fr/halshs-00836422.

for economic development. Evidence for these dilemmas can be seen, for instance, in the United Nations Educational, Scientific and Cultural Organization's (UNESCO's) threatening to put certain European cultural sites on its endangered heritage list after the planned construction of large infrastructural projects such as bridges or tunnels nearby, or the creation of Europe's annual 'most endangered heritage' list produced by Europa Nostra. In an attempt to mitigate these tensions, the EU's cultural policy, which prominently marked 2018 the 'European year of cultural heritage', not only lists the protection of artefacts and monuments as one of its four guiding principles, but also connects it to the other three principles of engagement (i.e., education), sustainability (reimagining sites, including tourism) and innovation (as in the use of science and technology).[44] In all of these attempts at justification and legitimisation, there becomes evident an EU governmentality approach that may be able to garner increased policy and material support for cultural actions through subtle interventions in national cultural policies, but simultaneously diminishes the intrinsic value and independence of the culture and arts sectors. Moreover, it hinders and delimits their creativity and artistic freedom by signalling strategic economic benchmarks to be followed.

Insofar as its involvement is concerned, the EU justifies its focus on cultural heritage preservation, aside from diffuse popular support for European culture, with the fact that about 5–7 per cent of Europeans work in the cultural and creative sectors, generating about 4 per cent of the EU's gross domestic product. While this is a significant and growing sector that includes the core artistic institutions as well as the entertainment and design branches, it is marked by precarious labour.[45] This precariousness is based on a number of factors, such as the structure of Europe's cultural and creative sectors, where 96 per cent of the organisations are small micro-organisations with fewer than ten employees, and 35–40 per cent of people are self-employed freelance workers. These were hardest hit when, during the outbreak of the Covid-19 pandemic in 2020, 80 per cent of cultural events had to be cancelled.[46] So, while on the one hand culture represents not only a symbolic European value but a means of making a living for a sizeable

44 European Commission, DG Education and Culture, 'New European Agenda for Culture 2018'.
45 European Parliament Research Service, 'Employment in the Cultural and Creative Sectors'.
46 E. Politseva, 'Culture, Creativity and Coronavirus: Time for EU Action', *Social Europe*, 19 January 2021, www.socialeurope.eu/culture-creativity-and-coronavirus-time-for-eu-action.

population across Europe, in the best of times it is marked by instability and retrenchment, which is only furthered in times of (Euro- or pandemic) crises. The Eurocrisis of 2009–12 had already significantly impacted the arts and culture sectors, with residual austerity cuts of 25 per cent or more across many European countries threatening the livelihood of many artists and employees in the creative sectors.[47] Therefore, in the 2020 run-up to the EU's negotiations of its multi-year budget and extraordinary Covid-19 emergency recovery fund, forty-five of Europe's most prominent artists and creatives, ranging from Björk to Marina Abramović, appealed for support of the shuttered cultural sectors disrupted by Covid-19-related closures in an open letter to Europe's leader.[48] However, in the June 2020 Council summit of EU leaders, a budget was proposed that included a 13 per cent cut to EU cultural funding over the following 7 years.[49] The plans to reduce support for EU culture spending were criticised by the European Parliament, as well as by two of Europe's largest cultural associations, Culture Action Europe and IETM, the international network for contemporary performing arts, as hitting one of the most Covid-19-affected societal sectors the hardest.

Discussion and Outlook for the Future

Looking towards the future, two larger issue areas emerge that are likely to have a significant impact on the narrative conceptualisation and practical manifestation of European culture (policies): the first, broader issue relates to the stability and expansion of the EU's cultural reach on political and societal levels across Europe; the second pertains to increasing environmental degradation and the corresponding need for preservation and digitalisation of artefacts. Each of these issues presents complex challenges in its own right, and thus accordingly will leave an imprint on the politically assigned value of culture.

The first issue area concerns the EU's ambition to strengthen a common European culture narrative through its pan-European connecting of national arts, culture and heritage sectors, and the linking of culture to socio-economic

---

47 L. Rother, 'In Europe, Where Art Is Life, Ax Falls on Public Financing', *The New York Times*, 3 March 2012, www.nytimes.com/2012/03/25/world/europe/the-euro-crisis-is-hurting-cultural-groups.html.

48 Forty-Five Signatories, 'Bjork, Abba & 43 Others Call on Summit to Save European Arts', *EUobserver*, 17 July 2020, https://euobserver.com/opinion/148946?utm_source=euobs&utm_medium=email.

49 European Parliament, 'Long-Term EU Budget: MEPs Slam Cuts to Culture and Education' (2020), www.europarl.europa.eu/news/en/press-room/20200619IP R81615/long-term-eu-budget-meps-slam-cuts-to-culture-and-education.

gains. With the increasing populist contestation of the EU and the EU's ongoing enlargement in membership, its core values of (cultural) rights and the narrative maintenance of a common 'European' culture enveloping national ones have come under pressure. While enlargement to culturally dissimilar regions such as the Balkans can be potentially enriching as a way to move away from a uniform 'western' Eurocentric conception, it exemplifies how culture and history are not necessarily perceived as jointly European and can be instrumentalised for political purposes. For instance, the Former Yugoslav Republic of Macedonia (FYROM), in order to become a future EU member state, struggled for over 25 years to satisfy Greece's demand for the country's name to change, so as not to conflict with its own Macedonian region and the historical role of Alexander the Great regarding Greek national identity. After FYROM had finally changed its name to North Macedonia in 2019, the EU candidate state now faces Bulgaria's demand to successfully conclude a common history committee session to determine the textbook status of their historical interactions.[50] This is just a small example of the difficulties of imagining an inclusive European culture within an increasingly fragmented EU; let alone the 'othering' of the Balkans in continental Europe, ranging from the 'powder keg' depiction to the delay of EU enlargement proceedings on the basis of an alleged 'enlargement fatigue' in western Europe. This type of ideological resistance and focus on an exclusionary national culture – all culture is local while simultaneously much of it is hybridised, to begin with – in its extreme form might not only undermine the pan-European narrative binding cultures together. Taken a step further, it could also lead to the destruction of material and intangible heritage that should otherwise be preserved.

The other major point in this regard refers to the need for a societal broadening and diversifying of European cultural policies on the national level as well as on the EU level. As mentioned above, despite the socioculturally diverse richness in the arts and creative sectors, more can be done by state actors and EU institutions to advance policy frameworks that include more strongly race, religious and ethno-racial and sexual minorities, as well as immigrants and women. These have been institutionally overlooked, despite their significant contributions to domestic and pan-European culture(s). More generally, a conscious decentring of the region's Eurocentric civilisational exceptionalism discourse that recognises Europe's conflictual

---

50 Euractiv, 'Bulgaria Could Block North Macedonia's EU Path over "Common" History Interpretation' (5 May 2020), www.euractiv.com/section/all/short_news/bulgaria-could-block-north-macedonias-eu-path-over-common-history-interpretation.

imperialist role in this regard is necessary.[51] This includes a stronger recognition of the detrimental impact of colonialism – including by the EU itself, which seems to largely express historical amnesia in this regard by viewing it as a 'national' issue.[52] This extends to the repatriation of non-European cultural heritage to its owners, more colonial restitution policies and the stronger highlighting of contemporary social exclusion for cultural and social minorities. These are not distinct areas of grappling with Europe's historical memory, but as van Huis states they are connected,[53] as the way in which the colonial past is remembered has consequences for the in/exclusion of foreigners in European societies. Yet states generally avoid non-favourable narratives, and the same can be said about the EU.

At least on a narrative level, though, the EU's new House of European History problematises colonialism and the world wars, expressing in its summary view the possibility of changing the historical narrative that is often guarded and delimited on national levels. A narrow re-nationalisation trend focused on cultural exceptionalism, as pronounced by state leaders from France's President Macron to Hungarian Prime Minister Orbán, only adds to the critical challenges of degradation, commodification, national disparities and societal inequalities that culture in its various forms faces. A possible way out of this dilemma could be provided by current movements in research, such as the scholarly recognition of the geopolitical imprint of transnational powers on regional culture, and an emerging public discourse about the appropriation of cultural heritage by 'modern' powers (the discussions surrounding the validity of colonial monuments across Europe, the EU's House of European History in Brussels and Turkish President Erdoğan's appropriation of Byzantine sites such as the Hagia Sophia come to mind). Moreover, the social and spatial significance of production and circulation sites across Europe, from bodies of water to ancient pathways, as contributing factors for the development of cultures in their various forms equally points to a transnational element inherent in many domestic cultural heritage sites. By highlighting these countervailing aspects to cultural chauvinism

---

51 R. Balfour, 'Against a European Civilization: Narratives about the European Union', Carnegie Europe (2021), https://carnegieeurope.eu/2021/04/06/against-european-civilization-narratives-about-european-union-pub-84229.

52 A. Sierp, 'EU Memory Politics and Europe's Forgotten Colonial Past', *Interventions* 22, no. 6 (2020): 686–702.

53 I. van Huis, 'Contesting Cultural Heritage: Decolonizing the Tropenmuseum as an Intervention in the Dutch/European Memory Complex', in T. Lähdesmäki, L. Passerini, S. Kaasik-Krogerus and I. van Huis (eds.), *Dissonant Heritages and Memories in Contemporary Europe* (London, Palgrave, 2019), pp. 215–48.

more strongly in education and tourism and in exchange with policy-makers, it would be possible to counteract a limiting national lens on culture.

On the other hand, environmental degradation and climate change argu-ably present more difficult challenges because of their extended time hori-zons. Yet climate change is already under way across Europe, and increasing desertification, flooding, storms and fires are visible signs of a disruptive process by which all cultural heritage is potentially threatened. In the double challenge of preserving cultural heritage from decline on the one hand through the weight of history and ongoing economic development, and on the other hand from climate change, preservation needs will probably further drive the digitalisation of artefacts and monuments. These technology-driven developments are not limited to preservation, but in a broader sense also help to advance technologies that might help mitigate the corrosive effects of short-term climatic events and of more subtle long-term climate change. Here, the role of international organisations working in tandem, such as UNESCO, the EU and the Council of Europe, to bind and support states in their attempts to manage these drawn-out environmental challenges is evident.[54] Just as the discursive broadening of sectors impacted by culture has been a worthwhile strategy in terms of justifying EU culture policies and funding, so it is the widening of supportive measures by interlocking institutions working together that stands the best chance of tackling the most urgent environmental challenges. It is commendable that the EU Commission provided €18 million in its Horizon 2020 programme to increase environmental resilience and support reconstruction of historic sites.[55] While it also set up a European competence centre for digital preservation and conservation in 2021, in addition to more financial aid spent on general preservation, the total sum is rather small for twenty-seven member states aiming to address the complex challenges of climate change mitigation.

The final objective of such mitigation, however, should be not solely the preservation of the digitised artefacts, but rather their maintenance and public revitalisation, as they provide primary evidence and serve as an essential reminder of Europe's rich and connected tapestry of histories. Similarly to the institutional promotion of 'public humanities' in recent

54 C. Sabbioni, M. Cassar, P. Brimblecombe and R. A. Lefevre, 'Vulnerability of Cultural Heritage to Climate Change', Council of Europe (2008), www.coe.int/t/dg4/majorhazards/activites/2009/Ravello15-16may09/Ravello_APCAT2008_44_Sabbioni-Jan09_EN.pdf.

55 Cordis, 'Heritage at Risk', https://cordis.europa.eu/article/id/400947-heritage-at-risk-eu-research-and-innovation-for-a-more-resilient-cultural-heritage.

years, a public history using digitalisation and virtual arts as a means for preservation and engagement will become more important in a future set between a crumbling physical cultural infrastructure and technology-driven artistic developments. This trend is reinforced by the EU's 'Creative Europe' funding, in which slightly over half of all funding is apportioned to audio-visual services and technologies.[56] While this potentially increases the reach and equity of audiences, with additional support provided for Europe's rich but threatened cultural heritage, less funding is likely to be available in the future for the contemporary arts and creative sectors in a policy area as 'expendable' as culture. Environmental design and architecture, while linking policy issues in complementary ways as envisioned by the current European Commission's 'green Bauhaus' concept, can only be a partial solution as not all cultural manifestations can be, or ought to be, conceptualised under an environmental scope. The latter example is obviously linked to the EU's envisioned 'Green Deal', and once again the EU's governmentality in the cultural heritage sector is evidenced by a recently published position paper by leading European heritage institutions, in which cultural preservation becomes primarily a means in support of the EU's environmental goals.[57]

Finally, in terms of its broader societal meaning, culture is regularly being touted as essential by leading elites, while at the same time policy support for cultural activities and heritage has mostly been precariously under-funded, impacted by crises and often over-bureaucratised as detailed above. The social and financial repercussions of the extended Covid-19 pandemic have further imperilled the public recognition and funding for culture, which will make it less likely that governmental support for European cultural activities and heritage will remain sufficient to maintain Europe's status as a global cultural power. More so than in other world regions, cultural heritage and the living arts are vital parts of Europe's socio-economically important culture and tourism industries. The prolonged Covid-19 pandemic makes it more likely that any available funds from the EU's regular or recovery budgets will have to be apportioned according to a 'triage' system whereby less urgent interventions are under-prioritised and -funded. In the author's adopted home, the United States, the EU is viewed with adoration and envy over the symbolic importance that national and EU leaders attach to

56 M. Pasikowska-Schnass, 'Employment in the Cultural and Creative Sectors' (2019), www.europarl.europa.eu/RegData/etudes/BRIE/2019/642264/EPRS_BRI(2019)642264_EN.pdf.
57 Europa Nostra, 'European Cultural Heritage Green Paper' (2021), https://issuu.com/europanostra/docs/20210322-european_cultural_heritage_green_paper_fu.

European culture; especially during the pandemic,[58] but it remains to be seen whether Europe is willing to 'put the Euro where its mouth is'. The digitising shift to online performances during the pandemic showed the flexibility, creativity and resilience of the cultural sectors, but they were neither cost-effective nor as widely accessible or accepted as pre-Covid-19 performances and exhibitions in public spaces. Hence, European culture experts have been calling for an EU framework on the working conditions of European artists, in order to sustain Europe's rich cultural ecosystem by recognising and subsidising their contributions.[59] An awareness of the multifaceted challenges of the European arts and culture sectors exists, but even in EU research reports only vague recommendations about 'establishing a fair working system', together with increased digitalisation and a stronger acknowledgement of the society-supporting relevance of those policy sectors, are highlighted.[60] If even Europe, which arguably inhabits, cherishes and profits from the world's most expansive cultural heritage and creative sectors, cannot appropriately sustain them sufficiently, then future proclamations of 'European culture(s)' are likely to perpetuate a rather hollow narrative caught between solutionism and governmentality. Lasting sustainability ought to encompass a broader set of objectives that includes not only environmental protection, but more public funding, as well as social inclusion and a reassessment of Europe's cultural exceptionalism.

Recommended Reading

Friedman, R. and M. Thiel (eds.). *European Identity and Culture* (London, Ashgate, 2012).
Halle, R. 'European Art, Culture, and Politics', special issue of *EuropeNow* 33 (2020).
Shore, C. *Building Europe: The Cultural Politics of European Integration* (New York, NY, Routledge, 2000).

58 *New York Times*, 'The Arts Are in Crisis. Here's How Biden Can Help', 13 January 2021, www.nytimes.com/2021/01/13/arts/design/arts-stimulus-biden.html.
59 Politseva, 'Culture, Creativity and Coronavirus'.
60 M. Pasikowska-Schnass, 'Creative Europe Programme 2021–2027', European Parliament (2021), www.europarl.europa.eu/RegData/etudes/BRIE/2018/628229/EPRS_BRI(2018)628229_EN.pdf.

25

The Catholic Narrative of European Integration

MADALENA MEYER RESENDE

Introduction

The multilateral regional system built in post-war western Europe became the world's most robust and integrated such system, both economically and politically. This chapter proposes that the birth, development and sustainability of European integration that occurred in the period spanning from the late 1940s to 1989 benefited from a synthesis of Christian, nationalist and liberal ideas, and that this synthesis underscored the emergence of European integration and legitimated its development in the four decades of the Cold War.

The synthesis describing Europe's regime and historical evolution – termed here the 'Catholic narrative' – served as the analytical and prescriptive basis for the generation of Christian Democrats that played a crucial role in the reconstruction of the democratic order after the Second World War. To add to the understanding of the history of post-war Europe, this chapter describes the emergence of this synthesis in the early days of the Cold War, its consolidation in the four decades that followed, its demise after 1989 and the reconfiguration it has undergone since 2015. The specific religious origins of the post-war Catholic narrative are uncovered, and its functions in the context of the emerging bipolar system are established. In a historical moment when political actors were in dire need of innovative solutions to overcome Europe's security dilemma, the Catholic Church set the ground for new avenues of action by using its narrative power to rally liberal, religious and nationalist identities to counter the communist threat.

The Catholic narrative was formulated as a response to communist expansion and aligned Christian universalism with nationalism and liberalism. This new constellation of ideas then served as a roadmap for the restoration of

Germany as a state and its reconciliation with France, and as agreement on a formula for the integration of western Europe's liberal democracies. The narrative's synthesis of religious, nationalist and liberal ideas resulted in the transformation of its parts. Christians, especially Catholics, whose political doctrine required the overcoming of nation-states, recognised the need to restore states to defend western Europe from the Soviet threat. This implied the defeat of post-national federalism and the Vatican's adoption of Christian realism. In 1948, Pope Pius XII launched a campaign for the unification of Europe on the basis of the premise that the future of Europe lay in a gradual process of integration of the re-founded nation states, rather than on the building of a post-state federation. In the European integration project, the Christian Democratic parties found an ambiguous formula that enabled them to reconcile their universalist vision with their desire for nation-state autonomy. Christian Democrats then became the trustees of the new synthesis. Liberals and nationalists, in order to resist the force of communist movements, were forced to formulate a project with greater appeal and vision than the mere reinstatement of nation-states. In 1949, General de Gaulle's political party, Rassemblement du Peuple Français (the Rally of the French People), albeit refusing supranational institutions, declared the need for a European Union as 'an imperative necessity for the maintenance of peace and the safeguarding of the [. . .] future of France and the French Union'.[1] As the Cold War began, the leading liberal conservative French writer Raymond Aron advocated the inclusion of West Germany in a western European union.[2]

The engagement of the Catholic Church in the European post-war order was part of a wider anti-communist strategy adopted by Pope Pius XII. The post-war Christian internationalism broke with the anti-liberal papal internationalism of the inter-war years (when the Vatican campaigned for the strengthening of ties with national authoritarian regimes in order to defend Catholicism, and from which derived a host of concordats sealing the relationship with fascist regimes, including that of Nazi Germany).[3] In the post-war period, the Church's stance changed to that of allying with liberal democratic regimes, with Pope Pius XII devising a new Catholic internationalism. In the immediate post-war period of 1945–8, the Vatican adopted a position of neutrality towards the Soviet Union

1 Rassemblement du Peuple Français, 'Party Document: Between Federation and Confederation (February 1949)', in W. Lipgens and W. Loth (eds.), *Documents on the History of European Integration* (Berlin, De Gruyter, 1988), vol. III, p. 87.
2 R. Aron, *Le grand schisme* (Paris, Gallimard, 1948), pp. 66–8; R. Aron, 'L'idée de l'europe', *La Fédération* 39 (1948): 6–9.
3 G. Chamedes, *A Twentieth-Century Crusade: The Vatican's Battle to Remake Christian Europe* (Cambridge, MA, Harvard University Press, 2019).

and of fostering a peaceful international order based on the United Nations. However, at the start of the Cold War in 1947–8, Pope Pius XII sided with the United States and enrolled Christianity as an ideological legitimation of the United States' containment policy.[4] On the European front, Church internationalism was translated into a policy urging Franco-German reconciliation and regional integration. The Pope's pragmatism led European leaders to forsake post-national federalism and to establish a system of cooperation between nation states grounded on their common Christian bonds.

This chapter traces the emergence, consolidation, death and reconfiguration of the Catholic synthesis. The next section summarises the literature and the theoretical framework. The third section, on the emergence of the Catholic narrative, outlines its articulation, from the Second World War through to the establishment of the European Coal and Steel Community in 1950. The fourth section, on the narrative's consolidation, traces its institution as the basis for a generation of Christian Democrats practising an extroverted nationalism while establishing and deepening the European Community's institutions during the Cold War. The fifth section outlines the decline and death of the Catholic synthesis, from 1989 to the constitutional crisis of 2005. Despite Popes John Paul II and Benedict XVI investing heavily in a renewal of the Catholic narrative of Europe, the constitutional drafters refused to refer to the Christian religion as an essential basis of European integration, making official the death of the Catholic constellation. The sixth section, on the narrative's reconfiguration, describes the radical right's appropriation of Christian symbols in a new synthesis of nationalism and Christianity that serves an anti-democratic and anti-integration agenda.

Literature Review and Theoretical Framework

While the role of Christian Democracy in the establishment of European integration is well recognised,[5] a description of its narrative dimension is still lacking.[6] This chapter thus adds to the understanding of the symbolic and narrative

---

4 See W. A. McDougall, *Promised Land, Crusader State: The American Encounter with the World since 1776* (Boston, MA, Houghton Mifflin, 1998).

5 See, for example, M. Gehler and W. Kaiser, *Christian Democracy in Europe since 1945*, vol. II (London, Routledge, 2004); W. Becker, 'The Emergence and Development of Christian Democratic Parties in Western Europe', in E. Lamberts (ed.), *Christian Democracy in the European Union: Proceedings of the Leuven Colloquium 1995* (Leuven, Leuven University Press, 1997); S. Van Hecke and E. Gerard (eds.), *Christian Democratic Parties in Europe since the End of the Cold War* (Leuven, Leuven University Press, 2004).

6 See R. Forlenza, 'The Politics of the *Abendland*: Christian Democracy and the Idea of Europe after the Second World War', *Contemporary European History* 26, no. 2 (2017): 261–86; J. Lacroix and K. Nicolaïdis, *European Stories: Intellectual Debates on European Integration in National Contexts* (Oxford, Oxford University Press, 2010).

dimensions of European integration, while engaging with the transnational approach to European history.

In accordance with Paul Ricœur's view of narratives as a particular form of historical representation, the Catholic narrative and its new synthesis of ideas is positioned as an essential element of the history of post-war Europe.[7] Two aspects of Ricœur's narrative theory sustain our argument regarding the centrality of Catholic narratives in the history of European integration. First, Ricœur's theory highlights the capacity of narratives to create a 'synthesis of the heterogeneous',[8] including of previously unreconciled ideologies. By 'redescribing reality and combining elements dispersed in time and space',[9] the Vatican used the start of the Cold War to define the narrative on Europe. By asserting that the medieval Carolingian Empire was the origin of modern Europe, Catholic forces positioned Christianity as the central element of a culturally defined western Europe. Secondly, Ricœur's theory explains how narratives possess a performative power. Ricœur's elements of narration – persuasion, vision and initiative – outline the function of certain stories in transforming an idea from the realm of fortune to a project of political consequence.[10] Thus, narratives provide support to political leaders in overcoming political dilemmas, such as Germany's reconciliation with France and its integration in western Europe, and can inspire the bringing together of former enemies into a framework of cooperation.

Formulation of the Catholic Narrative as a Basis for European Integration

Building on the criticism of nationalism during the Second World War, Catholic forces embraced pacifism and federalism as a remedy for ending the cycle of wars that endangered the survival of Europe. The emerging Cold War prompted the Vatican to formulate a new narrative of the Christian West. While acknowledging nation-states' autonomy, Pope Pius XII prompted their integration in multilateral regional cooperation structures. The revised policy – inscribed in a broad Christian internationalism – was of key practical importance for the reconciliation of France and Germany and

---

7 P. Ricœur, 'Narrative Time', *Critical Inquiry* 7, no. 1 (1980): 169–90.
8 P. Ricœur, *Temps et Récit*, 2 vols. (Paris, Éditions du Seuil, 1983–5).
9 R. Kearney and J. Williams, 'Narrative and Ethics', *Proceedings of the Aristotelian Society, Supplementary Volumes* 70 (1996): 29–61.
10 P. Ricœur, *Hermeneutics and the Human Sciences: Essays on Language, Action and Interpretation* (Cambridge, Cambridge University Press, 1981).

for the formulation of a functionalist and gradual policy for the integration of Europe.

This section first outlines progressive Catholicism's criticism of nationalism during the Second World War. Secondly, it analyses the dilemmas present in French policy towards Germany in the immediate post-war period and the progressive resolution of these. Thirdly, it describes how the Vatican, in response to the onset of the Cold War, adapted its internationalism to the new circumstances and formulated a new synthesis between nationalism, Christian universalism and democracy that facilitated the emergence of a new formula for the unification of Europe. Fourthly, it explains how this formula assisted the reconciliation of the French Mouvement Républicain Populaire (Popular Republican Movement, MRP) and the German Christlich Demokratische Union (Christian Democratic Union, CDU) and the adoption of plans for a multilateral cooperation system.

Catholic Reckoning with Nationalism and Embrace of Liberal Democracy

The origins of the post-war Catholic narrative can be traced back to a Catholic reckoning with the role that nationalism and secularism played in causing the 'total war' waged by the Nazis. The condemnation of nationalism by Catholic progressives during the Second World War presaged the post-war deliberation that marked the search for a sustainable peace in Europe. In the words of E. H. Carr, the rise of extreme nationalism resulted from the loss of the 'sense of obligation deriving from the unity of Christendom and the validity of natural law [. . .] survived in the secular trappings of the Enlightenment', which 'sovereigns could not afford openly and flagrantly to flout [. . .] in their relations with one another'.[11]

During the Second World War, the Church attributed responsibility for the ascendance of an unbridled and deadly nationalism to the rise of secularist positivism in Western culture. Pope Pius XII concluded that the decline of religion and the disappearance of 'God's natural law' had created the context for the rise of unbounded nationalism in European politics. This narrative helped to conceal the Church's alliance with fascism in the inter-war period, and created the grounds for Catholicism's subsequent role in the formulation of the new form of nationalism that was to emerge from the ashes of the

---

11 E. H. Carr, *Nationalism and After* (London, Macmillan, 1968).

war.[12] As stated by E. H. Carr, 'Just as the movement for religious toleration sprang up from the religious wars of the 16th and 17th century Europe, also the movement for national toleration [. . .] could emerge from the destructive 20th century wars of nationalism.'[13]

The deliberations about the ills that led to the war were anchored in the theological debates of the time. The devastation caused by fascism during the Second World War made it impossible for the Catholic Church to continue to support regimes based on concepts of corporatism, a 'system of social organization that has at its base the grouping of men according to the community of their natural interests and social functions, and as true and proper organs of the state' according to its definition proposed by a commission created by Pope Leo XIII in 1881.[14] The corporatist model had until then allowed the Church to combine its concern for social questions with the maintenance of its status and privileges. An alliance with fascism – which had been doctrinally condemned, but politically supported before the war[15] – was no longer a sustainable option. The Church had to accept that the alternative to liberal democracy was no longer *ancien régime* monarchy, but totalitarian revolution.

Pope Pius XII's Christmas message of 1944 was the first open statement from the Church in support of democracy:

> In the sinister light of the war that engulfs them, in the baking heat of the furnace in which they are shut up, people are at last awakening from a protracted slumber. They are adopting a new attitude in the face of states and government, questioning, critical, distrustful. Taught by bitter experience, they set their face against dictatorial, unaccountable, and untouchable monopolies of power, and they call for a system of government that is more compatible with the dignity and liberty of citizens.[16]

Although there was a general and official condemnation of nationalism and authoritarian rule among Catholics, the campaign for the federalisation of Europe was mainly carried out by progressive forces in the forefront of

12 Pope Pius XII, 'On the Supposed Sovereignty of States (20 October 1939)', in W. Lipgens (ed.), *Documents on the History of European Integration* (Berlin, De Gruyter, 1986), vol. II, p. 706.

13 Carr, *Nationalism and After*.

14 Quoted in H. J. Wiarda, *Corporatism and Comparative Politics: The Other Great 'Ism'* (Armonk, NY, M. E. Sharpe, 1997).

15 E. Gentile, *Pour ou contre César?: Les religions chrétiennes face aux totalitarismes* (Paris, Aubier, 2013).

16 Pope Pius XII, 'Sur la démocratie. Radio message au monde. 24 Décembre 1944', quoted in E. Perreau-Saussine, *Catholicism and Democracy: An Essay in the History of Political Thought* (Princeton, NJ, Princeton University Press, 2012), p. 133.

Catholic resistance to Nazism. In 1940, one of its leaders, Jacques Maritain, presented a vision of 'the end of the national sovereign nation state', adding that 'The distinction of nations is part of the Western heritage. Our aim is a confederation of European nations.'[17] During the war, Maritain prophesied a 'new Christianity' for the post-war period, a time when a new Christian community, oriented not to the sacred but to the profane, would emerge and serve as the basis for European unity.[18] Maritain reasoned that peace in Europe would take root only if a 'federal Germany would be integrated in a federal Europe'.[19]

Transformation of French Policy towards Germany and French Adoption of the Catholic Model of European Integration

While Jacques Maritain's post-national federalism was a revolutionary idea in the 1940s, by the end of the war, Europe had changed radically, and the idea of replacing national states by a federation seemed impracticable. The Red Army occupied all of central and eastern Europe, Germany had been annihilated as a state and the United States had become the guarantor of security in western Europe. To rebuild Europe, an alliance between Great Britain and France had to emerge. However, France, in a much weaker position than Britain due to its prior capitulation to Nazi Germany, needed time to regain its power. The realignment of French leaders with the West, the containment of German resurgence and the maintenance of European autonomy vis-à-vis the United States was thus a lengthy and thorny process.[20] Between 1945 and 1950, the stance of the French political elite towards Germany evolved from a revanchist to a reconciliatory stance, and they adopted a plan for unifying Europe.[21] This culminated in the formula for the European Coal and Steel Community presented in the Schuman declaration of May 1950.

The reasons for the French delay in accepting German restoration are threefold. First, despite the apparent death of nationalism during the war, conservative nationalism returned to European politics, with General de

17 J. Maritain, 'On Political Justice (Spring 1940)', in W. Lipgens (ed.), *Documents on the History of European Integration*, vol. 1: *Continental Plans for European Union 1939–1945* (Berlin, De Gruyter, 1985), pp. 274–5.
18 This term and idea was first proposed in J. Maritain, *Humanisme intégral: Problémes temporels et spirituels d'une nouvelle chrétienté* (Paris, Aubier, 1936).
19 Maritain, 'On Political Justice'.
20 C. Gaspar, *A Balança da Europa* (Lisbon, Alêtheia, 2017).
21 W. I. Hitchcock, *France Restored: Cold War Diplomacy and the Quest for Leadership in Europe, 1944–1954* (Chapel Hill, NC, University of North Carolina Press, 1998).

Gaulle's politics of intransigence towards Germany (1945–6) being the most prominent example. His government's foreign policy was based on the permanent division of Germany, with the separation of the Ruhr and the Saarland from the German state. Equally, the refusal of the German Social Democratic Party's Kurt Schumacher to accept the division of Germany was also based on traditional concepts of sovereignty. The resignation of General de Gaulle as premier of France's Fourth Republic in January 1946 enabled the emergence of a new French policy towards Germany and Europe. A coalition government between the socialists, Christian Democrats and communists was formed under socialist Prime Minister Léon Blum. Blum and the British Labour Prime Minister Clement Attlee agreed a new defence cooperation treaty, the Treaty of Dunkerque, that identified Germany as the main threat.

The Prague Coup of February 1948, which followed the announcement of the United States' containment policy in March 1947, triggered a change of dynamics in the American and British governments, who started pressing the French to accept the restoration of West Germany as an economically viable entity as part of the Marshall Plan. Communist movements were seen as an existential threat to democracies in western Europe. Their partial defeat at the ballot box – and the downfall of the tripartite governments in France and Italy in 1947–8 – was an essential condition for the rethinking of French policy towards Germany. This rethinking hinged on devising a pragmatic solution for the restoration of West Germany and the strengthening of the other western European states in order to resist Soviet expansionism.

The change of policy of the MRP (the French Christian Democratic party) regarding the restoration of and reconciliation with Germany in May 1948 also led the MRP to take a position on the European integration model. The search for a compromise between nationalist and Catholic ideas was clear in the MRP's foreign policy papers. Acknowledging the necessity to combine the restoration of national states (above all, Germany) with the pooling of supranational competences in the economic field in a European multilateral organisation, the MRP Congress stated that 'the future status of Europe is a truly democratic Germany [that] will only be attained within the framework of a federal Europe, which would preclude it being a cause or occasion of war'.[22] The MRP thus proposed the integration of key economic sectors supervised by supranational institutions – and rejected the purely intergovernmental institutions promoted by the United States, such as the Council of

---

22 MRP Foreign Policy Motion, 10 May 1948, cited in Lipgens and Loth (eds.), *Documents on the History of European Integration*, vol. III, p. 67.

Europe or the Organisation for European Economic Co-operation. French Christian Democrats also excluded Britain from plans for the institutional framing of Franco-German reconciliation.

During the negotiations on the Statutes of London in June 1948, French foreign policy reflected the MRP's U-turn regarding the restoration of Germany. After 'hesitating a long time', French Prime Minister Georges Bidault (of the MRP) accepted the Anglo-American proposal to restore German political and economic sovereignty, starting with the establishment of the Deutsche Mark. It then became imperative for the French elite to devise a formula for the integration of Germany into a new European system of states.

The Cold War and the Catholic Church's New Internationalism

The worsening of tensions between the Eastern and Western blocs in 1947–8 also prompted the Catholic Church and the Christian Democratic forces to adopt a position on the German question and the European system of states. The Vatican's new internationalism, initiated by Pope Pius XII in 1946, definitively broke with the Church's former alignment with nationalist and corporatist ideas, and the post-war Catholic political theology affirmed its affinity with the humanist values of political pluralism, laicism and human rights now depicted as laic translations of the Catholic conceptions of natural law.[23] The Church's new internationalism aimed for the formation of a pacifist and inclusive world order based on organic cooperation between states, in which 'Christ and his Church were the ultimate foundation and directing norm'.[24]

In early 1948, the Vatican abandoned its policy of neutrality and joined the Cold War on the side of President Truman's 'crusade' against the Soviet Union.[25] Pope Pius XII thus called for the urgent restoration of West Germany and the launch of a regional system of multilateral cooperation based on nation states. Containment of the Soviet threat became the Pope's paramount priority, thus prompting a realist turn. In 1948, Pope Pius XII pronounced that he was in favour of a defence alliance with the United

---

23 Pope Pius XII, speech made at the February 1946 consistory, quoted in Chamedes, *A Twentieth-Century Crusade*, 244, note 31.

24 Chamedes, *A Twentieth-Century Crusade*, p. 238.

25 P. Chenaux, *Une Europe vaticane?: Entre le Plan Marshall et les Traités de Rome* (Brussels, Éditions Ciaco, 1990), p. 32.

States and the creation of a broad coalition of the free world's moral and political forces in order to defeat atheistic communism. The Pope offered Christianity as a strengthening element for Western liberalism in the face of the religious aspects of the communist expansionist programme.

The Vatican's policy towards Europe also took a sharp turn. First, the Pope suspended the Church's 'just war' against nation states, which had developed from the criticisms of nationalism during the Second World War. Instead of the post-state federation proposed by progressive Catholics, the Pope adopted a realist acknowledgement that nation states were stepping-stones along the way to the unification of western Europe. Speaking to the European Federalist Movement in November 1948, Pius XII urged European states to organise a counter-offensive and strengthen the historical states of western Europe. To respond to Soviet aggression effectively, these would need 'to leave their grandeur behind and adopt a gradualist policy of cooperation that strengthens the western alliance'.[26] In his 1948 Christmas radio message, while rebuking the false pacifism of the Soviet Union, Pius XII emphasised the need to adopt a pragmatic plan for cooperation between European nations that would allow them to overcome a cycle of wars that would ultimately lead to the 'death of human civilization', and urged states to adopt a 'cooperative effort that would save individual states from the narrowness of a self-centred mentality'.[27]

As a replacement for post-state federalism, the Pope adopted a narrative centred on the idea of a return to a 'Carolingian Europe', where Christian faith and culture would be the glue binding together European states in a spirit of unity. This narrative also signified the Pope's support for the vision of a continental 'small Europe' and the final abandoning of plans for a pan-European or Atlantic European model. The Carolingian narrative represented the synthesis of nationalism and universalist ideas now being proposed by the Church. The Vatican's campaign to unify western European Christendom included mass events to celebrate the reopening of the ruined cathedrals of Cologne (August 1948) and Mainz (September 1948). In a potent symbol of the restoration of the continent's spiritual unity, the ecclesiastical hierarchy together with hundreds of thousands of the faithful joined in

---

26 Pope Pius XII, speech to the Delegates of the International Congress of the European Union of the Federalists, 11 November 1948, quoted in Chenaux, *Une Europe vaticane?*, p. 303.
27 Pope Pius XII, 'Radio Message of His Holiness Pope Pius XII, Christmas Eve, 1948', *The Irish Monthly* 77, no. 908 (1949): 75–80.

the celebrations for the rebuilding of the Christian tradition after its near annihilation in the wars.[28]

The Europeanist engagement of Christian Democrats also intensified. In March 1947, the first Christian Democratic conference in Switzerland addressed the objective of regrouping western Christianity against the communist threat. The creation of the Nouvelles Équipes Internationales (New International Teams, NEI) in June 1947, representing a gathering of western European Christian Democratic parties, was a direct response to the establishment of the Communist Information Bureau earlier in the same year.[29] The NEI's core mission was to defend the Christian values of western Europe through the integration of the re-established western European states into a system of regional multilateral cooperation. In the first cycle of the Geneva meetings between leading Christian Democratic parties (March 1948 to June 1949), Georges Bidault and Konrad Adenauer affirmed their clear agreement with the Pope's campaign for the unification of Europe under the banner of Catholic internationalism.[30]

The application of the new Catholic internationalism to European integration required an adaptation of its principles. The Church's evocation of the Carolingian Empire symbolised a combination of nationalist and universalist ethics. Instead of being based on a post-state and post-national federal order, Europe was to become a democratic and post-totalitarian version of the medieval Carolingian Empire. The unification of Europe would follow the example of the medieval supranational political, cultural and geographical space where Christian states and kings were bound by a common religious culture. Reference to the pre-modern Catholic West offered an answer to the problematic question of nationalism, not only for Germany, but for the whole of western Europe. In November 1948, Pope Pius XII evoked 'a time when Europe formed, in its unity, a compact and [. . .] it accomplished, in its union, great things', a time in which 'the soul of this unity was the religion that impregnated all society with the Christian faith'.[31] Reference to the Carolingian Empire inferred a double faithfulness – to national states and

28 Chenaux, *Une Europe vaticane?*, pp. 97–9.

29 W. Kaiser, *Christian Democracy and the Origins of European Union* (Cambridge, Cambridge University Press, 2007).

30 Secret conversation between Georges Bidault and Konrad Adenauer about the European Union in Geneva, minutes of the Geneva meetings held between 1948 and 1953, private papers of Robert Bichet, cited in Chenaux, *Une Europe vaticane?*, pp. 306–9.

31 Pope Pius XII, speech to the Delegates of the International Congress of the European Union of the Federalists, 11 November 1948, quoted in Chenaux, *Une Europe vaticane?*, p. 303.

to Christian universalism – as the solution for the European system of states. The Catholic formulation was thus critical to the emergence of a pragmatic solution to the question of how to unify European democratic national states.

Christian Democrat Adoption of the Catholic Narrative

French Prime Minister Bidault took advantage of the Vatican's narrative to legitimise his policy of realignment with Germany – a policy that implied acceptance both of Germany's restoration and of a limitation of France's sovereignty. Bidault referred to a fast and pragmatic action on European unity as being 'better than the best laid plans'.[32] Facing both opposition from the nationalist branch of his own party[33] and scepticism from his coalition partners in the Socialist Party, Bidault stated during a secret Geneva meeting with Konrad Adenauer on 22 December 1948 that 'the warm welcome given by the Holy See to this idea which should give substance to the forces of Christian civilisation in the world of the twentieth century' had convinced him that action must be taken.[34]

In the same meeting, Adenauer, the future West German Chancellor, made explicit that his plans for a European union were based on Christian Democratic principles, and warned that, if they failed, the socialist parties would take the lead in unifying Europe in 'another spirit'.[35] Adenauer also considered the plans for European unification to be integral to the strategy for the restoration of West Germany and its reorientation towards western Europe, stating that 'The CDU is in total agreement about the necessity of a European Union, whatever its form', for while it was natural that Germany would initially have 'fewer rights than the other countries, [. . .] the progressive evolution of things would lead to equality among countries'.[36] Adenauer's policy was clear: 'European federation is the only means to resolve the German problem, by bringing Germany into a European community that associates Germany peacefully with international cooperation, while immunising itself against its traditional temptations.'[37] However, like Bidault, Adenauer faced opposition from within and from outside his party regarding the sacrifices implied by this vision.

---

32 Secret conversation between Georges Bidault and Konrad Adenauer about the European Union in Geneva, minutes of the meeting of 22 December 1948, private papers of Robert Bichet, cited in Chenaux, *Une Europe vaticane?*, 306.

33 Jean Marie Mayeur, introduction to Chenaux, *Une Europe vaticane?*, p. 8.

34 Secret conversation between Georges Bidault and Konrad Adenauer about the European Union in Geneva, minutes of the meeting of 22 December 1948, private papers of Robert Bichet, cited in Chenaux, *Une Europe vaticane?*, p. 306.

35 Ibid., p. 307   36 Ibid., p. 307.   37 Ibid., p. 307.

Adenauer's acceptance of the double limitation of German sovereignty echoed the contributions of the German Protestant intellectual Karl Jaspers. In *The German Guilt* (1946), Jaspers shaped the Christian Democratic reckoning with the war and its horrors. According to Jaspers, German citizens, albeit bearing no individual guilt, nevertheless bore 'collective responsibility' and thus were obliged to repent and atone for German crimes against humanity.[38] National responsibility and atonement meant, in practical terms, the acceptance of Germany's division and its initially diminished sovereignty. Equally, the country was to play a constructive role in the rebuilding of the European order. The significance of Jaspers' contribution was in its use of secularised religious concepts of repentance and atonement as the basis for the legitimacy of Germany's rupture with its aggressive and expansionist nationalism and for its anchoring in the Western democratic and constitutional order.

Within the CDU, Adenauer faced resistance to this strategy on two fronts: the CDU's Catholic progressive faction resisted Anglo-American plans to divide Germany, argued for a cooperative attitude towards the Soviet Union and favoured a post-national federalism,[39] while its Protestant faction, led by Ludwig Erhard, maintained a nationalist/statist tradition and was sceptical about the supranational model. Outside the CDU, the *Westbindung* strategy based on the division of Germany was also condemned by the Social Democratic Party's leader, Kurt Schumacher. The push given by the Cold War for a convergence of Catholic, nationalist and liberal beliefs came to Adenauer's assistance. The future Chancellor's *Westbindung* strategy hinged on a solution that allowed the progressive restoration of West German sovereignty through integration in European and transatlantic institutions. The Catholic narrative was thus integral to the formulation of the German Christian Democrats' post-war European policy.

Other Christian Democratic leaders also adopted the Catholic Europeanist narrative and pushed it to the forefront of their fight against communism, while using it to legitimise plans to build European multilateral cooperation structures. The new synthesis was integrated in the new identities of Christian Democrats,[40] as reflected in the words of Italian Prime Minister Alcide De Gasperi: 'It is only if we can give this constructive and luminous

38 K. Jaspers, *Die Schuldfrage: Ein Beitrag zur deutschen Frage* (Zurich, Artemis-Verlag, 1946).
39 Walter Dirks, quoted in Chenaux, *Une Europe Vaticane?*, pp. 225–7.
40 S. N. Kalyvas and K. Van Kersbergen, 'Christian Democracy', *Annual Review of Political Science* 13 (2010): 183–209.

vision now that we will be able to attract the masses, inspire in them the necessary élan and win the spirits of the young generations of Europeans. The building of instruments and technical means and the administrative solutions are no doubt necessary [...] But are we not risking seeing them decompose if a vital breath does not enter into them to make them alive at the moment of their birth?'[41]

The synthesis of ideas underscoring Carolingian Europe was not only the blueprint for the particular method for unifying Europe adopted by the Schuman declaration of May 1950, but it also triggered the reformulation of nationalism, from a nationalism based on an aggressive and inimical attitude towards other nations to one that views neighbouring states as friendly entities with which the joint exercise of sovereignty is possible. In his 1948 Christmas message, Pope Pius XII urged Christians to refuse the 'aberrations of an intransigent nationalism which denies or spurns the common bonds linking the separate nations together' and urged instead 'imposing on each of them many and varied duties toward the great family of nations'.[42]

The Pope's intervention in the debate on the unity of Europe facilitated the conciliation between the functionalist plans of French social Christian Democrats and the post-state German federalists. The Catholic narrative was thus a common ground around which a compromise solution was found and a democratic and multilateral European post-war order was built. The role of the Church's new internationalism in producing this narrative suggests that there was a deeper reason for the crucial contribution of Christian Democrats to the re-establishment of the liberal order in post-war Europe. Rather than this contribution being based solely on their prominence in office, the Christian Democrats acted as trustees of the Christian narrative, reconciling nationalism with liberal democracy and multilateral cooperation. The Italian Christian Democratic leader, Alcide De Gasperi, stated that 'only the Catholic way of fraternity between the peoples can allow countries to support limitations of sovereignty in favour of an international society and in the name of peace'.[43] Working within and through the European supranational institutions, European statesmen accepted restraint in the exercise of sovereign rights.

41 Speech of President De Gasperi to the Consultative Assembly of the Council of Europe, 10 December 1951, quoted in Chenaux, *Une Europe vaticane?*, p. 308.
42 Pope Pius XII, 'Radio Message of His Holiness Pope Pius XII, Christmas Eve, 1948'.
43 Chenaux, *Une Europe vaticane?*, p. 307.

Consolidation of the New Synthesis as a Basis
for European Integration

Christian Democratic parties became the depositories of the Catholic narrative and its transformed nationalism, and Christian Democrats acted upon this new ideology by establishing and developing the new European supranational institutions. During the Cold War, Catholic double fidelity to the nation state and to Europe was consolidated into practice through the cooperation of states in the European Economic Communities. The establishment of the Common Market in 1957 was thus facilitated by the commitment of post-war politicians working within the ideological setting prepared in the late 1940s. This generation of Christian Democratic leaders served as the backbone to the efforts to establish the European Commission's authority in conflicts with traditional national-minded forces, such as those represented by French President Charles de Gaulle. De Gaulle's opposition to supranationalism led to several crises in the 1960s, culminating in the 'Empty Chair Crisis' of 1965.

Albeit diminished, the role of the Catholic Church during these decades continued to be relevant to the ideological legitimation of the European integration process. The major doctrinal updating that took place during the Second Vatican Council (1962–5) reinforced the ideological convergence between the Catholic Church and European institutions. Catholic political theology officially adopted liberal Catholicism's formula of a doctrinal *aggiornamento* (revision) with liberal democracy and human rights. On the basis of the Catholic understanding of religious freedom and the separation between the Church and the state, the new political theology also encouraged the participation of the Catholic laity in political life.[44]

Beginning in 1965, Pope Paul VI's strong links and ideological alignment with European Christian Democrats[45] and the Vatican's investment in relations with Brussels resulted in the establishment of informal meetings of the Episcopal Conferences of East and Western Europe. In 1971, these meetings were formalised as the Council of the Bishops' Conferences of Europe.

44 H. McLeod, *The Religious Crisis of the 1960s* (Oxford, Oxford University Press, 2013); L. Diotallevi, '1967/1969: The End, or (Just) a Pause of the Catholic Liberal Dream?', *Religions* 11, no. 11 (2020), unpaginated, www.mdpi.com/2077-1444/11/11/623.
45 B. Chelini-Pont, 'Papal Thought on Europe and the European Union in the Twentieth Century', *Religion, State and Society* 37, no. 1–2 (2009): 131–46; A. O'Mahony, 'The Vatican and Europe: Political Theology and Ecclesiology in Papal Statements from Pius XII to Benedict XVI', *International Journal for the Study of the Christian Church* 9, no. 3 (2009): 177–94.

In 1970, the Holy See appointed an Apostolic Nuncio to Brussels especially assigned to the European Communities, and in 1979, it established the Commission of the Bishops' Conferences of the European Union, which was aimed at exchanging information with the institutions of the European Communities.

During the 1960s and 1970s, the increased ideological convergence between the Church and the European Communities resulted in the mutual legitimation and reinforcement of the two institutions. The Church's commitment to integral human development and protection of human dignity was mirrored in the language of the European Commission and the Council documents.[46] This alignment temporarily obscured the significance of the Church's declining societal influence after the revolutionary events that took place in France in May 1968.[47]

From the mid 1960s, despite Catholicism's diminished influence within European Christian Democratic movements, and despite the centre-right no longer being dominated by Christian Democrats, the Catholic narrative remained a core feature of the generation of leaders building the new European institutions. In Germany, the increased standing of the CDU's Protestant Atlanticists from 1963 onwards triggered heated debates with the Catholic Europeanists. Debate ensued, for example, over enlargement of the European Communities to the mainly Protestant countries of Denmark, Great Britain and Norway.[48] The victory of the Atlanticists resulted in the northern enlargement of 1973, which brought, for the first time, countries that were neither Catholic (Britain and Denmark) nor had traditional Christian Democratic parties (Britain, Denmark and Ireland) into the European Communities. Nevertheless, the creation of the European People's Party (EPP) in the run up to the first direct elections to the European Parliament in 1979 consolidated the narrative based on post-war Catholic political theology. Despite including Protestant, liberal and conservative parties, the EPP adopted as its core ideology the post-war narrative forged by the Catholic Church.[49]

In the late 1970s, signs of tensions between the now established 'community spirit and method' and more conventional national-interest visions

46 P. Kratochvíl and T. Dolezal, *The European Union and the Catholic Church: Political Theology of European Integration* (London, Palgrave MacMillan, 2017).
47 O. Roy, *Is Europe Christian?*, trans. C. Schoch (Oxford, Oxford University Press, 2020).
48 J. Hien and F. Wolkenstein, 'Where Does Europe End? Christian Democracy and the Expansion of Europe', *Journal of Common Market Studies* 59, no. 6 (2021): 1623–39.
49 Kalyvas and Van Kersbergen, 'Christian Democracy'; Van Hecke and Gerard (eds.), *Christian Democratic Parties in Europe*.

became increasingly evident. Margaret Thatcher's taking office in 1979 resulted in an assertive defence of British national interests in the context of the European Community budget negotiations. This provided evidence in support of those who had predicted that enlarging the Communities beyond their Catholic core would result in a watering down of their original model. Thatcher's prioritisation of British national interests over the adoption of a common approach to European problems departed from the Christian Democrats' proclamation of 'community spirit' and their belief that negotiation should be based on the notion that national interests could naturally be articulated with those of other nations.[50]

The End of the Cold War and the Decline and Death of the Catholic Narrative

With the end of the Cold War, the Catholic narrative lost its pivotal position as the ideological underpinning of the continental European political system, and this gave way to a reassessment of the relationship between nationalism, Christianity and liberal democracy. European leaders – including Christian Democratic leaders – progressively dropped the Christian West narrative as an instrument for legitimating political choices. A decade after the fall of the Soviet Union, the European national states' foreign policies presented an increased autonomy from the constraints and burdens that European integration had previously imposed on national policy choices. Such autonomy – especially of the increasingly hegemonic Germany – led to a diminished capacity of the European institutions to solve collective problems. The unravelling of the ideological underpinnings of European integration, intimately bound to individual states' changing understandings of their own national interests, could be felt in the successive crises that afflicted Europe during the 2005–15 period.

However, the Catholic narrative did not die without a fight. Emboldened by the defeat of communism, Pope John Paul II developed the narrative of a united and expanding Christian Europe and offered a new impetus to the pan-European unification of Christianity on the basis of an ecumenical dialogue with other Christian churches, in particular the Orthodox churches of eastern Europe. Subsequently, Pope Benedict XVI intervened in debates on the drafting of the European Constitution in an attempt to reinstate the

---

50 For the concept of extroverted nationalism, see M. Meyer Resende, *Catholicism and Nationalism: Changing Nature of Party Politics* (London, Routledge, 2015).

model of Carolingian Europe centred on western Europe's Catholic states. Benedict's grand European narrative was the most compelling account of the specific origins of Christianity as the basis for liberal democracy and Western civilisation. His assertion that Christian theology is central to western European political identity was, however, not recognised by the European Constitution's drafters, who preferred a secularist preamble to the Constitution. This refusal sealed the death of the Catholic narrative, in a sequence of events described in more detail below.

Pope John Paul II's Call for the Deepening and Widening of Europe

The Vatican viewed the end of the division of Europe after the collapse of communism in 1989 as an opportunity for the revival of Christian identity and the unification of its eastern and western parts. Pope John Paul II launched a campaign for the enlargement of the European Union to central and eastern Europe, inspired by the vision of a reunified Christian Europe. In his first Apostolic visit to Poland in 1979, John Paul II established the unification of Europe as the main mission of his papacy: 'Does Christ not want [the unity of Europe]? Does the Holy Spirit not order so? That through this Polish Pope, the Slavic Pope, the spiritual unity of a Christian Europe is demonstrated, constituted by two great traditions, the Eastern and the Western?'[51] Europe would only be complete when the West and the East, the 'two lungs through which it should breathe', were united.[52]

In the mid 1980s, the hope of political change in central and eastern Europe brought by perestroika reinvigorated the Pope's determination to campaign for European reunification.[53] While supporting the opposition Solidarity movement in Poland, the Pope named Saints Cyril and Methodius – symbols of the Christianisation of the Slavs – as patron saints of Europe in 1984. Immediately after the 1989 revolutions, the Pope involved the European episcopates in efforts aiming for the integration into the European family of the central and eastern European Christian nations that had been victims of totalitarianism. Mirroring the Vatican's post-Second World War

---

51 Pope John Paul II, Homily at the Mass at Cathedral of Gniezno, Apostolic Visit to Poland (1979), www.vatican.va/content/john-paul-ii/en/homilies/1979/documents/hf_jp-ii_hom_19790603_polonia-gniezno-cattedrale.html.

52 Pope John Paul II, 'Messa per i fedeli della Provincia Ecclesiastica di Praga' (1990), www.vatican.va/content/john-paul-ii/it/homilies/1990/documents/hf_jp-ii_hom_19900421_praga.html.

53 S. Gregg, *Challenging the Modern World: Karol Wojtyla/John Paul II and the Development of Catholic Social Teaching* (Lanham, MD, Lexington Books, 2002), p. 202.

initiatives, John Paul II convoked two Synods of European Bishops, in 1991 and 1999, to prepare the celebration of the Church's millennium and to launch a wider integration of Europe stretching 'from the Atlantic to the Urals'.[54] The first Synod (sometimes referred to as 'the Church's Maastricht') included, for the first time, representatives from the Orthodox Church and other major Christian communities from central Europe. John Paul II stated that the Synod was 'ultimately motivated by the fact that, by the end of the second Millennium, Christianity emerges divided, but longing for a new unity'.[55] The Vatican considered the evangelisation of the east and the enlargement of the European Union as complementary goals: 'The nations are all founded on their Christian heritage, symbolized by their baptism.'[56] Jean Marie Lustiger, Cardinal of Paris and a close associate of John Paul II, evoked the 'cultural, spiritual and moral dimension' of the Catholic vision for the continent's unification.[57]

John Paul II also warned about the dangers associated with the resurgence of nationalism. Aware that in central and eastern Europe an entrenched and unreformed tradition of introverted and ethnic nationalism resulted in resistance to the European Union's supranationalism, the Pope called for the reconciliation of a nation's interests with those of its neighbours: 'On the one hand, national differences should be maintained as a basis for European solidarity, on the other hand, national identity can only be realized through openness to other nations and solidarity with them.'[58] The Pope promoted a concept of European unity based on the notion of a community of European nations, and pointed to the concept's dual identification with Christianity's universalism and with the reality of nation states: 'European integration should not lead to the levelling of states, but rather should result in the maintenance of the rights and duties of each people, in respect of its sovereignty [...] The rights of nations go hand-in-hand with the rights of man.'[59]

54 L. Salin, *Vers une Europe vaticane?: L'influence du Saint-Siège sur l'élargissement de l'Union européenne* (Paris, L'Harmattan, 2005).
55 Pope John Paul II, 'Discorso di Giovanni Paolo II alla conclusione dei lavori dell'Assemblea Speciale per l'Europa del Sinodo dei Vescovi' (1991), www.vatican.va/content/john-paul-ii /it/speeches/1991/december/documents/hf_jp-ii_spe_19911213_lavori-sinodo.html.
56 Pope John Paul II, *Post-Synodal Apostolic Exhortation, Ecclesia in Europa, of His Holiness Pope John Paul II to the Bishops, Men and Women in the Consecrated Life and All the Lay Faithful on Jesus Christ Alive in His Church the Source of Hope for Europe* (Vatican, Libreria Editrice Vaticana, 2003).
57 J.-M. Lustiger, *Nous avons rendez-vous avec l'Europe* (Paris, Mame Éditions, 1991).
58 Pope John Paul II, *Post-Synodal Apostolic Exhortation, Ecclesia in Europa.*
59 L. Salin, *Vers une Europe vaticane?*, p. 52.

European Union Legitimacy Crisis and Constitutional Debate

A decade after the end of the Cold War, it was increasingly evident that an existential questioning of the nature, borders and future of the European Union had emerged, despite the Vatican's best efforts. In the following years, successive crises concerning transatlantic relations and the European Constitution suggested that a structural change was under way in the foundations of European integration. The demise of the consensus on the compromise between federalism and nation-states led to a debate concerning the foundations of integration. In this ideological and political vacuum, and emboldened by the victory of liberalism, the federalist forces grew in ambition. The questioning of the European Union's legitimacy resulted in a formal debate on the finality of the Union and reopened the treaty revision process.[60]

A new federalist challenge was brought into the public arena by the German Foreign Minister Joschka Fischer in a speech at the Humboldt University, which called for the federalisation of the European institutions and the adoption of a European Constitution. In Habermasian fashion, Fischer called for the replacement of the system of states,[61] promising that European integration would allow the peoples of continental Europe to abandon national identities and adopt a post-national 'constitutional patriotism'.[62] Resistance to post-national German federalism came foremost from the French elite. President Jacques Chirac and Prime Minister Lionel Jospin adopted a 'federation of nation-states' formula,[63] thus defending nation states as the constituent elements of the integration process.[64]

This debate eventually evolved into a formal process – the Convention on the Future of Europe – tasked with drafting a European Constitution. During the convention, several narratives on integration were deployed as legitimation strategies for the various proposals made regarding the European

---

60 A. Follesdal and S. Hix, 'Why There Is a Democratic Deficit in the EU: A Response to Majone and Moravcsik', *Journal of Common Market Studies* 44, no. 3 (2006): 533–62.

61 J. Habermas, *The Postnational Constellation: Political Essays* (Cambridge, MA, Polity Press, 1998).

62 J. Habermas, 'Citizenship and National Identity: Some Reflections on the Future of Europe', *Praxis International* 12, no. 1 (1992): 1–19.

63 J. Delors, 'Ma vision d'une Fédération des États-nations', *Le Monde des Débats* July–August (2000): 5–6, https://institutdelors.eu/wp-content/uploads/2021/05/article-federation-etats-nations-monde-debat-2000.pdf.

64 Speech by Jacques Chirac, President of the French Republic, to the Bundestag on 27 June 2000, in Dehousse (ed.), *Une constitution pour l'Europe?* (Paris, Presses de Sciences Po, 2002), pp. 245–52; speech by Prime Minister Lionel Jospin on 'The Future of an Enlarged Europe' on 28 May 2001, in Dehousse (ed.), *Une constitution pour l'Europe?*, pp. 253–66.

political regime.[65] While the federalists' narrative drew on a Habermasian post-foundational moral contractualism, the Catholic narrative sustained the original compromise between nation states and supranational institutions.

Federalists portrayed the constitution drafting exercise at the Convention as an example of an 'inter-subjective process of deliberative communication'[66] among the citizens of Europe, which, they claimed, fostered a sense of belonging and dispensed with a value-based community as the basis of a political entity. The drafting process – leading to the creation of a new legal instrument personifying the norms and values of Europeans – was deemed to be an example of such moral contractualism.[67] Federalists thus argued that the process was a sufficient basis of legitimacy for the emerging constitutional order.

Christian and religious-friendly intellectuals challenged the federalists and contested their assumption that moral contractualism was an adequate replacement for an existing value-based community.[68] The moral identity of Europe, based on the historical Christian identity of the continent, was the only 'value-based community' capable of legitimating the European political community.[69] These intellectuals and prelates maintained that the Christian spiritual tradition was the foundation of the Western political regime. Only the recognition of the Christian tradition could serve as an antidote against the degeneration of Europe caused by the 'distorting effect of communal governance, the de-personalisation of the market and the commercialisation of values'.[70] Thus, to build an ethical community, Europe should not suppress its Christian heritage, but rather make use of it.

Within this tradition, Cardinal Joseph Ratzinger's and later Pope Benedict XVI's rebuttal of the secularist and post-foundational thesis was the most fundamental attempt to reinstate the Catholic narrative and the post-war synthesis of Catholic, nationalist and liberal ideas. Through his historical, theological and philosophical essays on the basis of European unity, Cardinal Ratzinger made the most explicit connection between Christianity and the modern identity of Europe. His reinstatement of the Carolingian Empire as

65 A. Kutter, *Legitimation in the European Union: A Discourse and Field-Theoretical View* (London, Palgrave Macmillan, 2021), pp. 261–77.

66 Habermas, *The Postnational Constellation*; J.-M. Ferry, *Europe, la voie kantienne: Essai sur l'identité postnationale* (Paris, Éditions du Cerf, 2006).

67 Kutter, *Legitimation in the European Union*, p. 277.

68 L. Siedentop, *Democracy in Europe* (New York, NY, Columbia University Press, 2011); J. Weiler, F. Reimer and E.-W. Böckenförde, *Ein christliches Europa: Erkundungsgänge* (Salzburg, Verlag Anton Pustet, 2004); J. H. Weiler, 'A Christian Europe? Europe and Christianity: Rules of Commitment', *European View* 6, no. 1 (2007): 143–50.

69 Siedentop, *Democracy in Europe*.   70 Weiler et al., *Ein christliches Europa*.

the model for post-war Europe not only reiterated the Church's double fidelity to nation-states and to universalism, but also affirmed the essential nature of the link between European religious identity and the liberal democratic Western tradition.

Ratzinger's plotting of European history quoted Oswald Spengler and Arnold Toynbee's natural law of cultures[71] and presented a sequence of Europe's birth, growth, decline and death in close association with the development of Christianity. The foundation of Europe as a political identity was defined by its origin in the Carolingian Empire. Modern Europe's foundations were in 'a theology of history' and resulted from a willingness 'to express an awareness of both the continuity and the novelty of this new aggregate of states', while this 'emerging sense of self-consciousness expressed an awareness of finality and of mission'.[72] The Carolingian Empire, as the heir of the Roman Empire, not only manifested its Christian identity, but also inherited its system of separation of the spiritual and temporal orders, 'the foundations for what is specifically typical of the Western world'.[73] Christianity's elective affinity with liberal democracy was thus presented as the essential matrix of western European identity. According to Ratzinger, liberal values, despite being universal in nature, are also specifically European.[74]

While saluting the European Constitution's recognition of human rights as pre-constitutive elements of the European political tradition,[75] Ratzinger argued that these cannot be properly understood apart from the Christian tradition: 'The value, dignity, freedom, equality and solidarity of man in the basic affirmations of democracy and rule of law implies an image of man, a moral option and an idea of law, all of which are by no means obvious.' Therefore, the recognition of the divine origin of these ideas through revelation is the very 'constituent spiritual force' of Europe.[76] Christianity's contribution to forging the universal values that constitute European identity means that the religion has a 'role that is not only historical, but also foundational in relation to Europe'.[77]

---

71 A. Toynbee, *A Study of History* (Oxford, Oxford University Press, 1955); O. Spengler, *The Decline of the West* (New York, NY, Alfred A. Knopf, 1973).

72 J. Ratzinger, 'Europe: Its Spiritual Foundation: Yesterday, Today and in the Future', *Inside the Vatican* June–July (2004): 44–51.

73 Ibid.

74 Ibid.; L. Siedentop, *Inventing the Individual: The Origins of Western Liberalism* (Harmondsworth, Penguin Books, 2015).

75 Ratzinger, 'Europe: Its Spiritual Foundation'.   76 Ibid.

77 Pope Benedict XVI, 'Address of His Holiness Benedict XVI to the Participants in the Convention Organized by the Commission of the Bishops' Conferences of the

Finally, Ratzinger's narrative attributes the death of European civilisation and the crisis of the West to the victory of the secularist demand for a strict separation between the political and the religious. The 'emergence of a completely secular or non-denominational state, which abandoned and set aside the divine warranty and divine regulation of the political element'[78] pairs with the European Constitution drafters' rejection of the recognition of Europe's Christian roots in the preamble to the constitution. Pope Benedict took this ultimate refusal as confirmation of the estrangement of the Church. At the fiftieth anniversary of the Treaty of Rome in 2007, the Pope spoke of Europe's strange 'self-hate'[79] and accused it of being an 'apostasy from itself, even before [being an apostate] from God', to the point of 'doubting its very identity'.[80]

The rejection of the European Constitution in the French and Dutch referenda (in May and June 2005, respectively) demonstrated the limits of the European integration process and confirmed that the moderate approach based on nation-states devised in the late 1940s could not be overcome. The sovereign debt crisis (2009–15) further demonstrated that European states – and Germany in particular – were unwilling to go beyond the status quo and take on additional responsibilities for resolving the financial crisis.[81]

Reconfiguration of the Catholic Narrative: Appropriation of Christianity by the Radical Right

The demise of the Catholic narrative opened the way for the nationalist radical right's appropriation of Christianity and for the radical reconfiguration of the post-war synthesis of nationalism and Christianity. The radical right's narrative on the Christian West not only purged the religious-inspired universalism of Christianity, but also set it in opposition to liberal democracy. This section outlines the key steps in the articulation of a sectarian nationalism, a process initiated in central and eastern Europe, where a tradition of ethnic and introverted nationalism that sees other

European Community (COMECE)' (2007), www.vatican.va/content/benedict-xvi/en/speeches/2007/march/documents/hf_ben-xvi_spe_20070324_comece.html.

78 Ratzinger, 'Europe: Its Spiritual Foundation'.

79 Pope Benedict XVI, *Europe Today and Tomorrow: Addressing the Fundamental Issues* (San Francisco, CA, Ignatius Press, 2007).

80 Pope Benedict XVI, 'Address to the Participants in the Congress'.

81 Gaspar, *A balança da Europa*, p. 173.

nations as natural enemies[82] continues to shape national and societal attitudes,[83] and where the conflation of religion and national identity has high societal acceptance.[84] Using the backdrop of the refugee crisis (2014–16), the nationalist right used Christianity – transformed into a cultural marker and a criterion of exclusion – to strengthen its nationalist core. From Viktor Orbán to Matteo Salvini, the new nationalists portrayed themselves as the saviours of Christian European civilisation from Islamic invaders.

The arrival of hundreds of thousands of refugees from Islamic countries via the Mediterranean, coinciding with a wave of terrorist attacks across Europe, facilitated the subjugation of Christian universalism to nationalism and the use of the Christian narrative in support of an autocratic and anti-European agenda. Hungarian Prime Minister Viktor Orbán, borrowing heavily from the historical conflation evident in the nationalistic Catholicism of neighbouring Poland, articulated the narrative that Christian Europe and the Hungarian nation were threatened by an Islamic invasion aiming at the destruction of its soul. The European Union, in particular the European Commission's proposal regarding a system for the distribution of asylum seekers and refugees, was invoked by Orbán as constituting part of the threat to a vulnerable Christian Europe.[85]

In Orbán's narrative, the Christian element was de-sacralised and instrumentalised into an identitarian marker, losing its role as a source of social norms. According to Orbán, we cannot 'let masses of people from different religious backgrounds – who have been raised with different morals and different traditions, and who have no idea about Europe – come and teach us a lesson'.[86] Most notably, the post-war *aggiornamento* of Catholicism with democracy was ignored. Identitarian Christianity was used to legitimate the autocratic practices of the ruling Polish and Hungarian governments. At the

---

82 P. F. Sugar, *East European Nationalism, Politics and Religion* (Farnham, Ashgate, 1999); H. Kohn, *The Idea of Nationalism: A Study of Its Origins and Background* (London, Macmillan, 1955).
83 Pew Research Center, 'In EU, There's an East–West Divide over Religious Minorities, Gay Marriage, National Identity' (2017), www.pewresearch.org/fact-tank/2018/10/29/east-west-divide-within-the-eu-on-issues-including-minorities-gay-marriage-and-national-identity.
84 Pew Research Center, *Many Central and Eastern Europeans See Link between Religion and National Identity* (2017), www.pewresearch.org/fact-tank/2017/11/03/many-central-and-eastern-europeans-see-link-between-religion-and-national-identity.
85 R. Sata, 'Hijacking Religion for the Sake of the Nation: Illiberal Democracy in Hungary', in A. Hennig and M. Weinberg-Salzmann (eds.), *Illiberal Politics and Religion in Europe and Beyond: Concepts, Actors, Processes* (Frankfurt am Main, Campus, 2021), pp. 141–51.
86 Speech by Viktor Orbán, quoted in Sata, 'Hijacking Religion for the Sake of the Nation', p. 147.

core of the attack on liberal democracy was the radical right's replacement of a pluralist political community with an ascribed religious and ethnic nation as the basis of the political regime. As the self-identified defenders of the nation, the Polish and Hungarian leaders claimed to be the legitimate translators of the national interest, thus dispensing with traditional democratic balance-of-power mechanisms.

The explicit charting of the new nationalism's defensive nature was most effectively outlined by Donald Trump in his Warsaw speech of June 2017. Condensing a description of Poland's history of suffering and using the narrative of Polish resistance as an example of an attitude that all Western forces should emulate, Trump forcefully promoted the idea that each nation is permanently in existential danger and at risk of annihilation by its neighbours, by communism or by Islam. Simultaneously, Trump used the Polish national myth as the bulwark of Latin Christianity to elevate defensive nationalism to the guardianship of Western civilisation. While appropriating Pope Benedict XVI's conflation of liberal values and Christianity, Trump discarded these values (which had previously been the basis for universal solidarity) and used Christian civilisation to explicitly oppose enemy civilisations and, above all, Islam. In Trump's Warsaw speech, Christianity represents a call to arms: 'Our citizens did not win freedom together, did not survive horrors together, did not face down evil together, only to lose our freedom to a lack of pride and confidence in our values. We did not and we will not. We will never back down.'[87]

The Catholic Church was deeply divided by the appropriation of Catholicism by the nationalist right.[88] From 2015, Pope Francis campaigned to neutralise nationalistic Catholicism through a defence of human rights and more specifically of refugee rights. The intervention to discipline the anti-refugee Catholic clergy culminated in a visit to Poland in July 2016 and to the Mexican–US border in February 2016. During both visits, the Pope condemned restrictive refugee policies and preached Christian universalist solidarity. Pope Francis upheld the duty of the Church to maintain a 'spirit of readiness to welcome those fleeing from wars and hunger, and solidarity with those deprived of their fundamental rights'.[89]

87 D. Trump, 'Remarks by President Trump to the People of Poland' (2017), https://trump whitehouse.archives.gov/briefings-statements/remarks-president-trump-people-poland.

88 M. Meyer Resende and A. Hennig, 'Polish Catholic Bishops, Nationalism and Liberal Democracy', *Religions* 12, no. 2 (2021), unpaginated, www.mdpi.com/2077-1444/12/2/94.

89 J. Luxmoore, 'Eastern Europe's Church Leaders Face Growing Criticism over Refugees', *National Catholic Reporter*, 3 September 2017.

Conclusion

This chapter has traced the emergence, development, death and reconfiguration of the Catholic narrative of European integration. On the basis of Paul Ricœur's view of narratives as devices for the creation of new constellations of ideas, it establishes the Vatican's role in formulating a new synthesis of nationalist, Christian and liberal ideas that served to overcome the security dilemma posed by Germany in the post-war period and to find a compromise between European post-state federalism and a mere restoration of the system of nation-states. At the outset of the Cold War, the Church modified its new internationalism and invested in the legitimation of an emerging model for Europe's system of states.

This chapter has thus added to the literature on the centrality of Christian Democracy in the process of European integration by pointing to a deeper reason for its prominence. Rather than resulting merely from the prominence of Christian Democrats in the founding member states' governments, the importance of Christianity in shaping the post-war system of states was due to its role in reconciling nationalism with liberal democracy and multilateral cooperation. The Christian narrative emerges as a crucial legitimating device for the institutional consolidation of European integration during the Cold War.

With the end of the Cold War, and despite the best efforts of Popes John Paul II and Benedict XVI, the narrative's power diminished, and the refusal to include Christianity as one of the sources of European unity by the European Constitution's drafters marked its final demise. The loss of the post-war constellation of nationalist, Christian and liberal ideas underpinning European integration enabled an increased autonomy of nation-states from the European 'community spirit' and facilitated the succession of crises that came to batter relations between European states. The nationalist right used these crises to reconfigure the narrative into a form of sectarian nationalism opposing both liberal democracy and European integration.

Recommended Reading

Chamedes, G. *A Twentieth-Century Crusade: The Vatican's Battle to Remake Christian Europe* (Cambridge, MA, Harvard University Press, 2019).

Chenaux, P. *Une Europe Vaticane?: Entre le Plan Marshall et les Traités de Rome* (Brussels, Éditions Ciaco, 1990).

Forlenza, R. 'The Politics of the *Abendland*: Christian Democracy and the Idea of Europe after the Second World War', *Contemporary European History* 26, no. 2 (2017): 261–86.

Gehler, M. and W. Kaiser. *Christian Democracy in Europe since 1945*, vol. II (London, Routledge, 2004).

Ratzinger, J. 'Europe: Its Spiritual Foundation: Yesterday, Today and in the Future', *Inside the Vatican* June–July (2004): 44–51.

Salin, L. *Vers une Europe vaticane?: L'influence du Saint-Siège sur l'élargissement de l'Union européenne* (Paris, L'Harmattan, 2005).

26

European Integration and the Churches

SERGEI A. MUDROV

Introduction

The principal theories of European integration (neo-functionalism, intergovernmentalism and social constructivism) have been rather silent about the presence and role of the religious factor in the process of unification of Europe. Such an approach, based on a certain underestimation of religion, seems to be unjustifiable nowadays, since it has become evident that the religious component of European integration appears in various forms and formats. For instance, some Protestants regard this integration as a religious 'plot', usually of the Roman Catholic Church, aiming at the construction of a new European Catholic empire and the undermining of Protestantism.[1] It is therefore not surprising to encounter an opinion that the integration was 'sanctioned by the Vatican',[2] while the Vatican (and the Catholic Church more broadly) were closely connected with the Christian Democratic parties in western Europe. Furthermore, from the perspectives of certain religious groups, the European Union (EU) has been seen as 'playing a destructive role in an imminent global apocalypse'.[3]

The Catholic 'plot' and similar deliberations have constituted only a small part of the European religious story. Religion also appears in the life of the EU from a different angle. We could recount, for example, the reasoning against the accession of Turkey to the Union. Indeed, one of the arguments was

---

This chapter relies on my previous publications, particularly the monograph *Christian Churches in European Integration* (Abingdon and New York, NY, Routledge, 2016).

1 A. Noble, 'The Conspiracy behind the European Union: What Every Christian Should Know' (1998), www.contreculture.org/Blog de Ian Paisley.html.

2 J. Casanova, 'Religion, European Secular Identities, and European Integration', in T. A. Byrnes and P. J. Katzenstein (eds.), *Religion in an Expanding Europe* (Cambridge, Cambridge University Press, 2006), pp. 65–92, 66.

3 B. F. Nelsen and J. L. Guth, 'European Union or Kingdom of the Antichrist? Protestant Apocalyptic Narratives and European Unity', *National Identities* 19, no. 2 (2017): 251–67, 252.

explicitly religious: the membership of Turkey in the EU was regarded as undesirable, because this large Muslim country professes a religion alien to the Union, considered by some to be a 'Christian club'.[4] Also the religious dimension was one of the most controversial and fiercely debated issues at the time of the drafting of the European Constitution, namely the inclusion in the text of the reference to the Christian inheritance of Europe, or the reference to God. Furthermore, religious or religion-related arguments played an important role in the debates on the EU membership of the largest 'newcomer' of the 2004 enlargement, namely Poland, and in the discussion in Ireland on the referendums on the Lisbon Treaty in 2008 and 2009.[5] Indeed, in Poland some members of the Catholic Church's hierarchy presented the integration of Europe as a 'wonderful chance, difficult challenge and great apostolic task for the Church to achieve'. On the other hand, the integration process was depicted as 'attempts to de-Christianize and to divest Poles of their national character'. For example, 'one of the best known Polish priests' emphasised that 'making so-called Europeans of us means to create an enigmatic collection of individuals subordinated to bureaucratic decisions made by commissaries of the United Europe in Brussels, and to achieve the goal the communists wanted to achieve for 44 years'.[6] In the Republic of Ireland, the hierarchy of the Catholic Church was publicly more in favour of the ratification of the Treaty of Lisbon, whereas some representatives of the Catholic Church, organised in the civil society organization Coir, took the opposite stance. Crucially, Coir's Eurosceptic arguments were explicitly religious, with the intention of defending traditional Christian values, including the rights of unborn children, which, in their view, were threatened by the provisions of the Lisbon Treaty.[7]

4 B. F. Nelsen, 'Europe as a Christian Club: Religion and the Founding of the European Community, 1950–1975. The Ideological Dimension', www.researchgate.net/publica tion/228359486_Europe_as_a_Christian_Club_Religion_and_the_Founding_of_the_E uropean_Community_1950-1975_The_Ideological_Dimension.

5 S. Burdzej, 'Religion and Politics: Religious Values in the Polish Public Square since 1989', *Religion, State and Society* 33, no. 2 (2005): 165–74; D. Dinan, 'Institutions and Governance: Saving the Lisbon Treaty – An Irish Solution to a European Problem', *Journal of Common Market Studies* 47, Suppl. s1 (2009): 113–32; J. O'Brennan, 'Ireland Says No (Again): The 12 June 2008 Referendum on the Lisbon Treaty', *Parliamentary Affairs* 62, no. 2 (2009): 258–77.

6 P. Załęcki, 'Polish Roman Catholic Church and European Union. Selected Cultural Issues' (1999), https://repozytorium.umk.pl/bitstream/handle/item/1651/PZ7_Polish %20Roman%20Catholic%20Church%20and%20European%20Union_www.pdf? sequence=1.

7 'Irish Voters Reject EU Treaty', *The Guardian*, 13 June 2008, www.theguardian.com/w orld/2008/jun/13/ireland; 'Coir Anti-treaty Posters "Trade on People's Fears"', *Irish Examiner*, 1 September 2009, www.irishexaminer.com/news/arid-20099927.html.

The European Parliament adopted some resolutions which referred to Churches directly, requiring, for instance, that women be granted access to Mount Athos – an autonomous monastic territory in Greece, which women have been prohibited from entering, in accordance with Athonite tradition, for about 1,000 years.[8] Finally, the importance of religion has been confirmed in the referendums on EU membership, including the 2016 'Brexit' referendum in the UK. According to Kolpinskaya and Fox, in the UK non-religious individuals 'tend to be more supportive of EU membership and integration than religious respondents', and the vote at the referendum was defined, inter alia, by belonging to a particular religious denomination (i.e., 59.5 per cent of Anglicans voted to leave the EU, while for Catholics 47.6 per cent did so).[9] As Zsolt Enyedi claims, national identity in Europe 'is often built around religious values and is linked to Church-state regimes'.[10] It is therefore pertinent to claim that the presence of religion, or, to be more precise, Christian Churches, in the process of European integration is not disputable; we can only discuss how this presence has been seen, analysed and interpreted. This will be addressed in this chapter, in accordance with the following structure. First I shall discuss how the role of Churches in European integration has been described in the relevant literature. Then I shall analyse the role of Churches at the beginning of integration, in terms of their role as non-state actors and identity formers, as well as the Churches' influence and their presence at the supranational level. The final pages of this chapter will be devoted to discussion of the practical cooperation of the Churches and EU institutions.

The Role of Churches: The Main Approaches

Although the number of publications on the role of Churches in European integration is growing, there is hardly an identifiable pattern of agreement among scholars in this field. We instead encounter some contradictory approaches, forming polar perspectives. This polarity is normally confined to the following sets of positions.

---

8 European Parliament, 'European Parliament Resolution on the Situation Concerning Basic Rights in the European Union (2001) (2001/2014(INI))', 15 January 2003.
9 E. Kolpinskaya and S. Fox, 'Praying on Brexit? Unpicking the Effect of Religion on Support for European Union Integration and Membership', *Journal of Common Market Studies* 57, no. 3 (2019): 580–98.
10 Z. Enyedi, 'Conclusion: Emerging Issues in the Study of Church–State Relations', *West European Politics* 26, no. 1 (2003): 218–32, 223.

On the one hand, Christian Churches (or religion in general) are at times assigned a rather limited role, with emphasis on the claim that the impact of religion in Europe 'does not change the usual rules of the game'.[11] It is argued by the proponents of this approach that the Churches' role has become more noticed mainly due to the EU's initiatives, since the Union has sought new methods and means for its legitimisation. These means and methods embrace attempts to put citizens at the centre of the decision-making process and to improve the dialogue with civil society, including Churches. François Foret assumes that 'the European Commission proposes a strictly consultative role for churches', which allegedly does not equip them with a realistic chance to influence decision-making processes.[12] Foret's perspective is partly echoed by Martin Steven, who insists that the EU is 'an inherently secular body with no mention of Christianity in any of its other treaties or directives'.[13] At the same time, in his theorising Steven does not substantially develop his idea of the constrained role of Churches in the EU. He admits that they act, first, within some dimensions of the Church–state relations, exercising their influence on voting behaviour and European values, and, secondly, as 'political interest groups, lobbying decision-makers on aspects of social policymaking which concern them'.[14] Benoît Challand, taking a legalistic approach, identifies the presence of religion in the EU legislation as very limited and argues that 'the collocation of Europe and religion is only a very recent construction'.[15] Furthermore, in his view, even if the interest of the EU in religion has been increasing, this has happened for purely pragmatic reasons, such as the desire to separate the Union from its Islamic neighbours.[16]

However, the presence of religion in EU legislation does not always need to come in obvious and explicit forms. Keith Jenkins specifies that EU secondary legislation 'directly refers to and impacts on religion in many areas of law, including non-discrimination, labour law, data protection, culture, media law, animal welfare, cooperation, finances, customs, and

---

11 F. Foret, 'Religion: A Solution or a Problem for the Legitimisation of the European Union?', *Religion, State and Society* 37, no. 1 (2009): 37–50, 38.

12 Ibid., 39.

13 M. Steven, 'Religious Lobbies in the European Union: From Dominant Church to Faith-Based Organisation?', *Religion, State and Society* 37, no. 1 (2009): 181–91, 181.

14 Ibid., 183.

15 B. Challand, 'From Hammer and Sickle to Star and Crescent: The Question of Religion for European Identity and a Political Europe', *Religion, State and Society* 37, no. 1 (2009): 65–80, 66.

16 Ibid., 70.

economic law'.[17] Some scholars have even developed the concept of a 'European "common law" on religion', which includes eight fundamental principles: the value of religion, subsidiarity in matters of religion, the principle of cooperation (dialogue with religion), religious freedom, the autonomy of religious associations, religious equality (non-discrimination), the principle of the special protection of religion and the principle of religious privilege.[18] Religious organisations are also exempt from some regulations of non-discrimination directives, since they are allowed to introduce requirements for religion or beliefs of prospective employees.[19] Ronan McCrea suggests that the EU limits the role of religion in important aspects of the political and law-making area, but he also admits that the Union 'permits religion to exercise influence over law as an element of civil society and, perhaps more importantly, as an element of a public morality'.[20]

Lucian Leustean observes an increase in the level of importance of religious issues in the EU, even though the 'contacts between European institutions and religious communities have officially been made relatively late in the life of the European Community'.[21] The turning point appeared at the Treaty of Maastricht, with the prominent role of Jacques Delors' initiative on cooperation between Churches and the EU, known as the 'Soul for Europe project'. At present, according to Leustean, the Commission is open to dialogue with religious communities, with the likelihood that the benefits from this dialogue will be mutual, with religious communities 'becoming more assertive in influencing the agenda of European institutions' and encouraging 'the European Union to become a world player, rather than to remain a regional one'.[22] The growing Churches–EU cooperation has led to increasing discussion of European integration issues in the Churches, with the subsequent identification of their attitudes towards the EU and European integration.

---

17 K. Jenkins, 'The Churches and Europe: Relating to the European Institutions', in J. Barnett (ed.), *A Theology for Europe: The Churches and the European Institutions* (Oxford, Peter Lang, 2005), pp. 77–8.
18 N. Doe, 'Towards a "Common Law" on Religion in the European Union', *Religion, State and Society* 37, no. 1 (2009): 147–66.
19 Ibid., 152–3.
20 R. McCrea, *Religion and the Public Order of the European Union* (Oxford, Oxford University Press, 2011), p. 103.
21 L. N. Leustean, 'What Is the European Union? Religion between Neofunctionalism and Intergovernmentalism', *International Journal for the Study of the Christian Church* 9, no. 3 (2009): 165–76, 167.
22 Ibid., 174.

Overall, we can suggest that there are three main sets of ideas, emanating from the various approaches of scholars who analyse the role of Churches in European integration. First, religion is present in the EU legislation in various forms. Secondly, Churches exercise their influence in different formats, including those of the interest groups. Finally, the role of Churches has become more visible and important after the Treaty of Maastricht, and the cooperation between Churches and EU institutions is beneficial to both sides. These ideas, reflecting certain aspects of the Churches' activities, do not provide a comprehensive vision of the Churches' involvement in European integration. In my view, they also do not fully reflect the Churches' character. Since we recognise the growing role of Churches in European integration, it is pertinent to argue that Churches should be regarded as special and unique participants in European integration. To prove this claim, I shall address three issues: the participation of Churches at the beginning of integration, the role of Churches in the formation of European identities and their role as non-state actors in the process of European integration.

In this regard, on the theoretical level the introduction of Churches into studies of European integration can be based on the following arguments. First, there should be an acceptance of the social constructivist inclusion of identity and non-state actors into the analysis of European integration. Identity comes both in the form of European identity and in the form of national identities in the member states.[23] Secondly, there is an argument that Churches can be regarded as identity formers and non-state actors, and religion is viewed as part of identity, as one of its constituent elements.[24] However, the identification of the role and place of Churches in European integration is not confined solely to the above-mentioned arguments. Certainly, social constructivism allows us to look at Churches via the lenses of non-state actors and identity. Churches contribute to the formation of both European and national identities, directly and indirectly (via the system of values). Churches also embrace, in their relations with the outside world, the features of non-state actors, using mechanisms of influence which are similar

---

23 F. Mayer and J. Palmowski, 'European Identities and the EU – The Ties That Bind the Peoples of Europe', *Journal for Common Market Studies* 42, no. 3 (2004): 573–98.

24 J. Warhurst, 'The Catholic Lobby: Structures, Policy Styles and Religious Networks', *The Australian Journal of Public Administration* 67, no. 2 (2008): 213–30; P. Djupe and C. Gilbert, *The Political Influence of Churches* (Cambridge, Cambridge University Press, 2009).

to those of regular non-state actors (e.g., petitions, negotiations, etc.).[25] There are, however, some other features which allow us to see the Churches as unlike the ordinary actors introduced via social constructivism, but instead as unique participants in European integration. These are historical circumstances and Church–state relations. Indeed, only Churches are able to enter into specific relations with the state, acting within certain Church–state models, including an established Church, full separation and cooperation.[26] The above-mentioned features originate mainly from the essence of Churches as religious and spiritual institutions. I shall discuss these features in more detail, starting from the analysis of the Churches' role at the early stages of the integration process.

Christian Churches at the Beginning of Integration

Overall, the degree of involvement of Churches and the level of their influence at the creation of the European Community (EC) has remained a matter for discussion. Leustean admits the influence of religion (through Christian Democratic parties) on the establishment of the EC, but also states that 'without the political support of other parties, the ratification of the treaties of Paris (1951) and Rome (1957) would not have been possible'.[27] Speaking about the introduction of Churches, one should realise that the main role is normally given to the Roman Catholic Church, or the institutions which reflect the values and ideas existing in this Church. Daniel Philpott and Timothy Samuel Shah state that 'the Catholic Church actively inspired, promoted, and shaped European integration', while other Churches 'played a relatively weak and sporadic role in promoting and shaping European integration'.[28] According to Nelsen and Guth, 'a network of Catholic activists and statesmen were at the heart of the European project', and the Catholic Church 'also bolstered the European project'.[29] Bryan Hehir

25 C. Mandry, 'Instrument of Mobilization or a Bridge towards Understanding? Religion and Values in the Reform Process of the European Union', *Journal of Religion in Europe* 2 (2009): 257–84.

26 See, for a discussion of the phenomena of Church–state relations, S. Mudrov, 'Church–State Relations in the Post-Communist World: The Cases of Belarus and Estonia', *Journal of Church and State* 59, no. 4 (2017): 649–71.

27 Leustean, 'What Is the European Union?', 165.

28 D. Philpott and T. S. Shah, 'Faith, Freedom and Federation: The Role of Religious Ideas and Institutions in European Political Convergence', in Byrnes and Katzenstein (eds.), *Religion in an Expanding Europe*, pp. 34–64, 51.

29 B. Nelsen and J. Guth, 'Losing Faith: Religion and Attitudes toward the European Union in Uncertain Times', *Journal of Common Market Studies* 58, no. 4 (2020): 909–24, 911.

underlines that 'The EU is built on the EC and the EC was powerfully influenced by Christian Democracy, a political movement but one directly rooted in Catholic social thought and close collaboration with the Holy See's role in postwar Europe.'[30]

Also, a number of the founding fathers of the EC were devout Catholics, including the French Foreign Minister Robert Schuman, German Chancellor Konrad Adenauer and Italian Foreign Minister Alcide De Gasperi. Schuman believed that the project of European unification 'cannot do without the inspiration of its Christian sources'. As he also emphasised, 'Europe is the implementation of a universal democracy, in the Christian sense of the word.' Rocco Buttiglione states that 'faith in Jesus Christ [was] at the centre of the life of Alcide De Gasperi'. The tendency of De Gasperi to make 'constant reference to the holy texts as an element of salvation constituted the main feature of his actions, especially in moments of pain and uncertainty'.[31]

Gary Wilton mentions that the Christian faith of Robert Schuman (along with the faith of De Gasperi, Monnet and Adenauer) was not somehow restricted to the private sphere but was 'the inspiration for a life dedicated to public service and to the rebuilding of Europe upon secure Christian foundations'. Wilton finds it rather surprising that the educational materials of the European Commission about Schuman make no reference to his Christian convictions, despite the fact that they deeply inspired his political vision for Europe.[32] Linda Risso notes that the Christian Democratic parties of post-war Europe 'based their political programme on the radical view that western civilisation was embedded in Christian values and that it needed to be protected both from the seduction of modern lifestyles and from the even greater dangers of communism'.[33] Accepting the view that Christianity made Europe its home, it is understandable in this vein that Paul Gallagher

30 B. J. Hehir, 'The Old Church and the New Europe: Charting the Changes', in Byrnes and Katzenstein (eds.), *Religion in an Expanding Europe*, pp. 93–116, 103.
31 G. Venneri and P. O. Ferrara, 'Alcide De Gasperi and Antonio Messineo: A Spiritual Conception of Politics and a Pragmatic Idea of Religion?', *Religion, State and Society 37*, no. 1–2 (2009): 115–29.
32 House of Bishops' Europe Panel, 'The Enduring Legacy of Robert Schuman: A Vision and Values for Europe in the 21st Century' (2010), accessed online in 2020, but no longer available.
33 L. Risso 'Cracks in a Facade of Unity: The French and Italian Christian Democrats and the Launch of the European Integration Process, 1945–1957', *Religion, State and Society 37*, no. 1–2 (2009): 99–114, 100.

finds that 'Catholics in particular' should be enthusiastic about any project which 'emphasises the European dimension, be it political or otherwise'. In this case, possible indifference from the Catholic Church towards the European project would mean rejection of the Church's calling and history. On the contrary, the Church's close cooperation with the European institutions would be regarded as 'part of its contribution to the well-being of the world'.[34]

Interestingly, Madeley discusses the idea of European integration as a Catholic, rather than a Christian Democratic, project, since the creation of a supranational body (to administer the European Coal and Steel Community) was in agreement with the Catholic criticism of the nation state.[35] Indeed, it is not accidental that in the early 1950s Protestants and Social Democrats often viewed European integration 'as a Catholic conspiracy of conservatives, an ideologically tainted attempt to revive clerical politics as a hand-maiden of big business, orchestrated by the Vatican',[36] while Catholics were supportive of the project. However, Leustean notes that as early as 1950 a transnational reflection group was formed, which included leading Protestant politicians and churchmen. This group, named the Ecumenical Commission on European Cooperation, was designed 'to offer expertise on European issues for Protestant Churches'. In fact, one of the presidents of the European Commission (Jean Rey, 1967–70) was a member of this group. There were even suggestions that it was a Protestant man who allegedly stood behind the Schuman declaration – Andre Philip, French Economic Minister in 1946–7 and President of the Commission on International Affairs at the Protestant Federation of France.[37] Bearing these facts in mind, it looks pertinent to recognise a substantial meaning and contribution of Churches during the initial stages of the process of European integration.

34 P. Gallagher, 'The Holy See and Europe: An Enduring Commitment', in Barnett (ed.), *A Theology for Europe*, pp. 97–9.

35 J. T. S. Madeley, 'E unum pluribus. The Role of Religion in the Project of European Integration', in J. Haynes (ed.), *Religion and Politics in Europe, the Middle East and North Africa* (Abingdon, Routledge, 2010), pp. 113–36, 119.

36 P. Katzenstein, 'Multiple Modernities as Limits to Secular Europeanization?', in Byrnes and Katzenstein (eds.), *Religion in an Expanding Europe*, pp. 1–33, 17.

37 L. N. Leustean, 'The Ecumenical Movement and the Schuman Plan, 1950–54', *Journal of Church and State* 53, no. 3 (2011): 442–71, 444–7.

The Role of Churches as Non-state Actors

Christian confessions are well represented at the EU level, with offices in Brussels. The Christian organisations in Brussels play a twofold role: they inform their leaders about the main developments in the EU and try to influence the decision-making process. In the latter case, they seem to be operating like other organisations of civil society, but this similarity is superficial. One of the differences, highlighted by Thomas Jansen, is related to the scope of the areas of work. On the one hand, the organisations which represent economic, social and cultural sectors are more worried about specific EU policies, within the competence of the appropriate Directorates-General. On the other hand, the concerns of Churches and religious communities are 'more general and based on the ethical and moral aspects of European unification and European policy'. Therefore their dialogue with the European Commission is aimed more at the meaning, spiritual direction and ethical dimension of European integration and related policies. Consequently, the European Commission values Churches as, in the first instance, partners which may assist 'when it comes to weighing up the ethical dimension of the process of European unification and giving it meaning and identity'.[38]

Having said that, we do not need to assume that the role of Churches is limited to dealing with some broad issues that have solely ethical dimensions. At times Churches need to be more specific and even to defend their interests, or interests originating from their moral and social doctrines (especially if the EU elaborates legislation related to the scope of these doctrines). The methods that may be in use by Churches are similar to the regular methods of non-state actors. First, direct or indirect lobbying, with the help of different organisations/individuals, can be used.[39] The second method includes political mobilisation (especially among parishioners) and more actively exerting influence on the formation of public opinion. Mobilisation is a particularly strong method in countries where trust in the

38 T. Jansen, 'Europe and Religions: The Dialogue between the European Commission and Churches or Religious Communities', *Social Compass* 47, no. 1 (2000): 103–12, 104.
39 F. Foret and M. Markoviti, 'New Challenge, Old Solutions? Religion and Counter-radicalisation in the European Parliament and the Radicalisation Awareness Network', *European Politics and Society* 21, no. 4 (2019): 434–51.

Church is significant, and where either the masses can be mobilised easily, or influential political groups are willing to act in accordance with the Church's recommendations or requests. The mobilisation of the masses is useful to form strong public opinion, with which the government, claiming to be democratic, cannot deal formally. Of course, public opinion is changeable, as has been demonstrated especially in the referendums on important EU issues, but even these changeable instruments can be efficient in forcing governments to make decisions which would not be possible otherwise. As Zsolt Enyedi suggests, 'in the democratic era, the ability of Churches to put pressure on the state depends to a large extent on how skilled they are in mobilising public opinion'.[40]

Christof Mandry explains that the Churches (or, to put it better, the governing bodies of the Churches) possess adequate resources to operate and to shape public political debate: 'The decisive question, however, is how far they succeed in activating allies and influencing neutral third persons', which, in its turn, brings to the surface the mobilising potential of the religious theme itself, that is, reflection on the relationship between (political) identity and religion.[41] One can point out that 'organised Christianity' has indeed established itself as 'an important, publicly recognized, legitimate interlocutor in the institutional space of the EU', but this establishment is not necessarily a guarantee of success.[42] Rather, the real level of success is dependent on the mobilising potential of the theme chosen and advocated by the Churches and those acting on their behalf (and this often involves identity-related issues). As an example, we can point to the introduction of further restrictions to abortion in Poland – a measure supported by the Catholic Church (the issue of abortion, in the context of the protection of the rights of unborn children, is of significance for most Christian Churches). Thus, the contribution of Churches to identity formation (both at the national level and at EU level) underlines their additional distinctive feature. This will be explored in the next pages of the chapter.

---

40 Enyedi, 'Conclusion', 228.   41 Mandry, 'Instrument of Mobilization', 279.
42 P. Schlesinger and F. Foret, 'Political Roof and Sacred Canopy? Religion and the EU Constitution', *European Journal of Social Theory* 9, no. 1 (2006): 59–81, 60.

Churches, Identity and the EU

The relevance of identity to European integration is broadly accepted and is normally learnt through the national and European identities.[43] Since the EU is an association of nation-states, the concept of national identity needs to be taken into consideration. On the other hand, the EU is often referred to as an 'emerging polity'; thus the concept of European identity naturally appears on the agenda. Therefore, in order to reveal an additional feature of the role of Churches in European integration, we need to look at their possible contribution to the formation of both national and European identities. Since religion is regarded as a part of identity, Churches are able to contribute directly to the process of identity formation. This is especially true for areas where religion is an important part of everyday life. Certainly, this contribution is determined by European history, by its distinct features which demonstrate the meaningful role of Christianity. Indeed, Europe was not created from nothing, nor did it appear as a result of random coincidences. Rather, we can suggest that Europe (as a continent and as an idea) achieved its status because it was marked by Christian values and Christian faith.

In this vein, Sara Silvestri emphasises that 'classical culture was preserved and educational institutions were founded in Europe thanks to the work of religious orders [...] the much respected universities of Oxford and Cambridge were established as religious (Christian) institutions in first instance'.[44] Monasteries were centres of scientific research and important educational establishments. Christian architecture, embodied in magnificent cathedrals and public buildings, became a constituent part of European cities. Furthermore, the presence of Christianity was visible among the representatives of the ruling elite. Many emperors, especially after the fourth century AD, were devout Christians for whom the Gospel values played a very important role. The mood of that time could be discovered through the words of Saint Gregory of Nazianzus, who wrote to one of the emperors: 'You rule with Christ, and you command with Christ. So you should imitate God's love of man. This is the most divine feature of man, namely to do

43 J. Caporaso and M. Kim, 'The Dual Nature of European Identity: Subjective Awareness and Coherence', *Journal of European Public Policy* 16, no. 1 (2009): 19–42; S. Carey, 'Undivided Loyalties: Is National Identity an Obstacle to European Integration?', *European Union Politics* 3 (2002): 387–413; L. Cram, 'Identity and European Integration: Diversity as a Source of Integration', *Nations and Nationalism* 15, no. 1 (2009): 109–28; Mayer and Palmowski, 'European Identities and the EU'.

44 S. Silvestri, 'Does Islam Challenge European Identity?', in L. Faltin and M. Wright (eds.), *The Religious Roots of Contemporary European Identity* (London, Continuum International Publishing Group, 2007), pp. 14–28, 15.

good.'[45] It is therefore not accidental that one of the statements of the Holy Synod of the Church of Greece underlines that 'Europe cannot, and should not forget that its spiritual foundations lie in the Gospel of Christ.'[46] These Gospel foundations of Europe formed some of the distinct features of European societies. This fact was explicitly admitted by the French poet and philosopher Paul Valéry:

> The European person is not determined by his race, language and national- ity, since Europe is the motherland of many languages, nationalities and traditions. The European is whoever belongs to a people that has embraced the Roman rule of justice, has comprehended well Greek education and has accepted and assimilated Christian teaching.[47]

Apart from this direct contribution of Christianity, as shown above, one should bear in mind the existence of the indirect contribution to the process of identity formation. This is connected with values as a parameter of identity. Indeed, values are related, at least partly, to religion, and there is a well-grounded viewpoint that 'the identity of individual Europeans, and of Europe as a Union, continues to be heavily influenced by Christian values'.[48] In the Europe of today one can observe the existence of two sets of values: secular and religious. They are in conflict with each other; and this clash of values is the reflection of the desire to construct a certain type of European identity, based on either a religious or a non-religious dimension. When speaking about Christian values in terms of their application to Europe, we need to emphasise that they are, by and large, conservative ones, not eroded by the modernist trends found within some Christian factions. These values contain a clear moral and ethical message, where, inter alia, the family is seen as the union between man and woman; human life exists and should be protected from the moment of conception to the moment of natural death; and honesty, chastity and mutual help should be promoted, rather than criticised or even mocked. These conser-vative values have been contested by European secularism.

A clash of values has become the everyday reality of the contemporary EU. In this clash most Churches take a clear stance: as defenders of conservative

45 Archbishop Christodoulos, 'The Presence of the Church on the Horizon of Europe' (2003), www.orthodox-christian-comment.co.uk/news-presence_of_the_church_ on_the_ho.htm.
46 Church of Greece, 'The Holy Synod of the Church of Greece on the Future of Europe' (2003), www.ecclesia.gr/English/EnHolySynod/messages/europe_declaration.html.
47 Archbishop Christodoulos, 'The Word and Role of Orthodoxy in the European Union' (2000), www.ecclesia.gr/English/EnArchbishop/EnSpeeches/role_of_orthodoxy.html.
48 A. J. Menéndez, 'A Christian or a Laïc Europe? Christian Values and European Identity', Ratio Juris 18, no. 2 (2005): 179–205, 185.

Christian values. In fact, this ongoing clash of values in the EU often leaves Churches no option other than active participation on one side or other of the conflict. For Churches, it is very important to ensure that those values that will be laid down at the foundation of European identity will not promote a secular vision of the EU. Logically, Churches see themselves as the defenders and promoters of certain values (and a particular lifestyle) not only because of their theological doctrines and the inclinations of moral theology, but also out of a desire to contribute to identity formation, to ensure that the identity is more in conformity with Christian values. The type of values defended by Churches correlates with their respective theological doctrines. Thus, Churches have become involved also in the process of European integration, becoming identity formers and influencing the debates on both European and national identities. This was visible, for instance, in the debates on the EU Constitution, when Churches argued in favour of the reference to God and the Christian roots of Europe in the Preamble. It was also visible in the support of changes to the Constitution of Hungary, to define marriage as the union of a man and a woman. This adds an important feature to their unique role in the policy-making and integration processes in the EU.

A Level of Influence

The very fact that Churches can be regarded as unique participants in European integration forms a foundation for the further progression of the argument of this chapter. It allows for a detailed exploration of how Churches are incorporated into the life of the EU, and the assessment of their possible level of influence. An important note in that respect is that the process of secularisation which is occurring in some parts of the Union is not applicable to the same degree to the EU as a whole. Indeed, the countries of western Europe diverge considerably in religious matters, with religious participation higher in the southern Catholic parts and lower in the northern Protestant parts. Moreover, the importance of Churches has increased in some parts of Europe, such as the countries of the former Soviet bloc, after the fall of Communist regimes. Overall, there is no reason to expect that Churches in the EU at large will substantially lose their influence or will be driven into 'private space'. The survey data demonstrate that most people in the EU regard themselves as believers, belong to a particular confession and express rather positive attitudes towards Churches. The Treaty of Maastricht and the subsequent treaties (particularly Nice), which opened the doors of 'an ever closer union' to the nations in the east and south of Europe, have implicitly contributed to the overall increase of religiosity in the EU. It was related to the process of enlargement, which brought into the Union former Communist states with a higher level of religiosity than in the 'old' EU (for instance, such large countries as Poland and Romania, where the local population is very religious). This is especially important in view of the fact that religion influences people's views, 'their perception of events and their actions', including, of course, the views of the policy-makers.[49]

However, one should not assume that Churches have been active and influential in all policy areas. In fact, they might be active only on selected issues that they regard as particularly important. Such an approach is explained by the fact that the limited resources of Churches do not allow them to monitor carefully all aspects of the EU's activity. The issues which are regarded as the most important for Churches are mainly value-based, that is, involving concepts of identity, morality and the rights of vulnerable and oppressed groups. Taking into account the areas of importance for Churches and their social concepts and doctrines, it seems plausible that Churches do not act for self-centred aims but mainly in reflection of more common interests. It is logical that altruism and the desire to serve humankind are the main traits of their activity. Indeed, Churches aim at the promotion of moral norms and values which are based on the Gospel, as the source of divine wisdom and truth, even if these values do not always encounter overwhelming support in society. To an extent, the role of Churches is also dependent on how the theme of European integration is discussed and perceived in various confessions. It is, undoubtedly, an issue of high interest for the Catholics, with the Vatican trying to express rather optimistic views on the process of European unification. These views are not always shared by some representatives of the Roman Catholic Church, who may be critical of what they see as moral corruption in the EU. This criticism of the EU is partly echoed by some adherents of Orthodox Churches, who warn that Europe has lost its soul, denying its Christian roots. On the Protestant side, a clear Eurosceptic stance is taken by Free Churches, while mainstream Protestants remain largely pro-European.[50] However, in spite of the existence of various approaches, no mainstream Christian Church refrains from cooperation with EU institutions, as is made evident by their presence at the EU level.

---

49 J. Fox, 'Religion as an Overlooked Element of International Relations', *International Studies Review* 3, no. 3 (2001): 53–73, 59.

50 S. Mudrov, 'Religion and the European Union: Attitudes of Catholic and Protestant Churches toward European Integration', *Journal of Church and State* 57, no. 3 (2015): 507–28.

Churches at the Supranational Level

The presence of Churches at the supranational level is an important indicator of how actively and successfully Churches can monitor EU policy-making. It is of particular significance in their attempts to influence the decision-making process. The work of representations in Brussels is also a reflection of the Churches' interest in EU developments and their desire to participate in European integration.

First, it is important to underline that only the Roman Catholic Church has established its presence in the EU at the diplomatic level. This exists in two forms: the Embassy of the Holy See to the EU, and the mission of the Sovereign Military Order of Malta. Of course, the Papal Nuncio (appointed first in the capacity of a Nuncio for the EC in 1970) takes it as a natural task to defend, using diplomatic means, the Vatican's interests at the European level. The Sovereign Order of Malta's circumstances are not as favourable as for the Holy See: the representation of the Order is recognised as a diplomatic entity by the European Commission, but not by the EU member states. However, no other religious representation is regarded as a diplomatic mission; none could even acquire this status.

The Transparency Register website of the European Commission lists fifty-two organisations (as of April 2021) registered under Section V, 'Organisations representing churches and religious communities'.[51] However, not all religious organisations have chosen to register under this section. Some religious organisations (e.g., the 'International Catholic Migration Commission – Europe', 'Christian Aid' and some others) chose to register under Section III – 'Non-governmental organisations' and a small number of organisations did not register at all. The religious representations are mainly Christian. Certainly, not all of these organisations have a functioning staff, a clear agenda and an ability to monitor developments in the EU, let alone to influence its decision-making processes. In our view, it is pertinent to classify these representations along denominational lines. Lucian Leustean also suggests making a distinction in terms of the following functional parameters: the official representation of Churches; inter-Church or confessional organisations or networks; religious orders; and single-issue organisations.[52] The Catholic organisations, working on a wide range of issues, include the Commission of the Bishops' Conferences of the European Union

---

51 Transparency Register, https://ec.europa.eu/transparencyregister/public/homePage
.do?redir=false&locale=en.
52 Leustean, 'The Ecumenical Movement and the Schuman Plan', 307.

(COMECE), the Jesuit European Social Centre and Caritas Europa. Single-issue organisations are normally concerned about issues of immigration and refugees (one can mention here the International Catholic Migration Commission and the Jesuit Refugee Service Europe). Orthodox representations tend to concentrate on broader issues, and include representations of the Churches of Greece, Romania and Cyprus, the Moscow Patriarchate and the Liaison Office of the Orthodox Church (Ecumenical Patriarchate). Finally, Protestants are represented by the Evangelical Church in Germany (Evangelische Kirche in Deutschland, EKD) office, the European Evangelical Alliance, Christian Action, Research and Education (CARE for Europe) and the Lutheran Churches of Finland and Sweden. There are also representations of Free Churches. The ecumenical organisations are best represented by the Conference of European Churches (CEC).

Practical Cooperation

The analysis of practical cooperation between Churches and the EU institutions is important in order to see in more detail how the work of representations in Brussels is organised. Practical cooperation between Christian organisations and European institutions usually takes the form of consultations and meetings. Lucian Leustean distinguishes two main types of meetings: working groups (when experts from both sides work together on specific issues), and '"photo opportunities" between the highest levels of political and religious leadership in Europe' (when the Presidents or Vice-Presidents of the Council, Parliament and Commission are present, as well as Church leaders and leaders of other religions).[53] Although 'photo opportunity' style meetings are the most visible to the press and general public, they seem to be largely ceremonial, with few practical consequences. There have been fifteen such meetings since the first meeting in 2005 (see Table 26.1).[54] There was no high-level meeting in 2019, officially due to the 'transition between the outgoing and incoming Commission with European elections in the middle'.

---

53 Ibid., pp. 309–10.
54 European Commission – BEPA, 'Dialogue under Article 17: Dialogue with Churches, Religious Associations or Communities and Philosophical and Non-confessional Organisations', https://ec.europa.eu/archives/bepa/activities/outreach-team/dia logue/index_en.htm; European Commission, Justice and Consumers DG, 'Dialogue with Churches, Religious Associations or Communities and Philosophical and Non-confessional Organisations', https://ec.europa.eu/newsroom/just/item-detail.cfm? item_id=50189.

Table 26.1 High-level meetings between religious and political leaders in the EU

Date	Theme	Confessions present
July 2005	Rejection of terrorism and ongoing EU integration	Catholic, Protestant, Orthodox, Judaism and Islam
May 2006	Fundamental rights and mutual respect	Catholic, Protestant, Orthodox, Judaism, Islam and Buddhism
May 2007	Building a Europe based on human dignity	Catholic, Protestant, Orthodox, Judaism and Islam
May 2008	Climate change and reconciliation	Catholic, Protestant, Orthodox, Judaism and Islam
May 2009	Economic and financial crisis: ethical contributions for European and global economic governance	Catholic, Protestant, Orthodox, Judaism and Islam
July 2010	Combating poverty and social exclusion	Catholic, Protestant, Orthodox, Judaism, Islam, Hinduism and Sikhism
May 2011	A partnership for democracy and shared prosperity: a common willingness to promote democratic rights and liberties	Catholic, Protestant, Orthodox, Judaism, Islam and Buddhism
July 2012	Intergenerational solidarity: setting the parameters for tomorrow's society in Europe	Catholic, Protestant, Orthodox, Judaism, Islam, Hinduism and Baha'ism
May 2013	Putting citizens at the heart of the European project in times of change	Catholic, Protestant, Orthodox, Judaism, Islam and Hinduism
June 2014	The future of the EU	Catholic, Protestant, Orthodox, Judaism, Islam, Hinduism, Sikhism and Mormonism
June 2015	Living together and disagreeing well	Catholic, Protestant, Orthodox, Judaism, Islam, Hinduism, Buddhism and Mormonism
November 2016	Migration, integration and European values	Catholic, Protestant, Orthodox, Judaism, Islam, Hinduism and Mormonism
November 2017	The future of Europe: a value-based and effective Union	Catholic, Protestant, Orthodox, Judaism, Islam, Buddhism and Mormonism
October 2018	The future of Europe: addressing challenges through concrete actions	Catholic, Protestant, Orthodox, Judaism and Islam
November 2020	The European way of life	Catholic, Protestant, Orthodox, Judaism and Islam

What can be concluded from the particularities of these meetings? If we take into account the list of Churches which have participated in the annual high-level meetings, we can find that there are some established partners in the dialogue, who are normally invited each year. These include COMECE and CEC representatives (from the Catholic Church and ecumenical organisations, respectively). From the Protestant side, representatives of the EKD are generally invited. From Orthodox Churches, representatives of the Greek Orthodox Church attended most meetings, and representatives of the Moscow Patriarchate were officially present at the 2005, 2007, 2008, 2009 and 2011 meetings. A representative of the Church of Cyprus was present at the meetings in 2007, 2010, 2011, 2012 and 2014, and representatives of the Romanian Orthodox Church have attended most meetings since 2008. A representative of the Bulgarian Orthodox Church attended only one meeting, in 2010. The Ecumenical Patriarchate was represented at all of the meetings, usually by Metropolitan Emmanuel (Adamakis), who was until 2014 the head of the representation to the EU. Some smaller Churches were also invited from time to time, such as the United Protestant Church in Belgium.

Meetings of this type do not give much opportunity either for discussion or for substantial interventions from the participants. Indeed, it is hardly possible to have a deep and profound discussion in a meeting which takes place only once a year, lasts for 2 hours and is attended by ten to twenty participants. In contrast to these photo-op meetings, the working groups are more practical and provide more opportunity for exerting influence, especially if the Church experts are good professionals in their field. However, there are no formal rules to oversee the special involvement of Christian organisations in the EU's policy-making. Church experts work alongside experts from secular organisations, and there is unlikely to be any preference for the former among European institutions. Moreover, in certain cases, their Church affiliation may even lead to some uneasiness, if the partners in dialogue have strong anti-Church views or are opposed to any sort of religious involvement in policy-making, even if this involvement comes in the form of expertise not related to a religious agenda.

In principle, after the Treaty of Lisbon entered into force in 2009, it had been expected that Churches would have better opportunities to exercise their influence on the supranational (European) level. It was in agreement with the logic of developments in Europe, both in the west and in the east, which provided opportunities in the early 1990s for the increasing involvement of Christian Churches in the process of European integration. The

Treaty of Maastricht made integration less economic in nature, with a more substantial involvement of non-economic areas and actors. Jacques Delors' 1992 initiative 'to give a Soul to Europe, to give it spirituality and meaning', articulated in a speech to Churches, underlined the growing interest in religious communities from European institutions. It was therefore quite natural that the Lisbon Treaty, as noted by Leustean, gave religious communities 'a more significant position' and instituted 'a consultation framework with the European institutions'.[55] Indeed, Article 17(3) of the Treaty on the Functioning of the European Union (TFEU) envisages 'open, transparent and regular dialogue' with Churches (as well as with philosophical and non-confessional organisations). In April 2010, COMECE and the Church and Society Commission (CSC) of the CEC articulated their 'General considerations' on the implementation of this provision of the Treaty of Lisbon. They emphasised, in particular, that the Churches' dialogue partners should include the Council, Commission and Parliament, but also 'other EU institutions and bodies', and that opportunities for dialogue should be given to both minority and majority Churches.[56]

Explaining the characteristics of such dialogue, COMECE and the CSC of the CEC noted the following important aspects. Openness, according to them, means that the EU institutions should be willing 'to work with citizens towards the goal of *"involvement in the lawmaking and governance"* of the EU'.[57] One more feature of this openness is that no policy field which is within the EU's legislative and governmental competence should be excluded from this dialogue. It should also be 'frank' and can focus, inter alia, on the promotion of universal values, as mentioned in the Preamble of the Treaty on European Union, as well as 'the respect of human dignity of every human being, reconciliation and intercultural understanding, as well as on the realization of the principles of subsidiarity and solidarity in EU policy'. Transparency is explained as a good opportunity to allow the interested public to know the Churches' perspectives on EU issues and an opportunity for the EU institutions to disseminate their views to a bigger audience. The provision for a regular dialogue is particularly developed, with Christian organisations emphasising that regular dialogue 'goes above and beyond sporadic ad-hoc meetings between representatives of

---

55 Leustean, 'What Is the European Union?', 175.
56 COMECE and CSC of the CEC, 'Article 17 of the Treaty on the Functioning of the European Union. General Considerations on the Implementation of the Dialogue Foreseen by Its paragraph 3' (2010), p. 3, www.comece.eu/wp-content/uploads/sites/2/2022/04/20100521-Article-17-of-the-Treaty-on-the-Functioning-of-the-European-Union.pdf.
57 Ibid., p. 4, emphasis in the original.

Churches and EU institutions'. The Churches stressed that the future dialogue framework should improve and enhance the existing one, at all levels: working contacts, consultations, dialogue seminars and high-level meetings. In fact, these high-level and most visible meetings need 'common content preparation prior to the events as well as any subsequent follow-up'. Regarding the European Commission, regular dialogue 'should contribute to consolidate the frequency of meetings with the Churches'. In reality, this may well depend on the Commission's strategic annual planning, and therefore it concedes that such a meeting might even be necessary before the Commission declares its legislative and work programme for the coming year. Also, COMECE and the CSC of the CEC pointed out that they would welcome participating in the hearings organised by the European Parliament. All this confirms the Churches' readiness to cooperate closely with EU institutions.[58]

In contrast, however, the European Commission's official website does not provide such substantial and inclusive definitions of the characteristics of this dialogue as those elaborated by Christian Churches. To the EU, openness means that 'Dialogue partners can be churches, religious associations or communities, as well as philosophical and non-confessional organizations that are recognized or registered as such at national level and adhere to European values.' Transparent dialogue means that the European Commission, on a dedicated website, 'conveys to the public all relevant information about the activities within the dialogue'. Finally, regular dialogue means that 'The European Commission maintains a regular dialogue with interlocutors at various levels in the form of written exchanges, meetings, or specific events,' without specification of how regularly.[59]

This rather reserved tone on the part of the European Commission can possibly be viewed as a confirmation of Ronan McCrea's claim that the EU, while not being strictly secular, may in practice impose some limitations on the impact of the return of religion to the political arena.[60] It appears that the European institutions do not show the same degree of openness and eagerness to interact with Christian Churches as Churches express about interacting with the EU. Certainly, it was the Churches' achievement that in the text of the Lisbon Treaty the provisions for their dialogue with the EU were separated from the dialogue with civil society. However, it was partially

---

58 Ibid., pp. 4–5.
59 European Commission, 'Guidelines on the Implementation of Article 17 TFEU by the European Commission', https://commission.europa.eu/system/files/2017-06/guidelines-implementation-art-17_en.pdf.
60 McCrea, *Religion and the Public Order of the European Union*, p. 13.

watered down by the inclusion of 'philosophical and non-confessional organ-izations' in this dialogue. Moreover, the Churches initially requested 'struc-tured' dialogue, but this word does not appear in the wording of Article 17. Consequently, Article 17, if fully applied, simply means dialogue with almost everyone, without any specific obligations from the EU. In fact, putting Article 17 into practice still remains an issue of practical concern, since it is very difficult to organise the dialogue with hundreds of different denomin-ations. If all of them are invited at the same time, there would be, in the best case, a chance for short interventions from religious leaders, without a realistic opportunity for a lengthy and productive discussion. It appears, therefore, that for Churches there would be a greater chance of increasing their influence if the cooperation at the policy level were to acquire more intensive forms. However, the very fact that all EU institutions, including the Council and the Parliament, are now obliged to hold meetings and seminars with the representatives of the Churches is a testimony to the growing visibility of religious communities at the EU level.[61]

Conclusion

Having analysed the role of Churches in the uniting of Europe, I have identified that Churches should be regarded as special and unique partici-pants in European integration. This notion comes from within the frame-work of social constructivism, which introduces non-state actors into the analysis of European integration. Churches are unique, because they are different in their essence from other non-state actors (indeed, most Churches have a very old history and may include as their members the majority of the population in a state). Churches are special participants, because they made a visible contribution to the integration process in its initial stage, because they embrace the features of identity-formers and aim at providing values and a spiritual dimension to European integration. Thus, they deserve their own, separate place among other actors taken into account by social constructivists.

Despite their similarity to other actors (such as non-governmental organisations) in some respects, Churches retain their specific nature as religious, spiritual organisations. This difference is demonstrated by their contribution to European and national identities, by their role

---

61 S. Mudrov, 'Religion in the Treaty of Lisbon: Aspects and Evaluation', *Journal of Contemporary Religion* 31, no. 1 (2016): 1–16.

during the initial stages of integration and, finally, by the existence of the phenomena of Church–state relations. Churches influenced (through Christian Democratic parties) the establishment of the EC, and the Catholic Church inspired and promoted European integration. A number of the founding fathers of the EC were devout Catholics, including Schuman, Adenauer and De Gasperi. National identity in Europe has often been built around religious values, and the European person, according to Valéry, is someone who 'has accepted and assimilated Christian teaching'. Nowadays Churches continue to promote Gospel values in different European countries, including the Christian understanding of the family (as the union between a man and a woman) and the protection of the rights of unborn children. Their influence at national level was particularly noticeable in Poland and Hungary, where legislation was changed to reflect more the Christian approach towards family values. Religious arguments were also present in the discussions on the important referendums in the EU member states, including the 2008 and 2009 referendums in Ireland on the Lisbon Treaty and the 2016 referendum in the UK on withdrawal from the EU.

Also, it is important to note that there is a growing presence of Churches at the European level. All three Christian confessions – Orthodox, Catholic and Protestant – have established representations in Brussels, interacting with the EU institutions. Since the Roman Catholic Church has the most resources at its disposal, it is obvious that its activities at the supranational level are the most visible, and its influence is the strongest. Indeed, the largest and most influential representation in Brussels is that of the Catholic Church – COMECE. However, the Orthodox and Protestants have also found their way into the corridors of power in Brussels, especially the Church of Greece, the Romanian Orthodox Church and the EKD. To enhance their visibility and efficiency, the Orthodox Churches established the Committee of the Representatives of the Orthodox Churches in the European Union (CROCEU), which aims at bringing their voices together, especially on important moral and ethical issues.

Apart from acting on their own, the Orthodox, Protestants and Old Catholics interact with the EU institutions via ecumenical organisations, of which the CEC is the best known and most influential one. The CEC (as well as COMECE) has been regarded as a professional and reliable interlocutor by the officials in Brussels. The regular dialogue with the EU institutions, conducted at the highest level, involves representatives of all three Christian confessions, although preference is understandably given to the larger and more-established Churches, which continue to be influential actors both at the European level and at the national level. Indeed, as the survey data demonstrate, most people in the EU regard themselves as believers and express positive attitudes towards Churches. It is therefore logical that the Churches in the EU at large will not be put aside, but will continue to exercise their influence, using also the opportunities provided by Article 17 of the Treaty of Lisbon. Overall, it is obvious that the Churches continue to provide a positive contribution to the process of European integration, bringing Christian values and norms, and endeavouring to add to the integration process important ethical and value-based dimensions.

Recommended Reading

Leustean, L. N. (ed.). *Representing Religion in the European Union: Does God Matter?* (London and New York, NY, Routledge, 2012).

Mudrov, S. *Christian Churches in European Integration* (Abingdon and New York, NY, Routledge, 2016).

Mudrov, S. 'Did They Define the Outcome? Churches and the Independence Referendum in Scotland', *Journal of Religion in Europe* 11, no. 1 (2018), 20–45.

Nelsen, B. and J. Guth. *Religion and the Struggle for European Union: Confessional Culture and the Limits of Integration* (Washington, DC, Georgetown University Press, 2015).

Royce, M. *The Political Theology of European Integration: Comparing the Influence of Religious Histories on European Policies* (London, Palgrave McMillan, 2017).

Index